THE BIBLE IN ENGLISH DRAMA

AN ANNOTATED LIST OF PLAYS INCLUDING TRANSLATIONS
FROM OTHER LANGUAGES
FROM THE BEGINNINGS TO 1931

THE BIBLE IN ENGLISH DRAMA

AN ANNOTATED LIST OF PLAYS INCLUDING TRANSLATIONS
FROM OTHER LANGUAGES
FROM THE BEGINNINGS TO 1931

Compiled by EDWARD D. COLEMAN

A SURVEY OF RECENT MAJOR PLAYS
(1968)
By ISAIAH SHEFFER

NEW YORK
THE NEW YORK PUBLIC LIBRARY
and
KTAV PUBLISHING HOUSE, INC.

The Bible in English Drama was originally published in the *Bulletin of The New York Public Library,* Oct.-Dec. 1930 and Jan.-March 1931, and it was reprinted in book form by The New York Public Library in 1931.

This new printing, by offset, is jointly published by The New York Public Library and Ktav Publishing House, Inc., with the addition of "A Survey of Major Recent Plays" by Isaiah Sheffer.

MANUFACTURED IN THE UNITED STATES OF AMERICA
LIBRARY OF CONGRESS CATALOG CARD NUMBER: 67-11900

TABLE OF CONTENTS

A Survey of Major Recent Plays
(1968)

by ISAIAH SHEFFER

Edward Coleman's *The Bible in English Drama,* like its companion volume, *The Jew in English Drama,* is an enduring bibliographical work which deserves to be re-issued and to remain in print and thus available to scholars despite the fact that its entries go only up to the year 1931. It would no doubt take comparably intensive scholarship to extend the coverage of Coleman's work through the succeeding thirty-five years. What follows is merely the briefest of surveys of some of the more important and typical works of the recent decades, a highly selective sampling of the entries which would have come under the scrutiny of the bibliographer undertaking this task. *

In his introduction to the 1931 edition of this annotated bibliography, Coleman noted that "with the possible exception of Milton's *Samson Agonistes,* none of the English plays based on the Bible can be considered a great masterpiece of literature. Though not called upon to ascribe a reason for it, one ventures to suggest that it is due to the difficulty of improving on the Bible." [1] A survey of British and American drama since 1931 shows that this criticism has remained true. No very great work for the theatre has been drawn from a biblical source, nor has the total number of significant plays based upon the Bible been large. A cursory examination of the records of theatrical production of the last four decades in London and New York reveals that history, mythology, and the novel have each been the source of many more dramatic creations than the Bible.

If fewer playwrights have been looking towards the Bible for material (possibly because they have come to believe in the truth of the reason suggested by Mr Coleman) it might be pointed out in passing that there has been no such restraint or fear on the part of writers for the motion pictures. As biblical plays have continued to dwindle in number, biblical movies have proliferated. Motion picture producers have not doubted their ability to improve upon the Bible, not merely by adding other words to those taken from Scripture, but by adding pictures to those

---

* A critical study which appeared recently was Murray Roston *Biblical Drama in England: from the Middle Ages to the Present Day* (London, Faber and Faber 1968; Evanston, Northwestern University Press 1968) 335 p.

[1] Edward D. Coleman, in his Introduction to *The Bible in English Drama.* See p 1 below.

words, featuring genuine outdoor scenery and often in technicolor. The quality of these motion pictures whose varieties have included the Hollywood melodrama such as *David and Bathsheba*, the inspirational epic such as *The Greatest Story Ever Told*, experimental films such as *The Gospel According to St. Matthew*, and a recent extravaganza of a film modestly entitled *The Bible*, would be the subject of a separate study.

The biblical plays that have appeared in the years since the publication of the first edition of this volume also show considerable diversity of purpose and method. The publishers' catalogues indicate a continuing flow of the sort of juvenile school or festival play which Mr Coleman dismissed as of small literary merit. A sampling of these plays suggests that in addition to furnishing some non-ceremonial means of celebrating Christmas, Easter, or Chanukah in the schools their main purpose seems to be to introduce and explain the Bible through simple and understandable renderings of Bible stories. An obvious criticism of many plays of this genre is that all too often in them history, significance, or beauty are sacrificed in order to achieve this simple understandability. Examples abound of an old mode of speech that might be described as "biblical-colloquial": "Come here, Isaac. Now listen carefully. There's something I have to tell you."

The more ambitious and adult efforts to create theatre out of biblical material fall into two main types: the serious poetic drama and the comic biblical parody. In the following pages, several examples of each of these types will be examined in an effort to describe some of the specific techniques employed by the dramatist who turns to the Bible for inspiration.

In *The Theatre of the Absurd*, describing divergent trends in the avant-garde drama, the critic Martin Esslin points out the existence of one trend which insists on the *non*-absurd character of language:

> Even more important is its different attitude towards language: the 'poetic avant-garde' relies to a far greater extent on consciously 'poetic' speech; it aspires to plays that are in effect poems, images composed of a rich web of verbal associations. The theatre of the absurd, on the other hand, tends toward a radical devaluation of language. . . .[2]

It is in this "poetic" branch of the modern drama, the branch that seeks to depart from the realistic mode of dramatic expression that has been dominant for most of the first half of the twentieth century and to explore the use of poetry in stage speech, that most of the serious biblical dramas are found. One can only speculate whether this is because the

---

[2] Martin Esslin *The Theatre of the Absurd* (Garden City, New York, Doubleday 1961) p xxi.

poetically inclined playwright looks to the Bible for subject matter that will permit poetic exaltation or whether it is simply that the author who has for one reason or another already chosen a biblical story to dramatize very often finds himself then impelled to write in a poetic vein.

For the playwright Paddy Chayefsky whose earlier works, *Marty,* *Middle of the Night* and *The Tenth Man,* owed much of their success to their author's acute skill in recording and reproducing realistic, idiomatic modern speech, the play *Gideon*[3] represented a move in a new direction. While *Gideon* is actually written in prose with only occasional, though important, lyrical outbreaks, the prose is elevated — an attempt at a "classical," formal idiom of sufficient weight for a serious play on the subject of man's relation to God.

But this attempt evokes very uneven results. The play's language continually wavers between the rhetorically awkward:

> *The Angel:* (speaking to Gideon who is sulking) Now what occasions this new petulance?;

the forced colloquial:

> *One of Gideon's Officers:* As Gods go, this Lord Yahweh has a whimsical turn of mind, don't you think?;

and the deliberately anachronistic use of modern scientific terms:

> *Malchiel:* We have been told that this Gideon is a charismatic man. . . .

None of these three devices — the attempt at grandeur of utterance, the fanciful colloquialism, or the use of anachronism — are invalid and all three are among those most frequently used by all the playwrights under consideration. But each is a powerful instrument which gives a very definite tone to a dramatic work. It takes great skill to use more than one such instrument freely without risking the creation of a text that seems confused and uncertain in its intent. In the language of Chayefsky's *Gideon* grandiosity and small-talk sit uneasily side by side.

The dramatic content of *Gideon* centers around the question of man's belief in God, or rather man's lack of such belief. In the first scene of the play a personage appears to the farmer Gideon. Chayefsky refers to the visitor, rather coyly, as "The Angel" and describes him as "A man with a black beard, almost entirely enshrouded in long black mosaic robes." But despite the modest label this is no mere angel, as his first line makes clear:

> *The Angel:* I am the Lord your God, Gideon . . .

When this announcement fails to impress Gideon, the Angel reiterates:

[3] Paddy Chayefsky *Gideon* (New York, Random House 1962).

> *The Angel:* I am the Lord your God who brought you out of the house
> of Egypt! With signs and wonders I delivered you from bondage!

Gideon, after listening to a catalogue of his visitor's miracles, manages a
reply:

> *Gideon:* Suddenly a black-bearded stranger appears at my elbow and
> shouts at me: "I am your God!" Well I find this all an unusual
> business . . . I will tell you plainly — I do not believe in gods.

So the issue of the play is joined and throughout his retelling of the
biblical story of the conquests of Gideon's armies Chayefsky simultane-
ously depicts God's continuing efforts to win Gideon's belief by granting
him prestige, victory, and loot, as well as God's continual demand that
Gideon demonstrate his faith by executing the Lord's seemingly arbitrary
instructions to the last detail. In the end, Gideon announces what he has
come to feel:

> *Gideon:* I do not love you, Lord . . . I tried to love you, but it is too
> much for me. You are too vast a concept for me. I cannot love you,
> God, for it makes me a meaningless thing . . . My Lord, it is
> elemental in me to aspire to be greater than myself . . . So I beg of
> you, my Lord — go from my sight. Make not your presence known
> to me again that I might say: "God is a dream, a name, a thought,
> but not a real thing."
> *The Angel:* But I am a real thing.
> *Gideon:* I would pretend that you were not.

Lest the play should end on this rather fearful note of man's rejection
of God, Chayefsky adds a final twist that has the intended result of leaving
God—and Chayefsky's Broadway audience—smiling and unperturbed.
In one brief moment the playwright turns man's disbelief in God into a
favor granted by God himself! Gideon, in his climactic torment, cries out:

> *Gideon:* Oh God, I cannot believe in you! If you love me let me believe
> at least in mine own self! If you love me, God!

And the Angel's upraised arm, about to strike the rebellious mortal, falls
to his side as he replies: "I love you, Gideon." A few moments later, God
ends the play with a resigned and amused chuckle, saying:

> *The Angel:*   God no more believes it odd
>   That man cannot believe in God.
>   Man believes the best he can,
>   Which means, it seems, belief in man.

Chayefsky's play purports to show how man has come to worship himself instead of God. But this popular playwright never attempts a true
dramatic depiction of so serious an idea as man's realization that he exists

for himself, alone in a godless universe. He concentrates instead on the appealing entertainment value of a fanciful and folksy relation between a man and a storybook patriarch-God who may be cranky and ridiculous but who is really as human and lovable as you and me.

In an article written for *The New York Times* before the opening of his drama *J.B.*,[4] which was awarded the Pulitzer prize as the best play of 1959, the poet-dramatist Archibald MacLeish explains why, in his case at least, it was essential that he make use of the Bible.

> A man may be forgiven for dramatizing an incident from the Bible and even for modernizing it in the process. But what I have done is not so easy to excuse. I have constructed a modern play inside the ancient majesty of the Book of Job much as the Bedouins, 30 years ago, used to build within the towering ruins of Palmyra their shacks of gasoline tins roofed with fallen stones.
>
> The Bedouins had the justification of necessity and I can think of nothing better for myself. When you are dealing with questions too large for you which, nevertheless, will not leave you alone, you are obliged to house them somewhere — and an old wall helps. . . . I badly needed an ancient structure in which to build the contemporary play which has haunted me for five years past and the structure of the poem of Job is the only one I know into which our modern history will fit. Job's search, like ours, was for the meaning of his afflictions.[5]

The form of MacLeish's *J.B.* is more complex than that of *Gideon*. If the dramatist, as he tells us, has housed his contemporary play about the meaning of affliction within the walls of the biblical story of Job, he has also located that story within another theatrical framework intended to make the story more vivid to modern American audiences. The scene of the play is described as "a travelling circus which has been on the roads of the world for a long time." Two broken-down actors, now vendors of popcorn and balloons, Mr Zuss and Mr Nickles, enact the roles of God and Satan in a version of the Job story played out in the circus ring.

There is no need then, in this play, to imagine and represent in any degree of naturalistic detail the actual world of the Old Testament events. The Bible story is used, in a modernized American setting, but the author avoids many of the awkwardnesses of biblical dramatization described earlier by not having to suggest that this is how people talked or behaved in ancient days. The language can be the freely expressive modern verse of an American poet and need not be an impossible mixture of King James Version sonorities and twentieth century rhythms. When Nickles and Zuss, as Satan or God, speaks actual lines from the Book of Job, it is in an

---

[4] Archibald MacLeish *J.B.* (New York, Samuel French 1958).

[5] Reprinted in *J.B.* p 6.

artificial manner, through actors' masks. These lines are treated as what they are, quotations from an ancient text, rather than in the usual unbelievable fashion of biblical drama, as anyone's, even God's, spontaneous utterance.

The most significant part of the story of Job for the dramatist MacLeish is the very end in which God restores the repentant Job. This restoration, or more precisely, the reasons for Job's *acceptance* of it after all he has been through are the playwright's central concerns.

> *Nickles:* Live his life again?
> Not even the most ignorant, obstinate,
> Stupid or degraded man
> This filthy planet ever farrowed,
> Offered the opportunity to live
> His bodily life twice over, would accept it —
> Least of all Job, poor trampled bastard!
> It can't be borne twice over!
> Can't be!
>
> *Zuss:* It is though. Time and again it is.
> Every blessed generation.
> Time and again!
> Time and again!

How can Job accept this? How can he agree to begin to live again? In the scene that follows, the final scene of the play, he searches for an answer. Mr Zuss has this to offer:

> *Zuss:* There is no resolution of the mystery
> Of unintelligible suffering but the dumb
> Bowed head that makes injustice just
> By yielding to the Will that willed it —
> Yielding to the Will that willed
> A world where there can be injustice.

But Job does not find this mute yielding acceptable or sufficient. He turns on Zuss and on Nickles as well who has counseled an opposite course of suicidal negation:

> *J.B.:* Neither the bowing nor the blood
> Will make an end for me now!
> Neither the
> Yes in ignorance . . .
> the No in spite . . .
> Neither of them!

At that point J.B.'s wife Sarah returns; it is through her that he finds an answer. And just as in the final moments of *Gideon*, it is the invocation of the magic word love that turns the tide.

J.B.:   We *are* and that is all our answer.
We are and what we are can suffer.
But . . .
        what suffers loves . . .
                And love
Will live its suffering again,
Risk its own defeat again,
Endure the loss of everything again
And yet again and yet again
In doubt, in dread, in ignorance, unanswered.
Over and over, with the dark before,
The dark behind it . . . And still live . . . Still love.

An example of a more formal verse play containing neither anachronistic colloquialisms as in *Gideon* nor devices aimed a very modern theatrical perspective, such as MacLeish's circus ring, is Christopher Fry's drama *The Firstborn*.[6] In this play about Moses, the Pharaoh, and their families, the author's intent is to set on stage an actual, theatrically believable, unsatirized Old Testament world. The stage directions tell us that the play's action takes place in the summer of 1200 BC, alternating between Pharaoh's palace and the tent of Miriam, the sister of Moses.

It goes without saying that the attempt at this sort of "believability" is itself a theatrical convention. Mr Fry, writing in the twentieth century, is no more interested in, nor capable of creating an historically authentic depiction of Egypt before the Exodus than Racine in the seventeenth century could have or would have wanted to bother with research into the precise military details of the Trojan war or the decor of Agamemnon's palace. Plays like *The Firstborn* are representative of what might be called a "classical-biblical" theatrical mode whose more or less formalized stage settings, costumes, and acting level, and whose tendency toward verse derive from some unique mixture of nineteenth-century romantic costume plays and modern psychological melodramas.

In its poetic language, *The Firstborn* exemplifies perfectly Esslin's description of the poetic avant-garde; it is made up of "images composed of a rich web of verbal associations." The playwright unashamedly seeks lyrical beauty for its own sake:

    Teusret: (The daughter of the Pharaoh, speaking to the body of her
        brother, the Pharaoh's firstborn son who has been struck dead,
        telling him of the arrival of his bride:)
        I have seen her. How can she be

---

[6] Christopher Fry *The Firstborn* (Cambridge, The University Press 1946; London, Oxford University Press 1952; London and New York, Oxford University 1958). Also in *Religious Drama* vol 1 ed, Martin Halverson (New York, Meridian Books 1957).

> Too late? Is beauty not a wand? Then
> We shall live again. Oh Ramases,
> I'm Teusret. Are you so taken with the dark
> That what has dazzled me won't open your eyes?
> I have whispered into your sleep at other times
> And you've heard me — Ramases,
> She has come so gifted for you, possessing
> A fable of rubies, and pearls like seeds of the moon,
> With metal and strange horns, ebon and ivory,
> Spilling chalcedonyx and male sapphires.
> Doesn't their brightness come to you? Do they glimmer
> Nowhere in the cupboards of your sleep?

The student of the techniques of biblical dramaturgy will note that whereas what the authors of *Gideon* and *J.B.* took from the Bible was a story, the author of *The Firstborn* has taken mainly the single character of Moses. To be sure, certain biblical events in the life of Moses are referred to in the course of the play, but virtually all of the play's plot—Moses' complex relations with the members of Egypt's ruling house and with his own sister Miriam and her son, as well as the specific events that surround the death of the Pharaoh's firstborn—are the work of the author's imagination. It is not only for a dramatizable story that a playwright may turn to the Bible but also for an idea of a character who may inspire what is actually, without absolutely ignoring or distorting the biblical tale, a new and original narrative of his own.

It takes only sixteen verses in the fourth chapter of Genesis to narrate the story of Cain and Abel, yet many short and even long plays have been written on the subject. A recent example is the one-act verse play *Cain* by the American poet Howard Nemerov. What Nemerov[7] takes from the Bible is not so much a plot as a single incident: Cain, jealous of his brother's favor in the eyes of God, kills Abel.

The dramatist does two things with this bare incident to transform it into the play he wishes to write. First, and relatively less important, he elaborates the details of the stark narrative furnished by Genesis. For example, the Bible simply says: "Cain was a tiller of the ground." And Nemerov opens his play with the following speech by Cain who enters the stage alone, carrying vegetables:

> *Cain:*   The corn is coming along,
>   tomatoes ripening up nicely, in a week
>   there should be melons. The apples
>   are still green, but, then, after what happened
>   it might be as well if apples were not mentioned.

---

[7] Howard Nemerov *Cain* in *The Tulane Drama Review* vol 4, no 2 (winter 1959) 12-26.

There is a good deal I don't understand
about that story, often as I've heard it told.
Mother doesn't like to discuss it, of course,
and I suspect that even my father
is not entirely clear as to what happened
though he wears a very wise expression.

In this same ironic and skeptical vein, the author makes his second and more important contribution. About the central incident itself he asks, in effect, "what might it *really* have been like? Why *did* Cain kill Abel?" This is a dramaturgy based on not taking the Bible at face value when it comes to explaining the *motives* for actors in the biblical narrative. A first inkling of what Nemerov is up to and what the point of his play will be comes when we learn to our surprise that God *encourages* Cain to commit mankind's first murder!

> God: Cain, Cain, I am trying to tell you.
> All things can be done, you must only
> do what you will. Things are as they are
> until you decide to change them.

And later in the play we see more fully the dramatist's personal view of the true significance of Cain's act. To Nemerov Cain is not a criminal but a necessary instrument of God in fulfilling man's destiny. As God banishes Cain, he tells him:

> God: I send you away, Cain. You are one
> of My holy ones, discoverer of limits,
> your name is the name of one of the ways,
> and you must bear it. . . .
> You are the discoverer of power, and you
> shall be honored among men that curse you.

In this manner the biblical dramatist urges and lures his audience into taking a fresh and wondering look at the possible meanings of an old and familiar Bible incident. His main tools are the believable, realistic details which make the reader feel that he is enjoying an unaccustomed close-up view of a story he has only known from afar and the deliberately theatrical shock of supplying unexpected motives for biblical actions which the reader has long supposed he understood.

As we have seen, there are comic elements in most of the serious poetic biblical dramas we have been examining. Chayefsky's picture of a cranky Old Testament deity; MacLeish's depiction of Job's three comforters as a priest, a Marxist, and a psychiatrist; Nemerov's speculations on the domestic relations of Adam and Eve—all are in some degree parodies of the conventional images of these biblical characters. In plays like the late

Clifford Odets' *The Flowering Peach*[8] or Wolf Mankowitz's *It Should Happen to a Dog*[9] the element of parody becomes dominant.

Though these two plays—one American and one English—differ considerably from each other, they have in common one idea which serves as the starting point for their parody. It must have occurred to the authors of these plays, and no doubt to other writers as well, that many biblical characters, especially in the Old Testament, are *Jewish,* and that there might be comic potential in depicting them as one or another type of modern, twentieth-century Jew.

That Noah lived at a time when there were not yet any Jews did not seem to bother Clifford Odets. He made the hero of *The Flowering Peach* into a recognizably American-Jewish first-generation immigrant paterfamilias. Odets' Noah is a henpecked but loving husband who occasionally drinks a little too much, addresses his wife as "old friend of mine" and has troubles with his sons, especially that ne'er do well Ham and that sensitive baby Japheth.

Odets is very skillful with his limited and controlled use of anachronism. Noah's home, as the author describes the play's first act setting, resembles an apartment in the Bronx more than it depicts any imaginary antedeluvian dwelling place, yet no one in it actually asks for a glass of seltzer. It is mostly through their speech rhythms, their emotionalism, and their behavior in family situations that Odets makes his characters modern Jewish parodies of biblical personages. The Broadway production of *The Flowering Peach* featured the veteran Yiddish theatre comedian Menasha Skulnik as Noah, which made Odets' parody all the more obvious. But even without such a performer to create the role, this Noah, as written, is a close relative of Mr Berger in Odets' drama of Jewish family life in the depression, *Awake and Sing!*

Both Odets' Noah and Mankowitz's Jonah B. Ammittai resemble the Yiddish writer Sholom Aleichem's immortal character Tevya the Dairyman in that they engage in conversations with God that are meant to show a relationship at once intimate and long suffering, a relationship in which the browbeaten little man is not afraid to take the Lord to task and to scold Him for His irritating and impossible demands, like building an ark, or going to preach against Nineveh. Unfortunately, neither Odets nor Mankowitz (nor Chayefsky who also attempts something along this line) is the equal of Sholom Aleichem in creating such dialogues.

[8] Clifford Odets *The Flowering Peach* (New York, Brandt & Brandt Dramatic Department 1954) [typescript]. Unpublished manuscript is property of the author's estate.

[9] Wolf Mankowitz *It Should Happen to a Dog* in *Religious Drama* vol 3 ed, Martin Halverson (New York, Meridian Books 1959).

It Should Happen to a Dog, which its author calls a "serio-comic strip," is perhaps the broadest parody among our examples. It presents Jonah as a Jew from London's East End, a travelling salesman, the modern equivalent of a wandering preacher. When it comes to the use of anachronism, Mankowitz goes all the way:

> *Jonah:* (to God) Certainly, I'm on my way. By ship. You expect me to fly? If you are so clever and in such a hurry, make me sprout a couple of wings so I'll take off. It's quicker by air. But so far is only invented the ship.

Jonah's climactic exchange with the archangel who informs him that the Lord will spare Nineveh after all reads like a scene from a vaudeville comedian's routine:

> *Jonah:* If you don't mind a question . . .
> *Angel:* Any help I can give you.
> *Jonah:* If God knew right from the start exactly what He is going to do about everything — right?
> *Angel:* That's right.
> *Jonah:* Then he knows he isn't going to destroy Nineveh. Right?
> *Angel:* Right!
> *Jonah:* Then what does he want of my life? What's the point of all this expensive business with whales and palm trees and so on?
> *Angel:* You mankind, you can't see no further than your nose.
> *Jonah:* So what's the answer?
> *Angel:* You see — (long pause) frankly, I don't know.
> *Jonah:* It should happen to a dog.

A play that is worthy of special notice — though it would be found in this volume only as a foreign play in English translation — is *Barabbas*,[10] written in 1928 by the late Belgian dramatist Michel de Ghelderode (1898-1962). In what may very well prove to be one of the outstanding biblical dramas of this century, this unusual playwright cuts across the categories we have employed in our brief survey, creating a serious poetic drama which, however, makes use of some grotesquely comic biblical parody.

Commissioned to write an Easter play for a Flemish folk theatre in Brussels, Ghelderode, as was often his wont, approached the traditional materials in an unique and startling way. No conventional passion play, *Barabbas* pictures the events leading up to the crucifixion from the point of view of Jerusalem's underworld. The king of that underworld, the notorious bandit and killer Barabbas, becomes the central figure of this

---

10 Michel de Ghelderode *Barabbas* in *Seven Plays* (New York, Hill and Wang 1960)

Easter play, rather than Jesus who is seen briefly and who never speaks. The progress of the play is the gradual awakening of human consciousness in the mind and heart of the murderer Barabbas. In the first act he is a caged beast. He shares a prison cell with some men who, like himself, are condemned to die the next morning. He rages, sings, drinks, defies his jailers, and cruelly taunts his cellmates, all except the strange and silent Jesus whose presence unsettles him and upsets his bravado.

The language of *Barabbas*, even in translation from the original French, is extremely powerful. Though not in verse, the play is a colorful, flamboyant poetic work, the author attempting a richness of language that would be the literary equivalent of the paintings of the Flemish masters Pieter Breughel and Hieronymus Bosch in whose artistic tradition Ghelderode placed himself.

The second act of *Barabbas* contains the one scene based on actual biblical material, the Gospels' account of the crowd's choice of Barabbas as the one who will be set free and Jesus as the one who will be crucified. While Ghelderode does make use of this scene it is noteworthy that he places the crowd offstage and the actual choosing off to one side so as to focus the main theatrical attention on the private, off-the-record manipulations of the corrupt authorities who are determined to sway the populace and assure the death of Jesus.

The play's third act is one of the most remarkable creations in the more than thirty plays comprising Ghelderode's collected drama. Its setting is the *bottom* of the hill of Calvary at the hour of the crucifixion — once again the exact opposite of the inevitable locale of the final scene in conventional passion plays. At the foot of the hill, while the crowds have gathered up above, a circus barker (called by Ghelderode, in French, *le Barnum*) and his clown have set up a sideshow tent in which they proceed to present a hideously comic parody of what is taking place on the hill.

Barabbas arrives on the scene. He is only beginning to understand what has happened. He is confused by his freedom and does not know what to do. Thus the central dramatic and philosophical question of the play is posed: if man is free (and what Ghelderode has drawn from the Bible is the character of Barabbas who is nothing else but the man set free) then what is he to do with his freedom? What will give his life meaning?

The scenes that follow present Barabbas with a series of alternative answers. The barker and clown offer the now famous Barabbas a chance to make a fortune by joining in their act, converting his celebrity into cash. The apostle Peter offers him religious faith as an alternative, just as the decadent King Herod suggests a life of escape into sensual pleasure. Barabbas is finally brought to a deep awareness of his own spirit's awakening, only to be betrayed and killed by the little clown who is the mocker and the mockery of Jesus, the symbol of light towards which Barabbas has been moving.

In *Barabbas* Ghelderode has recapitulated and employed almost all of the dramaturgical techniques we have seen in the work of other biblical playwrights. He has taken characters and incidents directly from scripture and placed them on stage. But he has also imagined and furnished new characters and realistic detail to elaborate with his own imagination what the biblical narrative might only imply. He has succeeded better than most in finding a language that is believable for his characters and rich enough in color and poetic power for his theatrical purposes. He has used anachronism with careful control. He has turned traditional material upside down and inside out to cause his audience to see new and provocative possibilities in an already well known story. He has *used* a biblical framework to convey a highly personal play on the subject of man's freedom. Ghelderode's *Barabbas* may stand as a model of what is possible in making use of the Bible as a source and an inspiration for modern drama.

THE BIBLE IN ENGLISH DRAMA

INTRODUCTION

EVERY student of the Bible as literature has discerned in it nearly all the archtypes of literary forms — epic prose, lyric poetry, the short story, and historical narrative. There is a decided attempt at drama in the Song of Songs, and particularly in the Book of Job. Some scholars [1] have maintained in recent times that the Book of Job is a Greek tragedy in Hebrew, modeled after Euripides. But while it may be doubted, as is done by a certain eminent authority, whether the Bible contains a perfect drama,[2] it has in all ages and all languages served as a great source for dramatic compositions. The multiplicity of plots in the Bible and the variety of human emotions, vices, and virtues portrayed in them account for the multitude and diversity of Biblical plays throughout English literature.[3] Every type of the drama is represented, from the earliest liturgical plays to the most recent marionette plays and plays for radio presentation. Moreover, the availability of the Bible as a source book is obvious. Even the unschooled have always been more or less aware of the Bible and it has been better known than any other classic possibly could be. Biblical plays were also used for didactic and dogmatic purposes. By means of Bible stories, dramatized, a large number of religiously-minded authors aimed not only at inculcating moral truths but also at preaching certain religious dogmas.

In modern times the Old Testament rather than the New was used, because the less sacred character of the former, from the Christian point of view, encouraged its use for secular literary treatment. After the period of the miracle plays, the central character of the New Testament was felt, by the average author, to be too awe-inspiring for literary treatment, let alone stage production. With the possible exception of Milton's *Samson Agonistes*, none of the English plays based on the Bible can be considered a great masterpiece of literature. Though not called upon to ascribe a reason for it, one ventures to suggest that it is due to the difficulty of improving on the Bible. One may wonder why Shakespeare, well acquainted as he is considered to have been with the contents of the Sacred Scriptures, did not attempt to base a play on a Biblical episode. Perhaps he did well to steer clear of religious topics at a time when religion was in the arena of bitter politics, but it is not unlikely that some one of the host of Shakespearean scholars has answered the question more satisfactorily.

---

[1] See H. M. Kallen, *The book of Job as a Greek tragedy*. New York, 1918.

[2] See D. B. Macdonald, "The drama in Semitic literature," in *Biblical World*, 1895, n.s., v. 5, p. 16–28.

[3] No dramatization in English of the majestic story narrated in Judges, ch. 19 is known to the writer. Prof. H. A. Wolfson has called his attention to two Hebrew dramas based on this episode, each named *Pillegesh ba-Gibeah* ("The concubine in Gibeah"), one by David Samosćz, Breslau, 1818, and another by Leo Mekler, described as a historic tragedy, in four acts, Warsaw: Tuschijah, 1899.

If there be any virtue in the first of anything, it is not amiss to point out here that the first attempt at the dramatization of a Biblical topic was made before the Christian era — the *Exodus* of the Jewish Hellenistic poet Ezekielos (fl. 200–100 B. C.), preserved to posterity in fragments in the writings of Eusebius who in turn copied it from the lost work of Alexander Polyhistor. The episode of Mak and his sheep-stealing in the *Secunda Pastorum* of the Towneley cycle is the first comedy in the English language. Mrs. C. C. Stopes points out [4] that the comedy of *Jacob and Esau,* written sometime between 1537 and 1568, is the first English play that has dispensed with the allegorical treatment which characterized the earlier Moralities, the first to be divided into acts and numerous scenes, and the first one that has given a list of dramatis personae and has prescribed suitable attire for them.

The beginnings of English drama have their foundation not in classical or humanist models but in the liturgical services of the mediaeval Christian church. The liturgical drama was created, partly because of instinctive need for it, and partly through the desire of the clergy to supplement by means of mimic action the Latin service not completely understandable by the masses — "in order to fortify the unlearned people in their faith." The church occasions for such dramatic renditions, especially in the later period, were various and numerous, but originally they took place on the three cardinal dates of the Church — Christmas, Good Friday, and Easter, commemorating the birth, the death, and the resurrection of Jesus.

A series of rules, known to us as *Concordia Regularis,* devised by Ethelwold, Bishop of Winchester, during the reign of Edgar (959–979) describes the ceremony which is to form a part of the Easter service, and gives a liberal scenario and stage directions for three priests who are to simulate the three Marys in their search for Jesus in his tomb. A priest arrayed in white, representing an angel, sitting in the tomb greets them:

> Whom do you seek in the sepulchre?
>
> They: Jesus of Nazareth.
>
> He: He is not here; He has risen even as He predicted.
> Go and announce that He has risen from the dead.

At the turn of his bidding, the three turn to the choir and say: "Alleluja! the Lord has risen." This said, the angel recalls them with the anthem, "Come and see the place." He lifts the veil, shows them the sepulchre, bare of the cross, with only the cloth in which the cross was wrapped. The three priests take the cloth, lift it up in face of the congregation to demonstrate that the Lord is no longer on the cross, then sing the anthem *Surrexit Dominus,* and lay the cloth on the altar. A *Te Deum laudamus* is sung, and all the bells chime out together. Dialogued chanting and mimic action have here come together. The two essentials of true

---

4 In *Athenæum,* London, 1900, v. 115, p. 538–540.

drama have been fulfilled — the presentation of a story in action and the impersonation of the character concerned — and the mystical liturgy has thus been recreated into a liturgical mystery. Of course, it never entered the minds of the priests or the deacons, whoever the performers may have been, that they were acting or performing, feigning or playing, but it is in fact exactly what they were doing.

Similar to the passion-play *Quem quaeritis in sepulchro* described above, in which the sepulchre was the central property, is the *Quem quaeritis in praesepe* on Christmas in which the manger is the central point of interest. A praesepe or crib is placed behind the altar, facing the image of the Virgin. Boys representing angels, perched aloft, sing the "good tidings" and *Gloria in excelsis*. The shepherds, three or more in number, come to the crib and are met with *Quem quaeritis* by two priests representing midwives. A colloquy ensues. Finally the shepherds turn to the audience saying or chanting: "Now we know in very truth that the Christ is born into the world," and the drama ends. Besides the Sepulchre and the Pastores plays — the former exist in no less than 228 varying manuscripts — other liturgical plays have come down to us. Such are the *Lamentatio Rachel,* motivated on the Biblical planctus: "Rachel weeping for her children refused to be comforted" (Jeremiah 31.15), and associated in the church liturgy with the Slaughter of the Innocents episode for performance on Epiphany or Innocents Day (December 28); the *Tres Reges, Magi, Herodes,* variations of the *Stellae* group in which the characters are Herod, the wise men, sometimes also a messenger and a soldier, as narrated in Matthew 2: 1–15; the *Peregrini* play of varying content, sometimes confined to the Journey to Emmaus and the supper there, sometimes joined to the episode of the Incredulity of Thomas and the apparition to him, and at still other times where Christ himself and the three Marys appear as speakers; the *Prophetae* group, in which the characters are the prophets of the Old Testament, each of whom, together with Virgil and the Sibyl, are called upon to testify from their respective writings to the divinity of Christ. Other plays of lesser frequence on themes which the clerics probably considered as of minor significance are available, such as *Isaac et Rebecca,* or *Conversio Beati Pauli Apostoli,* designed for the feast on January 25, and numerous others. One such play, significant because of snatches of vernacular introduced into the body of the Latin text, is the *Suscitatio Lazari* by Hilarius, a pupil, about 1125, of the famous Abelard, and considered by many scholars to have been an Englishman. This last play is the only one which bears an author's name; all the others are anonymous.

Professor Adolphus W. Ward enumerates [5] three stages in the gradual development of the mystery-drama. The first stage is the substitution of the vernacular for the Latin tongue, in which hitherto all plays were composed. The second stage is the detachment of a given play from the church service of which it originally formed a part and its enactment as an independent play. The third

---

5 In his *A history of English dramatic literature to the death of Queen Anne.* London, 1899, v. 1, p. 40–41.

stage consisted in joining together different plays based on Scriptural themes into a series or group of plays to form a collective mystery or, as we know them in English literature, into a cycle. The first stage is exemplified so far as England is concerned, in the three *Shrewsbury Fragments,* discovered in 1890 by Professor W. W. Skeat.[6] The first fragment, an *Officium Pastores* of 50 lines, is an actor's copy and gives therefore only the words of the character he plays — that of the third shepherd. The second fragment is an *Officium Resurrectionis* and the words are those of the third Mary. The third fragment is a *Peregrini* liturgical drama and the words, according to Professor Skeat, are those of Cleophas. There is no evidence that the *Shrewsbury Fragments* can be ascribed to the town of Shrewsbury; the suggestion has been made that they are the remains of the lost Beverley cycle. Our main interest concerns the third stage spoken of by Professor Ward, the combination of the individual liturgical plays into a collection forming a cycle. Unlike the early liturgical plays common to all Christian countries of continental Europe, these cycles are neither translations from nor copies of foreign models. In their development and formation they constitute the main characteristic of the English religious drama. Each cycle embraces the entire course of Biblical history from Creation to the Day of Judgment and each was performed annually by the guilds or trade companies of a particular town on Corpus Christi day or on other Church festival days. Four such cycles have come down to us — York, Chester, Towneley or Wakefield, and the so-called "Coventry," by some scholars called "Hegge" or "N-towne." Other cycles, such as Beverley and Dublin, are known to us only by the surviving registers of titles. Professor Edmund K. Chambers gives a list of 36 plays dated 1520 for the first and a list of 17 dated 1498 for the second.

Besides the four Middle-English cycles, Cornwall has a group of pageants written in the native Cymric dialect. Because of its comprehensive compass of Biblical history it is by some scholars considered as a cycle group. With the exception of an epic poem on the Passion of Christ it constitutes the sole remains of the ancient Cymric language; and it bears the same relation to this epic poem as does the York cycle to the epic narrative *Cursor Mundi.* In each case the group of plays exhibits a close parallel to the respective epics. The Cornish drama is divided into three parts: *Origo Mundi, Passio Domini Nostri,* and *Resurrexio Domini Nostri,* designed to occupy three days in the presentation. The first part begins with Creation and ends with the building of the temple by Solomon, who rewards the workmen with Cornish parishes and consecrates a bishop to take care of it. This anachronism is typical of all the English cycles; some of them are of a most curious and amusing but historically instructive nature. There follows a long skip of Biblical narrative after Solomon; the birth and childhood of Jesus are not treated. Instead, the second part begins with the Temptation of Christ and the events from the Entry into Jerusalem onward through its third part ending with the Ascension of Christ. Running through all the three parts, but especially detailed in the first, is the legend of the origin of the wood of the Cross.

---

6 See his letter in *The Academy,* v. 37, p. 10–11.

The York plays though not mentioned before 1378 were in progress for a considerable time before. The stations assigned to the various pageants of the cycle in the year 1394 are spoken of as *assignatis antiquis* (in ancient times). The Chester cycle is believed to have originated in 1328 although there is no actual record of it till 1462. The principal part of the so-called Coventry cycle manuscript was written in 1468. No date for the Towneley cycle is available, except that the preserved manuscript is deemed to be of the late fourteenth or early fifteenth century. Three of the four cycles exist in complete form in single manuscripts. The Chester plays are available in five slightly varying manuscripts. The Towneley manuscript is owned in this country, having been acquired in 1922 by Henry E. Huntington.[7] It is now one of the treasures of the Huntington Library and Art Gallery, San Marino, California.

The occasions on which the cycle plays were performed were various. The most popular was Corpus Christi day instituted in 1264 but not strictly enjoined till 1311 by a decree of the Council of Vienne. Since this day falls within a few weeks of the longest day of the year it became highly convenient for the presentation of the long cycles. The Chester and the Coventry cycles were performed annually on Whitsuntide. Certain single plays were staged on certain holy or Saints' days. Evidence, both philological and external, points to East Anglia as the district where the religious drama was most assiduously cultivated. However, nearly every section of England is well represented, not to speak of Edinburgh in Scotland and Dublin across the Irish Sea. Cornwall in the southwest and Newcastle-upon-Tyne in the far north, York, Wakefield, and Beverley to the north, Chester to the west, and Coventry in the Midlands, all testify to the geographical ubiquity of the miracle plays.

Besides the collected series we possess isolated plays two of which, the *Harrowing of Hell* and the *Brome Abraham and Isaac,* are worth passing mention. The first, apocryphal in its subject, dates from the reign of Edward III, if not earlier, and is considered the first dramatic poem in the English language. It is preserved among the Harleian manuscripts in the British Museum, and differs in minute particulars from two other and even more ancient manuscripts — one in the Advocates' Library at Edinburgh, and the other among the Digby manuscripts in the British Museum. The *Brome Abraham and Isaac* play is one of six plays on that subject. Each of the four great cycles includes one, and a separate version exists at Trinity College, Dublin, known as the *Dublin Abraham.* No two are alike. The popularity of the theme may be accounted for by the human and pathetic interest of the story and by the mystic mediaeval interpretation of Isaac as a type of the suffering Christ. Others ascribe the variety of its versions to the Church's desire to inculcate obedience as a cardinal virtue. Two other *Abraham and Isaac* titles are extant in the lost Beverley and Dublin cycles. Besides these, Arthur Golding translated one from the French of Theodore Beza, in 1575. The Brome version is superior to all the others "in touches of child nature and the varied play

---

[7] See *Modern Language Association of America, Publications.* Menasha, Wisconsin, 1928, v. 42, p. 137–152.

of feeling skilfully shown — the dear coquetting between the love of his child and the committal of the deed by the obedient but agonized father." [8] The Dublin text, unlike all the others, introduces Sarah as a character.

The early English religious drama offers to the literary student a wide field for research and study. What were the processes that were responsible for the secularization of liturgical plays which involved the changes from Latin into English, and performance by the laity of the guilds instead of by the ecclesiastics in the church building, as formerly? What was the nature of that theological bias which even then objected to the staging of sacred plays outside the church (Robert Mannyng in his *Handlyng Synne*)? How were they staged, by whom, and at exactly what part of the service in the church or on what days of the year in the case of the cyclical plays? Then there are the literary questions connected with the cycles and the non-cycle plays, such as the introduction of comic elements and apocryphal matter from Christian legends into themes patently copied from the Scriptures, or the development of the characteristics which became the distinguishing marks of each cycle as to language, locality, and literary worth. These and a host of other problems are well known to every student of this period of our literature. They have been masterfully discussed and in good part solved in the works of J. P. Collier, A. W. Ward, E. K. Chambers, A. W. Pollard, and the editors of the various cycles in the editions of the Early English Text Society.[9] It would be superfluous to repeat the discussion here.

In the cyclical plays the Old Testament is subordinated to the New. Each cycle begins with *Creation* followed by the *Temptation of Adam and Eve*. Then come the episodes of *Cain and Abel* and the *Sacrifice of Isaac*, which well suited certain Christological interpretations, and the subject matter of the New Testament is soon reached. Thus, in the York cycle only eleven out of forty-eight plays treat of the Old Testament; in the Coventry cycle, six out of forty-two; in the Towneley, six out of thirty; and in the Chester, six out of twenty-five. This is perhaps as it should have been. The mediaeval church which inspired these plays was not interested primarily in the Old Testament. It was the New Testament which supplied its inspiration, and from it streamed all ecclesiastical authority — that of the highest prince of the Church as well as that of the most humble priest or monk. The Old Testament characters in the early English religious drama were treated reverently, at rarer times humorously, but never contemptuously. This atmosphere changes suddenly as soon as the Jewish characters in the New Testament are reached, i. e., those who were not the disciples or followers of Jesus. To understand the reason for this change a few remarks are not out of place.

That the Jew should figure in the religious plays in the inimical and hostile attitude of the Gospel towards him (Caiaphas, Annas, Judas) was to be expected. But in addition he figures therein as presented in literature to the mediaeval man of culture. From the *Cursor Mundi* he was known as a bloody usurer; from

---

[8] See L. T. Smith, *A Common-place book of the fifteenth century.* London, 1886, p. 48.

[9] The present survey of the miracle plays is based largely on A. W. Ward, cited *ante*, v. 1, p. 48–99 and Sir E. K. Chambers, *The Mediaeval stage.* Oxford, 1903, v. 2.

Gower's *Confessio Amantis,* as a swindler and thief ("I am a Jew and be mi lawe I schall to noman be felawe") ; and from the *Miracles of Our Lady,* as stiff-necked and obstinate in his theology ("for no gold that mihte him geve, chaunge wolde not he"). In the current legends of the Jews' desecration of the Host he carried his theological obstinacy into action. England, moreover, was the original home of the libel of blood-accusation (Little St. William of Norwich, 1144; Harold of Gloucester, 1168; Little Robert of Bury-St.-Edmunds, 1181; and Little St. Hugh of Lincoln, 1255). This wretched business was immortalized by none less than the father of English poetry in the Prioress' tale of the *Canterbury Tales* ("Our first foe, the serpent Satan that hath in Jews his wasp's nest," "Cursed Jew, cursed folk").

One more illuminating bit of psychology. In the year 1211 King John is said to have ordered the teeth of a certain Jew from Bristol pulled out, one each day, till he should make contribution of ten thousand marks to the royal treasury. Thomas Fuller (1608–1661) commenting on this episode 444 years later, in 1655, characteristically remarked, "Condemn we here man's cruelty, and admire Heaven's justice; for all these sums extorted from the Jews by temporal kings are but paying their arrearages to God for a debt they can never satisfy; namely, the crucifying of Christ." [10] This instance is cited as a not unfair commentary on the Christian attitude towards things Jewish in earlier days. If so notable a Christian historian and poet permitted himself to pen such thoughts at the time he did, it need surprise us little to behold such notions holding sway over the clerical mind in the much less enlightened age when the miracle plays had their being.

There were no Jews in England, at least none recognizable as such, during the period of the rise and progress of the miracle plays in that country, their expulsion having taken place in 1290 and their return in 1656. No living models, therefore, were at hand and none were needed. The author of the plays conceived the Jews in the light of the Gospel story of the Crucifixion. They had a further authority in St. Paul's Epistle to the Romans (2: 21–25). Did not the apostle enumerate therein the vices of the Jews — stealing, adultery, sacrilege, blasphemy? Whichever way the Christian turned, his senses were fed with atrocities of which the Jew was the reputed author. The church art, such as it then was in England, contributed to the vicious picture of the Jew. What the monk and the priest preached and described and what the sculptor and the carver reproduced in their grotesquely distorted figures, the author and the performer of the miracle play represented on the stage as it then existed.[11]

One can accordingly appreciate the full force of the allusions to the Jews in the liturgical plays — *nequam gens Judaica* ("vile race of Jews"), *plebs execranda* ("detestable people"), *gens dampnanda* ("accursed race"), *Judaeorum turbae*

---

10 Thomas Fuller, *The Church history of Britain, edited by J. S. Brewer.* Oxford, 1845, v. 2, p. 147.

11 See Paul Weber, *Geistliches Schauspiel und kirchliche Kunst in ihrem Verhältnis erläutert an einer Ikonographie der Kirche und Synagoge.* Stuttgart, 1894.

fallaces ("lying host of the Jews"), "that Judaea the guilty is destroyed this choir is rejoiced" (a refrain sung a dozen times in one of the *Prophetae* plays). Space forbids pointing out all the references in the Passion episodes of the English cycles which testify to their rabid anti-Jewishness. The so-called Coventry cycle, the most ecclesiastical and least literary of all, is truest to type. In the *Crucifixion* pageant of that cycle the stage directions provide for a dance around the Cross, which an eminent scholar describes as "a comic intermezzo, a grotesque dance, performed with the accompaniment of music." In the Latin register of plays of the York cycle as staged in the year 1415, reproduced by L. T. Smith in her *York plays* and translated by A. W. Pollard in his *English miracle plays,* no less than fifty references are given to the word "Jews" and to Jewish names. All the harrowing details of Jews scourging, binding, flogging, and otherwise maltreating Jesus are enumerated in the fashion of a very detailed working scenario.

Professor Wilhelm M. A. Creizenach in his *Geschichte des neueren Dramas* [12] tells how certain German municipalities enacted provisions for the protection of the Jews against the populace during the season of the performance of religious plays. In some cases decrees were promulgated that no plays were to be written about the Jews which may cause "inen laster oder schande." Apparently the Seligmanns and the Liebermanns, contemporary names used for the Jewish dramatis personae in the German miracle and mystery plays, must have protested to or pleaded with the Frankfort and Freiburg city fathers. No such untoward incidents took place in England, for the very good reason that there were no Jews in England to be protected against Christian pillage as a result of a too realistic passion play. No physical massacre could possibly be visited upon Jews in merrie England from 1290 to 1656. Instead, a more grievous result ensued. The seeds of a higher form of anti-Jewishness were planted deep and wide in the rich domain of English drama. Barabas and Shylock and a host of others coming down well towards the end of the nineteenth century are, in their viciousness and comicality, their more than ludicrous dress and execrable dialect, but the direct heirs of the Jew as portrayed in the early miracle plays.

The Biblical stories of Samson and David and the Josephus account of Herod and Mariamne have at all times provided favorite material for dramatizations. These are selected here for brief comment.

From Henslowe's *Diary* we know that Samuel Rowley (d. 1633) in collaboration with William Bourne or one Edward Juby, wrote a *Sampson* play. Another diary entry by a German nobleman traveling in England states that on September 15, 1602, he witnessed the performance of "eine tragica comoedia von Samsone und den halben Stamm Benjamin." The Stonyhurst pageant of *Samson* dates also from about the same time. The most notable dramatization of the subject, however, is the *Samson Agonistes* of Milton, 1671. It has a threefold interest: first, as an important experiment in English poetry, in that it attempts to transplant Attic tragedy in its most perfect form into English literature; second, as a dramatic poem of intrinsic literary merit; and third, as shadowing the personal

---

[12] Halle a.S., 1893–1916, 6 vol.

history and feelings of the poet himself. The blind and lonely Danite is an almost perfect prototype of the balked and apparently defeated Milton of the Restoration.

In addition to the many incidents in David's life as narrated in I and II Samuel, there arose many legends about him originating in Jewish and Christian tradition. These sources gave rise to many plays on the David theme: David and Saul, David and Goliath, David and Jonathan, David and Bathsheba, David and Absalom, and David and Nabal.

The theme of the love of Herod for Mariamne, combined with the struggles of the Herodian and Maccabaean families, has been a favorite topic for the dramatists from the earliest days to the present time. The first English version is the drama entitled *The Tragedie of Mariam the faire queene of Jewry,* printed 1612, by Lady Elizabeth Cary. Among the modern Herod plays Stephen Phillips' beautifully poetic drama enjoys a deservedly high reputation. It has much of the majestic quality of an Elizabethan drama:

> I dreamed last night of a dome of beaten gold
> To be a counter glory to the Sun
> There shall the eagle blindly dash himself
> There the first beam shall strike, and there the moon
> Shall aim all night long her argent archery;
> And it shall be the tryst of sundered stars
> The haunt of dead and dreaming Solomon
> Shall send a light upon the lost in Hell
> And flashings upon faces without hope.[13]

The improbable Herod of the Gospel story is left far behind and a more human Herod, no better but no worse than the rulers of his time, takes his place. Having been an actor, Phillips had a flair for the theatre and stagecraft, and his *Herod* produced by Sir Herbert Beerbohm Tree in 1901 had a long run on the English, and later, the American stage. Phillips' *Sin of David,* 1904, based on a love-story of the Civil Wars in England, may be mentioned here as indicative of a vogue among dramatists, and fiction writers as well, to give Biblical titles to otherwise non-Biblical works.

The last section in this bibliography lists Jewish Festival plays. The most popular of them, the Purim plays, mostly based on the book of Esther may be taken as typical of the rest. The story of the vindictive hatred of Haman, directed not against an individual, but against a whole nation, the dramatic suddenness of Haman's downfall and the delivery of the Jews through the rise of one of their own to royal favor, vividly impressed mediaeval Jews who were exposed daily to similar national dangers in the diasporas of Europe, and the date thereof was seized upon as the one occasion of the religious year for tomfoolery and

---

[13] Herod speaking, act III.

merriment. Unlike the miracle plays of Christian Europe, the Esther or Purim plays of the Jews did not originate among the religious leaders nor were they performed in or near the synagogue. They were not deemed of a sacred character, and were produced in the presence of the people assembled at the home of some leading member of the community. The ten sons of Haman provided the comic characters, while Mordecai, Esther, and Harbonah were cast as the heroes. Along with the story of Esther another favorite theme for dramatic presentation during the Purim period was the story of the sale of Joseph by his brothers, Joseph's subsequent rise to glory and the revelation of himself to his brothers in Egypt.

Up to within the last two decades of the last century the Esther and Joseph plays existed only in Hebrew, Judaeo-German, and German. With the establishment of a large number of Jewish communities in this country and the consequent rise of a younger American-born and English-speaking generation arose the need for festival plays in English. A large and varied assortment of such plays is now in existence. They are mostly juvenile in character, being designed for production by school children, and are based on the holidays commemorating the early history of the Israelites, such as Passover, Feast of Tabernacles (Succoth), Shabuoth (the giving of the Law on Mt. Sinai), Hanukkah (the Maccabaean victory over the Hellenic Syrians), Chamisho Osor (the Jewish traditional new year for trees), and other dates in the Jewish religious calendar. Their authorship has been inspired largely by Jewish educational and patriotic organizations under the influence of the Zionist movement and the Hebrew renaissance in Palestine. These festival plays cannot be considered as a continuation of the early Purim plays, being different in spirit, in method and literary form. Very few of them can lay claim to high literary merit.

*   *   *   *   *

The scope and plan of arrangement of this bibliography on the Bible in the English Drama need explanation. Originally it formed part of a larger work dealing with the Jew as a subject in English drama; it is now given here as an independent work. Its aim is to offer a complete and annotated list of English plays dealing with Biblical themes, including translations from other languages, based on the material available at The New York Public Library and in the compiler's own collection. Whenever a copy of a desired play was not available at either of these two sources, the Library of Congress and the catalogue of the British Museum were made use of. A very limited number of entries from other libraries were also included, for the sake of completeness. All entries bear the class-mark of The New York Public Library or the name of the library from which they were taken. Those not so marked are from the compiler's own collection. When an entry was recorded from an outside source only one edition, the earliest, was listed. The term "dramatic composition" was used in its most comprehensive sense. Any errors of judgment will be found to be in the direction of too great inclusiveness, rather than that of rejections. The test of any work for its inclusion was the existence of speeches in character, provided it had an inherent dramatic element in it, or was primarily intended for the stage or public entertainment. Mere dialogues which postulate no mimic accompaniment were excluded, but monologues designed primarily for public or stage presentation were included. The object being to dig out the less known and the less formally dramatic pieces to illustrate the ramifications of Biblical interest throughout the entire range of English dramatic literature, this list is designed to afford a place for every possible work which can lay claim to any of the criteria of a drama. It was not, however, easy to adhere to a definite rule, and certain exceptional cases were decided on their own merits.

The Old Testament plays are arranged according to the Hebrew canon of the Scriptures, beginning with Genesis and ending with Nehemiah. Under each book the plays are again arranged under incidents in the order given in each book. Thus, under Genesis are placed *Creation, Adam and Eve, Cain and Abel,* etc. Between the Old and New Testaments are placed those plays based on the Jewish Apocrypha (arranged according to the English Protestant version). No plays based on the Christian Apocrypha were found excepting several miracle plays about the Virgin Mary based largely on early Christian tradition. Due to the fact that the history of some of the more important characters, such as Moses and David, is contained in more than one book, it has been necessary, in the case of the Moses plays, to combine the last four books of the Pentateuch into one section, Exodus-Deuteronomy; and, in the case of the David plays, to combine the two books of Samuel into one. It was also found necessary to place several of the plays based on minor incidents out of chronological order and arrange them at the beginning of a given book along with those plays based on the book as a whole. The intention was to avoid many headings for which only a few plays were discovered.

The books of the Old Testament provided for the purposes of the list a chronological sequence of the events dramatized in the plays based upon them. Not so, however, is the case with the New Testament. The four Gospels containing a record of the life of Jesus largely supplement each other. The incident or incidents in one Gospel on which a play has been written has its parallel in many instances in one or all of the Gospel narratives. Therefore it has not been possible to arrange the plays in the order of the several Gospels, Matthew, Mark, Luke, and John. A connected view of the Gospel narrative was made necessary. Such a harmony for the purposes of the bibliography was found in the chapter headed "A synopsis of Gospel history," in *The Cambridge companion to the Bible,* published by the Cambridge University Press, 1905, p. 334–346. All the events recorded in the four Gospels are there numbered, and 180 incidents are chronologically set down. The New Testament plays are arranged in the order of incident as given in this Cambridge Harmony.

Some of the miracle plays on the Virgin are based not on incidents in the New Testament but on early tradition of the Church. On this account the plays about the Virgin, even those based on incidents occurring after the death of Jesus, were all brought together at the beginning of the New Testament. Following this is the Nativity group. Then comes the Infancy and Childhood of Jesus. This was divided into five sections: "Visit of the Magi," "Flight into Egypt," "Slaughter of the Innocents," "Presentation in the Temple," and "Jesus and the Doctors," the latter incident taking place when He was twelve years old. From this time until Jesus was thirty years old there is a period about which we know nothing whatever. These are the hidden years of Jesus. Next comes the "Ministry of Jesus," from the "Calling of St. John the Baptist" to the "Supper at Bethany." This period is covered by incidents 17–152; and, of the 135 incidents recorded, 34 have been discovered to provide a basis for ascertainable plays. Then comes the "Passion." It begins with the "Conspiracy of the Jews" and in order are placed "Last Supper," "Gethsemane," "Jesus before Caiaphas," "Jesus before Herod," "Pilate's Wife," "Judas Iscariot," "Condemnation," "Bearing of the Cross," "Crucifixion," and "Burial." In equal rank with the "Ministry of Jesus" and the "Passion" plays come the "Descent into Hell," "Resurrection," "Mary Magdalene," "Pilgrims and Thomas," and the "Ascension." Next follow those plays on the books of the New Testament which do not readily lend themselves to classification into the life of Jesus. Discoverable plays on St. Mark and St. John the Evangelist come here. Then follows the "Acts of the Apostles," under which are several subdivisions, such as "Descent of the Holy Spirit," "Stephen," "Peter," and "Paul." Two plays have been found on the book of Philemon. The final subject in the New Testament is designated "Last Things." Plays on the Antichrist and Judgment were placed under this heading.

The existence of the English cycles and the lesser collections of early miracle plays aggravated the problem of the arrangement of the Biblical plays. Because of the unique nature of the early religious plays, differing as they do from modern plays in their very language, anonymity of authorship and manner of construction, it did not seem desirable to place them side by side with the modern plays. They have, therefore, within any given incident, been placed first. Following them, the modern plays were arranged alphabetically by authors. The term modern in this connection was made to apply to plays dating as far back as 1496–1563 (John Bale). The four great cycles were given the following order: York, Towneley, Chester, and Coventry, while the lesser groups were arranged in the order of the number of plays each contains — Stonyhurst pageants, Cornwall, Digby, the three Shrewsbury fragments, and the two Coventry Corpus Christi plays — a rather arbitrary arrangement, but one for which there seemed to be no better alternative.

In the course of the preparation of this work four groups of plays, designated here "Babylonian Captivity," "Herod," "Wandering Jew," and "Fall of Jerusalem," were met with, which, although based on imaginative events not Biblical, were yet deemed within the scope of this bibliography, because of their quasi-Biblical nature. The first group embraces plays the milieu of which is during the first captivity of Judah and Israel, 586–537 B. C., which in itself is a Biblical event. The second deals with the loves and struggles of the Herodian and Hasmonean families, based largely on Josephus. The third is motivated on the New Testament phrases to be found in Matt. xvi: 28, and John xxi: 22–23. The fourth deals with episodes centering around the destruction of Jerusalem by Titus, 70 A. D. These four categories of plays could not be placed under any given book of the Bible for they are founded on events not recorded in the Bible. Neither could they be placed in the compiler's forthcoming bibliography of modern Jewish plays without doing violence to a sense of historical sequence. The first two, therefore, have been placed between the Apocrypha and the New Testament plays, and the last two at the end of the bibliography.

A section headed "Bible" has been provided to accommodate plays which have in them characters from various and widely scattered books of the Bible, both Old and New Testaments. Plays based on subjects outside of the Bible and in which Jesus is a character are placed in a section headed "Jesus," just before the "Virgin Mary" plays. Opera librettos and scores of oratorios have been excluded as not properly belonging here. Modern pageants where the text is in dialogue spoken by the actors and not recited by a reader to the accompanying action of the performers are included. Non-printed plays based on pre-existing published novels, or those which served as the basis for subsequently-published novels, as well as plays which exist only in an extensive and detailed prose synopsis, or those the text of which is available in substantial and numerous extracts were considered as printed plays and, therefore, included. A number of early Elizabethan Biblical lost plays, culled largely from W. C. Hazlitt's *Manual* and Professor Furnivall's *Dictionary,* are recorded. These may have existed in book form or they may be the surviving titles of formerly produced plays. Some of them are possibly not lost at all, and are available to us under different names. The authority for the information and such other facts as are known about this class of plays is stated. In case of translated plays only English reviews are included; of dramas originally written in English, however, reviews in all languages are recorded. All ascertainable translations into other languages of an English original are given, together with such reviews of them as could be found.

There remains the pleasant duty of acknowledging the help received by the compiler. Dr. Joshua Bloch, who fathered and nursed the idea of this bibliography, has throughout its preparation evinced an interest far beyond his official rôle of Chief of the Jewish Division of The New York Public Library. Dr. H. A. Wolfson, Professor of Jewish Literature and Philosophy in Harvard University, has helped with suggestions too varied to be enumerated. Miss Dora Steinglass of the Staff of the Jewish Division of the Library has catalogued most of the books and typed the greater part of the list. Mr. Daniel C. Haskell, Assistant Bibliographer of the Library, has fashioned this material into the form in which it here appears, and is also responsible for the indices. To all of them, as well as to numerous friends who have called attention to entries which otherwise might have escaped him, the compiler is grateful indeed. But above all and beyond all he is indebted to Mr. Frank A. Peterson, who for three years has given unsparingly of his time and enthusiasm and, by his continuous searching of the resources of the Library, has contributed largely to the completeness of this work. He is also responsible for the system of classification adopted.

THE LIST

GENERAL WORKS

Bible on the stage. (New review. London, 1893. 8°. v. 8, p. 183–189.) *** DA**
Three answers by Alexandre Dumas fils, F. W. Farrar, and Henry Arthur Jones to the question: Is it desirable that plays founded upon or connected with Biblical history should be introduced upon the English stage?
The discussion is continued in *The Spectator*, London, v. 70, p. 155–156, * *DA*.

Borden, Lucie Page. Discussion of the Biblical drama; possibility of presenting scriptural scenes and themes on a scale of magnificence. (The Flaming sword. Estero, Fla., 1905. f°. v. 18, no. 47, p. 6–7.) **† ZZY**

Bundy, Sarah Elizabeth. Religion and the drama. (Homiletic review. New York, 1917. 8°. v. 73, p. 93–99.) **ZIXD**

Candler, Martha. Drama in religious service... Illustrated with photographs. New York and London: Century Co., 1922. xv, 259 p. illus. 8°. **NAFM**
Bibliography, p. 239–259.

—— The everyday mission of the church; indoor and outdoor play; Biblical dramatics and pageantry. (Christian herald. New York, 1921. f°. v. 44, p. 749–750.) **† ZEA**
Abstracted in *Literary digest*, New York, Oct. 29, 1921, v. 71, p. 31, * *DA*.

Delfour, L. Clodomir. La bible dans Racine... Paris: Ernest Leroux, 1891. 3 p.l., xxv, 261 p. 8°. *** PZB**
Reviewed by Jean Réville in *Revue de l'histoire des religions*, Paris, 1892, tome 26, p. 100–101, *ZAA;* and by Émile Faguet in *Revue politique et littéraire, Revue bleue*, Paris, 1892, tome 49, année 29, semestre 1, p. 442–443, * *DM*.

The **Dramatic** element in the Bible. (Atlantic monthly. Boston, 1859. 8°. v. 4, p. 137–153.) *** DA**

Edland, Elisabeth. Bible dramatizations with small children. illus. (Church school. New York, 1923. 4°. v. 4, p. 230–231.)

Findon, B. W. A plea for the religious drama. (Fortnightly review. London, 1905. 8°. v. 84, p. 708–715.) *** DA**

Gabriel, Gilbert Wolf. Bible into drama. (Menorah journal. New York, 1928. 8°. v. 14, p. 188–193.) *** PBD**

Galloway, Thomas Walton. How to construct a Biblical drama. illus. (Church school. New York, 1923. 4°. v. 4, p. 465–466, 478.)

George, Walter Lionel. Religious drama [modern]. (In his: Dramatic actualities. London, 1914. 12°. p. 95–124.) **NAFD**

Heller, Max. Dramatizing the Old Testament. The discovery of human values in the Bible. Illustrated by Lesser Ury. (B'nai B'rith magazine. Chicago, 1925. 4°. v. 39, p. 226–228, 255.) *** PYP**

Hoffman, Chas. I. Religion on the stage. By Publius [pseud.]. (Jewish exponent. Philadelphia, 1902. f°. v. 36, no. 7, Dec. 5, 1902, p. 4.) *** PBD**

Hughes, Thomas P. The Biblical play; a new development of the drama. (Critic. New York, 1904. 8°. v. 45, p. 307–312.) *** DA**

Lamers, William Mathias. A few words on sacred drama. (Practical stage work. Sleepy Eye, Minn., 1928. 4°. v. 3, no. 3, Oct., 1928, p. 5–6, 8.) **MWA**

Lanier, Henry Wysham. Bible teaching through drama. (Homiletic review. New York, 1918. 8°. v. 76, p. 439–444.) **ZIXD**

Lemon, W. P. Biblical pageantry and dramatics. (Homiletic review. New York, 1923. 8°. v. 85, p. 395–404.) **ZIXD**

Lewis, Winifred. The religious drama; a selected bibliography. (Drama. Chicago, 1919. 4°. v. 10, p. 36–41.) **NAFA**

Museus, pseud. Christ in English literature. (Contemporary review. London, 1908. 8°. v. 93, literary supplement no. 4, p. 1–5.) *** DA**

General Works, continued

Reinstein, H.   Dramatization ' manual. Suggestions for dramatization of Bible stories, by H. Reinstein. Costume sketches by Rose Krupnick. Chicago: Board of Jewish Education, Dramatic Department [1929?]. [15] f. diagrams. 4°.
Cover-title.
Mimeographed.

Rudens, S. P. The substance of Biblical tragedy. (Reflex. Chicago, 1930. 8°. v. 6, May, 1930, p. 26–32.)   *** PBD**

The **Scripture** in drama. (Modern theatre. New York, 1907. 8°. v. 1, no. 2/3, p. 5–8.)   **NAFA**

Shillman, Bernard. Some Biblical episodes in literature. (Jewish chronicle supplement. London, 1924. f°. no. 44, August, 1924, p. iv–vi.)   *** PBE**

Spitz, Leon. The Bible, Jews and Judaism in American poetry. New York: Behrman's Jewish Book Shop, 1923. 118 p. 8°.   *** PZB**

Wright, Louis B. The Scriptures and the Elizabethan stage. (Modern philology. Chicago, 1928. 8°. v. 26, no. 1, p. 47–56.)   **NAA**

COLLECTED PLAYS AND COLLECTIONS

Andersen, Olivia Donaldson (Cushing). Creation and other Biblical plays. Geneva: Albert Kundig, 1929. 2 p.l., (1)8–361 p., 1 l. 4°.   **NBM**
Preface by Hendrik Christian Andersen. Each play is preceded by an "argument" by Lucille Gulliver.
Partial contents: Creation. Moses the lawgiver. The judge, King Saul and the singer. Jesus of Nazareth. The early Christian.

Bale, John, bishop of Ossory. ...The dramatic writings of John Bale, bishop of Ossory...edited by John S. Farmer. London: Privately printed for subscribers by the Early English Drama Society, 1907. 4 p.l., (1)4–347 p. illus. 12°. (Early English dramatists.)   **NCO (Early)**
Partial contents: A comedy concerning three laws, of Nature, Moses, and Christ. A tragedy or interlude manifesting the chief promises of God unto man. A comedy or interlude of John Baptist's preaching in the wilderness. A comedy or interlude concerning the temptation of Our Lord. Note-book and word-list.

Benton, Rita. ...Bible plays. New York, Cincinnati: The Abingdon Press [cop. 1922]. 237 p. illus. 8°. (The Abingdon religious education texts.)   **NASH**
Contents: Joseph and his brethren. The golden calf. The daughter of Jephthah. Ruth and Boaz. Esther. Daniel. The burning fiery furnace. The Christmas story.

—— ...Shorter Bible plays. New York, Cincinnati: The Abingdon Press [cop. 1922]. 3 p.l., (1)4–135 p. illus. 8°. (The Abingdon religious education texts.)   **NASH**
With music.
Contents: Noah's flood. The proving of Abraham. Moses in the bulrushes. Up, up from Egypt to the promised land. The call of Samuel. David and Goliath. The judgment of Solomon (longer version). The judgment of Solomon (shorter version). The good Samaritan. Manger service.

Boxer, James. Sacred dramas. I. Naaman the Syrian. II. The finding of Moses. III. Jephthah's daughter. Boston: Lee and Shepard; New York: Lee, Shepard, and Dillingham, 1875. 174 p. 8°.

Boyd, Charles Arthur. Worship in drama. A manual of methods and material for young people and their leaders. Philadelphia: Judson Press [cop. 1924]. 5 p.l., 175 p. 8°.   **NAFM**
Partial contents: Micaiah the truthful. Elijah the uncompromising. Isaiah the statesman. Paul the far-sighted. The hymn of the helper. A festival of light.

Boyd, Zachary. Excerpts from "The flowers of Zion." (In: Gabriel Neil, Biographical sketch of the Rev. Mr. Zachary Boyd. Glasgow, 1832. 8°. Appendix, p. vii–xxxii.)   **A p.v. 144**
Contents: David and Goliath. The historie of Jonah. The historie of Samson. The historie of Jephta. The flood of Noah. The towre of Babylon. The destruction of Sodom. Abraham commanded to sacrifice Isaac. The historie of John the Baptist.
The contents, here given, are from a ms. "The flowers of Zion" in possession of the University of Glasgow.

—— Four poems from ."Zion's flowers"; or, "Christian poems for spiritual edification." Printed from his manuscript in the Library of the University of Glasgow with an introduction containing some notices of his life and writings. Edited by Gabriel Neil. Glasgow: Printed by George Richardson, 1855. 157 p., 1 port. facsim. sq. 8°.   **NCL**
Partial contents: The historie of Jonah. Joseph tempted to adultery. David and Goliath. Dinah ravished by Shechem.

Burns, Mary Modena. Good things for Sunday schools; a complete entertainer containing recitations, monologues, dialogues, exercises, drills, tableaux and plays... Chicago: T. S. Denison & Co. [cop. 1916.] 146 p. illus. (music.) 12°.   **ZICS**
Partial contents: The beautiful story of Ruth the gleaner. The first Christmas.

Carman, Bliss, and MARY PERRY KING. Daughters of dawn. A lyrical pageant or series of historic scenes for presentation with music and dancing...with fifteen illustrations. New York: Mitchell Kennerley, 1913. 3 p.l., v–viii, 118 p. illus. 12°.   **NCM**
Contents: Eve. Deborah. Balkis. Mary.
Reviewed in *Boston Evening Transcript,* Boston, April 19, 1913, part 3, p. 8, * A, and in *New York Times review of books,* New York, 1913, v. 18, p. 288, † *NAA.*

Collected Plays and Collections, continued

Carvalho, Naomi Nunes. Vox humana. London: Kegan Paul, Trench, Trübner & Co., Ltd., 1912. vi p., 1 l., 157 p. 12°.

NRD p.v.9

Partial contents: Terah and Abraham. Abraham and Hagar. Rebekah and Jacob. Miriam and Pharaoh's daughter. Miriam and Pharaoh. Moses and an old Egyptian priest. The king of Moab and a scribe. Ruth and Orpah. Delilah and a Philistine lord. King David and a counsellor of the king. Isaiah and a watchman. Ezekiel and a sceptic. Conversation between Ezechiel and an Athenian actor. The death of Philo, the Græco-Judaic philosopher.

Christmas plays... Boston, Chicago: Pilgrim Press [cop. 1927]. 26 p. 12°.

Partial contents: The first Christmas morning, by Maud Lindsay. What child is this? by Martha Race.

Cobb, Mary L., compiler. Poetical dramas for home and school. Boston: Lee and Shepard; New York: Lee, Shepard and Dillingham, 1873. 189 p. 12°.   **MZB**

Partial contents: The Spanish gypsy, arranged from George Eliot. Moses in the bulrushes, Hannah More. Feast of Tabernacles, Rev. Henry Ware. The coming of the Messiah, Rev. S. H. Winkley. Deborah and Barak, Anonymous. Queen Vashti, Anonymous.

"Some of the pieces have never before appeared in print; others are abstracts or compilations from standard authors."

Cole, Edna Earle. The good Samaritan, and other Bible stories dramatized, illustrated with photographs by Harold Wagner. Boston: R. G. Badger [cop. 1915]. 7 p., 3 l., 13–133 p. illus. 12°.

Contents: The good Samaritan. Paul and the jailer. The king's life spared. Esther, the brave young queen. Peter and the Roman captain. Two journeys to Bethlehem. The story of the twelve spies. The story of Joseph. Naaman and Gehazi.

Collett, John. Sacred dramas; intended chiefly for young persons. To which is added, An elegy in four parts. Evesham: Printed for the author, 1805. 2 p.l., v p., 2 l., 224 p. 12°.

Contents: Ehud (from Judges iii.). Naboth (1. Kings xxi.). Esther.

Reviewed in *Annual review,* London, 1805, v. 4, p. 639, *NAA; British critic,* London, 1805, v. 26, p. 567–568, *DA;* and in *Monthly review,* London, 1807, series 2, v. 52, p. 94–95, *NAA.*

Converse, Florence. Garments of praise. A miracle cycle. New York: E. P. Dutton & Co. [cop. 1921.] vi, 208 p. 12°. **NAFM**

Partial contents: The blessed birthday; a Christmas miracle play. Thy Kingdom come; a dream for Easter even...

Eleven short Biblical plays, from the Drama League-Longmans, Green and Co. playwriting contest for 1928... New York: Longmans, Green and Co., 1929. v, 239 p. 12°.

NBL p.v.216

Contents: Betrayal, by C. E. Van Norman. Cleopas, by A. L. Barton. The door, by H. C. Crew. Elisha, by L. M. Dunning. For His name's sake, by H. L. Todd. The friend of Potiphar's wife, by C. A. Rollins. The gift of Jehovah, by E. Pettey. The light upon the way, by M. H. Johnson. Maundy Thursday, by E. K. Doten. The third shepherds' play, by R. Mansel. The woman from Nod, by E. F. Taylor.

Evans, Mrs. Florence (Wilkinson). Two plays of Israel: David of Bethlehem, Mary Magdalen. New York: McClure, Phillips & Co., 1904. 4 p.l., 5–333 p. 8°. ***PSQ**

Fearless men, by various authors; dramatizations from the prophets. [Chicago, cop. 1923.] 72 p. 8°.   **NBF p.v.60, no.6**

Contents: Amos, by S. H. Fritchman. Hosea, by Grace E. Middleton. Isaiah, by Florence Reeves. Jeremiah, by Elizabeth Hormell. The herald of the restoration, by Helen Galleher.

"Prepared to accompany 'Men unafraid' by Rollin H. Walker. These dramatizations were written by students in Professor Walker's class in Bible at Ohio Wesleyan University." — *Publisher's note.*

Gaw, Allison. Pharaoh's daughter, and other Biblical plays of the contest, 1927: Pharaoh's daughter, by Allison Gaw and Ethelean Tyson Gaw; The making of a king, by Lindsey Barbee; Ruth of Moab, by Mina R. Maxfield. New York: Longmans, Green and Co., 1928. xi, 261 p. illus. 8°.

NBL

These plays were submitted in the Drama League-Longmans Green play-writing contest, 1927, and *Pharaoh's daughter* was the prize-winner of the Non-sectarian Biblical group.

Reviewed in *Drama,* Mt. Morris, Ill., 1928, v. 18, p. 117, 122, *NAFA.*

Genlis, Stéphanie Félicité Ducrest de Saint Aubin, comtesse de, afterwards marquise de Sillery. Sacred dramas, written in French, by Madame la comtesse de Genlis. Translated into English by Thomas Holcroft. London: G. G. J. and J. Robinson, 1786. xv, 347 p. 8°.   **NKO**

Contents: The death of Adam. Hagar in the wilderness. The sacrifice of Isaac. Joseph made known to his brethren. Ruth and Naomi. The widow of Sarepta. The return of Tobias.

For bibliographical notes on this edition and on previous translations of her *Theatre of education* see Elbridge Colby, A Bibliography of Thomas Holcroft (*New York Public Library Bulletin,* v. 26, p. 672–674), **HND.* Also issued separately, **RB–NCC.*

Reviewed in *English review,* London, 1786, v. 8, p. 35–40, **DA;* and *Monthly review,* London, 1786, v. 75, p. 397, *NAA.*

———— Fredericksburg: Printed by L. A. Mullin, for the Rev. Mason L. Weems, 1797. viii, 136 p. 12°.   ***KD**

Githens, Harry W. Dramatized stories from the Old Testament. Cincinnati: Standard Pub. Co. [cop. 1927.] 200 p. 12°.

NASH

Twenty-four dramatizations of Old Testament stories for children.

Contents: A father of nations. Searching for a wife. A bad bargain. A long courtship. The coat of many colors. A prisoner promoted. Saved to serve. An adopted son. From palace to prairie. Delivered from bondage. The golden calf. A rash vow. A faithful daughter. A mother's gift. The shepherd king. A giant story. A wise king. A captive maid. A woman who dared. An interpreter of dreams. The fiery furnace. The handwriting on the wall. A persecuted prophet. A fish story.

Collected Plays and Collections, continued

—— New Testament stories dramatized; fresh, colorful, instructive. Cincinnati: Standard Pub. Co. ₍cop. 1929.₎ 216 p. 12°.
Contents: The star of the East. The fisherman. The wanderer. Opened eyes. An unexpected guest. Down through the roof. The magic touch. For thirty pieces of silver. Delivered from prison. At the beautiful gate. A captain's confession. The first martyr. At the feet of the apostles. The wrath of Israel. A stricken traveler. An interrupted coronation. A herald of the cross. A labor riot. An ambassador in bonds. The last journey.

Glover, Lydia May. ...Friends of Jesus; dramatizations from the New Testament. A little collection of brief plays, designed for devotional use by young people. New York, Cincinnati: The Abingdon Press ₍cop. 1923₎. 80 p. illus. 8°. (Biblical drama series.)
NAC p.v.113, no.5
Contents: Suggestions for directors. The seeing heart. The living water. Love's utmost. Whom Jesus loved. Simon of Cyrene. In His strength.

Grossman, Samuel S. Holiday and other plays for Jewish children. ₍v. p., n. d.₎ 14 pamphlets in 1 v. 4°. **NASH**
Contents: Arrows to the east. The Beduin fight. The call of Samuel. Hiding in the Sukkah. The jester's gift. The judgment of the shepherd. The light of love. The masque of the new land. Playing Noah. The ten commandments. The trusted jewels. Vote for Haman! Who built the Sukkoh? Chalutzim life.
Mimeographed.

Hale, Harris Grafton, and N. M. HALL, editors. Biblical dramas arranged by Harris G. Hale and Newton M. Hall. ₍nos. 1–12.₎ Boston: The Pilgrim Press, 1906. 12°.
NBL (Biblical)
Contents: The story of Joseph and his brethren. The story of Jacob. Moses the liberator. Samuel and Saul. David the king. The story of David and Jonathan. The story of Solomon. The story of Job. The story of Elijah. The messages of the prophets. Nehemiah the builder. Paul the prisoner of the Lord.
Library possesses [nos. 1–3, 6–7, 11].

Henderson, Mrs. Alice (Corbin). Adam's dream, and two other miracle plays for children, by Alice Corbin; with illustrations after the manner of the old English woodcuts, by Wm. P. Henderson, and music for the little songs and choruses in the plays, by Roy McWilliams. New York: C. Scribner's Sons, 1909. 2 p.l., vii–xii p., 1 l., 55 p. illus. 12°.
NASH
Contents: Adam's dream. The star of Bethlehem. Easter morning.

Heron, Henrietta, compiler. Pageants for the year... Chapter on costuming by J. H. Shonkwiler. Cincinnati: Standard Publishing Co. ₍cop. 1928.₎ 192 p. illus. 8°. **NAFM**
Partial contents: Dallas, M., Dawn of the third day. Parish, R. M., Saul in the desert.

Hinkson, Katharine (Tynan), "Mrs. H. A. Hinkson." Miracle plays: Our Lord's coming and childhood. London: John Lane; Chi-

cago: Stone and Kimball, 1895. 97(1) p., 1 l., 16 p. (advertisements), 6 pl. 12°. **NCR**
Contents: The Annunciation. The Visitation. The Nativity. The presentation in the Temple. The flight into Egypt. The finding in the Temple.

Hobbs, Mabel, and HELEN MILES. Six Bible plays; issued under the auspices of the Bureau of Educational Dramatics, Playground and Recreation Association of America. New York and London: The Century Co. ₍cop. 1924.₎ vi p., 3 l., 3–128 p. illus. 8°. **NASH**
Contents: Ruth and Naomi. Joseph and his brethren. Moses. Esther. The healing of Naaman. David and Jonathan. Old Hebrew melodies.

Kemp, Harry. Boccaccio's untold tale, and other one-act plays. New York: Brentano's ₍cop. 1924₎. 5 p.l., 252 p. 8°. **8 – NBM**
Partial contents: Solomon's song. Judith.

Kennedy, Anna R. Bible plays out of the East; being seven episodes related to the life of Christ from Christmas to Easter... New York: The Womans Press, 1929. 62 p. 8°.
Partial contents: The virgin's tree. Locusts and wild honey. A boy finds the kingdom. The women from Galilee. Easter night.

Kimball, Rosamond. The wooing of Rebekah and other Bible plays; a new method of dramatization. New York: C. Scribner's Sons, 1925. x p., 2 l., 268 p. illus. 8°. **ZICS**
Contents: The wooing of Rebekah. Jacob's journey. The story of Joseph. Moses in the bulrushes. Ruth. Samuel in the House of the Lord. David and Jonathan. Elijah and Elisha. The nativity. The prodigal son. The resurrection.
"The stories here dramatized...follow the text of the Bible itself." — *Preface.*

Kohut, George Alexander, editor. A Hebrew anthology; a collection of poems and dramas inspired by the Old Testament and post Biblical tradition gathered from writings of English poets, from the Elizabethan period and earlier to the present day. Edited by George Alexander Kohut; with an introduction by Hudson Maxim... Cincinnati: S. Bacharach, 1913. 2 v. 8°. ***PSO**
Paged continuously.
Contents: v. 1. Lyrical, narrative and devotional poems. v. 2. Selections from the drama.
Contents of v. 2: Lucifer, Joost van den Vondel [extract]. Cain, Lord Byron. Heaven and earth: a mystery, Lord Byron. Moses in the bulrushes, Hannah More. Samson Agonistes, John Milton. David and Goliath, Hannah More. Jonathan, Thomas Ewing, jr. David and Bathshua, C. W. Cayzer. Hadad, J. A. Hillhouse [extract]. Elijah, Robert Davidson. Athaliah, J. B. Racine. The Song of songs which is Solomon's, Ann Francis. Belshazzar, H. H. Milman. Belshazzar, Hannah More. The Jewish captives, J. M. Leavitt. Daniel, Hannah More. Judas Maccabaeus, H. W. Longfellow [extract]. The fall of Jerusalem, H. H. Milman [abridged]. Herod and Mariamne, Amélie Rives (Princess Troubetzkoy). Nathan the Wise, G. E. Lessing. Torquemada, Victor Hugo [extract]. The Spanish gypsy, George Eliot (selections from book II). The merchant of Venice, Shakespeare [extract].
Reviewed by Julian Morgenstern in *American citizen,* New York, 1913, v. 3, p. 155–156, **PBD;* by Joseph Jacobs in *The American Hebrew,* New York,

Collected Plays and Collections, continued

Kohut, G. A. A Hebrew anthology, *cont'd*

1913, v. 93, p. 120, * *PBD;* by David Philipson in the *American Israelite,* Cincinnati, v. 59, May 15, 1913, p. 4, * *PBD;* by J. D. Eisenstein in *Hatoren,* New York, 1913, v. 1, p. 137–138, * *PBA;* by A. M. Friedenberg in the *Hebrew standard,* New York, v. 61, May 2, 1913, p. 12, * *PBD;* by Israel Abrahams in *Jewish chronicle,* London, July, 1913, supplement, p. v–vi, * *PBE;* by Edward N. Calisch in *Jewish quarterly review,* Philadelphia, 1914, new series, v. 5, p. 263–266, * *PBE; New York Tribune,* May 24, 1913, p. 8, cols. 2–3, * *A;* and *Sunday school times,* Philadelphia, 1913, v. 55, p. 642–643, † *ZICN.*

Also reviewed in *Academy,* London, 1913, v. 85, p. 110–111, * *DA; Athenæum,* London, June 28, 1913, p. 694, * *DA; Outlook,* New York, 1913, v. 104, p. 824–825, * *DA; New York Times book review,* 1913, v. 18, p. 353, † *NAA.*

Levinger, Elma C. (Ehrlich.) Entertaining programs for the assembly in the Jewish religious school... Cincinnati: Department of Synagogue and School Extension of the Union of American Hebrew Congregations [cop. 1930]. xv, 198 p. 8°.   * **PSY**
Bibliography, p. 195–198.
Partial contents: The Hebrew's Friday night. A day in a Jewish home. In our synagogue. Class contests. The shepherd psalm. The magic circle. The Jewish community. The prayers of Israel. Pilgrims to Palestine. The boy who broke the idols. The girl who was good to strangers. The poor student. The heathen who stood on one foot. Palestine spring song, by A. Burstein. The carob tree. The tree song. The kings of Israel. The precious water. Samuel, by Walter Brown. The golden ring. The message of the prophets. Our Jewish mothers' hall of fame.

—— Jewish festivals in the religious school; a handbook for entertainments. Cincinnati: The Union of American Hebrew Congregations, 1923. xi, 587 p. illus. 8°.
      * **PSY**
Partial contents: 1. The Chanukah lights. 2. Over the Chanukah lights, by Miriam Myers. 3. The youngest son. 4. Purim prologue — "My basket." 5. A set of Purim pictures. 6. For love of Torah, by Jessie E. Sampter. 7. Ruth — a story of the harvest, by Leona Bachrach. 8. How Succoth came to Chayim. 9. The golden staff. 10. The unlighted menorah. 11. The light of Israel. 12. A sick Purim. 13. The star of Judah. 14. The pageant of Esther. 15. The silver cup. 16. Out of Egypt. 17. Ruth of Moab. 18. "Let there be light."

Lobingier, Mrs. Elizabeth Erwin (Miller). The dramatization of Bible stories; an experiment in the religious education of children. Chicago, Ill.: The University of Chicago Press [cop. 1918]. xiv, 162 p. illus. 12°. (The University of Chicago publications in religious education... Principles and methods of religious education.)   * **YIR**
Partial contents: Dramatizations of "Joseph," "David and Goliath," "Moses in the bulrushes," "Ruth," "Queen Esther," "Abraham and the three guests," "Daniel in the lions' den," and of "New Testament parables."

Lyndsay, David. Dramas of the ancient world. Edinburgh: W. Blackwood, 1822. vi p., 1 l., 278p. 8°.
Dialogues in verse.
Contents: The deluge. The plague of darkness. The last plague. Rizpah. Sardanapalus. The destiny of Cain. The death of Cain. The Nereid's love.
Reviewed in *European magazine,* London, 1822, v. 81, p. 256–259, * *DA,* and in *Literary gazette,* London, 1822, v. 4, p. 17–19, * *DA.*

Manley, William Ford. Bible dramas. Radio plays adapted for church and social gatherings. New York, Chicago: Fleming H. Revell Co. [cop. 1928.] 225 p., 1 pl. 8°.
      NBM
Contents: James of Galilee. Cain and Abel. Diana of the Ephesians. Samson and Delilah. Saul of Tarsus. Ruth. The message from Sinai. Courage. Sacrifice. Ishmael. The mess of pottage. Judith.

—— A second book of Bible dramas... New York: Fleming H. Revell Company [cop. 1930]. 206 p. 8°.   **NBM**
Partial contents: The first gift. Judas Iscariot. The unconquered. The prodigal. The comeback. Naaman's cloak. Number one on the docket. The king dreams. Naboth's vineyard.
"Written originally for production over the radio... Printed without revision as they were originally produced over the radio" from WEAF and associated radio stations.

More, Hannah. Sacred dramas, chiefly intended for young persons: the subjects taken from the Bible. To which are added: Reflections of King Hezekiah, Sensibility, a poem. And essays on various subjects, principally designed for young ladies. Philadelphia: Printed for Thomas Dobson, 1787. vii(i), 9–191(1) p. 8°.   * **KD**
The dramas are: Moses; David and Goliath; Belshazzar; Daniel.
For reviews of the 1st ed., 1782, see *Critical review,* London, 1782, v. 53, p. 199–204, *NAA; London chronicle,* London, 1782, v. 51, p. 185, * *A,* and *Monthly review,* London, 1782, v. 67, p. 31–35, *NAA.*
See also John Genest, *Some account of the English stage,* Bath, 1832, v. 6, p. 247–251, *NCOM.*

—— Sacred dramas: chiefly intended for young persons. The subjects taken from the Bible to which is added Sensibility: an epistle. London: Printed for J. Cadell, and W. Davies, 1810. 294 p., 1 l. 16. ed. 12°.

—— Sacred dramas, chiefly intended for young persons: the subjects taken from the Bible, to which are added, Reflections of king Hezekiah; — Sensibility, a poem; — and Search after happiness. Boston: J. West & Co., 1811. vi, 7–191 p. 16°.   * **PSQ**

Moulton, Arthur Wheelock. It came to pass. Boston: Richard G. Badger, The Gorham Press, 1916. 90 p. 12°.   **ZFHK**
Six "dramatic situations" (dialogues) are developed: Across the table; On the Galilean lake; Tears of a man; The precious ointment; The silver pieces; Joseph of Arimathea.

New sacred dramas for young persons. London, 1820. 8°.
Title from British Museum Catalogue.

Opal, pseud. The cloud of witnesses. New York: J. Miller, 1874. 522 p. 12°.   **NBM**
Partial contents: Creation. Abel's widow. The benedicite. St. Paul in Athens.

Osgood, Phillips Endecott. Old-time church drama adapted; mystery plays and moralities of earlier days for sundry churchly uses to-day. New York and London: Harper

Collected Plays and Collections, continued

& Brothers, 1928. 5 p.l., 3–291 p. illus. 12°.
NAFM
Partial contents: Quem quaeritis. Melchizedek,
Abraham, and Isaac [Chester play]. Nativity cycle
of the York mystery plays. Elijah [adapted from
Mendelssohn]. Judas Maccabaeus [adapted from
Handel].
Reviewed in *Homiletic review*, New York, 1928,
v. 95, p. 517, *ZIXD*.

—— Pulpit dramas; a series of dramatizations for church, pulpit or parish house use.
New York and London: Harper & Brothers,
1929. xxxi p., 2 l., 3–191(1) p. illus. 12°.
NAFM
Contents: Destiny. Under authority. Rejected of
Nazareth. In Herod's dungeon. Outcast. Lazarus
tells of his death. Judas of Kerioth. Gabbatha. Naked
evil. "Without a city wall." The first day of the week.

—— The sinner beloved, and other re-
ligious plays, for use in church and parish
house. New York and London: Harper &
Brothers, 1928. 5 p.l., 247 p. illus. 12°.
NAFM
Partial contents: The sinner beloved. Shepherds all?
John Mark, his witness. The fears of Nicodemus.
City walls and open plains. The story of a story.

Overton, Grace Sloan. Dramatic activities
for young people... New York & London:
Century Co. [cop. 1927.] ix, 83 p. 12°.
Partial contents: The living Christ. Youth's prophetic vision. The eternal quest.
Reviewed in *Homiletic review*, New York, 1927,
v. 94, p. 432, *ZIXD*.

P., Br. Three plays, scriptural and his-
torical. For male characters only. Trans-
lated from the French, for the use of St.
Mungo's Academy, Glasgow. London:
Samuel French; New York: Samuel French
& Son [1871]. v. p. 12°. **NKM p.v.229, no.5**
Partial contents: Joseph and his brethren. Daniel
in the lions' den.

Parsons, Mrs. Margaret Colby (Getchell).
Ten stirring Bible plays... Franklin, O.,
Denver, Col.: Eldridge Entertainment
House, 1927. 69 p. 12°.
Partial contents: The babe in the bulrushes. The
little prophet Samuel. David, the shepherd boy.
Joseph, the dreamer of dreams. Benjamin and the
silver cup. Ruth. Daniel and the lions. The widow's
cruse (Elijah). Boy heroes of the Bible.

Pennie, John Fitzgerald. Scenes in Pal-
estine; or, Dramatic sketches from the Bible.
To which is added the Fair Avenger; or the
Destroyer destroyed, an academic drama [in
four acts and in verse]. London, 1825. 12°.
Title from British Museum Catalogue.

Pinski, David. King David and his wives.
Translated from the Yiddish by Isaac Goldberg. New York: B. W. Huebsch, Inc., 1923.
186 p. 12°. ***PTP**
Contents: Michal. Abigail. Bathsheba. In the
harem. Abishag.

Raine, James Watt. Bible dramatics...
New York & London: The Century Co. [cop.
1927.] vii, 372 p. 12°.

Religious dramas, 1924–[1925] selected by
the Committee on Religious Drama of the
Federal Council of the Churches of Christ
in America. New York & London: The
Century Co. [cop. 1923–26.] 2 v. 8°.
NAFM (Religious)
Partial contents: [v. 1]: The rock, by M. P. Hamlin.
Good Samaritan, by A. B. Ferris. A sinner beloved,
by P. E. Osgood. The resurrection, by R. Kimball.
Pilgrim and the Book, by Percy Mackaye. v. 2: Quest
divine, by M. N. Goold. Two thieves, by E. W. Bates.
St. Claudia, by M. N. Goold. Alabaster box, by A. J.
Harnwell and I. J. Meaker. Whither goest thou? by
C. H. Currie. At the gate beautiful, by H. S. Mason.
Barabbas, by Dorothy Leamon. The Shepherds, by
M. N. Goold.

Russell, Mary M. Dramatized Bible
stories for young people. New York: G. H.
Doran Co. [cop. 1921.] xiii (i), 17–92 p. 12°.
Contents: A mother's faith (Moses). In quest of a
great treasure (Naaman). A woman who dared (Esther). The outcome of a secret (Bartimeus). Easter
morn, by Annie M. Darling. Easter morning. A
search for a wife (Isaac and Rebecca). The value of
preparation (Ten virgins). The secret of success (Nehemiah). A neighbor and his work (Good Samaritan).
A girl who knew how to be a friend (Ruth). A thanksgiving service (Miriam). The first Christmas.

Savage-Armstrong, George Francis. The
tragedy of Israel. London: Longmans,
Green and Co., 1892. 3 v. new ed. 12°. **NCR**
Part one: King Saul. Part two: King David. Part
three: King Solomon.
Library has part 3 only, in the 1876 edition.

Sherman, Josephine Ballou. Worship in
pantomime and pageant. Some pre-sermon
pictures of sacred themes... Franklin, O.:
Eldridge Entertainment House, Inc. [cop.
1926.] 32 p. 12°.
Partial contents: Faithfulness [the Talents]; Moses;
The Babe in the manger; The ten virgins; Who is my
neighbor? [The Good Samaritan]; The testing of
Abraham; A man and his two sons [the Prodigal Son];
Ruth and Naomi; Belshazzar's Feast.

Smith, Roy L. Pantomimes and pageants
for pulpit use... Cleveland: F. M. Barton
Co., Inc. [cop. 1928.] 115 p. 8°.
Partial contents: As Mary told it. Joseph and the
inn-keeper.

Soble, Mae Stein. Bible plays for children,
by Mae Stein Soble (Mrs. John J. Soble)...
New York: J. T. White & Co., 1919. 136 p.
12°. **NASH**
Partial contents: The first temptation. Mother love
finds a way. The call of God. The golden calf. The
promised land. The might of right.

Stackhouse, Perry James. Bible dramas
in the pulpit. Philadelphia, Boston: The
Judson Press [cop. 1926]. 6 p.l., 3–153 p. 8°.
NBM
Contents: Joseph, the dreamer. Joseph, the interpreter of dreams. Joseph's dreams come true. A queen
who saved a nation from death. The babe of Bethlehem: a Christmas drama. The disciple of the. night:
a drama sermon. The conversion of a dishonest tax-
collector. Facts are stubborn things. The rich young
ruler. The man of Kerioth. Thomas, the twin: an
Easter drama.

Collected Plays and Collections, continued

Stillingfleet, Benjamin. Joseph. ₁Moses and Zipporah. David and Bathsheba. Medea. Four dramas in verse.₁ ₁London? 1765?₁ 138 p. 8°.

Not published. Only 18 copies were privately printed. Title from British Museum Catalogue.

Sunday school and church entertainments designed for anniversaries, celebrations, Christmas...and the full round of entertainments. Philadelphia: Penn Pub. Co., 1914. vi, 7–184 p. 12°. **ZICS**

Published in 1888 by the National School of Elocution and Oratory.
Partial contents: Clara J. Denton, From captivity to power. E. Murray, Elijah and the rain. Mrs. L. M. Willis, Naaman, the leper. Clara J. Denton, While shepherds watched.

Sweeny, Nelson D. Bible character impersonations; a chronological collection of costumed biographical readings... Franklin, O.: Eldridge Entertainment House, Inc., cop. 1927. 145 p. 12°.

Contains twenty-five Old Testament impersonations, and twenty-seven from the New Testament.

Tennant, William. Hebrew dramas: founded on incidents of Bible-history. Edinburgh, 1845. 16°.

Title from British Museum Catalogue.
"His 'Hebrew dramas' — Jephthah's daughter, Esther, Destruction of Sodom — not without a degree of freshness and vigor...are somewhat lacking in sustained interest." — *Dictionary of National Biography.*
Reviewed in *The Athenæum,* London, March 22, 1845, p. 289, * *DA;* and in *Gentleman's magazine,* London, 1845, v. 178, p. 612–613, * *DA.*

Thomas, M. W., editor. Old Testament drama; or, Dramatic readings from Hebrew literature. Selected and edited by M. W. Thomas... London: Thomas Nelson &

Sons, Ltd. ₁1927.₁ ix, 11–198 p., 1 pl. 12°. (The "Teaching of English" series. no. 112.)
Contents: Introduction. Abraham. Jacob and Esau. The adventures of Joseph. The exodus. Samson. Saul. The two prophets. Job the patient. Daniel the seer.
Text of dialogue largely in Biblical language.

Whiffen, Edwin Thomas. Jephtha sacrificing and Dinah; two dramatic poems. New York: Grafton Press ₁cop. 1908₁. 89 p. 12°. **NBI**

——— Tamar, and other poems. New York: Broadway Publishing Co., 1914. 321 p. 12°.

Whiting, Isabel Kimball. Dramatic services of worship. Introduction by Samuel McChord Crothers... Boston: Beacon Press, Inc., 1925. xiii, 220 p., 1 pl. 8°. **NBM**

Partial contents: The anointing of David by Samuel. Armistice day service adapted from Isaiah. The nativity. The renewal of spirit. The sword of Gideon. On the road to Jerusalem.

Whitney, Mary Ellen. Bible plays and how to produce them. New York, Chicago: Fleming H. Revell Company ₁cop. 1927₁. 176 p. illus. 12°.

Partial contents: Abraham and Isaac. The crowning of Saul. David and Goliath. The crowning of Solomon. Naaman the leper. Esther. Daniel in the lion's den. Ruth. The parable of the good Samaritan. The imprisonment of Peter and John. The martyrdom of Stephen. The conversion of Saul. Paul and Silas at Philippi. The shipwreck of Paul.

Wilder, Thornton Niven. The angel that troubled the waters, and other plays. New York: Coward-McCann, Inc., 1928. xvi p., 1 l., 19–149 p. 12°. **NBM**

Partial contents: And the sea shall give up its dead. Now the servant's name was Malchus. Hast thou considered thy servant Job? The flight into Egypt.
Reviewed by Isabel Paterson in *Books,* New York, v. 5, Nov. 18, 1928, p. 2, † *NAA; New York Times book review,* Nov. 18, 1928, p. 2, 16, † *NAA; Saturday review,* London, 1928, v. 146, p. 615, * *DA; Times literary supplement,* London, 1928, v. 27, p. 826, † *NAA;* by M. E. M. in *Boston Transcript,* Dec. 8, 1928, Book section, p. 11, col. 6, * *A.*

MIRACLE PLAYS

BIBLIOGRAPHY

Bates, Katharine Lee. Outlines and references. (In her: English religious drama. New York, 1893. 12°. p. 240–254.) **NAFM**
Also in the New York edition of 1902, *NCOD.*

Candler, Martha. Bibliography. (In her: Drama in religious service. New York and London, 1922. 8°. p. 239–259.) **NAFM**

Carey, Millicent. Bibliography. (In her: The Wakefield group in the Towneley cycle ... Göttingen, Baltimore, 1930. 8°. p. 245–251.) **NAFM**

Chambers, Sir Edmund Kerchever. Texts of mediaeval plays. I. Miracle plays. (In his: Mediaeval stage. Oxford, 1903. 8°. v. 2, p. 407–435.) ***R – NAFM**

Creizenach, Wilhelm Michael Anton. ₁A bibliography of₁ mysteries and miracle plays. (In: Cambridge history of English literature. Cambridge, 1907–27. 8°. v. 5, p. 388–391.) ***R – NCB**

Crum, Mason. Descriptive list of plays and pageants suitable for use in churches, Sunday schools and other religious organizations. (In his: A guide to religious pageantry. New York, 1923. 12°. p. 79–134.) **NAFM**

Greg, Walter Wilson. Bibliographical and textual problems of the English miracle cycles. Lectures delivered as Sandars Reader in Bibliography in the University of Cambridge, 1913... London: Alexander Moring,

Miracle Plays — Bibliography, continued

Limited, 1914. 2 p.l., (1)4–143(1) p., 1 folded table. 8°. **NAFM**
Contents: I. — Introduction: Bibliography and literature. II. — The coming of Antichrist: relation of the manuscripts of the Chester cycle. III. — Christ and the doctors: interrelation of the cycles. IV. Ludus Coventriae: the fabrication of a cycle.
Reprinted from *The Library*, London, series 3, v. 5, p. 1–30, 168–205, 280–319, 365–399, * *HA.*

Kress, Leona L. (Sister M. Clarissa.) Bibliography of medieval English religious drama. (Emerson quarterly. Boston, 1928. 4°. v. 8, May, 1928, p. 12.) † **NANA**

Mysteries, miracle plays, moralities, and religious drama. (Boston Public Library. Bulletin. Boston, 1879–80. 8°. v. 4, p. 131–135, 244.) * **GW (Boston)**

Overton, Grace Sloan. [Bible plays, bibliography.] (In her: Drama in education. New York [cop. 1926]. 12°. p. 228–272.) **ZICS**

Rudwin, Maximilian J. Passion play literature; being a partial list of books and magazine articles relating to the passion play in Oberammergau and other villages in Catholic Germany, Austria and Switzerland. (Bulletin of bibliography. Boston, 1916–18. 4°. v. 9, p. 66–67, 90–93; v. 10, p. 6–10.) * **GAA**
Arranged chronologically in accordance with consecutive decennial production.

Stoddard, Francis H. References for students of miracle plays and mysteries... Berkeley, 1887. 68 p., 1 folded table. 8°. (University of California. — Library. Bulletin no. 8.) * **HND (California)**

Utesch, Hans. Literatur. (In his: Die Quellen der Chester-Plays... Kiel, 1909. 8°. p. i–v.) **NAFM p.v.4**

GENERAL WORKS

Agius, Ambrose. Mystery plays in an English village. (Downside review. Bath, 1929. 8°. v. 47, p. 246–250.) * **DA**

Albright, Victor Emanuel. [Staging the miracle plays.] 5 pl. (In his: The Shakesperian stage. New York, 1909. 8°. p. 11–28.) **NCOM**

The **Ancient,** mediaeval and modern stage. (Edinburgh review. Edinburgh, 1883. 8°. v. 158, p. 57–89.) * **DA**

Bain, Ebenezer. [The Aberdeen craftsmen and the miracle plays.] (In his: Merchant and craft guilds; a history of the Aberdeen incorporated trades. Aberdeen, 1887. 8°. p. 47–61.) **SKD**

Bates, Katharine Lee. The English religious drama. New York and London: Macmillan and Co., 1893. 4 p.l., 254 p. 8°. **NAFM**
Contents: Latin passion plays and saint plays. Miracle plays; description, enumeration, dramatic values. Moralities. Appendix: topical outline and references.
Reviewed in *New-Shakespeareana*, New York, 1906, v. 5, p. 73–74, * *NCK (New); and by Charles Davidson in *Modern language notes*, Baltimore, 1894, v. 9, p. 114–116, *RAA.*

——— New York: Macmillan Co., 1902. 4 p.l., 254 p. 8°. **NCOD**

Beverley, England. [Orders for the governance of the Corpus Christi play in Beverley, England, 1390, 1411, 1431, 1392, 1457, 1391.] (In: Beverley town documents, ed. by Arthur F. Leach. London, 1900. 4°. verso p. 33–37, Latin text; recto p. 33–37, English translation.) **XAA (Selden)**
Selden Society. Publications. v. 14.
See also the Index for other orders for Corpus Christi day.
See also note by F. Liebermann in *Archiv für das Studium der neueren Sprachen und Litteraturen*, Braunschweig, 1903, Bd. 110, p. 426–427, *RAA.*

Bourne, Edward G. Miracle plays. (Modern language notes. Baltimore, 1896. 4°. v. 11, p. 62–63.) **RAA**
Regarding the earliest presentation of the miracle plays. Answered by William H. Hulme, *ibid.*, p. 125–126.

Brink, Bernhard Aegidus Konrad ten. [English religious drama.] (In his: Geschichte der englischen Litteratur. Strassburg, 1893. 8°. Bd. 2, p. 243–309.) * **R – NCB**

Broadbent, R. J. [Pantomime in the English religious cyclic plays.] (In his: A history of pantomime. London [1901]. 12°. p. 77–86.)

Cady, Frank W. Towneley, York, and True-Coventry. (University of North Carolina. — Philological Club. Studies in philology. Chapel Hill, N. C., 1929. 8°. v. 26, p. 386–400.) **RNA (North Carolina)**
Further support for the author's theory as to the common liturgical source of the Nativity and Passion groups of plays in the York, Towneley and Coventry cycles.

Cahour, A. Dramatic mysteries of the fifteenth and sixteenth centuries. (Catholic world. New York, 1865. 8°. v. 1, p. 577–598.) * **DA**

Carroll, K. M. Miracle plays as guides to mediaeval life. (Contemporary review. London, 1929. 8°. v. 135, p. 81–89.) * **DA**

Carson, W. R. Miracle plays. (Ecclesiastical review. Philadelphia, 1902. 8°. v. 27 [series 3, v. 7], p. 141–160.) **ZLF**

Carstensen, Cathrine. Kvindetyper i Middelalderens religiøse Skuespil, særlig de engelske. København: Kleins Forlag, 1901. 105 p. 8°. (Studier fra Sprog- og Oldtidsforskning udgivne af det Philologisk-historiske Samfund. Nr. 50.) **RAA (Filologisk)**

Miracle Plays — General Works, continued

Chambers, Sir Edmund Kerchever. Religious drama. (In his: Mediaeval stage. Oxford, 1903. 8°. v. 2, p. 1–176.)   *** R – NAFM**

Clarke, Sidney W. The miracle play in England; an account of the early religious drama. London: W. Andrews & Co. [1897.] 5 p.l., 94 p. illus. 12°.   **NAFM**

Clodd, Edward. Miracle plays. (Longman's magazine. London, 1890. 8°. v. 15, p. 621–629.)   *** DA**
Reprinted in *Eclectic magazine,* New York, 1890, new series, v. 51, p. 742–746, ** DA,* and in *Living age,* Boston, 1890, v. 185, p. 431–436, ** DA.*

—— Mysteries and moralities. (Knowledge. London, 1885. 4°. v. 8, p. 2–4, 43–45, 83–85, 131–133, 172–174, 219–220, 243–244, 260–262, 285–286, 312–313.)   **OA**

Coffman, George Raleigh. The miracle play in England; some records of presentation, and notes on preserved plays. (University of North Carolina. Studies in philology. Chapel Hill, 1919. 8°. v. 16, p. 56–66.)   **RNA (North Carolina)**

—— The miracle play in England — nomenclature. (Modern Language Association of America. Publications. Baltimore, 1916. 8°. v. 31 [new series, v. 24], p. 448–465.)   **RAA**

—— ...A new theory concerning the origin of the miracle play... Menasha, Wis.: George Banta Pub. Co., 1914. vi, 84 p. 8°.   **NAFH p.v.3**

—— A plea for the study of the Corpus Christi plays as drama. (University of North Carolina. — Philological Club. Studies in philology. Chapel Hill, 1929. 8°. v. 26, p. 411–424.)   **RNA**
Cf. additional note, *ibid.,* v. 27, p. 688. *Cf. also* Robert Withington, *The Corpus Christi plays as drama, ibid.,* v. 27, p. 573–582.

Coit, Davida. The poetic element in the mediæval drama. (Atlantic monthly. Boston, 1885. 8°. v. 56, p. 407–415.)   *** DA**

Coleman, Alexis Irénée du Pont, and A. D. Compton. Miracle-plays, mysteries, moralities. (Encyclopædia of religion and ethics. ed. James Hastings. New York, Edinburgh, 1916. 4°. v. 8, p. 690–695.)   *** R – ZAB**

Collier, John Payne. The performance of dramas by parish clerks and players in churches. (Shakespeare Society. Papers. London, 1847. 8°. v. 3, p. 40–47.)   *** NCK (Shakespeare)**

—— Printed religious plays [of the sixteenth century]. (In his: The history of dramatic poetry. London, 1831. 12°. v. 2, p. 236–257.)   **NCOM**

—— The Widkirk, Chester, and Coventry miracle-plays. [A comparative view.] (In his:

The history of dramatic poetry. London, 1831. 12°. v. 2, p. 155–229.)   **NCOM**
Introduction to miracle-plays, p. 123–154.

Cook, Albert Stanburrough. A remote analogue to the miracle play. (The Journal of English and Germanic philology. Bloomington, Ind., 1902. 8°. v. 4, p. 421–451.)   **RKA**
"In the first part of Cynewulf's Christ, that dealing with the Advent, there is a passage of 49 lines which various writers have imagined to constitute a precursor of the English drama."
The passage is given in prose, together with five homiletical expansions from the Fathers to which it is related.

Courthope, William John. The rise of the drama in England. (In his: A history of English poetry. London, 1895. 8°. v. 1, p. 393–425.)   *** R – NCID**

Craig, Hardin. The Corpus Christi procession and the Corpus Christi play. (Journal of English and Germanic philology. Urbana, Ill., 1914. 8°. v. 13, p. 589–602.)   **RKA**
"It is now pretty generally agreed that the English religious plays grew from their liturgical origins on English soil and were not translated from the French."

—— The origin of the Old Testament plays [in the religious drama]. (Modern philology. Chicago, 1913. 8°. v. 10, p. 473–487.)   **NAA**
"I venture to offer the following materials in support of another theory; namely, that the Old Testament plays, particularly those derived from the Book of Genesis and those relating to the Fall of Lucifer and the angels, in other words, the stock plays of the English cycles and of the popularly developed Continental cycles, did not originate from the Processus Prophetarum, but from the addition to the Passion play of a body of epical and homiletic material derived, in the first instance, from the lectiones and accompanying ritual of the church."

Creizenach, Wilhelm Michael Anton. The early religious drama. [Miracle plays.] (In: Cambridge history of English literature. Cambridge, 1907–27. 8°. v. 5, p. 36–51.)   *** R – NCB**

—— [Die englischen Mysterien.] (In his: Geschichte des neueren Dramas. Halle a.S., 1893. 8°. Bd. 1, p. 281–298.)   *** R – NAF**

—— Religious dramas. (New Schaff-Herzog encyclopedia of religious knowledge. New York and London [cop. 1911]. 4°. v. 9, p. 475–479.)   *** R – ZAB**

Crosse, Gordon. The miracle plays. illus. (In his: The religious drama. London [1913]. 16°. p. 58–96.)   **NAF**

Crowley, Timothy J. Character-treatment in the liturgical drama [and] in the cyclic drama. (In his: Character-treatment in mediaeval drama. Notre Dame, Ind., 1907. 8°. p. 41–117.)   **NAFD**

Cushman, L. W. [The devil in the English miracle plays.] (In his: The devil and the vice in the English dramatic literature before Shakespeare. Halle a. S., 1900. p. 4–44. 8°. (Studien zur englischen Philologie. Heft 6.)   **NCOD**

Miracle Plays — General Works, continued

Davidson, Charles. Concerning English mystery plays. (Modern language notes. Baltimore, 1892. 4°. v. 7, col. 339–343.) **RAA**

—— Studies in the English mystery plays. [New Haven, Conn.,] 1892. 125–297 p. 8°.
NAFM
Dissertation, Yale University.
Bibliography, p. 127–129.
Extr.: Connecticut Academy of Arts and Sciences. Transactions. v. 9, part 1.
Reviewed in *Academy*, London, 1893, v. 43, p. 80, * *DA;* and by H. Ungemach in *Anglia: Beiblatt,* Halle a.S., 1894, Bd. 4, p. 257–260, *RNA.*

—— —— 173 p. 8°. **NAFM**

Dearmer, Geoffrey. Miracle plays. (Saturday review. London, 1924. f°. v. 137, p. 8–9.) * **DA**

Dustoor, P. E. Some textual notes on the English mystery plays. (Modern language review. Cambridge, 1926. 8°. v. 21, p. 427–431.) **NAA**
On the York, Towneley, Newcastle, and non-cycle mystery plays.

Eckhardt, Eduard. Clownartige Gestalten in den Misterien und ältesten Mirakelspielen. (In his: Die lustige Person im älteren englischen Drama. Berlin, 1902. 8°. p. 27–97.)
NCOD

The **Educational Alliance.** — The Dramatic Club of the Thomas Davidson School. [Program and explanation of the miracle plays.] [New York: F. V. Strauss & Co.,] 1905. 2 l. 8°. **NAFM p.v.3, no.9**

English mystery ..miracle [and morality] plays. (In: Alfred Bates, editor. The drama. London [cop. 1903]. 8°. v. 4, p. 39–110.)
NAF (Bates)

Frank, Grace. Revisions in the English mystery plays. (Modern philology. Chicago, 1917. 8°. v. 15, p. 565–572.) **NAA**

Gaaf, W. van der. Miracles and mysteries in south-east Yorkshire. (Englische Studien. Leipzig, 1906. 8°. Bd. 36, p. 228–230.) **RNA**
For a further notice (by Edward Sorg) see *ibid.,* 1906, Bd. 37, p. 172–173.

Gayley, Charles Mills. The earlier miracle plays of England. (International quarterly. New York, 1905. 4°. v. 10, p. 108–129.) * **DA**

—— Plays of our forefathers; and some of the traditions upon which they were founded... New York: Duffield and Co., 1907. xi p., 1 l., 349 p. illus. 8°. **NAFM**

Genée, Rudolph. Die englischen Mirakelspiele und Moralitäten als Vorläufer des englischen Dramas. Berlin: Verlag von Carl Habel, 1878. 32 p. 8°. (Sammlung gemeinverständlicher wissenschaftlicher Vorträge. Serie 13, Heft 305.) * **C**

Gerould, Gordon Hall. Saints' lives in drama. (In his: Saints' legends. Boston and New York, 1916. 12°. p. 300–308.) **ZDK**

Gilbert, Allan H. Milton and the mysteries. (University of North Carolina. — Philological Club. Studies in philology. Chapel Hill, N. C., 1920. 8°. v. 17, p. 147–169.) **RNA (North Carolina)**
Traces the similarities to Milton's *Paradise lost* and *Paradise regained* in some of the larger cycle plays.

Gollancz, Israel. Mr. Israel Gollancz on the "early drama." [Abstract of a lecture delivered Dec. 16, 1888.] (Jewish chronicle. London, 1888. f°. Dec. 21, 1888, p. 12.)
* **PBE**

Grabo, Carl H. The mystery plays. (Chautauquan. Chautauqua, N. Y., 1906. 8°. v. 44, p. 98–106.) * **DA**

Greene, Antoinette. An index to the non-Biblical names in the English mystery plays. (In: Studies in language and literature in celebration of the seventieth birthday of James Morgan Hart. New York, 1910. 12°. p. 313–350.) **NCB**

Harris, Herbert. Was Paradise Lost suggested by the mystery plays? (Modern language notes. Baltimore, 1895. 4°. v. 10, p. 223.) **RAA**

Hase, Karl August von. Miracle plays and sacred dramas, a historical survey... Translated from the German by A. W. Jackson and edited by the Rev. W. W. Jackson... London: Trübner & Co., 1880. x p., 1 l., 273 p. 8°.
"Lectures...delivered at Jena and Weimar in the winter of 1857–58."

Hastings, Charles. [Liturgical drama, miracle plays and religious drama in England.] (In his: The theatre; its development in France and England. Translated by Frances A. Welby. London, 1901. 8°. p. 107–113, 118–126, 135–142, 156–165.) * **R – NAF**

Hohlfeld, Alexander Rudolf. Die altenglischen Kollektivmisterien, unter besonderer Berücksichtigung des Verhältnisses der York- und Towneley-Spiele. (Anglia. Halle a. S., 1889. 8°. Bd. 11, p. 219–310.) **RNA**

Hudson, Henry Norman. Miracle plays. (In his: Shakespeare. Boston, 1872. 12°. v. 1, p. 55–71.) **NADB**

Hughes, Elizabeth A. The use of the drama by the church as an instrument of social control. The ideals and standards which she tried to have work down to people. The drama in the hands of the crafts. (In her: A study of a mediaeval agency of social control. Chicago, 1915. 4°. p. 14–53.)
† **NAC p.v.145, no.2**

Hughes, T. Cann. Miracle play. (Notes and queries. London, 1896. 8°. series 8, v. 10, p. 364–365.) * **R – * DA**

Jusserand, Jean Adrien Antoine Jules. Les mystères. (In his: Le théâtre en Angleterre depuis la conquête. Paris, 1881. 2. ed. 12°. p. 39–106.) **NCOM**

Miracle Plays — General Works, continued

Jusserand, J. A. A. J., *continued*

—— A note on pageants and 'scaffolds hye.' 2 pl. (English miscellany, presented to Dr. Furnivall. Oxford, 1901. 8°. p. 183–195.) **RNB (English)**

—— ₍Religious drama in mediaeval England.₎ (In his: A literary history of the English people. New York, 1895. 8°. v. 1, p. 456–489.)   *** R – NCB**
Library also has 3. ed., 1926, *NCB.*

Keltie, John S. ₍The origins of English drama.₎ (In his: The works of the British dramatists. Edinburgh, 1870. 8°. p. xiv–xxvii.)   **NCO**

Kirtlan, Ernest J. B. The mystery and miracle plays. (London quarterly review. London, 1920. 8°. v. 134, p. 117–119.) *** DA**

Klein, Julius Leopold. ₍Chester, Towneley and Coventry plays.₎ (In his: Geschichte des englischen Dramas. Leipzig, 1876. 8°. Bd. 1, p. 711–754.)   **NAF**

Kress, Leona L. (Sister M. Clarissa.) Religious motive in English mediaeval drama. (Emerson quarterly. Boston, 1928. 4°. v. 8, Jan., 1928, p. 11–12, 28; March, 1928, p. 11–12, 28; May, 1928, p. 11–12.)   **† NANA**

Kretzmann, Paul Edward. The liturgical element in the earliest forms of the medieval drama with special reference to the English and German plays. Minneapolis: Bulletin of the University of Minnesota, 1916. vii, 170 p. table. 4°. (University of Minnesota. Studies in language and literature. no. 4.)   **STG (Minnesota)**

Leach, Arthur F. Some English plays and players, 1220–1548. (English miscellany, presented to Dr. Furnivall. Oxford, 1901. 8°. p. 205–234.)   **RNB (English)**
Refers principally to the presentation of miracle plays at Beverley and Lincoln, England.
"I suspect and suggest that the origin of the Corpus Christi play in England is to be sought in the developments of the great town democracies and craft gilds of Flanders, whether French or Teutonic."

Lyle, Marie Caroline. The original identity of the York and Towneley cycles... ₍Minneapolis, Minn., 1919.₎ iv p., 1 l., 113 p. 4°.   **NCE p.v.28, no.4**
Issued also as Research publications of the University of Minnesota, v. 8, no. 3, June, 1919; Studies in language and literature no. 6. This issue is identical with that with the addition of the cover-title with thesis note.
Cf. E. G. Clark, "The York plays and the gospel of Nicodemus," in *Publications of the Modern Language Association of America,* v. 43, p. 153–161, *RAA;* Grace Frank, "On the relation · between the York and the Towneley plays," v. 44, p. 313–319, and the rejoinder by Miss Lyle, v. 44, p. 319–328.

Manly, John Matthews. The miracle play in mediaeval England. (Royal Society of Literature of the United Kingdom. Transactions. London, 1927. 8°. new series, v. 7, p. 133–153.)   **NAA**

Matthews, Brander. The medieval drama. (In his: The development of the drama. New York, 1903. 12°. p. 107–146.) **NADB**

Mediæval theatricals. (Knickerbocker. New York, 1864. 8°. v. 63, p. 237–247.) *** DA**

Medley, Dudley Julius. The setting of the miracle plays. (Glasgow Archaeological Society. Transactions. Glasgow, 1906. 8°. new series, v. 5, part 2, p. 59–67.)   **CPA**
Deals largely with the staging of the miracle plays. Read at a meeting of the Society held on 23rd February 1905.

Mill, Anna Jean. ₍Miracle plays in Scotland.₎ (In her: Mediaeval plays in Scotland ... Edinburgh and London, 1927. 8°. p. 60–85.)   **NCOD**
St. Andrews University publications, no. 24.

The **Modern** church and miracle plays. (Literary digest. New York, 1912. f°. v. 44, p. 336.)   *** DA**
Abstract of several articles occasioned by the production of *The Miracle* at the Olympia, London, Dec. 23, 1911. For a further discussion see the twenty-one articles, letters, and editorials in the *Tablet,* London, 1912, v. 119, p. 82, 139, 162–164, 184, 202, 224–225, 263, 304–306, 345–346, 385, † *ZLF.*

Moore, E. Hamilton. The apocryphal element in mediaeval drama. (International journal of apocrypha. London, 1907. 4°. no. 11, p. 15–16.)   *** YLY**

—— English miracle plays and moralities. London: Sherratt & Hughes, 1907. vi p., 1 l., 199 p. 8°.   **NAFM**
Contents: Foreword. I. The liturgical drama. II. Church plays in England. III. The great cycles. IV. The actors and the stage. v. Comedy and tragedy. VI. The Gospel story. VII. The Cornish mysteries. VIII. Later development. IX. The early morality. X. Protestant moralities. Conclusion. Students' list (p. 197–199).
Reviewed by W. W. Greg in *Modern language review,* Cambridge, 1908, v. 3, p. 396, *NAA.*

Moore, Edward R. Mediaeval religious drama. (Fordham monthly. New York, 1913. 8°. v. 31, p. 328–333.)   **STG**

Moore, John Robert. The tradition of angelic singing in English drama. (Journal of English and Germanic philology. Urbana, Ill., 1923. 8°. v. 22, p. 89–99.)   **RKA**

Mysteries, moralities and other early dramas. (Retrospective review. London, 1820. 8°. v. 1, p. 332–357.)   *** DA**
English miracle plays, p. 332–340.

Mystery or passion plays. (Blackwood's Edinburgh magazine. New York, 1869. 8°. v. 106, p. 671–693.)   *** DA**

Nicoll, Allardyce. The growth of native drama: tropes and liturgical plays. illus. (In his: British drama. London ₍1925₎. 8°. p. 20–40.)   *** R – NCOD**
Also printed in 1927.

Miracle Plays — General Works, continued

Oelrich, Wilhelm. Die Personennamen im mittelalterlichen Drama Englands... Kiel: A. F. Jensen, 1911. 108 p., 1 l. 8°.
Dissertation, Erlangen. **NCO p.v.381**
Literaturverzeichnis, p. 7–9.

O'Neill, Francis. Ballad influence on miracle plays. (American Catholic quarterly review. Philadelphia, 1911. 8°. v. 36, p. 28–38.) ***DA**

—— The English miracle play. (Catholic University. Bulletin. Washington, 1909. 8°. v. 15, p. 464–473.) **STG**

P., J. Mysteries, or miracle plays. (Dublin University magazine. Dublin, 1871. 8°. v. 78, p. 361–373.) ***DA**

Patch, Howard R. The Ludus Coventriae and the Digby massacre. (Modern Language Association of America. Publications. Baltimore, 1920. 8°. v. 35, p. 324–343.) **RAA**

Peele, D. D. The history of religious pageantry. (In: Mason Crum, A guide to religious pageantry. New York, 1923. 12°. p. 16–31.) **NAFM**

Pennington, Jo. Mystery and miracle plays; primarily religious they were the foundations, laid and abandoned by the Church, of modern drama. illus. (International studio. New York, 1924. 4°. v. 80, p. 207–213.) **† MAA**

A **Poem** against the friars and their miracle-plays. (In: Reliquiæ antiquæ. Edited by T. Wright and J. O. Halliwell. London, 1841. 8°. v. 1, p. 322–323.) **NCE**
"From MS. Cotton. Cleop. B. ii, of the fifteenth century."

Pollard, Alfred William. Old Christmas plays. illus. (Universal review. London, 1889. 4°. v. 5, p. 517–534.) ***DA**

Roosval, Johnny. The reredoses and the theatre of the fifteenth century. (Mask. Florence, Italy, 1910–11. 4°. v. 3, p. 1–5.) **† NAFA**

Rudwin, Maximilian Josef. Modern Passion plays. (Open court. Chicago, 1916. 8°. v. 30, p. 278–300.) ***DA**

Sanborn, Katherine Abbott. The old miracle plays. (In her: My favorite lectures of long ago, for friends who remember. Boston, 1898. 8°. p. 174–216.) **NBQ**

Schaff, David Schley. The religious drama. (In: Philip Schaff, History of the Christian Church. New York, 1907. 8°. v. 5, part 1, p. 869–875.) *** R – ZDB**

Schelling, Felix Emmanuel. Old English sacred drama. illus. (Lippincott's monthly magazine. Philadelphia, 1904. 8°. v. 74, p. 441–453.) ***DA**

Schwab, Moïse. Mots hébreux dans les mystères du moyen âge. (Revue des études juives. Paris, 1903. 8°. v. 46, p. 148–151.) ***PBF**

A **Sermon** against miracle plays. (In: Reliquiæ antiquæ. Edited by T. Wright and J. O. Halliwell. London, 1843. 8°. v. 2, p. 42–57.) **NCE**
"From a ms. volume of English sermons, written at the latter end of the fourteenth century, and now preserved in the library of St. Martin's-in-the-Fields, London."
Reprinted in W. C. Hazlitt, editor, *The English drama and stage under the Tudor and Stuart princes, 1543–1664*, [London], 1869, p. 73–95, *NCOD*, and in G. G. Coulton, editor, *Life in the Middle Ages*, Cambridge, 1928, v. 1, p. 191–196, *BTH*.

Sharp, Thomas. A dissertation on the pageants or dramatic mysteries anciently performed at Coventry, by the trading companies of that city: chiefly with reference to the vehicle, characters, and dresses of the actors. Compiled, in a great degree, from sources hitherto unexplored. To which are added; the Pageant of the Shearmen & Taylors' Company, and other municipal entertainments of a public nature. Coventry: Merridew and Son, 1825. 3 p.l., 114 p., 115–118 f., 119–226 p., 2 l., 1 facsim., 9 pl. f°. **† NAFM**
Reviewed in *Retrospective review*, London, 1825, v. 13, p. 297–316, * *DA*.

Sheppard, Thomas. Miracle plays [in Hull, England]. (In his: Evolution of the drama in Hull and district. Hull, 1927. 8°. p. 7–32.) **NCOM**

Snell, Frederick John. Miracle plays. (In his: The customs of old England. London [1911]. 12°. p. 49–60.) **CN**
Library also has the London [1919] edition.

Solomon, Benvenuta. Some aspects of the devil in English dramatic literature. (Gentleman's magazine. London, 1907. 8°. v. 302, p. 583–601.) ***DA**
The devil in the cyclical miracle-plays, p. 583–587.

Spencer, Matthew Lyle. Corpus Christi pageants in England... New York: Baker & Taylor Co., 1911. 5 p.l., 276 p. 12°. **NCOM**
Bibliography, p. 263–269.

Strutt, Joseph. Ancient plays called miracles taken from Scripture. The Coventry play. Mystery described. How enlivened. (In his: Glig-gamena angel-deod; or, The sports and pastimes of the people of England. London, 1810. 2. ed. 4°. p. 136–139.) **† MVB**

Taylor, George C. The relation of the English Corpus Christi play to the Middle English religious lyric. (Modern philology. Chicago, 1907. 8°. v. 5, no. 1, July, 1907, p. 1–38.) **NAA**

Miracle Plays — General Works, continued

Thomas Davidson Dramatic Circle. The Thomas Davidson Dramatic Circle presents a revival of... English medieval miracle plays... 1. The creation and fall of man; 2. Noah's ark; 3. The sacrifice of Isaac; 4. The shepherds.·.. May 11, 1907... Carnegie Lyceum... ₍New York, 1907.₎ Poster: 10½ x 8½ in. †† **NAC p.v.8, no.25**

Tisdel, Frederick Monroe. The influence of popular customs on the mystery plays. (Journal of English and Germanic philology. Baltimore, 1903–05. 8°. v. 5, p. 323–340.) **RKA**

Verney, F. P. Mysteries, moralities, and the drama. (Contemporary review. London, 1875. 8°. v. 25, p. 595–609.) ***DA**

Ward, Adolphus William. ₍Religious drama in England.₎ (In his: A history of English dramatic literature. London, 1899. new ed. 8°. v. 1, p. 40–98.) ***R-NCOD**

Wesley, Edmund Alfred. The English miracle play. (Literary and Philosophical Society of Liverpool. Proceedings. London and Liverpool, 1899. 8°. v. 53, p. 133–152.) ***EC**

Whitmore, Charles Edward. The mediaeval sacred drama. Origin and growth of the liturgical drama. (In his: The supernatural in tragedy. Cambridge, 1915. 8°. p. 113–176.) **NAF**

Williamson, Claude C. H. Early religious drama. (American Catholic quarterly review. Philadelphia, 1921. 8°. v. 46, p. 225–242.) ***DA**

Winslow, Ola Elizabeth. Low comedy in the scripture cycles. (In her: Low comedy as a structural element in English drama. Chicago, 1926. 8°. p. 1–43.) **NCOD**

Wright, Thomas. On the history of the drama in the middle ages. (In his: Essays on archaeological subjects. London, 1861. 12°. v. 2, p. 169–193.) **CBA**
Repr.: Bentley's miscellany, London, 1855, v. 38, p. 298–309, * *DA.*

Young, Karl. Concerning the origin of the miracle play. (In: The Manly anniversary studies in language and literature. Chicago, 1923. 8°. p. 254–268.) **NCB (Manly)**

—— Observations on the origin of the mediaeval passion-play. (Modern Language Association of America. Publications. Baltimore, 1910. 8°. v. 25, p. 309–354.) **RAA**

—— The origin of the Easter play. (Modern Language Association of America. Publications. Baltimore, 1914. 8°. v. 29, p. 1–58.) **RAA**

COLLECTIONS

General Collections

Adams, Joseph Quincy, editor. Chief pre-Shakespearean dramas; a selection of plays illustrating the history of the English drama from its origin down to Shakespeare... Boston, New York: Houghton Mifflin Co. ₍cop. 1924.₎ vii, 712 p. illus. 12°. ***R-NCO**
Partial contents: Sources of the liturgical drama. Liturgical plays. Sources of the vernacular (Shrewsbury fragments). The craft cycles (selections). Noncycle plays (Conversion of St. Paul, Magdalene).

Collier, John Payne. Five miracle plays, or Scriptural dramas. Privately printed under the care of J. Payne Collier, F. S. A. London: ₍F. Shoberl, Jun.,₎ 1836. v. p. 12°.
Contents: Introduction The harrowing of hell, from Ms. Harl. 2253. The harrowing of hell, from Auchinleck Ms. The sacrifice of Abraham, Trin. Col. Dublin. The adoration of the shepherds, from the Towneley Ms. The marriage of the Virgin, from the Coventry cycle. The advent of Antichrist, from the Chester cycle. Glossary.
This volume contains six, instead of five, plays; the sixth being the second Harrowing of hell play. Each play has a preface initialed J. P. C. followed by the legend "only twenty-five copies printed"; each is separately paged, and each bears the imprint of F. Shoberl, Jun. The second Harrowing of hell play is prefaced by another hand, is dated July, 1835, and bears the imprint Edinburgh: Ballantyne and Co.
This copy has bookplates of Russell and R. F. B. Hodgkinson, on inside cover. Signature of Mitford, 1837, and E. S. Dallas, 1864 on second fly-leaf. Inserted is a colored slip reading "The Rev. J. Mitford, with the editor's sincere regards."

Everyman. "Everyman," with other interludes, including eight miracle plays. London: J. M. Dent & Sons; New York: E. P. Dutton & Co. ₍1909.₎ xxi, 198 p. 12°. (Everyman's library, ed. by Ernest Rhys. Poetry and the drama.) **NAFM**
Introduction by Ernest Rhys.
Partial contents: Deluge. Abraham, Melchisedec, and Isaac. The Wakefield second Shepherds' play. The Coventry Nativity play. The Wakefield miracle-play of the crucifixion. The Cornish mystery-play of the three Maries. The mystery of Mary Magdalene and the apostles. The Wakefield pageant of the harrowing of hell. God's promises.

Everyman, & other plays. Decorated by John Avsten. ₍London:₎ Chapman & Hall, Ltd., 1925. 6 p.l., 201 p. illus. 4°. **NAFM**
Partial contents: Nativity [Shearmen and tailors]. [Second Towneley] Shepherds' play.

Harvard Dramatic Club miracle plays. *See* **Robinson,** Donald Fay, editor.

Hemingway, Samuel Burdett, editor. English Nativity plays. Edited with introduction, notes, and glossary by Samuel B. Hemingway... New York: Henry Holt and Co.,

Miracle Plays — General Collections, cont'd

1909. 3 p.l., xlviii, 319 p. 8°. (Yale studies in English. no. 38.) **NAFM**
Contents: History and development of the Nativity plays. Chester plays, nos. 6, 7. Coventry plays, nos. 11, 12, 13, 15, 16. York plays, nos. 12, 13, 14, 15. Towneley plays, nos. 10, 11, 12, 13. Notes. Glossary.
Reviewed in *The Nation,* New York, 1909, v. 89, p. 311–312, * *DA;* and by Sir E. K. Chambers in *Modern language review,* Cambridge, 1912, v. 7, p. 546, *NAA.*

Hone, William. Ancient mysteries described; especially the English miracle plays, founded on apocryphal New Testament story, extant among the unpublished manuscripts in the British Museum; including notices of ecclesiastical shows... With engravings on copper and wood... London: Printed for W. Hone, 1823. 1 p.l., x p., 1 l., 13–298 p. illus. 8°. **NAFM**
Contents: The birth of Mary. Mary's education in the Temple, and being saved by angels. The miraculous espousal of Joseph and Mary. A council of the Trinity and the Incarnation. Joseph's jealousy. Visit of Mary to Elizabeth. The trial of Mary and Joseph. The miraculous birth and the midwives.
Reviewed in the *European magazine,* London, 1823, v. 84, p. 161–163, * *DA.*

Manly, John Matthews. Specimens of the pre-Shaksperean drama with an introduction, notes and a glossary by John Matthews Manly. Boston and London: Ginn & Co., 1897. 2 v. 12°. (Athenaeum Press series.) **NCO**
Partial contents: [Shrewsbury fragments]. Norwich Creation and fall. Towneley Noah's flood. [Coventry] Noah and Lamech. Brome Abraham and Isaac. Towneley Isaac. Towneley Jacob. Chester De Mose et Rege Balaak et Balaam Propheta. [Coventry] The Salutation and conception. Towneley The second shepherds' play. Coventry The pageant of the Shearmen and taylors (The Nativity and the slaughter of the Innocents). York Resurrection. Chester Antichrist (Hengwrt version). York Judgment day. Digby The conversion of St. Paul. The play of the sacrament. Nice wanton. David and Bethsabe (by Peele).

Marriott, William. A collection of English miracle-plays or mysteries; containing ten dramas from the Chester, Coventry, and Towneley series, with two of latter date. To which is prefixed, An historical view of this description of plays. Basel: Schweighauser & Co., 1838. lxiii(i), 271 p. 8°. **NAFM**
Contents: Chester miracle-plays: The deluge; Antichrist. Coventry miracle-plays: Joseph's jealousy; The trial of Mary and Joseph; The Pageant of the Company of shearmen and tailors. Towneley miracle-plays: Pharao; Pastores; Crucifixio; Extractio animarum ab inferno; Juditium. Candelmas-day, or the killing of the children of Israel. God's promises.

Osgood, Phillips Endecott. Old-time church drama adapted. Mystery plays and moralities of earlier days for sundry churchly uses to-day... New York and London: Harper & Brothers, 1928. 5 p.l., 3–291 p. illus. 12°. **NAFM**
Partial contents: The Quem Quaeritus. Melchizedek, Abraham and Isaac [Chester]. The Nativity cycle of the York mystery plays.

Parry, W. Dyfed, editor. Old plays for modern players. Selected and modernized by W. Dyfed Parry. London: Edward Arnold & Co. [1930.] 156 p., 1 pl. 12°.
Partial contents: [Chester] Noah's flood. [Brome] Abraham and Isaac. [Towneley second] shepherds' play.

Pollard, Alfred William. English miracle plays, moralities and interludes. Specimens of the pre-Elizabethan drama edited, with an introduction, notes, and glossary, by Alfred W. Pollard. Oxford: At the Clarendon Press, 1890. lx, 250 p. 12°. **NAFM**
Partial contents: York play no. 1, The creation and Fall of Lucifer. Chester play no. 2, Noah's flood. Chester play no. 4, The sacrifice of Isaac. Towneley play no. 13, Secunda pastorum (abridged). Coventry play no. 11, The salutation and conception. Digby plays, Mary Magdalen (abridged). The harrowing of hell [Middle-English, Harley Ms. Text L]. [Brome play of] Abraham and Isaac.
The Library also has the 4th, 7th and 8th editions (1904, 1923, 1927).
Reviewed by E. Kölbing in *Englische Studien,* Bd. 16, 1892, p. 278–282, *RNA.* See also his article "Kleine Beiträge zur Erklärung und Textkritik vor-Shakespeare'scher Dramen," Bd. 21, 1895, p. 162–167. For an index to the textual notes in these two articles, arranged by the respective plays, see the *General-register zu Bd. 1–25* of *Englische Studien,* p. 52–53, 77–84.
Also reviewed in *The Athenæum,* London, Jan. 24, 1891, p. 130–131, * *DA,* and by J. M. Garnett in *American journal of philology,* Baltimore, 1891, v. 12, p. 92–94, *RAA.*
For a review of the 2d edition, 1895 (by E. Kölbing) see *Englische Studien,* Bd. 22, p. 288–289; for reviews of the 4th ed. see *Englische Studien,* Leipzig, 1904, Bd. 34, p. 103–105, *RNA,* and *Notes and queries,* London, 1904, series 10, v. 2, p. 278, * *R* – * *DA.*
On "the locality of the Towneley plays" by W. W. Skeat see *Athenæum,* London, 1893, v. 102, p. 779, * *DA.*

Robinson, Donald Fay, editor. The Harvard Dramatic Club miracle plays; ten plays translated and adapted by various hands, edited with notes on production and music by Donald Fay Robinson. Preface by George Pierce Baker. New York City: S. French; London: S. French, Ltd. [cop. 1928.] xiii, 247 p. 8°. **NAFM**
Contents: Produced plays: The pageant of the shearmen and the tailors, the Coventry play adapted by J. M. Brown. The Towneley play adapted by R. C. Burrell. The nativity, the Chantilly play translated and adapted by E. Sanchez and D. F. Robinson. The Benediktbeuren play translated and adapted by D. F. Robinson. The wisemen, the Spanish play translated and adapted by D. F. Robinson. The Provençal play, translated and adapted by D. F. Robinson. Unproduced plays, translated and adapted by D. F. Robinson: The Hessian Christmas play. The Maastricht play. The star, the Bilsen play. The Umbrian play.

Schweikert, Harry Christian, editor. Early English plays. New York: Harcourt, Brace and Co. [cop. 1928.] vi p., 1 l., 845 p. illus. 8°. **NCO**
Partial contents: The fall of Lucifer. Noah. Abraham and Isaac. The second Shepherds' play. The judgment day.
See also introduction, p. 17–22: Miracle plays; p. 22–31: The great cycles and their production.

Miracle Plays — General Collections, continued

The **Second** shepherds' play; Everyman and other early plays. Translated with introduction and notes by Clarence Griffin Child. Boston: Houghton Mifflin Co. ₍cop. 1910.₎ xlviii, 138 p. 16°. (Riverside literature series.)   **NCO p.v. 556**

Partial contents: The Quem Quaeritis from the Regularis Concordia Monachorum. The Brome Abraham and Isaac. The second Shepherds' play of the Towneley cycle.

Tickner, Frederick James, editor. Earlier English drama from Robin Hood to Everyman. Edited and arranged for acting.

American edition revised by Thomas Whitfield Baldwin... New York: Thomas Nelson & Sons ₍cop. 1929₎. xx, (1)18–304 p. illus. 16°. (Nelson's English series.)
NCO (Tickner)

Partial contents: Noah's flood (Newcastle); The Flood (Towneley); Abraham's sacrifice of Isaac (York); Sacrifice of Isaac (Brome); Creation (Ludus Coventriæ); Prophets (Ludus Coventriæ); Pageant of Shearmen and Taylors; Shepherds' play (Chester); Secunda pastorum; Massacre of the innocents (Chester); Salutation (Ludus Coventriæ); Raising of Lazarus (Ludus Coventriæ); Christ betrayed (Chester); Trial of Christ (Ludus Coventriæ); Condemnation and crucifixion (Ludus Coventriæ); Harrowing of hell (Chester); Resurrection (Chester); Doomsday (Ludus Coventriæ); Conversion of Saint Paul (Digby).

INDIVIDUAL CYCLES

YORK PLAYS

York plays. York plays; the plays performed by the crafts or mysteries of York on the day of Corpus Christi in the 14th, 15th, and 16th centuries now first printed from the unique manuscript in the library of Lord Ashburnham. Edited with introduction and glossary by Lucy Toulmin Smith... Oxford: At the Clarendon Press, 1885. lxxviii p., 1 l., 557 p. illus. 8°.   **NAFM**

p. xi–lxxviii: Introduction.
p. 529–557: Glossary.
"Written about 1340–50, if not even earlier...the bulk of it [is] the work of a single hand."

Reviewed in *Anglia*, Halle a. S., 1885, v. 8, Anzeiger, p. 159–163 (by Ludwig Proescholdt), *RNA; The Athenæum*, London, 1885, v. 86, p. 187–188, * DA; Deutsche Litteraturzeitung, Berlin, 1885, Jahrg. 6, col. 1304–1306 (by Julius Zupitza), *NAA; American journal of philology*, Baltimore, 1886, v. 7, p. 518–520 (by James M. Garnett), *RAA; Revue critique d'histoire et de littérature*, Paris, 1885, nouv. série, tome 20, p. 466–471 (by J. J. Jusserand), *NAA; The Nation*, New York, 1885, v. 41, p. 242, * DA; Saturday review, London, 1885, v. 60, p. 233–234, * DA; and Scottish review, London, 1885, v. 6, p. 220–248, * DA.

Also reviewed in *Englische Studien*, Heilbronn, 1886, Bd. 9, p. 448–453 (by Joseph Hall), *RNA*. For an index to the textual notes, arranged by the respective plays, see *Generalregister zu Band 1–25*, p. 77–84.

See also the article by E. Kölbing "Beiträge zur Erklärung und Textkritik der York plays" in *Englische Studien*, Bd. 20, p. 179–220.

Mooney, Margaret Sullivan, compiler. A rosary of mystery plays. Fifteen plays selected from the York cycle of mysteries performed by the crafts on the day of Corpus Christi in the 14th, 15th and 16th centuries. Translated from the Middle English of the originals into our mother tongue by Margaret S. Mooney... Albany: Frank H. Evory & Co., 1915. 150 p., 15 pl. 8°. **NAFM**

Contents: The annunciation. The visit of Mary to Elizabeth. The nativity. The presentation of the child Jesus. Christ with the doctors in the Temple. The agony in the Garden of Gethsemane. The scourging of Jesus by Pilate's orders. The crowning of Jesus with thorns. Christ led up to Calvary bearing his cross. The crucifixion of Christ. The resurrection. The ascension. The descent of the Holy Spirit. The

assumption of the Virgin. The coronation of the Virgin.
Reviewed in the *Catholic world*, New York, 1916, v. 102, p. 685–686, * DA.

Wright, Paul H. The word of God: a miracle play adapted from the mediaeval York cycle ₍plays 1–18, 41₎, by Paul H. Wright; with an introduction by the Rev. Arnold Pinchard... York: The Church Shop, 1926. 39(1) p. 12°. **NAFH p.v.16, no.6**
Produced at All Saints Church, York, England.

The **ASHBURNHAM** ms. of the York mystery plays. (Academy. London, 1882. f°. v. 22, July 1, 1882, p. 9–10.)   *** DA**

CLARK, Eleanor Grace. The York plays and the gospel of Nicodemus. (Modern Language Association of America. Publications. Menasha, Wis., 1928. 8°. v. 43, p. 153–161.)
RAA

COBLENTZ, H. E. A rime index to the "Parent cycle" of the York mystery plays, and of a portion of the Woodkirk Conspiracio et Capito. (Modern Language Association of America. Publications. Baltimore, 1895. 8°. v. 10, p. 487–557.)   **RAA**

COOPER, Thomas Parsons. The armorial bearings of the old craft guilds and companies ₍of York₎. Colored plates. (In: The book of the York pageant 1909... York, 1909. 4°.)

CRAIGIE, William Alexander. The gospel of Nicodemus and the York mystery plays. (In: An English miscellany. Presented to Dr. Furnivall. Oxford, 1901. 8°. p. 52–61.) **RNB**

DUSTOOR, P. E. Textual notes on the York Old Testament plays. (Anglia. Halle a. S., 1928. 8°. Bd. 52, p. 26–36.)   **RNA**

HERTTRICH, Oswald. Studien zu den York plays... Breslau: Buchdruckerei Lindner, 1886. 2 p.l., 31 p., 1 l. 8°.   **NAFH p.v.20**

HOLTHAUSEN, Ferdinand. Beiträge zur Erklärung und Textkritik der York Plays. (Archiv für das Studium der neueren

Miracle Plays — Individual Cycles: York Plays, continued

Sprachen und Litteraturen. Braunschweig, 1890. 8°. Bd. 85, p. 411–428.) **RAA**
Continued under title "Nachtrag zur den Quellen der York Plays" in Bd. 86, p. 280–282.

—— ₁Textual criticism.₎ (Anglia. Halle a.S., 1899. 8°. Bd. 21, p. 443–452.) **RNA**

—— Zur Erklärung und Textkritik der York plays. (Englische Studien. Leipzig, 1910. Bd. 41, p. 380–384.) **RNA**

KAMMAN, Paul Julius Gustav. Die Quellen der York-Spiele. (Anglia. Halle a. S., 1888. 8°. Bd. 10, p. 189–226.) **RNA**

—— Über Quellen und Sprache der York Plays. Halle a. S.: Ehrhardt Karras, 1887. 2 p.l., 75 (1) p. 8°.
Title from Columbia University Library.

KOELBING, Eugen. Beiträge zur Erklärung und Textkritik der York Plays. (Englische Studien. Leipzig, 1895. 8°. Bd. 20, p. 179–220.) **RNA**

LUICK, Karl. Zur Textkritik der Spiele von York. (Anglia. Halle a.S., 1899. 8°. Bd. 22, p. 384–391.) **RNA**

ROWE, Henry Kalloch. The Corpus Christi plays at York. (Brown magazine. Providence, 1892. 8°. v. 3, p. 110–114.) **STG (Brown)**

ZUPITZA, Julius. ₁Textual studies.₎ (Deutsche Literaturzeitung. Berlin, 1885. 4°. Bd. 6, cols. 1304–1306.) **NAA**

TOWNELEY PLAYS

A group of Towneley plays were produced by the Norwich Players, Old Music House, Norwich, England, 1919.

Towneley plays. The Towneley mysteries. London: J. B. Nichols and Son ₁1836₎. xx p., 1 l., 352 p. illus. 8°. (Surtees Society. Publications. ₁no. 3.₎) **CA (Surtees)**
Thirty-two mysteries, supposed to have been acted at Wakefield; printed from a manuscript formerly in the possession of the Towneley family; edited by James Raine, compared with manuscript by Joseph Stevenson. *cf.* Dict. nat. biog. and pref. (p. xviii). *cf. also* Lowndes, Bibliographer's manual.
Reviewed in *Gentleman's magazine*, London, 1836, new series, v. 6 [v. 160], p. 563–572, * DA.

—— The Towneley plays. Re-edited from the unique ms. by George England, with side-notes and introduction by Alfred W. Pollard, M. A. London: Published for the Early English Text Society by K. Paul, Trench, Trübner & Co., 1897. xxxiv p., 1 l., 416 p., 1 l. 8°. (Early English Text Society. Extra series. no. 71.) **NCE (Early)**
Appendix. The Secunda pastorum of the Towneley plays and Archie Armstrang's aith, by E. Kölbing: p. xxxi–xxxiv.
Reviewed in *Athenæum*, London, 1899, v. 114, p. 769, * DA, and in *Notes and queries*, London, 1898, series 9, v. 1, p. 179, * R – * DA.

BUNZEN, Asmus. Ein Beitrag zur Kritik der Wakefielder Mysterien... Kiel: H. Fiencke, 1903. 3 p.l., 58 p., 1 l. 8°. Litteratur, p. 55–58. **NAFM p.v.1, no.2**
Reviewed by K. Luick in *Anglia: Beiblatt*, Halle a.S., 1906, Bd. 17, p. 161–163, *RNA*.

CADY, Frank W. The couplets and quatrains in the Towneley mystery plays. (Journal of English and Germanic philology. Urbana, Ill., 1911. 8°. v. 10, p. 572–584.) **RKA**

—— The liturgical basis of the Towneley mysteries. (Modern Language Association of America. Publications. Baltimore, 1909. 8°. v. 24, p. 419–469.) **RAA**

—— The Passion group in Towneley. (Modern philology. Chicago, 1913. 8°. v. 10, p. 587–600.) **NAA**

—— The Wakefield group in Towneley. (Journal of English and Germanic philology. Urbana, Ill., 1912. 8°. v. 11, p. 244–262.) **RKA**

CAPES, F. M. The poetry of the early mysteries. (Nineteenth century. London, 1883. 8°. v. 14, p. 654–673.) ***DA**
Extracts translated into modern English.
Reprinted in *Eclectic magazine*, London, 1884, new series, v. 39, p. 1–16, * DA.

CAREY, Millicent. The Wakefield group of the Towneley cycle; a study to determine the conventional and original elements in four plays commonly ascribed to the Wakefield author... Göttingen: Vandenhoeck & Ruprecht; Baltimore: The Johns Hopkins Press, 1930. 4 p.l., 251 p. 8°. (Hesperia. Ergänzungsreihe: Schriften zur englischen Philologie. Heft 11.) **NAFM**
Bibliography, p. 245–251.

COATES, Sir Edward Feetham, bart. Catalogue of the Towneley mysteries and the York missal, the property of the late Sir Edward F. Coates... which will be sold by auction by Messrs. Sotheby, Wilkinson & Hodge... on Wednesday, the 8th of February, 1922... ₁London:₎ Dryden Press ₁1922₎. 8 p., 1 facsim. 4°. **NAC p.v.76, no.10**

DUSTOOR, P. E. Textual notes on the Towneley Old Testament plays. (Englische Studien. Leipzig, 1928. 8°. Bd. 63, p. 220–228.) **RNA**

EBERT, Adolf. Die englischen Mysterien, mit besonderer Berücksichtigung der Towneley-Sammlung. (Jahrbuch für romanische und englische Literatur. Berlin, 1859. 8°. Bd. 1, p. 44–82, 131–170.) **NAA**

FRANK, Grace. St. Martial of Limoges in the York plays. (Modern language notes. Baltimore, 1929. 8°. v. 44, p. 233–235.) **RAA**

GAYLEY, Charles Mills. The later miracle plays of England. I. The Wakefield master of comedy. (International quarterly. New York, 1905. 4°. v. 12, p. 67–88.) ***DA**

Miracle Plays — Individual Cycles:
Towneley Plays, continued

HOLTHAUSEN, Ferdinand. Studien zu den Towneley plays. (Englische Studien. Leipzig, 1924. 8°. Bd. 58, p. 161–178.)   **RNA**

PEACOCK, Matthew H. Towneley, Widkirk, or Wakefield plays? (Yorkshire archaeological journal. Leeds, 1898–1900. 8°. v. 15, p. 94–103.)   **CO**

—— The Wakefield mysteries. (Anglia. Halle a. S., 1901. 8°. Bd. 24, p. 509–524.)   **RNA**

"The object of this paper will be to show that there are important reasons for believing that they were performed in Wakefield, and should therefore be called 'The Wakefield mysteries'."

—— The Wakefield mysteries. (Anglia. Beiblatt. Halle a. S., 1925. 8°. Bd. 36, p. 111–114.)   **RNA**

—— The Wakefield mysteries. [Two letters.] (Times literary supplement. London, March 5, 1925, p. 156; June 7, 1928, p. 431.)   ***A**

Adduces further proof that the so-called Towneley plays were written and acted at Wakefield.
For an answer by Russell Potter to his letter of March 5, see p. 300.

SHARPE, Lancelot. Remarks on the Towneley mysteries [elucidating some passages of Shakespeare], in a letter...addressed to Thomas Amyot. (Archaeologia; or, Miscellaneous tracts relating to antiquity. London, 1838. 4°. v. 27, p. 251–256.)   **† CA**

WANN, Louis. The influence of French farce on the Towneley cycle of mystery plays. (Wisconsin Academy of Sciences, Arts and Letters. Transactions. Madison, 1918. 8°. v. 19, part 1, p. 356–368.)   ***EA**

—— A new examination of the manuscript of the Towneley plays. 1 folded facsim. (Modern Language Association of America. Publications. Menasha, Wis., 1928. 8°. v. 43, p. 137–152.)   **RAA**

The Chester Plays

Chester plays. Chester mysteries... London: Bensley and Sons, 1818. 5 p.l., xxii p., 1 l., 70 p., 1 pl. 4°. (Roxburghe Club.)   **NAFM**

Contents: Introduction (by J. H. Markland), p. i–xvi. Postscript, p. xvii–xxii. Proclamation, p. 1–2. The Banes, or Prologue, p. 3–12. De Deluvio Noe, p. 15–37. De Occisione Innocentium, p. 41–70.
The introduction is reprinted in William Shakespeare, *Plays and poems*, ed. E. Malone, London, 1821, v. 3, p. 525–549, *NCM (Malone)*.

—— The Chester plays: a collection of mysteries founded upon Scriptural subjects, and humorously represented by the trades of Chester at Whitsuntide. Edited by Thomas Wright... London: Printed for the Shakespeare Society, 1843–47. 2 v. illus. 8°.   **NAFM (Chester)**

Contents: 1. The Fall of Lucifer. 2. The Creation and Fall, and Death of Abel. 3. Noah's flood. 4. The

histories of Lot and Abraham. 5. Balaam and his ass. 6. The salutation and Nativity. 7. The play of the shepherds. 8. The three kings. 9. The offering and return of the three kings. 10. The slaughter of the innocents. 11. The purification. 12. The temptation and the woman taken in adultery. 13. Lazarus. 14. Christ's entry into Jerusalem. 15. Christ betrayed. 16. The Passion. 17. The Crucifixion. 18. The harrowing of hell. 19. The Resurrection. 20. The pilgrims of Emaus. 21. The Ascension. 22. The emission of the Holy Ghost. 23. Ezechiel. 24. Antichrist. 25. Doomsday.

—— —— London: Printed for the Shakespeare Society, 1843–47. 2 v. in 1. illus. 8°. (In: Thomas Amyot, A supplement to Dodsley's Old plays. [London,] 1853. v. 1.)   ***NCK (Shakespeare)**

Shakespeare Society. Publications, no. 17, 35.

—— The Chester plays. Re-edited from the mss. by the late Dr. Hermann Deimling. London: Published for the Early English Text Society by K. Paul, Trench, Trübner & Co., 1893–1916. 2 v. 8°. (Early English Text Society. Extra series. no. 62, 115.)

Paged continuously.   **NCE (Early)**
v. 2 edited by Dr. Matthews.
Final section issued "without the usual apparatus."
— *Prefatory note,* v. 2.

—— The Chester miracle plays, done into modern English and arranged for acting by I. and O. Bolton King. With an introduction by Sir Barry V. Jackson. London: Society for Promoting Christian Knowledge [1930]. xvii p., 1 l., 3–177 p. music. 12°.   **NAFM**

Partial contents: The childhood of man; The Nativity; The Passion; Epilogue, On the road to Emmaus.
"Perhaps the nearest modern parallel to the spirit of these old plays is to be found in the...American play 'The green pastures.'"
Reviewed in *Times literary supplement,* London, 1930, v. 29, p. 1041, † *NAA.*

BAUGH, Albert C. The Chester plays and French literature. (In: Schelling anniversary papers, by his former students. New York, 1923. 8°. p. 35–63.)   **NBP**

BRIDGE, Joseph C. The Chester miracle plays; some facts concerning them, and the supposed authorship of Ralph Higden. (Chester & North Wales Archeological and Historic Society. Journal. Chester, 1903. 8°. new series, v. 9, p. 59–98.)   **CO (Chester)**

DALE, Darley. The Chester plays. An appreciation. (Month. London, 1906. 8°. v. 107, p. 266–278.)   ***DA**

DEIMLING, Hermann Wilhelm Eduard. Text-Gestalt und Text-Kritik der Chester plays... Berlin: Mayer & Müller, 1890. 2 p.l., 32 p., 1 l. 12°.

Title from Columbia University Library.

DUSTOOR, P. E. Textual notes on the Chester Old Testament plays. (Anglia. Halle a.S., 1928. 8°. Bd. 52, p. 97–112.)   **RNA**

GOLLANCZ, Hermann. The Chester mystery plays. (Chester and North Wales Archaeological and Historic Society. Journal. Chester, 1908. 8°. new series, v. 14, p. 18–28.)   **CO (Chester)**

Miracle Plays — Individual Cycles:
Chester Plays, continued

HUME, A. ₍On the Chester mystery play, presented before the Congress of the British Archaeological Association, 1849.₎ (British Archaeological Association. Journal. London, 1849. 8°. v. 5, p. 317–320.) **CA**

MATHEWS, Godfrey W. The Chester mystery plays. Liverpool: E. Howell, Ltd., 1925. 2 p.l., 85 p., 2 pl. 8°. **NAFM**
"Reprinted from the 'Transactions of the Historic Society of Lancashire and Cheshire' vol. lxxvi, with an appendix and an additional plate."

UNGEMACH, Heinrich. Die Quellen der fünf ersten Chester Plays. Erlangen: A. Deichert, 1890. 1 p.l., x p., 1 l., 198 p. 8°. (Münchener Beiträge zur romanischen und englischen Philologie. Heft 1.) **RDTA**
Benützte Literatur, p. vii–x.

UTESCH, Hans. Die Quellen der Chester-Plays... Kiel: Druck der Kieler Tagespost, 1909. 2 p.l., v, 94 p., 1 l. 8°. **NAFM p.v.4**
"Literatur," p. i–v.

COVENTRY PLAYS

Coventry plays. Ludus Coventriae A collection of mysteries, formerly represented at Coventry on the feast of Corpus Christi. Edited by James Orchard Halliwell. London: Printed for the Shakespeare Society, 1841. xvi, 434 p. 8°. **NAFM**
The first five plays were first printed in John Stevens, *History of the antient abbeys, monasteries, hospitals, cathedrals and collegiate churches*, London, 1722, v. 1, p. 139–157, and reprinted in 1830 in Sir William Dugdale, *Monasticon Anglicanum*, new ed., v. 6, part 3, p. 1537–1543, † *CAB*.

—— —— London: Printed for the Shakespeare Society, 1843. xvi, 434 p. 8°. (In: Thomas Amyot, editor, A supplement to Dodsley's Old plays. ₍London,₎ 1853. v. 2, no. 1.) *** NCK (Shakespeare)**
[Shakespeare Society. Publications. no. 4.]

—— Ludus Coventriæ; or, The plaie called Corpus Christi, Cotton ms. Vespasian D. VIII, by K. S. Block... London: Published for the Early English Text Society, by H. Milford, Oxford University Press, 1922. lx, 402 p., 1 l. facsims. 8°. (Early English Text Society. Extra series no. 120.) **NCE (Early)**
Numbered as 42 plays in the ms. (omitting 17 and 22 and repeating 10) preceded by a "Proclamation" which describes the "pageants."
"The title Ludus Coventriæ has been retained... [though] it is now recognized that there is no connexion between The plaie called Corpus Christi and the Coventry civic cycle." — *cf.* p. vi and xxxix.
Reviewed by A. H. T. in *Modern language review*, Cambridge, 1924, v. 19, p. 256–257, *NAA*.
For textual notes by F. Holthausen see *Anglia; Beiblatt*, Halle a. S., 1924, Bd. 35, p. 37–40, *RNA*.

BIRT, Henry Norbert. The ancient mystery plays of Coventry. (Downside review. Wes-

ton-super-Mare, Eng., 1897. 8°. v. 16, p. 1–20.) *** DA**

BLOCK, Katherine Salter. Some notes on the problem of the 'Ludus Coventriæ.' (Modern language review. Cambridge, 1915. 8°. v. 10, p. 47–57.) **NAA**

CRAIG, Hardin. The Coventry cycle of plays. (The Athenæum. London, 1913. f°. Aug. 16, 1913, p. 166.) *** DA**
"There are good reasons for fixing upon Lincoln as the home of these plays."
For a letter by W. W. Greg disagreeing with this view see issue for Sept. 13, p. 262.

DODDS, Madeleine Hope. The problem of the 'Ludus Coventriae.' (Modern language review. Cambridge, 1914. 8°. v. 9, p. 79–91.) **NAA**
"The cycle of plays known as the 'Ludus Coventriae' exists in a single ms. (British Museum Cotton Ms. Vespasian D. viii) which bears the following notes:
(1) The date 1468.
(2) At the beginning the signature 'Robert Hegge, Dunelmensis,' and before the 29th play 'Ego R. H. Dunelmensis, Possideo.'
(3) On the fly-leaf in an Elizabethan hand 'The plaie called Corpus Christi.'
(4) On the fly-leaf in the hand of Richard James, Sir Robert Cotton's librarian c. 1630; 'Contenta Novi Testamenti scenice expressa et actitata olim per monachos sive fratres mendicantes: vulgo dicitur hic liber "Ludus Coventriae," sive ludus Corporis Christi: scribitur metris Anglicanis.' " — *p. 79.*

HARTMAN, Herbert. The home of the Ludus Coventriae. (Modern language notes. Baltimore, 1926. 8°. v. 41, p. 530–531.) **RAA**

KRAMER, Max. Sprache und Heimat des sogen. Ludus Coventriae; eine Untersuchung zur mittelenglischen Sprachgeschichte ... Halle a. S.: ₍C. Vogt,₎ 1892. 69(1) p. 8°.
Title from Columbia University Library.

SWENSON, Esther Lydia. An inquiry into the composition and structure of Ludus Coventriae...with a note on the home of Ludus Coventriae, by Hardin Craig... Minneapolis: the University, 1914. 2 p.l., 83 p. 4°. (University of Minnesota. Studies in language and literature 1.) **STG (Minn.)**
Reviewed by W. W. Greg in *Library*, London, 1920, series 4, v. 1, p. 182–184, ** HA;* and by Hardin Craig in *The Nation*, New York, 1913, v. 97, p. 308–309, ** DA.*

THOMPSON, Elbert N. S. The Ludus Coventriæ. (Modern language notes. Baltimore, 1906. 4°. v. 21, p. 18–20.) **RAA**

WELLS, Henry W. Ludus Coventriæ. (American church monthly. New York, 1927. 8°. v. 22, p. 273–286.) **ZRA**

WYNNE, Arnold. ₍On the Coventry plays.₎ (In his: The growth of English drama. Oxford, 1914. 12°. p. 25–38.) **NCOD**

Miracle Plays — Individual Cycles, continued

THE STONYHURST PLAYS

Brown, Carleton Fairchild, editor. . . . The Stonyhurst pageants, edited with introduction by Carleton Brown. . . Göttingen: Vandenhoeck & Ruprecht; Baltimore: The Johns Hopkins Press, 1920. 30*, 302 p. 8°. (Hesperia Ergänzungsreihe: Schriften zur englischen Philologie. . . Heft 7.) **NAFM**

Contents: Introduction. [The 6 Pagean] of Iacob. The 7 pagean of Ioseph. The eight pagean of Moyses. The 9 pagean of Iosue. The 10 pagean of Gedeon. The 11 pagean of Iephte. The 12 pagean of Samson. [The 14 pagean of Saul.] The 15 pagean of Dauid. The 16 pagean of Salomon. The 17 pagean [of Elias]. [The 18 pagean of Naaman.]

"The cycle of Old Testament plays here printed for the first time is preserved in MS. A. VI. 33 in the Library of Stonyhurst College in northern Lancashire . . . The manuscript in its present state begins and ends imperfectly. . . Even in its present fragmentary state the Stonyhurst cycle of pageants run to 8,740 lines, far exceeding in length any of the series of Old Testament plays occurring in the earlier English cycles. . . The fragment of the play of Jacob with which the ms. now begins is numbered "The 6 Pagean." The five lost plays which preceded were perhaps (1) The Creation, (2) The Temptation and Fall, (3) Cain and Abel, (4) Noah, (5) Abraham. Another lost play was the "13th Pageant". . . The ms. ends imperfectly in "The 18 Pageant of Naaman," and it is, of course, impossible to say how far the author carried his dramatization of Old Testament history, if, indeed, he did not continue his cycle into the New Testament. The author was a Roman Catholic, probably a Jesuit priest. . . It can easily be shown that he used the Douay Bible, published 1609–10, as his source. In view of the linguistic evidence we can determine the dates of these pageants to be 1610–1625. . . From the earlier plays. . . the author has rigorously excluded all humor. The Pageant of Naaman differs radically from all the others [in this respect]. . . The Cycle has a distinct interest for the student of literature as a curiously belated survival of an earlier form of drama." — *From the introduction by the editor.*

Reviewed by F. Holthausen in *Anglia: Beiblatt,* Halle a. S., 1922, Bd. 33, p. 84–88, *RNA;* by M. Weyrauch in *Literarisches Zentralblatt für Deutschland,* Leipzig, 1921, Bd. 72, p. 707, *NAA;* by R. Ackermann in *Literaturblatt für germanische und romanische Philologie,* Leipzig, 1923, Bd. 44, p. 350–351, † *RAA;* and briefly in *Archiv für das Studium der neueren Sprachen,* Braunschweig, 1921, Bd. 141, p. 312, *RAA.* Also reviewed by W. W. Greg in *Modern language review,* Cambridge, 1920, v. 15, p. 440–446, *NAA.* For the editor's answer to this review see v. 16, p. 167–169.

THE CORNWALL PLAYS

Norris, Edwin, editor. The ancient Cornish drama, edited and translated by Mr. Edwin Norris. Oxford: At the University Press, 1859. 2 v. 8°. **NAFM**

Contents: Origo mundi. Passio domini nostri. Resurrexio domini nostri.

The three dramas. . . constitute the most important relic known to exist of the Celtic dialect once spoken in Cornwall.

Text in old Celtic and modern English printed on opposite pages.

The three parts of the Cornish drama are analyzed into twelve, twenty-one and ten scenes respectively by Sir E. K. Chambers in his *Mediaeval stage,* Oxford, 1903, p. 433–434, * *R – NAFM.*

Reviewed in *The Athenæum,* London, June 25, 1859, p. 838–839, * *DA.*

JENNER, Henry. The Cornish drama. (Celtic review. Edinburgh, 1907. 8°. v. 3, p. 360–375; v. 4, p. 41–68.) **NDK**

PETER, Thurstan Collins. The old Cornish drama; with illustrations from ancient Cornish sacred poems and miracle plays of other lands. (A lecture.) London: Elliot Stock, 1906. 49 p. illus. 8°. **NAFM**

STOKES, Whitley. A collation of Norris' Ancient Cornish drama. ⌊By Whitley Stokes.⌋ (Archiv für celtische Lexikographie. Halle, 1898–1900. 8°. Bd. 1, p. 161–174.) **RPA**

THE DIGBY PLAYS

Digby plays. The Digby mysteries. . . Edited from the mss. by F. J. Furnivall. . . London: Publisht for the New Shakspere Society, by N. Trübner & Co., 1882. xxxii, 239(1) p. 4°. *** NCK (New)**

Partial contents: Forewords. Appendix: Notes on the Chester plays and midsummer show. Herod's killing of the children. The conversion of St. Paul. Mary Magdalene. Christ's burial and resurrection. Glossary and index (mainly by S. J. Herrtage).

Reviewed by Richard Wülcker in *Anglia,* Halle a.S., 1883, Bd. 6, Anzeiger, p. 74–76, *RNA.*

—— The Digby plays, with an incomplete 'morality' of Wisdom, who is Christ (part of one of the Macro moralities). Re-issued from the plates of the text edited by F. J. Furnivall for the New Shakspere Society in 1882. London: Publisht for the Early English Text Society by K. Paul, Trench, Trübner & Co., 1896. 4 p.l., v–xxxii, 239 p. 8°. (Early English Text Society. Extra series ⌊no.⌋ 70.) **NCE (Early)**

COLLIER, John Payne. The Digby miracle-plays. (In his: The history of English dramatic poetry. London, 1831. 12°. v. 2, p. 230–235.) **NCOM**

SCHMIDT, Karl. The Digby-Spiele; Einleitung Candlemas day and the kyllynge of the children of Israell; The conuersion of Seynt Paule. Berlin: G. Bernstein, 1884. 30 p., 2 l. 8°.

Title from Columbia University Library.

—— Die Digby-Spiele. (Anglia. Halle a. S., 1885. 8°. Bd. 8, p. 371–404.) **RNA**

This study is a continuation of the previous entry. No text is given.

For comments see Sir E. K. Chambers, *Mediaeval stage,* v. 2, p. 429–431, * *R – NAFM.*

TOWNELEY and Digby mysteries. (Gentleman's magazine. London, 1836. 8°. new series, v. 6 ⌊v. 160⌋, p. 563–572.) *** DA**

Miracle Plays — Individual Cycles, continued

SHREWSBURY FRAGMENTS

Shrewsbury fragments. Fragments of Yorkshire mysteries. (Academy. London, 1890. 4°. v. 37, p. 27–28.)   * **DA**
The angels and the shepherds (Officium pastorum). The three Maries at the sepulchre (Officium resurrectionis). The two disciples going to Emmaus (Officium peregrinorum).
See letter from W. W. Skeat in *The Academy*, v. 37, p. 10–11 in which the discovery is first announced of these fragments "demonstrably older than the earliest of the large cycles [York]."
Also printed in J. M. Manly, *Specimens of the pre-Shaksperean drama*, 1897, v. 1, p. xxviii–xxxvii, *NCO;* and in the Early English Text Society, Extra series, no. 104 (ed. Waterhouse), p. 1–7, with notes on p. xv–xxvi, *NCE (Early)*.

COVENTRY CORPUS CHRISTI PLAYS

Coventry plays. Two Coventry Corpus Christi plays: 1. The shearmen and taylors' pageant, re-edited from the edition of Thomas Sharp, 1825; and 2. The weavers' pageant, re-edited from the manuscript of Robert Croo, 1584; with a plan of Coventry, and appendixes containing the chief records of the Coventry plays. By Hardin Craig. London: Published for the Early English Text Society by K. Paul, Trench, Trübner & Co., 1902. xxxviii, 133(1) p., 1 folded plan. 8°. (Early English Text Society. Extra series. [no.] 87.)   **NCE (Early)**

OLD TESTAMENT PLAYS

Bale, John, bishop of Ossory. A tragedye or enterlude, manyfestyng the chefe promyses of God unto man by all ages in the old lawe, from the fall of Adam to the incarnacyon of the Lorde Jesus Christ. Compyled by Johan Bale, Anno Domini MDXXXVIII. In the worde (which now is called the eternall sonne of God) was lyfe from the begynnynge, and that lyfe was the lyght of men. This lyght yet shyneth in the darknesse, but the darknesse comprehendeth it not. Joan i. (In: Robert Dodsley, editor, Select collection of old plays. London: J. Dodsley, 1780. 2. ed. 12°. v. 1, p. 1–40.)   **NCO (Dodsley)**
Among the interlocutors are Justus Noah, Abraham fidelis, Moses sanctus, David rex pius, Esaias propheta, and others. The "Promises" are those made by God to them. Each of them in an *Actus* devoted to him holds discourse with Pater Coelestis.

—— God's promises. (In: Robert Dodsley, editor, A select collection of old plays. London, 1825–27. 12°. v. 1, p. 1–42.)   **NCO (Dodsley)**

—— —— (In: William Marriott, editor, Collection of English miracle-plays or mysteries. Basel, 1838. 8°. p. 221–257.)   **NAFM**

—— —— (In: Robert Dodsley, editor, A select collection of old English plays. 4th edition by W. C. Hazlitt. London, 1874–76. 8°. v. 1, p. 277–322.)   **NCO (Dodsley)**

—— The chief promises of God unto man. [1538.] (In his: The dramatic writings of John Bale, edited by J. S. Farmer. London, 1907. 16°. p. 83–125.)   **NCO (Early)**
Early English dramatists.

—— ...The chief promises of God unto man <God's promises> by John Bale, bishop of Ossory. 1538. London, W. C. and Edinburgh: T. C. & E. C. Jack, 1908. vii p., facsim. (1 p.l., [38] p.) 4°. (The Tudor facsimile texts...)   **NCO (Tudor)**
Facsimile reprint of the only known copy of the

first edition, in the British Museum, with t.-p. mutilated (lower half wanting).
Facsimile interleaved.

—— The interlude of "God's promises." (In: "Everyman," with other interludes including eight miracle plays. London [1909]. 16°. p. 153–182.)   **NAFM**

JONES, Emrys Edward. John Bale's drama God's promises. Erlangen: Junge & Sohn, 1909. xx, 40 p., 1 l. 8°.   **NCO p.v.310, no.12**

Bale, John. A comedy concernynge thre lawes, of nature, Moses, & Christ. (Anglia. Halle a.S., 1882. 8°. Bd. 5, p. 160–225.)   **RNA**
Edited by Arnold Schroeer, who adds, *ibid.,* "Literarhistorisches," p. 137–159, 232–238; "Lexicalische Anmerkungen," p. 225–232; and "Excurs über die Metrik," p. 238–264.
See also emendations by F. Holthausen, *Anglia*, 1892, Bd. 14, p. 322, *RNA*.

—— —— Halle: Max Niemeyer, 1882. 3 p.l., 128 p. 8°.

—— A comedy concernynge thre lawes of nature, Moses, and Christ, corrupted by the Sodomytes, Pharysees and Papystes. Compyled by Johan Bale. Anno M.D.XXXVII. (In his: The dramatic writings of John Bale, edited by J. S. Farmer. London, 1907. 16°. p. 1–82.)   **NCO (Early)**
Early English dramatists.
t.-p. is a reduced facsimile of the t.-p. of the Bodleian copy.
An anti-Catholic play. One of the interlocutors is the Law of Moses. In the directions given for apparelling of the vices, Covetousness is to be decked like a pharisee or spiritual lawyer.

—— ...A comedy concerning three laws of Nature, Moses and Christ, compiled by John Bale, bishop of Ossory. 1538. London and Edinburgh: T. C. & E. C. Jack, 1908. vi p., facsim. (1 p.l., [101] p. incl. port.) 4°. (The Tudor facsimile texts)   **NCO (Tudor)**
Facsimile of the copy in the British Museum which lacks t.-p., preceded by facsimile of t.-p. taken from the copy in the Bodleian Library.

Old Testament Plays, continued

Bayard, Lyman R. "Out of the Bible"; a pageant for children's day, promotion day, or any other special day. Los Angeles: Pageant Publishers, cop. 1922. 23 p. illus. music. 8°.

"Religious education and imagination call the Bible children out of a great Bible on the platform."

Bellamy, Frederica Le F. The jongleur's story, a history and demonstration of religious drama. New York: The Womans Press ⌈cop. 1926⌉. 41 p. 12°. **NAFH p.v.10**

A series of tableaux introduced by the Jongleur's story (Le tombeor de Nostre Dame).

Burr, Amelia Josephine. A masque of women poets. (Stratford journal. Boston, 1917. 8°. v. 1, March, 1917, p. 13–33.) *** DA**

Hannah, Deborah, Judith.

Bynner, Witter. Cake; an indulgence. New York and London: Alfred A. Knopf, 1926. 169 p., 1 l. 12°. **NBM**

Ultra modernistic play. The Biblical characters introduced are Mary Magdalene, Judas, and Adam and Eve.

Reviewed in *Independent,* New York, 1926, v. 117, p. 364, * *DA;* by W. P. Eaton in *New York Herald Tribune, Books,* v. 3, Oct. 3, 1926, p. 5, † *NAA;* by P. A. Hutchinson in *New York Times Book review,* v. 31, Dec. 26, 1926, p. 7, † *NAA; Theatre arts monthly,* New York, 1926, v. 10, p. 874, *NBLA.*

Children of the Bible ⌈in six scenes⌉. (In: Three Biblical pageants with music for churches, Sunday schools and community organizations. Philadelphia, 1922. 8°. p. 3–6.) **NAC p.v.10**

The **Chronothanatoletron** or old times made new. An entertainment for female characters only. Written for the class-day exercises at Dana Hall School, Wellesley, Mass., by two members of the class of '87, and first performed before members of the school and their friends, June 18, 1887. Boston: W. H. Baker & Co., 1889. 23 p. 12°.

NBL p.v.34, no.1

A pageant of historic women. The chronothanatoletron, or time and death annihilator, brings forth on the stage Sarah, and Pharaoh's daughter as the foster mother of Moses.

Class contests, based on dialogue, "Books of our Bible" ⌈for three contests⌉. (In: Elma C. E. Levinger. Entertaining programs for the assembly. Cincinnati ⌈cop. 1930⌉. 8°. p. 37–41.) *** PSY**

Connelly, Marcus Cook. The green pastures, a fable suggested by Roark Bradford's Southern sketches "Ol' man Adam an' his chillun," by Marc Connelly. New York: Farrar & Rinehart, Inc. ⌈cop. 1929.⌉ xvi p., 1 l., 3–173 p. 12°. **NBM**

First produced at the Mansfield Theatre, New York, Feb. 26, 1930, with an all-negro cast; Richard B. Harrison as the Lord, Daniel L. Haynes as Adam, and Tutt Whitney as Noah.

Reviewed in *Times literary supplement,* London, 1930, v. 29, p. 410, † *NAA.* See also *Collection of newspaper clippings of dramatic criticism,* 1929–30, volume G, † *NBL.* The compiler of this list has in his

collection of dramatic clippings two hundred and eighty mounted newspaper and magazine reviews and illustrations of the production, and biographical sketches of the author and actors.

Reprinted in *Best plays of 1929–1930,* New York, 1930, p. 33–70, *NAFH,* and in *Six plays,* London, 1930, p. 9–112, *NCO.*

Damon, Samuel Foster. The judging of God ⌈a dramatic poem⌉. (In his: Astrolabe, infinitudes and hypocrisies. New York and London, 1927. 12°. p. 41–42.)

The characters are Adam, Judas, and Jesus.

Grossman, Samuel S. A pageant of Jewish "costumes". . . ⌈Philadelphia? 1922?⌉ 10 f. 4°. **†* PBM p.v.112**

Mimeographed.

Some of the characters are the heroes of the Old Testament coming out of the pages of a story book.

Hale, Harris G., and N. M. HALL. . . . The Messages of the prophets. Arranged by Harris G. Hale and Newton M. Hall. Boston: The Pilgrim Press, 1907. iv, 22 p. 12°. (Biblical dramas. ⌈no. 10.⌉)

Hare, Walter Ben. The women of the Bible; a dramatic entertainment in three parts. Boston: Walter H. Baker Co., 1922. 25 p. 12°. (Baker's novelty plays.)

The women characters in parts one and two are from the Old Testament; in part three, from the New Testament.

Kidder, Jerome. The drama of earth. ⌈In three parts.⌉ New York: Adolphus Ranney, 1857. 360 p. 12°. **NBM**

Among the dramatis personae are Christ, Lucifer, Adam and Eve, Noah, Herod, Columbus, Iago, a Southern planter, Uncle Tom, and a medley of others. The action ranges back and forth through Ararat, Calvary, Spain, a London gin-shop, Pennsylvania, the Blue Ridge Mountains (1620), Massachusetts (1845), Cincinnati, etc.

Notes to the drama on p. 299–360.

Lamkin, Nina B. The passing of the kings; a pageant. Illustrations of costumes in colors by Buckton Nendick. Chicago: T. S. Denison & Co. ⌈cop. 1920.⌉ 86 p., 10 l. illus. 8°.

Illustrations at the end, 10 l. **NBM**

A pageant of history from 490 B. C. to 1918, in eight episodes. Preceding each episode is a prologue, spoken by the prophet of Israel, words from the Old Testament.

Levinger, Elma C. Ehrlich. "Let there be light." A pageant in seven episodes. (In her: Jewish festivals in the religious school. Cincinnati, 1923. 8°. p. 517–549.) *** PSY**

Time: episodes depicting Jewish history from Abraham to Jewish life in America.

—— The message of the prophets. ⌈In one scene.⌉ (In her: Entertaining programs for the assembly. Cincinnati ⌈cop. 1930⌉. 8°. p. 169–175.) *** PSY**

Among the characters are Amos, Jeremiah, and Isaiah.

—— Our Jewish mothers' hall of fame. ⌈In one scene.⌉ (In her: Entertaining programs for the assembly. Cincinnati ⌈cop. 1930⌉. 8°. p. 177–182.) *** PSY**

The characters are: a Jewish child, Sarah, Hannah, Ruth, Esther, Hannah, mother of the Maccabaean martyrs, Beruria, and Emma Lazarus.

Old Testament Plays, continued

Linsky, Fannie Barnett. The alphabet story. illus. (Young Israel. Cincinnati, 1928. f°. v. 20, Feb., 1928, p. 13.)   *** PBD**

M., H. C. Heavens! or, Peter the politician. (Princeton tiger. Princeton, N. J., 1922. 4°. v. 32, no. 5, Nov. 4, 1922, p. 23.)   **STG**

Outside the gates of Heaven, 1922 A. D. Several Biblical characters in burlesque.

Mackaye, Percy Wallace. The pilgrim and the book. A dramatic service of the Bible [in seventeen actions]. (In: Religious dramas 1924. New York and London: Century Co. [1923.] 8°. p. 213–252.)   **NAFM**

Characters: characters from the Bible, individual books of the Old and of the New Testament, Spirit of the Old and of the New Testament.

—— The Sistine eve; fragments of an oratorio written for the beginning of the twentieth century. (In his: Poems. New York, 1909. 8°. p. 51–86.)   **NBI**

The dramatis personae are figures in the paintings by Michelangelo and Botticelli on the ceiling and walls of the Sistine Chapel, among which are Biblical characters.

Reprinted in his *Sistine eve and other poems*, New York, 1915, *NBI*, and *Poems and plays*, New York, 1916, v. 1, *NBG*.

Marble, Annie (Russell). Boys and girls from Hebrew history; a children's day pageant... (With directions for its production.) [In three parts.] New York: Century Co. [cop. 1923.] 16 p. music. 8°.

Marks, Milton, and others. God is one; an historical pageant of Israel's loyalty, by Milton Marks, Henry Hart, Martin A. Meyer. New York: Bloch Publishing Company, 1914. 30 p. 12°.

The pageants cover the range of Jewish history from the time of Pharaoh to modern America.

Morrow, Martina. The prophets; a Biblical representation [in a prelude and one act]. New York: E. S. Werner Pub. & Supply Co., cop. 1902. 6 p. 8°.

The characters are the major and minor prophets from Moses to Malachi.

Newman, Louis Israel. A vision of Jewish womanhood; a series of tableaux. New York: Bloch Pub. Co., 1920. 15 p. 16°.

Written in 1915 for the Women's Circle of the First Hebrew Congregation of Berkeley, Cal.

Pageant of the Bible among the nations, celebrating the centennial of the American Bible Society, first presented under the direction of Marie Moore Forrest by churches and Sunday schools at Washington, D. C., May 6, 1916... New York: American Bible Society, 1916. 24 p. illus. 4°. (Centennial pamphlets. no. 7.)

The pageant is in fourteen scenes, portraying episodes connected with the successive translations of the Bible. Scene I is the Septuagint translation. The members of the cast are Ptolemy II and seventy-two rabbis in white robes.

Parsons, Margaret Colby (Getchell). Boy heroes of the Bible (or Boy heroes). [In one scene.] (In her: Ten stirring Bible plays. Franklin, Ohio, cop. 1927. 12°. p. 62–67.)

The characters are Tom, a boy of today, and six Biblical boy heroes. The latter narrate their adventures to Tom.

Ranking, Boyd Montgomerie Maurice. The mead of much desire [a dramatic poem]. (In his: Fair Rosamond, and other poems. London, 1868. 16°. p. 113–150.)   **NCM**

Several Biblical women speaking.

Riley, Mrs. Alice Cushing (Donaldson). ...The brotherhood of man; a pageant of international peace for pageantry class, institute of 1921, the Drama League of America. New York: A. S. Barnes and Company, 1924. 3 p.l., 9–50 p., 1 illus. 8°. (Pageants with a purpose, L. Taft, editor.)   **NBM**

A pageant presenting the development of the ideal of brotherhood from its personal to its international phases through a prologue and eight episodes.

The prologue presents Love, Law, and Justice, and their relation to the Promised Land envisioned by Moses, the Lawgiver.

Episode I. Individual friendship — David and Jonathan (1 Samuel, chapters XVI to XX).

Episode II. Brotherhood in faith. The disciples of Christ. (Acts I, and Matthew XXVIII).

The *Brotherhood of man* was worked out as a laboratory exercise in the class in pageantry of the Drama League of America Institute, 1921.

Samuels, Maurice Victor. A pageant of the strong. [In a prelude and five scenes.] New York: Jarvis-Maxwell Pub. Co., 1923. 58 p. 8°.   **NBL p.v.125**

" 'A pageant of the strong' is a revelation of Jewish idealism" as exemplified in five episodes of Jewish history. Scene I is that of Abram in Chaldea; scene 2, Moses in the wilderness; scene 3, the expulsion from Spain, 1492; scene 4, the year 1648 in Poland; and scene 5, modern America. Presented for the first time at the Hotel Astor's Grand Ballroom on the evenings of Dec. 26, 27, 28, 1921.

Schulman, Samuel, and SARA MILLER. The spirit of Judaism; a pageant [in eight parts]. Cincinnati, Ohio: Dept. of Synagog and School Extension of the Union of American Hebrew Congregations [cop. 1926]. 35 p. 12°.

The characters are from Jewish history. The first part is the promise to Abraham; the last part is the synagogue in America.

Swann, Mona. At the well of Bethlehem; a drama [in three parts] arranged from the Authorized Version of the Bible. London: Privately printed by L. B. Hill [cop. 1930]. xiii, 1–32 p. music. 8°.

"The stories of Ruth the gleaner, David the shepherd, and of Mary the mother...united by a group of narrators."

Reviewed in *Drama*, London, Dec., 1930, v. 9, p. 42, *NAFA*.

Tarrant, William George, and LYMAN R. BAYARD. Marching with the heroes; a hymn by William George Tarrant, dramatized by Lyman R. Bayard. Los Angeles: Pageant Publishers, 1927. 14 p. illus. music. 8°.

A pageant of universal history in which appear certain Old Testament characters.

Old Testament Plays, continued

Tomes, Margaret Otey. The children and the evangelists; a Nativity play written for the Christmas eve festival of St. Andrew's Church, Detroit, Mich., 1918. ₍In eight scenes.₎ (Drama. Mt. Morris, Ill., 1920. 4°. v. 11, p. 58–60.)   **NAFA**

Torch of civilization. ₍A pageant in five episodes.₎ (Emerson quarterly. Boston, 1927. 4°. v. 8, Nov., 1927, p. 7–8, 22.)   † **NANA**
Produced by the Emerson College of Oratory. Elmer Bryan as the Hebrew shepherd.

Vicente, Gil. ₍A synopsis, with extracts, by J. B. Trend, of Vicente's Mystery of the sibyl Cassandra, a dramatic eclogue presented before the Court on Christmas Eve 1503?, based on an earlier liturgical drama in vogue at Palma, Majorca, Spain.₎ (Music & letters. London, 1929. 8°. v. 10, p. 124–140.)   * **MA**
The setting is modern. The patriarchs Abraham, Moses and Isaiah are introduced, in an effort to persuade the unwilling Cassandra to marry her wooer, Solomon.

KING, Georgiana Goddard. The play of the sibyl Cassandra. Bryn Mawr, Pa.: Bryn Mawr College; New York: Longmans, Green and Co., 1921. 2 p.l., 55(1) p., 1 pl. 16°. (Bryn Mawr notes and monographs. no. 2.)   **NAC p.v.80**

GENESIS

Austin, Alfred. The tower of Babel: a poetical drama ₍in five acts₎. Edinburgh and London: William Blackwood and Sons, 1874. 5 p.l., (1)4–256 p. 8°.
Interludes, p. 237–256.
Based on Genesis XI: 2–4.
The scene: Plain of Shinar. Time: the twenty-third century B. C.
Reviewed in *The Athenæum*, London, Jan. 2, 1875, p. 28–29, * *DA; Saturday review*, London, 1875, v. 39, p. 87–88, * *DA;* and in *The Spectator*, London, 1875, v. 48, p. 249–250, * *DA*.

—— The tower of Babel; a celestial love-drama ₍in five acts₎. London and New York: Macmillan and Co., 1890. ix, 182 p. 8°. **NCR**
Reviewed in *Literary world*, London, 1891, new series, v. 43, p. 33, * *DA*.

Beverley, Robert Mackenzie. Jubal, a dramatic poem. London: John Hatchard and Son, 1827. 1 p.l., 239 p. 12°.

Boyd, Zachary. Towre of Babylon. ₍A dramatic poem. Excerpt of about 400 out of 930 lines from the ms. "Flowers of Zion."₎ (In: Gabriel Neil, Biographical sketch of the Rev. Mr. Zachary Boyd. Glasgow, 1832. 8°. Appendix, p. xxi–xxv.)   **A p.v. 144**
Seven speakers.

Byron (6th baron), George Gordon Noël Byron. Heaven and earth; a mystery. Founded on ₍Genesis VI: 2₎. (Liberal. London, 1822. 8°. v. 1, p. 165–206.)   **NDH (Liberal)**
Reprinted in *Museum of foreign literature and science*, Philadelphia, 1823, v. 2, p. 410–431, * *DA;* in

Lord Byron's *Miscellaneous works*, London, 1830, p. 197–258, and his *Poetical works*, new ed., London, 1856, v. 4, p. 183–221, *NCM;* and in G. A. Kohut, *A Hebrew anthology*, Cincinnati, 1913, v. 2, p. 727–747, * *PSO*. A selection under the title "Anah and Aholibamah" is printed in *The Poet and the painter*, New York, 1869, p. 121–126, † *NCI (Poet)*.
Reviewed in *Blackwood's magazine*, London, 1823, v. 13, p. 72–77, * *DA; Edinburgh review*, Edinburgh, 1823, v. 38, p. 27–48, * *DA; Monthly magazine*, London, 1823, v. 55, p. 35–39, * *DA; New monthly magazine*, London, 1823, v. 7, p. 353–358, * *DA*.

—— Ĉielo kaj tero. (The heaven and the earth.) Mistero de Lord Byron. Esperantigis Doktoro Noël. Nancy'o: E. Thomas, 1906. 54 p. 8°.   **RAXF p.v.16**

שמים וארץ. מיסטריום מאת לורד בירון... מתרגם מאנגלית... על ידי דוד פרישמאן. (התקופה) Warsaw, 1920. 4°. v. 6, p. 151–212.)   * **PBA**

Небо и земля. (Переводъ Бунина.) (In: I. A. Bunin, Сочиненія. Petrograd, 1915. 8°. v. 3, p. 221–244.)   * **QDB (Bunin)**

CHEW, Samuel Claggett. Byron and Croly. (Modern language notes. Baltimore, 1913. 4°. v. 28, p. 201–203.)   **RAA**

—— Cain and Heaven and earth. (In his: Dramas of Lord Byron. Göttingen, 1915. 8°. p. 118–143.)   **NCC**

EIMER, Manfred. Das apokryphe Buch Henoch und Byrons Mysterien. (Englische Studien. Leipzig, 1912. 8°. Bd. 44, p. 18–31.)   **RNA**

—— Astronomie; Kosmogonie und Paläontologie; Zur Weltanschauung ₍of Cain, Heaven and earth, and other works₎. (In his: Byron und der Kosmos. Heidelberg, 1912. 8°. p. 98–180.)   **RNB (Anglistische)**
Anglistische Forschungen. Heft 34.

MAYN, Georg. Über Byrons "Heaven and earth." Breslau: Anton Schreiber ₍1887₎. 2 p.l., 66 p., 1 l. 8°.

Cooper, W. Ralph, and ALFRED DUNNING. The heritage. (In their: Six craft plays. London, 1928. 12°. p. 107–118.)   **NASH**
Tubal Cain, of "The maker of swords."

—— The maker of swords. ₍In one act.₎ illus. (In their: Six craft plays. London, 1928. 12°. p. 19–38.)   **NASH**
Tubal Cain: the first smith.

Jacobs, Thornwell. The journey of Nimrod. ₍In four acts.₎ illus. (In his: Islands of the blest, and other poems. Oglethorpe University, Ga., 1928. 8°. p. 273–335.)   **NBI**

Jameson, Robert William. Nimrod, a dramatic poem in five acts... ₍By R. W. Jameson.₎ London: William Pickering, 1848. 2 p.l., 251, 2 p. 8°.

Old Testament Plays — Genesis, continued

Lesley, or **Lesly,** George. Fire and brimstone; or, The destruction of Sodom. ₍A drama in verse, not divided into acts.₎ ₍London, 1675.₎ 8°.
Title from British Museum Catalogue.

Levinger, Elma C. (Ehrlich). The lost path; a Jewish fairy play for little children. (Jewish child. New York, 1917. f°. v. 5, no. 43, p. 1–3.) *** PBD**

Reznikoff, Charles. Genesis. (In his: Nine plays. New York ₍1927₎. 8°. p. 104–113.) **NBM**

Rolt-Wheeler, Francis William. Nimrod; a drama. Boston: Lothrop, Lee and Shepard Co. ₍cop. 1912.₎ vii p., 3 l., 90 p. 8°. **NBM**
" 'Nimrod' was begun in the winter of 1901, and in its first form, as a dramatic poem, was completed in 1903. Later it was prepared for stage production, and on July 19, 1906, was copyrighted as such under its present title. In the winter of 1911 an advantageous change in the first act suggested itself to the author and the drama was again entirely rewritten... The story is not based on any legend, but is suggested by the necessary type of warfare in the Tigris and Euphrates valleys in the days whereof the Hebrew Bible speaks concerning Nimrod, son of Cush, the mighty hunter before the Lord. The double conflict between democracy and aristocracy and between superstition and monotheism is of direct modern application." — *From Prefatory note, p. vii.*
Reviewed in *The Nation,* New York, 1913, v. 96, p. 190, * DA.

Saltus, Francis Saltus. Lot's wife. ₍A dramatic poem.₎ (In his: The witch of En-dor, and other poems. Buffalo, 1891. 12°. p. 281–331.) **NBI**

Wortley, Lady Emmeline Charlotte Elizabeth Stuart. Jairah, a dramatic mystery ₍in two acts₎; and other poems. London, 1840. 12°.
Title from British Museum Catalogue.
Reviewed in *The Athenæum,* London, Jan. 2, 1841, p. 14, * DA.

LUCIFER

Miracle Plays

The **Fall** of Lucifer. The tanners playe... ₍Chester play no. 1.₎ (In: The Chester plays, ed. by Wright. London: Shakespeare Society, 1843. 8°. v. 1, p. 8–19.) **NAFM (Chester)**
Also printed in 1893 (ed. Deimling) in Early English Text Society, Extra series no. 62 (*The Chester plays*), p. 9–20, *NCE (Early)*.

₍Fall of Lucifer.₎ ₍Part of Coventry play no. 1.₎ (In: Sir William Dugdale, Monasticon Anglicanum. London, 1830. f°. v. 6, part 3, p. 1537–1538.) **† CAB**
First printed in John Stevens, *History of the antient abbeys, monasteries, hospitals, cathedrals and collegiate churches,* London, 1722, v. 1, p. 144–145. Also printed in J. Q. Adams, *Chief pre-Shakespearean dramas,* Boston, 1924, p. 86–87, * R – NCO, and in H. C. Schweikert, *Early English plays,* New York [cop. 1928], p. 71–73, *NCO.*

Modern Plays

Blunt, Wilfrid Scawen. Satan absolved; a Victorian mystery. With a frontispiece after George Frederick Watts R. A. London and New York: John Lane, The Bodley Head, 1899. viii, 52 p., 1 pl. 8°. **NAFM**
Satan, the Lord God, angels.
Reprinted in his *Poetical works,* London, 1914, v. 2, p. 254–294, *NCM,* and in his *Poems,* New York, 1923, p. 131–170, *NCM.*

Santayana, George. Lucifer; a theological tragedy ₍in five acts₎. Chicago and New York: H. S. Stone and Co., 1899. 4 p.l., 187 p., 1 l. 12°. **NBM**
First appeared, in abbreviated form, in his *Sonnets and other verses,* New York, 1896, p. 99–118, *NBI.*
Reviewed in *Harvard graduates magazine,* Boston, 1899, v. 8, p. 297–298, *STG;* and in *The Independent,* New York, 1899, v. 51, p. 1958, * DA.
"Mr. Santayana's method is to embody the various attitudes of man towards life in the persons of Lucifer, Hermes, Mephistopheles, and Christ, and to show how they all, except the last, fail and die through their imperfections."

Vondel, Joost van den. Vondel's Lucifer. Translated from the Dutch by Leonard Charles Van Noppen. Illustrated by John Aarts. New York: Continental Publishing Co., 1898. 3 p.l., 9–438 p., 1 port. illus. 8°. (Holland Society art edition.) **NHM**
Contents: Translator's Preface. Introduction, W. H. Carpenter. Vondel and his Lucifer, Dr. G. Kalff. Vondel: his life and times, the translator. The "Lucifer": an interpretation, the translator. Bibliography. Parallelisms between Vondel and Milton. Lucifer.
Issued in an edition of 1250 numbered copies.
Selections are printed in Julian Hawthorne, editor, *The Masterpieces and the history of literature,* New York, 1906, v. 6, p. 280–284, *NAB; Warner's Library of the world's best literature,* v. 25, p. 15494–15498, * R – NAC; G. A. Kohut, *A Hebrew anthology,* Cincinnati, 1913, v. 2, p. 685–689, * PSO, and in Edwin Markham, compiler, *The book of poetry,* New York, 1927, v. 2, p. 3003–3004, *NAEM.*
Reviewed in *The Critic,* New York, 1898, v. 33, p. 521–523, * DA; *The Nation,* New York, 1899, v. 69, p. 55–56, * DA; and in *The Saturday review,* London, 1898, v. 86, p. 540–541, * DA.
See A. J. Barnouw, *Vondel,* New York, 1925, p. 141–153, *NHC (Vondel).*

—— —— Greensboro, N. C.: Chas. L. Van Noppen, 1917. 3 p.l., 9–458 p., 1 port. illus. 12°. **NHM**

CURRIE, Charles Warren. Joost van den Vondel, the Catholic. (Catholic world. New York, 1898. 8°. v. 68, p. 309–316.) *** DA**
His masterpiece Lucifer, p. 313–314.

G., E. W. A Dutch Milton. (Cornhill magazine. London, 1877. 8°. v. 35, p. 596–615.) *** DA**
Reprinted in *Living age,* Boston, 1877, v. 133, p. 550–562, * DA.

GRABO, Carl Henry. Milton and Vondel. (Chautauquan. New York, 1909. 12°. v. 54, p. 114–123.) *** DA**

REPPLIER, Agnes. Joost van den Vondel. (Catholic world. New York, 1886. 8°. v. 42, p. 595–607.) *** DA**

Old Testament Plays — Genesis, continued

Lucifer, continued

THOMPSON, Elbert N. S. ₁Lucifer as a source of Milton's Paradise Lost.₁ (In his: Essays on Milton. New Haven, 1914. 8°. p. 171–174.) * **NCC**

WOODHULL, Marianna. "Lucifer," Vondel. (In her: The epic of Paradise Lost. New York & London, 1907. 12°. p. 211–234.) * **NCH**

THE CREATION

Miracle Plays

The **Creation,** and the fall of Lucifer. The barkers. ₁York play no. 1, 160 lines.₁ (In: Lucy T. Smith, editor, York plays. Oxford, 1885. 8°. p. 1–7.) **NAFM**

Reprinted in A. W. Pollard,˙ editor, *English miracle plays,* Oxford, 1890, p. 1–7, 177–179, *NAFM* (other editions issued in 1904, 1923, and 1927).

The **Creation,** to the fifth day. Playsterers ₁play₁. ₁York play no. 2, 86 lines.₁ (In: Lucy T. Smith, editor, York plays. Oxford, 1885. 8°. p. 8–13.) **NAFM**

Creatio. ₁Towneley play no. 1.₁ (In: The Towneley mysteries. London, 1836. 8°. p. 1–7.) **CA (Surtees)**

Surtees Society. Publications. [v. 3.]

Also printed in 1897 (ed. England) in Early English Text Society, Extra series no. 71 (*The Towneley plays*), p. 1–9, *NCE (Early).*

The **Creation** and Fall, and Death of Abel. The drapers playe... ₁Chester play no. 2.₁ (In: The Chester plays, ed. by Wright. London: Shakespeare Society, 1843. 8°. v. 1, p. 20–44.) **NAFM**

Also printed, 1893 (ed. Deimling) in Early English Text Society, Extra series no. 62 (*The Chester plays*), p. 20–47, *NCE (Early).*

The **Childhood** of man. ₁In ten scenes.₁ ₁Chester plays 1–4, adapted.₁ (In: Chester miracle plays, done...by I. and O. Bolton King. London ₁1930₁. 12°. p. 1–57.) **NAFM**

The **Creation.** ₁Coventry play no. 1.₁ (In: Ludus Coventriæ, ed. Halliwell. London: Shakespeare Society, 1841. 8°. p. 19–23.) **NAFM (Coventry)**

Also printed in 1922 (ed. Block) in Early English Text Society, Extra series no. 120 (*Ludus Coventriæ*), p. 16–20, lines 1–52 (Creation of Heaven and the angels), lines 53–82 (Fall of Lucifer), lines 83–142 (Creation of the world and man), *NCE (Early),* and in F. J. Tickner, editor, *Earlier English drama from Robin Hood to Everyman,* New York [cop. 1929], p. 99–103, *NCO (Tickner).*

...The **Beginning** of the world. ₁2846 lines.₁ (In: Edwin Norris, editor, Ancient Cornish drama. Oxford, 1859. 8°. v. 1, p. 2–217.) **NAFM**

The temptation. Cain and Abel. Birth of Seth. Death of Adam. Noah. Abraham. Moses and Pharaoh. David. Bathsheba. Solomon. Maximilla.

Begins with the creation and ends with the building of the Temple by Solomon, who consecrates a bishop to take care of it.

' Cornish text and English translation on opposite pages.

For an analysis of the drama by Henry Jenner

see his article "Cornish drama" in *Celtic review,* Edinburgh, 1907, v. 4, p. 41–46, *NDK.*

Jordan, William. The Creation of the world, with Noah's flood; written in Cornish in the year 1611, by William Jordan; with an English translation, by John Keigwin. Edited by Davies Gilbert. London: Printed for J. B. Nichols, 1827. viii, 186 p. 8°. **NDR**

Gwreans an bys. The creation of the world, a Cornish mystery, edited, with a translation and notes, by Whitley Stokes. Berlin: Published for the Philological Society by A. Asher & Co., 1863. 208 p. 8°. (Philological Society. Transactions. 1864.) **RAA**

Cornish text and English translation on opposite pages. Edited from Ms. Bodley 219.

Adam and his progeny, Noah and his sons, Eve, Tubal, and Lamech figure in the play.

—— London and Edinburgh: Williams and Norgate, 1864. 208 p. 8°.

For an analysis of the drama by Henry Jenner see his article "Cornish drama" in *Celtic review,* Edinburgh, 1907, v. 4, p. 64–68, *NDK.*

Modern Plays

Andersen, Olivia Donaldson (Cushing). Creation. ₁In three acts.₁ (In her: Creation and other Biblical plays. Geneva, 1929. 4°. p. 11–67). **NBM**

In *Creation* the author wished to proclaim "that man as an individual came into this world a spiritual being... Through the instinct of possession [the gold digger in the play]...he falls from the ideal man." Place: in celestial places and somewhere on the young earth. Time: in the beginning.

The **Creation** of the world.

A droll which was very popular at Bartholomew Fair at the close of the seventeenth and commencement of the eighteenth century. It concluded with a scene of "Noah and his family coming out of the ark, with all the beasts, two by two, and all the fowls of the air seen in a prospect sitting upon the trees." This droll is alluded to in *Wit and Drollery, Jovial Poems,* 1682, and is there called the World's Creation. See Hazlitt, *Manual,* p. 54.

Newman, Louis Israel. The alphabet and the creation. ₁Illustrated by A. Goodelman.₁ San Francisco: ₁The Temple Publications,₁ 1927. 8 p. 8°.

Derived from the story in *The Jewish anthology* (edited by Edmund Fleg; translated by Maurice Samuel), New York, 1925, p. 196–198, which gives as its source Louis Ginsberg, *The Legends of the Jews,* i; Zohar, i, 2b–3b. The playlet appeared for the first time in *Young Israel,* Cincinnati, v. 19, Sept., 1926, p. 6–7, 22, * *PBD.* It was presented at the dedication of the Temple House of Congregation Emanu-El, San Francisco, by the Religious School, Sunday, Feb. 6, 1927.

Opal, pseud. The creation. Metamorphic period. ₁Drama 1.₁ (In his: The cloud of witnesses. New York, 1874. 12°. p. 10–50.) **NBM**

Based on Gen. 1:1–11:25.

Oppenheim, James. Prelude (to "Creation" — a drama). (Seven arts. New York, 1917. 8°. v. 1, p. 240–259.) * **DA**

Old Testament Plays — Genesis, continued

ADAM AND EVE

Miracle Plays

God creates Adam and Eve. The cardmakers [play]. [York play no. 3, 96 lines.] (In: Lucy T. Smith, editor, York plays. Oxford, 1885. 8°. p. 14–17.) **NAFM**

God puts Adam and Eve in the Garden of Eden. The regynall of the fullers' pagyant [play]. [York play no. 4, 99 lines.] (In: Lucy T. Smith, editor, York plays. Oxford, 1885. 8°. p. 18–21.) **NAFM**

Man's disobedience and fall from Eden. The cowpers [play]. [York play no. 5, 175 lines.] (In: Lucy T. Smith, editor, York plays. Oxford, 1885. 8°. p. 22–28.) **NAFM**

Adam and Eve driven from Eden. The armourers [play]. [York play no. 6, 168 lines.] (In: Lucy T. Smith, editor, York plays. Oxford, 1885. 8°. p. 29–34.) **NAFM**

The **Fall** of man. [Coventry play no. 2.] (In: Ludus Coventriæ, ed. Halliwell. London: Shakespeare Society, 1841. 8°. p. 24–32.) **NAFM (Coventry)**

First printed in John Stevens, *History of the antient abbeys, monasteries, hospitals, cathedrals and collegiate churches,* London, 1722, v. 1, p. 145–147. Also printed in Sir William Dugdale, *Monasticon Anglicanum,* new ed., London, 1830, v. 6, part 3, p. 1538–1540, † *CAB.*

Also printed in 1922 (ed. Block) in Early English Text Society, Extra series no. 120 (*Ludus Coventriæ*), p. 20–29, lines 143–416, *NCE (Early),* and in F. J. Tickner, editor, *Earlier English drama from Robin Hood to Everyman,* New York [cop. 1929], p. 103–109, *NCO (Tickner).*

The **Adam**. [An Anglo-Norman play, translated by Sarah F. Barrow.] (In: The mediaeval religious plays Antichrist and Adam. Cleveland, O., 1925. 8°. p. 33–68.) **NAC p.v.142, no.5**

Western Reserve University bulletin. v. 28, no. 8.

Adam, Cain and Abel, Moses, Solomon, Isaiah, Jeremiah, and Nebuchadnezzar figure in this mystery.

"The immediate source of the Adam seems undoubtedly to have been the pseudo-Augustinian sermon concerning the Creed and against Jews, Pagans and Arians, probably written in the Middle Ages... Studer arrives at the 'conclusion that the Mystère d'Adam was originally written in England about the middle of the twelfth century...within the period 1146–1174'." — *From the prefatory introduction.*

For a bibliographical and critical study see Paul Studer, editor, *Le mystère d'Adam,* Manchester [Eng.], 1918, p. xi–lviii, 59–63, *NAFM (Adam).*

...**Adam,** a religious play of the twelfth century, also known as the Repraesentatio Adae and Le mystère d'Adam and containing three parts: Adam and Eve, Cain and Abel, and the Processus prophetarum, translated from the Norman French and Latin into English verse by Edward Noble Stone. Seattle, Wash.: University of Washington Press, 1926. 3 p.l., 159–193 p. 4°. (University

of Washington. Publications in language and literature. v. 4, no. 2.) **NAA (Washington)**

Reviewed by George R. Coffman in *Speculum,* Cambridge, Mass., 1927, v. 2, p. 351–353, † *BTA.*

Norwich pageants. The grocers' play. From a manuscript in the possession of Robert Fitch... Norwich: Charles Muskett, 1856. 2 p.l., 24 p. 8°.

With critical notes.

Also in *Norfolk archaeology,* Norwich, 1859, v. 5, p. 8–31, *CO.*

Two texts are given, both copied from an eighteenth century transcript of the lost Grocers' book of Norwich. The first is dated June 16, 1533 and is headed, The story of ye creacion of Eve, with ye expellyng of Adam & Eve out of paradyce. It consists of 90 lines and is apparently incomplete. The second text is dated 1565, and is headed, The storye of ye temptacion of man in paradyce, beyng therin placyd, & the expellynge of man & woman from thence, newely renvid [renewed] & accordynge unto ye Sk=ypture, begon thys yere anno 1565, anno 7. Eliz. 153 lines.

Both texts begin with the creation of Eve and end with the expulsion from paradise. The dramatis personae are Pater, Adam, Eve, and Serpens; in the second text, Angel is added, together with some abstract characters. Under title of Paradise, it was staged by the Norwich Players, in Norwich, 1922.

Reproduced, with textual emendations, under title Norwich Whitsun plays by J. M. Manly in his *Specimens of pre-Shaksperean drama,* Boston, 1897, v. 1, p. 1–12, *NCO (Manly).*

Re-edited (transcribed and collated anew from the ms. used by Fitch) by Osborn Waterhouse in Early English Text Society, Extra series 104 (*Non-cycle mystery plays*), London, 1909, p. 8–18, *NCE (Early).*

J. Q. Adams prints the second text, based on Waterhouse's edition, in his *Chief pre-Shakespearean dramas,* Boston [cop. 1924], p. 88–93, * *R – NCO,* with emendations from Fitch and Manly.

HARROD, Henry. A few particulars concerning early Norwich pageants. (Norfolk archaeology. Norwich, 1852. 8°. v. 3, p. 3–18.) **CO**

Modern Plays

Andreini, Giovanni Battista. Adam: a sacred drama [in five acts and in verse], translated from the Italian of Gio. Battista Andreini. (In: John Milton, Cowper's Milton. Chichester [Eng.], 1810. 8°. v. 3, p. 1–199.) * **NCF (1810)**

First Italian edition published at Milan in 1613.

William Hayley in his *Life of Milton,* London, 1796, p. 281–323, †* *NCC,* prints extracts both in Italian and in English translation.

A review of the 2d Italian edition, Lugano, 1834, in *American quarterly review,* Philadelphia, 1834, v. 16, p. 308–324, * *DA,* gives numerous translated extracts.

The "ADAM" of Andreini. (Catholic world. New York, 1870. 8°. v. 11, p. 602–612.) * **DA**

WOODHULL, Marianna. "L'Adamo," Andreini. (In her: The epic of Paradise Lost. New York & London, 1907. 12°. p. 188–210.) * **NCH**

Benacense, Troilo Lancetta. [Analysis of the drama entitled Adam and Eve, in four acts.] (In: William Hayley, Life of Milton. London, 1796. 4°. p. 324–328.) †* **NCC**

Old Testament Plays — Genesis, continued

Adam and Eve, continued

Browning, Elizabeth (Barrett). A drama of exile. (In her: A drama of exile, and other poems. New York, 1845. 12°. v. 1, p. 13–131.) **NCM**

The characters are Adam and Eve, Gabriel, Lucifer, angels, and Christ (in a vision).
First published, 1844.
Also printed in various editions of her poetical works.
For reviews see *American Whig review*, New York, 1845, v. 1, p. 38–48, * *DA; Edinburgh review*, London, 1861, v. 114, p. 522–523, * *DA; The Examiner*, London, Oct., 1844, p. 628, * *DA; Graham's magazine*, Philadelphia, 1845, v. 26, p. 46–47, * *DA.*

Čapek, Karel, and J. Čapek. ...Adam the creator, a comedy in six scenes and an epilogue. Translated by Dora Round. London: George Allen & Unwin, Ltd. ₁1929.₎ 187 p. 12°. *** Q p.v.168**

A satire.

Carman, Bliss, and Mary Perry King. Eve ₁a dramatic poem₎. illus. (In their: Daughters of dawn. New York, 1913. 12°. p. 7–14.) **NCM**

Clough, Arthur Hugh. Fragments of the mystery of the Fall. ₁In fourteen scenes.₎ (In his: Poems and prose remains...edited by his wife. London, 1869. 12°. v. 2, p. 43–69.) **NCG**

Unfinished.
Reviewed in *Westminster review*, London, 1869, v. 92, p. 180–181, * *DA.*

Doughty, Charles Montagu. Adam cast forth. ₁A sacred drama in five songs.₎ London: Duckworth & Co., 1908. 4 p.l., 124 p. 12°. **NCR**

Judaeo-Arabian legend.
"Adam and Hawwa, cast forth from the Paradise, fell down in several places of the Earth; whence they, after age-long wandering, meet together again, upon a mountain." — *p.* [v].
Reviewed in *The Times literary supplement*, London, 1926, v. 25, p. 85–86, † *NAA;* by John Freeman in the *London mercury*, London, 1926, v. 14, p. 371–375, * *DA; The Academy*, London, 1908, v. 74, p. 634–635, * *DA;* and in *Athenæum*, London, 1908, v. 132, p. 11, * *DA.*
For a critical study see Barker Fairley, *Charles M. Doughty; a critical study*, New York [1927], p. 162–182, *NCC (Doughty),* and for an account of its composition, D. G. Hogarth, *The life of Charles M. Doughty*, London, 1928, p. 160–167, *AN.*

Downie, Robert Mager. The marriage of the dawn, an idyl of Eden ₁in four parts₎. (In his: The marriage of the dawn, an idyl of Eden, and other verse. Beaver Falls, Pa. ₁Camden, Pa., printed, cop. 1922.₎ 8°. p. 1–66.) **NBI**

"Adam's soliloquy," "Eve's awakening," "The tryst" are the titles of parts 1, 2 and 3 respectively. In part 4, "The meeting," Adam and Eve speak.

Dryden, John. The state of innocence, and Fall of man: an opera ₁in five acts₎, written in heroick verse, and dedicated to Her Royal Highness the Dutchess... London: Printed by H. H. for Henry Herringman, 1678. 10 p.l., 44 p. 4°.

First published, 1677.
Improperly termed *opera;* it is rather a dramatic poem.
Reprinted in his *Works*, London, 1808, v. 5, p. 89–166, *NCF,* and Edinburgh, 1821, *NCF.*

Genlis, Stéphanie Félicité Ducrest de St. Aubin, comtesse de. The death of Adam, a sacred drama, in three acts. (In her: Sacred dramas. London, 1786. 8°. p. xi–xv, 1–77.) **NKO**

Characters: Adam, Cain, Seth, Eve, Selima.
"My piece is only an imitation of the drama (The death of Adam) of M. Klopstock. It was not designed for the theatre by the author nor was it ever performed; but it has been translated into all languages." — *Preface.*

Groot, Hugo de. The Adamus exul of Grotius; or the prototype of Paradise lost. ₁A tragedy in five acts.₎ Now first translated from the Latin, by Francis Barham, London: Sherwood, Gilbert, and Piper, 1839. xii, 51 p. 2. ed. 8°. **NHM**

Originally published at Leyden, 1601.
Prolegomena by the translator [on the indebtedness of Milton's Paradise lost to the Adamus exul], p. 1–8.
Reviewed in *The Athenæum*, London, 1840, v. 13, p. 126, * *DA,* and in *The Spectator*, London, 1839, v. 12, p. 1119, * *DA.*

Lauder, William. An essay on Milton's imitation of the moderns. (Gentleman's magazine. London, 1747. 8°. v. 17, p. 24–26, 82–86, 285–286.) *** DA**

Enlarged and reprinted as *An essay on Milton's use and imitation of the moderns in his Paradise lost,* London, 1750, * *NCH.*
For a reply see John Douglas, *Milton vindicated,* London, 1751, * *NCH (Lauder).*

Woodhull, Marianna. Man's fall in tragedy: "Adamus exsul," Grotius. (In her: The epic of Paradise lost. New York & London, 1907. 12°. p. 144–164.) *** NCH**

Henderson, Alice (Corbin). Adam's dream; a miracle play for children. (In her: Adam's dream, and two other miracle plays. New York, 1909. 12°. p. 1–12.) **NASH**

Scene: A pleasant place in the garden of Eden.

Klopstock, Friedrich Gottlieb. The death of Adam, a tragedy; in three acts ₁and in verse₎, from the German ₁by R. Lloyd₎. London, 1763. 12°.

Title from British Museum Catalogue.
Review, accompanied by numerous extracts, in *Monthly review*, London, 1763, v. 29, p. 95–99, *NAA.*

Lucas, H. The revolution which began in heaven; or, Cœlo-tartaro-terra. A dramatic vision of time, from the fall of the angels to the redemption of man. London: J. Watson, 1850. 39 p. 12°. **ŽEY p.v.91**

In three acts.
The dramatis personae are celestials, infernals, and two terrestials, Adam and Eve.

Old Testament Plays — Genesis, continued

Adam and Eve, continued

Macleish, Archibald. Nobodaddy: a play ₁in three acts₁. Cambridge: Dunster House, 1926. 67(1) p. 8°.　　**＊KP (Pynson)**
Illustrated t.-p. in color.
The characters are Adam, Eve, Cain, Abel, and a Voice, in the Garden of Eden.
Reviewed by Léonie Adams in *The New republic,* New York, 1926, v. 48, p. 100, ＊*DA;* by R. P. Blackmur in *Poetry,* Chicago, 1926, v. 28, p. 339–342, ＊*DA;* by Stephen Vincent Benét in *Saturday review of literature,* New York, 1926, v. 2, p. 934, † *NAA;* and in *The Times literary supplement,* London, June 10, 1926, v. 25, p. 396, † *NAA.*

Madách, Imre. The tragedy of man; dramatic poem. Translatèd from the original Hungarian by William N. Loew. New York: Arcadia Press ₁introd. 1908₁. 224 p. 8°. **NWF**
A poem of the type of Goethe's Faust. The scene is laid in Eden. Adam, Eve, Lucifer.
Extracts, accompanied by biographical and critical note by G. A. Kohut, printed in Warner's *Library of the world's best literature,* v. 16, p. 9515–9530, ＊ *R – NAC.*

Monro, Harold. Outside Eden ₁a dramatic poem₁. (In his: Real property.￣ New York and London ₁1922₁. 8°. p. 46–48.) **NCM**

Moody, William Vaughn. The death of Eve; a fragment. (In his: Poems and plays. Introduction by John Matthews Manly. Boston and New York, 1912. 12°. v. 1, p. 393–448.)　　　**＊R – NBI**
The fragment is one of a proposed trilogy. Only the first act was completed. "In 'Death of Eve' it was intended to set forth the impossibility of separation, the complete unity of the Creator and his creation... Eve, being the means of separation of man from God, is the appropriate and necessary means of reconciliation." The characters are all from the book of Genesis.

The **Progenitors;** or, Our first parents, a morality. An old Irish religious poem, done into English verse by Alfred Perceval Graves and dramatised ₁in four scenes₁ by Mona Douglas. Oxford: Basil Blackwell, 1929. 23 p. 12°.

Raleigh, Stephen Walter. The beginning of time and things ₁a dramatic poem in two acts₁. (In his: Dramatic and poetical works. Philadelphia ₁1904?₁. 8°. p. 50–103.) **NBI**
"This poem constitutes Book vii, Drama i of an epic poem entitled Humanity lost." Among the characters are Adam, Eve, Cain, and Abel.

Read, Elizabeth Day. Garden of Eden; or, Disobedience and retribution. Boston: American Unitarian Association, n.d. 2 l. 4°.
Typewritten.

Sachs, Hans. The children of Eve. ₁A morality in one scene.₁ (In his: Shrovetide plays, translated and adapted by E. U. Ouless. London ₁cop. 1930₁. 8°. p. 10–19.) **NGC**
Original title: "Wie Gott der Herr Adam und Eva ihre Kinder segnet." Dated Sept. 23, 1553. The details of the theme are based on a fable by Philipp Melanchthon. Lord God appears as a messenger.
Reviewed in *Times literary supplement,* London, 1930, v. 29, p. 685, *NAA.* "The translator has adapted rather than translated."

―― The unlike children of Eve: how God the Lord talks to them. ₁In five acts.₁ Translated by Frank Sewall. ₍In: Warner's Library of the world's best literature. New York, 1917. 8°. v. 21, p. 12616–12631.)
　　　　　　　　　　　　　　　＊R – NAC
The nineteen dramatis personae are the Lord God, two angels, Satan and a messenger, Adam and Eve, six obedient, and six disobedient sons of Eve.

Schneor, Zalman. Eve, a play ₁in one act₁. (Reflex. Chicago, 1930. 8°. v. 6, Aug./ Sept., 1930, p. 74–85.)　　　**＊PBD**
The characters are Adam, Eve, two serpents, lions and apes, male and female each. "Eden has ended; the world begins."

Shaw, Bernard. Back to Methuselah. A metabiological pentateuch. New York: Brentano's, 1921. ciii p., 1 l., 300 p. 12°. **NCR**
Part i. In the beginning. (Two acts.) Time **b.** c. 4004; Afternoon in the Garden of Eden. The characters are Adam, Eve, Cain, and the serpent.
Reviewed by Edward Shanks in *Outlook,* London, 1924, v. 53, p. 143, ＊ *DA.*
The play was produced by the Theatre Guild at the Garrick Theatre, New York, parts 1 and 2 Feb. 27, parts 3 and 4 March 6, and part 5 on March 13, 1922. Reviewed in the *New York Clipper,* 1922, v. 70, March 22, p. 20, and April 5, p. 20, *MVA;* by Walter Prichard Eaton in *The Freeman,* New York, v. 5, March 29, 1922, p. 63–64, ＊ *DA,* and by Kenneth Macgowan in *Theatre arts magazine,* New York, 1922, v. 6, p. 180–187, *NBLA.* See also *Collection of newspaper clippings of dramatic criticism,* New York, 1921–22, volume A–D, † *NBL.*
A synopsis of the plot is given in C. Lewis Broad and Violet M. Broad, *Dictionary to the plays and novels of Bernard Shaw,* London [1929], p. 21–30, *NCC (Shaw).*

―― ―― New York: Brentano's, 1922. ciii p., 1 l., 300 p. 12°.　　　**NCR**

―― ―― Leipzig: B. Tauchnitz, 1922. 295 p. 16°. (Tauchnitz edition. Collection of British and American authors. no. 4578.)
　　　　　　　　　NCO p.v.541, no.6

בראשית. עברית מאת אלכסנדר מלחי. (הדים.) Tel Aviv, 1923. 16°. ₁v. 2,₁ no. 10, p. 3–23.)
　　　　　　　　　　　　　　　＊PBA
Hebrew translation of part 1, act 1.

BALMFORTH, Ramsden. Bernard Shaw's "metabiological" plays. (In his: The ethical and religious value of the drama. London ₁1925₁. 12°. p. 165–175.) **NAFD**

BAUGHAN, E. A. "Back to Methuselah." (Fortnightly review. London, 1923. 8°. v. 120 ₁new series, v. 114₁, p. 827–834.) **＊DA**

GREIN, Jacob Thomas. About Shaw's "Back to Methuselah." (In his: The new world of the theatre. London, 1924. 8°. p. 229–231.) **NAF**

LOWENTHAL, Marvin. Bernard Shaw among the rabbis. (Menorah journal. New York, 1921. 4°. v. 7, no. 5, Dec., 1921, p. 282–286.) **＊PBD**

Old Testament Plays — Genesis, continued
Adam and Eve, continued

Soble, Mae Stein. The first temptation: a· dramatization. (In her: Bible plays for children. New York, 1919. 12°. p. 23–38.)
NASH

Untermeyer, Mrs. Jean (Starr). Eve before the tree [a dramatic poem]. (In her: Dreams out of darkness. New York, 1921. 8°. p. 25–36.)
NBI

CAIN AND ABEL

Miracle Plays

BONNELL, John Kester. Cain's jaw bone. 6 illus. (Modern Language Association. Publications. Menasha, Wis., 1924. 8°. v. 39, p. 140–146.)
RAA
"The artists took the idea of the jaw-bone from mystery plays..."

EMERSON, Oliver Farrar. Legends of Cain, especially in old and middle English. (Modern Language Association of America. Publications. Baltimore, 1906. 8°. v. 21, p. 831–929.)
RAA

Sacrificium Cayme and Abell. The originall perteynyng to the craft of gloueres. [York play no. 7, 138 lines.] (In: Lucy T. Smith, editor, York plays. Oxford, 1885. 8°. p. 35–39.)
NAFM

Mactacio Abel. [Towneley play no. 2.] (In: The Towneley mysteries. London, 1836. 8°. p. 8–19.)
CA (Surtees)
Surtees Society. Publications. [v. 3.]
Also printed in 1897 (ed. England) in Early English Text Society, Extra series no. 71 (*The Towneley plays*), p. 9–22, *NCE (Early)* and in 1924 in J. Q. Adams, editor, *Chief pre-Shakespearean dramas*, p. 94–100, *R – NCO.* An extract is printed in Allardyce Nicoll, editor, *Readings from British drama*, New York [1928], p. 27–29, *R – NCO.*
Translated into German by Theodor Vatke and published in *Archiv für das Studium der neueren Sprachen und Literaturen,* Braunschweig, 1875, Bd. 54, p. 39–54, *RAA;* translated, with introduction and notes, by F. Holthausen in *Englische Studien,* Leipzig, 1927, Bd. 62, p. 132–151, *RNA.*

CAREY, Millicent. [Phraseology. Plot. Characterization. Humor and realism. Authorship.] (In her: The Wakefield group in the Towneley cycle. Göttingen, 1930. 8°. p. 9–48, 210–217.)
NAFM

HAMELIUS, Paul. The character of Cain in the Towneley plays. (Journal of comparative literature. New York, 1903. 8°. v. 1, p. 324–344.)
NAA

Cain and Abel. [Coventry play no. 3.] (In: Ludus Coventriæ, ed. Halliwell. London: Shakespeare Society, 1841. 8°. p. 33–39.)
NAFM (Coventry)
First printed in John Stevens, *History of the antient abbeys, monasteries, hospitals, cathedrals and collegiate churches,* London, 1722, v. 1, p. 147–149. Also printed in Sir William Dugdale, *Monasticon Anglicanum,* new ed., London, 1830, v. 6, part 3, p. 1540–1541, † *CAB.*
Also printed in 1922 (ed. Block) in Early English Text Society, Extra series no. 120 (*Ludus Coventriæ*), p. 29–35, *NCE (Early).*

Modern Plays

Alfieri, Vittorio. Abel. [A tragedy in five acts.] (In his: Tragedies. London: G. Bell, 1876. v. 2, p. 469–523.)
NNR
Characters: Adam, Eve, Abel, Cain.
The original title of this play was Cain; a musical tragedy. The characters are divided into two classes — one comprising the first four denizens of the earth after creation, and the second consisting of supernatural beings.

Battine, William. Another Cain; a mystery. [A dramatic poem, in five acts and in verse.] London, 1822. 12°.
Title from British Museum Catalogue.

Byron (6th baron), George Gordon Noël Byron. Sardanapalus, a tragedy. The two Foscari, a tragedy. Cain, a mystery. By Lord Byron. London: J. Murray, 1821. viii, 439(1) p. 8°.
First edition.
Cain occupies p. 331–439.
Dedicated to Sir Walter Scott. The author, in the preface, disclaims acquaintance with other dramas on the subject.
Reprinted in G. A. Kohut, editor, *A Hebrew anthology,* Cincinnati, 1913, v. 2, p. 691–725, *PSO.* Act III, scene I is reprinted in *New-England galaxy,* Boston, v. 5, no. 228, Feb. 22, 1822, p. 1. A selection under the title "Adah and Cain" is printed in *The poet and the painter,* New York, 1869, p. 69–74, † *NCI (Poet).*
Reviews: *Eclectic review,* London, 1822, new series, v. 17, p. 418–427, * *DA; European magazine,* London, 1822, v. 81, p. 64–69, * *DA; Literary gazette,* London, 1821, v. 3, p. 808–812, * *DA; London magazine,* London, 1822, v. 5, p. 70–71, * *DA; Monthly magazine,* London, 1822, v. 53, p. 10–15, * *DA; Monthly review,* London, 1822, v. 97, p. 96–98, * *DA; Quarterly review,* London, 1822, v. 27, p. 508–524, * *DA; United States literary gazette,* Boston, 1824, v. 1, p. 54–56, * *DA.*
The play was produced by the Manhattan Players at the Lenox Little Theatre, New York, April 8, 1925, with Wm. P. Carleton as Cain. For reviews see Collection of newspaper clippings of dramatic criticism, 1924–25, volume A–E, † *NBL.*

—— Cain; a mystery. To which is added a letter from the author to Mr. Murray, the original publisher. London: R. Carlile, 1822. iv, (1)6–23(1) p. 8°.
NCO p.v.310, no.4
The correspondence between Byron and his publisher, Murray, is also printed in the *Literary gazette,* London, 1822, v. 4, p. 166–167, * *DA.*

—— Cain; a mystery. By the Right Hon. Lord Byron. Paris: A. and W. Galignani, 1822. 4 p.l., (i)vi–viii p., 1 l., (1)12–137 p. 12°.
NCM
Bd. with v. 5 of his *Works.* Paris, 1821, with binder's title reading: Byron, Vol. v & vi.

—— Cain; a mystery. To which is added a letter from the author to Mr. Murray, the original publisher. London: R. Carlile, 1826. iv, 5–24 p. 8°.
ZEY p.v.1

—— Cain; a dramatic mystery in three acts by Lord Byron; translated into French verse and refuted in a series of philosophical and critical remarks preceded by a letter addressed to Lord Byron, upon the motives and the purpose of this work, by Fabre d'Olivet, MDCCCXXIII; done into English by Nayán Louise Redfield... New York &

Old Testament Plays — Genesis, continued

Cain and Abel, continued

London: G. P. Putnam's Sons, 1923. xi, 265 p. 8°.   **NCR**

—— Kain; dramatická báseň lorda Byrona. Přeložil Josef Durdík. V Praze: E. Grégr, 1871. 117 p. 16°. (Poesie světová. ₁Svazek₁ 1.)   *** QVK**

—— Kain. Mistero de Lord Byron (Bajron.) Tradukis A. Kofman. Nurnbergo: W. Tümmel, 1896. ix, 102 p. 16°. **RAXF p.v.19**
Translation into Esperanto.

—— Caïn, mystère dramatique en trois actes... Traduit en vers français, et réfuté dans une suite de remarques philosophiques et critiques; précédé d'une lettre adressée à Lord Byron, sur les motifs et le but de cet ouvrage, par Fabre D'Olivet. Paris: Servier, 1823. 2 p.l., 248 p., 1 l. 8°.
First French translation.

—— Cain, ein Mysterium. Aus den Englischen. ₁Deutsch von Gustav Friedrich Constantin Parthey.₁ Berlin u. Stettin: Nicolaische Buchhandlung, 1831. viii, 120 p. 12°.
First German translation.

—— Kains. Misterje 3 zehleenos. Tulkojis ₁into Lettish₁ J. Rainis. Riga: A. Gulbis ₁1924₁. 95 p. 8°. (Uniwesala biblioteka. no. 258/259.)
Title from Berliner Titeldrucke. 24.37442.

קין. שיר חזיון על פי כתבי הקדש. תרגם
מאנגלית לעברית דוד פרישמן.
Warsaw: "Tuschijah," 1900. 2 parts in 1 v. xl, 128 p. 12°.   *** PSN**

Каинъ. (Переводъ Бунина.) (In: I. A. Bunin, Сочиненія. Petrograd, 1915. 8°. v. 3, p. 133–185.)
  * QDB (Bunin)

BLUMENTHAL, Friedrich. ...Lord Byron's mystery "Cain," and its relation to Milton's "Paradise lost" and Gessner's "Death of Abel." Oldenburg: Gerhard Stalling, 1891. 12 p. sq. 4°. (Beilage zum 48. Jahresbericht der städtischen Ober-Realschule zu Oldenburg. Ostern 1891.)
Reviewed by E. Kölbing in *Englische Studien,* Leipzig, 1892, Bd. 16, p. 310, **RNA**.

"BRITANNICUS," pseud. Revolutionary causes: with a notice of some late publications, and a postscript containing strictures on ₁Lord Byron's₁ Cain... London, 1822. 8°.
Title from British Museum Catalogue.

BROOKE, Stopford. Byron's "Cain." (Hibbert journal. Boston, 1919. 8°. v. 18, p. 74–94.)   **ZAA**

CHEW, Samuel Claggett. The dramas of Lord Byron, a critical study. Göttingen: Vandenhoeck & Ruprecht; Baltimore: The

Johns Hopkins Press, 1915. 3 p.l., 181(1) p. 8°. (Hesperia. Ergänzungsreihe: Schriften zur englischen Philologie... Heft 3.)   **NCC**
Cain, and Heaven and earth, p. 118–143.

₁DISCUSSION concerning Byron's Cain, in form of a dialogue. A letter from Lord Byron to his publisher, Murray, dated Pisa, Feb. 8, 1822, assuming all responsibility against possible damages in the publication of Cain, together with a poem, "Byron to Murray," satirizing the same.₁ (Blackwood's magazine. Edinburgh, 1822. 8°. v. 11, p. 375–376, * 359.)   *** DA**
Reprinted in John Wilson and others, *Noctes Ambrosianæ,* New York, 1866, v. 1, p. 138–140, † *NCZ.*

EIMER, Manfred. Byron und der Kosmos. Ein Beitrag zur Weltanschauung des Dichters und den Ansichten seiner Zeit. Heidelberg: C. Winter, 1912. xiii, 233(1) p. 8°. (Anglistische Forschungen. Heft 34.)
  RNB (Anglistische)
Astronomie; Kosmogonie und Paläolontologie; Zur Weltanschauung [of Cain, Heaven and Hell, and other works], p. 98–180.
Vorbilder und Parallelen zu "Kain," p. 212–225.

GRANT, Harding. Lord Byron's Cain, a mystery; with notes; wherein the religion of the Bible is considered, in reference to acknowledged philosophy and reason. London: William Crofts, 1830. xvi, 432 p. 12°.
Reviewed in *Fraser's magazine,* London, 1831, v. 3, p. 285–304, * *DA,* and *Imperial magazine,* London, 1830, v. 12, col. 950–953, * *DA.*

GREEFF, A. Byron's Lucifer. (Englische Studien. Leipzig, 1906. 8°. Bd. 36, p. 64–74.)
  RNA

"HARROVIENSIS,'" pseud. A letter to Sir Walter Scott...in answer to the remonstrance of Oxoniensis on the publication of Cain, a mystery, by Lord Byron. London: Rodwell and Martin, 1822. 85 p. 8°.
Title from British Museum Catalogue.

HOLTERMANN, Adolph. Cain, a mystery by Lord Byron, critically examined by Adolph Holtermann. Brunswick: Frederic Vieweg and Son, 1869. 27 p. 8°.   *** C p.v.996**
"The drama contains essentially nothing else and nothing less, than the author's own relation to the theology of his day... Cain is a religious sceptic and as such in conflict with the society of all those who adhere to the orthodox creed."

HOWELL, Owen. Abel; written, but with great humility, in reply to Lord Byron's Cain. London: J. Mardon, 1843. 2 p.l., 22 p. 12°.   **NCI p.v.42, no.6**
"The object of Lord Byron...was to embody all the emotions of despair as they act upon the human mind; in the present poem, the author has endeavored to personify Hope, and to bring together as many pleasing expectations as possible..." — *From introductory note.*

LORD Byron's tragedies. (Edinburgh review. Edinburgh, 1822. 8°. v. 36, p. 437–444.)   *** DA**
"We regret very much that it should ever have been published. It will give great scandal and offence to pious persons in general..."

Old Testament Plays — Genesis, continued

Cain and Abel, continued

MAUROIS, André. A propos du Cain de Lord Byron. (Europe. Paris, 1924. 8°. tome 4, p. 235–239.)   *** DM**

MESSAC, Régis. Cain et le problème du mal dans Voltaire, Byron et Leconte de Lisle. (Revue de littérature comparée. Paris, 1924. 8°. année 4, p. 620–652.)   **NAA**

MORTIER, Alfred. Manfred et Cain. (In his: Le démon dans ses incarnations dramatiques. Paris, 1924. 12°. p. 55–62.)   **NAC p.v.122**

OXONIENSIS, pseud. A remonstrance addressed to Mr. John Murray, respecting a recent publication [Lord Byron's Cain]. London, 1822. 8°.
Title from British Museum Catalogue.

"PHILO-MILTON," pseud. A vindication of the Paradise lost from the charge of exculpating "Cain, a mystery." London, 1822. 8°.
Title from British Museum Catalogue.

SCHAFFNER, Alfred. Lord Byron's Cain und seine Quellen... Strassburg: K. J. Trübner, 1880. 48 p. 8°.
Reviewed by Felix Bobertag in *Englische Studien*, Heilbronn, 1881, Bd. 4, p. 335–338, *RNA*.

URIEL, a poetical address to the Right Honorable Lord Byron... An examination into his assertion that "If Cain is blasphemous, Paradise Lost is blasphemous"... London: The author, 1822. x p., 1 l., 128 p. 8°.   **NCI p.v.58, no.2**
Authorship ascribed to Henry Smithers, Liverpool, England.

WILKINSON, Henry. Cain; a poem; intended to be published in parts. Containing an antidote to the impiety and blasphemy of Lord Byron's Cain; with notes, etc. Part 1. London: Baldwin, Cradock and Joy, 1824. 8°.
No more published.
Title from British Museum Catalogue.

DIXIE, Lady Florence Caroline (Douglas). Abel avenged: a dramatic tragedy [in three acts]... London: E. Moxon, Son, and Co. [1877.] 122 p. 16°.
Based on Genesis IV: 23–24.
"It is the tradition of the Hebrews, that Lamech, in hunting, slew Cain, mistaking him for a wild beast; and that having discovered what he had done, he beat so unmercifully the boy by whom he was led into the mistake that the lad died of the blows."
"Written in the author's sixteenth year .. It has been read through and approved by Lord Lytton." — *Preface.*

The **First** murderer, a dramatic sketch. (Bolster's quarterly magazine. Dublin, 1826. 8°. v. 1, p. 203–210.)   *** DA**
Cain, Adah, A voice.
"I have endeavored to shew that without the existence of evil man could not possess free will..."

Harper, William. Cain and Abel: a dramatic poem; and minor pieces. London, Manchester [printed], 1844. 8°.
Title from British Museum Catalogue.

Lodge, George Cabot. Cain; a drama. Boston and New York: Houghton, Mifflin & Company, 1904. 6 p.l., 154 p., 1 l. 12°.   **NBM**
In three acts. Dedicated "to the deathless memory of Jesus of Nazareth who...was at last brought to his death by the priesthood of the orthodox church through the operation of the established courts of social justice."
Reprinted in his *Poems and dramas*, Boston, 1911, v. 1, p. 229–339, *NBI*.

Lyndsay, David. The death of Cain. (In his: Dramas of the ancient world. Edinburgh, 1822. 8°. p. 209–256.)

—— The destiny of Cain. (In his: Dramas of the ancient world. Edinburgh, 1822. 8°. p. 177–208.)

Manley, William Ford. Cain and Abel. (In his: Bible dramas. New York [cop. 1928]. 8°. p. 26–42.)   **NBM**

Morland, Henry. The restoration of Cain; a mystery in three acts. London: Potter-Sarvent Pub. Co., 1916. vii, 9–40 p. 12°. **NCR**
The characters are Adam, Cain, Hárasha (wicked one), Spirit of Abel, Eve, and the four daughters of Adam and Eve, Tehillah, Mirzach, Makor, and Zitsah. Scene in various parts of Asia. Cain is forgiven.

Morley, Christopher. East of Eden. Genesis IV: 16 — a play in one act. (New republic. New York, 1924. 4°. v. 39, Aug. 13, 1924, p. 318–323.)   *** DA**
Scene: the home of Cain and his wife, in "the land of Nod."
Reprinted in his *One act plays*, Garden City, N. Y., 1924, p. 143–174, *NBM*.

Opal, pseud. Abel's widow. (Drama II) [In two scenes]. (In his: The cloud of witnesses. New York, 1874. 12°. p. 50–55.)   **NBM**

Read, Elizabeth Day. Cain and Abel; or, Devine [sic!] Nemesis. Boston: American Unitarian Association, n.d. 7 l. 4°.
Typewritten.

Reade, John Edmund. Cain the wanderer. [In a prologue and twelve scenes.] (In his: Cain the wanderer; A vision of heaven; Darkness; and other poems. London, 1829. 8°. p. 21–154.)
It bears traces of Byron's influence. The volume is dedicated to Goethe.

Taylor, Edith Foreman. The woman from Nod. [In one act.] (In: Eleven short Biblical plays. New York, 1929. 12°. p. 223–239.)   **NBL p.v.216**

Old Testament Plays — Genesis, continued

NOAH

Miracle Plays

The **Building** of the Ark. The shipwrites
[play]. [York play no. 8, 151 lines.] (In: Lucy
T. Smith, editor, York plays. Oxford, 1885.
8°. p. 40–44.) **NAFM**

Noah and his wife, the Flood and its wan-
ing. The fysshers and marynars [play]. [York
play no. 9, 322 lines.] (In: Lucy T. Smith,
editor, York plays. Oxford, 1885. 8°. p. 45–
55.) **NAFM**

Processus Noe cum filiis. [Towneley play
no. 3.] (In: The Towneley mysteries. London, 1836. 8°. p. 20–34.) **CA (Surtees)**
Surtees Society. Publications. [v. 3.]
Also printed in 1897 (ed. England) in Early English
Text Society, Extra series no. 71 (*The Towneley plays*),
p. 23–40, *NCE (Early)*; in J. M. Manly, *Specimens
of the pre-Shaksperean drama*, Boston, 1897, v. 1,
p. 13–30, *NCO*; in J. S. P. Tatlock and R. G. Martin,
editors, *Representative English plays*, New York, 1916,
p. 5–12, * *R – NCO*; in J. Q. Adams, editor, *Chief
pre-Shakespearean dramas*, Boston, 1924, p. 101–110,
* *R – NCO*; and in H. C. Schweikert, *Early English
plays*, New York [1928], p. 74–89, *NCO*.
Extracts are printed in *Chester mysteries*, London,
1818, p. xviii–xx, *NAFM*, and an abbreviated form in
F. J. Tickner, editor, *Earlier English drama from
Robin Hood to Everyman*, New York [cop. 1929], p. 59–
73, *NCO (Tickner)*.

CAREY, Millicent. [Phraseology. Plot.
Characterization. Humor and realism.] (In
her: The Wakefield group in the Towneley
cycle. Göttingen, 1930. 8°. p. 49–109.)
NAFM

De Deluvio Noe. The water-leaders, and
the drawers of Dee playe. [The Deluge.
Chester play no. 3.] (In: Chester mysteries.
London, 1818. 4°. p. 13–37.) **NAFM**
Also printed in William Marriott, *A collection of
English miracle-plays*, Basel, 1838, p. 3–15, *NAFM*;
The Chester plays, ed. Wright, London, 1843, v. 1,
p. 45–56, *NAFM*; Early English Text Society, Extra
series no. 62 (*The Chester plays*), 1893, p. 48–63, *NCE
(Early)*; A. W. Pollard, *English miracle plays*, Oxford, 1890, p. 8–20, 180–184, *NAFM* (also editions of
1904, 1923, 1927); Samuel Smallwood, *Some ancient
mystery towers remaining in England*, [Hitchin, England, 1916], p. 57–72, *NAFH p.v.5*; J. Q. Adams,
editor, *Chief pre-Shakespearean dramas*, Boston, 1924,
p. 111–116, * *R – NCO*; and in *Everyman, with other
interludes, including eight miracle plays*, London
[1909], p. 26–36, *NAFM*.
Selections are printed in John S. Keltie, *The works
of the British dramatists*, Edinburgh, 1870, p. xl–xlii,
NCO, and in Julian Hawthorne, editor, *The Masterpieces and the history of literature*, New York, 1906,
v. 4, p. 332–335, *NAB*. A modern arrangement of it
constitutes episode IV of a Chaucerian festival celebrated at Wheaton College, May 23, 1925 (see "*May
Day in Canterbury; a Chaucerian festival. Arranged
by Anne Throop Maury. Boston: W. H. Baker &
Co., 1925.*" p. 27–36, *NBL p.v.143, no. 14)*.
A modern presentation, with interpolations from the
Towneley series, was given at the New Theatre, New
York, under the auspices of Columbia University on
March 27, 1911. It was accompanied by an illustrative
lecture by Prof. Brander Matthews. See *New York
Dramatic mirror*, March 29, 1911, v. 65, p. 7, * *DA*.

—— The Chester play of the Deluge, edited by J. Isaacs, with engravings on wood

by David Jones. Waltham Saint Lawrence,
Berkshire: Printed and published at the
Golden Cockerel Press, 1927. iv, 16 p., 1 l.
illus. f°. †* **KP**
Text in double columns.
Half-title: The thirde pagent of Noyes flood. The
waterleaders and drawers in dye.
Colophon: This book was printed by Robert Gibbings
at the Golden Cockerel Press, Waltham Saint Lawrence,
Berkshire, & completed on the XVI. day of November,
MCMXXVII. The text is based, by permission, on that
established by Professor A. W. Pollard for his 'English
miracle plays', with variants from the manuscripts
edited by the late Dr. Hermann Deimling for the
Early English Text Society... The edition is limited
to CCLXXV copies, of which this is number 272.
Reviewed in *Times literary supplement*, London,
1928, v. 27, p. 217, † *NAA*.

Noah's flood. (In: W. Dyfed Parry, editor, Old plays for modern players, selected
and modernized by W. Dyfed Parry. London [1930]. 12°. p. 13–25.)

SHEPPARD, Thomas. "Noah's ark" at Hull.
3 illus. (In his: Evolution of the drama in
Hull and district. Hull, 1927. 8°. p. 24–29.)
NCOM

Noah's flood. [Coventry play no. 4.] (In:
Ludus Coventriæ, ed. Halliwell. London:
Shakespeare Society, 1841. 8°. p. 40–48.)
NAFM (Coventry)
First printed in John Stevens, *History of the antient
abbeys, monasteries, hospitals, cathedrals and collegiate
churches*, London, 1722, v. 1, p. 149–151. Also printed
in Sir William Dugdale, *Monasticon Anglicanum*, new
ed., London, 1830, v. 6, part 3, p. 1541–1542, † *CAB*.
Also printed in 1922 (ed. Block) in Early English
Text Society, Extra series no. 120 (*Ludus Coventriæ*),
p. 35–43, *NCE (Early)*, and in J. M. Manly, *Specimens
of pre-Shaksperean drama*, Boston, 1897, v. 1, p. 31–
40, *NCO*.

Noah's ark. Noah's ark, or, The Shipwrights' ancient play, or dirge. [The New-
castle shipwrights' play.] (In: John Brand,
History and antiquities of... Newcastle upon
Tyne. London, 1789. 4°. v. 2, p. 373–379.)
† **CO**
Particulars concerning the Corpus Christi plays,
anciently performed by the trading companies of New-
castle upon Tyne, *ibid.*, p. 369–372.
Reprinted from Henry Bourne, *History of New-
castle-upon-Tyne*, 1736.
Also printed in Thomas Sharp, *A dissertation on the
pageants or dramatic mysteries anciently performed at
Coventry*, Coventry, 1825, p. 223–225, † *NAFM*; F. J.
Tickner, editor, *Earlier English drama from Robin
Hood to Everyman*, New York [cop. 1929], p. 53–59,
NCO (Tickner); in Early English Text Society, Extra
series no. 104 (*Non-cycle mystery plays*), London,
1909, p. 19–25, and editorial introduction, p. xxxv–
xliii, *NCE (Early)*; and in *County folk-lore. Examples
of printed folk-lore concerning Northumberland*, London, 1904, v. 4, p. 160–167, *ZBA (County)*.

—— Das Noahspiel von Newcastle upon
Tyne. Herausgegeben von Ferd. Holt-
hausen. Göteborg: Wald. Zachrissons bok-
tryckeri, 1897. 42 p., 1 l. 8°. (Göteborgs
högskolas årsskrift. Band 3 [no.] 3.)
NIMA (Göteborg)
The text of the play occupies p. 3–11.
See also a note by Holthausen in *Anglia: Beiblatt*,
Halle a.S., 1920, Bd. 31, p. 90–92, *RNA*.
Reviewed in *Athenæum*, London, 1898, v. 111,
p. 512, * *DA*, and by H. Logeman in *Englische Studien*,
Leipzig, 1900, Bd. 28, p. 115–117, *RNA*.

Old Testament Plays — Genesis, continued

Noah, continued

—— 'Noah's ark.' The Newcastle Shipwrights play. With a modernized version by M. S. D. Newcastle-upon-Tyne: Printed by M. S. Dodds [1925?]. 20 p.

Title taken from a short notice in *Notes and queries*, London, 1926, v. 150, p. 18, * R - * DA.

BROTANEK, Rudolf. Noahs Arche. Ein Misterium aus Newcastle upon Tyne. (Anglia. Halle a. S., 1899. 8°. Bd. 21, p. 165–200.) **RNA**

The text of the play is printed on p. 170–183.
The Sharp text, 1825, and the original in the northern dialect of the second quarter of the fifteenth century are printed on opposite pages.

DUSTOOR, P. E. Notes on the E. E. T. S. edition. (Modern language notes. Baltimore, 1928. 8°. v. 43, p. 252–255.) **RAA**

Noah's flood. [Extract from the Cornish Origo mundi.] (In: F. J. Tickner, editor, Earlier English drama from Robin Hood to Everyman. New York [cop. 1929]. 16°. p. 44–52.) **NCO (Tickner)**

Modern Plays

Benton, Rita. Noah's flood. [A play in two scenes.] (In her: Shorter Bible plays. New York [cop. 1922]. 8°. p. 11–36.) **NASH**

Boyd, Zachary. Flood of Noah. [A dramatic poem. Excerpt of about 390 lines out of about 860 lines from the ms. "Flowers of Zion."] (In: Gabriel Neil, Biographical sketch of the Rev. Mr. Zachary Boyd. Glasgow, 1832. 8°. Appendix, p. xvii–xxi.)

Seven speakers. **A p.v.144**

Dall, Ian. Noah's wife, an archaic incident. [A dramatic poem.] illus. (In his: Noah's wife. Oxford, 1925. 12°. p. 3–8.) **NCM**

Characters: Noah, Mrs. Noah, their three sons and their wives.

Ecclestone, Edward. Noah's flood; or, The destruction of the world, an opera [in five acts and in verse]. London, 1679. 4°.

Title from British Museum Catalogue, which should be consulted for other editions.

Grossman, Samuel S. Playing Noah. A Biblical dramatization in two scenes. [New York: Young Judaea.] 6 l. 4°. (In his: [Holiday and other plays for Jewish children].)

Mimeographed. **NASH**

The characters are a boy and a girl, with boys and girls representing the animals in Noah's Ark.

Hursten, Zora Neale. "The first one," a play in one act. (In: Charles S. Johnson, editor, Ebony and topaz, a collectanea. New York [1927]. 4°. p. 53–57.) **810.8–J**

In the Schomburg Collection.
Scene: valley of Ararat, three years after the flood. Noah curses Ham with blackness; hence, Ham's color.

Lyndsay, David. The deluge. (In his: Dramas of the ancient world. Edinburgh, 1822. 8°. p. 1–64.)

Noah's flood. In 1662 a license was granted to George Bayley, of London, musitioner, to make show of a play called Noah's flood.

Hazlitt, *Manual*, p. 167.

Pierce, Frederick Erastus. The world that God destroyed. [In five acts.] (In his: The world that God destroyed, and other poems. New Haven, Conn., 1911. 12°. p. 1–118.) **NBI**

Reade, John Edmund. The deluge; a drama in twelve scenes. London, 1839. 8°.

Title from British Museum Catalogue.

Seiffert, Marjorie Allen. Noah's Ark; a play for toys. (Poetry. Chicago, 1928. 8°. v. 32, p. 1–14.) *** DA**

Whitworth, Geoffrey Arundel. Father Noah. (In his: Father Noah, and other fancies. New York, 1919. 12°. p. 11–42.) **NCM**

Scene: in the hold of the ark during the flood.
Reprinted in A. M. Sharp, editor, *Modern plays in one act*, London [1929], p. 15–39, *NCO.*
Presented by the Unnamed Society of Manchester, England, at the Margaret Morris Theatre, Chelsea, Feb. 25, 1922, and revived at a matinee in aid of the British Drama League Library Fund at the Savoy Theatre, London, June 12, 1923. Mr. Winfrid Walter as Noah. For an illustration of a stage setting by William Grimmond see *English review*, London, 1922, v. 34, p. 351, * DA.

Worrell, Edna Randolph. The toy's rebellion. [In one scene.] Music. (Ladies' home journal. Philadelphia, 1902. 4°. v. 20, Dec., 1902, p. 16.) *** DA**

Mr. Noah.

ABRAHAM

Miracle Plays

Abraham's sacrifice of Isaac. The parchemyners and bokebynders [play]. [York play no.10, 380 lines.] (In: Lucy T. Smith, editor, York plays. Oxford, 1885. 8°. p. 56–67.) **NAFM**

Also, in abbreviated form, in F. J. Tickner, editor, *Earlier English drama from Robin Hood to Everyman,* New York [cop. 1929], p. 73–82, *NCO (Tickner).*
Illustration, drawn by A. Forestier, in *Illustrated London news,* London, 1910, v. 136, p. 344, * DA.

Abraham. [Towneley play no. 4.] (In: The Towneley mysteries. London, 1836. 8°. p. 35–42.) **CA (Surtees)**

Surtees Society. Publications. [v. 3.]
Also printed in 1897 (ed. England) in Early English Text Society, Extra series no. 71 (*The Towneley plays*), p. 40–49, *NCE (Early).*

HUGIENIN, Julian. An interpolation in the Towneley Abraham play. (Modern language notes. Baltimore, 1899. 4°. v. 14, col. 255–256.) **RAA**

Old Testament Plays — Genesis, continued

Abraham, continued

The **Histories** of Lot and Abraham. The barbers and the waxe chaundlers playe. [Chester play no. 4.] (In: The Chester plays, ed. Wright. London: Shakespeare Society, 1843. 8°. v. 1, p. 57–76.) **NAFM**

Also printed in 1893 (ed. Deimling) in Early English Text Society, Extra series no. 62 *(The Chester plays),* p. 63–83, *NCE (Early);* in *"Everyman," with other interludes including eight miracle plays,* London [1909], p. 37–51, *NAFM;* and, adapted, in P. E. Osgood, *Old-time church drama adapted,* New York, 1928, p. 99–123, *NAFM.*

The episode of the Sacrifice of Isaac is printed in A. W. Pollard, *English miracle plays,* Oxford, 1890, p. 21–30, 184–187, *NAFM* (other editions in 1904, 1923, 1927).

An adaptation of this play forms scene I of part III entitled "Bacon at Oxford" in John Erskine, *A pageant of the thirteenth century for the seven hundredth anniversary of Roger Bacon,* New York, 1914, p. 51–55, *NBM.* "Though a liberty has been taken with the facts, in dating this particular play so early and locating it at Oxford, it furnishes a scene typical of the thirteenth century English town." *p. 50.*

Produced at the Charterhouse by the Elizabethan Stage Society, July, 1901. See *Athenæum,* London, July 20, 1901, p. 103, * *DA.*

Abraham's sacrifice. [Coventry play no. 5.] (In: Ludus Coventriæ, ed. Halliwell. London: Shakespeare Society, 1841. 8°. p. 49–57.) **NAFM (Coventry)**

First printed in John Stevens, *History of the antient abbeys, monasteries, hospitals, cathedrals and collegiate churches,* London, 1722, v. 1, p. 151–153. Also printed in Sir William Dugdale, *Monasticon Anglicanum,* new ed., London, 1830, v. 6, part 3, p. 1542–1544, † *CAB.*

Also printed in 1922 (ed. Block) in Early English Text Society, Extra series no. 120 *(Ludus Coventriæ),* p. 43–51, *NCE (Early).*

Abraham and Isaac, a mystery play; from a private manuscript of 15th century. [Edited by] L. Toulmin Smith. [The Brome ms.] (Anglia. Halle a. S., 1884. 8°. Bd. 7, p. 316–337.) **RNA**

The text of the play is printed on p. 323–337.

The Brome ms. dates from 1499, and is the first example of English drama found in East Anglia. Containing 466 lines, it is the longest of the miracle plays on this topic.

"Five [old] English plays on the subject of Abraham's sacrifice are known, the Brome ms. gives a sixth, and no two are alike. Each of the four great collections of plays, the Chester, York, Towneley, and Coventry, includes it; one is also found in a separate form at Trinity College, Dublin... It was a favourite piece, both on account of its human and pathetic interest, and its capabilities of conveying instruction, either of the mystic-typical kind familiar to the early centuries, or of a directly religious and moral nature." — *p. 317.*

Reviewed in the *American journal of philology,* Baltimore, 1885, v. 6, p. 375–376, *RAA.* For textual emendations by F. Holthausen, see *Anglia,* Halle a. S., 1891, Bd. 13, p. 361–362, *RNA.*

Later printed by Miss Smith in her *A common-place book of the 15th century,* London, 1886, p. 46–69, *NCE.*

Reprinted in J. M. Manly, *Specimens of pre-Shaksperean drama,* Boston, 1897, v. 1, p. 41–57, *NCO;* Early English Text Society, Extra series no. 104 *(Non-cycle mystery plays),* London, 1909, p. 36–53, editorial introduction, p. xliii–liv, *NCE (Early);* J. S. P. Tatlock and R. G. Martin, editors, *Representative English plays,* New York, 1916, p. 13–19, * *R – NCO;* J. Q. Adams, editor, *Chief pre-Shakespearean dramas,* Boston, 1924, p. 117–124, * *R – NCO;* Brander

Matthews and P. R. Lieder, editors, *Chief British dramatists,* Boston, 1924, p. 1–9, *NCO;* J. B. Hubbell and J. O. Beaty, compilers, *An introduction to drama,* New York, 1927, p. 99–106, *NAFM;* H. C. Schweikert, editor, *Early English plays,* New York [cop. 1928], p. 90–103, *NCO;* F. J. Tickner, editor, *Earlier English drama from Robin Hood to Everyman,* New York [cop. 1929], p. 82–99, *NCO (Tickner).*

Printed in adapted form in *The second shepherds' play; Everyman and other early plays,* Boston [cop. 1910], p. 7–26, *NCO p.v.556.*

An extract, giving the denouement, is printed in A. W. Pollard, *English miracle plays,* Oxford, 1890, p. 173–176, *NAFM* (other editions 1904, 1923, 1927).

See *Theatre magazine,* New York, 1908, v. 8, p. 176 for an illustration of a scene from the play as produced by the students of the University of Illinois.

Abraham and Isaac. A miracle play adapted from the pageant of the Barbers and Wax-chandlers in the Chester cycle of miracles and from the Book of Brome found at Brome Hall, Suffolk... (In: S. A. Eliot, editor, Little theater classics. Boston, 1920. 12°. v. 2, p. 71–112.) **MZB**

Presented in a version by Sam Hume at The Greek Theatre, Berkeley, Cal., October, 1907; The Auditorium, St. Paul, Minn., Christmas, 1915; The Arts and Crafts Theater, Detroit, Mich., Jan., 1917, and The Artists' Guild Theater, St. Louis, Mo., Christmas, 1917; and in the present version at the Municipal Theater, Northampton, Mass., Christmas, 1918.

The **Old** English miracle play of Abraham and Isaac. London: De La More Press, 1905. 33 p., 1 l. 24°.

A modernized version of the Brome Abraham and Isaac play.

Abraham and Isaac. (In: W. Dyfed Parry, editor, Old plays for modern players, selected and modernized by W. Dyfed Parry. London [1930]. 12°. p. 26–36.)

DUSTOOR, P. E. [Textual] notes. (Modern language review. Cambridge, 1928. 8°. v. 23, p. 211–212.) **NAA**

The **Sacrifice** of Abraham, a miracle play. Now first printed from Ms. Trin. Coll. Dublin. [The Dublin ms.] 19 p. 12°. (In: J. P. Collier, Five miracle plays. London, 1836.)

The ms. of this play bears no title, the name "Sacrifice of Abraham" having been first given to it by Collier.

Printed (ed. Brotanek) in *Anglia,* Halle a. S., 1898, Bd. 21, p. 21–55, *RNA;* also printed in Early English Text Society, Extra series no. 104 *(Non-cycle mystery plays),* London, 1909, p. 26–36, editorial introduction, p. xliii–liv, *NCE (Early).*

FORT, Margaret Dancy. The metres of the Brome and Chester Abraham and Isaac plays. (Modern Language Association of America. Publications. Menasha, Wis., 1926. 8°. v. 41, p. 832–839.) **RAA**

HARPER, Carrie A. A comparison between the Brome and Chester plays of Abraham and Isaac. (In: Studies in English and comparative literature. Boston, 1910. 8°. p. 51–73.) **NABM**

Radcliffe College monographs. no. 15.

Old Testament Plays — Genesis, continued

Abraham, continued

HOHLFELD, Alexander Rudolf. Two old
English mystery plays on the subject of
Abraham's sacrifice. [Chester and Brome
versions.] (Modern language notes. Baltimore, 1890. 4°. v. 5, col. 222–237.) **RAA**
    The agreeing parts of the two versions are printed in
parallel columns.

Sacrifice of Abraham. (In: Three Cretan
plays. London, 1929. 8°. p. 61–99.) **NSRM**
    A Greek miracle play, "un véritable mystère, du
genre de ceux que l'on représentait par tout l'Europe
au moyen âge," first published according to E. Legrand
in 1535 at Venice, or, as is argued in the present
introduction, in 1668. "It has usually been said to
fall naturally into two acts of 544 and 609 lines
respectively, but I have suggested a division into four
acts."
    "Produced in Athens on March 28, 1929, apparently
for the first time in Greece." The translation, by F. H.
Marshall, is made from the text of Émile Legrand in
Bibliothèque grecque vulgaire, Paris, 1880, v. 1, p. 226–
268. *Cf.* introduction and analysis, by John Mavrogor-
dato, p. 6–31.
    Reviewed in *Times literary supplement*, London,
1930, v. 29, p. 492, † *NAA.*

Modern Plays

Abraham. [In six scenes.] (In: M. W.
Thomas, editor, Old Testament drama. London [1927]. 12°. p. 11–28.)

Abraham and Lot: a Scriptural drama thus
noticed in Henslowe's Diary: "received at
Abrame and Lotte, the 9 of Jeneuary, 1593,
lij. s."
    Noted in W. C. Hazlitt, *Manual*, p. 1.

Barnum, Madalene Demarest. Brethren;
a play for Peace Day. (In her: School plays
for all occasions. New York [cop. 1922]. 12°.
p. 139–154.) **MZB**
    The covenant of peace between Abraham and
Abimelech (Genesis XXI).

Benton, Rita. The proving of Abraham.
(In her: Shorter Bible plays. New York
[cop. 1922]. 8°. p. 38–42.) **NASH**
    The sacrifice of Isaac.

Bèze, Théodore de. A tragedie of Abrahams sacrifice written in French by Theodore Beza, and translated into English by
Arthur Golding. Edited, with an introduction, notes and an appendix containing the
Abraham sacrifiant of Theodore Beza, by
Malcolm W. Wallace... [Toronto:] University of Toronto Library, 1906. lxi, <127>
p., 5 pl. 4°. (University of Toronto studies.
Philological series.) *** PSQ**
    Golding's translation is reprinted from the first
English edition, London, T. Vantroullier, 1577. (With
facsimile reproduction of original t.-p.)
    First printed at Geneva in 1550.
    "In the present edition I have attempted to reproduce
as accurately as possible the copy which is in the
Bodleian (black letter, 18mo.) except in one particular,
viz. the abbreviated words are written in full." —
p. [*v*].
    "Appendix [p. [89]–<127>]: Abraham sacrifiant
(reprinted from the edition of J. G. Fick, Geneva,
1874)".

Boyd, Zachary. Abraham commanded to
sacrifice Isaac. [A dramatic poem. Excerpt
of about 300 lines out of about 840 lines from
the ms. "Flowers of Zion."] (In: Gabriel
Neil, Biographical sketch of the Rev. Mr.
Zachary Boyd. Glasgow, 1832. 8°. Appendix, p. xxvii–xxx.) **A p.v.144**
    Five speakers.

——— The destruction of Sodom. [A dramatic poem. Excerpt of about 200 lines out
of about 2000 lines from the ms. "Flowers of
Zion.") (In: Gabriel Neil, Biographical
sketch of the Rev. Mr. Zachary Boyd. Glasgow, 1832. 8°. Appendix, p. xxv–xxvii.)
    Nine speakers. **A p.v.144**

Carvalho, Naomi Nunes. The first mi-
gration. [A dialogue between Terah and
Abraham.] (In her: Vox humana. London,
1912. 12°. p. 5–9.) **NRD p.v.9, no.2**

——— Separation (Hebrew). [A dialogue between Abraham and Hagar.] (In her: Vox
humana. London, 1912. 12°. p. 11–15.)
    NRD p.v.9, no.2

Drucker, Aaron Phinias. The sacrifice of
Isaac; a drama — paraphrased from Genesis
XV and XXII. [In three acts.] (Young Judaean.
New York, 1914. 8°. v. 4, Jan., 1914, p. 19–
21.)
    Copy in Dropsie College.

Farrer, E., of Oundle. The trial of Abraham, a dramatic poem. Stamford [Eng.],
1790. 8°.
    Title from British Museum Catalogue.

Genlis, Stéphanie Félicité Ducrest de St.
Aubin, comtesse de. Hagar in the desert; a
dramatic dialogue. (London magazine. London, 1781. 8°. v. 50, p. 9–12.) *** DA**
    Characters: Hagar, Ishmael.
    Reprinted in her *Sacred dramas*, London, 1786,
p. 79–98, *NKO*, and in her *The Theatre of education*,
London, 1787, v. 1, p. 1–12, *NKO.*

——— The sacrifice of Isaac, a sacred drama
in two acts. (In her: Sacred dramas. London, 1786. 8°. p. 99–157.) **NKO**

Githens, Harry W. A father of nations.
[Abraham.] [In six scenes.] (In his: Dramatized stories from the Old Testament. Cincinnati [cop. 1927]. 12°. p. 15–22.) **NASH**

Hare, Walter Ben. Hagar in the desert.
(In his: Costume monologues. Boston, 1919.
12°. p. 97–99.) **NBM**

Hunt, James Henry Leigh. Abraham and
the fire-worshipper, a dramatic parable. (In
his: Poetical works, ed. by S. Adams Lee.
Boston, 1859. 24°. v. 1, p. 132–135.) **NCM**
    Characters: Abraham, a Persian traveller, and a
voice.

Lesley, George. Abraham's faith. [A tragi-
comedy, in verse. London, 1675.] 59–77 p.
8°.
    Part of a book. Title from British Museum Cata-
logue.

Old Testament Plays — Genesis, continued

Abraham, continued

Levinger, Elma C. (Ehrlich). The boy who broke the idols, a little play about Abraham ₍in one scene₎. (In her: Entertaining programs for the assembly. Cincinnati ₍cop. 1930₎. 8°. p. 81–84.)   *** PSY**

Levy, Leah. Abraham. ₍A play in five acts.₎ New York: Bloch Pub. Co., 1901. 22 p. 16°. (Bible plays for the Sabbath school.)   *** PSQ**

Lobingier, Elizabeth Erwin (Miller). Abraham and the three guests. (In her: The dramatization of Bible stories. Chicago ₍cop. 1919₎. 12°. p. 84–92.)   *** YIR**

MacQueen, Lawrence I. Sacrifice; a play, in one act. (Drama. Chicago, 1921. 4°. v. 11, p. 216–219.)   **NAFA**

Manley, William Ford. Ishmael. (In his: Bible dramas. New York ₍cop. 1928₎. 8°. p. 166–184.)   **NBM**

—— Sacrifice. (In his: Bible dramas. New York ₍cop. 1928₎. 8°. p. 147–165.)   **NBM**
Abraham and Isaac.

Metastasio, Pietro Antonio Domenica Buonaventura. Isaac; a type of the redeemer. ₍In two parts, translated with some omissions by Robert Charles Sands.₎ <From Metastasio.> illus. (In: Talisman for 1828. New-York, 1827. 16°. p. 145–166.)   **NBA**
Reprinted in Robert C. Sands, *Writings*, New York, 1834, v. 1, p. 117–135, *NBG.*

The **Offering** of Isaac; a sacred drama. ₍In three parts and in verse.₎ (In: Poems on various subjects...and the Offering of Isaac. London, 1811. 16°. p. 129–221.)
Title from British Museum Catalogue.
Usually ascribed to Sir Thomas Noon Talfourd.
Reviewed in *British critic,* London, 1811, v. 38, p. 291–292, * *DA.*

Osgood, Phillips Endecott. City walls and open plains, an allegory of spiritual venture ₍in one scene₎. illus. (In his: The sinner beloved, and other religious plays. New York and London, 1928. 12°. p. 194–214.)   **NAFM**
Abram's departure from Ur.

Radcliff, Ralph. The Burning of Sodom: a tragedy by Ralph Radcliff. Not printed.
Noted in W. C. Hazlitt, *Manual,* p. 32.

Reznikoff, Charles. Abram in Egypt. ₍A dramatic sketch.₎ (Menorah journal. New York, 1924. 4°. v. 10, p. 514–515.)   *** PBD**
Characters: Abraham, Sarai, Pharaoh's messengers.
Reprinted in his *Nine plays*, New York, 1927, p. 20–22, *NBM.*

Russell, Mary M. How love made a father cruel; or, Hagar and Ishmael sent into the wilderness. ₍In three scenes.₎ (In her: Drama as a factor in social education. New York ₍cop. 1924₎. 12°. p. 98–112.)   **SSI**
Genesis xvi.

Tennant, William. Destruction of Sodom. (In his: Hebrew dramas. Edinburgh, 1845. 16°.)
Title from British Museum Catalogue.

Wells, Rollin John. Hagar; a dramatic poem in three acts; illustrated by William L. Hudson. New York: Broadway Publishing Co., 1903. 4 p.l., 125 p., 8 pl. 12°.
Reviewed in *New York Dramatic mirror,* v. 52, Dec. 3, 1904, p. 12, * *DA.*

Whitney, Dorothea U. Story of Abraham. ₍In four parts.₎ Boston: American Unitarian Association ₍1916?₎. 7 l. 4°.
Typewritten.
First presented by the First Parish Church, Watertown, Mass., March, 1916.

Whitney, Mary Ellen. Abraham and Isaac. ₍A play in three scenes.₎ (In her: Bible plays and how to produce them. New York ₍cop. 1927₎. 12°. p. 13–19.)
Place: the house of Abraham.

Zacuto, Moses ben Mordecai. Foundation of the world. ₍Translation by Israel Abrahams of the beginning of the first scene.₎ (Jewish chronicle. London, 1892. f°. Aug. 26, 1892, p. 7.)   *** PBE**
The translated extract is from the first dramatic poem in modern Hebrew, written in the forties of the seventeenth century, and first published by A. Berliner in 1874. The speakers are Abram and Terah. The episode narrated is based on a Midrash which tells how Abram smashed the idols of his father, and mischievously placed the hammer in the hands of the biggest of the images.

ISAAC

Miracle Play

Isaac. ₍The Towneley play no. 5.₎ (In: The Towneley mysteries. ₍London,₎ 1836. 8°. p. 43–44.)   **CA (Surtees)**
Surtees Society. Publications. [v. 3.]
The fragmentary condition of the play is due to the loss of two leaves of the ms.
Also printed in 1897 (ed. England) in Early English Text Society, Extra series no. 71 *(The Towneley plays)*, p. 49–51, *NCE (Early),* and in J. M. Manly, *Specimens of the pre-Shaksperean drama,* Boston, 1897, v. 1, p. 58–60, *NCO.*

Modern Plays

Githens, Harry W. Searching for a wife ₍for Isaac₎. ₍In four scenes.₎ (In his: Dramatized stories from the Old Testament. Cincinnati ₍cop. 1927₎. 12°. p. 23–29.)   **NASH**

Hobart, Marie Elizabeth Jefferys. Rebekah; an Old Testament mystery play. New York: Domestic and Foreign Missionary Society, 1920. 47 p. illus. 12°.
Deals with the wooing of Rebekah by Eliezer for Isaac.
"Rebekah was written for the 1920 Conference for Church Work at Wellesley, Mass., and the 1920 Summer School for Churchworkers at Geneva, New York. It was given at Wellesley and at Geneva."

Iliowizi, Henry. Isaac's blessing. A drama in four parts. n.p., n.d. 14 p. 12°.

Old Testament Plays — Genesis, continued

Isaac, continued

Kimball, Rosamond. The wooing of Rebekah. ₁A play in five scenes.₁ (In her: The wooing of Rebekah and other Bible plays. New York, 1925. 8°. p. 23–36.)   **ZICS**

Levinger, Elma C. (Ehrlich). The girl who was good to strangers, a dialogue ₁in one scene₁. (In her: Entertaining programs for the assembly. Cincinnati ₁cop. 1930₁. 8°. p. 85–87.)   *** PSY**
The characters are Eliezer, Abraham's servant, and Rebekah.

Lobingier, Mrs. Elizabeth Erwin (Miller). Isaac and Rebekah; its dramatization. ₁In three acts.₁ illus. (Church school. New York, 1922. 4°. v. 3, p. 521–523, 534.)
Reprinted in her *Dramatization in the church school*, Chicago [1923], p. 76–85, * YIR.
"The dramatization...is the work of intermediate girls of United Church, Oberlin, Ohio."

Russell, Mary M. A search for a wife. ₁In three scenes.₁ (In her: Dramatized Bible stories for young people. New York, 1921. 12°. p. 53–58.)
Eliezer finding Rebekah as wife for Isaac.

Yates, James Stanley. Genesis xxvii. ₁A dramatic poem.₁ (In his: War lyrics and other poems. Oxford, 1919. 12°. p. 7–13.)
Isaac, Jacob, and Esau.   **BTZI**

JACOB

Miracle Plays

Jacob. Sequitur Jacob. ₁The Towneley play no. 6.₁ (In: The Towneley mysteries. ₁London,₁ 1836. 8°. p. 45–48.) **CA (Surtees)**
Surtees Society. Publications. [v. 3.]
Also printed in 1897 (ed. England) in Early English Text Society, Extra series no. 71 (*The Towneley plays*), p. 52–56, *NCE (Early)*, and in J. M. Manly, *Specimens of the pre-Shakspearean drama*, Boston, 1897, v. 1, p. 60–65, *NCO*.

₁The **6 Pagean**₁ of Jacob. ₁106 lines.₁ (In: C. F. Brown, editor, Stonyhurst pageants. Göttingen, 1920. 8°. p. 1–4.)   **NAFM**

Modern Plays

Beer-Hofmann, Richard. From Jaákobs Traum (Jacob's dream). Translated by A. B. ₁A fragment.₁ (Hebrew Union College monthly. Cincinnati, 1927. 4°. v. 14, no. 6, June, 1927, p. 24.)   *** PBD**

Boyd, Zachary. Dinah ravished by Shechem. ₁A dramatic poem.₁ (In his: Four poems from "Zion's flowers." Glasgow, 1855. 8°. p. 141–157.)   **NCL**
Seven speakers.

Carvalho, Naomi Nunes. The mother's son. ₁A dialogue between Rebekah and Jacob.₁ (In her: Vox humana. London, 1912. 12°. p. 17–21.)   **NRD p.v.9, no.2**

Cooper, Miriam Denness. The wrestler at Jabbok; an Old Testament mystery play ₁in three acts₁. Hartford, Conn.: Church Missions Publishing Co., 1927. 30 p. 8°. (The Church in story and pageant. Publication. no. 15.)   **NBL p.v.223**

Githens, Harry W. A bad bargain. ₁In three scenes.₁ (In his: Dramatized stories from the Old Testament. Cincinnati ₁cop. 1927₁. 12°. p. 30–35.)   **NASH**
The selling of Esau's birthright.

—— A long courtship. ₁In four scenes.₁ (In his: Dramatized stories from the Old Testament. Cincinnati ₁cop. 1927₁. 12°. p. 36–41.)   **NASH**
Jacob's wooing of Rachel.

Hale, Harris G., and NEWTON M. HALL. ...The story of Jacob. Arranged by Harris G. Hale and Newton M. Hall. Boston: The Pilgrim Press, 1906. iv, 20 p. 12°. (Biblical dramas. ₁no. 2.₁)   **NBL (Biblical)**

Hauptmann, Gerhart. Pastoral ₁Das Hirtenlied. In two acts. Translated by Ludwig Lewisohn.₁ (In his: Dramatic works. New York, 1917. 12°. v. 7, p. 349–384.)   **NGE**
Love story of Jacob and Rachel.
Original German first appeared in *Neue Rundschau*, Jahrg. 15, Bd. 1, p. 1–26, * *DF*.

Jacob and Esau. ₁In two scenes.₁ (In: M. W. Thomas, editor, Old Testament drama. London ₁1927₁. 12°. p. 29–46.)

Jacob and Esau. The history of Jacob and Esau. (In: Robert Dodsley, editor. A select collection of old English plays. 4th ed. by W. C. Hazlitt. London, 1874–76. 8°. v. 2, p. 185–264.)   **NCO (Dodsley)**
Also printed in J. S. Farmer, editor, *Six anonymous plays (Second series)*, London, 1906, p. 1–90, *NCO (Early)* (published by Early English Drama Society).

—— ...Jacob and Esau. 1568. London: Issued for subscribers by T. C. & E. C. Jack, 1908. v p., facsim. (₁56₁ p.) 4°. (The Tudor facsimile texts...)   **NCO (Tudor)**
"Licensed in 1557–8; date of earliest known edition, 1568; reproduced in facsimile, 1908."
Original title: A newe mery and wittie Comedie or Enterlude, newely imprinted, treating vpon the Historie of Iacob and Esau, taken out of the xxviJ. Chap. of the first booke of Moses entituled Genesis... Imprinted at London by Henrie Bynneman...1568.
Mrs. C. C. Stopes in *Athenæum*, London, April 28, 1900, p. 538–540, * *DA*, points out that this is one of the first English plays that has dispensed with all allegorical treatment; the first that is constructed with regard to the unities and is divided into five acts and numerous scenes; the first that has given a descriptive list of the dramatis personae and determined suitable attire. The authorship of the play is here claimed for Wm. Hunnis, d. 1597.
Produced by the Elizabethan Stage Society at the Little Theatre, London, March 6, 1911; at Oxford in 1912; and at Crosby Hall, London, May 28, 1924.

Kimball, Rosamond. Jacob's journey. ₁A play in three scenes.₁ (In her: The wooing of Rebekah, and other Bible plays. New York, 1925. 8°. p. 37–46.)   **ZICS**

Old Testament Plays — Genesis, continued

Jacob, continued

Manley, William Ford. The mess of pottage. (In his: Bible dramas. New York ₁1928₁. 8°. p. 185–204.) **NBM**

Moore, Thomas Sturge. At Bethel. ₁A dramatic poem.₁ (In his: The sea is kind. Boston and New York, 1914. 8°. p. 156–165.) **NCM**
The speakers are the angels mentioned in the story of Jacob's dream, Genesis 28.

Plieksans, Janis. The sons of Jacob. ₁A play in five acts₁ by J. Rainis ₁pseud.₁. Translated by Grace Rhys ₁from the Latvian₁. London and Toronto: J. M. Dent & Sons, Ltd., 1924. xiii p., 1 l., 227 p., 1 port. 12°. **** QYN**
Produced by the International Theatre Society at the Scala Theatre, London, May 22, 1925.
Reviewed in *Era,* London, v. 88, May 30, 1925, p. 8, † *NAFA,* and in *The Mask,* Florence, Italy, v. 11, p. 91, *NAFA.*

Robinson, James G. Jacob and Esau; a pantomime, written and designed for children's and young people's entertainments. ₁In four scenes.₁ Franklin, O.: Eldridge Entertainment House, Inc. ₁cop. 1926.₁ 12 p. 12°. (Eldridge popular plays.)

Whiffen, Edwin Thomas. Dinah. (In his: Jephtha sacrificing, and Dinah. New York ₁cop. 1908₁. 12°. p. 43–89.) **NBI**

—— Dinah. ₁Dramatic poem.₁ (In his: Tamar and other poems. New York, 1913. 12°. p. 174–223.)

JOSEPH

Miracle Play

The **7 pagean** of Ioseph. ₁1048 lines.₁ (In: C. F. Brown, editor, Stonyhurst pageants. Göttingen, 1920. 8°. p. 5–40.) **NAFM**

Modern Plays

For a discussion of Joseph as a dramatic subject see *Jewish chronicle,* London, May 16, 1890, p. 5–6, * *PBE.*

The **Adventures** of Joseph. ₁In eight scenes.₁ (In: M. W. Thomas, editor, Old Testament drama. London ₁1927₁. 12°. p. 47–72.)

Atchinson, Frances Elizabeth. Story terrace. ₁In one act.₁ New York: H. W. Wilson Co., 1926. 21 p. illus. music. 12°.
Also issued in 1927. **NBL p.v.113**
Written for Children's book week. Produced at Evansville, Ind., 1925. Among the story characters is Joseph from the Bible.

Baker, Clara M., and others. Joseph and his brethren. ₁In four acts.₁ Based on Genesis, chapters 37 and 41–45 inclusive. By a committee composed of Clara M. Baker, Estella E. Bryant, Anne M. Boyd, Henrietta

P. Eckhard, and a class of boys. (In: T. W. Galloway, The dramatic instinct in religious education. Boston ₁cop. 1922₁. 12°. p. 94–115.)

Beale, William Thomas. The chancellor of Egypt; a dramatization of the Bible story of Joseph and his brethren, in four acts. Boston: The author, 1905. 1 p.l., 55(1) p. 8°. **NBL p.v.11, no.11**

Beardsley, Harry J. Joseph; or, Zaphnath Paaneah; a tale of ancient Egypt. ₁In four acts.₁ ₁n. p.,₁ cop. 1923. 23 p. 8°.
Title from Library of Congress.
Time: BC. 1729–1706.

Benton, Rita. Joseph and his brethren. ₁A drama in five acts.₁ (In her: Bible plays. New York ₁cop. 1922₁. 8°. p. 13–51.) *** PSQ**

Boyd, Zachary. Joseph tempted to adultery. ₁A dramatic poem.₁ (In his: Four poems from "Zion's flowers." Glasgow, 1855. 8°. p. 47–104.) **NCL**
Seven speakers.

Cole, Edna Earle. The story of Joseph. ₁In five acts.₁ (In her: The good Samaritan and other Bible stories dramatized. Boston ₁cop. 1915₁. 12°. p. 85–107.)

Crippen, Thomas George. Joseph in Egypt. A Biblical drama in five acts. Edited by C. J. Hanssen. New York: The Dramatic Pub. Co. ₁18–?₁ 28 p. 16°. (The wizard series.) **NBL p.v.144, no.1**

—— —— Chicago: The Dramatic Pub. Co., n.d. 28 p. 12°. (Sergel's Acting drama. no. 536.)

Dearmer, Mabel (White). The dreamer; a poetical drama. (In her: Three plays. London, 1916. 12°. p. 103–201.) **NCR**
In a prologue and three acts.
Produced at the King's Hall Theatre, Covent Garden, London for the first time Nov. 28, 1912.

Dell, Floyd. The chaste adventures of Joseph, a comedy ₁in one act₁. (In his: King Arthur's socks, and other village plays. New York, 1922. 12°. p. 15–42.)
First produced at the Liberal Club, New York, 1914, Floyd Dell as Joseph.

Denton, Clara Janetta (Fort). From captivity to power. A drama in five short acts, interspersed with tableaux. (In: Sunday school and church entertainments. Philadelphia, 1914. 12°. p. 9–23.) **ZICS**

Dunn, Fannie Wyche. The story of Joseph. (Dramatized from the Bible.) In five scenes. illus. (In her: What shall we play? New York, 1916. 12°. p. 67–92.)
Also published in 1926. **NASH**

Ebb, Sophie B. Joseph, a Biblical play ₁in three acts₁. New York: Bloch Pub. Co., 1903. 7 l. 8°. *** PSQ**
Reprinted from *Jewish home,* New York, 1903, v. 10, p. 127–137, * *PBD.*

Old Testament Plays — Genesis, continued

Joseph, continued

Gairdner, William Henry Temple. Joseph and his brothers, an Old Testament passion play in four acts. London: Society for Promoting Christian Knowledge; New York: The Macmillan Company, 1921. xii, 13–72 p. illus. 12°. **NCO p.v.471, no.2**
Reviewed in *Jewish guardian,* London, Nov. 25, 1921, p. 6, * PBE.

Genlis, Stéphanie Félicité Ducrest de St. Aubin, comtesse de. Joseph made known to his brethren. A sacred drama, in two acts. (In her: Sacred dramas. London, 1786. 8°. p. 159–214.) **NKO**
The scene: Memphis, in the palace of Joseph, minister to Pharaoh, under the name of Oratis.

Githens, Harry W. The coat of many colors. ₁In two scenes.₁ (In his: Dramatized stories from the Old Testament. Cincinnati ₁cop. 1927₁. 12°. p. 42–51.) **NASH**

—— A prisoner promoted. (In his: Dramatized stories from the Old Testament. Cincinnati ₁cop. 1927₁. 12°. p. 52–57.) **NASH**
Joseph raised to the premiership in Egypt.

—— Saved to serve. ₁In three scenes.₁ (In his: Dramatized stories from the Old Testament. Cincinnati ₁cop. 1927₁. 12°. p. 58–66.) **NASH**
Joseph as custodian of the harvest in Egypt.

Groot, Hugo de. Hugo Grotius Sophompaneas, or Joseph. A tragedy ₁in five acts and in verse₁. With annotations by Francis Goldsmith. London: Printed by W. H., 1652. xxii, 102, 3 p. 8°.
Copies in the British Museum and the Amsterdam University Library.
First published at Amsterdam in Latin, 1635. For the name Sophampaneas, see Genesis XLI: 45. "An allegory on his own life, the Hebrew Joseph at the court of Egypt being the Hollander Grotius on the point of entering the service of the crown of Sweden, hopeful of being able, on his Swedish post, to serve his native country, even as Joseph, in Egypt, had been of service to his own people." — E. F. Walbridge, in his *Drames à clef*, citing A. J. Barnouw as his authority.

Haas, Harlow Edgar. Joseph and his brethren. A Biblical play ₁in four acts₁. Franklin, Ohio: Eldridge Entertainment House, cop. 1924. 20 p. 12°. (Eldridge popular plays.)

Hale, Harris G., and N. M. HALL. ...The story of Joseph and his brethren. Arranged by Harris G. Hale and Newton M. Hall. Boston: The Pilgrim Press, 1906. iv, 26 p. 12°. (Biblical dramas. ₁no. 1.₁) **NBL (Biblical)**

Hamilton, Sarah. The liberation of Joseph, a sacred dramatic poem... London, 1827. 12°.
Title from British Museum Catalogue.
Reviewed in *New monthly magazine,* London, 1827, v. 21, p. 189, * DA.

Herford, I. S. A. Joseph and his brethren: a modern Yorkshire mystery. (New Englander and Yale review. New Haven, 1889. 8°. v. 51, p. 294–299.) * **DA**
Contains the scenario of a play of the above title "given...in a mill district of Yorkshire, a few years ago."

Hobbs, Mabel, and HELEN MILES. Joseph and his brethren. (In their: Six Bible plays. New York, 1924. 8°. p. 19–38.) **NASH**

Iliowizi, Henry. Joseph, a dramatic representation in seven tableaux. Minneapolis, Minn.: Tribune Job Printing Co., 1885. 46 p. 12°. **NBL p.v.24, no.6**

Jacobson, Janie. Joseph and his brethren. A Scriptural play in four acts. ₁New York: Stettiner Bros.,₁ cop. 1905. 16 p. nar. 8°.
Title from cover. * **PSQ**

Joseph and his brothers. A Biblical drama, or, mystery play ₁in two acts, and in verse₁. London, Derby ₁printed₁: T. Richardson and Son, 1864. 32 p. 16°.
Title from British Museum Catalogue.

Jukes, Richard. Joseph and his brethren: a poem. Third thousand. Re-written. London, 1863. 8°.
Title from British Museum Catalogue.
For an account of the presentation of this drama by the people of Gornal, Staffordshire, England, see *Cornhill magazine,* London, 1891, v. 63 [new series, v. 16], p. 282–288, * DA.

Katzenelson, Isaac. Joseph and his brethren; a Biblical drama in three acts. (Young Judaean. New York, 1912. 8°. v. 3, Nov., p. 4–5, 22; Dec., p. 10–13.)
Copy at Dropsie College.
Adapted from the Hebrew by Barnett R. Brickner. Third act not published. Produced at the People's Theatre, New York, by the Dr. Herzl Zion Club in Hebrew, April 27, 1911. A. H. Silver as Judah, M. Seltzer as Jacob, I. S. Chipkin as Reuben, Jesse Schwartz as Simeon, M. Melicow as Ephraim, Miriam Hindes as Benjamin, and Benjamin Friedman as Joseph.
See Dr. Herzl Zion Club. Keepsake, ed. E. D. Coleman, p. 8, * PZX p.v.22.

Kimball, Rosamond. The story of Joseph. ₁A play in five parts.₁ (In her: The wooing of Rebekah, and other Bible plays. New York, 1925. 8°. p. 47–97.) **ZICS**

Lobingier, Elizabeth Erwin (Miller). Joseph. (In her: The dramatization of Bible stories. Chicago ₁cop. 1919₁. 12°. p. 17–43.) * **YIR**

Miller, J. Joseph and his brethren. A drama in three acts ₁in three parts, and in verse₁ by J. Miller. London: For J. Watts, 1757. 27 p. 4°.
Title from British Museum Catalogue.

More, Hannah. Joseph made known to his brethren: a sacred drama, in two acts. (In her: The search after happiness, to which is added, Joseph made known to his brethren. Philadelphia, 1811. 16°. p. 52–72.) **NCM**

Old Testament Plays — Genesis, continued

Joseph, continued

Okmulgee, Okla. — Robert E. Lee School. The story of Joseph; a dramatization project. Worked out by the 5 B grade of the Robert E. Lee School, Okmulgee, Okla., under the direction of the teacher, Miss Helen Dixon. ₍In four scenes.₎ illus. (Normal instructor and primary plans. Dansville, N. Y., 1923. f°. v. 32, May, 1923, p. 44, 78–79, 81.)   † **SSA**

P., Brother. Joseph and his brethren. A drama. In three acts. London ₍1871?₎. 26 p. (In: P., Three plays...for male characters only. Translated from the French... By Br. P. London ₍1871?₎. 12°.)
NKM p.v.229, no.5

Parker, Louis Napoleon. Joseph and his brethren; a pageant play. New York: John Lane Company, 1913. 8 p.l., 3–154 p. illus. 12°.   * **PSQ**

The compiler owns a prompter's copy having two ms. notes by the author.

Produced at the Century Theatre, New York, Jan. 11, 1913, with James O'Neill as Jacob, Howard Kyle as Simeon, Brandon Tynan as Joseph, and Pauline Frederick as Zuleika. Reviewed by Clayton Hamilton (with illus.) in *The Bookman,* New York, v. 37, p. 63–64, * *DA;* by Arthur Ruhl (with illus.) in *Collier's,* New York, v. 50, Feb. 22, 1913, p. 23, * *DA;* in the *Dramatist,* Easton, Pa., v. 4, p. 348, *NAFA;* by Clayton Hamilton (with illus.) in *Everybody's magazine,* New York, v. 28, p. 520, * *DA;* by Channing Pollock (with illus.) in *Green book album,* Chicago, v. 9, p. 566–568, 628–630, *NAFA;* by Mabel Lyon in *Jewish exponent,* Philadelphia, v. 57, no. 4, May 2, 1913, p. 1–2, * *PBD;* by J. S. Metcalfe in *Life,* New York, v. 61, p. 200, * *DA;* by Matthew White, jr., in *Munsey's magazine,* New York, v. 48, p. 1014–1015, * *DA;* by Ann Randolph in *National magazine,* Boston, v. 39, p. 417–420, * *DA;* in the *New York dramatic mirror,* New York, v. 69, Jan. 22, 1913, p. 7, * *DA;* in the *Theatre magazine,* New York, v. 17, p. 37–38, by Eva vom Baur, v. 17, p. 94–96 (with illus.) and by Max J. Herzberg, v. 18, July, 1913, p. xx, † *NBLA;* and by Louis Lipsky in *Young Judaean,* New York, v. 3, Feb., 1913, p. 3–5. *Current opinion,* New York, v. 54, no. 3, March, 1913, p. 206–209, * *DA,* contains a resumé of various reviews. The author, in the *New York dramatic mirror,* v. 69, Jan. 8, 1913, p. 10 describes how he came to write the play. For additional illustrations see *Harper's weekly,* New York, v. 57, Feb. 1, 1913, p. 18, * *DA; New York dramatic mirror,* front covers (colored) of the issues for Feb. 12 and April 16, 1913; and *Theatre magazine,* v. 19, p. 133 (two portraits of Maxine Elliott as Potiphar's wife).

An extract from act iv, scene 1 is printed in *Young Judaean,* New York, v. 3, April, 1913, p. 11–12.

Produced at His Majesty's Theatre, London, Sept. 2, 1913, with Herbert Tree as Jacob, George Ralph as Joseph, and H. A. Saintsbury as Simeon. Reviewed in *The Times,* London, Sept. 3, 1913, p. 6, * *A.* For illustrations of the production see *The Graphic,* London, v. 88, p. 421, 424–425, 547, * *DA,* and the *Illustrated London news,* v. 143, p. 446, * *DA.* A synopsis of the play, accompanied by an illustration of the production, appeared in *The Play pictorial,* London, v. 22, no. 135, p. 101–120, † *NCOA.*

A novelized version of the play by George Vaux Bacon appeared in the *Green book album,* Chicago, v. 9, p. 1085–1104, *NAFA.*

Parsons, Margaret. Benjamin and the silver cup. ₍In one act.₎ (In her: Ten stirring Bible plays. Franklin, Ohio, cop. 1927. 12°. p. 33–40.)

Reprinted from *John Martin's book, "The child's magazine."*

—— Joseph, the dreamer of dreams. ₍In one act.₎ (In her: Ten stirring Bible plays. Franklin, Ohio, cop. 1927. 12°. p. 26–32.)

Reprinted from *John Martin's book, "The child's magazine."*

Peay, Ida S. Joseph sold into Egypt. ₍Boston: American Unitarian Association, n. d.₎ 8 l. 4°.

Typewritten.

Procter, W. T. Joseph, a sacred drama ₍in five acts and in verse₎. Burton-upon-Trent, 1802. 8°.

Title from British Museum Catalogue.

Reviewed in *British critic,* London, 1803, v. 21, p. 313–314, * *DA,* and in *Poetical register, and repository of fugitive poetry for 1802,* London, 1803, 2. ed., p. 451, *NCI.*

Raine, James Watt. The selling of Joseph. ₍In one scene.₎ (In his: Bible dramatics. New York & London ₍cop. 1927₎. 12°. p. 67–71.)

Read, Elizabeth Day. The sons of Jacob; a play in one act. Boston: American Unitarian Association, n. d. 4 l. 4°.

Typewritten.

Rollins, Cecil A. The friend of Potiphar's wife. ₍In one act.₎ (In: Eleven short Biblical plays. New York, 1929. 12°. p. 105–127.)
NBL p.v.216

Russell, Mary M. ₍The dreamer of dreams, in three scenes.₎ (In her: How to produce plays and pageants. New York ₍cop. 1923₎. 12°. p. 38–50.)   **MZB**

Dramatized by school children.

Stackhouse, Perry J. Joseph, the dreamer. ₍A play in four scenes.₎ (In his: Bible dramas in the pulpit. Philadelphia ₍cop. 1926₎. 8°. p. 1–14.)   **NBM**

—— Joseph, the interpreter of dreams. ₍A play in three scenes.₎ (In his: Bible dramas in the pulpit. Philadelphia ₍cop. 1926₎. 8°. p. 15–29.)   **NBM**

—— Joseph's dreams come true. ₍A play in four scenes.₎ (In his: Bible dramas in the pulpit. Philadelphia ₍cop. 1926₎. 8°. p. 31–44.)   **NBM**

Stillingfleet, Benjamin. Joseph. (In his: Joseph. ₍London? 1765?₎ 8°.)

Title from British Museum Catalogue.

Swift, Fletcher Harper. Joseph, a drama for children, in one act and three scenes... with an introduction by Richard Morse Hodge... New York: W. B. Harison, cop. 1907. 1 p.l., 5–31 p. 12°.

Illustrated cover; text of play printed on one side of leaf only.

Taft, Linwood. Joseph; a play in five acts based upon the story of Joseph as found in Genesis. New York & London: The Century Co. ₍cop. 1925.₎ 3 p.l., 3–80 p. 12°.
NBL p.v.117, no.7

Old Testament Plays — Genesis, continued

Joseph, continued

Walker, Marion Mitchell. The book in Sally's cupboard; a play for Good Book week. ₍In one scene.₎ (Primary education — Popular educator. Boston, 1928. f°. v. 46, p. 194–195, 219, 238, 247.) † **SSA**
Joseph, a book character.

Watts, Harvey Maitland. The wife of Potiphar; dramatic episode in one scene. (In his: The wife of Potiphar, with other poems. Philadelphia, 1911. 12°. p. 197–228.) **NBI**

Wells, Charles Jeremiah. Joseph and his brethren, a Scriptural drama, in two acts ₍and in verse₎. By H. L. Howard ₍pseud. of C. J. Wells₎. London, 1824. 8°.
"The Bible story is followed very closely and the time included extends through the whole life of Joseph."
Reviewed in *New monthly magazine*, London, 1824, v. 12, p. 172–173, * *DA*, and *Monthly repository*, London, 1837, new series, v. 11, p. 158–163, *ZXDA*.
For brief comment by D. G. Rossetti see Alexander Gilchrist, *Life of William Blake*, London, 1863, v. 1, p. 381–382, *AN*.

—— Joseph and his brethren; a dramatic poem ₍in four acts₎. With an introduction by Algernon Charles Swinburne. London: Chatto and Windus, 1876. xix, 252 p. 8°.
Reviewed in *British quarterly review*, New York, April, 1876, v. 63, p. 271–272, * *DA*, and in *Westminster review*, New York, 1876, v. 105, p. 281–282, * *DA*.
In *Literary anecdotes of the nineteenth century*, London, 1895, [v. 1], p. 289–318, *NCB*, H. Buxton Forman prints a dramatic scene intended by Wells to be placed between the two scenes which are now the fifth and sixth of act iv, to be inserted between p. 228 and 229 of the 1876 edition, but which was never included in any printed edition. Reprinted also as a pamphlet, *NCO p.v.339*.

—— Joseph and his brethren, a dramatic poem; by Charles Wells. With an introduction by Algernon Charles Swinburne, and a note on Rossetti and Charles Wells by Theodore Watts-Dunton. London, New York: H. Frowde ₍1908₎. lviii, 230 p. 16°. (The world's classics. ₍no.₎ 143.) * **PSQ**
See "Joseph [a poem] (after reading Charles Wells' 'Joseph and his brethren')," by Vincent Starrett, in *Estrays*, Chicago, 1918, p. [19], *NBF p.v.15*.

HERZBERG, Max John. A poetic play on "Joseph and his brethren." (Maccabaean. New York, 1910. 8°. v. 19, p. 1–5.) * **PBD**
Reprinted in *Jewish record*, Richmond, Va., July 8, 1910, v. 2, p. 1–5, 9, * *PBD*.

SWINBURNE, Algernon Charles. An unknown poet. (Fortnightly review. London, 1875. 8°. v. 23 ₍new series, v. 17₎, p. 217–232.) * **DA**
A review with numerous extracts.

Whitmore, H. F. The story of Joseph. ₍In a prologue, seven scenes, and an epilogue.₎ Boston: American Unitarian Association, n.d. 10 l. 4°.
Typewritten.

Willan, Edmund. Joseph ₍a dramatic poem₎. (In his: Odes and a drama. Guildford, 1918. 12°. p. 27–39.) **NCM**

Willy, John. The story of Asenath, daughter of Potipherah, High Priest of On. ₍In five acts.₎ Chicago: The Hotel Monthly, cop. 1913. 82 p. 8°.
Based on Genesis XLI: 45.
"The play...was written by me during the years, 1884 and 1885..."
Reviewed in *Hotel monthly*, Chicago, 1913, v. 21, no. 246, p. 4–5, *KBB*, and in *Open court*, Chicago, 1913, v. 27, p. 640, * *DA*.

Zoleikha; a dramatic tale from Holy Writ. ₍In five acts and in verse.₎ London, 1832. 8°.
Title from British Museum Catalogue.
Reviewed in *New monthly magazine*, London, 1832, v. 36, p. 439, * *DA*.

EXODUS-DEUTERONOMY

Backus, Irene Garrett. The great commandment. ₍Boston: American Unitarian Association,₎ n.d. 14 l. 4°.
Typewritten.
A series of dramatic episodes depicting the commandment "Thou shalt love thy neighbor as thyself," as it appeared in five great religions of the world. Prepared for the Young People's Religious Union of Los Angeles, Calif.

Broome, Frederick Napier. A temple service. (Ordained in Israel after the deliverance from Moab.) ₍A colloquy between the priests and the people.₎ (In: W. F. Alexander and A. E. Currie, compilers, A treasury of New Zealand verse," being a new edition of "New Zealand verse." Auckland ₍1926₎. 12°. p. 280–287.) **NCI (Alexander)**

Cole, Edna Earle. The story of the twelve spies. ₍In three acts.₎ (In her: The good Samaritan, and other Bible stories dramatized. Boston ₍cop. 1915₎. 12°. p. 75–83.)
Based on Numbers XIII; XIV: 1–39.

David, Edward, and SAMUEL S. GROSSMAN. A pageant of old Israel. (An operetta-picture in one scene.) Music by Samuel E. Goldfarb. New York: Young Judaea. 5 l. f°.
Words only.
Mimeographed.
This is a dramatization in spectacular form of chapter three of Mishnah Bokerim, dealing with the pilgrimage to Jerusalem. The text used here is from reconstructed Biblical phrases, mainly from Psalms and the Prophets.

Dembitz, Arthur A. The daughters of Zeloph'had. ₍In six scenes.₎ (In his: The letters of Akiba to Rachel. Philadelphia, 1922. 12°. p. 49–67.) * **PHI**
Based on the episode narrated in Numbers XXVII:1–11.

Dobbs, Sir Henry Robert Conway. Korah. ₍In three acts.₎ London: Grant Richards, 1903. xi, 124 p. 16°.
The characters are from Numbers XXXVI.

Old Testament Plays — Exodus-Deuteronomy, continued

Levinger, Elma C. (Ehrlich), and EDWARD DAVIS. In the days when the Temple stood. (A play-and-pageant of old Israel for Shovuoth.) ₍In two acts.₎ Edited by Samuel S. Grossman. (In: Jewish festival plays. Shovuoth. New York: Bureau of Jewish Education. 8°. p. 7-25.)

The scene is laid in Biblical days when Jews made pilgrimage to Jerusalem on the Feast of Weeks. Deuteronomy XVI: 9-12.

Linsky, Fannie Barnett. Pictures from the book of Exodus, for Passover. New York: Bloch Pub. Co., 1930. 15 p. 12°.

A dramatization of part of the Seder service.

McKenzie, Beatrice M. A pageant of Thanksgiving. Given at Unity Centre, Des Moines, Iowa. Boston: American Unitarian Association ₍1924₎. 5 l. 4°.

Mimeographed.

Group I — the Hebrew group.

Ware, Henry, jr. The feast of tabernacles. A poem for music. ₍A play in two scenes.₎ (In his: Works. Boston, 1846. 12°. v. 1, p. 288-308.) **ZEP**

Based on Leviticus XXIII: 33-44. Place: the temple at Jerusalem. Time: the last day of the feast. The author's preface to the play is dated March 14, 1837.

—— The feast of tabernacles. ₍In two scenes.₎ (In: M. L. Cobb, compiler, Poetical dramas for home and school. Boston, 1873. 12°. p. 147-159.) **MZB**

MOSES

Ezekielos

Ezekielos. ₍The Exodus; fragments of a drama preserved by Eusebius who in turn copied from the lost work of Alexander Polyhistor.₎ (In: Eusebius Pamphili, bishop of Caesarea, Preparation for the Gospel. Translated from a revised text, by Edwin Hamilton Gifford. Oxford, 1903. 8°. part 1, p. 467-475.)

The fragments are in book IX, chapters 28-29.

The characters are Moses, Zipporah, Chum, Jethro, God, and a messenger.

The first drama written by a Jew, an Alexandrine poet of the second century B. C. Also the first drama on a Biblical subject.

Reprinted, with an introduction, by Joshua Bloch, in *Jewish tribune*, New York, v. 94, April 19, 1929, p. 18-19, 60, †* PBD.

An extract of forty-one lines is printed in *Ante-Nicene Christian library*, Edinburgh, 1867, v. 4 (*Clement of Alexandria*), p. 452-453, ZEL, and reprinted in *Ante-Nicene fathers*, Buffalo, N. Y., 1887, v. 2, p. 335-336, * R – ZEL. Specimens of the drama are also printed in Alfred Edersheim, *History of the Jewish nation*, London, 1896, p. 528-531, * PXH.

ABRAHAMS, Israel. The phoenix of Ezekielos. (In his: By-paths in Hebraic bookland. Philadelphia, 1920. 8°. p. 46-52.) ***PAT**

Identification of the remarkable bird (phoenix) mentioned in the drama.

BAYLE, Pierre. ₍Ezekiel, a Jewish poet.₎ (In his: Dictionary, historical and critical. London, 1735. f°. v. 2, p. 880.) †**AA**

Library also has other editions of the Dictionary.

CARVALHO, Naomi Nunes. A pseudo-classic play. ₍A conversation between Ezechiel (an Alexandrian poet) and an Athenian actor on the former's Exodus.₎ (In her: Vox humana. London, 1912. 12°. p. 135-140.) **NRD p.v.9**

Time: 100 B.C.

HONE, William. Origin of religious plays. (In his: Everyday book and table book. London, 1830. 8°. v. 1, p. 743.) ***AY**

"Written...as a political spectacle to animate his dispersed brethren with the hopes of a future deliverance."

JEWISH drama. (In: Richard Ryan, Dramatic table talk...in theatrical history and biography. London, 1825. 24°. v. 1, p. 32.) **NCOM**

SCHUERER, Emil. Ezekiel the tragic poet. (In his: History of the Jewish people in the time of Jesus Christ. Edinburgh, 1886. 8°. Division II, v. 3, p. 225-228.) ***PXH**

A list of references is given on p. 228.

SOME account of the Greek Christian poets. (Athenæum. London, 1842. 4°. v. 15, p. 190, cols. 2-3.) ***DA**

Miracle Plays

The **Departure** of the Israelites from Egypt, the ten plagues, and the passage of the Red Sea. The hoseers ₍play₎. ₍York play no. 11, 406 lines.₎ (In: Lucy T. Smith, York plays. Oxford, 1885. 8°. p. 68-92.) **NAFM**

Pharao. ₍The Towneley play no. 8.₎ (In: The Towneley mysteries. London ₍1836₎. 8°. p. 55-65.) **CA (Surtees)**

Surtees Society. Publications. [v. 3.]

Also printed in William Marriott, *A collection of English miracle-plays*, Basel, 1838, p. 93-108, *NAFM*; in 1897 (ed. England) in Early English Text Society, Extra series no. 71 (*The Towneley plays*), p. 64-78, *NCE (Early)*; and in J. Q. Adams, editor, *Chief pre-Shakespearean dramas*, Boston, 1924, p. 125-131, * R – NCO.

LIPSKY, Abram. An old English Haggada. The Exodus in the form of a morality play. (Maccabaean. New York, 1907. 8°. v. 12, p. 125-131.) ***PBD**

The Towneley Pharaoh play adapted and modernized; the christological conclusion of the original here omitted.

Moses and the two tables. ₍Coventry play no. 6.₎ (In: Ludus Coventriæ, ed. Halliwell. London: Shakespeare Society, 1841. 8°. p. 58-64.) **NAFM (Coventry)**

Also printed in 1922 (ed. Block) in Early English Text Society, Extra series no. 120 (*Ludus Coventriæ*), p. 51-57, *NCE (Early)*.

DUSTOOR, P. E. The origin of the play of 'Moses and the tables of the law.' (Modern language review. Cambridge, 1924. 8°. v. 19, p. 459-462.) **NAA**

The **Eight** pagean of Moyses. ₍1589 lines.₎ (In: Carleton Brown, editor, Stonyhurst pageants. Göttingen, 1920. 8°. p. 41-95.) **NAFM**

Old Testament Plays—Exodus-Deuteronomy,
continued

Moses, continued

Modern Plays

FREED, Clarence I. Drama of the Exodus. Plays sacred and profane inspired by story of the Mosaic epic. illus. (American Hebrew. New York, 1925. f°. v. 116, p. 698, 710–711, 722–723.) †*PBD

Andersen, Olivia Donaldson (Cushing). Moses the lawgiver. ₁In three acts.₁ (In her: Creation and other Biblical plays. Geneva, 1929. 4°. p. 105–148.) NBM
"In *Moses the lawgiver,* a god, the one God, is recognized... From God there comes through Moses — who in himself may serve as an example of the expression of the divine speaking through the human soul — the word of God, a code of life, the laws for daily living." Place: Egypt and the Wilderness. Time: 1531–1491 B. C.

Baker, Clara. The child Moses. ₁In two acts.₁ (In: T. W. Galloway, The dramatic instinct in religious education. Boston ₁cop. 1922₁. 12°. p. 68–78.)

Benton, Rita. The golden calf. ₁A play in three acts.₁ (In her: Bible plays. New York ₁cop. 1922₁. 8°. p. 53–77.) *PSQ

┌── Moses in the bulrushes. (In her: Shorter Bible plays. New York ₁cop. 1922₁. 8°. p. 43–51.) NASH

── Up, up from Egypt to the promised land. (In her: Shorter Bible plays. New York ₁cop. 1922₁. 8°. p. 52–61.) NASH

Bloomgarden, Solomon. Zethro and Zipporah; a dialogue translated ₁from the Yiddish of Jehoash, pseud. of Solomon Bloomgarden₁ by J. Rolnick. (East and West. New York, 1915. 4°. v. 1, no. 6, p. 160.) *PBD

Boxer, James. Finding of Moses. ₁In two acts.₁ (In his: Sacred dramas. Boston, 1875. 12°. p. 75–101.)

Brown, Charles Hovey. Moses: a drama. Boston: Gorham Press, 1902. 69 p. 8°.
In five acts. *PSQ

Carpenter, Edward. Moses: a drama in five acts. London: E. Moxon, Son and Co. ₁1875.₁ 126 p. 16°.
Reviewed in *Athenæum,* London, 1875, v. 66, p. 432–433, *DA.
Issued with alterations in 1910 as:

── The promised land; a drama of a people's deliverance. In five acts ₁and in verse₁. (In the Elizabethan style.) London: S. Sonnenschein & Co., Lim., 1910. 126 p. new ed. 12°. NCR
Among the dramatis personae are Moses, Miriam, Aaron, Joshua, Korah, and Dathan.

Carvalho, Naomi Nunes. Childhood. ₁A dialogue between Miriam and Pharaoh's daughter.₁ (In her: Vox humana. London, 1912. 12°. p. 23–27.) NRD p.v.9

── The climax. ₁A dialogue between Miriam and Pharaoh.₁ (In her: Vox humana. London, 1912. 12°. p. 29–34.) NRD p.v.9

── Concession. ₁A dialogue between Moses and an old Egyptian priest.₁ (In her: Vox humana. London, 1912. 12°. p. 35–39.) NRD p.v.9

Clibborn, Edward. בתיה Pharaoh's daughter: an ΑΝΘΡΟΠΟΛΟΓΙΚΑΛ drama, on the plan of the mystery and parable play, developed from Herodotus's narrative of the spoliation of the treasury of Rhampsinitus, the monuments of Thothmes III., the "Song of songs," etc...₁Evidence, Greek, Hebrew, and Egyptian in favor of the original reality of the story of stories as developed in the parable play of Pharaoh's daughter.₁ ₁By Edward Clibborn.₁ London: Williams and Norgate, 1868. cxxviii p., 1 l., 384 p. 12°.
In five acts, 3323 lines.

Dowling, Paul Henry. The child Moses. (Jewish child. New York, 1917. f°. v. 5, no. 11, March 16, 1917, p. 3.) *PBD
Also printed in the issue for April, 1919, v. 8, no. 1, p. 7.

The Exodus. ₁In three scenes.₁ (In: M. W. Thomas, editor, Old Testament drama. London ₁1927₁. 12°. p. 73–96.)

Gairdner, William Henry Temple. Passover-night; a Bible mystery-play in three scenes. London: Society for Promoting Christian Knowledge; New York: The Macmillan Co., 1921. 24 p. 12°.
During the life-time of Moses. The characters are divided into two groups: Israelites and Egyptians.

Gaw, Allison, and ETHELEAN TYSON GAW. Pharaoh's daughter, a romantic drama in three acts. illus. (In their: Pharaoh's daughter, and other Biblical plays of the contest, 1927. New York, 1928. 8°. p. 1–146.) NBL
Prize-winning play. "The theme is Moses' choice between a throne and his kinspeople, the Jews." First produced by the Pasadena, Calif., Community Players, Oct. 15, 1925. Arthur Lubin as Prince Rameses-Moesis.
For a review and illustrations of the stage settings see *Drama,* Mount Morris, Ill., 1928, v. 18, p. 117, 122, *NAFA.*

Githens, Harry W. An adopted son. ₁In two scenes.₁ (The childhood of Moses.) (In his: Dramatized stories from the Old Testament. Cincinnati ₁1927₁. 12°. p. 67–74.) NASH

── Delivered from bondage. ₁In five scenes.₁ (The plagues of Egypt.) (In his: Dramatized stories from the Old Testament. Cincinnati ₁1927₁. 12°. p. 83–88.) NASH

── From palace to prairie. ₁In four scenes.₁ (The calling of Moses.) (In his: Dramatized stories from the Old Testament. Cincinnati ₁1927₁. 12°. p. 75–82.) NASH

── The golden calf. (In his: Dramatized stories from the Old Testament. Cincinnati ₁1927₁. 12°. p. 89–99.) NASH
In three scenes.

Old Testament Plays—Exodus-Deuteronomy, continued

Moses, continued

Goldberg, Israel. The desert generation. A dramatic poem in one scene, by Rufus Learsi ₁pseud.₁. ₁New York: Young Judea, n. d.₁ 3 l. 4°.
Mimeographed.
Time: During the journey in the desert.

Gray, Terence. A royal audience. Rameses the Great. An ostracon of the new empire. A play ₁in one act₁ for Bible students who know not Egypt. (In his: "And in the tomb were found..." New York, 1923. 8°. p. 93–122.) *** OBT**
Mose, "Elder of the Israilu." Time: ca. 1200 B.C., during the reign of Rameses the Great. See p. 83–89.

Grossman, Samuel S. The ten commandments. Playlet in one scene. ₁New York: Young Judaea.₁ 5 l. 4°. (In his: ₁Holiday and other plays for Jewish children.₁) **NASH**
Typewritten.
The characters are the ten commandments and Moses; at the top of Mt. Sinai.

Hale, Harris G., and N. M. HALL. ...Moses the liberator. Arranged by Harris G. Hale and Newton M. Hall. Boston: The Pilgrim Press, 1906. iv, 25 p. 12°. (Biblical dramas. ₁no. 3.₁) **NBL (Biblical)**

Hasty, John Eugene. If it were today; a playlet written by John Eugene Hasty for John Henry Nash on the occasion of his attempt to tell the Advertising Club of San Francisco "why is the poor printer," as suggested by his friend Wallace Kibbee... San Francisco: Printed by John Henry Nash, 1925. 1 p.l., 5 p. f°. **†††* KP (Nash)**
Printed in lavendar and black.
"Dramatis personae: the dynamic advertising manager, the alert sales manager; a go-getter salesman, an efficient office boy, and Moses."
Scene: the conference chamber of the Children of Israel, Incorporated. Moses comes from Mount Sinai with the Ten Commandments as a live slogan for the new commandments.

Hobbs, Mabel, and HELEN MILES. Moses. (In their: Six Bible plays. New York, 1924. 8°. p. 39–52.) **NASH**
In two scenes.

Judah, Samuel Benjamin Herbert. The maid of Midian, a tragedy, in four acts; founded on the massacre of the Midian captives, by order of Moses: as recorded in the thirty-first chapter of the Book of Numbers ... Philadelphia: A. E. Armstrong, 1833. 24 p. 12°.
For full collation see A. S. W. Rosenbach, *An American Jewish bibliography*, 1926, p. 288–289, from which this entry is taken.
Copy located: Lee M. Friedman, Esq., Boston.

Kimball, Rosamond. Moses in the bulrushes. (In her: The wooing of Rebekah, and other Bible plays. New York, 1925. 8°. p. 99–104.) **ZICS**

Koven, Joseph. In the desert. ₁A play in four scenes.₁ (In his: The miracle of Saint Masha, and other plays. New York ₁cop. 1924₁. 12°. p. 5–47.) **NBM**
Place: Mt. Sinai and the Desert. Time: during the Exodus.

Langner, Lawrence. Moses; a play, a protest and a proposal. New York: Boni and Liveright, 1924. xlix, 5–187 p. 8°. **NBM**
Reviewed in *American Hebrew*, New York, 1924, v. 115, p. 830, * *PBD*, and by Elliott E. Cohen in *The Menorah journal*, New York, 1925, v. 11, no. 1, Feb., 1925, p. 89–91, * *PBD*. A synopsis, with extracts, was printed in *B'nai B'rith magazine*, Chicago, 1925, v. 39, p. 132–135, * *PYP*.

Leaman, Lily M. The child Moses; a Biblical play ₁in two scenes₁. Philadelphia: Penn Pub. Co., 1923. 21 p. 12°.
"The play is based upon the story told in the first chapter of Exodus."
Produced by the Pilgrim Players before the Drama League of America at Chicago, April 23, 1919.

Levinger, Elma C. Ehrlich. The favorite of Pharaoh. A satire of old Egypt ₁in one act₁. illus. (The American Hebrew. New York, 1925. f°. v. 116, p. 684, 718–719, 728–729, 734.) *** PBD**

—— From the waters; a one-act play on the finding of Moses. (In: Jewish festival books. Passover. New York: Bureau of Jewish Education. 8°. p. 7–14.)

—— The golden staff. A Succoth operetta ... Music Samuel Goldfarb. (In her: Jewish festivals in the religious school. Cincinnati, 1923. 8°. p. 279–303.) *** PSY**
Time: in the days of the Kings. Place: in Penuel and Jerusalem.

Lobingier, Mrs. Elizabeth Erwin (Miller). The baby Moses. ₁In three scenes.₁ (As dramatized by junior girls.) (In her: Dramatization in the church school. Chicago ₁1923₁. 12°. p. 72–75.) *** YIR**

—— Moses in the bulrushes. (In her: The dramatization of Bible stories. Chicago ₁cop. 1919₁. 12°. p. 52–58.) *** YIR**
In three acts.

Lyndsay, David. The last plague. (In his: Dramas of the ancient world. Edinburgh, 1822. 8°. p. 91–100.)

—— The plague of darkness. (In his: Dramas of the ancient world. Edinburgh, 1822. 8°. p. 65–90.)

Manley, William Ford. The message from Sinai. (In his: Bible dramas. New York, 1928. 8°. p. 115–130.) **NBM**
In five scenes.

Margrie, William. Moses; a cosmic drama in 3 acts. London: A. H. Stockwell ₁1922₁. 91 p. 12°. **NCR**
"This play is based on a chemical principle."
"The elements here are Darwinism and the Salvation Army. The resulting compound may be called Creative Rationalism. It is simple, but magnificent." — *From the preface.*

Old Testament Plays—Exodus-Deuteronomy, continued

Moses, continued

Miller, Harriet Mann. A vision of Moses. ₁A play.₁ Syracuse, N. Y.: Craftsman Press ₁cop. 1924₁. 18 p. 12°.

Miller, May. Graven images; a ₁one-act₁ play, adapted to the capacity of children of the eighth grade. illus. (In: Willis Richardson, compiler, Plays and pageants from the life of the negro. Washington ₁cop. 1930₁. 8°. p. 107–137.)   **NBL (Richardson)**
Motivated on the episode of racial color prejudice mentioned in Numbers 12:1.

More, Hannah. Moses in the bulrushes; a sacred drama. By Miss More. (London magazine. London, 1782. 8°. v. 51, p. 160–164, 206–207.)   *** DA**
The subject taken from the second chapter of Exodus.
Reprinted in her *Sacred dramas,* Philadelphia, 1787, p. 16–37, * *KD,* and in Mary L. Cobb, compiler, *Poetical dramas for home and school,* Boston, 1873, p. 127–145, *MZB,* and in G. A. Kohut, *A Hebrew anthology,* Cincinnati, 1913, v. 2, p. 749–759, * *PSO.* Caleb Bingham prints a scene in his *Columbia orator,* Boston, 1799, 2. ed., p. 137–142, * *KD* (Library also has other editions).

Murray, Alfred L. The childhood of Moses; a dramatization, written by a group of children in a vacation school ₁of the Calvary Baptist Church, Rochester, N. Y.₁. ₁In four acts.₁ (International journal of religious education. Mount Morris, Ill., 1929. 4°. v. 6, Oct., 1929, p. 29, 47.)

Mygatt, Tracy Dickinson. Children of Israel, a play in three acts...with an introduction by Clara Fitch. New York: George H. Doran Company ₁cop. 1922₁. x p., 2 l., 15–92 p. 12°. (The Drama League series.)   **NBL p.v.85, no.5**
Time: during the sojourn of the Israelites in Egypt. Before the Exodus.

Ordway, Priscilla. The baby Moses. A play ₁in one scene₁ for older primary or first-grade junior children which would be suitable for presentation at the close of a daily vacation church school. (Church school. New York, 1924. 4°. v. 5, p. 522–523.)

Overton, Grace Sloan. The age-old dream. A masque for mother-and-daughter week. ₁In one act.₁ (Church school journal. Cincinnati, 1927. 4°. v. 59, p. 209–211.)
The mother of Moses is one of the characters.

Parsons, Margaret. The babe in the bulrushes. ₁In one act.₁ Reprinted from John Martin's book. (In her: Ten stirring Bible plays. Franklin, Ohio, cop. 1927. 12°. p. 9–14.)

Pickthall, Marjorie Lowry Christie. Mons Angelorum. Moses, Joshua, the Three Angels of the Universe. (In her: The lamp of poor souls. New York, 1916. 12°. p. 124–138.)   **NCM**
Also printed in her *Complete poems,* Toronto [cop. 1927], p. 238–249, *NCM.*

Rosenberg, Isaac. Moses; a play ₁in two scenes₁. (Menorah journal. New York, 1922. 4°. v. 8, no. 3, June, 1922, p. 149–161.) *** PBD**
The play was first issued, privately, in London in 1916. Later appeared in his *Poems,* published by Heinemann, London, 1922.
An appreciation of Isaac Rosenberg as poet and soldier, by Laurence Binyon, is printed on p. 139–148 of the *Menorah journal.*
Reviewed by Samuel Roth in *Voices,* London, 1921, v. 5, p. 74–75, * *DA.*

Rubinstein, Harold F., and HALCOTT GLOVER. Exodus, a dramatic sequence in five episodes. London: E. Benn, Limited, 1923. 109(1) p. 12°. (Contemporary British dramatists. v. 1.)   **NCO (Contemporary)**
Contents: Episode I. The dreamer. Scene: the seat of Joseph before Pharaoh. Episode II. The Ark of bulrushes. Scene: by the river Nile. Episode III. Moses the Egyptian. Scene: by the brickfields of Rameses. Episode IV. The Passover. Scene: in Aaron's house. Episode V. Prophecy. Scene: in the wilderness.
Produced by the Jewish Literary and Social Society of Manchester, England, at the Lesser Free Trade Hall, April 5, 1930. Reviewed in *Jewish guardian,* London, April 11, 1930, p. 21, * *PBE.* Cf. also issue of April 18, p. 7–8.

Russell, Mary M. A mother's faith. ₁In three scenes₁ (In her: Dramatized Bible stories for young people. New York ₁1921₁. 12°. p. 17–21.)
Jochebed at the abandoning of the infant Moses.

—— A Thanksgiving service. ₁In two scenes₁. (In her: Dramatized Bible stories for young people. New York ₁1921₁. 12°. p. 83–87.)
Moses and Miriam at the crossing of the Red Sea.

Schwartz, Jacob. The golden calf. ₁A play in three acts₁. London: C. W. Daniel, Ltd., 1922. 69 p. 12°. (Plays for a people's theatre. no. 22.)   **NCO p.v.490, no.6**
Scene: wilderness of Sinai.

Silver, Sheindel Klein. A pantomime on the Exodus. ₁In three acts₁. (Young Judaean. New York, 1923. 8°. v. 13, no. 4, p. 106–111.)   *** PBD**

Soble, Mae Stein. The call of God. A dramatization. (In her: Bible plays for children. New York, 1919. 12°. p. 77–87.)   **NASH**
Scene: the Mount of God, in the land of the Midianites.

—— The golden calf. A dramatization. (In her: Bible plays for children. New York, 1919. 12°. p. 89–94.)   **NASH**
Scene: the mountain-side.

—— Mother love finds a way: a dramatization ₁in two scenes₁. (In her: Bible plays for children. New York, 1919. 12°. p. 49–68.)   **NASH**
Scene: Egypt. Finding of Moses.

—— The promised land A dramatization. (In her: Bible plays for children. New York, 1919. 12°. p. 95–108.)   **NASH**
Scene: the Tabernacle.
Persons: Moses, Joshua, Caleb, who have returned from Hebron.

Old Testament Plays—Exodus-Deuteronomy,
continued

Moses, continued

Stanfield, Claribel Leontine. The marriage of Moses. [In five scenes.] (In her:
Book of verses. New York [1906]. 12°. [part
2], p. 25–38.) **NBI**

Stillingfleet, Benjamin. Moses and Zip-
porah. (In his: Joseph. [London? 1765?] 8°.)
Title from British Museum Catalogue.
"Intended to be set as an oratorio by John Christopher
Smith, the successor of Handel." — *Dictionary of Na-
tional Biography.*

Strachey, Lytton. A dialogue between
Moses, Diogenes and Mr. Loke. (In his:
Books and characters, French & English.
London, 1922. 8°. p. 133–135.) **NCZ**

BALAAM

Miracle Play

Balaam and his ass. The cappers and lyn-
nan drapers playe... [Chester play, no. 5.]
(In: The Chester plays, ed. by Wright. London: Shakespeare Society, 1843. 8°. v. 1,
p. 77–93.) **NAFM (Chester)**
Also printed in 1893 (ed. Deimling) in Early English Text Society, Extra series no. 62 (*The Chester
plays*), p. 84–103, *NCE (Early)*; in J. M. Manly,
Specimens of the pre-Shaksperean drama, Boston,
1897, v. 1, p. 66–81, *NCO;* and in J. Q. Adams, editor,
Chief pre-Shakespearean dramas, Boston, 1924, p. 132–
138, * *R — NCO.*

Modern Plays

Balaam's dying prayer. [In verse.] (Ex-
tracted from an unpublished drama.) [Lon-
don, 1862.] 16°.
Title from British Museum Catalogue.

Lowe, Helen. The prophecy of Balaam,
The Queen's choice, and other poems. Exeter, London [printed], 1841. 8°.
Title from British Museum Catalogue.
Reviewed in *English review,* London, 1850, v. 14,
p. 323, 332–333, *ZPD.* " 'The prophecy of Balaam' is
...one of the grandest dramatic poems in existence."

Schapiro, Benjamin Aaron Moses. Moses
and Balaam; a true prophet and a false priest.
A scenario [in twelve scenes]. (Jews and
Christians. New York, 1927. 8°. v. 1, no. 1,
p. 43–47.) **PBD**
Incomplete.

JOSHUA

Miracle Play

The **9 pagean** of Iosue. [552 lines.] (In:
C. F. Brown, editor, Stonyhurst pageants.
Göttingen, 1920. 8°. p. 95–114.) **NAFM**

Modern Plays

Burton, Richard. Rahab; a drama in three
acts. New York: H. Holt and Company,
1906. 4 p.l., 5–119 p. 8°. * **PSQ**
Based on Joshua, chap. 2.
The whole action takes place in Jericho, capital
city of the Canaanites, about 1500 B.C.

—— —— With four scenes and playbill
from Donald Robertson's production...
New York: Henry Holt and Co., 1909. 119 p.
illus. 8°. **NBM**
Produced at the Ravinia Theatre, Highland Park,
Ill., Wednesday, Sept. 9, 1908.

Friedman, Lillian Frances. The walls of
Jericho; a one act play. (Jewish tribune.
New York, 1925. f°. v. 44, Sept. 18, 1925,
p. 32, 45.) * **PBD**
Based on Joshua VI:20. ●

Morell, Thomas. Joshua; a sacred drama.
[By Thomas Morell.] As it is perform'd at
the Theatre-Royal in Covent-Garden. Set
to musick by Mr. Handel... Printed in the
year 1761. 20 p. 8°.
Words only.

Raine, James Watt. [Jael and Sisera.] [In
two scenes.] (In his: Bible dramatics. New
York & London [cop. 1927]. 12°. p. 76–81.)
Judges V and VI.

—— Joshua's decision. [In one scene.] (In
his: Bible dramatics. New York & London
[cop. 1927]. 12°. p. 238–248.)
Based on Joshua IX. Story of the Gibeonites.

Rowley, Samuel. Joshua: by Samuel Rowley. Acted by the Lord Admiral's Servants,
1602. Not now known.
On Sept. 27, 1602, Henslowe paid Rowley for a
play of Joshua.

JUDGES

Collett, John. Ehud, a sacred drama [in
seven scenes]. (In his: Sacred dramas. Evesham, 1805. 12°. p. 1–67.)

The **Parable** of the trees and its prophecy.
[In one scene.] (In: Jewish Education Committee, Chicago. Portfolios for holy days and
festivals. Chamishoh Osor bi-Shevat. Chicago
[1929?]. 2 f. 4°.
Mimeographed.
Based on Judges IX:7–15.

Sackler, Harry. The legend of Luz. A
play. (Menorah journal. New York, 1924.
4°. v. 10, no. 3, p. 258–266.) * **PBD**
Place: Luz. The trysting-place of the elders near
the gate.
An episode based on a quotation from Judges I:
26 and an interpretative midrashic comment, (Elijah
Zuto). The episode placed in the time of the Judges.
Translated by the author from his own original
Hebrew, which appeared, under the title of "Eternal
City," in *Hatoren,* New York, v. 6, no. 9, May 16,
1919, p. 6–10, * *PBA.*
Produced by the Religious School Students' Associ-
ation of Temple Emanu-El, at the Temple Playhouse,
San Francisco, April 13, 1929.

Old Testament Plays — Judges, continued

Deborah

Carman, Bliss, and MARY PERRY KING. Deborah, twelfth century B. C. ₜA dramatic poem.₎ illus. (In their: Daughters of dawn. New York, 1913. 12°. p. 15–24.)   **NCM**

Deborah. ₜAn anonymous play in three scenes.₎ (In: M. L. Cobb, compiler, Poetical dramas for home and school. Boston, 1873. 12°. p. 177–182.)   **MZB (Cobb)**

Ford, Alfred. Jael and Sisera: a woman's rights drama. (In his: Scenes and sonnets. New York ₜcop. 1872₎. 12°. p. 1–14.)   **NBH p.v.33**

Frank, Florence (Kiper). Jael; a poetic drama in one act. ₜChicago:₎ The Chicago Little Theatre, 1914. 29(1) p., 1 l. 12°.   **NBL p.v.222**

Cover-design and tail-piece by C. Raymond Johnson. Jael was originally produced at the Chicago Little Theatre, Oct. 20, 1914 with the following cast: Jael, Miriam Kiper; Sisera, Louis Alter; Abigail, Lou Wall Moore.

Norris, Charles Gilman. The rout of the Philistines; a forest play; music by Nino Marcelli; the 20th grove play of the Bohemian Club of San Francisco, as performed by its members in the Bohemian Grove, Sonoma county, Cal., on the 29th of July 1922. San Francisco: Bohemian Club, 1922. 5 p.l., 13–82 p. illus. 8°.   **NBL p.v.96**

Gideon

Miracle Play

The **10 pagean** of Gedeon. ₜ310 lines.₎ (In: C. F. Brown, editor, Stonyhurst pageants. Göttingen, 1920. 8°. p. 114–124.)   **NAFM**

Modern Plays

Raine, James Watt. ₜThe sword of Gideon.₎ ₜIn one scene.₎ (In his: Bible dramatics. New York & London ₜcop. 1927₎. 12°. p. 71–76.)

Judges VII and VIII.

Whiting, Isabel Kimball. The sword of Gideon. ₜIn three scenes.₎ (In her: Dramatic services of worship. Boston, 1925. 8°. p. 117–136.)   **NBM**

Jephthah's Daughter

Miracle Play

The **11 pagean** of Iephte. ₜ292 lines.₎ (In: C. F. Brown, editor, Stonyhurst pageants. Göttingen, 1920. 8°. p. 125–134.)   **NAFM**

Modern Plays

Alexander, William. Ella; or, The prince of Gilead's vow. A dramatic poem ₜin five acts₎. (In his: Poetical works. Philadelphia, 1847. 8°. p. 175–200.)   **NBHD**

Asch, Shalom. Jephthah's daughter... ₜTranslated by Isabel Shostac.₎ (East and West. New York, 1915. 4°. v. 1, p. 108–117.)   * **PBD**

In a prologue, two acts, and an epilogue.

See *Menorah journal*, New York, v. 2, 1916, p. 46–50, * PBD, for a partial translation and comments by Percy B. Shostac.

Reviewed by T. D. O'Bolger in *East and West*, v. 1, p. 129–130, * PBD.

Baddeley, Wilbore St. Clair. The daughter of Jephthah; a lyrical tragedy. (In his: The daughter of Jephthah, and other poems. London, 1879. 12°. p. 1–30.)

Reviewed in *The Athenæum*, London, Dec. 27, 1879, p. 847, * DA.

Benton, Rita. The daughter of Jephthah. ₜA play in one scene.₎ (In her: Bible plays. New York ₜcop. 1922₎. 8°. p. 78–95.)   * **PSQ**

Place: outside the tent of Jephthah, pitched on the Mizpah.

Boxer, James. Jephthah's daughter. ₜIn four acts.₎ (In his: Sacred dramas. Boston, 1875. 12°. p. 103–174.)

Boyd, Zachary. Historie of Jephta. ₜA dramatic poem. Excerpt of about 60 lines out of about 720 lines from the ms. "Flowers of Zion."₎ (In: Gabriel Neil, Biographical sketch of the Rev. Mr. Zachary Boyd. Glasgow, 1832. 8°. Appendix, p. xvii.)   **A p.v.144**

Thirteen speakers.

Buchanan, George. A tragedy called Jephthah; or, The vow... Newly translated into English by William Tait... Edinburgh, 1750. 12°.

A prose translation.

Copy in Library of Faculty of Advocates, Edinburgh.

—— Jephtha; or, The vow: a tragedy by ₜGeorge₎ Buchanan. Translated from the Latin by C. C. ₜCharles Chorley.₎ Truro, 1854. 48 p. 12°.

Title from British Museum Catalogue.

—— The Jephtha, and Baptist... translated by A. Gibb. Edinburgh, 1870. 8°.

Title from British Museum Catalogue.

"Among the pupils [of Buchanan] who' took part in acting [Jephtha] was Montaigne." — *Dictionary of national biography.*

—— Jephtha; a drama from the Latin of George Buchanan by A. Gordon Mitchell. Paisley: Alex. Gardner ₜpref. 1902₎. 130 p. illus. 12°.

The author's preface and dedication, dated at Paris the 27th of July, 1554, is printed on p. 18–21. The argument, p. 23, is taken from the book of Judges.

—— Jephthah; or, The vow. (In his: Sacred dramas. Translated by Archibald Brown. Edinburgh, 1906. 8°. p. 1–88.)   **NCP**

For a bibliography of the early Latin editions, English and foreign translations, see *George Buchanan; Glasgow quatercentenary studies, 1906*, Glasgow, 1907, p. 402–405, *AN*.

Fries, Carl. Quellenstudien zu George Buchanan. (Neue Jahrbücher für klassische Altertum Geschichte und Litteratur. Leipzig, 1900. 4°. Jahrg. 3, Bd. 6, p. 177–192, 241–261.)   † **NAA**

Old Testament Plays — Judges, continued

Jephthah's Daughter, continued

Bunston, Anna. Jephthah's daughter... ₍A drama in five acts.₎ London: Erskine Macdonald ₍1914₎. 78 p. 12°. **NCR**
Reviewed by W. G. Hole in *Poetry review*, London, 1914, v. 5, p. 190–193, * *DA.*

Campbell, James. Scene from an unfinished dramatic poem on the subject of Jeptha's rash vow. (In his: Judgment of Babylon; The siege of Massada, with other poems. London, 1826. 8°. p. 157–179.)
Myra, the name given here to Jephtha's daughter, and Azariah, her lover, are the two characters.

Christopherson, John. Jephthah; the Greek text edited and translated into English by Francis Howard Fobes... with an introduction by Wilbur Owen Sypherd... Newark, Del.: University of Delaware Press, 1928. vii, 157 p. 12°. **NSRM**
Greek text and English translation on opposite pages. The only English academic play in Greek known to have survived. "The exact date of composition is unknown, probably 1544."
Reviewed in *The Times literary supplement*, London, March 7, 1929, p. 189–190, † *NAA.* See also F. S. Boas, *University drama in the Tudor age*, Oxford, 1914, p. 45–62, *NCOD.*

Wagner, Bernard M. The tragedy of Iephte. (Times literary supplement. London, 1929. f°. v. 28, p. 1097.) † **NAA**
Cf. v. 29, p. 78, as to the existence at the Bodleian Library of a Latin translation of the Greek original.

Cromer, James Monroe. Jeptha's daughter; a drama in five acts. Boston: The Gorham Press, 1916. 103 p., 1 port. 12°. **NBM**

Crowley, Aleister. Jephthah; a tragedy. (In his: Jephthah, and other mysteries, lyrical and dramatic. London, 1899. 8°. p. 1–71.) **NBM**

Edison, John Sibbald. Jephtha; a dramatic poem. With a brief dissertation touching the question which has arisen as to the fate of Jephtha's daughter. London, 1863. 8°.
Title from British Museum Catalogue.

Githens, Harry W. A rash vow. ₍In five scenes.₎ (In his: Dramatized stories from the Old Testament. Cincinnati ₍cop. 1927₎. 12°. p. 100–109.) **NASH**

Graves, Mrs. Adelia Cleopatra (Spencer). Jephthah's daughter; a drama in five acts, founded on the eleventh chapter of Judges. Memphis, Tenn.: South-western Publishing Co., 1867. 144 p., 4 pl. 12°.
Title from Library of Congress.

Hoadly, John. Jephtha, an oratorio: in two parts. Compos'd by Dr. Greene. ₍The words by J. Hoadly.₎ London, 1737. 8°.
Words only.
Title from British Museum Catalogue.

Hull, Phin. G. Libretto of Jephthah and his daughter. A dramatic cantata in three

acts. New York, Cincinnati, Chicago: John Church Co., cop. 1883. 23 p. 16°.
Words only.

Jacobson, Janie. Jephthah's vow; a scriptural play in two acts. (In her: Ruth, the Moabitess. New York, 1910. nar. 8°. p. 10–16.) **NBL p.v.13, no. 9**

Jephtha; a drama in five acts ₍and in verse₎. By a lady. London, 1846. 8°.
Title from British Museum Catalogue. The ff. entry is given in Halkett and Laing: Jeptha; a dramatic poem. By a lady. [Mrs. —Salmon.] London, 1846. 8°.

Jephtha's daughter, a Scriptural drama, in three acts ₍and in verse₎ by a lady ₍pseud.₎. (In: V. Alfieri, Saul, a tragedy. London, 1821. 8°. p. 115–152.) **NNR**

Jeptha's rash vow; or, The virgin sacrifice. As it is acted at Lee and Harper's great theatrical booth, over against the Hospital-Gate in West Smithfield... Southwark, 1733. 8°.
Title from British Museum Catalogue.
According to Hazlitt, this piece is mentioned in Sorbiere's *Journey to London in 1698*, as having been performed that year as a puppet-show at Bartholomew Fair. Its alternative title was given it, when acted again at the same fair, in 1701.

Levinger, Elma C. Ehrlich. Jephthah's daughter. A play in one act. (The Ark. Cincinnati, 1913. 8°. v. 3, p. 407–415.) * **PBD**

—— Jephthah's daughter; a Biblical drama in one act. Prize play, Drama League of America... New York: S. French, cop. 1921. 1 p.l., 5–36 p., 7 l. illus. 8°. **NBF p.v.41, no.3**
Also printed in H. L. Cohen, *The junior play book*, New York [1923], p. 123–157, *NAFH;* and in C. S. Thomas, *The Atlantic book of junior plays*, Boston [1924], p. 185–215, *NAFH.*

Morell, Thomas. Jeptha, an oratorio, or, Sacred drama as it is perform'd at the Theatre-Royal in Covent-Garden. ₍By Thomas Morell.₎ Set to musick by Mr. Handel. London: J. Watts ₍1770?₎. 20 p. 8°.

Munday, Anthony, and Thomas Decker. Jeptha: a play by Anthony Munday and Thomas Decker, acted in May, 1602.
Ascribed by J. Barker to Chettle.

Nelson, Lucy H. Jephthah's daughter; a Biblical drama in three acts. Chicago: A. Flanagan Co. ₍cop. 1909.₎ 32 p. 8°.

Pember, Edward Henry. Jephthah's daughter, a tragedy in three acts. (In his: Jephthah's daughter, and other poems. London, 1904. 8°. p. 1–103.)

Pierce, Sarah. Jephthah's daughter. ₍In four acts.₎ Copied from the original mss. given by Mrs. Asa Gray, grandniece of Miss Pierce, to the Litchfield Historical Society. (In: E. N. Vanderpoel, compiler, Chronicles of a pioneer school from 1792 to 1833, being the history of Miss Sarah Pierce and her Litchfield School. Cambridge, Mass., 1903. 8°. p. 119–145.) **IQM (Litchfield)**
"Mostly, as far as I can judge, in Miss Sarah Pierce's hand-writing." (Mrs. Gray.)

Old Testament Plays — Judges, continued

Jephthah's Daughter, continued

Tennant, William. Jephthah's daughter. (In his: Hebrew dramas. Edinburgh, 1845. 16°.)

Title from British Museum Catalogue.

Vartie, John. Jephtha: a dramatic fragment ₍in five acts₎. London: Sampson Low, and C. & J. Ollier, 1820. xviii p., 1 l., 51 p. 8°.
NCO p.v.93, no.1

p. v–xiii: biographical sketch of the author.

Whiffen, Edwin Thomas. Jephtha sacrificing. ₍A dramatic poem.₎ (In his: Jephtha sacrificing, and Dinah. New York ₍cop. 1908₎. 12°. p. 3–41.)   **NBI**

Also printed in his *Tamar and other poems,* New York, 1913, p. 224–264.

Wilson, Mrs. Ann. Jephthah's daughter, a dramatic poem ₍in five acts and in verse₎. London, 1783. 8°.

Title from British Museum Catalogue.
Reviewed in *Monthly review,* London, 1783, v. 69, p. 439, * DA.

SAMSON

Miracle Play

The 12 **pagean** of Samson. ₍392 lines.₎ (In: C. F. Brown, editor, Stonyhurst pageants. Göttingen, 1920. 8°. p. 135–149.)   **NAFM**

Modern Plays

Andreyev, Leonid Nikolayevich. Samson in chains; posthumous tragedy ₍in five acts₎, by Leonid Andreyev; authorized translation from the original manuscript, and a preface by Herman Bernstein. London: Brentano's, Ltd. ₍pref. 1923.₎ xi p., 2 l., 3–207 p. 12°.
The characters are mostly Biblical.   **** QDK**
The fourth act was translated and published in the *Jewish tribune,* New York, v. 42, Sept. 7, 1923, p. 14–15, 66, 68–69, * PBD.

Aste, Ippolito Tito d'. Samson. A play in five acts by Ippolito d'Aste. The English translation prepared expressly for the American tour of Signor Salvini and his Italian company, under the management of Mr. Maurice Grau. New York: G. F. Nesbitt & Co., 1873. 79 p. 8°.   **NNO p.v.147, no.1**
Text in Italian and English on opposite pages.
The argument from the book of Judges. Period 1117 B. C.

—— Samson. A tragedy, in five acts, by Ippolito d'Aste. Translated by W. D. Howells. With the English and Italian words, as performed by Signor Salvini, during his farewell American tour, under the direction of Mr. A. M. Palmer. New York: C. D. Koppel, cop. 1889. 2 p.l., (1)4–51 p. 8°.
* C p.v.1718, no.3

Bloch, Regina Miriam. Samson and Delilah. A fantastic version ₍in one act₎. Illus-

trations by H. C. Rude. (B'nai Brith magazine. Chicago, 1927. 4°. v. 41, p. 342–345.)
* PYP
Reprinted in *Jewish times,* Baltimore, Sept. 23, 1927, v. 17, p. 193–198, †* PBD.

Boyd, Zachary. Historie of Samson. ₍A dramatic poem. Excerpt of about 360 lines out of about 2100 lines from the ms. "Flowers of Zion."₎ (In: Gabriel Neil, Biographical sketch of the Rev. Mr. Zachary Boyd. Glasgow, 1832. 8°. Appendix, p. xiii–xvii.)
Thirteen speakers.   **A p.v.144**

Carvalho, Naomi Nunes. The Greek and Hebrew marriage. ₍A dialogue between Delilah and a Philistine lord.₎ (In her: Vox humana. London, 1912. 12°. p. 55–59.)
NRD p.v.9

Levinger, Elma C. Ehrlich. Snaring the lion; a one-act play based upon an incident in Judges. (The Drama. Washington, 1919. 8°. v. 9, no. 34, p. 60–83.)   **NAFA**

Lounsbery, Grace Constant. Delilah, a drama in three acts. New York: Scott-Thaw Company, 1904. 128 p. 16°.   **NBM**

Manley, William Ford. The comeback. ₍In three scenes.₎ (In his: A second book of Bible dramas. New York ₍cop. 1930₎. 8°. p. 119–135.)   **NBM**
Cast: Two guards, Samson, and Delilah.

—— Samson and Delilah. (In his: Bible dramas. New York ₍cop. 1928₎. 8°. p. 63–79.)   **NBM**
In four scenes.

Milton, John. Paradise Regain'd. A Poem. In IV Books. To which is added Samson Agonistes. The Author John Milton. London, Printed by J. M. for John Starkey... MDCLXXI. 1 p.l., 111, 101(1) p., 1 l. 8°.   **Reserve**
Lacks leaf preceding title-page.
First edition.
For a list of editions see *Contributions to a catalogue of the Lenox Library,* no. 6 (*Works of Milton*), New York, 1881, * GW. See card catalogue for later entries.
Also printed in *Select plays,* Baltimore, 1804, v. 6, [no. 3], *NCO (Select).*
For translations into foreign languages see D. H. Stevens, *Reference guide to Milton, from 1800 to the present day,* Chicago, 1930, items 1614–1625, *RB–* NCB.
First produced by the Elizabethan Stage Society, April 7, 1900, at the South Kensington Museum, London, with F. Rawson Buckley in the part of Samson. Reviewed by Max Beerbohm in *Saturday review,* London, v. 89, p. 489, * DA, and in *Athenæum,* London, v. 115, p. 475, * DA.
Produced by the British Academy, under direction of W. Poel, at the Theatre, Burlington Gardens, London, Dec. 15, 1908 with Ian Maclaren as Samson, Evelyn Weeden as Delilah. Reviewed in *Athenæum,* London, 1908, v. 132, p. 799–800, * DA, and by Max Beerbohm in *Saturday review,* London, 1908, v. 106, p. 754–755, * DA.
Performed by the sixth grade boys of the Queen Elizabeth Grammar School, Wakefield, England, April 8 and 9, 1930. Produced at Fellows' Garden, Exeter College, Oxford, May 22, 1930; Mr. Bodington as Samson, Mrs. Coghill as Delilah. For reviews see *The Times,* London, May 23, 1930, p. 14 b, * A, and Eric Evans in *Drama,* London, 1930, v. 8, p. 163, *NAFA.*

Old Testament Plays — Judges, continued

Samson: Milton's Samson Agonistes, continued

—— ΣΑΜΨΩΝ ΑΓΩΝΙΣΤΗΣ. Johannis Miltoni Samson Agonistes. Graeco carmine redditus cum versione Latina, a Georgio Henrico Glasse... Oxonii: e typographeo Clarendoniano, 1788. xl, 266 p., 1 l. 8°.
*NCG
The Greek translation, p. 1–136; the Latin, p. 142–266.
Not in Stevens.
Reviewed in *Critical review*, London, 1788, v. 66, p. 212–215, *NAA*, and in *Monthly review*, London, 1789, v. 81, p. 1–19, 97–111, *NAA*.

ABRAHAMS, Israel. Samson Agonistes. (Jewish chronicle. London, 1908. f°. Dec. 18, p. 18.)
*PBE

BAUM, Paull Franklin. Samson Agonistes again. (Modern Language Association of America. Publications. Baltimore, 1921. 8°. v. 36, p. 354–371.)
RAA

BREWER, Wilmon. Two Athenian models for Samson Agonistes. (Modern Language Association of America. Publications. Menasha, Wis., 1927. 8°. v. 42, p. 910–920.)
RAA
Contends that Milton took his plot "almost entirely" from Aeschyles' *Prometheus bound* and Sophocles' *Oedipus Coloneus*.

BRIDGES, Robert. "Extraordinary." [On use of the word in line 1383 of the Agonistes.] (Athenæum. London, 1903. 4°. July 18, 1903, p. 93–94.)
*DA

CLARK, Evert Mordecai. Milton's conception of Samson. (University of Texas. Studies in English. Austin, Tex., 1928. 8°. no. 8, p. 88–99.)
NABM (Texas)

—— Milton's earlier Samson. (University of Texas. Studies in English. Austin, Tex., 1927. 8°. no. 7, p. 144–154.)
NABM (Texas)
Apropos of Milton's earlier interest in the story of Samson as a possible subject for heroic song.

COOK, Albert Stanburrough. Samson Agonistes, lines 1665–1666. (Modern language notes. Baltimore, 1906. 8°. v. 21, p. 78.)
Parallels with classical literature.

COSGROVE, Isaac K. The Hebraic influences in Samson Agonistes. (The Jewish chronicle. London, 1925. f°. no. 58, Oct., 1925, supplement, p. vii.)
*PBE

CURRY, Walter Clyde. Samson Agonistes yet again. (Sewanee review. Sewanee, Tenn., 1924. 8°. v. 32, p. 336–352.)
*DA
"It is a subjective drama of spiritual development and achievement rather than a play of incident."

DUPUY, Ernest. Les origines littéraires d'Alfred de Vigny. (Revue d'histoire littéraire de la France. Paris, 1903. 8°. année 10, p. 373–412.)
NKBA
Pages 391–401 contain a comparison of De Vigny's Samson with that of Milton.

EPPS, P. H. Two notes on English classicism. (University of North Carolina. — Philological Club. Studies in philology. Chapel Hill, N. C., 1916. 8°. v. 13, p. 190–196.)
RNA (North Carolina)
"We have found that the Samson agrees with classical theory and practice... Even the length...is about the same as that of Greek tragedy."

FRAENKEL, Ludwig. Klassisches (Shakespeare, Milton) auf der heutigen Londoner Bühne. (Englische Studien. Leipzig, 1900. 8°. Bd. 28, p. 479–480.)
RNA
On the occasion of its London production in 1900.

FRETZ, Grace Faulks. Samson Agonistes: an appreciation. (Methodist review. New York, 1927. 8°. v. 110, p. 103–108.)
*DA
"One cannot but be impressed by the analogy between Milton's situation and that of Samson."

GILBERT, Allan A. [Conjectural emendation of line 1096.] (Modern language notes. Baltimore, 1914. 8°. v. 29, p. 161–162.)
RAA

GRIERSON, Herbert John Clifford. A note upon the "Samson Agonistes" of John Milton and "Samson of Heilige Wraeck" by Joost van den Vondel. (In: Mélanges d'histoire littéraire générale et comparée offerts à Fernand Baldensperger. Paris, 1930. 8°. tome 1, p. 332–339.)
NABM

HANFORD, James Holly. Samson Agonistes and Milton in old age. (University of Michigan. Studies in Shakespeare, Milton and Donne. New York and London, 1925. 8°. p. 165–189.)
RAE

JEBB, Sir Richard Claverhouse. Samson Agonistes and the Hellenic drama. n. t.-p. [London,] 1908. 8 p. 8°. ***NCF p.v.1, no.7**
"However Greek the drama may be in structure, Milton's mind was Hebraic."

KILGO, Mrs. J. W. The Hebrew Samson and Milton's Samson. (Methodist quarterly review. Nashville, Tenn., 1924. 8°. v. 73, p. 312–316.)

KNOWLTON, E. C. Causality in Samson Agonistes. (Modern language notes. Baltimore, 1922. 8°. v. 37, p. 333–339.)
RAA

KREIPE, Christian Friedrich Emil Edzard. Milton's "Samson Agonistes." Halle (Saale): M. Niemeyer, 1926. ix, 69(1) p. 8°. (Studien zur englischen Philologie. Heft 70.)
NCE p.v.76, no.7
Reviewed by S. B. Liljegren in *Anglia: Beiblatt*, Halle a. S., 1928, Bd. 39, p. 366, *RNA*.

POWELL, Chilton L. Milton Agonistes. (Sewanee review. Sewanee, Tenn., 1926. 8°. v. 34, p. 169–183.)
*DA

ROBERTS, R. Ellis. Samson Agonistes yet again. (Sewanee review. Sewanee, Tenn., 1924. 8°. v. 32, p. 336–356.)
*DA

Old Testament Plays — Judges, continued

Samson: Milton's Samson Agonistes, continued

SCHMIDT, Alexander. Milton's dramatische Dichtungen. (In his: Gesammelte Abhandlungen. Berlin, 1889. 8°. p. 134–176.) **NCB**
[Simson Agonistes], p. 161–176.
"Nicht in [gewissen] Personen, sondern in den allgemeinen Verhältnissen, in der Aehnlichkeit der historischen Situationen, liegt der Schlüssel zu der polemischen Absicht des Dichters."

STENGERS, Jeanne. Le "Samson" de Milton et de Vondel. (Revue de l'Université de Bruxelles. Bruxelles, 1905. 8°. année 10, p. 261–284.) *** EM**

THALER, Alwin. [The stage history of Milton's Samson.] (University of North Carolina. — Philological Club. Studies in philology. Chapel Hill, N. C., 1920. 8°. v. 17, p. 269–279.) **RNA**
Reprinted in his *Shakspere's silences*, Cambridge, 1929, p. 214–221, * NCV *(Thaler).*

THOMPSON, Edward J. Samson Agonistes. (London quarterly review. London, 1916. 8°. v. 125, p. 244–254.) *** DA**
The poets alone, not the critics, rightly understood and appreciated Milton and his Samson.

TILLYARD, Eustace Manderville Wetenhall. Samson Agonistes: its origin, quality, dramatic motive [and] relation to Milton's experience and thought. (In his: Milton. London, 1930. 8°. p. 328–354.) *** R – * NCC**

TUPPER, James Waddell. The dramatic structure of Samson Agonistes. (Modern Language Association of America. Publications. Baltimore, 1920. 8°. v. 35, p. 375–389.) **RAA**

Pottle, Emery Bemsley. Delilah, a tragedy by Emery Gilbert [pseud.]. (In: Kenyon Nicholson, editor, The Appleton book of short plays. Second series. New York and London, 1927. 8°. p. 313–333.)

Read, Elizabeth Day. Samson and the Philistines; or, Evil begets evil. Boston: American Unitarian Association, n.d. 5 l. 4°.
Typewritten.

Samson. [In four scenes.] (In: M. W. Thomas, editor, Old Testament drama. London [1927]. 12°. p. 97–107.)

Watson, Edward Willard. By Gaza's gate; a cantata. Words based on the text of the Polychrome Bible. (In his: Old lamps and new. Philadelphia [1905]. 12°. p. 103–114.) **NBI**

Whiffen, Edwin T. Samson marrying, Samson at Timnah, Samson hybristes, Samson blinded; four dramatic poems. Boston: R. G. Badger, 1905. 190 p. 8°. **NBM**
Also printed in his *Tamar and other poems*, New York, 1913, p. 5–173.

I. AND II. SAMUEL

Andersen, Olivia Donaldson (Cushing). The judge, King Saul and the singer. [In six acts.] (In her: Creation and other Biblical plays. Geneva, 1929. 4°. p. 149–224.) **NBM**
"In *The judge* [Samuel], *King Saul and the singer* [David] spiritual conceptions progress"... The Israelites "are taught obedience to that code which they received in the tables of the law." Place: Canaan. Time: 1120–1056 B. C.

Gilmore, Alice F. Our library; a Dewey decimal play [in one scene]. illus. (Wilson, H. W., firm, publishers. Wilson bulletin. New York, 1930. 8°. v. 5, p. 186–191.) *** HA**
Eli, little Samuel, and the three wise men constitute the group Religion, 200.

Keefe, William Randolph. Nabal, a dramatic poem based on the twenty-fifth chapter of First Samuel. [n. p.,] 1901. 20 p. 8°.
Title from Library of Congress.

Young, Andrew John. The death of Eli, a dramatic poem. (In his: The death of Eli, and other poems. London, 1921. 12°. p. 19–30.)
In the courtyard of the Temple, outside Shiloh. *Cf.* I. Samuel, ch. 4.

SAMUEL THE PROPHET

Benton, Rita. The call of Samuel. (In her: Shorter Bible plays. New York [cop. 1922]. 8°. p. 63–72.) **NASH**
Place: Shiloh, before the door of the tabernacle.

Brown, Walter. Samuel. [In three acts.] (In: Elma C. E. Levinger, Entertaining programs for the assembly. Cincinnati [cop. 1930]. 8°. p. 154–156.) *** PSY**

Githens, Harry W. A mother's gift. [In four scenes.] (In his: Dramatized stories from the Old Testament. Cincinnati [cop. 1927]. 12°. p. 115–120.) **NASH**
Hannah and her son Samuel.

Grossman, Samuel S. The call of Samuel. [New York: Young Judaea.] 5 l. 4°. (In his: [Holiday and other plays for Jewish children.]) **NASH**
Typewritten.

Hale, Harris G., and N. M. HALL. ...Samuel and Saul. Arranged by Harris G. Hale and Newton M. Hall. Boston: The Pilgrim Press, 1907. iv, 17 p. 12°. (Biblical dramas. [no.4.])

Hannah, the mother of Samuel the prophet and judge of Israel; a sacred drama. Boston, 1839. xiii, 94 p. 12°.
Title from Roden's *Later American plays*, p. 2.
Reviewed in *New-York mirror*, New York, 1839, v. 16, p. 255, * DA.

Kimball, Rosamond. Samuel in the House of the Lord. [A play in five scenes.] (In her: The wooing of Rebekah, and other Bible plays. New York, 1925. 8°. p. 121–135.) **ZICS**

Old Testament Plays — I. and II. Samuel, continued

Samuel the Prophet, continued

Parsons, Margaret. The little prophet, Samuel. ₍In one act.₎ (In her: Ten stirring Bible plays. Franklin, Ohio, cop. 1927. 12°. p. 15–21.)

Valentine, Cloyd Hampton. Samuel; a pageant ₍in nine scenes₎. Boston: Young People's Religious Union, n.d. 2 p.l., 20 l. 4°. Mimeographed.

SAUL

Miracle Play

The **14 pagean** of Saul. ₍1445 lines.₎ (In: C. F. Brown, editor, Stonyhurst pageants. Göttingen, 1920. 8°. p. 149–198.) **NAFM**

Modern Plays

Alfieri, Vittorio. Saul, a tragedy. (In his: Tragedies, translated from the Italian by Charles Lloyd. London, 1815. 12°. v. 3, p. 60–126.) **NNR**
Written in 1782–83 at the suggestion of the Countess of Albany. It is in five acts and contains 1567 lines. "All critics agree in considering this the finest of Alfieri's tragedies."
Reprinted in the 2. ed., London, 1821, v. 4, p. 60–126, *NNR*, and in G. Bell's London ed., 1876, v. 2, p. 107–164, *NNR*.
Selections are printed in Julian Hawthorne, editor, *Masterpieces and the history of literature*, New York, 1906, v. 7, p. 181–190, *NAB*.
Reviewed in *Monthly review*, London, 1816, series 2, v. 80, p. 40, *NAA*.

—— Saul, a tragedy ₍in five acts and in verse₎. (In his: Saul...and Jephtha's daughter, by a lady. London, 1821. 8°. p. 9–112.) **NNR**
The translation is by a lady, authoress of *Jephtha's daughter*, in the same volume. Cf. advertisement.

WINTER, William. Salvini as King Saul and King Lear. (In his: Shadows of the stage. New York, 1893. 24°. p. 339–344.) **NADB**
Saul, played by Salvini, is the only one of Alfieri's plays seen on the English stage.

Bloch, Regina Miriam. The witch of En-Dor. ₍In one scene.₎ Illustrated by Saul Raskin. (B'nai B'rith magazine. Cincinnati, 1927. 4°. v. 42, p. 102–103.) *** PYP**

Brooks, Byron Alden. King Saul. A tragedy. New York: Nelson & Phillips; Cincinnati: Hitchcock & Walden, 1876. 144 p., 1 pl. 12°.
Reviewed in *The Christian advocate*, New York, Jan. 25, 1877, p. 56–57, †† *ZTA*, and in *Frank Leslie's Sunday magazine*, New York, 1877, v.1, p. 252–253, *** DA*.

Brown, John. The cure of Saul. A sacred ode ₍in three parts₎, as it is performed at the Theatre-Royal in Covent Garden. Written by Dr. Brown... London: L. Davis and C. Reymers, 1763. vi, (1)8–22 p. 4°.

Chaloner, John Armstrong. "Saul"; a tragedy in three acts... Roanoke Rapids, N. C.: Palmetto Press, 1915. 66, 4 p. 8°. In three acts. **NBL p.v.71, no.3**
Reprinted in his *The Scarlet women, and other sonnets*, New York, 1924, p. 275–343, *NBI*.

Cole, Edna Earle. A king's life spared. ₍In two acts.₎ (In her: The good Samaritan, and other Bible stories dramatized. Boston ₍cop. 1915₎. 12°. p. 31–39.)
Based on i. Samuel xxiv: 1–22.

Coxe, Arthur Cleveland. Saul, a mystery ...by the author of "Christian ballads," "Athanasion," etc... ₍Arthur Cleveland Coxe₎. New York: D. Appleton & Co., 1845. x p., 1 l., (1)14–297(1) p. 12°. **NBM**
"The character of Saul appears to me to combine those attributes in which the Tragic Muse has heretofore found her noblest material." — *From the dedicatory epistle to John Jay, p. v.*

Crane, Edward. Saul and Jonathan. (In his: Collection of poetical miscellanies. Manchester ₍Eng.₎, 1761. 8°.)
Title from D. E. Baker, *Biographia dramatica*, 1812, v. 4, p. 241.

Fulford, William. Saul, a dramatic poem ... London, 1862. 8°.
Title from British Museum Catalogue.
Reviewed in *Athenæum*, London, July 12, 1862, p. 47–48, *** DA*.

Heavysege, Charles. Saul. A drama. In three parts. ₍By Charles Heavysege.₎ Montreal: H. Rose, 1857. iv, (1)6–315 p. 8°.
Reviewed, by Coventry Patmore, in *North British review*, Edinburgh, 1858, v. 29, p. 143–147, *** DA*. "What much adds to the startling effect of this poem, is the manifest fact that the writer is some person who has received little or no education... There are two things, however, which he proves that he knows, namely, the Bible and human nature."
The second ed., 1859, was reviewed in *Literary gazette*, London, 1859, new series, v. 3, p. 421–423, *** DA*. "In the author of 'Saul', the poetic and the philosophic intellect have combined to form a dramatist of no common order." The reviewer states that the book was introduced to England by Nathaniel Hawthorne.

—— —— A new and rev. ed. Boston: Fields, Osgood, & Co., 1869. 436, 5 p. 12°. *** PSQ**
The three parts are in five, four and six acts respectively, and a different set of dramatis personae is given for each part. Pages 1–5 at the end of the book are a review of the first edition of Saul, from the *North British review* for Aug., 1858.

—— —— New York: Lovell Print. & Pub. Co., 1876. 436, 5 p. 12°. *** PSQ**
Reviewed by Louisa Murray in *Canadian monthly*, Toronto, 1876, v. 10, p. 250–254, *** DA*.

BURPEE, Lawrence Johnstone. Charles Heavysege. port. (Royal Society of Canada. Transactions. ₍Montreal,₎ 1901. 8°. 1901, section 2, p. 17–60.) *** EC**

CLARK, Daniel. The poetry of Charles Heavysege. (Canadian monthly. Toronto, 1876. 8°. v. 10, p. 127–134.) *** DA**

GREENSHIELDS, E. B. A forgotten poet. (University magazine. Montreal, 1908. 8°. v. 7, p. 343–359.) **† STK (McGill)**

Old Testament Plays — I. and II. Samuel, continued

Saul, continued

Hill, Aaron. Saul; a tragedy ₁in one act₁. (In his: Dramatic works. London, 1760. 8°. v. 2, p. 177–185.)   **NCP**

Kōri, Torahiko. Saul and David; an epic drama ₁in five acts₁. London: Arthur L. Humphreys, 1918. 3 p.l., 79 p. 12°. ***OSH**
Translated from the Japanese by the author with the assistance of H. M. Sainsbury.

Logan, Algernon Sydney. Saul: a dramatic poem. Philadelphia: J. B. Lippincott & Co., 1883. 80 p. 12°.   **NBM**
Saul's death on Mount Gilboa.

Norwood, Robert Winkworth. The witch of Endor; a tragedy. New York: George H. Doran Company ₁cop. 1916₁. 121 p. 12°.
In five acts.   **NCR**

Raine, James Watt. Saul's awakening. ₁In one scene.₁ (In his: Bible dramatics. New York & London ₁cop. 1927₁. 12°. p. 248–256.)
Based on I. Samuel ix.

—— The witch of Endor. ₁In two scenes.₁ (In his: Bible dramatics. New York & London ₁cop. 1927₁. 12°. p. 269–277.)
I. Samuel xxviii.

Roworth, W. S. Saul: a dramatic poem. London: E. Stock ₁1865₁. 2 p.l., 90 p. 16°.   **NCM**
Reviewed in *Athenæum*, London, April 21, 1866, p. 529, * *DA*.

Saul. ₁In nine scenes and epilogue.₁ (In: M. W. Thomas, editor, Old Testament drama. London ₁1927₁. 12°. p. 109–142.)

Saul, a dramatic sketch. (American monthly magazine. Boston, 1829. 8°. v. 1, p. 200–203.)   *** DA**
The characters are Saul, Samuel, and the witch of Endor. Wegelin in his *Early American plays, 1714–1830*, p. 6, states that "the piece is probably by N. P. Willis," who was the editor of the magazine in which it appeared.

Saul; a dramatic sketch...with other poems and translations. London, 1844. 8°.
Title from the British Museum Catalogue.
Reviewed in *Athenæum*, London, Feb. 8, 1845, p. 149, * *DA*.

Savage-Armstrong, George Francis. The tragedy of Israel. Part I. King Saul. London, 1872. 8°.
Reviewed in *Athenæum*, London, June 14, 1873, p. 755, * *DA*.

—— —— London: Longmans, Green and Co., 1892. 156, 19 p. 12°.

Storrs, Lewis Austin. The tragedy of Saul, first king of Israel. New York: G. W. Dillingham Co. ₁1904.₁ 2 p.l., (1)8–124 p. 8°.
A drama in five acts.   **NBM**
Reviewed in *Jewish tribune*, Portland, Ore., Feb. 3, 1905, v. 4, p. 4, * *PBD*.

Thorndike, Arthur Russell. Saul, a historical tragedy in five acts. Depicting the life and death of King Saul. London: ₁R. Flint and Co.,₁ 1906. 88 p., 1 port. 8°.
Title from the Library of Congress.
"The triumph of the House of David over that of Saul seems to me to be a foreshadowing of the great triumph of the New Testament over the Old, that is (David being the direct ancestor of the Messiah) the triumph of the doctrines of Christ over the carefully lettered statutes of the Mosaic Dispensation."

The **Tragedy** of King Saul. Written by a deceas'd person of honour, and now made publick at the request of several men of quality who have highly approv'd of it... London: H. Playford, 1703. 5 p.l., 67 p. 8°.
Title from Library of Congress.
Sometimes attributed to Joseph Trapp. W. S. Clark, citing Horace Walpole, attributes it to Roger Boyle, Earl of Orrery. See *Review of English studies*, v. 2, p. 282, *RNA*.

Tully, James. King Saul; a tragedy ₁in four acts₁. London: A. H. Stockwell ₁1922?₁. 119 p. 12°.   **NCR**

V., G. Saul; a dramatic poem ₁in four acts₁, by G. V... Paisley: A. Gardner, Ltd., 1924. 117 p. 12°.   **NCR (Saul)**

Whiting, Isabel Kimball. The renewal of spirit. Adaptation of the Bible and Robert Browning's "Saul" ₁in one scene₁. (In her: Dramatic services of worship. Boston, 1925. 8°. p. 91–116.)   **NBM**

Whitney, Mary Ellen. The crowning of Saul. ₁A play in four scenes.₁ (In her: Bible plays and how to produce them. New York ₁cop. 1927₁. 12°. p. 20–26.)

DAVID

Miracle Play

The **15 pagean** of Dauid. ₁690 lines.₁ (In: C. F. Brown, editor, Stonyhurst pageants. Göttingen, 1920. 8°. p. 199–223.)   **NAFM**

Modern Plays

Absalom: a scriptural drama alluded to in Henslowe's Diary, ed. Collier, p. 241 — "paid for poleyes and workmanshipp for to hange Absolome, xiiijd."
See W. C. Hazlitt, *Manual*, p. 1.

Austin, Grace Jewett. Abigail. A play in five acts. Bloomington, Ill.: George A. Brown, Frontier Press, 1924. 48 p. 12°.   **NBL p.v.120, no.8**
Historical basis: I. Samuel, chap. 25. Time: 1060 B. C.

Bale, John. Absalom: a drama by John Bale. No longer known.
See W. C. Hazlitt, *Manual*, p. 1.

—— David and Absolom: a tragedy, in five acts, by Bishop Bale, not mentioned in the catalogue of his Works. A ms. copy of

Old Testament Plays — I. and II. Samuel,
continued

David, continued

this play, supposed to be in the author's
handwriting, and certainly contemporary,
containing 62 pages in quarto, is among the
Stowe mss. Mr. Fleay conjectures that it
may be the play of the Two sins of King
David.

See W. C. Hazlitt, *Manual*, p. 59.

Barbee, Lindsey. The making of a king;
a Biblical drama [in three acts]. (In: Allison
Gaw and E. T. Gaw, Pharaoh's daughter,
and other Biblical plays of the contest, 1927.
New York, 1928. 8°. p. 147–184.) **NBL**
Prize-winning play.
Dramatization of the story of Jonathan and David
in opposition to King Saul.

Bentley, John. The royal penitent; a sacred drama [in three acts and in prose, with
songs]. London, 1803. 12°.
Title from British Museum Catalogue.
Reviewed in *British critic*, London, 1803, v. 22,
p. 434, * *DA*.

Benton, Rita. David and Goliath. [A play
in two acts.] (In her: Shorter Bible plays.
New York [cop. 1922]. 8°. p. 73–97.) **NASH**
Place: Bethlehem.

Bloomgarden, Solomon. The Shunamite:
a one-act Biblical play by Yehoash [pseud.].
Authorized translation from the Yiddish by
Henry T. Schnittkind. (Stratford journal.
Boston, 1919. 8°. v. 4, p. 313–320.) * **DA**
Based on the episode, narrated in I. Kings, I: 1–4.
Produced by the Menorah Societies of Harvard and
Radcliffe at the Agassiz House, Cambridge, on April
10, 1926. L. H. Weinstein and Harold Rose as King
David, Sylvia Schlafer as the Shunamite.
Reprinted in Frank Shay, editor, *Twenty-five short
plays, international*, New York [1925], p. 363–370,
NAFH (Shay).

Boyd, Henry. Poems, chiefly dramatic
and lyric, etc. Dublin, 1793. 8°.
Title from British Museum Catalogue.
Contains a play on the subject of David and Uriah.
Reviewed in *British critic*, London, 1795, v. 6,
p. 57–59, * *DA*.

Boyd, Zachary. David and Goliah [a dramatic poem]. (In his: Four poems from
"Zion's flowers." Glasgow, 1855. 8°. p. 107–
138.) **NCL**
Eight speakers.
An excerpt is printed in Gabriel Neil, *Biographical
sketch of the Rev. Mr. Zachary Boyd*, Glasgow, 1832,
appendix, p. vii–x, *A p.v. 144.*

Carvalho, Naomi Nunes. Despair. [A dialogue between King David and a counsellor
of the King.] (In her: Vox humana. London, 1912. 12°. p. 61–65.) **NRD p.v.9**

Cayzer, Charles William. David & Bathshua; a drama in five acts by Charles Whitworth Wynne [pseud.]. London: Kegan Paul,
Trench, Trübner & Co., Ltd., 1903. 3 p.l.,
116 p. 8°.

—— —— New York: The Knickerbocker
Press, 1903. 4 p.l., 100 p. 8°. **NCR**
Reprinted in his *By the way of the gate*, London,
1911, v. 2, p. 1–99, *NCM*. Also printed in G. A.
Kohut, *A Hebrew anthology*, Cincinnati, 1913, v. 2,
p. 855–890, * *PSO*.

DANNENBERG, Max. Die Verwendung des
biblischen Stoffes von David und Bathseba
im englischen Drama. (G. Peele: David and
Bethsabe; Ch. W. Wynne: David and Bathshua; St. Phillips: The sin of David.) Königsberg i. Pr.: Hartung, 1905. 2 p.l., 70 p.,
1 l. 8°. **NCO p.v.308, no.8**

Chaloner, John Armstrong. "Saul and
David"; a tragedy in two acts. [Roanoke
Rapids, N. C.: Palmetto Press, 1915.] 67 p.,
1 l. 8°. **NBL p.v.71, no.3**
Reprinted in his *The Scarlet women, and other
sonnets*, New York, 1924, p. 345–411, *NBI*.

Cogswell, Warren H. The Hebrew prince;
or, Jonathan and David, a tragedy in five
acts. Concord, N. H.: Printed by the Re-
publican Press Association, 1885. 22 p. 8°.
Title from Library of Congress.
The cover-title adds: Written for Cogswell and
Mackenzie, and played only by them.

Connelly, Marcus Cook. Little David, an
act which the author loved most, but which
nevertheless was omitted from "The Green
pastures" [because it did not fit into the
chronological sequence of the play]. illus.
(Hearst's international cosmopolitan. New
York, 1930. 4°. v. 89, Sept., 1930, p. 30–31,
197–198.) * **DA**
A Negro version of how David killed Goliath. The
characters: David, Samuel, and Goliath.

Cook, Mrs. Alice (Carter). Michal; a playlet of the time of David. [In two acts.] Boston: The Four Seas Company, 1922. 3 p.l.,
9–66 p. 12°. **NBM**

Cross, Norman. David and Bathsheba [a
dramatic poem]. (In his: Songs after sunset.
Oxford, n.d. 12°. p. 19–23.) **NCM**

David and Uriah; a drama in five acts.
Philadelphia, 1835. 34 p. 12°.
Title from Robert F. Roden, *Later American plays*,
p. 2.

David's madness. (Jewish child. New
York, 1914. f°. v. 2, no. 38, p. 2–3.) * **PBD**
Based on the episode narrated in I. Samuel, XXI:
11–14.

Drachman, Julian M. Jonathan's raid
[upon the Philistines]. Dramatization...
port. (Jewish forum, New York, 1921–22.
4°. v. 4, p. 1066–1069; v. 5, p. 109–114.) * **PBD**
Based on the incident narrated in I. Samuel, ch. 14.

Ehrmann, Max. David and Bathsheba. [In
three acts.] (The Drama. Washington, 1917.
8°. no. 28, p. 485–569.) **NAFA**
"Max Ehrmann [an appreciation]," by Vandervoort
Sloan, *ibid.*, p. 485–491.

Old Testament Plays — I. and II. Samuel,
continued

David, continued

Evans, Florence (Wilkinson). David of
Bethlehem. ₁A play in five acts.₁ (In her:
Two plays of Israel. New York, 1904. 12°.
p. 1–202.)   * **PSQ**
Characters: David, Saul, Jonathan, etc.

Ewing, Thomas. Jonathan; a tragedy ₁in
five acts, in verse and prose₁. New York and
London: Funk & Wagnalls Company, 1902.
148 p. 12°.   * **PSQ**
Reprinted in G. A. Kohut, *A Hebrew anthology,*
Cincinnati, 1913, v. 2, p. 817–853, * PSO.

Fowle, William Bentley. David and
Goliath. (In his: The hundred dialogues.
New York, 1861. 12°. p. 134–135.)   **MZB**

——— Nathan and David. (In his: The hundred dialogues. New York, 1861. 12°.
p. 206–208.)   **MZB**

Freeman, John. Prince Absalom. ₁A dra-
matic poem.₁ London: Macmillan and Co.,
Limited, 1925. vii, 47(1) p. 8°.   **NCR**
In verse.
Reviewed by Francis Bickley in *The Bookman,* Lon-
don, 1925, v. 69, p. 185–186, †* *GDD,* and in *The
Times literary supplement,* London, Dec. 31, 1925,
p. 906, *NAA.*

Gilbert, Robert Warren. Amnon and
Tamar. ₁A dialogue.₁ (In his: Golden rod and
lilies. Boston, 1908. 8°. p. 155–160.) **NBI**

Githens, Harry W. A giant story. ₁In two
scenes.₁ (In his: Dramatized stories from the
Old Testament. Cincinnati ₁cop. 1927₁. 12°.
p. 131–137.)   **NASH**
David and Goliath.

——— The shepherd king. ₁In four scenes.₁
(In his: Dramatized stories from the Old
Testament. Cincinnati ₁cop. 1927₁. 12°.
p. 121–130.)   **NASH**
David and Saul.

Grossman, Samuel S. The shepherd and
the prince. A play within a play in one act.
(The Ark. Cincinnati, 1914. 8°. v. 4, p. 689–
697.)   * **PBD**
David and Jonathan are the main characters.
Reproduced, under title of "The judgment of the
shepherd," in his *Holiday and other plays for Jewish
children,* ₁no. 6₁, *NASH.*

Hale, Harris G., and NEWTON M. HALL.
...David the King. Arranged by Harris G.
Hale and Newton M. Hall. Boston: The
Pilgrim Press ₁cop. 1906₁. iv, 21 p. 12°.
(Biblical dramas. ₁no. 5.₁)

———... The story of David and Jonathan.
Arranged by Harris G. Hale and Newton M.
Hall. Boston: The Pilgrim Press, 1906. iv,
23 p. 12°. (Biblical dramas. ₁no. 6.₁)
                                NBL (Biblical)

Hamilton, Mrs. C. L. David. ₁A sacred
drama in three acts, by Mrs. C. L. Hamilton.₁
Hartford: Church Missions Publishing Co.
₁1914.₁ 40 p. 12°. (Soldiers and servant series. no. 46.)   **NBL p.v.220**

Heaton, Augustus George. David and
Abigail. A writing in five parts. From ıst
Samuel; ch. xxv. illus. (In his: The heart of
David the psalmist king. Washington, D. C.,
1900. 8°. p. 171–253.)   **NBM**

——— David and Abishag. From ı Kings,
ch. 1st and 2nd, and ı Chronicles, ch. xx to
xxix. illus. (In his: The heart of David the
psalmist king. Washington, D. C., 1900. 8°.
p. 345–389.)   **NBM**

——— David and Bathsheba. A writing in
five parts. From ıı Samuel, xı–xıı. illus. (In
his: The heart of David the psalmist king.
Washington, D. C., 1900. 8°. p. 255–344.)
                                      NBM

——— David and Michal. A writing in five
parts. From 1st Samuel; xvı–xvııı chs. illus.
(In his: The heart of David the psalmist
king. Washington, D. C., 1900. 8°. p. 13–
169.)   **NBM**

Hillhouse, James Abraham. Hadad, a dra-
matic poem. New York: E. Bliss & E.
White, 1825. x p., 1 l., (1)14–208 p. 8°.
                                     NBHD
Hadad is a Syrian king, contemporary of David,
according to the poem.
Reprinted in his *Dramas, discourses and other pieces,*
Boston, 1839, v. 1, p. 87–217, *NBM.* Selections are
printed in W. C. Bryant, *Selections from the American
poets,* New York, 1840, p. 44–49, *NBH;* in G. B.
Cheever, *The American common-place book of poetry,*
Boston, 1831, p. 22–25, 72–76, 152–156, 340–341, *NBM,*
and in G. A. Kohut, *A Hebrew anthology,* Cincinnati,
1913, v. 2, p. 891–896, * PSO. The Library also has
other editions of both Bryant and Cheever.
Reviewed in *Christian examiner,* Boston, 1825, v. 2,
p. 301–307, * *DA; New York review and Athenaeum
magazine,* New York, 1825, v. 1, p. 1–13, * *DA;* in
United States literary gazette, Boston, 1825, v. 2, p. 96–
103, * *DA;* and, with numerous extracts, in *North
American review,* Boston, 1826, v. 22, p. 13–27, * *DA.*

——— Scena quarta dell atto quinto di Adad,
poema dramatico... Tradato in verso ita-
liano de L. Da Ponte. New York: Gray e
Bunce, 1825.
Title from Wegelin.

Hobbs, Mabel, and HELEN MILES. David
and Jonathan. (In their: Six Bible plays.
New York ₁cop. 1924₁. 8°. p. 95–121.) **NASH**
In four scenes.

Kimball, Rosamond. David and Jonathan.
₁A play in four parts.₁ (In her: The wooing
of Rebekah, and other Bible plays. New
York, 1925. 8°. p. 137–186.)   **ZICS**

Kinsolving, Sally (Bruce). David and
Bath-Sheba. ₁In one act.₁ (In her: David
and Bath-Sheba, and other poems. Balti-
more, 1922. 12°. p. 1–23.)
The other characters in the play are Uriah, Joab, and
Nathan, the prophet.

Old Testament Plays — I. and II. Samuel,
continued

David, continued

Kōri, Torahiko. Absalom. A tragedy in three acts and a prologue. (In his: Absalom, and other plays and poems. London, 1920. 12°. p. 11–69.) *** OSH**
Translated from the Japanese by the author, with the assistance of H. M. Sainsbury.

Lawrence, David Herbert. David, a play by D. H. Lawrence. London: M. Secker ₁1926₁. 128 p. 8°. **NCR**
The play is in 16 scenes. Among the characters are Merab and Michal, daughters of Saul, Jonathan, Abner, Samuel, and Agag, king of Amalek.
Reviewed by Bonamy Dobrée in *The Nation and the Athenæum,* London, 1926, v. 39, p. 103–104, * *DA;* by Percy A. Hutchison in *New York Times Book review,* New York, Dec. 26, 1926, p. 7, † *NAA;* and in *The Times literary supplement,* London, March 25, 1926, p. 232, † *NAA.*
Presented by the Incorporated Stage Society at the Regent Theatre, London, May 22, 1927. Reviewed in the *Spectator,* London, 1927, v. 138, p. 939–940, * *DA,* and in *Jewish chronicle,* May 27, 1927, p. 34, * *PBE.*

—— —— London: Martin Secker, 1930. 127(1) p. 12°. (New Adelphi library. no. 55.)

Levinger, Elma C. Ehrlich. In the night watches. (The Jewish child. New York, 1914. f°. v. 2, no. 39, p. 1–2.) *** PBD**
The characters are King David and his harpist, Judah, during the reign of David in Jerusalem.

—— The kings of Israel. (A pageant based on the stories of the first three kings of Israel.) ₁In eight scenes.₁ (In her: Entertaining programs for the assembly. Cincinnati ₁cop. 1930₁. 8°. p. 142–149.) *** PSY**

—— The precious water. ₁In one scene.₁ A story of David and his mighty men. (The Jewish child. New York, 1913. f°. v. 1, no. 24, p. 3.) *** PBD**
Reprinted in her *Entertaining programs for the assembly,* Cincinnati ₁cop. 1930₁, p. 149–154, * *PSY.*
Based on the episode narrated in II. Samuel, XXIII: 15–17 and I. Chronicles, XI: 17–19.

Lobingier, Elizabeth Erwin (Miller). David and Goliath. (In her: The dramatization of Bible stories. Chicago ₁cop. 1919₁. 12°. p. 44–51.) *** YIR**
In three scenes.

Lubicz-Milosz, O. W. de. Mephiboseth. A mystery in three scenes with an epilogue. Translated from the French by Edward J. O'Brien. (The Stratford journal. Boston, 1916. 8°. v. 1, no. 2, Christmas, 1916, p. 40–80.) *** DA**
The scene is laid at Jerusalem.
A note on mystery plays, by the translator, p. 37–39.

Lyndsay, David. Rizpah. (In his: Dramas of the ancient world. Edinburgh, 1822. 8°. p. 101–123.)

Manley, William Ford. Courage. (In his: Bible dramas. New York ₁cop. 1928₁. 8°. p. 131–146.) **NBM**
In four scenes.
David and Goliath.

Michal, Saul's daughter. A romance. ₁A dramatic poem.₁ By Lydia Jane ₁pseud.₁. (Southern literary messenger. Richmond, 1840. 4°. v. 6, p. 320–324.) *** DA**

Moore, Thomas Sturge. Absalom; a chronicle play in three acts. London: At the sign of the Unicorn, 1903. 2 p.l., xci p. 12°. *** KP (Unicorn)**
Colophon: Here ends Absalom, a chronicle play, printed by Strangeways & Sons, Tower Street Cambridge Circus, for The Unicorn Press, Ltd., VII Cecil Court, St. Martin's Lane, London, W. C., MDCCCCIII.

Morax, René. King David, a play in two parts. Taken from the Bible by René Morax; translated by Dennis Arundell. Cambridge: At the University Press, 1929. xii, 132 p. 16°. **NKM p.v.**
"First performed at the Théâtre du Jorat, Mezières, on June 11, 1921... This translation has been made for a performance in Cambridge, by the University Musical Society, on May 10, 1929."

More, Hannah. David and Goliath; a sacred drama ₁in five parts₁. (In her: Sacred dramas. Philadelphia, 1787. 24°. p. 38–88.) *** KD**
The subject taken from the 17th chapter of the first book of Samuel.
Reprinted in G. A. Kohut, *A Hebrew anthology,* Cincinnati, 1913, v. 2, p. 795–816, * *PSO.*
A selection is printed in Caleb Bingham, *Columbia orator,* Boston, 1799, 2. ed., p. 278–281, * *KD,* and in John W. S. Hows, *Junior ladies' reader,* Philadelphia, 1861, p. 127–129, *NANV.*

Morland, Henry. The story of David; a dramatic poem. (In his: Restoration of Cain. London, 1916. 12°. p. 41–60.) **NCR**
David on the night succeeding his confession to the prophet Nathan.

A 'Mystery play' in the Black Country. (Chambers's journal. London and Edinburgh, 1895. 8°. v. ₁72₁, p. 401–403.) * **DA**
Contains the scenario of the *Sacred drama of Absalom,* in eleven scenes, performed near Birmingham, England.
Reprinted in *Littell's Living age,* Boston, 1895, v. 206, p. 251–254, * *DA.*

Parsons, Margaret. David, the shepherd boy. ₁In one act.₁ (In her: Ten stirring Bible plays. Franklin, Ohio, cop. 1927. 12°. p. 21–25.)
Reprinted from *John Martin's book,* "The child's magazine."

Peele, George. The love of King David and fair Bethsabe. 1599. ₁Edited by W. W. Greg. London:₁ Malone Society, 1912. ix p., 30 l., 3 facsims. 8°. (Malone Society. Reprints.) **NCO (Malone)**
Contains facsimile of original title-page: The love of King David and fair Bethsabe. With the tragedie of Absolon... London: Printed by Adam Islip, 1599.
Previously printed in various editions of his works as follows: London, 1828, ed. by Dyce, v. 1, p. 249–326, *NCP;* London, 1829, ed. by Dyce, 2. ed., p. 1–80, *NCP; Plays and poems,* London, 1887, ed. by Morley, p. 79–167, *NCL;* London, 1888, ed. by Bullen, v. 2, p. 1–86, *NCP;* and in *Dramatic and poetical works of Robert Greene and George Peele,* London, 1861, ed. by Dyce, p. 459–486, *NCP (Greene).*
Also printed in Thomas Hawkins, editor, *The origin of the English drama,* Oxford, 1773, v. 2, p. 123–193,

Old Testament Plays — I. and II. Samuel,
continued

David, continued

Peele, George. The Love of King David,
continued

*NCO; J. S. Keltie, editor, The works of the British
dramatists, Edinburgh, 1870, p. 59–75, NCO; A. H.
Thorndike, editor, The minor Elizabethan drama, London, New York [1910], v. 1, p. 125–182, NCO; and in
J. M. Manly, editor, Specimens of the pre-Shaksperean
drama, Boston, 1897, v. 2, p. 419–486, NCO.*
    Short extracts printed in Charles Lamb, *Specimens
of English dramatic poets, who lived about the time of
Shakespeare*, London, 1808, p. 13–15, * KL. Also in
the edition edited by Israel Gollancz, London, 1893,
v. 1, p. 60–65, 295.

    BULAND, Mable. ₁The presentation of time
in George Peele's David and Bethsabe.₁ (In
her: The presentation of time in the Elizabethan drama. New York, 1912. 8°. p. 229–
232.)   **NCOD**

    BURBAGE. ₁A letter tracing the resemblance
of the invocation of M. G. Lewis' play, Al-
fonso, to that in Peele's David and Bathseba.₁
(Monthly mirror. London, 1802. 8°. v. 13,
p. 266–267.)   ***DA**

    DANNENBERG, Max. Die Verwendung des
biblischen Stoffes von David und Bathseba
im englischen Drama. (G. Peele: David and
Bethsabe; Ch. W. Wynne: David and Bathshua; St. Phillips: The sin of David.) Königsberg i. Pr.: Hartung, 1905. 2 p.l., 70 p.,
1 l. 8°.   **NCO p.v.308, no.8**
    "The situations in the play are suggestive of Eliza-
beth and Leicester as David and Bathsheba, Uriah as
Leicester's first wife, and Absalom as Mary, Queen
of Scots." — *Prof. Ward, quoting Fleay.*

    SAMPLEY, Arthur M. The version of the
Bible used by Peele in the composition of
David and Bethsabe. (University of Texas.
Studies in English. Austin, Tex., 1928. 8°.
no. 8, p. 79–87.)   **NABM (Texas)**
    "Peele made use of the Bishops' Bible," 1568.

Pinski, David. Abigail; in one act. (In his:
King David and his wives. New York, 1923.
12°. p. 43–96.)   ***PTP**
    From I. Samuel, ch. 25.
    First appeared in Isaac Goldberg, translator, *Six
plays of the Yiddish theatre*, Boston [1916], p. 5–49,
* PTP.
    Presented at the David Lewis Theatre, Liverpool,
by the University Jewish Students' Society, May 19,
1927, with Miss S. Applebaum as Abigail and A.
Haselton as David.
    For a notice of the presentation see *Jewish chronicle*,
London, May 27, 1927, p. 35, * PBE.

    —— Abishag. ₁In one act.₁ (In his: King
David and his wives. New York, 1923. 12°.
p. 153–186.)   ***PTP**
    From I. Kings, ch. 1.

    —— Bathsheba. ₁In one act.₁ (In his: King
David and his wives. New York, 1923. 12°.
p. 97–126.)   ***PTP**
    From II. Samuel, ch. 11.

    —— In the harem. ₁In one act.₁ (In his:
King David and his wives. New York, 1923.
12°. p. 127–151.)   ***PTP**
    From II. Samuel, xx:3
    First written in 1914.

    —— Michal. ₁A play in one act.₁ (In his:
King David and his wives. New York, 1923.
12°. p. 7–41.)   ***PTP**
    From I. Samuel, ch. 17 and 18.
    Reprinted from the *Stratford journal*, Boston, 1918,
v. 2, April, 1918, p. 25–35, * DA.

Rice, Cale Young. David, a tragedy ₁in
four acts and in verse₁. New York: McClure,
Phillips & Co., 1904. 1 p.l., vi, 116 p. 4°.
                                           NBM

    —— —— New York: The McClure Co.,
1909. 1 p.l., 128 p. 12°.
    Reprinted in his *Plays and lyrics*, London, 1906,
p. 233–317, NBI; *Collected plays and poems*, New
York, 1915, v. 2, p. 519–650, NBI; and *Selected plays
and poems*, New York [1926], p. 201–270, NBI.

Sampter, Jessie Ethel. The story of David;
a dramatic sketch in seven scenes for out-of-
door performance. New York: Dept. of Education, Zionist Organization of America, cop.
1920. 12 p. 4°.
    Typewritten.

Savage-Armstrong, George Francis. The
tragedy of Israel. Part II. King David, in
five acts. London: Longmans, Green and
Co., 1892. 275, 19 p. 12°.

Sevringhaus, Grace. The kingmaker's
choice. ₁In one scene.₁ (Church school. New
York, 1923. 4°. v. 4, p. 468–469, 480.)
    The choosing of David.

    —— —— Music by Lyman R. Bayard.
Los Angeles: Pageant Publishers, cop. 1927.
14 p. illus. music. 8°.

Sheppard, William Ffranck. Urijah the
Hittite; a tragedy ₁in four acts₁ by W.
ffranck. Lincoln ₁Eng.₁: J. W. Ruddock &
Sons, 1927. 81(1) p. 12°.   **NCO p.v.549, no.1**
    "He [David] was...a great sinner. The chief theme
now treated is the doom which followed the great fall."

Soble, Mae Stein. The might of right. A
dramatization in six scenes. (In her: Bible
plays for children. New York, 1919. 12°.
p. 109–136.)   **NASH**
    David and Goliath.

Stillingfleet, Benjamin. David and Bathsheba. (In his: Joseph. ₁London? 1765?₁ 8°.)
    Title from British Museum Catalogue.

Sullivan, Vincent Philamon. Son of Bathsheba, the original bathing beauty...supple-
mented with Ballads of us fellers no. 2 and
seven illustrations. New York: Trend Publishing Co., cop. 1920. 1, ₁1₁, 2–67 p. illus.
16°.   **NBL p.v.74, no.6**

Untermeyer, Louis. Goliath and David ₁a
poetic dialogue₁. (In his: Burning bush. New
York, 1928. 8°. p. 99–101.)   **NBI**

Voltaire, François Marie Arouet de. Saul:
a drama, in five acts. Translated from the
French of M. de Voltaire, by Oliver Martext

THE BIBLE IN ENGLISH DRAMA

Old Testament Plays — I. and II. Samuel, continued

David, continued

₁pseud.₁ of Arden. London: J. Carlile, 1820. 28 p. 8°.   **ZEY p.v.2**

"The whole passes within the space of two or three generations, in order to render the action more tragic by the number of deaths, in conformity to the true Jewish spirit." — *From the note by the translator, p. 3.*

Despite its name, the play concerns itself largely with King David and his love affairs. David is pictured as a most despicable character; cruel, rapacious, treacherous and licentious.

By means of anachronism, the author attributes to David the Jew (the reference is always to Jews, not Israelites) all characteristics, which popular anti-Jewish prejudice, in Voltaire's time, would ascribe to the contemporary Jews. Saul has a minor rôle in the play.

Waters, Howard. A tragedy-drama entitled Jonathan and David, in four acts. ₁By Howard Waters.₁ ₁Stockwell, Ind., 1902.₁ 61 p. 24°.

Title from Library of Congress.

Whiffen, Edwin T. Tamar ₁a dramatic poem₁. (In his: Tamar, and other poems. New York, 1913. 12°. p. 265–312.)

Based on the episode of Tamar and Amnon. *Cf.* II. Samuel, ch. 13.

Whiting, Isabel Kimball. The anointing of David by Samuel. ₁In one scene.₁ (In her: Dramatic services of worship. Boston, 1925. 8°. p. 1–18.)   **NBM**

Whitney, Mary Ellen. David and Goliath. ₁A play in five scenes.₁ (In her: Bible plays and how to produce them. New York ₁cop. 1927₁. 12°. p. 27–33.)

Wise, Joseph. The coronation of David. ₁A drama in two acts and in verse.₁ Lewes, 1766. 8°.

Title from British Museum Catalogue.

Reviewed in *Monthly review,* London, 1766, v. 34, p. 406, *NAA.*

Young, Andrew John. Rizpah; a dramatic poem. (In his: The adversary. London, 1923. 12°. p. 53–80.)   **NCM**

Based on II. Samuel, ch. 21.

I. AND II. KINGS

Ashton, Winifred. Naboth's vineyard; a stage piece, by Clemence Dane ₁pseud.₁. London: W. Heinemann, Ltd., 1925. 4 p.l., 90 p. 8°.   **NCR**

Based on I. Kings, ch. 21.

—— New York: Macmillan Co., 1926. 4 p.l., 90 p. 8°.

Reviewed by E. V. Odle in *The Bookman,* London, 1926, v. 69, p. 288, †* *GDD.*

Boyd, Charles Arthur. Micaiah the truthful; a Biblical drama in four scenes. (In his: Worship in drama. Philadelphia ₁cop. 1924₁. 8°. p. 51–57.)   **NAFM**

Carvalho, Naomi Nunes. The poet as historian (The Moabite stone). ₁A dialogue between the king of Moab and a scribe.₁ (In her: Vox humana. London, 1912. 12°. p. 41–45.)   **NRD p.v.9**

The Moabite stone dates from the time of Omri.

Collett, John. Naboth, a sacred drama ₁in five scenes₁. (In his: Sacred dramas. Evesham, 1805. 12°. p. 69–116.)

Harnwell, Mrs. Anna Jane (Wilcox). The sin of Ahab, a drama in one act, with an introduction by Clara Fitch. New York: George H. Doran Company ₁cop. 1922₁. vii p., 2 l., 13–28 p. 8°. (The Drama League series.)   **NBL p.v.86, no.6**

Scene: Samaria, capital of Israel, the latter part of the tenth century B. C.

Krass, Nathan. The lost scroll. New York: Bloch Pub. Co., 1919. 6 p. 12°.

In the time of King Josiah

Leach, William H. Naboth's vineyard. ₁In three acts.₁ (In: Church plays and entertainments for young people. Franklin, Ohio, cop. 1924. 12°. p. 19–26.)

Manley, William Ford. Naboth's vineyard. ₁In four scenes.₁ (In his: A second book of Bible dramas. New York ₁cop. 1930₁. 8°. p. 189–206.)   **NBM**

Parsons, Margaret. The widow's cruse. ₁In one scene.₁ (In her: Ten stirring Bible plays. Franklin, Ohio, cop. 1927. 12°. p. 58–61.)

II. Kings, ch. 4.

Reprinted from *John Martin's book, The child's magazine.*

Raine, James Watt. Ahaz casts away the heritage. ₁In two scenes.₁ (In his: Bible dramatics. New York & London ₁cop. 1927₁. 12°. p. 171–200.)

Based on II. Kings, XVI: 1–9, II. Chronicles, XXVII and XXVIII, and Isaiah VII and VIII.

—— The king forgets. ₁In one scene.₁ (In his: Bible dramatics. New York & London ₁cop. 1927₁. 12°. p. 152–168.)

Based on II. Kings XII. In the reign of Jehoash, or Joash, king of Judah, 878–841 B. C.

—— Naboth's vineyard. ₁In one scene.₁ (In his: Bible dramatics. New York & London ₁cop. 1927₁. 12°. p. 44–57.)

Sadler, Anthony. The Subjects joy for the King's restoration, cheerfully made known in a sacred masque ₁in verse₁. By the author of Inquisitio Anglicana ₁Anthony Sadler₁. London, 1660. 4°.

Title from British Museum Catalogue.

The plot of this piece is founded on I. Kings, xi:12 and II. Chronicles, xlii. Scene: Bethel in Canaan. The character of Charles is borrowed from that of Jeroboam. See W. C. Hazlitt, *Manual,* p. 220.

Old Testament Plays — I. and II. Kings,
continued

SOLOMON

Miracle Play

The **16 pageant** of Salomon. ₁370 lines.₁
(In: C. F. Brown, editor, Stonyhurst pag-
eants. Göttingen, 1920. 8°. p. 224–235.)
NAFM

Modern Plays

Benton, Rita. The judgment of Solomon
(longer version). (In her: Shorter Bible
plays. New York ₁cop. 1922₁. 8°. p. 99–114.)
Place: Gibeon.   **NASH**

—— The judgment of Solomon (shorter
version). (In her: Shorter Bible plays. New
York ₁cop. 1922₁. 8°. p. 116–121.)   **NASH**

Bottomley, Gordon. Solomon's parents ₁a
dramatic poem₁. (In his: Poems of thirty
years. London, 1925. 8°. p. 87–93.) **NCM**
Chief speaker, Bathsheba. Poems dated 1906.

Carman, Bliss, and MARY PERRY KING.
Balkis; tenth century B. C. ₁A dramatic poem.₁
illus. (In their: Daughters of dawn. New
York, 1913. 12°. p. 25–33.)   **NCM**

Cox, Robert. King Solomon's wisdom.
₁An interlude.₁ ₁By Robert Cox.₁ (In: Francis
Kirkman, editor, Wits; or, Sport upon sport.
London, 166–?. 8° in fours. part 2. ₁2₁ p.)
NCO
Deals with the episode of the two mothers.

Githens, Harry W. A wise king (Solomon). ₁In five scenes.₁ (In his: Dramatized
stories from the Old Testament. Cincinnati
₁cop. 1927₁. 12°. p. 138–145.)   **NASH**

Hale, Harris G., and N. M. HALL. ...The
story of Solomon. Arranged by Harris G.
Hale and Newton M. Hall. Boston: The
Pilgrim Press, 1906. iv, 26 p. 12°. (Biblical
dramas. ₁no. 7.₁)   **NBL (Biblical)**

Hanssen, C. J. The Queen of Sheba; a
Biblical drama in three acts for young ladies.
Chicago and New York: The Dramatic Pub.
Co., cop. 1899. 24 p. 16°. (Sergel's acting
drama.)
Scene: First and third act, Jerusalem; second act,
the Land of Sheba.

Joseph, Leon Edward. The widow of
Naphtali; a Masonic play in one act. New
York: S. French, cop. 1927. 19 p. 12°.
(French's international copyrighted...ed. of
the works of the best authors. no. 580.)
NBL p.v.173, no.8
Time: the eleventh year of the reign of King
Solomon.
Repr.: National Masonic Research Society. The
Builder.

Karadja, Mary Louise (Smith), princess.
King Solomon; a mystic drama in five acts
and an epilogue, with commentaries... London: K. Paul, Trench, Trübner & Co., Ltd.,
1912. 4 p.l., (1)12–242 p. 12°.   **＊PSQ**
"The drama represents synthesis; the commentaries,
analysis.
"The Royal Arch uniting the two columns is Good-
will: the Light emerging from the Spiritual Temple
herein erected is generated through my intense desire
to serve God and my fellow-creatures." — *p. 87.*

Klopstock, Friedrich Gottlieb. Solomon:
a sacred drama ₁in five acts and in verse₁.
Translated from the German...by R. Huish.
London, 1809. 8°.
Title from British Museum Catalogue.
Reviewed in *British critic,* London, 1811, v. 36,
p. 299, ＊ *DA,* and in *Monthly review,* London, 1811,
series 2, v. 64, p. 319–321, *NAA.*

Lindsay, Nicholas Vachel. King Solomon
and the Queen of Sheba. A poem game. (In
his: The Chinese nightingale, and other
poems. New York, 1922. 12°. p. 112–123.)
NBI
Reprinted in his *Collected poems,* New York, 1923,
p. 167–174, *NBI.*

Manley, William Ford. Number one on
the docket. ₁In three scenes.₁ (In his: A second book of Bible dramas. New York ₁cop.
1930₁. 8°. p. 153–168.)   **NBM**
The story of Solomon and the two mothers, each
claiming to be the mother of the same child.

Mary Agnes, Sister. The Queen of Sheba,
a Biblical drama ₁in three acts₁. By S. M. A.
Winnipeg, Man.: St. Mary's Academy, cop.
1915. 32 p. 12°.

Paul, Adolf Georg. The language of the
birds; a comedy by Adolf Paul. Only authorized English translation ₁from the
Swedish₁ by Arthur Travers-Borgstroem.
Scenic music by Jean Sibelius, introduction
by Henry C. Shelley. London: A. Montgomery, 1922. 71 p. illus. 16°.   **NIR**
Without music.
"The germ of the story he derived from Biblical
history... The tragic case of the man who is lacking
in self-mastery" is the moral of the play. Produced
at the Royal Burg Theatre, Vienna, Nov. 29, 1911.

Russell, E. Phillips. A parcel for King
Solomon. ₁In one scene.₁ (New masses. New
York, 1930. 4°. v. 5, May, p. 10–12.) **＊DA**

Ruthenburg, Grace Hutchinson. Solomon.
₁One-act play.₁ (Poet lore. Boston, 1925. 8°.
v. 36, p. 600–609.)   **＊DA**
The characters of the play are Solomon, the Shulam-
mite maid, an elder, three priests, and a slave. Centered
around the episode of the division of Israel into two
kingdoms in the latter part of the reign of Solomon.

Savage-Armstrong, George Francis. The
tragedy of Israel. Part 3: King Solomon.
London: Longmans, Green, Reader and
Dyer, 1876. 3 p.l., 13, (1)4–240 p., 1 l. 16°.
NCR

—— —— London: Longmans, Green and
Co., 1892. 240, 19 p. 12°.
Reviewed in *Jewish chronicle,* London, July 21, 1876,
p. 251.

Old Testament Plays — I. and II. Kings, cont'd

Solomon, continued

Seavey, Martha M. Judith of Tyre, a drama in three acts. New York: J. T. White & Co. ₍cop. 1924.₎ 120 p., 1 l. 12°. **NBM**
Solon, merchant prince of Tyre, and his daughter Judith representing the Israelites in struggle with the Phoenician sun-god Melkart.

Symons, Arthur. The lover of the Queen of Sheba. ₍A dramatic poem.₎ (Dome. London, 1899. sq. 8°. new series, v. 5, p. 5–12.) ***DA**
Reprinted in his *Images of good and evil*, London, 1899, p. 30–41, *NCM*.

Whitney, Mary Ellen. The crowning of Solomon. ₍A play in four scenes.₎ (In her: Bible plays and how to produce them. New York ₍cop. 1927₎. 12°. p. 34–41.)

ELIJAH AND ELISHA

Miracle Play

The **17 pageant** ₍of Elias₎. ₍815 lines.₎ (In: C. F. Brown, editor, Stonyhurst pageants. Göttingen, 1920. 8°. p. 236–262.) **NAFM**
No title is given to this pageant in the ms.

Modern Plays

Boyd, Charles Arthur. Elijah the uncompromising. ₍In five acts.₎ (In his: Worship in drama. Philadelphia ₍cop. 1924₎. 8°. p. 58–73.) **NAFM**

Davidson, Robert. Elijah, a sacred drama. (In his: Elijah, and other poems. New York, 1860. 12°. p. 7–101.) ***PSQ**
Reprinted in G. A. Kohut, *A Hebrew anthology*, Cincinnati, 1913, v. 2, p. 897–921, ** PSO.*

Dunning, Luella M. Elisha, the prophet of God. ₍In one act.₎ (In: Eleven short Biblical plays. New York, 1929. 12°. p. 71–88.) **NBL p.v.216**

Ellet, Mrs. Elizabeth Fries (Lummis). The trial by fire; a fragment. (Godey's lady's book. Philadelphia, 1842. 8°. v. 24, p. 41–43.) ***DA**
Based on I. Kings, ch. 18.

Genl's, Stéphanie Félicité Ducrest de St. Aubin, comtesse de. The widow of Sarepta. A sacred drama in one act. (In her: Sacred dramas. London, 1786. 8°. p. 283–312.) **NKO**

Hale, Harris G., and N. M. HALL. ...The story of Elijah. Arranged by Harris G. Hale and Newton M. Hall. Boston: The Pilgrim Press, 1907. iv, 19 p. 12°. (Biblical dramas. ₍no. 9.₎)

Hirschbein, Perez. Elijah the prophet. ₍A comedy in 1 act.₎ Translated by Elias Lieberman. (East and West. New York, 1915. 4°. v. 1, p. 261–266.) ***PBD**
Elijah in the rôle of a stranger and guest at a Sabbath meal in the home of a poor country Jew.

Kimball, Rosamond. Elijah and Elisha. ₍A play in three parts.₎ (In her: The wooing of Rebekah, and other Bible plays. New York, 1925. 8°. p. 187–218.) **ZICS**

Manley, William Ford. Naaman's cloak. ₍In six scenes.₎ (In his: A second book of Bible dramas. New York ₍cop. 1930₎. 8°. p. 136–152.) **NBM**
Based on II. Kings v: 20–27.

Murray, E. Elijah and the rain. ₍In three acts.₎ (In: Sunday School and church-entertainments. Philadelphia, 1914. 12°. p. 35–43.) **ZICS**

Osgood, Phillips Endecott. Elijah, an oratorio (part one). The music by Felix Mendelssohn. A dramatized adaptation in the form of a sung miracle play ₍in three episodes₎. illus. (In his: Old-time church drama adapted. New York and London, 1928. 12°. p. 243–270.) **NAFM**

Pettey, Emmy. The gift of Jehovah. ₍In one act.₎ (In: Eleven short Biblical plays. New York, 1929. 12°. p. 129–154.) **NBL p.v.216**

S., C. G. The Shunamite. ₍A dramatic poem.₎ London: William Poole ₍1883?₎. 2 p.l., 101 p. 12°.

The **Two** prophets. ₍In three scenes.₎ (In: M. W. Thomas, editor, Old Testament drama. London ₍1927₎. 12°. p. 143–153.)

NAAMAN

Miracle Play

₍The 18 pageant of Naaman.₎ ₍1136 lines.₎ (In: C. F. Brown, editor, Stonyhurst pageants. Göttingen, 1920. 8°. p. 263–302.) **NAFM**
The title is supplied from the page headings in the ms.

CRAIG, Hardin. Terentius Christianus and the Stonyhurst pageants. (Philological quarterly. Iowa City, Iowa, 1923. 8°. v. 2, no. 1, p. 56–62.) **NAA**
"The pageant of Naaman [in the Stonyhurst pageants] is a translation of the play *Naaman* in Terentius Christianus of Cornelius Schonaeus. It is by no means an accurate or faithful translation, but it is unmistakable."

Modern Plays

Boxer, James. Naaman the Syrian. ₍In four acts.₎ (In his: Sacred dramas. Boston, 1875. 12°. p. 9–74.)

Cole, Edna Earle. Naaman and Gehazi. ₍In three acts.₎ (In her: The good Samaritan, and other Bible stories dramatized. Boston ₍cop. 1915₎. 12°. p. 109–115.)
Based on II. Kings v: 9–27.

Donovan, Alice V. A little maid of Israel: a play ₍in three scenes₎. (International journal of religious education. Mount Morris, Ill., 1927. 4°. v. 3, July/Aug., 1927, p. 31–33.)

Old Testament Plays — I. and II. Kings,
continued

Naaman, continued

Githens, Harry W. A captive maid. [In
five scenes.] (In his: Dramatized stories
from the Old Testament. Cincinnati [cop.
1927]. 12°. p. 146–153.) **NASH**
Naaman and the captive Israelite maid.

Hitchcock, Mary S. The slave maid of
Israel; a Biblical drama in three acts...
Chicago: T. S. Denison & Co. [cop. 1930.]
85 p. 12°.
Twelve men and eleven women. Time: 894 B. c.,
at the palace of Naaman, near Damascus in Syria.
Based on II. Kings v.

Hobbs, Mabel, and HELEN MILES. The
healing of Naaman. (In their: Six Bible
plays. New York [cop. 1924]. 8°. p. 75–93.)
In three scenes. **NASH**

Leach, William H. Miriam, the captive
maiden. [In two acts.] (In: Church plays and
entertainments for young people. Franklin,
Ohio, cop. 1924. 12°. p. 11–18.)
Based on II. Kings, ch. 5.

Naaman's quest. [In four acts.] By a class
of girls. (In: T. W. Galloway, The dramatic
instinct in religious education. Boston [cop.
1922]. 12°. p. 79–93.)

Raine, James Watt. [Naaman the Syrian.]
[In three scenes.] (In his: Bible dramatics.
New York & London [cop. 1927]. 12°.
p. 137–151.)
Based on II. Kings v.

Rea, John. A captive maiden in Damascus.
San Francisco: Whitaker & Ray-Wiggin
Co., 1915. 32 p. 12°. **NBL p.v.34, no.6**

Russell, Mary M. In quest of a great
treasure. [In three scenes.] (In her: Dramatized Bible stories for young people. New
York [1921]. 12°. p. 22–28.)

Van Dyke, Henry. The house of Rimmon;
a drama in four acts... New York: C. Scribner's Sons, 1908. 5 p.l., 5–121 p., 1 pl. 12°.
* PSQ
First printed in *Scribner's magazine,* New York,
1908, v. 44, p. 129–147, 283–300, * DA. Reprinted in
his *Poems,* New York, 1920, p. 473–548, NBI.
Reviewed by Sidney A. Farbish in *Jewish exponent,*
Philadelphia, v. 47, no. 23, p. 9, * PBD.
Produced as a copyright performance at the Bays-
water Bijou Theatre, London, March 16, 1908.

Whitney, Mary Ellen. Naaman the leper.
[A play in five scenes.] (In her: Bible plays
and how to produce them. New York [cop.
1927]. 12°. p. 42–49.)

Willis, Mrs. L. M. Naaman, the leper. [In
four scenes.] (In: Sunday school and church
entertainments. Philadelphia, 1914. 12°.
p. 88–93.) **ZICS**

JEZEBEL

Barbor, Herbert Reginald. Jezebel; a
tragedy in three acts. London: A. Brenton
[cop. 1924]. 5 p.l., (1)8–151 p. 8°. **NCR**

Barnard, P. Mordaunt. Jezebel; a drama
[in three acts]. London: Francis Griffiths,
1904. 61 p. 12°.
Reviewed in *Academy and literature,* London, 1904,
v. 67, p. 229–230, * DA.

Bayne, Peter. The days of Jezebel; an historical drama [in five acts]. London: Strahan
& Co., 1872. xxvi p., 1 l., 212 p. 12°.
Reviewed in *Athenæum,* London, May 25, 1872,
p. 647–648, * DA, and in *Literary world,* London, 1872,
new series, v. 5, p. 297–300, * DA.

Bradley, Richard Beadon. The portion of
Jezebel. A sacred drama [in five acts and in
verse]. London, 1843. 2. ed. 8°.
Title from British Museum Catalogue.

Lally, Gwen. Jezebel; a play [in four acts].
London: A. L. Humphreys, 1918. vii, 72 p.
16°. **NCR**
" 'Jezebel' was licensed for public representation by
the Lord Chamberlain in 1912, being the first Biblical
play 'passed' by the censor in this country. A copyright
performance of 'Jezebel' was given at the Comedy
Theatre, by the courtesy of Mr. Arthur Chudleigh, in
March, 1912."

McDowall, H. M. Jezebel; a tragedy [in
three scenes]. Oxford: B. Blackwell, 1924.
30 p. 12°. **NCO p.v.511, no.3**

Masefield, John. A king's daughter; a
tragedy in verse. [In five acts.] New York:
The Macmillan Company, 1923. 4 p.l., 170 p.
12°. **NCR**

―――― ―――― London: William Heinemann,
Ltd., n.d. 4 p.l., 127 p. 12°.
Reprinted in his *Verse plays,* New York, 1925,
p. 209–313, NCR.
Reviewed in *Yale literary magazine,* New Haven,
1924, v. 89, p. 195–196, STG.
Performed at the Oxford Playhouse, May 25th and
26th, 1923, by the Hill Players. Miss Penelope Wheeler
as Jezebel, Dudley Barlow as Naboth, Leslie Davey
as Ahab.

CLARKE, George Herbert. John Masefield
and Jezebel. (Sewanee review. Sewanee,
Tenn., 1924. 8°. v. 32, p. 225–242.) *** DA**

Stockbridge, Dorothy. Jezebel; a play.
(In: Frank Shay, editor, Contemporary one-
act plays of 1921, American. Cincinnati [cop.
1922]. 8°. p. 541–569.) **NBL (Shay)**
First produced at Vassar College.

Trowbridge, William Rutherford Hayes.
Jesebel. Eine Studie im Stile Oscar Wildes.
Aus dem Englischen frei übertragen von Sil-
Vara. (Bühne und Welt. Berlin, 1909. 4°.
v. 11, p. 994–1009.) **† NGA**
The ms. of the original English has not been pub-
lished.

Welsh, Robert Gilbert. Jezebel. [A play
in one act.] (The Forum. New York, 1915.
8°. v. 53, p. 647–660.) *** DA**

Old Testament Plays — I. and II. Kings,
continued

ATHALIAH

Racine, Jean Baptiste. Athaliah, a tragedy.
Translated from the French of Monsieur
Racine, by Mr. ₁William₁ Duncombe. The
third edition, revised and corrected. London:
J. Watts, 1746. 7 p.l., 64 p., 1 pl. 12°.
Translator's dedication dated Nov., 1722.

—— Athaliah, a sacred drama, translated
₁by J. Sheppard₁. Edinburgh, 1815. 12°.
Title from British Museum Catalogue.

—— Athaliah, a tragedy... Translated...
with notes by J. C. Knight. London, 1822.
12°.
Title from British Museum Catalogue.

—— Athaliah, a sacred drama. Translated
...by C. Randolph. London, Lyme ₁printed₁,
1829. 8°.
Title from British Museum Catalogue.

—— Athaliah, a sacred drama, translated
from Racine and original poems. By...T.
Fry. London, 1841. 8°.
Title from British Museum Catalogue.

—— The death of Athaliah, a Scriptural
drama ₁in verse₁, founded on ₁or rather translated from₁ the "Athalie" of Racine: to which
are added a few fugitive pieces of sacred
poetry. By...W. Trollope... London: H.
Wix, 1844. xii, 115 p. 2. ed. 12°.
Title from British Museum Catalogue.

—— Racine's Athalie... Literally translated. By R. Mongan. ₁Dublin, 1880.₁ 54 p.
12°. (Kelly's classical keys.)
Title from British Museum Catalogue.

—— Joash and Athaliah. Scenes in the
chambers of Solomon's Temple. Translated
from Racine's...Athalie by Mrs. A. F. Foster. Edinburgh: Ballantyne, Hanson & Co.,
1880. 64 p. 8°.
Title from British Museum Catalogue.

—— Athaliah, a tragedy. 1691. ₁In five
acts.₁ (In his: Dramatic works. Translated
by R. B. Boswell. London, 1890. 8°. v. 2,
p. 327–403.)
"It is now universally acknowledged to deserve either
first or second place among Racine's masterpieces." —
The translator in the introduction.
Boswell's translation is reprinted in G. A. Kohut,
A Hebrew anthology, Cincinnati, 1913, v. 2, p. 923–
962, * *PSO.*

—— Athalie, tragédie, tirée de l'Écriture
Sainte par Jean Racine. Traduite en anglais
par F. C. de Sumichrast. Avec quatre illus-
trations. Cambridge, 1897. xxvii p., 2 l.,
189(1) p., 1 l., 1 port., 3 pl. 8°. * **PSQ**
Added t.-p. in English; French and English texts
on opposite pages.
"Printed for the Department of French, Faculty of
Arts and Sciences, of Harvard University, by the
Cooperative Printing Society of Cambridge, Mass."
"The translation has been made from the text of the

edition of 1697, the latest published during Racine's
life time" — *p. xiii.*
Performed in English in Sanders Theatre, Harvard
University, Dec. 6, 1897, by students, graduates, and
instructors of Harvard University and Radcliffe College.

—— Athalie... Translated into English
verse, by W. P. Thompson. London:
Hachette & Co., 1897. 102 p. 8°.
Title from British Museum Catalogue.
Selections are printed in *Rachel's Readings in both
French and English, first series,* New York, 1855,
NKM p.v. 18, and in Julian Hawthorne, editor, *Master-
pieces and the history of literature,* New York, 1906,
v. 5, p. 301–304, *NAB.*

FISHER, Dorothea Frances Canfield. ₁Racine's
Athalie.₁ (In her: Corneille and Racine in
England. New York, 1904. 12°. p. 249–255.)
* **R – NKC**

TROLLOPE, Henry M. Athalie. (In his: Corneille and Racine. Edinburgh, 1881. 12°.
p. 193–214.) * **R – NAC (Foreign)**
Foreign classics for English readers. Edited by Mrs.
Oliphant.

HEZEKIAH

Allen, William, warden of Dulwich College. Hezekiah, king of Judah; or, Invasion
repulsed, and peace restored: a sacred drama
of national application at this awful crisis.
Inscribed to the most noble the Marchioness
of Stafford. London, 1798. 8°.
Authorship ascribed to William Allen in Halkett &
Laing, 1928. British Museum Catalogue enters under
W., W. A.
Reviewed in *British critic,* London, 1799, v. 13, p. 74,
* *DA;* in *Monthly review,* London, 1799, series 2, v. 28,
p. 350–351, *NAA;* and in *Critical review,* London, 1799,
series 2, v. 27, p. 112–114, *NAA.* "It is poorly planned
and feebly executed."

Gairdner, William Henry Temple. King
Hezekiah; a tragical drama in a prologue and
four acts. London: Society for Promoting
Christian Knowledge ₁1923₁. x, 11–84 p. 12°.
NCR
The scene is in Jerusalem throughout, except in act
IV, scene I, where it is laid in Sennacherib's pavilion
at his camp in the plains. Time, the closing years of
the eighth century B. C.

Stead, William Force. Hezekiah. ₁A one-
act playlet.₁ (Voices. London, 1921. 8°. v. 5,
p. 41–44.)   * **DA**
Founded on II. Kings, XX: 1–6.

ISAIAH

Boyd, Charles Arthur. Isaiah the statesman. ₁In five acts.₁ (In his: Worship in
drama. Philadelphia ₁cop. 1924₁. 8°. p. 74–
92.)   **NAFM**

Carvalho, Naomi Nunes. Time, the one
and indivisible. ₁A dialogue in Jerusalem
between Isaiah and a watchman.₁ (In her:)
Vox humana. London, 1912. 12°. p. 79–84.)
NRD p.v.9

Old Testament Plays — Isaiah, continued

Glazebrook, Michael George. Deutero-Isaiah's drama of exile. ₁In a prelude and three acts.₎ (In his: Studies in the book of Isaiah. Oxford, 1910. 12°. p. 225-260.)
* YLRB

Goold, Marshall N. The quest divine. ₁A play in three acts.₎ (In: Religious dramas. New York: Century Co. ₁cop. 1926.₎ 8°. v. 2, p. 1–51.)
NAFM
Prize play in the Religious drama contest, 1925.
Time: 740 B. C. Place: Samaria. Characters: Hosea, Amos, Isaiah, Jezreel.

Kennedy, Katherine. Isaiah; prince and prophet. ₁In prologue, five episodes and epilogue.₎ London: Society for Promoting Christian Knowledge, 1924. 32 p. 12°.
NCO p.v.512, no.2

Layton, Frank George. The prophet; a play. London: C. W. Daniel, Ltd., 1922. 91 p. 12°. (Plays for a people's theatre. no. 18.)
NCO p.v.486, no.5
In six scenes.
Action is laid in Jerusalem at the time of Sennacherib's adventure against King Hezekiah.

Levinger, Elma C. Ehrlich. The plowshare or the sword. ₁In one scene.₎ (In her: Through the schoolyear; an anthology of original plays. Boston, 1925. 12°. p. 11–17.)
NAFH p.v.37
Isaiah, prophet of peace, and the nations of the world are the characters. A peace play.

Reeves, Florence. Isaiah, the prophet. A dramatization in three acts. (In: Fearless men. ₁Chicago, cop. 1923.₎ 8°. p. 29–46.)
NBF p.v.60, no.6

Whiting, Isabel Kimball. Armistice day service adapted from Isaiah ₁in one scene₎. (In her: Dramatic services of worship. Boston, 1925. 8°. p. 45–67.)
NBM

Whitman, Eleanor Wood. The drama of Isaiah. ₁In three acts.₎ Boston, Chicago: Pilgrim Press ₁cop. 1917₎. xi, 64 p. illus. 12°.
The action of the play covers the reigns of the three kings Uzziah, Ahaz, and Hezekiah.
First presented in Boston, May 17, 1916.

JEREMIAH

Hormell, Elizabeth. Jeremiah. A dramatization in two acts. (In: Fearless men. ₁Chicago, 1923.₎ 8°. p. 47–60.) **NBF p.v.60, no.6**

Leavitt, Nason W., and B. E. LEAVITT. ...Tea Tephi: a romantic and historic opera; words by Nason W. and Burton E. Leavitt (father and son). Putnam, Conn.: B. E. Leavitt, 1911. 55 p. illus. 16°.
NBL p.v.119, no.1
At head of title: Libretto only.
On cover: Supplement to Our race quarterly, Sept., 1911.
Time: 600 B. C. Jeremiah — main character.
Theme: Anglo-Israelism.

Whitman, Mrs. Eleanor Wood. Jeremiah; a drama in five acts, based upon the story of Jeremiah as found in the Bible. New York & London: The Century Co. ₁cop. 1925.₎ xvi, 125 p. illus. 12°. **NBL p.v.125, no.3**
Among the fifty-odd characters of the play are Jeremiah; Zebidah, his mother; Hamutal, his sister; Hilkiah, high-priest; Hananiah, false prophet; King Jehoiakim, and Nebuchadnezzar. Jeremiah is interpreted not as a man of sorrows, but as a brave hero.

—— Jeremiah and the Rechabites; a Bible parable in pantomime. illus. (Church school. New York, 1924. f°. v. 5, p. 163–164, 189.)
Jeremiah xxxv.

Zweig, Stefan. Jeremiah; a drama in nine scenes, translated from the author's revised German text by Eden and Cedar Paul. New York: T. Seltzer, 1922. 6 p.l., 5–336 p. 8°.
NGE
Reviewed by Marvin Lowenthal in *Menorah journal*, New York, 1923, v. 9, p. 250, * PBD.

G., I. "Jeremiah:" a drama in nine scenes. ₁A review.₎ (The Freeman. New York, 1923. f°. v. 7, p. 478.) *** DA**
"The passion of Jeremiah is a passion of pacifism... It required rare courage to write such a play between the Easter of 1915 and the Easter of 1917. It is somewhat freely adapted from the source."

ROLLAND, Romain. The cry of humanity. A review of Stephen Zweig's poetic drama "Jeremias." Translated by Amelia V. Ende. (Jewish exponent. Philadelphia, 1922. f°. v. 69, March 3, 1922, p. 1, 6.) *** PBD**

—— The voice of suffering. A review of Stefan Zweig's drama, "Jeremiah." (The American Hebrew. New York, 1922. f°. v. 111, no. 1, May 19, 1922, p. 18, 33, 38, 40, 42.) *** PBD**

EZEKIEL

Carvalho, Naomi Nunes. The choice of evil. ₁A dialogue in Babylon between Ezekiel and a sceptic.₎ (In her: Vox humana. London, 1912. 12°. p. 85–90.) **NRD p.v.9**

Glenn, Mendel G. The valley of the dried bones; a playlet ₁in one scene₎. illus. (Young Judaean. New York, 1929. 4°. v. 19, Feb., 1929, p. 6–7.) *** PBD**
Ezekiel xxxvii: 1.

HOSEA

Izachak, pseud. The marriage of Hosea, a passion play in three acts. New York: Halcyon Publishing Company, 1929. 174 p. 12°.
The action at Samaria, 735–725 B. C.

Middleton, Grace E. Hosea. A dramatization in two scenes. (In: Fearless men. ₁Chicago, cop. 1923.₎ 8°. p. 17–27.)
NBF p.v.60, no.6

Old Testament Plays — Hosea, continued

Osgood, Phillips Endecott. A sinner beloved — a morality play and pageant. Using the book of the prophet Hosea as its imaginative basis. Minneapolis, Minn., n.d. 8 l. 8°.

Time: that of Jeroboam, the son of Joash, the king of Israel.

Reprinted in *Religious dramas,* New York [cop. 1923], v. 1, p. 77–102, *NAFM,* and, in revised form, in his *The sinner beloved, and other religious plays,* New York, 1928, p. 23–73, *NAFM.*

Schoonmaker, Edwin Davies. The prophet. An interpretation of the strange life of Hosea, prophet of Israel. A scene [scene six] from an unpublished drama. (The Hue and cry. Woodstock, N. Y., 1926. 4°. v. 4, no. 10, p. 33–39.) ***DA**

AMOS

Fritchman, Stephen H. Amos. A dramatization in two scenes. (In: Fearless men. [Chicago, cop. 1923.] 8°. p. 7–16.) **NBF p.v.60, no.6**

Place: Beth-el. Time: the latter part of Jeroboam's reign, about 755 B. C.

Overton, Grace Sloan. Youth's prophetic vision; a dramatization of Amos [in three episodes]. (In her: Dramatic activities for young people. New York [cop. 1927]. 12°. p. 23–45.)

Raine, James Watt. Amos. [In three scenes.] (In his: Bible dramatics. New York & London [cop. 1927]. 12°. p. 102–112.)

—— [Amos and his message.] [In one scene.] (In his: Bible dramatics. New York & London [cop. 1927]. 12°. p. 114–129.)

University of Oklahoma. — Class in Old Testament. Amos; a play in two acts, written by students in Old Testament in the University of Oklahoma, under the direction of Miss Mary De Bardeleben, and based upon a plot by Harold Keith. New York: Womans Press [cop. 1926]. 28 p. 12°.

JONAH

Boyd, Zachary. The historie of Jonah [a dramatic poem]. (In his: Four poems from "Zion's flowers." Glasgow, 1855. 8°. p. 3–43.) **NCL**

Speakers: The Lord, Jonah, The shipmaster, The sailors, The king of Ninive, The men of Ninive.

An excerpt is printed in Gabriel Neil, *Biographical sketch of the Rev. Zachary Boyd,* Glasgow, 1832, p. x–xiii, *A p.v.144.*

Githens, Harry W. A fish story. [In four scenes.] (In his: Dramatized stories from the Old Testament. Cincinnati [cop. 1927]. · 12°. p. 195–200.) **NASH**

Greene, Robert. A looking glass for London and England. (In his: Dramatic works, ed. by A. Dyce. London, 1831. 12°. v. 1, p. 55–140.) **NCP**

Also printed in his *Life and complete works in prose and verse,* ed. by A. B. Grosart, London, 1881–86, v. 14, p. 1–113, *NCF;* in his *Plays and poems,* ed. by J. C. Collins, Oxford, 1905, v. 1, p. 137–214, *NCP;* and in *Robert Greene,* ed. by T. H. Dickinson, London, 1910, p. 77–164 (The Mermaid series), *NCP;* also in *Dramatic and poetical works of Robert Greene and George Peele,* ed. by Dyce, London, 1861, p. 113–147, *NCP.*

First printed 1594. Thos. Lodge, 1558?–1625, is usually regarded as joint author. Ward calls it "a peculiar Elizabethan variation of the old religious drama." The action takes place after the overthrow of Jeroboam, king of Judah. The story of Jonah is woven into the play, and the moral applied to London.

Herbert, Alan Patrick. The Book of Jonah. (As almost any modern Irishman would have written it.) (London Mercury. London, 1921. 8°. v. 3, p. 601–605.) ***DA**

Timothy James O'Leary, Mrs. T. J., and Michael Flannigan Joner (in the role of Jonah).

Maynard, John A. Jonah; a play in five episodes. [Boston: American Unitarian Association, n.d.] 14 l. 4°.

Typewritten.

Nineveh's repentance. A tragi-comedy mentioned in the list annexed to the Careless Shepherdess, 1656. A lost play.

See W. C. Hazlitt, *Manual,* p. 166.

Radcliff, Ralph. Jonas: a tragedy by Ralph Radcliff. Not printed.

See W. C. Hazlitt, *Manual,* p. 122.

Ritchie, John. The life of Jonah, the prophet... [A dramatic poem.] London: Partridge and Co. [1872.] 48 p. 12°. ***PSQ**

Snowman, Leonard Victor. A second chapter of "Jonah." [One scene.] (Jewish chronicle. London, 1924. f°. Sept. 26, 1924, p. 26–28.) **PBE**

MICAH

Friedlaender, David. Letters on the reading of the sacred Scriptures. New era. New York, 1874. 8°. v. 4, p. 305–307, 326–328.) ***PBD**

Chapters 6 and 7 of the book of Micah cast in a dialogue form. The speakers are the Lord, the prophet, and the people.

HABAKKUK

Stine, Wilbur Morris. Habakkuk, a poem. Philadelphia: Acorn Press, 1923. xvi, 302 p. 12°. **NBI**

"Vengeance," a celestial visitant, and Habakkuk are the two characters.

Old Testament Plays, continued

PSALMS

Boyd, Charles Arthur. The hymn of the helper. A dramatic setting for Psalms 42 and 43 ₍in two scenes₎. (In his: Worship in drama. Philadelphia ₍cop. 1924₎. 8°. p. 120–125.) **NAFM**

The characters are Shallum b. Ezra and Heman ben Joel.

Levinger, Elma C. Ehrlich. The shepherd psalm. ₍In one scene.₎ (In her: Entertaining programs for the assembly. Cincinnati ₍cop. 1930₎. 8°. p. 44–47.) *** PSY**

JOB

General Works

Balmforth, Ramsden. The drama of Job. (In his: The ethical and religious value of the drama. London ₍1925₎. 12°. p. 11–40.) **NAFD**

Bradley, George Granville. ₍Job not a drama.₎ (In his: Lectures on the Book of Job, delivered in Westminster Abbey. Oxford, 1888. 2. ed. 12°. p. 14–15.) *** PDW**

Delitzsch, Franz Julius. The dramatic art of the plot and execution. (In his: Biblical commentary on the Book of Job. Translated by Francis Bolton. Edinburgh, 1866. 8°. v. 1, p. 14–18.) *** PDW**

Dickinson, Thomas Herbert. The book of Job on the stage. illus. (Play book. Madison, Wis., 1914. 8°. v. 2, Dec., 1914, p. 12–17.) **NAFA**

Flory, John Samuel. The Book of Job. (In his: Dramas of the Bible; a literary interpretation of the Book of Job and the Song of Solomon. Boston, 1923. 12°. p. 11–162.) *** YLN**

Gaertner, Hersch. Der dramatische Charakter des Buches Hiob und die Tendenz desselben. Berlin: Druck von H. Itzkowski, 1909. 120 p., 1 l. 8°. *** PDW**

Litteratur, p. 9.

Green, William Henry. The dramatic character and integrity of the Book of Job. (Presbyterian and Reformed review. Philadelphia, 1897. 8°. v. 8, p. 683–701.) *** DA**

Hanby, Claude S. Drama of Job. ₍A description of a dramatic presentation.₎ (Homiletic review. New York, 1922. 8°. v. 84, p. 175–183.) **ZIXD**

Jastrow, Morris. The literary form of Job — a symposium, not a drama. (In his: The book of Job; its origin, growth and interpretation. Philadelphia, 1920. 8°. p. 174–181.) *** PDW**

Kallen, Horace Meyer. Dramatic literature among the Jews. Job and the Euripidean tradition. (Play-book. Madison, Wis., 1913–14. 8°. v. 1, no. 9, p. 3–7; no. 10, p. 15–24; no. 12, p. 12–18.) **NAFA**

——— The original form of Job. (In his: The Book of Job as a Greek tragedy, restored. New York, 1918. 12°. p. 3–38.) *** PDW**

L., D. Is the book of Job a drama? (In: Drama; or, Theatrical pocket magazine. London, 1821. 16°. p. 318–320.) **NCOA**

Lowth, Robert. Poema Jobi non esse justum drama. (In his: De sacra poesi Hebraeorum. Goettingae, 1768. 2. ed. 12°. p. 706–717.) *** PDF**

Reprinted from Blasius Ugolinus, *Thesaurus antiquitatum sacrarum,* Venetiis, 1766, tom 31, cols. 559–566, †* *PBR.*

Also in his *Lectures on the sacred poetry of the Hebrews,* new ed., Andover, Mass., 1829, p. 273–293, *PDF,* and London, 1847, p. 372–381, *NADB.*

Lowth, judging the book by the Aristotelian criteria of a drama, holds that although Job has all the marks of tragedy, it lacks the essential requirement of "action." He concludes that it may be called a dramatic poem, but not a drama.

Macdonald, Duncan Black. The original form of the legend of Job. (Journal of Biblical literature. Norwood, Mass., 1895. 8°. v. 14, p. 63–71.) *** DA**

Owen, John. The book of Job ₍as a drama₎. (In his: Five great skeptical dramas of history. London, 1896. 8°. p. 107–167.) **YBO**

Phillips, Forbes. Is 'Job' a problem play? (Nineteenth century and after. London, 1906. 8°. v. 60, p. 414–426.) *** DA**

Abstracted in *Current literature,* New York, 1906, v. 41, p. 560–562, * *DA.*

Rauch, Joseph. A study in early Hebrew dramatics. (Jewish comment. Baltimore, 1918. 4°. v. 51, p. 249–251.) †* **PBD**

Sabine, Charles. The Hebrew drama. (Voice of Jacob. London, 1847. f°. v. 7, p. 162–163.) . * **PBD**

Repr.: Oswald's well, July, 1848.

Stubbs, W. H. The drama of Job. (London quarterly review. London, 1930. 8°. Oct., 1930, p. 213–219.) *** DA**

"It is a religious book, but it is cast in dramatic form... The dramatis personae are: Job, the Heretic; Eliphaz, the Religious Neurotic; Bildad, the Traditionalist; Zophar, the Man-in-the-Street."

Wright, George Henry Bateson. ₍The Book of Job a drama.₎ (In his: The Book of Job; a new critically revised translation. London, 1883. 8°. p. 1–3.) *** PDW**

Modern Plays

Ashford, John. Job: a sacred drama ₍in verse₎. London, 1866. 8°.

Title from British Museum Catalogue.

Reviewed in *The Athenæum,* London, May 26, 1866, p. 703, * *DA.*

Old Testament Plays — Job, continued

The **Book** of Job. ₍Dramatized.₎ (In: R. M. Smith, editor, Types of philosophic drama. New York, 1928. 12°. p. 1–83.)   **NAFH**

Clements, Colin Campbell. Job; a play in one act adapted by Colin Campbell Clements ... New York and London: Samuel French, cop. 1923. 36 p. 12°. (French's International copyrighted...edition of the works of the best authors. no. 453.)

Czarnomska, Elizabeth. The genesis of the Book of Job. ₍In one scene.₎ (In: The authentic literature of Israel, freed from the disarrangements, expansions and comments of early native editors... Edited by Elizabeth Czarnomska. New York, 1928. 8°. part 2, p. xxv–xxvi.)   *** PDP**
Scene: a study of a doctor of law, in Jerusalem.

Dunning, Alfred. ...Job, a dramatic version. London: Society for Promoting Christian Knowledge, 1928. iv, 5–16 p. 8°.
At head of title: Parish plays, no. 16.
First performed at Kirkstall Road Demonstration School, Leeds, England, Dec. 21, 1927.

The **Epic** of "Job" ₍in five scenes₎. (Divine life. Edited by Celestia Root Lang. Chicago, 1907. 8°. v. 1, Aug., 1907, p. 15–22.)
"Job, a candidate for the Perfect Life."   **YVA**

Giran, Étienne. A modern Job; an essay on the problem of evil... With introduction by Archdeacon Lilley, authorised translation by Fred Rothwell. Chicago and London: Open Court Publishing Co., 1916. 92 p., 1 port. 8°.
    * YLN
A restatement in modern language and in dialogue form of the book of Job.
Reviewed, by J. V. Nash, in *Open court,* Chicago, 1926, v. 40, p. 424–431, * DA.

Greene, Robert. Job: the history of Job, by Robert Greene. Entered at Stationers' Hall, 1594, but not printed. This piece is in Warburton's list.
See W. C. Hazlitt, *Manual,* p. 121.

Hale, Harris Grafton, and N. M. HALL. ...The story of Job. Arranged by Harris G. Hale and Newton M. Hall. Boston: The Pilgrim Press, 1907. iv, 27 p. 12°. (Biblical dramas. ₍no. 8.₎)

Haynes, Henry W. Job, a lyrical drama; and other poems. London, 1845. 2. ed. 12°.
Title from British Museum Catalogue.
Reviewed in *The Athenæum,* London, March 22, 1845, p. 289, * DA.

Jennings, William. The dramatic poem of Job; a close metrical translation, with critical and explanatory notes. London: Methuen & Co., Ltd., 1912. xvii p., 1 l., 112 p. 8°.
Reviewed in *Poetry review,* London, 1912, v. 1, p. 335, * DA.

Job. A play which Collier makes out to be "Jube the Sane" is described in one of the injured Cotton mss. as having been performed at the marriage of Lord Strange to the daughter of the Earl of Cumberland, temp. Edward VI. See Collier's *Annals of the stage,* v. 1, p. 146. The title should possibly be Job the Saint.
See W. C. Hazlitt, *Manual,* p. 121.

Job the patient. ₍In one scene.₎ (In: M. W. Thomas, editor. Old Testament drama. London ₍1927₎. 12°. p. 155–178.)

Kallen, Horace Meyer. The tragedy of Job. (In his: The Book of Job as a Greek tragedy restored. New York, 1918. 12°. p. 85–163.)   *** PDW**
Reviewed, by W. P. Eaton, in *The Bookman,* New York, 1918, v. 47, p. 638–639, * DA; by Claude G. Montefiore in *Harvard theological review,* 1919, v. 12, p. 219–224, *ZEA;* and in *The Nation,* New York, 1918, v. 107, p. 662, * DA.
"In 1913 Mr. [T. H.] Dickinson...of the Wisconsin Dramatic Society gave two performances of the Tragedy, one in Milwaukee, and one in Madison; and in 1916 [May 8] the Harvard Menorah Society...gave a performance of the Tragedy in Boston." — *Preface.*
"Text used...is that of the American Revised Version." — *p. 81.*

Moulton, Richard Green. The Book of Job ₍arranged in verse by R. G. Moulton₎ presented as a play ₍by Stuart Walker at the Booth Theatre, New York, March 7, 1918, with George Gaul as Job₎. (Current opinion. New York, 1918. f°. v. 64, no. 5, May, 1918, p. 341–342.)   *** DA**
For notices and comments on the production see Arthur Row in *The Bellman,* Minneapolis, 1918, v. 24, p. 487–489, * DA; J. Ranken Towse in *The Literary digest,* New York, v. 57, April 6, 1918, p. 40–41 (abstracted from his review in the *New York Evening Post),* * DA; *New York dramatic mirror,* New York, v. 78, March 16, 1918, p. 5, * DA; and *The Outlook,* New York, 1918, v. 118, p. 480–481 (illus.), * DA.

Peterson, Henry. The modern Job. ₍A dramatic poem in three parts.₎ (In his: Poems... Second series. Philadelphia, 1883. 12°. p. 111–227.)   **NBI**
Among the characters are Job, Judas, and Paul.

Radcliff, Ralph. Job's afflictions: a tragedy by Ralph Radcliff. Not printed.
See W. C. Hazlitt, *Manual,* p. 121.

Stevens, James Stacy. A dramatization of the Book of Job, the problem of human suffering. Boston: The Stratford Company ₍cop. 1917₎. 41 p. 8°.   *** PD p.v.20**

Young, Andrew John. The adversary. ₍In two parts.₎ London: J. G. Wilson ₍1923₎. 80 p. 12°.   **NCM**
The adversary is Satan; he and Job are the main characters.

SONG OF SONGS

General Works

Archer, Ruby. The idyl of Israel known as the Song of Solomon or Song of Songs. (Poet lore. Boston, 1907. 8°. v. 18, p. 97–106.) ***DA**

Budde, Karl. The Song of Solomon. (New world. Boston, 1894. 8°. v. 3, p. 56–77.)   *** DA**

Old Testament Plays — Song of Songs, cont'd

Cannon, William Walter. The Song a dramatic poem. (In his: The Song of songs, edited as a dramatic poem. Cambridge, 1913. 8°. p. 9–18.) *** PDW**

Delitzsch, Franz Julius. ["The Song is a dramatic pastoral."] (In his: Commentary on the Song of Songs and Ecclesiastes. Edinburgh, 1877. 8°. p. 8–11.) *** YLP**

Falconer, Hugh. The maid of Shulam. London: Hodder and Stoughton, 1904. x p., 1 l., 155 p. 12°.

Flory, John Samuel. The Song of Solomon. (In his: Dramas of the Bible; a literary interpretation of the Book of Job and the Song of Solomon. Boston, 1923. 12°. p. 163–202.) *** YLN**

Griffis, William Elliot. The lily among thorns; a study of the Biblical drama entitled the Song of Songs. Boston and New York: Houghton, Mifflin and Co., 1890. x, 11–274 p. 12°. *** YLP**

Hyde, Walter Woodburn. Greek analogies to the Song of Songs [as regards its literary structure and purpose]. (In: M. L. Margolis, The Song of Songs, a symposium. Philadelphia, 1924. 8°. p. 31–42. *** YLP (Margolis)**

Lowth, Robert. Canticum Salomonis non esse justum drama [with "Notae editoris" by J. D. Michaelis]. (In his: De sacra poesi Hebraeorum... Goettingae, 1768. 2. ed. 12°. p. 593–613.) *** PDF**
Reprinted from Blasius Ugolinus, *Thesaurus antiquitatum sacrarum...*, Venetiis, 1766, tom 31, cols. 493–504, †* *PBR*.

Martineau, Russell. The Song of Songs. (American journal of philology. Baltimore, 1892. 8°. v. 13, p. 307–328.) **RAA**

—— The Song of Songs again. [Reply to Budde.] (American journal of philology. Baltimore, 1895. 8°. v. 16, p. 435–443.) **RAA**

Modern Plays

Alexander, James Bradun. King Solomon. A drama in five acts. Relating to incidents in the life of the wise king, derived from history and legend including his courtship of the beautiful Shulamite, as set forth in Solomon's Song. And introducing six songs... [Minneapolis?] 1899. vii, 10–112 p. illus. 12°. **ZEY p.v.65, no. 19**

Barlow, N. P. The Shunemite maid in the court of David and Solomon, in the mountains of Gilead, in the Song of Solomon. [Madison, Wis.: Tracy & Kilgore, printers, cop. 1916.] 43 p., 1 port. 8°.

Bible. — Song of Solomon: English. The Song of Songs. A Hebrew pastoral drama. Not by King Solomon. With notes and illustrations by Satyam Jayati [pseud. of H. A. Ouvry]. London: Williams and Norgate, 1867. vi, (1)8–87 p., 4 pl. 8°. *** PDW**
Dramatization of the Song in five acts. "An abridged paraphrase of the Song of Jayadeva called Gita Govinda, or the Celebration of the God of Crishna, has also been attempted, as a [dramatic] poem of a like nature to the Song [of Songs]." — *Preface.*

Bland, John. A grammatical version, from the original Hebrew; of the Song of Solomon, into English blank verse... The whole being a drama, in seven scenes... With notes on the whole. London: J. Wren, 1750. x p., 1 l., 46 p. 8°. *** C p.v.915**
Imperfect, part of Song of Moses, the Lamentation of David, and notes missing.

Bowdler, Elizabeth S. The Song of Solomon, paraphrased...also, A commentary and notes critical and practical [by Elizabeth S. Bowdler.] <Written in the year 1769.> Edinburgh: Printed for Drummond [etc.], 1775. 2 p.l., [v]–vi p., 1 l., 175 p. 8°. *** YLP**
Arranged in seven eclogues, corresponding to seven days' duration of the action in the poem. The characters: bridegroom, bride, virgins in chorus, and seven virgins individually.

Cannon, William Walter. The Song of Songs [as a dramatic poem in five cantos]. (In his: The Song of Songs. Cambridge, 1913. 8°. p. 99–115.) *** PDW**
The characters are named Solomon, Shulamith, court lady, and the poet.
Reviewed in *Corriere israelitico*, Trieste, 1913, anno 52, p. 149, * *PBH*; and by Israel Abrahams in the *Jewish chronicle*, London, 1913, July supplement, p. iv–v, * *PBE.*

Chapman, Matthew James. The bride: a dramatic idyl. (Hebrew idyls. no. 7.) (Fraser's magazine. London, 1836. 8°. v. 13, p. 324–332.) *** DA**
In seven scenes.

Croxall, Samuel. The fair Circassian; a dramatic performance. Done from the original by a gentleman-commoner of Oxford. (In his: The fair Circassian... To which are added several occasional poems. London, 1751. 9. ed. 12°. p. 17–39.)
"A licentious versification of the Song of Solomon." — *Lowndes.*

—— —— 3 pl. (In his: The fair Circassian ...with several occasional poems... London, 1765. 8. ed. 12°. p. 15–38.)
Preface, p. vii–xiv.

—— —— The Fair Circassian, a poem; imitated from the Songs of Solomon... New York: Printed for the Amateurs of the Fine Arts, 1795. vi p., 1 l., (1)8–32 p. 12°. *** KD 1795**
In the American edition, the prologue, beginning Virgins of Albion, is omitted The two characters He and She are, in the American edition, called Zephyrus and Saphyra.

Old Testament Plays — Song of Songs, cont'd

Dearness, William. A restoration of the drama of Canticles, with copious notes, also, an essay on The calf cult of northern Israel. Cincinnati: The Ebbert & Richardson Co., 1911. 77 p. 8°.   ***PDW**

"In Bible times there was a betrothal period which this book of ours contemplates, and gives us in scene and language all that may be purposely left out of the rest of the Scriptures."
Reviewed in *Open court,* Chicago, 1912, v. 26, p. 574–575, * *DA.*

Dietz, Ella. The song of songs. ₁A dramatic poem.₁ (In her: Triumph of life. London, 1885. 12°. p. 97–102.)   **NCM**
A paraphrase, in part, of the Biblical Song of Songs.

Falconer, Hugh. The Song of Songs ₁reconstructed in three scenes₁. (In his: The maid of Shulam. London, 1904. 12°. p. 27–62.)
"Maintains typical significance of Song of Songs over and above literal meaning. It is an erotic poem, but something more besides."

Fite, W. A. The Song of Songs, the Bible's greatest love story, a dramatization ₁in five acts₁... Cincinnati: Fillmore Music House, Powell & White ₁cop. 1923₁. 15 p. 8°.

Forrest, William Mentzel. King or shepherd? The Song of Solomon, newly rendered and for the first time given as a complete drama... Boston: The Stratford Company ₁cop. 1928₁. 3 p.l., ix, 54 p. 12°.   ***PDW**
Rearranged in Biblical phraseology into a drama of five acts. Time: 957 B. C. in March, month of flowers and weddings. Place: Shulam or Shunem, Galilee, and Jerusalem.
"Solomon is the unsuccessful wooer of a beautiful peasant girl... He restores her to the shepherd, who takes her home and weds her."

Fox, J. E. The Song of Songs. ₁A dramatization in three acts.₁ (Expository times. Edinburgh, 1895–96. 8°. v. 7, p. 105–107, 170–173, 224–225.)   **ZEA**
The paraphrase is based on F. Godet's *Study on the Song of Songs.* A Christological interpretation.

Francis, Ann. A poetical translation of the Song of Solomon from the original Hebrew; with a preliminary discourse and notes, his-. torical, critical, and explanatory... London: J. Dodsley, 1781. 2 p.l., ₁4₁, xix (i), 102 p. 4°.   *** YLP (Francis)**
In seven cantos. Time: seven days. A list of dramatis personae is given: Solomon, nobles of Zion, Egyptian spouse, Jewish Queen, choral virgins of Egypt, Jerusalem, and Zion.
Reprinted in G. A. Kohut, *A Hebrew anthology,* Cincinnati, 1913, v. 2, p. 963–981, * *PSO.*
Reviewed in *Critical review,* London, 1782, v. 53, p. 32–39, *NAA.*

Fry, John, rector of Desford. Canticles; or, Song of Solomon: a new translation, with notes; and an attempt to interpret the sacred allegories contained in that book... London: Printed for J. Hatchard, 1811. 277 p. 8°.   *** YLP (Fry)**
Paraphrased in twelve idyls. The characters: bride, bridegroom, virgins, and chorus.

Garstang, Walter. The sacred eclogue; being the poetic allegorical descriptions, or idylls, ("Song of Songs,") of the prophet Solomon, king of Israel. Opening the spiritual mystery of perfect nuptial love. A new version, in English, of the text in the Biblia Hebraica, edit. E. Van der Hooght. By Walter Garstang... Blackburn: James Douglas, 1882. 32 p. 12°.

Good, John Mason. Song of Songs: or, Sacred idyls. Translated from the original Hebrew, with notes critical and explanatory ... London: Printed for G. Kearsley, 1803. xxxvi, 210 p. 8°.   *** YLP (Good)**
In twelve idyls. The characters: royal bride, King Solomon, attendant virgins.
Reviewed in *British critic,* London, 1805, v. 26, p. 489–495, * *DA.*

Kemp, Harry. Solomon's song. A pastoral tragi-comedy in one act. (In: Frank Shay, editor, Contemporary one-act plays of 1921, American. Cincinnati ₁cop. 1922₁. 8°. p. 353–372.)   **NBL**
Reprinted in Kemp's *Boccaccio's untold tale, and other one-act plays,* New York [cop. 1924], p. 101–122, 8–*NBM.*

Latymer (5th baron), Francis Burdett Thomas Coutts-Nevill. The Song of Songs; a lyrical folk-play of the ancient Hebrew arranged in vii scenes by Francis Coutts. With illustrations by Henry Ospovat. London: J. Lane, 1906. 67 p., 6 pl. 24°. (Flowers of Parnassus. v. 27.)   ***YLP**

Levey, Sivori. ...Virginel (an ancient historical drama). The Song of Songs (which is of Solomon) — inasmuch as it portrayeth a lowly maiden — herein called Virginel — a Shunammite — an humble vine-dresser of Shunem — her constancy amid temptation, and her faithfulness to her lover, a shepherd, against the importunities of King Solomon, who has caused her, because of her beauty, to be brought into the Palace. Reconstructed by Sivori Levey. ₁Roehampton, London: Fountain Pub. Co., 1919.₁ 58 p. 8°. (Pilgrimage plays. no. 1.)   **NCO p.v.460**
Cover-title.

McLeod, Katheryn Congdon. My beloved is mine. (A Biblical drama.) (The Jewish forum. New York, 1927. 8°. v. 10, p. 306–309.)   ***PBD**

Osborne, Hubert. The Song of Solomon. ₁In four scenes.₁ New York and London: D. Appleton and Co., 1927. xii, 59 p. 12°.   **NBM**
"The text of the play consists of The Song of Solomon, together with certain passages from I. Kings, Proverbs and Ecclesiastes, the King James version of the Bible being adhered to, except in a few instances where the Revised Version, or Ernest Renan's translation were used."— *Note, p. vii.* "The Song of Solomon" was first produced in The Arts Theater of the Carnegie Institute of Technology, Pittsburgh, Pa., Oct. 12, 1921.

Old Testament Plays — Song of Songs, cont'd

Perrin, W. The Song of Songs, by Solomon. (In his: Hebrew canticles; or, A poetical commentary, or paraphrase on the various songs of Scripture. Philadelphia, 1820. 16°. p. 17–53.)   *** YIS**
Time: four days. Characters: spouse, bridegroom, and virgins.

Remsen, Henry R. Eros, a masque ₍in four acts₎. (In his: Daughter of Ypocas, and other verse. ₍Hartford, Conn., cop. 1897.₎ 12°. p. ₍20–28.₎)   **NBI**
A dramatic poem on the Song of Songs with the Shulamite maiden, "a Jew of her class," and a chorus of Jewish maidens as the characters.

The **Song** of Songs; a new metrical translation arranged as a drama, with introduction and notes by W. Jennings. Oxford: Parker & Co., 1914. 55(1) p. 12°.
* YCO (Song of Solomon, 1914)

The **Song** of Songs. Adapted by Walter Nugent Monck. In two scenes. Privately printed, English Drama Society.
Title from Violet Kent, *The players' library and bibliography of the theatre*, London, 1930, item no. 4992.
Produced by the English Dramatic Society at Queen's-gate Hall, South Kensington, March 4, 1908. For reviews see Warren C. Cawley, *Collection of about 100,000 clippings on plays*, Box Sha-So, *MWE*.

The **Song** of Songs ₍in dramatized form, in seven idyls₎. (In: Richard Green Moulton, Literary study of the Bible. Boston, 1895. 8°. p. 202–217.)   *** YIG**
See also Lyric idyl: 'Solomon's Song,' *ibid.*, p. 194–201.

The **Song** of Songs; seven scenes, one for each day of a wedding festival. (In: The Authentic literature of Israel, freed from the disarrangements, expansions and comments of early native editors... Edited by Elizabeth Czarnomska. New York, 1928. 8°. part 2, p. 334–342.)
* PDP (Bible. O. T. Eng.)

...The **Song** of Songs of Solomon. ₍A dramatic arrangement in 11 eclogues occurring on six consecutive days₎ and ₍illustrated₎ by means of engravings. (In: Augustin Calmet, Calmet's Dictionary of the Holy Bible, with the Biblical fragments of the late Charles Taylor... London, 1841. 8. ed. 4°. v. 3, p. 641–692; plates, v. 5, nos. 147–156.)
* YID (Calmet)

₍Spring; or, Phaireedaim. In five scenes.₎ (In: Songs of the Semitic in English verse, by G. E. W. London, 1877. 12°. p. 55–79.)
Introduction and synopsis, p. 19–54.   *** PDF**

Stolz, Karl Ruf. The Song of Songs. Dramatized and edited with introduction and notes, Karl R. Stolz. (University of North Dakota quarterly journal. Grand Forks, 1920. 8°. v. 10, p. 371–384.)
STG (North Dakota)

Williams, Thomas. The Song of Songs which is by Solomon. (In his: Song of Songs, which is by Solomon; a new translation. Philadelphia, 1803. 8°. p. 127–144.)
* YLP (Williams)
In fourteen sections. Time extends over seven mornings and seven evenings. Characters: spouse, bridegroom, and virgins.

Wright, Sidney Fowler. The Song of Songs ₍in five scenes₎. (In his: Song of Songs, and other poems. London ₍1925₎. 12°. p. ₍5–26₎.)   **NCM**
Also in the New York, 1929 ed., p. 1–23.

Young, Stark. The Queen of Sheba. ₍In one act.₎ (Theatre arts magazine. New York, 1922. 8°. v. 6, p. 152–164.)   **NBLA**
A youth and a maiden, both demented, address one another in the lovers' language of the Song of Songs.

RUTH

Bachrach, Leona, and others. Ruth — a story of the harvest. A play in three acts. By Leona Bachrach, Charles Pesorowsky and Eugene Solomon. (In: E. E. Levinger, Jewish festivals in the religious drama. Cincinnati, 1923. 8°. p. 255–260.)   *** PSY**

Benton, Rita. Ruth and Boaz. ₍A play in four acts.₎ (In her: Bible plays. New York ₍cop. 1922₎. 8°. p. 96–126.)   *** PSQ**

Boyd, Charles Arthur. Ruth the loyal; a Biblical drama ₍in four acts₎. Boston: Chicago: Pilgrim Press ₍cop. 1925₎. vi, 21 p., 1 pl. 12°.
"The Bible text in the drama usually follows the American Standard Edition of the Revised Bible." — *From Foreword.*

Browne, Frances Elizabeth. Ruth: a drama ₍in six scenes₎. (In her: Ruth, and other lyrical poems. New York, 1871. 12°. p. 5–30.)   **NBI**

Burns, Mary Modena. The beautiful story of Ruth the gleaner. ₍In three scenes.₎ (In her: Good things for Sunday schools. Chicago ₍cop. 1916₎. 12°. p. 13–15.)   **ZICS**

Carvalho, Naomi Nunes. Character. ₍A dialogue between Ruth and Orpah.₎ (In her: Vox humana. London, 1912. 12°. p. 47–53.)   **NRD p.v.9**

Demarest, Ada Rose. "When ye reap the harvest," a dramatization of incidents from the book of Ruth. (In her: Junior pageants. Cincinnati ₍cop. 1927₎. 8°. p. 75–79.)
Pageant no. 11. In two scenes.

Genlis, Stéphanie Félicité Ducrest de St. Aubin, comtesse de. Ruth and Naomi, a sacred drama, in two acts. (In her: Sacred dramas. London, 1786. 8°. p. 215–281.)
NKO

Githens, Harry W. A faithful daughter. ₍In two scenes.₎ (In his: Dramatized stories from the Old Testament. Cincinnati ₍cop. 1927₎. 12°. p. 110–114.)   **NASH**
Story of Naomi and her two daughters-in-law.

Old Testament Plays — Ruth, continued

Herbst, Eva. Ruth, a harvest pageant. Cincinnati: Department of Synagog and School Extension of the Union of American Hebrew Congregations ₍cop. 1921₎. 16 p. illus. 12°.
<small>Presented in June, 1920 on the grounds of the Rockdale Ave. Temple, Cincinnati, O.</small>

Hobbs, Mabel, and HELEN MILES. Ruth and Naomi. (In their: Six Bible plays. New York ₍cop. 1924₎. 8°. p. 1–18.)　　**NASH**
<small>In three scenes.</small>

Horne, Mary Blake. Ruth, a mystery play. ₍In three acts.₎ Milwaukee: The Young Churchman Co. ₍1929?₎ 22 p. illus. music. 8°.
<small>Cover-title.</small>

Jacobson, Janie. Ruth, the Moabitess; a scriptural play in three acts. ₍New York: Schoen & Kellerman, 1910.₎ 9 p. nar. 8°.
　　　　　　　　　　　　NBL p.v.13, no.9

Kimball, Rosamond. Ruth. ₍A play in seven scenes.₎ (In her: The wooing of Rebekah, and other Bible plays. New York, 1925. 8°. p. 105–120.)　　**ZICS**

Lawrence, Annabel. Ruth; a Biblical drama in three acts... Chicago: T. S. Denison & Co. ₍cop. 1916.₎ 1 p.l., 34 p., 1 pl. 12°.
　　　　　　　　　　　　　　NBL p.v.57

Leiser, Joseph. The girl from Moab; a harvest play in three acts. Cincinnati: Department of Synagog and School Extension of the Union of American Hebrew Congregations, cop. 1922. 32 p. 12°.

Levinger, Elma C. Ehrlich. Ruth; a little play for Shabuoth in one act. New York: Bloch Pub. Co., 1924. 4 p. 16°.

—— Ruth of Moab. A springtime play in one act. (In her: Jewish festivals in the religious school. Cincinnati, 1923. 8°. p. 503–515.)　　　　　　　　　　*** PSY**

—— The strange woman, a practical idyl of old Palestine ₍in one act₎. (B'nai B'rith news. Mount Morris, Ill., 1924. 4°. v. 15, p. 233–236.)　　　　　　　　**†* PYP**

Linsky, Fannie Barnett. The pageant of the law, a Sh'vuos program... New York: Bloch Pub. Co., 1930. 11 p. 12°.
<small>Cover-title.</small>

Lobingier, Elizabeth Erwin (Miller). Ruth. (In her: The dramatization of Bible stories. Chicago ₍cop. 1919₎. 12°. p. 59–67.)
<small>In three scenes.</small>　　　　　　*** YIR**

Manley, William Ford. Ruth. (In his: Bible dramas. New York ₍cop. 1928₎. 8°. p. 96–114.)　　　　　　　　**NBM**
<small>In four scenes.</small>

Maxfield, Mina R. Ruth of Moab; a pastoral of Canaan, 1300 B. C. ₍In seven scenes.₎ (In: Allison Gaw and E. T. Gaw, Pharaoh's daughter, and other Biblical plays of the contest, 1927. New York, 1928. 8°. p. 185–261.)
<small>Prize-winning play.</small>　　　　　　**NBL**

Mitchell, Myrtilla E. Ruth and Naomi, a Scriptural dialogue. (Hebrew watchword

and instructor. Philadelphia, 1897. 8°. v. 1, June, 1897, p. 15.)　　　　　　*** PBD**

Parsons, Margaret Colby (Getchell). Ruth. (A Biblical play, especially suited to the harvest season) ₍in three scenes₎. (In her: Ten stirring Bible plays. Franklin, Ohio, cop. 1927. 12°. p. 40–49.)

Pierce, Sarah. Ruth. ₍In one act of two scenes. From an unfinished manuscript in possession of the Litchfield Historical Society.₎ (In: E. N. Vanderpoel, compiler, Chronicles of a pioneer school from 1792 to 1833, being the history of Miss Sarah Pierce and her Litchfield School. Cambridge, Mass.: Printed by the University Press, 1903. 8°. p. 84–100.)　　**IQM (Litchfield)**
<small>Written by Miss Pierce for the amusement and edification of her pupils of the Litchfield, Conn., Female Academy. Her plays were usually given at the end of the school term, and the young men of the town were often invited to take part.
Judging from an entry in the diary of one of the pupils (see p. 48), this play was probably presented at the 1802 commencement exercises.</small>

Putnam, Edith Palmer. Ruth the gleaner. A dramatization of the scriptural story ₍in one act₎. Especially designed for a Thanksgiving entertainment. (Hints. New York, 1906. 8°. v. 8, no. 9, p. 22–28.)　　**MZA**

Read, Elizabeth Day. "Ruth"; or "Filial devotion"; in three scenes. Boston: American Unitarian Association, n.d. 5 l. 4°.
<small>Typewritten.</small>

Russell, Mary M. A girl who knew how to be a friend. ₍In two scenes.₎ (In her: Dramatized Bible stories for young people. New York, 1921. 12°. p. 78–82.)

Ruth. (In: Jewish Education Committee, Chicago. Portfolios for holy days and festivals. Shovuoth. ₍Chicago, 192–?₎ 2 f. 4°.)
<small>Mimeographed.</small>

Ruth the gleaner. ₍In four scenes.₎ (Young Judaean. New York, 1923. 8°. v. 13, p. 140–143.)　　　　　　　　　　　*** PBD**

Ruth the gleaner. ₍In three acts.₎ Adapted by Bureau of Jewish Education. (In: Jewish festival books. Shovuoth. New York: Bureau of Jewish Education, n.d. 8°. p. 26–38.)

Selden, Almira. Naomi. A sacred drama in five scenes. (In her: Effusions of the heart. Bennington, Vt., 1820. 16°.)
<small>Title from Oscar Wegelin, *Early American plays, 1714–1830,* New York, 1900, p. 86.</small>

Spence, Hersey Everett. Ruth; a dramatization of Biblical history. ₍In four acts.₎ Nashville, Tenn.: Cokesbury Press ₍cop. 1924₎. 67 p., 1 pl. 12°.　　**NBM**

₍**Summer;** or, Ruth. In nine brief scenes and songs.₎ (In: Songs of the Semitic in English verse, by G. E. W. London, 1877. 12°. p. 91–103.)　　　　　*** PDF**
<small>Introduction, p. 83–90.</small>

Whitney, Mary Ellen. Ruth. ₍A play in six scenes.₎ (In her: Bible plays and how to produce them. New York ₍cop. 1927₎. 12°. p. 74–81.)

Old Testament Plays — Ruth, continued

Young, Andrew John. Boaz and Ruth. (In his: Boaz and Ruth, and other poems. London, 1920. 12°. p. 20–31.)

Scene: the threshing-floor of Boaz, outside Bethlehem.

Reviewed in *Expository times,* Edinburgh, 1921, v. 32, p. 568.

ESTHER

Abelson, Anna Goldina. Mordecai's cousin; a Purim play in four acts. New York: Bloch Pub. Co., 1923. 14 p. 8°.
                                         * PSQ p.v.1

Reprinted from *Jewish forum,* New York, v. 6, no. 3, March, 1923, p. 239–245, * *PBD.*

Abercrombie, Lascelles. Vashti ₍a dramatic poem in four parts₎. (In his: Emblems of love. London, 1912. 12°. p. 16–74.) **NCM**

Bain, Donald. Queen Esther; a Purim play ₍in four acts₎. Buffalo, N. Y.: Union and Times Press, 1917. 63 p. 12°.

Time: 521–516 B. C.

Benton, Rita. Esther. (In her: Bible plays. New York ₍cop. 1922₎. 8°. p. 127–157.)

In one act.   *** PSQ**

Bien, Herman M. "Purim:" a series of character-poems in four parts and tableaux, containing the complete history from the Book of Esther. For recitations by young people, especially Sunday schools and Y. M. L. A. to all of whom this work is devotedly dedicated, by Rabbi H. M. Bien. Vicksburg, Miss.: Vicksburg Prtg. and Pub. Co., 1884. 18 p. 8°.

—————— Cincinnati: Bloch Pub. Co., 1889. 28 p. 2. rev. ed. 8°.   *** PSQ p.v.1**

Bliss, Frank Chapman. Queen Esther. A tragic poem ₍in four acts₎. (In his: Queen Esther, and other poems. Newark, N. J., 1881. 8°. p. 9–100.)   **NBM**

Brennan, John P. Esther, the Persian queen. A drama in five acts. Youngstown, O.: McNally Brothers ₍1897₎. 45 p. 12°.

Title from Library of Congress.

Browne, Mabel Montgomery. Esther; dramatization of Biblical history ₍in five acts₎ ... Nashville, Richmond: Cokesbury Press ₍cop. 1924₎. 37 p. music. 12°. **NBM**

"Action has been governed by descriptions given in the Bible and by Josephus in 'Antiquities of the Jews.' The added prayers of Esther and Mordecai (acts II and IV) are patterned from Greek manuscripts given in the Cambridge Bible. The Decree of Ahasuerus (act IV, sc. 2) is abridged from one recorded by Josephus." — *p. 5.*

Buchan, Alexander Winton. Esther: a drama in five acts. ₍By A. W. Buchan.₎ Glasgow, 1873. 103 p. 8°.

Title from Halkett & Laing, 1926, v. 2, p. 215.

Bursetown, Goodman. Haman, the Amalekite; a witty and very interesting Purim historical modern drama in three acts

for adults and minors, by Rabbi G. Bursetown... ₍Houston? Tex., cop. 1924.₎ 16 p. 8°.

Chapman, Edward M. Esther, the Jewish queen; a Purim play ₍in two scenes₎ for Young Israel. n.p., cop. 1911. ₍8₎ p. 8°.

The play opens after the downfall of Haman.

Cole, Edna Earle. Esther, the brave young queen. ₍In four acts.₎ (In her: The good Samaritan and other Bible stories dramatized. Boston ₍cop. 1915₎. 12°. p. 41–51.)

Title from Library of Congress.

Collett, John. Esther, a sacred drama ₍in nine scenes₎. (In his: Sacred dramas. Evesham, 1805. 12°. p. 117–210.)

Cox, Robert. King Ahasuerus and Queen Esther. ₍An interlude. By Robert Cox.₎ (In: Francis Kirkman, editor, The Wits; or, Sport upon sport. London, 1673–72. 8° in fours. part 2. ₍2₎ p.)   **NCO**

"The incomparable Robt. Cox...was not only the principal actor, but also the contriver and author of most of these farces." — *From the preface to part 2.*

Reprinted in *Jewish home,* New York, 1906, v. 12, p. 90, * *PBD.*

Cushing, Mrs. Eliza Lansford (Foster). Esther, a dramatic sketch. ₍In five acts.₎ (Godey's lady's book. Philadelphia, 1838. 8°. v. 16, p. 241–244; v. 17, p. 2–8, 73–81, 216–221, 260–264.)   *** DA**

Reprinted in her *Esther...with, Judith, a poem,* Boston, 1840, p. 6–103 (copy in Library of Congress).

Acts 1–2, and acts 4–5 in Godey's appear as acts 1, 2, and 3, respectively, in the published book form.

Daugherty, Sonia V. M. Esther, a drama in three acts. With a preface by Mrs. Starr A. Best. The winning Biblical play of the 1929 Drama League-Longmans, Green and Co. playwriting contest. New York: Longmans, Green and Co., 1930. xii, 3–118 p. 12°.

Davis, Emelia C. Esther; a Purim play ₍in nine acts₎. (Young Israel. London, 1899. 8°. v. 2, Supplement, Young Israel budget, Feb., 1899, p. 3–8.)   *** PBE**

Dembitz, Arthur A. Prologues to "Esther"; remarks of principal characters ₍Ahasuerus, Vashti, Mordecai, Haman, and Esther₎. Translated from the originals (Hebrew, Babylonian, Persian and Aramaic). (American Hebrew. New York, 1919. f°. v. 104, p. 434–435.)   *** PBD**

Elmaleh, Leon H. Esther the Queen; a Purim play ₍in four acts₎. New York: Bloch Pub. Co., 1921. 15 p. 3. ed. 12°.

Produced March 18, 1908 by the Mikveh Israel Association, Philadelphia, Pa. Reviewed in the *Jewish exponent,* Philadelphia, v. 46, no. 23, March 20, 1908, p. 10, * *PBD.*

Esther; a sacred drama ₍in three acts₎... Cambridge: Metcalfe and Palmer, 1844. iv p., 1 l., 46 p. 8°.

Ms. note on t.-p., where author's name is usually given, reads: By R. W. Essington, M. A. Fellow of King's College, Cambridge.

"I take the license of imagining that the heroine ₍Esther believed₎ that she was destined to be the mother of the Saviour." — *From the Introduction.*

Old Testament Plays — Esther, continued

Fite, W. A. Esther, a Bible dramatization [in eight acts]. Cincinnati: Fillmore Music House, Powell & White [cop. 1923]. 16 p. 8°.

Githens, Harry W. A woman who dared (Esther). [In five scenes.] (In his: Dramatized stories from the Old Testament. Cincinnati [cop. 1927]. 12°. p. 154–163.) **NASH**

Glenn, Mendel G. A Purim play [in two acts]. illus. (Young Judaean. New York, 1929. 4°. v. 19, March, 1929, p. 4–6, 20.) *** PBD**

Godly Queen Hester. A new enterlude of Godly Queene Hester edited from the quarto of 1561 by W. W. Greg. Louvain: A. Uystpruyst, 1904. xvi, 62 p. 8°. (Materialien zur Kunde des älteren englischen Dramas. Bd. 5.) **NCO**

Also printed in J. S. Farmer, editor, *Six anonymous plays (Second series)*, London, 1906, p. 245–287, *NCO (Early).*

A short selection is printed in *International journal of apocrypha*, London, 1908, no. 15, p. 16.

Reviewed by Wolfgang Keller in *Deutsche Shakespeare Gesellschaft, Jahrbuch*, Berlin-Schöneberg, 1905, Bd. 41, p. 220–221, * NCK.

"There is high probability that [William Hunnis] wrote 'The godly Queene Hester.' " — C. C. Stopes in *The Athenæum, 1909, v. 115, p. 540.*

ABRAHAMS, Israel. Queen Esther on the English stage. (In his: Festival studies. London, 1906. 16°. p. 124–131.) *** PKA**

A **PURIM** interlude. (Jewish messenger. New York, 1873. f°. v. 33, March 14, 1873, p. 1.) *** PBD**

Goethe, Johann Wolfgang von. Junkdump Fair, a moral and politick puppet play [in one scene]. illus. (In: Paul McPharlin, compiler, A repertory of marionette plays. New York, 1929. 4°. p. 243–273.) **NAFM (McPharlin)**

Translated from the German "Das Jahrmarktsfest zu Plundersweilern."

The scene is a market-place of a German town in the eighteenth century. In this mountebank play are introduced two scenes from Esther: Haman and Ahasuerus, and Mordecai and Esther.

Presented by young Goethe, at Frankfort in 1769, before a circle of friends.

Goldschmidt, William. Hadassah; or, the Persian queen. Operetta in three acts. Music by Sigmund Sabel. n. p. [cop. 1891.] 35 p. 8°. *** PSQ**

Words only.

Goody, A. Duncan. Esther; a drama in verse [in two acts]. London: Simpkin, Marshall, Hamilton, Kent, and Co., 1899. 2 p.l., 50 p. 8°.

Grant, Elsie V. B. The story of Purim in verse [in seven scenes]. illus. (Young Israel. Cincinnati, 1924. f°. v. 16, no. 7, p. 5–7, 15.) *** PBD**

Grillparzer, Franz. Esther. [Synopsis of the play with numerous extracts.] (In: Gustav Pollak, Franz Grillparzer and the

Austrian drama. New York, 1907. 12°. p. 333–350.) *** R – NGA**

" 'Esther,' in the opinion of most critics, bears the impress of the period of Grillparzer's maturest powers ... Grillparzer was familiar with Racine's drama, as well as with Lope de Vega's 'La hermosa Ester' and Godinez's 'Aman y Mardoqueo'... His Esther bears a certain resemblance to the character of Hero in 'Des Meeres und der Liebe Wellen.' "

Performed at the Burgtheater, Vienna, April 28, 1868.

BURGESS, Amy V. An analysis of the female characters of Grillparzer's dramas: Rahel and Esther. (University College of Wales. Aberystwyth studies. Aberystwith, 1912. 8°. v. 1, p. 104–107.) **STK (Wales)**

Gruenfeld, M. The feast of Esther (a fairy play on the past for the present). From the German of Dr. M. Gruenfeld by Oscar Leonard. (Young Israel. Cincinnati, 1911. 8°. v. 7, p. 447–449.)

—— —— Cincinnati: Young Israel, cop. 1911. 21. 8°.

Hare, Walter Ben. A dream of Queen Esther; a Biblical drama in three acts. Chicago: T. S. Denison & Co. [1920.] 79 p. illus. 12°. (Denison's select plays.) **NBL p.v.75, no.7**

Harnwell, Anna Jane. The star in the East; a Biblical drama, in four acts... Prize play, Drama League of America. New York, London: S. French, cop. 1921. 74 p., 4 l. diagrs. 8°.

With the exception of one Anna, handmaid to Esther, the characters are all from the book of Esther. The Bible narrative is closely followed except the Christological reference at the end.

Hellman, George Sidney. Esther, a drama in three acts. (Menorah journal. New York, 1917. 4°. v. 3, p. 76–89, 156–173, 218–233.) *** PBD**

Excerpts from it were previously published in his *The Hudson, and other poems*, New York, 1909, p. 115–144, *NBI.*

Hester and Ahasuerus: a Scriptural drama. A performance on June 3, 1594, is noticed by Henslowe. In the Prospectus of the New Shakespear Society it is said to survive in a German translation.

See W. C. Hazlitt, *Manual*, p. 106.

Hobbs, Mabel, and **HELEN MILES.** Esther. (In their: Six Bible plays. New York [cop. 1924]. 8°. p. 53–73.) **NASH**

In three scenes.

J., H. S. Esther, a dramatic sketch. In two scenes. (Purim gazette. New York: Hebrew Orphan Asylum Press, 1883. 4°. p. 25–29.)

Jacobson, Janie. Esther, queen of Persia. A Scriptural play in 5 acts. Philadelphia: Julius H. Greenstone, 1912. 16 p. 12°. **NBL p.v.181, no.13**

—— —— Philadelphia: Julius H. Greenstone, 1921. 16 p. 12°.

—— A maid of Persia. A Purim play in four acts. [New York,] 1905. 14 p. 8°. * PSQ

Produced by the Confirmation class of the Beth Israel Temple, Philadelphia, on March 19, 1916.

Old Testament Plays — Esther, continued

Kuhn, Samuel O. A Jewish maid of Shushan; a Purim play ₍in two acts₎. New York: Bloch Pub. Co., 1922. 12 p. 12°.

Leibson, Jacob J. Too much Haman. A Purim play in three acts. (Helpful thoughts. New York, 1903. 8°. v. 8, p. 137–144.) * **PBD**

—— —— New York: Bloch Pub. Co. ₍cop. 1903.₎ 13 p. 8°.		* **PSQ**

Leiser, Joseph. The belle of Shushan; a Purim play for children in three acts. Cincinnati: Department of Synagog and School Extension of the Union of American Hebrew Congregations ₍cop. 1923₎. 27 p. 12°.

The characters are from the book of Esther, and several fictitious characters. Presented by the San Francisco Emanu-El Temple House on March 11th, 1928.

Levinger, Elma C. Ehrlich. The pageant of Esther in 3 parts and 12 scenes, by E. C. Ehrlich. (The Ark. Cincinnati, Feb. 28, 1913. 8°. v. 3, no. 2, p. 103–118.) * **PBD**

—— The pageant of Esther; a Purim pageant in eleven scenes. With plates for costumes. Cincinnati: Department of Synagog and School Extension of the Union of American Hebrew Congregations ₍cop. 1923₎. 42 p., 3 l. illus. 12°.

Reprinted in her *Jewish festivals in the religious school*, Cincinnati, 1923, p. 407–448, * **PSY.** Except for "Notes to the producer," p. 409–412, this is a reprint of the text published in *The Ark*.

—— A set of Purim pictures; ten tableaux telling the chief events of the Purim story. (In her: Jewish festivals in the religious school. Cincinnati, 1923. 12°. p. 129–133.) * **PSY**

—— The star of Judah; a Purim play ₍in five acts₎. (Young Israel. Cincinnati, 1911. 8°. v. 7, p. 433–441.)		* **PBD**

—— —— ₍Cincinnati: Young Israel, 1911?₎ 9 p. 8°.		* **PSQ p.v.1**

—— —— Cincinnati: The Ark ₍1911?₎. 12 p. 8°.

Reprinted in her *Jewish festivals in the religious school*, Cincinnati, 1923, p. 375–405, * **PSY.**

Levy, Clifton Harby. Haman and Mordecai, a Purim-play, in five acts. Cincinnati: Bloch Pub. Co., 1886. 21 p. 12°. * **PSQ p.v.1**

Linsky, Fannie Barnett. A Purim fantasy; a play in one act. Cincinnati: Department of Synagog and School Extension of the Union of American Hebrew Congregations ₍cop. 1929₎. 19 p. 12°.

Represents the months of the Jewish year. The Purim story in woven in. Most of the play is in verse.

Lobingier, Elizabeth Erwin (Miller). Queen Esther. (In her: The dramatization of Bible stories. Chicago ₍cop. 1919₎. 12°. p. 68–83.)		* **YIR**

In five scenes.

Mackinnon, David. Ahasuerus; a Persian play ₍in one act₎, B. C. 500. London: A. H. Stockwell ₍1920?₎. 44 p. 12°.		**NCR**

Martin, Lena Prather. Vashti; a Biblical play in three acts. Franklin, O.: Eldridge Entertainment House, Inc., cop. 1929. 42 p. 12°. (Eldridge church entertainments.)

Mary Agnes, Sister. Queen Esther; a drama in three acts founded on Holy Scripture. Chicago: A. Flanagan Co. ₍cop. 1905.₎ 32 p. 12°.

—— Queen Esther, a drama founded on Holy Scriptures ₍in three acts₎. By S. M. A. ₍Winnipeg, Man.: St. Mary's Academy, cop. 1924.₎ 25(1) p. 12°.

Masefield, John. Esther and Berenice; two plays by John Masefield. New York: The Macmillan Company, 1922. ix p., 2 l., 205 p. illus. 12°.		**NCR**

"The play of Esther is an adaptation… Berenice is a translation [from Racine]." — *Preface.*

Esther occupies p. 1–107.

It was first produced by Miss Penelope Wheeler at Wootton, Berks, May 5, 1921.

Reprinted in his *Verse plays*, New York, 1925, p. 99–155, *NCR.*

Reviewed in *The Freeman*, New York, 1922, v. 5, p. 526, * *DA;* by A. Weiner in *Jewish exponent*, Philadelphia, v. 69, no. 26, March 24, 1922, p. 9, * *PBD;* by Israel Abrahams in *Jewish guardian*, London, March 14, 1924, p. 11, * *PBE;* by George S. Hellman in *Menorah journal*, New York, 1922, v. 8, p. 248–250, * *PBD;* in *The Nation & The Athenæum*, London, 1922, v. 31, p. 60, 62, * *DA;* by Edmund Wilson, jr., in *The New republic*, New York, 1922, v. 30, p. 291, * *DA;* by Robert Lynd in *The New statesman*, London, 1922, v. 18, p. 533–534, * *DA;* and by A. Williams-Ellis in *The Spectator*, London, 1922, v. 128, p. 598–599, * *DA.*

Mendes, Henry Pereira. Esther: a purim play. (For Sunday schools.) (American Hebrew. New York, 1894. 4°. v. 54, p. 461–465.)		* **PBD**

Reprinted in v. 64, 1899, p. 517–521.

—— —— New York: P. Cowen, 1899. 23 p. 16°.		* **PSQ p.v.1**

—— —— New York: Lincoln Prtg. Co., n. d. 24 p. 2. ed. 24°.

Reviewed in *The American Hebrew*, New York, v. 2, no. 6, March 26, 1880, p. 63.

—— Esther and Harbonah. Boston: The Gorham Press ₍cop. 1917₎. 118 p. 12°. **NBM**

"Nearly forty years have passed since I wrote this play. I wrote it for my young people, for the cause of religious Loyalty, to keep them strong therein… The play itself is founded on the Bible-Book of Esther, with suggestions from Xenophon and Herodotus, the Greek historians of that era; the Apocrypha, Medrashim or Legends two thousand years old, etc." — *From Author's preface.*

Moses, Anna Jonas. "Esther." A drama in five acts. By a lady of Mobile ₍i. e. Anna Jonas Moses₎. n.p., n.d. 23 p. 12°.

—— —— Cincinnati: Bloch Pub. and Prtg. Co., 1887. 27 p. 8°.		* **PSQ**

Reprinted in *Young Israel*, Cincinnati, 1909, v. 3, p. 435–439, 468–471, * *PBD.*

Old Testament Plays — Esther, continued

National Training School, New York. — Class in Religious Pedagogy. The drama of Esther ₍in three acts₎ written and given by the Class in Religious Pedagogy at the National Training School ₍of the Young Women's Christian Association₎, March, 1917. New York: Womans Press, 1919. 24 p. 12°.

Noe, Cotton. The blood of Rachel; a dramatization of Esther ₍in three acts₎. (In his: Blood of Rachel, and other poems. Louisville, Ky., 1916. 12°. p. 1–74.) **NBI**

Ochs, Julius. The Megilla; or, The story of Esther: an operatic medley ₍in three acts₎. Cincinnati: Bloch Pub. Co. ₍190–?₎ 32 p. nar. 12°. *** PSQ p.v.1**
"The opera is intended to be serio-comic, not burlesque."

Polack, Elizabeth. Esther, the royal Jewess: or, The death of Haman! An historical drama in three acts. London: S. French ₍18—?₎. 30 p., 1 pl. 12°. (Lacy's acting edition of plays. v. 120.) **NCO (Lacy)**

—— The only edition correctly marked, by permission from the prompter's book... Embellished with a fine engraving, by Mr. Findlay, from a drawing, taken in the theatre. London, New York: Samuel French ₍18—?₎. 30 p., 1 pl. 12°. (French's acting edition. no. 1799.)
First produced at the Pavilion Theatre, March 7, 1835.

The **Purim** play ₍in two scenes₎. (Young Israel. New York, 1878. 8°. v. 8, p. 145–156.) *** PBD**
A play (dramatization of the book of Esther) within a play.
The scene is laid in an American city of to-day.

Queen Hester. *See* **Godly Queene Hester.**

Queen Vashti. ₍An anonymous play in four scenes.₎ (In: M. L. Cobb, compiler, Poetical dramas for home and school. Boston, 1873. 12°. p. 183–189.) **MZB**

Racine, Jean Baptiste. Esther; or, Faith triumphant. A sacred tragedy ₍in three acts and in verse, from the French of Racine₎ by Thomas Brereton. London, 1715. 12°.
Title from the British Museum Catalogue.

—— The sacred dramas of Esther and Athalia... Edinburgh, 1803. 8°.
Title from British Museum Catalogue.

—— Esther. A drama. By Racine. Translated from the French. By Mrs. Caroline Andrews. Philadelphia, 1876. 63 p. 16°.
On p. 5 is printed a testimonial from Isaac M. Wise of Cincinnati to the faithfulness of the translator's version.

—— Esther; a tragedy... Literally translated by...J. Rice. Dublin ₍1882₎. 44 p. 12°. (Kelly's Classical keys.)
Title from British Museum Catalogue.

—— Esther, a tragedy ₍in a prologue and three acts₎ founded on Holy Scripture. (In his: Dramatic works. Translated by R. B. Boswell. London, 1890. 8°. v. 2, p. 269–325.)
Acted at the Maison de Saint Cyr in 1689. The incidents are in strict accordance with the Biblical narrative. The fictitious character of Elizabeth, friend to Esther, has Madame de Maintenon for its prototype.
Short selections are printed in S. N. Elrington, jr., *Original poems and lyrics*, Dublin, 1853, p. 185–194, *NCM; Young Judaean*, New York, v. 1, March, 1911, p. 12–15; and in *Rachel's Readings in both French and English, first series*, New York, 1855, 5 p., *NKM p.v.18*.

—— Esther... Translated from the French by A. P. Daril. Truro: Netherton & Worth, 1895. vi, 48 p. 8°.
Title from British Museum Catalogue.

Fisher, Dorothea Frances (Canfield). Esther and Athalie. (In her: Corneille and Racine in England. New York, 1904. 12°. p. 249–255.) *** R – NKC**

Spitz, Leon. Racine's Biblical drama. The tragedies of the great French poet owed considerably to the stories of the Bible. (Jewish tribune. New York, 1926. f°. v. 45, March 26, 1926, p. 34, 51.) *** PBD**

Russell, Mary M. A woman who dared. ₍In three scenes.₎ (In her: Dramatized Bible stories for young people. New York, 1921. 12°. p. 29–34.)

Sansom, John. Esther: a sacred drama. London ₍: Hatchard₎, 1845. 8°.
Title from British Museum Catalogue.

Schneider, Rose. The appeal of Esther. ₍In four acts.₎ (Young Israel. Cincinnati, 1911. 8°. v. 7, p. 461–462.)

Shultz, Eveline Spooner. Queen Esther at the palace. New York: Hints Pub. Co., cop. 1902. 8 p. 12°.
Cover-title.
Consists of twenty living pictures or explanations.

Stackhouse, Perry J. A queen who saved a nation from death. ₍A play in four scenes.₎ (In his: Bible dramas in the pulpit. Philadelphia ₍cop. 1926₎. 8°. p. 45–57.) **NBM**
Time: 473 b. c.

Tennant, William. Esther; or, The fall of Haman. (In his: Hebrew dramas. Edinburgh, 1845. 16°.)
Title from British Museum Catalogue.

Waldo, Edna La Moore. The story of Esther. Arranged in four short episodes for use in church schools. Franklin, Ohio: Eldridge Entertainment House, Inc., cop. 1926. 9 p. 12°. (Eldridge church entertainments.)

White, Edward Joseph. Esther, queen of Persia; a historical drama in three parts (adapted for the screen). ₍St. Louis, cop. 1924.₎ 62 p. illus. 4°.

Whitney, Mary Ellen. Esther. ₍A play in nine scenes.₎ (In her: Bible plays and how to produce them. New York ₍cop. 1927₎. 12°. p. 50–65.)

Old Testament Plays — Esther, continued

Wilcox, Ella Wheeler, and LUSCOMBE SEARELLE. Mizpah; a poetical play in four acts founded on the historical narrative of Esther. Written by Ella Wheeler Wilcox and Luscombe Searelle. Music composed by Luscombe Searelle. Produced by Elizabeth Kennedy and her company in New York and the leading theatres of America. New York: Klebold Press, Inc., 1906. 119 p. 12°.

The plot of this drama, other than the Biblical story, together with the scenario, situations, music and all lines not printed in italics are from the pen of Ella Wheeler Wilcox.

Selections are printed in her *Poems of progress,* Chicago [cop. 1909], p. 46–57, *NBI.*

Reviewed in *The Reader,* Indianapolis, 1906, v. 8, p. 97–98, * *DA.*

Produced at the Academy of Music, New York, Sept. 24, 1906. For reviews of the production see *New York dramatic mirror,* New York, v. 56, Oct. 6, 1906, p. 3, * *DA,* and *Theatre magazine,* New York, 1906, v. 6, p. 284, †† *NBLA.*

Willner, Wolff. The Book of Esther; dramatized [in three acts]... Cincinnati: American Hebrew Pub. House, Bloch Prtg. Co., 1892. 32 p. 8°.   * PSQ

The cast of characters, some of whom are fictitious, are humorously described.

Reviewed in *Jewish exponent,* Philadelphia, v. 10, no. 18, Feb. 5, 1892, p. 7, column 2, * *PBD.*

Wolf, Ruth E. Levi. A festival of feasts; a Purim fantasy. New York: Bloch Pub. Co. [cop. 1911.] 12 p. 16°.

The Jewish holidays, as well as the principal persons in the book of Esther, are the characters.

Woolf, Henry. Merry Purim; a tiny farce playlet for tiny tots, in two acts. Cincinnati: Department of Synagogue and School Extension of the Union of American Hebrew Congregations [cop. 1929]. 16 p. 12°.

Written in rhyme and prose.

Zeto, pseud. Vashti [a tragedy in five acts]. (In his: Vashti, and other poems. London, 1897. 16°. p. 1–91.)   **NCM**

DANIEL

Abelson, Alter. The undefiled. Biblical play in five acts. Scenes 12. (Jewish forum. New York, 1920. 8°. v. 3, p. 164–172, 221–226, 265–271, 361–370, 494–498, 501, 565–566, 569–570, 573–574.)   * PBD

Benton, Rita. The burning fiery furnace. [A play in three acts.] (In her: Bible plays. New York [cop. 1922]. 8°. p. 192–213.)   * PSQ

—— Daniel. [A play in three acts.] (In her: Bible plays. New York [cop. 1922]. 8°. p. 158–191.)   * PSQ

Chapin, Harry Lorenzo. Semeramus. A spectacular drama in six acts. (In his: Poems and plays. New York [cop. 1915]. 8°. p. 90–113.)   **NBI**

Daniel and Belshazzar.

Daniel; a play for children in three scenes. (Jewish child. New York, 1919. f°. v. 8, no. 7, p. 4, 6.)   * PBD

Daniel the seer. [In five scenes.] (In: M. W. Thomas, editor, Old Testament drama. London [1927]. 12°. p. 179–198.)

Githens, Harry W. The fiery furnace. [In two scenes.] (In his: Dramatized stories from the Old Testament. Cincinnati [cop. 1927]. 12°. p. 172–178.)   **NASH**

Shadrach, Meshach, and Abednego.

—— An interpreter of dreams. [In two acts.] (In his: Dramatized stories from the Old Testament. Cincinnati [cop. 1927]. 12°. p. 164–171.)

—— A persecuted prophet. [The prophet Daniel, governor of Babylon. In three scenes.] (In his: Dramatized stories from the Old Testament. Cincinnati [cop. 1927]. 12°. p. 185–194.)   **NASH**

Lobingier, Elizabeth Erwin (Miller). Daniel in the lion's den. (In her: The dramatization of Bible stories. Chicago [cop. 1919]. 12°. p. 93–97.)   * YIR

In three scenes.

Manley, William Ford. The king dreams. [In four scenes.] (In his: A second book of Bible dramas. New York [cop. 1930]. 8°. p. 169–188.)   **NBM**

More, Hannah. Daniel; a sacred drama [in seven parts]. (In her: Sacred dramas. Philadelphia, 1787. 24°. p. 131–169.) * KD

The subject taken from the sixth chapter of the book of Daniel.

Reprinted in G. A. Kohut, editor, *A Hebrew anthology,* Cincinnati, 1913, v. 2, p. 1083–1101, * *PSO.*

Nebuchadnezzar: a play first acted by the Lord Admiral's players in December, 1596. See Henslowe's Diary, ed. Collier, p. 83.

See W. C. Hazlitt, *Manual,* p. 163.

Opal, pseud. The benedicite. [In four scenes.] (Drama III.) (In his: Cloud of witnesses. New York, 1874. 12°. p. 56–61.)   **NBM**

Based on the furnace incident narrated in Daniel, ch. 1.

P., Brother. Daniel in the lion's den. A sacred drama. In five acts. London [1871?]. 36 p. (In: P., Three plays... For male characters only. Translated from the French... By Br. P. London [1871?]. 12°.)   **NKM p.v.229, no.5**

Parkhurst, Winthrop. Morraca; a play in one act. (Drama. Washington, 1918. 8°. v. 8, p. 536–574.)   **NAFA**

Based on Daniel, ch. 5.

David, a youth beloved by Morraca, wife of Belshazzar, acts the rôle of the historical Daniel. Apologies to Daniel, a preface, p. 524–535.

Parsons, Margaret. Daniel and the lions. [In three scenes.] (In her: Ten stirring Bible plays. Franklin, Ohio, cop. 1927. 12°. p. 50–58.)

Old Testament Plays — Daniel, continued

Raine, James Watt. Daniel's loyalty. ₁In two scenes.₁ (In his: Bible dramatics. London & New York ₁cop. 1927₁. 12°. p. 343–356.)

Russell, Mary M. Strangers in a strange land. (In her: How to produce plays and pageants. New York ₁cop. 1923₁. 12°. p. 185–215.) **MZB**

Whitney, Mary Ellen. Daniel in the lion's den. ₁A play in five scenes.₁ (In her: Bible plays and how to produce them. New York ₁cop. 1927₁. 12°. p. 66–73.)

Williams, Benjamin Harrover. Babylon; a drama. ₁Chicago: G. Garretson & Co., 1901.₁ 1 p.l., 65 p. 12°.

Title from the Library of Congress.

Daniel, the prophet, is one of the characters, as well as Nebuchadnezzar. The main plot, however, is not Biblical.

BELSHAZZAR

Calderon de la Barca, Pedro. Belshazzar's feast. (In his: Mysteries of Corpus Christi; from the Spanish. By Denis Florence Mac-Carthy. Dublin, 1867. 16°. p. 111–208.) **NPP**

First Spanish edition appeared in 1664.

Mac-Carthy's translation is reprinted in Alfred Bates, *The drama*, London, 1903, v. 4, p. 251–298, *NAF (Bates).*

CALDERON'S Autos sacramentales: Baltassar's feast. (Catholic world. New York, 1875. 8°. v. 21, p. 213–217.) *** DA**

Cole, Francis Richard. Love & fate; or, Triumph in destruction... A master drama of the ancient world; love romance of a beautiful Grecian maid and a warrior bold culminating at the feast of Belshazzar... Produced under the original title of Belshazzar and the writing on the wall... (In his: Plays... Chicago, cop. 1922. ₁12₁, 79(1) p. 12°.) **NBM**

Among the characters are Soloman, a Jew in the service of King Belshazzar, and Daniel, the prophet.

Dumas, William Charles. Belshazzar ₁a drama in five acts₁. Boston: R. G. Badger ₁cop. 1912₁. 120 p. 12°. *** PSQ**

Githens, Harry W. The handwriting on the wall. (In his: Dramatized stories from the Old Testament. Cincinnati ₁cop. 1927₁. 12°. p. 179–184.) **NASH**

Gómez de Avellaneda y Arteaga, Gertrudis. Belshazzar; a drama translated from the Spanish by William Freeman Burbank. London: B. F. Stevens & Brown; San Francisco: A. M. Robertson, 1914. 4 p.l., 64 p., 1 port. 12°.

Title from Library of Congress.

The scene of the play, which is in four acts, is Babylon. Time, 558 B. C. The events of the play precede the fall of the city into the hands of Cyrus. Among the characters are Daniel and Jehoiakim, deposed king of Judea.

Jacobson, Janie. Belshazzar; a Scriptural play in four acts. ₁New York: Schoen and Kellerman, 1911.₁ 11(1)₁ p. nar. 8°. *** PSQ**

Leavitt, John McDowell. The siege of Babylon. A tragedy, by the author of "Afranius," "The Idumean"... ₁J. M. Leavitt.₁ New York: Hurd and Houghton, 1869. 47 p. 16°. **NBL p.v.22**

Milman, Henry Hart. Belshazzar: a dramatic poem. London: J. Murray, 1822. iv, 162 p. 8°. **NCM**

"Though, in the following poem, I have adhered strictly to the outline in Scripture, I have availed myself of whatever appeared to my purpose in the profane historians. My general authorities, where I do not follow the Book of Daniel, are Herodotus and Diodorus Siculus..."

Reprinted in his *Poetical works*, London, 1839, and London, 1840, v. 1, p. 239–357, *NCM.* Also printed in *Poetical works of Milman, Bowles, Wilson, and Barry Cornwall*, Paris, 1829, p. 131–155, *NCI,* and in *The poetical works of Howitt, Milman, and Keats*, Philadelphia, 1847, p. 382–407, *NCI,* and G. A. Kohut, *A Hebrew anthology*, Cincinnati, 1913, v. 2, p. 983–1031, * *PSO.*

Reviewed in *British critic*, London, 1822, v. 60, p. 152–160; *Literary gazette*, London, 1822, v. 4, p. 319–321, **DA*; and in *New monthly magazine*, London, 1822, v. 5, p. 49–54, * *DA.*

More, Hannah. Belshazzar; a sacred drama ₁in three parts₁. (In her: Sacred dramas. Philadelphia, 1787. 24°. p. 89–130.) *** KD**

The subject taken from the fifth chapter of Daniel.

Reprinted in G. A. Kohut, *A Hebrew anthology*, Cincinnati, 1913, v. 2, p. 1033–1053, * *PSO.*

O'Neill, Eugene Gladstone. Belshazzar, a Biblical play in scenes. Destroyed by the author, 1915. Noted in H. L. Cohen, *More one-act plays*, p. 315.

Osgood, Phillips Endecott. Destiny. Belshazzar of Babylon asks for a revelation. ₁In one scene.₁ illus. (In his: Pulpit dramas. New York and London, 1929. 12°. p. 1–24.) **NAFM**

Saltus, Francis Saltus. Bel-shar-uzzur (Belshazzar). A dramatic poem. ₁In five scenes.₁ (In his: The witch of En-dor, and other poems. Buffalo, 1891. 12°. p. 183–279.) **NBI**

EZRA

GOLDSTEIN, Max. Darius, Xerxes und Artaxerxes im Drama der neueren Literaturen. Beitrag zur vergleichenden Literaturgeschichte. Naumburg a.S.: G. Pätz ₁1912?₁. xiv, 113(1) p. 8°. **NAFH p.v.1, no.5**

Benützte Literatur, p. ix–xiv.

—— —— Leipzig: A. Deichert, 1912. xiv, 113(1) p. 8°. (Münchener Beiträge zur romanischen und englischen Philologie. Heft 54.) **RDTA (Münchener)**

Browne, Laurence E. The first act of Judaism. (In his: Early Judaism. Cambridge, Eng., 1920. 12°. p. 113–122.) *** PNC**

A summary in dramatic form of the first five chapters of his book, dealing with the times of Ezra and Nehemiah. Time: 520 B. C.

Old Testament Plays — Ezra, continued

Osgood, Phillips Endecott. The story of a story. ₍In one scene.₎ (In his: The sinner beloved, and other religious plays. New York and London, 1928. 12°. p. 215–247.) **NAFM**

A play on the circumstances leading to the composition of the book of Ruth. Ezra is one of the characters.

Russell, Mary M. The secret of success. ₍In four scenes.₎ (In her: Dramatized Bible stories for young people. New York ₍cop. 1921₎. 12°. p. 63–73.)

NEHEMIAH

Bartlett, Edward R., and E. Ruth Bartlett. Release, a dramatic presentation of the Easter message ₍in two episodes₎. (International journal of religious education. Mount Morris, Ill., 1927. 4°. v. 3, March, 1927, p. 18–21.)

The scene of the first episode is laid at the ruins of ancient Jerusalem in the time of Nehemiah; the three scenes of the second, in Nazareth and Jerusalem in the time of Jesus.

Curryer, C. E. The building of the wall. A Biblical play in three acts arranged by C. E. Curryer. With an introduction by E. L. Ramsay. London: Christophers ₍1926₎. 31(1) p., 1 pl. 12°. **NCO p.v.543, no.7**

Galleher, Helen. The herald of the restoration. A dramatization in prologue, one scene and epilogue. (In: Fearless men. ₍Chicago, cop. 1923.₎ 8°. p. 61–72.) **NBF p.v.60, no.6**

Characters: Spirit of Judah, heralds, the prophet, Jews, merchants, etc.

Hale, Harris G., and N. M. Hall. ...Nehemiah the builder. Arranged by Harris G. Hale and Newton M. Hall. Boston: The Pilgrim Press, 1906. iv, 18 p. 12°. (Biblical dramas. ₍no. 11.₎) **NBL (Biblical)**

Mackett, John. Nehemiah, a sacred drama in six parts ₍and in verse₎. To which is added, A paraphrase on the seventy-third Psalm... Rochester ₍1793₎. 8°.

Title from British Museum Catalogue.

Tilston, Thomas. The return from the captivity, Isandula and other poems. London, 1879. 8°.

" 'The return from the captivity,' concerns the return of the Jews to their native land in the time of Cyrus. It is in the form of a drama interspersed with songs and choruses." — *Jewish chronicle, London, Sept. 5, 1879, p. 12.*

Whitman, Eleanor Wood. Nehemiah the builder; a Biblical drama with music ₍in four acts₎... Boston, Chicago: The Pilgrim Press ₍cop. 1926₎. 5 p.l., 32 p., 4 pl. 12°. Words only. **NBL p.v.149, no.1**

"The whole dramatic story comes from Nehemiah's own memoirs and therefore gives accurate historical data for his period ₍Nehemiah, chaps. 1–7; 12: 27–47; 13: 4–31₎." The first presentation of this drama was given in Jordan Hall, Boston, and the music was selected by Henry Gideon, director of music of Temple Israel, who included appropriate Hebrew music.

APOCRYPHA PLAYS

ESDRAS

King Darius. The story of King Darius, 1565. London: Issued for subscribers by T. C. and E. C. Jack, 1909. v p., 32 l. 4°. (Tudor facsimile texts.) **NCO (Tudor)**

Facsimile reprint of earliest known edition, reproduced from the copy in the British Museum.

Original title-page reads: A Pretie new Enterlude, both pithie & pleasaunt of the Story of the King Daryus, Beinge taken out of the third and fourth Chapter of the third booke of Esdras... Imprynted at London... by Thomas Colwell... MDLXV.

Also printed in John S. Farmer, editor, *Anonymous plays. 3rd series*, London, 1906, p. 41–92, *NCO (Early)*, and in *Quellen und Forschungen zur Sprach- und Culturgeschichte*, Strassburg, 1898, Heft 80, p. 359–418, notes, p. lxiii–lxx, *NFF.*

—— King Darius. An hitherto (1906) unknown edition. London: Issued for subscribers by T. C. & E. C. Jack, 1907. 35 l. 4°. **NCO (Tudor)**

Facsimile reprint of British Museum copy. Original title-page reads: A preaty new enterlude, both pythie and pleasaunt, of the story of King Darius... Imprinted at London... By Hugh Jackson. Anno Domini, 1577.

Short selections are printed in *International journal of apocrypha*, London, 1908, no. 13, p. 17 and no. 14, p. 5–6.

Gibbings, W. W. The 16th century Esdrasplay. (International journal of apocrypha. London, 1907. 4°. no. 11, p. 13–15.) ***YLY**

TOBIT

A list of stage properties for a Tobit play produced July, 1564 in Lincoln, England, is given in *County folk-lore... Examples of printed folk-lore concerning Lincolnshire*, London, 1908, v. 5, p. 387, *ZBA (County).*

Abrahams, Israel. The Tobit drama in the sixteenth century. (In: Judaica. Festschrift zu Hermann Cohens siebzigsten Geburtstage. Berlin, 1912. 8°. p. 25–30.) ***PBN**

Bates, Katharine Lee. The healing of Tobit; a play ₍in three acts₎ of Assyria. (In her: The pilgrim ship. New York, 1926. 8°. p. 145–210.) **NBI**

Reprinted in her *Selected poems, ed. by Marion Pelton Guild*, Boston and New York, 1930, p. 223–230, *NBI.*

Fiske, Isabella Howe. A comedy of the exile ₍in one act₎. (Poet lore. Boston, 1906. 8°. v. 17, no. 1, p. 51–58.) ***DA**

Genlis, Stéphanie Félicité Ducrest de St. Aubin, comtesse de. The return of Tobias, a sacred drama. (In her: Sacred dramas. London, 1786. 8°. p. 313–347.) **NKO**

In ten scenes.

Jacobson, James. Tobias, a dramatic poem. With other pieces. London: ₍Cadell,₎ 1818. 12°.

Title from British Museum Catalogue.

Apocrypha Plays — Tobit, continued

Lefevre, H. Tobias. [A dramatic poem.] (Frank Leslie's Sunday magazine. New York, 1886. 4°. v. 20, p. 126–127.) *** DA**

C. F. Gounod used the words for his oratorio.

The **Story** of Tobit, adapted from the Apocrypha by Doris Pailthorpe, Zoë Procter, and Dorothea Rock; a mime in the mediaeval manner. Illustrations by Doris Pailthorpe. London: Sidgwick & Jackson, Ltd. [1930.] 57 p. illus. 12°. **NCR**

Introduction by R. W. Chambers.
First produced at the Guildhouse, London, by the Guildhouse Players, October, 1925. Miss Maude Royden as reader.

Tobit: an old English mystery, acted at Lincoln in July, 1563. See some account of the properties used in it in Malone's Shakespear, iii.26.

See W. C. Hazlitt, *Manual*, p. 230.

Woolley, Olive Frank. Sara. [In one act.] (In: University of Utah plays, edited by B. R. Lewis. Boston [cop. 1928]. 12°. p. 83–100.) **NBL p.v.186**

JUDITH

Purdie, Edna. The story of Judith in German and English literature... Paris: Honoré Champion, 1927. vi, 161 p., 2 l. 8°. (Bibliothèque de la Revue de littérature comparée. tome 39.) **NKB (Bibliothèque)**

Reviewed in *Jewish chronicle*, London, v. 87, Feb. 10, 1928, p. 12, * *PBE.*

Sypherd, Wilbur Owen. "Judith" in American literature. (Modern Language Association of America. Publications. Menasha, Wis., 1930. 8°. v. 45, p. 336–338.) **RAA**

Lists American plays and poems not mentioned by Purdie.

Abercrombie, Lascelles. Judith [a dramatic poem in four parts]. (In his: Emblems of love. London, 1912. 12°. p. 127–187.) **NCM**

Aldrich, Thomas Bailey. Judith of Bethulia, a tragedy [in five acts]. Boston and New York: Houghton, Mifflin and Company, 1904. 4 p.l., 98 p., 1 l., 1 pl. 8°. *** PSQ**

Reprinted in his *Works*, Boston, 1915, v. 2, p. 169–248, *NBG.*

"This play — written for Miss Nance O'Neil and produced at the Tremont Theatre, Boston, October 13, 1904 — is in part a dramatization of the author's narrative poem 'Judith and Holofernes.' "
Reviewed in *International journal of apocrypha*, London, 1907, no. 8, p. 7–11, * *YLY.*
The *New York dramatic mirror*, New York, Oct. 22, 1904, v. 52, p. 14, * *DA*, contains a review, by Jay Benton, of the Boston production.
For additional reviews see the Warren C. Cawley collection of 100,000 clippings on plays, box J, *MWE.*

Bennett, Arnold. Judith, a play in three acts, founded on the apocryphal book of "Judith"... London: Chatto & Windus, 1919. 125 p., 1 l. 12°. **NCR**

—— —— New York: George H. Doran Company [cop. 1919]. 3 p.l., 9–96 p. 12°. **NCR**

Reviewed in *The Athenæum*, London, May 9, 1919, p. 310, * *DA;* by William Archer in *The Bookman*, London, 1919, v. 56, p. 105–106, ††* *GDD;* in *Illustrated London news*, London, 1919, v. 154, p. 692, * *DA;* in *The Nation*, New York, 1919, v. 109, p. 340–341, * *DA;* by Francis Hackett in *The New republic*, New York, 1919, v. 20, p. 268–269, * *DA;* and by William Archer in *The Review*, New York, 1919, v. 1, p. 109, * *DA.*
First presented at the Devonshire Park Theatre, Eastbourne, England, April 7, 1919. Produced in London at the Kingsway Theatre April 30, 1919 with Lillah McCarthy as Judith and Claude King as Holofernes.

Bickerstaff, Isaac. Judith: a sacred drama as performed in the Church of Stratford-on-Avon on occasion of the Jubilee, 6 Sept., 1769, in honour of the memory of Shakespeare. The music by Dr. Arne. London: W. Griffin, 1769. iv, 20 p. 4°.

Title and collation copied from Jaggard's *Shakespeare bibliography*, in which it is stated that a copy is in the Boston Public Library.

—— —— [Selections.] (London chronicle. London, 1769. 4°. v. 26, p. 229.) *** A**

Giacometti, Paolo. ...Tragedy of Judith: [in five acts] as presented by Madame Ristori and her dramatic company, under the management of J. Grau. The English translation by Isaac C. Pray. New York: J. A. Gray & Green, 1866. 40 p. 8°. **NNO p.v.132, no.7**

Words only. Italian and English texts printed in parallel columns. Time: 634 B. C.
"This play is from the book of Judith, to be found in the Apocrypha. The story is strictly followed, and all the chief characters of the drama are to be found in the Scriptural poem." — *From the Argument, p. 2.*
The play was produced at the Tremont Theatre, Boston, March 24, 1904, with Nance O'Neil as Judith. For comments see the Warren C. Cawley collection of about 100,000 clippings on plays, box J, *MWE.*

Hebbel, Christian Friedrich. Judith, a tragedy in five acts. Translated from the German by Carl Van Doren. (Poet lore. Boston, 1914. 4°. v. 25, p. 257–321.) *** DA**

First produced at the Court Theatre, Berlin, July 6, 1840.
For three reviews of the first American production at Tripler Hall, New York, April 4, 1864, with Avonia Jones Brooke in the title rôle, see *Daly's theatre scrapbooks*, v. 1, † *NBL.*

Newport, Clara Price. Judith. (In her: Woman in the thought and work of Friedrich Hebbel. Madison, Wis., 1912. 8°. p. 56–65.) **STG (Wisconsin)**

University of Wisconsin. Bulletin: Philology and literature series. v. 5, no. 3.

Robertson, J. G. Friedrich Hebbel. (Modern language review. Cambridge, 1913. 8°. v. 8, p. 145–159.) **NAA**

Contains a discussion of Hebbel's *Judith* and *Herod and Mariamne.*

Holofernes: an interlude acted at Hatfield in 1556.

See W. C. Hazlitt, *Manual*, p. 108.

Apocrypha Plays — Judith, continued

Holofernes: a play performed at Derby in 1572.

See W. C. Hazlitt, *Manual*, p. 108.

Judith and Holofernes: a droll mentioned by John Locke, the celebrated philosopher, in a letter dated 1664, as acted at Bartholomew Fair. It was acted at the same fair at least as late as 1732; and there is a picture of the booth, with some of the actors, in a curious fan of 1728, on which are represented some of the chief scenes of the fair.

See W. C. Hazlitt, *Manual*, p. 123.

Kemp, Harry. Judith. A one-act play. (In his: Boccaccio's untold tale, and other one-act plays. New York [cop. 1924]. 12°. p. 123–143.)   **8–NBM**

Time: During the reign of Nebuchadnezzar — B. C. 561 — twelfth year of his reign.

Levinger, Elma C. Ehrlich. In the tent of Holofernes. A play in one act. (The American Hebrew. New York, 1922. f°. v. 112, no. 5, Dec. 15, 1922, p. 165, 169, 172, 174.) * **PBD**

Manley, William Ford. Judith. (In his: Bible dramas. New York [cop. 1928]. 8°. p. 205–225.)   **NBM**

In three scenes.

Mills, Samuel Alfred. Judith; or, The wife of Manasseh; a fictional drama. New York: Hamilton Print [1902]. 112 p. 8°.

Title from Library of Congress.
In four acts.

Moore, Thomas Sturge. Judith. [In one act.] (In his: A Sicilian idyll and Judith. London, 1911. 8°. p. xli–lxxii.)   **NCR**

Reviewed in *Poetry review*, London, 1912, v. 1, p. 158–160, * *DA*, and in *Truth*, London, 1916, v. 79, p. 152, * *DA*.

Produced by the Stage Society, at Queen's Theatre, London, Jan. 23, 1916.

Pennie, John Fitzgerald. The fair avenger; or, The destroyer destroyed, an academic drama [in four acts and in verse]. (In his: Scenes in Palestine; or, Dramatic sketches from the Bible. London, 1825. 12°.)

Title from the British Museum Catalogue.

A short selection is printed in *International journal of apocrypha*, London, 1908, no. 13, p. 12–13.

Radcliff, Ralph. The Fortitude of Judith: a tragedy by Ralph Radcliff. Not printed.

See W. C. Hazlitt, *Manual*, p. 88.

Schonaeus, Cornelius. A play of Judith. (Modern language notes. Baltimore, 1917. 8°. v. 32, p. 1–6.)   **RAA**

"An incomplete play of 'Holofernes,' in Latin and English, is found in Hengwrt and Peniarth MS. 508, at the National Library of Wales... The original Latin, which proves to be a copy of a portion of the play of Judith by Cornelius Schonaeus is written on the even pages; the English translation is on the odd pages." The English translation is given in the body of the article, p. 2–4, which is by Gwen Ann Jones.

Schuetze, Martin. Judith; a tragedy in five acts. New York: Henry Holt and Co., 1910. 5 p.l., 5–306 p. 12°.   **NBM**

Reviewed by Edith J. R. Isaacs in *Drama*, Chicago, no. 3, Aug., 1911, p. 168–171, *NAFA*. "Holofernes is

conceived as a splendid warrior overcoming Judith — overwhelming her patriotism and her religion by a great love which wrecks Judith's life, after she has committed the murder."

SUSANNA

Jasper, Walter. Susanna; a drama in five acts. Boston: Mayhew Publishing Co., 1908. 2 p.l., 100 p. 8°.   **NBM**

Moeller, Philip. Sisters of Susannah. A Biblical farce. (In his: Five somewhat historical plays. New York, 1918. 12°. p. 71–99.)   **NBM**

Shortly after the trial of Susanna.

Produced at the Comedy Theatre, New York, Oct. 2, 1916 by the Washington Square Players, with Erskine Sanford as Job, and Arthur E. Hohl as Samson. See *New York dramatic mirror*, New York, Oct. 7, 1916, v. 76, p. 7, * *DA*.

Susanna: a droll on the subject of Susanna and the Elders was acted at Bartholomew Fair in the seventeenth century. It is mentioned in an old song on that fair.

See W. C. Hazlitt, *Manual*, p. 221.

Susanna's tears: a piece, so called, is included in the curious and valuable list at the end of Massinger's *Old Law*, 1656; and it is mentioned by Langbaine. Not otherwise known.

See W. C. Hazlitt, *Manual*, p. 221.

Tollet, Elizabeth. Susanna, or, Innocence preserv'd. Musical drama. (In her: Poems on several occasions. London, 1755. 12°.)

Title from British Museum Catalogue.

Warshaw, J. High lights in the story of Susanna. [A dramatic poem in four scenes.] (Poet lore. Boston, 1917. 8°. v. 28, p. 242–245.)   * **DA**

MACCABEES

Boylesve, Marin de. The Maccabees; a Biblical drama in three acts from the French of Marin de Boylesve. Chicago: Dramatic Pub. Co., cop. 1899. 41 p. 12°.

Cohn, Esther. Watch fires. A little story of Hannah's sons. (The Ark. Cincinnati, 1913. 8°. v. 3, p. 758–761.)   * **PBD**

—— —— n.p., n.d.

Mimeographed.

Esterman, Joseph. The martyr child. (A dramatization for young children of the scene between Antiochus, Hannah, and her youngest child.) [New York: Young Judaea.] 2 l. 4°.

Mimeographed.

Freed, Clarence I. The Maccabee; one-act play. (Council of Y. M. H. and Kindred Associations. Publication. New York, 1918. 8°. Nov., 1918, p. 19–28.)

Frishberg, J. S. Hannah and her seven sons. (A Chanukah play.) Written originally in Hebrew by J. S. Frishberg. New York: S. Druckerman, 1922. 16 p. 12°.

Apocrypha Plays — Maccabees, continued

Ginsberg, Jean Doris. Story of Hanukkah. ₍In four scenes.₎ (Young Israel. Cincinnati, 1930. 4°. v. 22, July, p. 17–18.) *** PBD**

Grossman, Samuel S. "The mother of martyrs." The story of Hannah and her seven sons ₍in one act₎ for Chanuckah presentation. New York: Young Judaean Pub. Association, cop. 1913. 8 p. 8°. *** PSQ p.v.1**
Repr.: Young Judaean, Dec., 1913, v. 4, p. 13–19.

Jacobson, Janie. For liberty, for school and home. Founded on Jewish patriotism. ₍In three acts.₎ (Hebrew standard. New York, 1903. f°. v. 44, Nov. 13, 1903, p. 2, 9–10.) *** PBD**

—— For liberty. A Chanucah play in four acts. ₍New York: Stettiner Bros.,₎ cop. 1905. 16 p. nar. 8°. *** PSQ**

—— —— ₍New York: Stettiner Press, cop. 1916.₎ 16 p. nar. 8°.

Katzenelson, Isaac. The Hasmoneans. ₍In one act.₎ Adapted from the Hebrew by Efraim Rosenzweig. (In: Jewish Education Committee, Chicago. Jewish child home library. Chanukah. Chicago ₍1930₎. p. 15–20.)

Kuhn, Samuel O. In defiance of Antiochus. (The Ark. Cincinnati, 1914. 8°. v. 4, p. 563–566.) *** PBD**

—— —— ₍Cincinnati: Ark Pub. Co.,₎ cop. 1914. 4 p. 8°.
Cover-title.

Lampe, John A. Sons of Mattathias; a drama. Chicago: J. A. Lampe, 1898. 1 p.l., 38 p. 8°.
Title from Library of Congress.

Leiser, Joseph. A make-believe Chanukah; a play for children in three acts, with prolog. Cincinnati: Department of Synagog and School Extension of the Union of American Hebrew Congregations ₍cop. 1922₎. 24 p. 12°. *** PBM p.v.98, no.6**
The prologue takes place in the living room of the Bergs (modern America). Acts ɪ, ɪɪ, and ɪɪɪ in Modin, 165 ʙ. ᴄ.

Levinger, Elma C. Ehrlich. The light of Israel. A Chanukkah play in four acts by E. C. E. (The Ark. Cincinnati, 1912. 8°. v. 2, p. 945–959.) *** PBD**

—— —— With plates for costumes. Cincinnati: Department of Synagog and School Extension of the Union of American Hebrew Congregations ₍cop. 1923₎. 32 p., 2 l. illus. 12°. *** PBM p.v.98, no.9**
Reprinted in her *Jewish festivals in the religious school*, Cincinnati, 1923, p. 317–349, * *PSY*, and in her *Chanukah entertainments*, p. 83–115, * *PKB*.

—— The young defender; a short sketch for Hanuka. New York: Bloch Pub. Co., 1922. 4 p. 16°.

Longfellow, Henry Wadsworth. Judas Maccabæus. ₍In five acts.₎ (In his: Three books of song. Boston, 1872. 12°. p. 111–174.) **NBI**
Reprinted in his *Complete poetical works*, Boston, 1876, p. 240–246, *NBI*. For later editions see the Library's catalogue.
Extracts are printed in G. A. Kohut, *A Hebrew anthology*, Cincinnati, 1913, v. 2, p. 1103–1110, * *PSO*, and an extract under the title "Hannah and her seven sons," in *Young Judaean*, New York, Dec., 1910, v. 1, p. 12–16.
Reviewed by Herbert Pentin in *Gentleman's magazine*, London, 1907, v. 303, p. 317–328, * *DA*.
The poem was read and illustrated in pantomime by Educational Alliance pupils, New York, Dec., 1900. See *Hebrew Standard*, New York, Jan. 4, 1901, p. 3, * *PBD*.

——

גבורות יהודה מכבי אדער גס־חנכה... א דראמא
אין פינף אקטען... איבערגיזעצט...אין יודיש
דיוטש פין מ. א. בעליניסאן...
Odessa: M. Belinson, 1882. 1 p.l., 18 p. 4°. *** PTW**
From the Russian translation of P. Weinberg.

——

יהודה המכבי ע"פ ה. ו. לנגפלאו. מתרגם מאת
יוסף מזל.
Manchester: Printed and published by the translator, 1900. 4 p.l., 60 p. 12°. *** PSN**

—— Iуда Маккавей. Драма. ₍Translated by P. Weinberg.₎ (Еврейская библіотека. St. Petersburg, 1875. 8°. v. 5, p. 1–33.) *** PBI**

Aʙʀᴀʜᴀᴍs, Israel. Longfellow's "Judas Maccabaeus." (In his: By-paths in Hebraic bookland. Philadelphia, 1920. 8°. p. 290–296.) *** PAT**

Lᴇᴠɪɴɢᴇʀ, Elma C. Ehrlich. The youngest son. ₍An extract adapted by E. E. Levinger.₎ (In her: Jewish festivals in the religious school. Cincinnati, 1923. 12°. p. 100–102.) *** PSY**

Mendes, Henry Pereira. A Chanukah play for Sunday schools ₍in three acts₎. (American Hebrew. New York, 1899. 4°. v. 64, p. 113–117.) *** PBD**
See communication by the author on p. 148.

—— Judas Maccabaeus. A Chanuka play for Sunday school children. New York: P. Cowen, 1898. 19 p. 16°. *** PSQ p.v.1**

Osgood, Phillips Endecott. A dramatic adaptation of the oratorio "Judas Maccabaeus," by G. F. Handel, for use as a sung miracle play in church. ₍In two parts.₎ illus. (In his: Old-time church drama adapted. New York and London, 1928. 12°. p. 271–291.) **NAFM**

Roth, Samuel. Uziel and Zephamah. (From the Hebrew) ₍in four scenes₎. illus. (Young Judaean. New York, 1913. 8°. v. 4, Dec., 1913, p. 2–5.)

Apocrypha Plays — Maccabees, continued

Silver, Sheindel Klein. A new Chanukah play ₁in three acts₎. (Young Judaean. New York, 1928. 4°. v. 18, Dec., 1928, p. 2–3, 25, 28.)   †* **PBD**

Silverman, Althea Osber. The romance of Judas Maccabeus; an historical romance of the Maccabean war ₁in two acts₎. New York: Bloch Pub. Co., 1924. 12 p. 12°.

Sisters of Mercy, St. Catharine's Convent, New York City. The martyrdom of the Maccabees. ₁In three scenes.₎ (In their: Poems for Catholics & convents and plays for Catholic schools. West Chester, New York, 1873. 12°. p. 239–254.)   **NBI**
"To the reader," p. iv–viii, signed Sr. M. A.

CAPTIVITY PLAYS

Buckton, A. M. Kings in Babylon, a drama ₁in two acts₎... London: Methuen & Co. ₁cop. 1906.₎ 4 p.l., 72 p. 12°. **NCO p.v.584**
Place: Babylon. Time: 572 B. C.
Parallels in part the fiery furnace story narrated in Daniel, chapter 3.

Hewetson, George Benson. Athali: a fragmentary tragedy ₁in six scenes₎. (In his: The strike, and other poems. New York, 1896. 16°. p. 105–120.)   **NBI**
An incident following the capture of Jerusalem.

Kosach, Larisa Petrovna. The Babylonian captivity, by Lésya Ukráinka ₁pseud.₎. (In: C. E. Bechhofer Roberts, Five Russian plays, with one from the Ukrainian. New York, 1916. 12°. p. 153–173.) ** **QDK (Roberts)**
"The translation of the Babylonian captivity from the Ukrainian is due mainly to Miss Sophie Volska." — *Preface.*
The Hebrew captivity typifies "the enslavement of modern Ukraine by its powerful neighbors."

Leavitt, John McDowell. Belshazzar. Fragments. (In his: Visions of Solyma, and other poems. New York, 1895. 12°. p. 120–131.)   **NBI**
An abbreviated version of his five-act play *Jewish captives,* published 1876.
Also printed in his *Our flag, with other poems,* New York, 1909, p. 179–232, *NBI.* The last speech of Eli in the last act differs in this issue from the one reprinted by Kohut.

—— The Jewish captives. (In: G. A. Kohut, A Hebrew anthology. Cincinnati, 1913. 8°. v. 2, p. 1055–1081.)   * **PSO**

Morgan, Arthur Middlemore. Israel in Babylon. ₁A dialogue.₎ (In his: Immanuel. London, 1875. 12°. p. 166–180.)   **NCM**
An aged captive Jew and his daughter; three days after the events in Daniel, chapter 3.

West, Emma Elise. The drama of Babylonian captivity. ₁Four parts₎ arranged as a dramatic reading. (Werner's magazine. New York, 1900. 8°. v. 24, p. 592–597.)   **MWA**

HEROD PLAYS

FLETCHER, Jefferson Butler. Herod in the drama. (University of North Carolina. — Philological Club. Studies in philology. Chapel Hill, N. C., 1922. 8°. v. 19, p. 292–307.)   **RNA (North Carolina)**

GREG, Walter Wilson. Herod the Great on the English stage. (Spectator. London, 1900. f°. v. 85, p. 657–658.)   * **DA**

Falkland, Elizabeth (Tanfield) Cary, viscountess. The tragedy of Mariam. 1613... ₁London: Printed for the Malone Society by H. Hart at the Oxford University Press,₎ 1914. xix, ₁67₎ p., 2 facsims. ob. 8°. (...The Malone Society reprints.)   **NCO (Malone)**
"This reprint of Lady Elizabeth Cary's Tragedy of Mariam has been prepared by A. C. Dunstan with the assistance of the general editor [W. W. Greg]."
With reproductions of original t.-p. and page A₃ recto.
Original title: The Tragedie Of Mariam, The Faire Queene of Iewry. Written by that learned, vertuous, and truly noble Ladie, E. C. [*Printer's mark*] London. Printed by Thomas Creede for Richard Hawkins... 1613.
A supplement ([4] p. and facsim.) inserted loose, includes collotype reproduction of a leaf containing dedicatory sonnet and list of characters. This leaf seems to have been issued with only a small part of the original edition, as only two copies are known in which it occurs.
The earliest English handling of the story of Herod and Mariamne, based on Josephus' *Antiquities of the Jews.*

DUNSTAN, Arthur Cyril. Examination of two English dramas: "The Tragedy of Mariam" by Elizabeth Carew; and "The True tragedy of Herod and Antipater: with the death of faire Marriam," by Gervase Markham, and William Sampson. Königsberg i. Pr.: Hartung, 1908. 97(1) p., 1 l. 8°.
Books referred to, p. 98.   **NCO p.v.308, no.6**

Farquhar, Edward. Mystery of King Herod. ₁A dramatic poem.₎ (In his: Poems. Boston, 1905. 12°. p. 23–30.)   **NBI**

Fenton, Elijah. Mariamne. A tragedy ₁in five acts₎. Acted at the Theatre Royal in Lincoln's-Inn-Fields. Written by Mr. Fenton ... London: Printed for J. Tonson, 1723. 4 p.l., 75 p., 2 l. 8°.   **NCP**
Based on the story in Josephus, books 14 and 15.
First produced at the Lincoln's-Inn-Fields Theatre, London, Feb. 22, 1723.

Herod Plays, continued

—— Mariamne. A tragedy. London: T. Ashley, 1728. 104 p., 1 l. 2. ed. 16°.
NCO p.v.52

—— —— London: J. R. Tonson, 1760. 3 p.l., 9–22 p. 12°. **NCO p.v.533**
An imperfect copy.

—— —— London: John Bell, 1794. 3 p.l., (1)8–88 p., 1 pl. 24°. **NCO p.v.361, no.5**

—— —— London: John Bell, 1794. v(i), (1)8–82 p., 2 pl. 12°. (Bell's British theatre. v. 26, ₍no. 1.₎) **NCO (Bell)**

—— —— London: G. Cawthorn, 1803. 88 p., 1 port. 24°. **NCO p.v.368, no.1**

GRACK, Walter. Studien über die dramatische Behandlung der Geschichte von Herodes und Mariamne in der englischen und deutschen Litteratur. (Massinger, Fenton, Hebbel, Stephen Phillips.) Königsberg i. Pr.: H. Jaeger, 1901. 135 p., 2 l. 8°.
Litteratur, p. 133–135. **NCO p.v.317, no.8**

Hebbel, Christian Friedrich. Herod and Mariamne, a tragedy in five acts. With appreciation "Christian Friedrich Hebbel" by Edith J. R. Isaacs. (Drama. Chicago, 1912. 8°. no. 6, p. 1–168.) **NAFA**
Translated by Edith J. R. Isaacs and Kurt Rahlson.

—— Herod and Mariamne; a tragedy in five acts, translated by L. H. Allen. (In his: Three plays. London ₍1914₎. 12°. p. 67–184.) **NGE**
Everyman's library.
First presentation at the Burgtheater, Vienna, April 19, 1849. The original German edition appeared in 1850.

CAMPBELL, Thomas Moody. Hebbel's Herodes und Mariamne. (Modern language notes. Baltimore, 1929. 8°. v. 44, p. 250–253.) **RAA**
Elucidation of 11. 1289–1295, in act ii, scene 5.

NEWPORT, Clara Price. Herodes and Mariamne. (In her: Woman in the thought and work of Friedrich Hebbel. Madison, Wis., 1912. 8°. p. 94–101.) **STG (Wisconsin)**
University of Wisconsin. Bulletin: Philology and literature series. v. 5, no. 3.

Heywood, Joseph Converse. Salome. A dramatic poem. New York: Hurd and Houghton, 1867. 222 p. 12°. **NBM**
An entirely different play from the author's *Salome, the daughter of Herodias*, published anonymously in 1862, and reissued in 1867 under title: *Herodias*.
Destruction of Jerusalem, 70 A. D. Among the characters are Titus, Josephus, and Kaliphilus, the Wandering Jew.

Iliowizi, Henry. Herod: a tragedy... Minneapolis, Minn.: ₍Tribune Book Rooms,₎ 1884. 80 p. 8°. *** PSQ**
In five acts.

Krantzhor, Max. Queen Mariamne and King Herod. ₍In three acts.₎ Santa Monica, Cal.: W. F. Behrman ₍cop. 1929₎. 55 p. 12°.
"The subject matter of this drama was taken from Josephus." The characters are all members of the Herodian and the Hasmonean families. The play is dedicated to Adolf Czukor.

Leavitt, John McDowell. Antipater. (In his: Our flag, with other poems. New York, 1909. 12°. p. 233–279.) **NBI**
A reprint of *The Idumean*, 1869.

—— The Idumean. ₍A tragedy in five acts.₎ (In his: Afranius, and The Idumean... New York, 1869. 12°. p. 55–105.) **NBM**
Abstracts of a number of reviews are published on p. 35–47 of his *The siege of Babylon*, New York, 1869, *NBL p.v.22*.
Reprinted as *Antipater*, 1909.

Mallarmé, Stéphane. Hérodiade. (From the French.) Translated by Arthur Symons. (Savoy. London, 1896. 8°. Dec., p. 67–68.) *** DA**

—— Herodiade ₍a dramatic poem₎. Translated by Joseph Twadell Shipley. (Poet lore. Boston, 1921. 4°. v. 32, p. 458–462.) *** DA**
A translation by Richard Hovey is printed in the latter's *Along the trail*, Boston, 1898, p. 41–44, *NBI* (also in the New York, 1907, edition, *NBI*).

FRY, Roger. Mallarmé's "Herodiade" ₍with extracts₎. (Criterion. London, 1923. 8°. v. 1, p. 119–126.) *** DA**

Markham, Gervase. The true Tragedy Of Herod And Antipater: With the Death of faire Marriam. According to Iosephvs, the learned and famous Iewe. As it hath beene, of late, diuers times publiquely Acted (with great Applause) at the Red Bull, by the Company of his Maiesties Revels.

Written by ⎱ Gervase Markham, And William Sampson. ⎰ Gentlemen.

₍Ornament₎ London: Printed by G. Eld, for Mathevv Rhodes, and are to bee sold at his Shop at the vpper end of the Old Bayly, neere Newgate. 1622. ₍83₎ p. 4°.
Title from Library of Congress.

DUNSTAN, Arthur Cyril. Examination of two English dramas: "The Tragedy of Mariam" by Elizabeth Carew; and "The True tragedy of Herod and Antipater: with the death of faire Marriam," by Gervase Markham, and William Sampson. Königsberg i. Pr.: Hartung, 1908. 97(1) p., 1 l. 8°.
NCO p.v.308, no.6

SILBERMANN, Abraham Moritz. Untersuchungen über die Quellen des Dramas "True Tragedy of Herod and Antipater with the death of faire Marriam" by Gervase Markham and William Sampson (1622). Wittenberg: Herrosé & Ziemsen ₍1930₎. 86 p., 1 l. 8°.
He concludes that Markham's drama is based not on Josephus, as stated on the title-page, but on Abraham Ibn Daûd's (RABAD I) Hebrew abstract of the Jossipon of Joseph ben Gorion (Gorionides). This he knew through Peter Morwyng's English translation of Sebastian Lepusculus' Latin translation of 1559. With not as good evidence the author concludes that Massinger's *Duke of Milan* is taken not from Josephus but from Markham's *Herod and Antipater*, and that both dramas show the influence of Shakespeare's *Othello*.
Reviewed by T. W. Baldwin in *Journal of English and Germanic philology*, Urbana, Ill., 1929, v. 28, p. 439–440, *RKA*.

Herod Plays, continued

Moore, Thomas Sturge. Mariamne. London: Duckworth and Co., 1911. lxxv p. 8°.
On cover: Mariamne, a conflict.   **NCR**
Drama in five acts in verse.
Reviewed in *Poetry review*, London, 1912, v. 1, p. 131–132, * *DA*.

Orrery (1st earl), Roger Boyle. Herod the Great. A tragedy. Written by the Right Honourable the Earl of Orrery. London: Printed by T. Warren for F. Saunders ₍etc.₎, 1694. 2 p.l., 40 p., 1 l. 4°.
This play was never acted. The plot is taken from Josephus.

CLARK, William S. The published but unacted "heroic plays" of Roger Boyle, Earl of Orrery. (Review of English studies. London, 1926. 8°. v. 2, p. 280–283.)   **RNA**

SIEGERT, ₍Eduard. Roger Boyle, Earl of Orrery und seine Dramen. Zur Geschichte des heroischen Dramas in England. Wien und Leipzig: Wilhelm Braumüller, 1906. 4 p.l., 75 p. 8°. (Wiener Beiträge zur englischen Philologie. Bd. 23.) **NCB (Wiener)**
Benutzte Werke, p.l. 4.

Osborn, Laughton. Mariamne, being the third of the tragedies of Jewish and Biblical history, and the second in continuation of volume VI of the dramatic series by L. C. New York: H. L. Hinton, 1873. 2 p.l., 167–269 p. 8°.   * *PSQ*

Peck, Francis. Herod the Great: a ₍dramatic₎ poem... London, 1740. iii, 4–34 p. 8°. (In his: New memoirs of the life and poetical works of John Milton. London, 1740.)
* *NCC*

Phillips, Stephen. Herod, a tragedy... London and New York: John Lane, 1901. 128 p. 12°.
First edition.
Madeleine Rolland in *Revue d'art dramatique*, Paris, 1901, v. 16, [part 1], p. 441–453, *NAFA*, gives a synopsis of the play with a translation into French of a part of the third act.
Reviewed by Abram Lipsky in *American Hebrew*, New York, 1909, v. 86, p. 4, * *PBD*; in *Everybody's magazine*, New York, 1910, v. 22, p. 127–128, * *DA*; by Israel Abrahams in *Jewish chronicle*, London, Dec. 7, 1900, p. 24, * *PBE*; in *The World to-day*, Chicago, 1909, v. 17, p. 1249, * *DA*; by Hamilton Clayton in *The Forum*, New York, 1909, v. 42, p. 578–579, * *DA*, and in *The Nation*, New York, 1909, v. 89, p. 414, * *DA*; by Harriet Quinby in *Leslie's weekly*, New York, 1909, v. 109, p. 462, * *DA*; in *The Spectator*, London, 1900, v. 85, p. 616–618, * *DA*; and in *The Times*, London, Nov. 1, 1900, p. 4, * *A*.
First produced at Her Majesty's Theatre, London, Oct. 31, 1900, with Herbert Beerbohm Tree as Herod and Miss Maud Jeffries as Mariamne. For a review see *Jewish chronicle*, London, Nov. 2, 1900, p. 10, * *PBE*.
Produced at the Lyric Theatre, New York, Oct. 26, 1909 with William Faversham as Herod and Julie Opp as Mariamne. Reviewed in *The Theatre*, New York, 1909, v. 10, p. 169–170, † *NBLA*, and in *New York dramatic mirror*, v. 62, Nov. 6, 1909, p. 5, * *DA*.

—— —— London: J. Lane, 1901. 128 p., 1 l. ₍2. ed.₎ 12°.   **NCR**

—— —— London and New York: John Lane, 1901. 1 p.l., 126 p. 6. ed. 12°.

—— —— New York: J. Lane Co., 1905. 3 p.l., (1)6–126 p. ₍7. ed.₎ 12°.   **NCR**

—— —— New York: J. Lane, 1909. 3 p.l., (1)6–126 p. ₍8. ed.₎ 12°.   * *PSQ*

—— Herodes; eine Tragödie von Stephen Phillips. Autorisierte deutsche Ausgabe. Mettmann: Hugo von der Heyden, 1902. 147(1) p. 8°.

ARCHER, William. Herod: a tragedy. (In his: Poets of the younger generation. London, 1902. 8°. p. 309–352.)   **NCID**

GRACK, Walter. Studien über die dramatische Behandlung der Geschichte von Herodes und Mariamne in der englischen und deutschen Litteratur. (Massinger, Fenton, Hebbel, Stephen Phillips.) Königsberg i. Pr.: H. Jaeger, 1901. 135 p., 2 l. 8°.
Litteratur, p. 133–135.   **NCO p.v.317, no.8**

GREEFF, A. Stephen Phillips als Dramatiker. (Englische Studien. Leipzig, 1909. 8°. Bd. 40, p. 47–78.)   **RNA**

GROPALLO, Laura. Herod. (Nuova antologia. Roma, 1901. 8°. v. 91, p. 721–731.)   **NAA**

GWYNN, Stephen Lucius. Mr. Phillips' "Herod." (Contemporary review. London, 1901. 8°. v. 79, p. 32–37.)   * *DA*

SOUVENIR of Stephen Phillips' historical play "Herod," produced at Her Majesty's Theatre, by Herbert Beerbohm Tree, on the 30th of October, 1900. ₍London and Glasgow: Langfier, Ltd., 1900?₎ 20 pl. 4°.

ZANGWILL, Israel. Two un-Jewish Jewish plays. (American Hebrew. New York, 1900. 4°. v. 68, p. 73–74.)   * *PBD*

—— —— (New century review. London, 1900. 8°. v. 8, p. 480–482.)   * *DA*

Pordage, Samuel. Herod and Mariamne. A tragedy. Acted at the Duke's Theatre... ₍By Samuel Pordage.₎ London: Printed for William Cademan, at the Popes-Head in the Lower Walk of the New Exchange in the Strand, 1673. 2 p.l., 65 p., 1 l. 4°.
Title from Library of Congress.
First edition.
Dedication signed by the editor, Elkanah Settle.

—— —— London, Printed for William Cademan, at the Popes-Head in the Lower Walk of the New Exchange in the Strand, 1674. 2 p.l., 65 p., 1 l. 4°.

CLARK, William S. Pordage's Herod and Mariamne. (Review of English studies. London, 1929. 8°. v. 5, p. 61–64.)   **RNA**
Argues that the play was produced at Dorset Garden, and not, as Prof. A. Nicol maintains, at Lincoln's Inn Fields.

Herod Plays, continued

Reznikoff, Charles. Coral, and Captive Israel; two plays. ₍New York City: For sale at the Sunwise Turn, cop. 1923.₎ 1 p.l., 40 p. 12°.

Captive Israel occupies p. 19–40.
Time: about 30 B. C. Place: Jerusalem, except the feast scene (in Egypt), the fourth (Babylon), and the fifth (Alexandria).
Reprinted in *Menorah journal*, New York, v. 10, no. 1, Feb., 1924, p. 38–45, * *PBD*, and in the author's *Nine plays*, New York [1927], p. 56–73, *NBM*.

Rich, Sir Henry. The daughter of Herodias, a tragedy ₍in five acts and in verse₎. London, 1831. 8°.

Title from British Museum Catalogue.
Reviewed in *New monthly magazine*, London, 1831, v. 33, p. 107, * *DA*.

Solly, Henry. Herod the Great, an historical drama in three parts. London: K. Paul, Trench, Trübner & Co., 1896. xx p., 1 l., 336 p. 12°.

The first two parts forming *Herod the Great* are in four and two acts respectively. The third part, with a list of dramatis personae of its own, is in three acts, and is called *Herod the despot*.
In the introduction to the play, the author defends the character of Herod, and begs to discount the account of him given by Josephus, as prejudiced and as coming from a personal enemy.

Symons, Arthur. Cleopatra in Judaea. (Forum. New York, 1916. 8°. v. 55, p. 643–660.) * **DA**

Reprinted in his *Tragedies*, New York, 1916, p. 123–151. *NCR*, and London, 1917, p. 123–151.
Reviewed by W. J. Turner in *London mercury*, London, 1922, v. 6, p. 89, * *DA*.
Produced by the Fortune Players at the Court Theatre, London, April 9, 1922. Noticed in *The Curtain*, London, 1922, v. 1, p. 54, *NAFA*.

Troubetskoy, Amélie (Rives) Chanler. Herod and Mariamne. A tragedy. Philadelphia: J. B. Lippincott Co. ₍cop. 1888.₎ 305–389 p. 8°. **NBM**

Repr.: Lippincott's monthly magazine, Philadelphia, 1888, v. 42, p. 305–389, * *DA*.
See "A few more words about Miss Rives" by Edgar Fawcett, *ibid.*, p. 390–394, in which he says "I should call 'Herod and Mariamne' the dramatic effort of a beginner... I find it a tragedy of uneven yet often astonishing vigor. Its gloom is unrelieved by any play of humor... The character of Herod is too unrelievedly ferocious and lurid."
Reprinted in G. A. Kohut, editor, *A Hebrew anthology*, Cincinnati, 1913, v. 2, p. 1147–1235, * *PSO*.

Voltaire, François Marie Arouet de. Mariamne. A tragedy. (In his: Dramatic works. Translated by Mr. Francklin. London, 1761. 16°. v. 1, p. 109–196.) **NKE**

This volume is no. 12 of the complete edition of Voltaire's Works.
The scene is laid in Jerusalem. "This piece was produced in 1724."
The play is also printed in the edition of Voltaire's Works edited by John Morley, v. 8, part 2, New York, 1901, p. 211–269, *NKE*. Voltaire's preface is printed in v. 10, part 1, p. 235–240.

Waller, William. Mariamne; or, The court of Herod the Great: a dramatic poem. A tragedy, in five acts... London: ₍J. Rogerson,₎ 1839. 3 p.l., 50 p. 12°. **NCO p.v.335, no.14**

Wilde, Oscar. Salome; a play. New York: F. M. Buckles & Company, 1906. 60 p. 12°.

Bound with his: Duchess of Padua. 1906. **NCR**

—— Salome, a tragedy in one act, translated from the French of Oscar Wilde. London: John Lane, The Bodley Head; New York: John Lane Company, 1906. 3 p.l., 66 p. 12°.

Also printed in *Poet lore*, Boston, 1907, v. 18, p. 199–223, * *DA*, and in B. H. Clark, editor, *Representative one-act plays by British and Irish authors*, Boston, 1921, p. 71–106, * *R – NCO*. A synopsis with many extracts was printed in *Current literature*, New York, 1906, v. 41, p. 308–312, * *DA*.
The play was originally written in French for Sarah Bernhardt. The English version was made by Lord Alfred Douglas, and a series of pictures was made by Aubrey Beardsley to illustrate the English edition, two of these being reproduced with the synopsis in *Current literature*.
First English production at the Bijou Theatre, London, May 10, 1905, with Miss Murby as Salome. Reviewed by Max Beerbohm in the *Saturday review*, London, 1905, v. 99, p. 623–624, * *DA*. For comments on this review by Robert Ross, T. Sturge Moore, and A. B. Clifton see p. 703–704, 738, and 807 respectively. Also reviewed in *The Sketch*, London, 1905, v. 50, p. 142, * *DA*.
Produced by the New Players Society, London, at the Court Theatre Feb. 27, 1911 with Adeline Bourne as Salome and Arthur Wontner as Jockanan the prophet. See *The Mask*, Florence, Italy, v. 3, 1911, p. 189–190, † *NAFA*.
Revived at the Comedy Theatre, New York by the Washington Square Players, April 22, 1918 with Mme. Yorska in the title rôle and Walter Hampden as Iokanaan. Reviewed by Channing Pollock in *Green book magazine*, Chicago, v. 20, July, 1918, p. 4–5, 10–11, 14–15, *NAFA;* by J. S. Metcalfe in *Life*, 1918, v. 71, p. 722, * *DA;* by Arthur Row in *Poet lore*, Boston, 1919, v. 30, p. 433–435, * *DA;* and in *New York dramatic mirror*, New York, 1918, v. 78, p. 620, * *DA*. For additional reviews see *Collection of newspaper clippings of dramatic criticism, 1917–18*, vol. P–Y, † *NBL*.
Revived at the Klaw Theatre May 22, 1922, with Noel Leslie as Johannen, Fred Eric as Herod, and Thelma Harvey as Salome. For reviews see *Collection of newspaper clippings of dramatic criticism, 1921–22*, vol. S–Z, † *NBL*.
Produced by the all-negro cast of the Art Theatre at the Frazee Theatre, New York, May 7, 1923 with Evelyn Preer as Salome. See *Collection of newspaper clippings of dramatic criticism, 1922–23*, vol. S–Z, † *NBL*.

—— Salomé; a tragedy in one act, by Oscar Wilde. ₍San Francisco: Grabhorn Press, 1927.₎ 21 l., col'd front. 4°. * **KP (Grabhorn)**

Caption title.
Printed in red, blue, and black; marginal ornaments in red and gray.
Colophon: One hundred and ninety-five copies printed in March, nineteen hundred and twenty-seven at the Grabhorn Press, San Francisco, by Edwin and Robert Grabhorn. Frontispiece and marginal decorations from wood blocks designed and cut by Valenti Angelo.

—————

שלומית. דראמה בת מערכה אחת מאת אוסקר
וילדה. עברית מאת א. שפר. (המעורר.)
London, 1907. 8°. v. 2, p. 135–144, 201–214.) * **PBA**

Bendz, Ernst. A propos de la Salomé d'Oscar Wilde. (Englische Studien. Leipzig, 1917. 8°. Bd. 51, p. 48–70.) **RNA**

Reprinted in his *Oscar Wilde; a retrospect*, p. 92–123, *A p.v.128, no.6*.

Herod Plays, continued

DE CHEVETTE, J. Salome — a review. (Jewish American. Detroit, 1907. f°. v. 14, May 10, 1907, p. 1–3.)   †* PBD

HAGEMANN, Carl. ₍Salome. A criticism.₎ (In his: Oscar Wilde, sein Leben und sein Werk. Berlin, 1925. 8°. p. 105–116.) NCC

HENDERSON, Archibald. The dramas of Oscar Wilde. (Arena. Trenton, N. J., 1907. 8°. v. 38, p. 134–139.)   * DA

LEDGER, Walter. Bibliography. (In: Oscar Wilde, Salomé; La sainte courtisane; A Florentine tragedy. London ₍1911₎. 16°. p. 93–109.)   NCR

LOPÈRE, Frédéric. An overture to "Salome." ₍Conversation between Arthure and

Heraklit on the significance of Wilde's play.₎ (Colonnade. New York, 1914. 4°. v. 7, p. 170–174.)   † NAFA

ROOF, Katherine Metcalf. Salomé — the play and the opera. ₍Illustrated with 8 plates, four of which in black and red, are by Frances Lea.₎ (Craftsman. New York, 1907. 4°. v. 11, p. 523–538.)   MAA

SALOME, Strauss and Sathanas. (Academy. London, 1907. 4°. v. 72, p. 438–439.)   * DA

SPENCER, Herman. The original of Salome's love-story. (Harper's weekly. New York, 1909. f°. v. 53, Jan. 30, 1909, p. 29.)   * DA

TANZIO, Silvio. "Salomè," dramma musicale de Oscar Wilde; musica di Riccardo Strauss. (Rivista teatrale italiana. Napoli, 1906. 8°. v. 11, p. 172–181.)   NNP

NEW TESTAMENT PLAYS

JESUS CHRIST

Andersen, Olivia Donaldson (Cushing). Jesus of Nazareth. ₍In four acts.₎ (In her: Creation and other Biblical plays. Geneva, 1929. 4°. p. 225–290.)   NBM

"By the presence of Jesus in the world, Mrs. Andersen exemplifies in *Jesus of Nazareth* the highest spiritual doctrine ever revealed to mankind." Place: Galilee and Judah. Time: 32–33 A. D.

Bacon, Josephine Dodge (Daskam). Twilight of the gods. ₍In two scenes.₎ (Forum. New York, 1915. 8°. v. 53, p. 7–20.)   * DA

The three persons of the Christian Trinity are the principal dramatis personae.

—— —— New York: Mitchell Kennerley, 1915. 43 p. 12°.   NBM

Barlow, Joseph. Jesus of Nazareth; a tragedy ₍in five acts₎. Westminster: Roxburghe Press, n.d. 188 p., 1 pl. 12°.

"It is this element — the 'sexual element'...which I have endeavored to restore to the narrative (of the Gospels)...and I maintain that the story...is thereby rendered not only more interesting, but also a thousand times more sweet and holy and 'sacred.'" — *From the preface.*

Bates, Esther Willard. The city of God; an Easter pageant of life everlasting. ₍In one act.₎ Music arranged and selected by Harry S. Mason. (International journal of religious education. Mt. Morris, Ill., 1925. f°. v. 1, March, 1925, p. 43–52.)

Bates, Katharine Lee. Joanna the wife of Chuza. (In her: The pilgrim ship. New York, 1926. 8°. p. 66–73.)   NBI
A dialogue.

Berenberg, David P. Glaucon & Sarai ₍a dramatic poem₎. (In his: The letters of Glaucon & Sarai, and other poems. Northampton, Mass. ₍cop. 1924.₎ 8°. p. 7–36.) NBI

Twenty-three poems, styled here as letters to each other, dealing with the times and personality of "Yeshua-bar-Miriam."

Boulter, Benjamin Consitt. ...The mystery of the epiphany... London: Society for Promoting Christian Knowledge, 1920. ix(i), 11–80 p. illus. 12°. (Parish plays.)

In eleven scenes, from the Annunciation to the Baptism. Produced in 1918 at the Church of St. Silas, Kentish Town.

Burns, John F. Vision, a tale of the time of Christ, historical mystery play. ₍Villanova? Pa., cop. 1924.₎ 4 p.l., (1)8–79(1) p. 8°.   NAC p.v.119, no.8

Added title-page: ...Historical mystery play in three acts by the Villanova Players, Villanova College, Pa.

Calderon de la Barca, Pedro. The divine philothea ₍in thirty-nine scenes₎. (In his: Mysteries of Corpus Christi, from the Spanish. By D. F. MacCarthy. Dublin, 1867. 16°. p. 209–344.)   NPP

Represents the struggle of the soul upon the earth against its enemies, of whom Judaism is one. "Philothea is the God-loving human soul which Christ, the Prince of Light, has chosen for his bride..." This *auto* was performed, evidently for the first time, in the year 1681.

Dana, Mary Stanley Bunce, afterward Shindler. Dialogue between the Savior and the mourner. (In her: The parted family, and other poems. New York, 1842. 12°. p. 186–188.)   NBHD

New Testament Plays — Jesus Christ, cont'd

Demarest, Ada Rose. "I love to tell the story." (In her: Junior pageants. Cincinnati ₍cop. 1927₎. 8°. p. 41–48.)
Pageant no. 5. In three scenes.

Dickerson, Penelope. The passers-by; a religious play in one act... Chicago: Dramatic Publishing Company ₍cop. 1928₎. 22 p. 12°. (Sergel's acting drama. no. 675.)
NBL p.v.204
The influence of Christianity on the followers of Christ, most of them bearing Hebrew names, soon after the Crucifixion. Iscah, a beggar-maid, is the central character.

Dimick, Elizabeth. The boy in the carpenter shop; a sacred reading. Franklin, O.: Eldridge Entertainment House, Inc., cop. 1929. 5 p. 12°. (Eldridge popular monologs.)

Doten, Edith Kinney. Maundy Thursday; a miracle play for a communion sermon on Holy Thursday ₍in three scenes₎. (In: Eleven short Biblical plays. New York, 1929. 12°. p. 183–204.) **NBL p.v.216**
Christ in the person of the great physician, in England during the reign of James I.

Durward, Bernard I. The strong man. ₍In nine scenes.₎ (In his: Poems. Milwaukee, 1882. 12°. v. 1, p. 87–107.) **NBI**
The infant Jesus is one of the characters.

Foley, Marie A. The gift; a play in one act. New York: S. French, cop. 1921. 1 p.l., 5–25 p. 8°. **NBF p.v.41, no. 2**
A symbolic play. Jesus performs miracles, although he does not appear as a character.
Scene: a little town of Judea, A. D. 30.
First performed in New York City, Nov. 5, 1920.

Gilbert, Robert Warren. Jesus and Nathan. ₍A dialogue.₎ (In his: Golden rod and lilies. Boston, 1908. 12°. p. 131–138.) **NBI**

Gregory, Isabella Augusta (Persse), lady. The travelling man; a miracle play. (In her: Seven short plays. Dublin ₍1911₎. 12°. p. 163–179.) **NCR**
The characters are a mother, a child, and a travelling man, who is Christ.
Also printed in Montrose J. Moses, editor, *A treasury of plays for children*, Boston, 1921, p. 441–452, *NASH*; in J. P. Webber and H. H. Webster, editors, *Short plays for young people*, Boston, 1925, p. 74–84, *NASH;* and in J. Compton, compiler, *The curtain rises; a collection of plays*, London [1927], p. 137–151, *NCO.*

Gregory, Odin. Jesus; the tragedy of man ₍in a prelude and five acts₎. New York: Colony Pub. Co., Inc. ₍cop. 1922.₎ 138 p. 2. ed. 8°. **NBM**
Among the non-Biblical characters in this play are Samuel, a merchant and member of the Sanhedrin; Isaac, his son; and Esther, his daughter.

Hamlin, Mary P. He came seeing; a one-act play. New York: Samuel French; London: Samuel French, Ltd., cop. 1928. 35 p. 8°. **NBL p.v.194**
The time passes during the last year of Jesus' life, near Jerusalem. Jesus himself does not appear as a character.

Hartmann, Sadakichi. Christ; a dramatic poem in three acts. By C. Sadakichi Hartmann. ₍Boston? The author,₎ 1893. 81 p. 12°. **NBL p.v.110, no.2**

Herts, Benjamin Russell. The son of man; a drama in four acts. New York: Frank Shay, 1916. 3 p.l., 9–77 p. 12°. **NBL p.v.59, no.20**

Hitchcock, Mary S. Whatsoever ye sow; a Biblical drama in three acts. Chicago: T. S. Denison & Co. ₍cop. 1928.₎ 52 p. 12°. (Religious plays.) **NBL (Religious)**
Time: about 29 A. D. Place: Prince Stephen's palace in Jerusalem. Among the characters is one Rabbi Joseph, a priest from the Temple.

Housman, Laurence. Nazareth; a morality in one act. New York: S. French ₍cop. 1916₎. 17 p. 12°. **NAC p.v.25, no.1**

Jenkinson, Margaret Clifford. Shadows of the Christ; being a succession of scenes ₍in a prologue and three acts₎ indirectly representing His Ministry, Passion, and Resurrection. With an introduction by Alexander Nairne ...and a woodcut by Madame Raverat. Cambridge: W. Heffer & Sons, Ltd., 1921. xii, 90 p. 12°. **NCR**
"The title...is meant to suggest that each scene contributes something towards a complete picture of Christ's life and teaching." — *From the prefatory note, p. v.*

Joplin, Frances Grigsby. The New Testament in the making. ₍In seven scenes.₎ A pageant of the Scriptures... Franklin, Ohio: Eldridge Entertainment House, Inc., cop. 1927. 13 p. 12°. (Eldridge church entertainments.)
The characters are some of the apostles, Mary of Bethany, and others.

Levi ben-Halpai, pseud. of Edward A. Guy? The true history and tragedy of Joshua, the Messiah. ₍A drama in prologue and five acts.₎ Washington, D. C.: Edward A. Guy, 1903. 1 p.l., 46 p. 8°. **ZFHH p.v.2**
Scene: various parts of Palestine and Egypt. Time: 5 B. C. — 28 A. D.

Longfellow, Henry Wadsworth. The divine tragedy. Boston: James R. Osgood and Co., 1871. iv, 150 p. 16°. **＊KL**
Contents: Introitus. The first Passover. The second Passover. The third Passover. Epilogue.
Reprinted as Part I of *Christus, a mystery*. Boston, 1872. 12°. *＊KL.*
First edition.

—— Boston: J. R. Osgood and Co., 1871. iv p., 1 l., 313 p. 8°. **＊KL**
Large-type first edition, in original binding.
Reviewed in *Canadian monthly*, Toronto, 1872, v. 1, p. 186–188, *＊DA; Dublin University magazine*, Dublin, 1872, v. 79, p. 331–336, *＊DA*; and by Edward C. Towne in *The Index*, Toledo, O., 1872, v. 3, p. 23, † *ZEY*. The last is a freethinker's view.

New Testament Plays — Jesus Christ, cont'd

Lorimer, Emilia Stuart. The poet. ₍A dramatic poem.₎ (In her: Songs of Alban. London, 1912. 12°. p. 31–35.)   **NCM**
Among the speakers is Christ.

McGiffert, Gertrude Huntington Boyce. The aged Christ. ₍In three scenes.₎ (In her: A Florentine cycle, and other poems. New York, 1915. 12°. p. 201–217.)   **NBI**

Norman, Carl Adolph. A Galilean; dramatic poem, in ₍a prologue₎ six acts ₍and an epilogue₎... ₍Columbus, Ohio: Phillips Printing Co., cop. 1929.₎ 1 p.l., 137 p. 12°.   **NBL p.v.219**

Pearse, Padraic H. Iosagan. ₍In two scenes.₎ (In his: The singer, and other plays. Dublin and London, 1918. 12°. p. 101–123.)   **NCR**
Translated from the Gaelic by Joseph Campbell. Iosagan, the child Jesus, at play with little Irish boys, beside the sea-coast village, in Iar-Connacht.

Riesner, Rebecca. Friends of Jesus, a pageant ₍in one act₎. Cincinnati: Powell & White, n.d. 8 p. 8°.

Sinclair, Upton Beall. Hell; a verse drama and photo-play ₍in four acts₎. Pasadena, Calif.: The author ₍cop. 1923₎. 128 p. 16°.   **NBL p.v.96**
Heavenly and earthly characters, among them "Comrade Jesus."

Vojnović, Ivo, knez. The resurrection of Lazarus. ₍In four acts and a concluding poem.₎ By Ivo Vojnovich. Authorized translation from the Croatian by John J. Batistich and George Rapall Noyes. (Poet lore. Boston, 1926. 8°. v. 37, p. 317–395.)   *****DA**
A Serbian patriotic play. "Christ, on the mount of His holy Transfiguration, raises from the dead the Eternal Lazarus, our People."

Von Herder, Alexandra. Jesus of Nazareth; a poetical drama in seven scenes. London: W. Heinemann, 1913. x, 249(1) p., 1 pl. 12°.   **NCR**
In verse.

—— —— Boston: J. W. Luce and Co., 1913. x, 249 p., 1 pl. 12°.
Reviewed by Edward Thomas in *The Bookman,* London, 1913, v. 44, p. 47, †* *GDD.* Also reviewed in *Poetry and drama,* London, 1913, v. 1, p. 501, * *DA.*

Wallace, Lewis. Klaw & Erlanger's production of Gen. Lew Wallace's "Ben-Hur," as presented at the Broadway Theatre, New York. Dramatized by William Young... ₍New York,₎ cop. 1900. 4 l., 17 pl. ob. 8°.   †**NBL**
Title on cover: Souvenir album; scenes of the play, Ben-Hur.
Produced at the Drury Lane Theatre, London, April 3, 1902. Reviewed in *The Times,* London, April 4, 1902,

p. 4, * *A,* and *To-day,* London, v. 34, p. 784, 786, * *DA.* The *Illustrated sporting and dramatic news,* London, has a full-page illustration of a stage setting of the 1912 revival in v. 77, p. 397, * *DA.*
See C. V. D. Runyon, *Clippings from the press,* v. 26, p. 302–305, †* *CZ,* for a miscellaneous collection of clippings, dated 1895–1900, partly dealing with the production of the play.

Davis, Glenmore. The most successful play ever produced. The story of "Ben Hur," and the fortunes it has made. (Green book magazine. Chicago, 1914. 8°. v. 11, Jan., 1914, p. 36–45.)   **NAFA**

Ellsworth, William W. Behind the scenes at "Ben Hur." ₍A descriptive account.₎ illus. (Critic. New York, 1900. 8°. v. 36, p. 245–249.)   *****DA**

Gunnison, Binney. Ben-Hur and Iras. Adapted from "Ben Hur," by Lew Wallace. (In his: New dialogues and plays. New York, 1900. 12°. ₍part 3:₎ Advanced dialogues, p. 149–156.)   **NACG (NDP)**
Also in the edition of 1905, *MZB.*

A **Remarkable** play. (Overland monthly. San Francisco, 1900. 8°. new series, v. 36, p. 38–46.)   *****DA**
A descriptive account with five full-page illustrations.

Robinson, M. N. The plot of Ben-Hur. (American notes and queries. Philadelphia, 1889. 8°. v. 2, p. 196–197.)   * **DA**

Smith, Benjamin E. The "Ben-Hur" chariot-race. illus. (St. Nicholas. New York, 1900. 8°. v. 28, part 1, p. 45–49.) * **DA**

Willcox, Helen Lida. Rome or the kingdom? ₍In one act.₎ (In: Lydia Glover Deseo, compiler, Four peace plays with worship services. New York ₍cop. 1929₎. 8°. p. 51–64.)
Running title: "They that take the sword."
Love, the ideal of Jesus, vs. War, the ideal of ancient Rome. Time: about 32 A. D., in a village in the Plain of Esdraelon.

Winkley, Samuel Hobart. The coming of Messiah. ₍In three scenes.₎ (In: M. L. Cobb, compiler, Poetical dramas for home and school. Boston, 1873. 12°. p. 161–175.) **MZB**
With the exception of Zachariah and John, the characters are all Jewish women, most of whom hail Jesus as the Messiah.

Younghusband, Sir Francis Edward. The reign of God; a drama. London: John Murray ₍1930₎. xxiv, 129 p. 12°.   **NCR**
In five acts and an epilogue.
"I have used the form of a drama as the better method of communicating the spirit of Jesus than the ordinary 'life.' " — *Preface, p. vii.*
Reviewed in *Times literary supplement,* London, 1930, v. 29, p. 396, † *NAA.*

New Testament Plays, continued

VIRGIN MARY

The cycle miracle plays on the Virgin Mary are classified in the following order adapted from Sir E. K. Chambers, *Mediaeval Stage*, 1903, v. 2, p. 321–323

PLAYS		CYCLES		
	YORK	TOWNELEY	CHESTER	COVENTRY
Prophetae	..	7	..	7
Birth of Mary	..	..	..	8
Education of Mary	..	..	..	9
Betrothal of Mary	..	..	..	10
Annunciation	12	10	..	11
Salutation of Elizabeth	..	11	..	13
Suspicion of Joseph	13	..	..	12
Purgation of Mary	..	..	..	14
Augustus & Cyrenius	..	9	..	..
Purification of Mary	41	17	11	18
Death of Mary	45	..	..	..
Assumption & Coronation	47	..	..	41

Miracle Plays

THIEN, Hermann. Über die englischen Marienklagen... Kiel: H. Fiencke, 1906. xii, 91(1) p. 8°.　　　　**NCI p.v.129**
Litteratur, p. vii–xi.
For the author's discussion of the Marienklagen as treated in the York, Towneley, Chester, and Coventry cycles, and the Digby plays, see p. 47–66.

VRIEND, J. The blessed Virgin Mary in medieval drama of England, with additional studies in Middle English literature... Purmerend, Holland: J. Muusses, 1928. xv, 160 p. 8°.　　　　**NAFH p.v.31**
Bibliography, p. xiii–xv.

The Prophetae

Processus Prophetarum. [Towneley play no. 7.] (In: The Towneley mysteries. London [1836]. 8°. p. 49–54.)　**CA (Surtees)**
Surtees Society. Publications. [v. 3.]
Also printed in 1897 (ed. England) in Early English Text Society, Extra series no. 71 (*The Towneley plays*), p. 56–64, *NCE (Early)*.

The **Prophets.** [Coventry play no. 7.] (In: Ludus Coventriæ, ed. Halliwell. London: Shakespeare Society, 1841. 8°. p. 65–69.)
　　　　NAFM (Coventry)
Also printed in 1922 (ed. Block) in Early English Text Society, Extra series no. 120 (*Ludus Coventriæ*), p. 57–72, *NCE (Early)*. A brief selection is printed in F. J. Tickner, editor, *Earlier English drama from Robin Hood to Everyman*, New York [cop. 1929], p. 110–112, *NCO*.

BONNELL, John K. The source in art of the so-called Prophets Play in the Hegge collection. (Modern Language Association of America. Publications. Baltimore, 1914. 8°. v. 29, p. 327–340.)　　　**RAA**

The Birth of Mary

The **Barrenness** of Anna. [Coventry play no. 8.] (In: Ludus Coventriæ, ed. Halliwell. London: Shakespeare Society, 1841. 8°. p. 70–78.)　　　**NAFM (Coventry)**
Also printed in 1922 (ed. Block) in Early English Text Society, Extra series no. 120 (*Ludus Coventriæ*), p. 62–71, *NCE (Early)*.
Extracts under the title "Birth of Mary" are printed in William Hone, editor, *Ancient mysteries described*, London, 1823, p. 13–19, *NAFM*. Interpolations by the editor wherever portions of the text are omitted.

The Education of Mary

Mary in the Temple. [Coventry play no. 9.] (In: Ludus Coventriæ, ed. Halliwell. London: Shakespeare Society, 1841. 8°. p. 79–89.)　　　**NAFM (Coventry)**
Also printed in 1922 (ed. Block) in Early English Text Society, Extra series no. 120 (*Ludus Coventriæ*), p. 71–82, *NCE (Early)*.
Extracts under the title "Mary's education in the Temple, and being saved by angels" are printed in William Hone, editor, *Ancient mysteries described*, London, 1823, p. 20–26, *NAFM*. Interpolations by the editor wherever portions of the text are omitted.

The Betrothal of Mary

The **Marriage** of the Virgin, a miracle play now first printed from MS. Cotton, Vesp. D.VIII. [Coventry play no. 10.] [London, 1836.] 24 p. 12°. (In: J. P. Collier, Five miracle plays. London, 1836.)

Mary's betrothment. [Coventry play no. 10.] (In: Ludus Coventriæ, ed. Halliwell. London: Shakespeare Society, 1841. 8°. p. 90–104.)　　　**NAFM (Coventry)**
Also printed in 1922 (ed. Block) in Early English Text Society, Extra series no. 120 (*Ludus Coventriæ*), p. 83–97, *NCE (Early)*.
Extracts from the play under the title "The miraculous espousal of Mary and Joseph" are printed in William Hone, editor, *Ancient mysteries described*, London, 1823, p. 27–37, *NAFM*. Interpolations by the editor are made wherever portions of the text are omitted.

New Testament Plays — Virgin Mary, cont'd

Miracle Plays, continued

The Annunciation

The **Annunciation**, and visit of Elizabeth to Mary. The Spicers [play]. [York play no. 12, 240 lines.] (In: Lucy T. Smith, editor, York plays. Oxford, 1885. 8°. p. 93–101.) **NAFM (Smith)**

The Prophets, the Annunciation, and the Visitation are printed in S. B. Hemingway, editor, *English Nativity plays*, New York, 1909, p. 121–129, *NAFM*. The Annunciation, lines 1–196, is reprinted in M. S. Mooney, *A rosary of mystery plays*, Albany, 1915, p. 21–27, *NAFM (Mooney)*. An adaptation of lines 145–192 is printed in P. E. Osgood, *Old-time church drama adapted*, New York, 1928, p. 137–139, *NAFM*.

Annunciacio. [Towneley play no. 10.] (In: The Towneley mysteries. London [1836]. 8°. p. 72–80.) **CA (Surtees)**

Surtees Society. Publications. [v. 3.]

Also printed in 1897 (ed. England) in Early English Text Society, Extra series no. 71 *(The Towneley plays),* p. 86–97, *NCE (Early)*, and in S. B. Hemingway, editor, *English Nativity plays*, New York, 1909, p. 155–166, *NAFM*.

The **Salutation** and conception. [Coventry play no. 11.] (In: Ludus Coventriæ, ed. Halliwell. London: Shakespeare Society, 1841. 8°. p. 105–116.) **NAFM (Coventry)**

Also printed in 1922 (ed. Block) in Early English Text Society, Extra series no. 120 *(Ludus Coventriæ),* p. 97–108, *NCE (Early)*.

Also printed in part in A. W. Pollard, *English miracle plays*, Oxford, 1890, p. 44–48, 191–193, *NAFM* (other editions issued in 1904, 1923, 1927); J. M. Manly, *Specimens of the pre-Shaksperean drama*, Boston, 1897, v. 1, p. 82–93, *NCO;* S. B. Hemingway, editor, *English Nativity plays*, New York, 1909, p. 71–83, *NAFM;* and in J. Q. Adams, editor, *Chief pre-Shakespearean dramas*, Boston, 1924, p. 139–141 (lines 188–340, the conclusion), * *R – NCO*. Lines 1–136 are reprinted in Lesley Frost, editor, *Come Christmas*, New York, 1929, p. 165–170, *NAEM*. Lines 188–340, *ibid.*, p. 144–150.

Extracts under the title "A council of the Trinity and the Incarnation" are printed in William Hone, editor, *Ancient mysteries described*, London, 1823, p. 38–45, *NAFM*. Interpolations have been made by the editor wherever portions of the text are omitted.

The Salutation of Elizabeth

The **Visitation.** [York play no. 12, lines 197–240.] (In: M. S. Mooney, A rosary of mystery plays. Albany, 1915. 8°. p. 28–30.) **NAFM (Mooney)**

Salutacio Elizabeth. [Towneley play no. 11.] (In: The Towneley mysteries. London, 1836. 8°. p. 81–83.) **CA (Surtees)**

Surtees Society. Publications. [v. 3.]

Also printed in 1897 (ed. England) in Early English Text Society, Extra series no. 71 *(The Towneley plays),* p. 97–100, *NCE (Early);* in S. B. Hemingway, editor, *English Nativity plays*, New York, 1909, p. 167–169, *NAFM;* and in F. J. Tickner, editor, *Earlier English drama from Robin Hood to Everyman*, New York [cop. 1929], p. 181–184, *NCO (Tickner)*.

The **Visit** to Elizabeth. [Coventry play no. 13.] (In: Ludus Coventriæ, ed. Halliwell.

London: Shakespeare Society, 1841. 8°. p. 124–130.) **NAFM (Coventry)**

Also printed in 1922 (ed. Block) in Early English Text Society, Extra series no. 120 *(Ludus Coventriæ),* p. 115–122, *NCE (Early)*, and in S. B. Hemingway, editor, *English Nativity plays*, New York, 1909, p. 92–100, *NAFM*.

Extracts are printed by William Hone in his *Ancient mysteries described*, London, 1823, p. 53–58, *NAFM*, with interpolations by the editor wherever portions of the text were omitted.

The Suspicion of Joseph

Joseph's trouble about Mary. The pewtereres and foundours [play]. [York play no. 13, 306 lines.] (In: Lucy T. Smith, York plays. Oxford, 1885. 8°. p. 102–111.) **NAFM (Smith)**

Also printed under the title "Joseph's return" in S. B. Hemingway, editor, *English Nativity plays*, New York, 1909, p. 130–140, *NAFM*.

Joseph's return. [Coventry play no. 12.] (In: Ludus Coventriæ, ed. Halliwell. London: Shakespeare Society, 1841. 8°. p. 117–123.) **NAFM (Coventry)**

Also printed in 1922 (ed. Block) in Early English Text Society, Extra series no. 120 *(Ludus Coventriæ),* p. 109–115, *NCE (Early)*, and in S. B. Hemingway, editor, *English Nativity plays*, New York, 1909, p. 84–91, *NAFM*.

Previously printed under the title "Joseph's jealousy" in William Marriott, *A collection of English miracle-plays*, Basel, 1838, p. 41–47, *NAFM*.

Extracts are printed in William Hone, *Ancient mysteries described*, London, 1823, p. 46–52, *NAFM*. With interpolations by the editor wherever portions of the text are omitted.

The Purgation of Mary

The **Trial** of Joseph and Mary. [Coventry play no. 14.] (In: Ludus Coventriæ, ed. Halliwell. London: Shakespeare Society, 1841. 8°. p. 131–144.) **NAFH (Coventry)**

Also printed in 1922 (ed. Block) in Early English Text Society, Extra series no. 120 *(Ludus Coventriæ),* p. 123–135, *NCE (Early)*. Lines 1–32, Prologue of summoner; lines 1–372, The trial of Joseph and Mary. Previously printed in William Marriott, *A collection of English miracle-plays*, Basel, 1838, p. 48–56, *NAFM*.

Extracts are printed in William Hone, editor, *Ancient mysteries described*, London, 1823, p. 59–66, *NAFM*. Interpolations made by the editor wherever portions of the text are omitted.

Augustus and Cyrenius

Caesar Augustus. [Towneley play no. 9.] (In: The Towneley mysteries. London, 1836. 8°. p. 66–71.) **CA (Surtees)**

Surtees Society. Publications. [v. 3.]

Also printed in 1897 (ed. England) in Early English Text Society, Extra series no. 71 *(The Towneley plays),* p. 78–85, *NCE (Early)*.

The Purification of Mary

The **Purification** of Mary: Simeon and Anna prophesy. Hatmakers, masons, and laborers [play]. [York play no. 41, 459 lines.] (In: Lucy T. Smith, York plays. Oxford, 1885. 8°. p. 433–447.) **NAFM (Smith)**

Printed, with the title "The presentation of the Child Jesus," in M. S. Mooney, *A rosary of mystery plays*, Albany, 1915, p. 36–51, *NAFM*.

New Testament Plays — Virgin Mary, cont'd

Miracle Plays, continued

Purificacio Mariæ. ₍Towneley play no. 17.₎
(In: The Towneley mysteries. London, 1836.
8°. p. 154–157.)   **CA (Surtees)**
Surtees Society. Publications. [v. 3.]
Also printed in 1897 (ed. England) in Early English
Text Society, Extra series no. 71 *(The Towneley
plays),* p. 181–185, *NCE (Early).*

The **Purification.** The blackesmythes
playe. ₍Chester play no. 11.₎ (In: The Chester
plays, ed. Wright. London: Shakespeare
Society, 1843. 8°. v. 1, p. 189–200.)
                                NAFM (Chester)
Also printed in 1893 (ed. Deimling) in Early English Text Society, Extra series no. 62 *(The Chester
plays),* p. 205–217, *NCE (Early).*

The **Purification.** ₍Coventry play no. 18.₎
(In: Ludus Coventriæ, ed. Halliwell. London: Shakespeare Society, 1841. 8°. p. 172–
178.)   **NAFM (Coventry)**
Also printed in 1922 (ed. Block) in Early English
Text Society, Extra series no. 120 *(Ludus Coventriæ),*
p. 162–169, *NCE (Early).*

The Death of Mary

The **Death** of Mary. The draperes ₍play₎.
₍York play no. 45, 194 lines.₎ (In: Lucy T.
Smith, York plays. Oxford, 1885. 8°. p. 473–
479.)   **NAFM (Smith)**

The Assumption and Coronation

The **Assumption** and coronation of the
Virgin. The osteleres ₍play₎. ₍York play no.
47.₎ (In: Lucy T. Smith, York plays. Oxford, 1885. 8°. p. 491–496.)   **NAFM (Smith)**
Reprinted in M. S. Mooney, *A rosary of mystery
plays,* Albany, 1915, p. 145–147, *NAFM.*

O'NEILL, Francis. The Blessed Virgin in
the York cycle of miracle plays. (American
Catholic quarterly review. Philadelphia,
1909. 8°. v. 34, p. 439–455.)   * **DA**

The **Assumption** of the Virgin. ₍Coventry
play no. 41.₎ (In: Ludus Coventriæ, ed. Halliwell. London: Shakespeare Society, 1841.
8°. p. 383–400.)   **NAFM (Coventry)**
Also printed in 1922 (ed. Block) in Early English
Text Society, Extra series no. 120 *(Ludus Coventriæ),*
p. 354–373, *NCE (Early).*

The **Assumption** of the Virgin. A miracle
play from the N-town cycle; edited by W. W.
Greg... ₍Coventry play no. 41.₎ Oxford:
The Clarendon Press, 1915. 75(1) p., 2 facsims. 8°. (Studies in the religious drama. 1.)
                               NAFM (Studies)
"My immediate...intention is to inquire whether any
marked difference in dialect or style of composition
exists between the Assumption play and the bulk of the
cycle, such as could be adduced in support of the
bibliographical evidence for an independent origin." —
Introduction, p. 5.
Reviewed by E. K. Chambers in *Modern language
review,* Cambridge, 1916, v. 11, p. 465–466, *NAA.*

Foreign Miracle Plays

De uno peccatore qui promeruit graciam..
₍Concerning a sinner who was promised
grace, a miracle play on the Virgin, from old
Swedish, from a ms. in the library of the
University of Copenhagen.₎ (Society for the
Advancement of Scandinavian Study. Pub-
lications. Scandinavian studies and notes.
Menasha, Wis., 1928. 8°. v. 10, p. 1–13.) **NIC**
First published at Lund, 1842, under title of *En
syndares omvändelse.* The old Swedish text is here
published with an English translation by M. S. Peterson
in parallel columns, under title of *A Swedish miracle
De notre dame.*

Guibour; a miracle play of Our Lady:
version from the Old French by Anna
Sprague Macdonald. New York: The Sunwise Turn, Inc., 1919. x, 64 p. 12°. (Neighbourhood Playhouse plays. no. 2.)   **NKN**
Known in the original as "Un miracle de Nostre
Dame, comment elle garda une femme d'estre arse," and
belongs to a collection of forty miracle plays, all
celebrating the intervention of Our Lady. Produced
at the Neighbourhood Playhouse, New York, Jan. 18,
1919; with Irene Lewisohn as Our Lady.

Marieken van Nijmejen. A marvelous history of Mary of Nimmegen, who for more
than seven year lived and had ado with the
devil. Translated from the Middle Dutch by
Harry Morgan Ayres... With an introduction by Adriaan J. Barnouw... The Hague:
Martinus Nijhoff, 1924. 3 p.l., xxv, 78 p. 16°.
(Dutch library. v. 3.)   **NAFM**
Emma and Moonen on Procession Day see the play
wherein Our Lady speaks. See p. 46, 53, 56.

Prophetæ. Christmas. (In: J. Q. Adams,
compiler, Chief pre-Shakespearean dramas.
Boston, New York ₍cop. 1924₎. 8°. p. 41–48.)
                                 * **R – NCO**
Latin text and English translation.
"Printed by U. Chevalier, *Ordinaires de l'Église
cathédrale de Laon,* 1897, p. 385, from a manuscript
of the thirteenth century."

Siège d'Orléans. Saint Joan of Orleans.
Scenes from the fifteenth century Mystère
du Siège d'Orléans. Selected and translated
by Joan Evans... The text edited by Paul
Studer... Oxford: Clarendon Press, 1926.
xxxi, 191 p. illus. 8°.   **NAFM (Siège)**
French text and English translation.
In the heavenly scenes Christ and "Our Lady" are
among the speakers.

Modern Plays

Assisium, Sister M. Homage to Our Lady
of the Blessed Sacrament. ₍A dramatic poem.₎
(Sentinel of the Blessed Sacrament. New
York, 1918. 8°. v. 21, p. 543–544, 629–631,
748–750.)   **ZLF**

Carman, Bliss, and MARY PERRY KING.
Mary. ₍A dramatic poem.₎ illus. (In their:
Daughters of dawn. New York, 1913. 12°.
p. 63–71.)   **NCM**

New Testament Plays — Virgin Mary, cont'd

Modern Plays, continued

Caswall, Edward. Drama angelicum: a masque of angels before Our Lady in the temple. (In his: Hymns and poems. London, 1873. 2. ed. 12°. p. 301–343.)   **NCI**
In four scenes.

Edland, Elisabeth. The children's king. ₁In one scene.₁ (In her: The children's king, and other plays for children, with chapters on dramatizing with children. New York and Cincinnati ₁cop. 1928₁. 12°. p. 41–49.)   **NASH**
A "Woman" (Virgin Mary) is the chief character.

Flecker, James Elroy. Joseph and Mary. ₁A dramatic poem.₁ (In his: Forty-two poems. London, 1911. 12°. p. 34–37.)   **NCM**
Reprinted in his *Collected poems*, London [1921], p. 83–86, *NCM*, and in *Georgian poetry, 1911–1912*, London, 1914, p. 87–88, *NCI*.

Graves, Frederick D. Our Lady of the olives. ₁In three acts.₁ Hartford: Church Missions Publishing Co., 1924. 39 p. 8°. (Church in story and pageant. Publication no. 2.)   **NBL p.v.223**

Greene, Henry Copley. Théophile; a miracle play. Boston: Small, Maynard & Co., 1898. viii, 32 p., 1 pl. 16°.   **NBM**
Produced at the Teatro Bambino, Dublin, N. H., July 18, 1898, with Eugenia Brooks Frothingham as the Virgin Mary.

Hinkson, Katharine (Tynan). The annunciation. ₁In two scenes.₁ illus. (In her: Miracle plays. London, 1895. 12°. p. 11–25.)   **NCR**

—— The visitation. ₁In two scenes.₁ illus. (In her: Miracle plays. London, 1895. 12°. p. 27–38.)   **NCR**

Maeterlinck, Maurice. Sister Beatrice: a miracle play in three acts. Done into English by A. Bernard Miall. (Anglo-Saxon review. London, 1900. 4°. v. 6, p. 90–119.)   **†* DA**
Scene: Louvain at the end of the thirteenth century. The Holy Virgin in the likeness of Sister Beatrice.
Reprinted in his *Sister Beatrice and Adriane & Barbe Bleue*, New York, 1913, p. 1–91, *NKP*.

Porter, Arthur Kingsley. The Virgin and the clerk... ₁In eight scenes.₁ Boston: Marshall Jones Company, 1929. 2 p.l., 96 p., 1 l. 12°.   **NBM**
The scene is placed in Adana, Cilicia. The Virgin voids and surrenders to the bishop coadjutor a contract he had signed with a Jew for the sale of his soul in return "for success to be delivered."

THE NATIVITY

Miracle Plays

Boyle, Peter A. The Christmas mystery play. (Xavier. New York, 1909. 8°. v. 21, p. 461–469.)   **† STG (St. Francis)**

Chesshire, John K. C. Bethlehem tableaux from behind the scenes; with prac-

tical hints and illustrations... With a preface by the Bishop of Worcester. London: J. M. Dent & Sons, Ltd., 1913. x, 101 p., 1 l. illus. sq. 8°.   **NAFM**

FitzPatrick, Francis L. A mediaeval Nativity play. (Holy Cross purple. Worcester, Mass., 1897. 8°. v. 4, p. 21–29.)   **STG**

Hemingway, Samuel Burdett. The history and development of the Nativity plays. (In his: English Nativity plays. New York, 1909. 8°. p. vii–xix.)   **NAFM**

Mackay, Constance D'Arcy. The miracle play comes back. Many churches are now reviving this beautiful old custom. 3 illus. (Delineator. New York, 1925. f°. v. 107, Dec., 1925, p. 5, 80.)   **† VSA**

Mangan, R. L. The Nativity in early pageants. (Catholic world. New York, 1909. 8°. v. 90, p. 294–304.)   *** DA**

Rosé, Grace Norton. A miracle play in a country house. From the old English Coventry or Chester cycles can be adapted a play for Christmas eve or that holiday house party. 6 illus. and diagrs. (House and garden. New York, 1919. f°. v. 36, Dec., 1919, p. 19–21, 62.)   **† MSA**

The **Journey** to Bethlehem; the birth of Jesus. The tille thekers ₁play₁. ₁York play no. 14, 154 lines.₁ (In: Lucy T. Smith, York plays. Oxford, 1885. 8°. p. 112–117.)   **NAFM (Smith)**
Also printed in S. B. Hemingway, editor, *English Nativity plays*, New York, 1909, p. 141–146, *NAFM;* M. S. Mooney, *A rosary of mystery plays*, Albany, 1915, p. 31–35, *NAFM;* J. Q. Adams, editor, *Chief pre-Shakespearean dramas*, Boston, 1924, p. 142–144, * R – NCO; in Lesley Frost, editor, *Come Christmas*, New York, 1929, p. 198–204, *NAEM*. An adaptation is printed in P. E. Osgood, *Old-time church drama adapted*, New York, 1928, p. 139–146, *NAFM*.
A presentation of the Nativity as arranged by E. K. Chambers from the York and Coventry cycles was given at the Everyman Theatre, Hampstead, England, Dec. 24, 1920, and a production of the Nativity and other episodes from the York plays was given at the York Everyman Theatre at Guildhall, York, Jan. 5, 1925.

Towneley ₁Nativity plays, part of nos. 10, 11, 13, 14, 15₁ adapted by Randall Cayford Burrell. (In: Harvard Dramatic Club, Miracle plays. Edited by D. F. Robinson. New York, 1928. 8°. p. 31–68.)   **NAFM**
Included is a part of the fourteenth play in the York cycle and a few lines of the thirteenth play of the Ludus Coventriæ. Produced by the Harvard Dramatic Club, Dec. 18 and 19, 1923.

The **Salutation** and Nativity. The wryghtes and sklaters plaie... ₁Chester play no. 6.₁ (In: The Chester plays, ed. Wright. London: Shakespeare Society, 1843. 8°. v. 1, p. 94–118.)   **NAFM (Chester)**
Also printed in 1893 (ed. Deimling) in Early English Text Society, Extra series no. 62 (*The Chester plays*), p. 104–132, *NCE (Early)*, and in S. B. Hemingway, editor, *English Nativity plays*, New York, 1909, p. 5–35, *NAFM*. Lines 513–736 are reprinted in Lesley Frost, editor, *Come Christmas*, New York, 1929, p. 205–213, *NAEM*.

New Testament Plays — The Nativity, cont'd

Miracle Plays, continued

The **Nativity**. ₁In sixteen scenes.₁ ₁Chester plays 6–10, adapted.₁ (In: Chester miracle plays, done...by I. and O. Bolton King. London ₁1930₁. 12°. p. 59–118.) **NAFM**

The **Nativity** and adoration cycle of the Chester mysteries as performed in New York on Christmas Eve at the Greenwich Village Theatre with a prefatory note on the sources and method of playing, including The Sheaphardes' play the Offering of the Sheaphardes the Adoration of the Magi. Edited by Frank M. Conroy and Roy Mitchell. New York: Egmont H. Arens, 1917. 23 p. 12°.
NAC p.v.25
The English Drama Society gave productions of the Nativity at Bloomsbury Hall, London in December, 1906 and at University College, London, in December, 1907. For an account of the 1906 production, together with illustrations, see *London illustrated news*, v. 129, p. 935–936, * DA. See also *The Athenæum*, London, v. 130, p. 835, * DA.

The **Birth** of Christ. ₁Coventry play no. 15.₁ (In: Ludus Coventriæ, ed. Halliwell. London: Shakespeare Society, 1841. 8°. p. 145–155.) **NAFM (Coventry)**
Also printed in 1922 (ed. Block) in Early English Text Society, Extra series no. 120 (*Ludus Coventriæ*), p. 135–145, *NCE (Early)*, and in S. B. Hemingway, editor, *English Nativity plays*, New York, 1909, p. 101–112, *NAFM*.
Extracts under the title "The miraculous birth and the midwives" are published in William Hone, editor, *Ancient mysteries described*, London, 1823, p. 67–72, *NAFM*. Interpolations made by the editor wherever portions of the text are omitted.
Produced at the Old Vic, London, Jan. 7, 1919 (first staged Dec., 1918).

The Shearmen and Taylors Play (Coventry)

The **Pageant** of the company of Shearmen and Taylors, in Coventry. (In: Thomas Sharp, A dissertation on the pageants or dramatic mysteries anciently performed at Coventry... Coventry, 1825. f°. p. 83–112.)
† NAFM
The words and music of the songs of this pageant are given on p. 113–114 and folios 115–118. Glossary and illustrations. p. 119–124.
"The Gild or Company of Shearmen and Taylors... took for the subject of their pageant the Birth of Christ and offering of the Magi, with the flight into Egypt, and Murder of the Innocents." — *p. 82.*

The **Pageant** of the company of Shearmen and Tailors, in Coventry: the Nativity. (In: William Marriott, editor, Collection of English miracle-plays or mysteries. Basel, 1838. 8°. p. 57–89.) **NAFM**

The **Pageant** of the Shearmen and Taylors. (In: J. M. Manly, editor, Specimens of the pre-Shaksperean drama. Boston, 1897. 12°. v. 1, p. 120–152.) **NCO**

The **Pageant** of the Shearmen and Taylors. (In: Two Coventry Corpus Christi plays. ₁Edited₁ by Hardin Craig. London, 1902. 8°. p. 1–32.) **NCE (Early)**
Early English Text Society. Extra series no. 87.

A **Miracle** play of the Nativity. ＜The Pageant of the Shearmen and Tailors, from the Coventry Corpus Christi plays.＞ (In: An English garner. ₁v. 12.₁ Fifteenth century prose and verse, with an introduction by A. W. Pollard. Westminster, 1903. 8°. p. 243–273.) **NCE (English)**

A **Christmas** miracle play adapted from the pageant of the Shearmen and Tailors in the Coventry cycle of miracles... (In: S. A. Eliot, editor, Little theatre classics. Boston, 1918. 12°. v. 1, p. 55–104.) **MZB**
Presented at the John Herron Art Institute, Indianapolis, Ind., December, 1915.

The **Magi**, Herod, and the slaughter of the innocents. (In: J. Q. Adams, editor, Chief pre-Shakespearean dramas. Boston, 1924. 8°. p. 158–166.) *** R – NCO**
Lines 475–900 of the Shearmen and Taylors' pageant.

Coventry Nativity play of the company of Shearmen and Tailors. (In: "Everyman," with other interludes including eight miracle plays. London ₁1909₁. 16°. p. 74–98.) **NAFM**

The **Nativity**. ₁Play of the company of Shearmen and Tailors.₁ illus. (In: Everyman, and other plays. London, 1925. 8°. p. 69–139.) **NAFM**

The **Pageant** of the Shearmen and Tailors. A miracle play adapted by John Mason Brown. (Theatre arts monthly. New York, 1925. 8°. v. 9, p. 824–835.) **NBLA**
"The time should be Corpus Christi 1534 or thereabouts, and the scene the streets of Coventry... The text has been cut and occasionally rearranged, but the dialogue remains close to the original, and wherever possible represents a simplification of the early spelling rather than any serious adaptation."
Reprinted in Harvard Dramatic Club, *Miracle plays*, New York, 1928, p. 3–29, *NAFM*.
Produced by the Harvard Dramatic Club, Dec. 20 and 21, 1922.

The **Christmas** mystery of Shearmen's guild of Coventry. ₁Adapted.₁ (American church monthly. New York, 1927. 8°. v. 22, p. 307–320.) **ZRA**

Pageant of Shearmen and Tailors. (In: F. J. Tickner, editor, Earlier English drama from Robin Hood to Everyman. New York ₁cop. 1929₁. 16°. p. 112–133.) **NCO (Tickner)**
In abbreviated form.

BURNS, Mary Modena. The first Christmas, or the Nativity. A miracle play. ₁Adapted.₁ (In her: Good things for Sunday schools. Chicago ₁cop. 1916₁. 12°. p. 139–146.) **ZICS**

Foreign Nativity Plays

The **Benediktbeuren** play. Translated and adapted by Donald Fay Robinson. Prologue adapted by Prof. Kuno Francke. (In: Harvard Dramatic Club miracle plays, edited by D. F. Robinson. New York, 1928. 8°. p. 87–97.) **NAFM (Robinson)**
Written in Latin for the use of the Bavarian abbey of Benediktbeuren. Produced by the Harvard Dramatic Club, Dec. 16 and 17, 1925.

New Testament Plays — The Nativity, cont'd

Miracle Plays, continued

The **Hessian** Christmas play. (In: Harvard Dramatic Club miracle plays, edited by D. F. Robinson. New York, 1928. 8°. p. 132–148.)
NAFM (Robinson)
The play is found ·in a late fifteenth century ms. Translated in abridged form and adapted by D. F. Robinson. In a prologue and nine scenes.

Little shepherds of Bethlehem. Los pastorcillos en Belen. ₁A drama in five acts.₁ Translated from the Spanish by Mrs. A. S. C. Forbes. Engrossed by J. F. Lloyd. Los Angeles, Cal.: Wetzel Pub. Co., 1929. ₁11₁, 78 l., 1 port. music. 4°.
"From Los pastorcillos and other Nativity plays of Spain there was evolved in California the popular Christmas plays known as Pastorela and Pastores... The last time that Pastorela was given in Los Angeles was on Christmas Eve 1861."

The **Maastricht** play. A Christmas miracle. Adapted by Donald Fay Robinson. (Theatre arts monthly. New York, 1927. sq. 8°. v. 11, Dec., 1927, p. 947–952.) **NBLA**
The play here given is a part of a greater play, which presents the history of the world from creation to judgment. Attributed to the early middle of the fourteenth century.
In thirteen scenes. The present version is a translation, with minor omissions, of lines 96–551 of the Maastricht 'Paachspel.'
Reprinted in *Harvard Dramatic Club miracle plays*, edited by D. F. Robinson, New York, 1928, p. 149–162, *NAFM (Robinson)*.

Mystère de la Nativité. The mystery of the Nativity. Translated from the Liégeois of the xvth century· and with a foreword by Richard Aldington. London: G. Allen & Unwin, Ltd. ₁1924.₁ 31 p., 1 pl. 24°. **NAFM**
"The text of this mystery is that published by Prof. Gustave Cohen in his *Mystères et moralités du ms. 617 de Chantilly*... The poem is a fragment of a longer play, the remainder of which is lost." — *Note, p. 9.*

The **Nativity.** <The Chantilly play.> Translated and adapted by Eduardo Sanchez and Donald Fay Robinson. (In: Harvard Dramatic Club miracle plays, edited by D. F. Robinson. New York, 1928. 8°. p. 69–85.)
NAFM (Robinson)
In eight scenes. "The ms. was written by a nun, one Katherine Bourlet."
Produced by the Harvard Dramatic Club, Dec. 16 and 17, 1924.

The **Provençal** play. Translated and adapted by Donald Fay Robinson. (In: Harvard Dramatic Club miracle plays, edited by D. F. Robinson. New York, 1928. 8°. p. 111–130.)
NAFM (Robinson)
In fourteen scenes. The translation is a very free one.
The play dates from the end of the thirteenth or beginning of the fourteenth century. Produced by the Harvard Dramatic Club, Dec. 19 and 20, 1927.

The **Star.** <Bilsen play.> (In: Harvard Dramatic Club miracle plays, edited by

D. F. Robinson. New York, 1928. 8°. p. 163–173.)
NAFM (Robinson)
In seven scenes. Translated and adapted by D. F. Robinson.
Assigned to the end of the eleventh century.

The **Umbrian** play. (In: Harvard Dramatic Club miracle plays, edited by D. F. Robinson. New York, 1928. 8°. p. 175–193.)
NAFM (Robinson)
In thirteen scenes.

The **Wisemen.** <The Spanish play.> Translated and adapted by Donald Fay Robinson. (In: Harvard Dramatic Club miracle plays, edited by D. F. Robinson. New York, 1928. 8°. p. 98–110.) **NAFM (Robinson)**
In five scenes. Freely elaborated. Motifs from the Chantilly, Orleans, and Umbrian plays and from other sources are incorporated.
Produced by the Harvard Dramatic Club, Dec. 16 and 17, 1926.

Modern Plays

Adams, Alice E. How the world keeps Christmas. ₁In one scene.₁ music. (Normal instructor and primary plans. Dansville, N. Y., 1919. f°. v. 29, Dec., 1919, p. 43–44.)
† SSA

Adams, May Belle. The coming of Christ; a Christmas pageant ₁in nine scenes₁. (Emerson quarterly. Boston, 1929. 4°. v. 10, Nov., 1929, p. 17–20, 26–28.) **† NANA**

Agius, Ambrose. The coming of Christ. (In his: Two mystery plays. London ₁1927₁. 12°. p. 5–32.) **NCO p.v.554, no. 7**
In nine scenes.

Bain, Ethel. ...Come ye to Bethlehem. ·₁In three parts.₁ Hartford: Church Missions Pub. Co., 1930. 18 p. 8°. (The church in story and pageant. Publications. no. 28.)
Cover-title. The three parts: The prophecy, The fulfillment, The bearer of the light.

—— The road to Bethlehem; a Christmas play for children in one scene. New York: The Avondale Press ₁cop. 1927₁. 3 p.l., 3–13 p. 12°. **NASH**

Bainbridge, Stella M. Bethlehem; the house of bread; a Christmas play...₁in a prologue, seven scenes, and an epilogue.₁ London: The Society of SS. Peter & Paul ₁1922?₁. 23(1) p. 16°. (Christmas plays. no. 3.) **NCO p.v.487, no.1**
Produced by the children of the parish of St. Columba, Montreal, on Holy Innocents' Day, 1920.

Baird, George M. P. The heart o'Mary. A mystery play done in English verse... New York and London: Samuel French, Ltd., cop. 1927. 36 p. 12°. (French's international copyrighted edition of the works of the best authors. no. 608.) **NBL p.v.167, no.1**

New Testament Plays — The Nativity, cont'd

Modern Plays, continued

Bartlett, Edward R., and E. RUTH BARTLETT. The child of prophecy. ₍In three acts.₎ Music by Lyman R. Bayard. Los Angeles: Pageant Publishers, 1926. 25 p. 8°.

Act one: Israel in exile. Act two: Bethlehem. Act three: the manger.
First appeared in *Church school*, New York, 1922, v. 4, p. 69–72.

—— Followers of the star. ₍In four scenes.₎ (International journal of religious education. Mount Morris, Ill., 1925. f°. v. 2, Nov., 1925, p. 24–27.)

Bates, Esther Willard. The Christmas flowers. A mystery play for children. Boston: W. H. Baker Company, 1924. 26 p. 12°.

On cover: Baker's royalty plays.

—— The promise of peace. A Christmas Nativity. (International journal of religious education. Mount Morris, Ill., 1926. 4°. v. 3, Dec., 1926, p. 14–17.)

—— —— Boston: Walter H. Baker Co. ₍cop. 1927.₎ 23 p. 12°. **NBL p.v.191**

On cover: Baker's royalty plays.

Bates, William Oscar. In the light of the manger, a prophetic fantasy in one act. (Drama. Chicago, 1920. 4°. v. 11, p. 102–103.) **NAFA**

The main characters are a mother, a son, and a Roman soldier. Time: the days of King Herod.
Reprinted in B. L. Schafer, editor, *A book of one-act plays,* Indianapolis [1922], p. 67–76, *NBL.*

Bayard, Lyman R. "When the stars shone"; a Christmas pageant. Los Angeles: Pageant Publishers, 1921. 31 p. illus. 4°.

First appeared in *Church school*, New York, 1921, v. 3, p. 80–89.

Benson, Robert Hugh. A mystery play in honour of the Nativity of Our Lord. London: Longmans, Green and Co., 1908. xiii, 101 p. illus. 12°. **NCR**

In a prologue and five scenes.
Produced at Cambridge, England, December, 1907 and January, 1908.

—— —— New York: Longmans, Green and Co., Ltd., 1926. 48 p. new impression. 12°.

Benton, Rita. The Christmas story. illus. music. (In her: Bible plays. New York ₍cop. 1922₎. 8°. p. 214–237.) **NASH**

Also issued separately, New York [cop. 1922]. 29 p. 8°.

Betzner, Era. Bringers of gifts. ₍In a prologue and one scene.₎ New York: The Womans Press ₍1930?₎. 15 p. 12°. (Program series. no. 20.)

Cover-title.

Bolton, Ivy. Guiding light, a Nativity play ₍in four acts₎. New York: Womans Press ₍cop. 1927₎. 20 p. 12°.

Bouchor, Maurice. Noël; or, The mystery of the Nativity. illus. Translated by Paul McPharlin. (In: Paul M₍c₎Pharlin, compiler, A repertory of marionette plays. New York, 1929. 4°. p. 122–183.) **NAFM**

Produced at the Signoret's Petit-Théâtre, Paris, in the autumn of 1890.

Bowie, Walter Russell. The soldier of Bethlehem; a Christmas pageant ₍in four scenes₎. New York: Abingdon Press ₍cop. 1927₎. 32 p. music. diagr. 8°.

First appeared in *Church school*, New York, 1922, v. 4, p. 33–37.

Brewster, Daniel O. "Fra Angelico." <A miracle play of the mystery of the Nativity.> ₍A pantomime in ten scenes.₎ (Emerson quarterly. Boston, 1928. 4°. v. 8, Nov., 1928, p. 5, 16.) **† NANA**

Bridgeman, Sidney. …The stable door; a mystery play of three scenes and four tableaux. London: Society for Promoting Christian Knowledge, 1919. 48 p. music. 12°. (Parish plays.)

Brooke, Audrey. The heavenly visitor; a Christmas mystery play. ₍In three acts.₎ London: Faith Press, Ltd. ₍1928.₎ 3 p.l., 26 p. 12°.

Foreword by the Lord Bishop of Johannesburg.
The play was given, Christmas, 1927, at St. Mary's Pro-Cathedral, Johannesburg.

Brown, Katharine S., and GLENNA SMITH TINNIN. One night in Bethlehem; a play of the Nativity, in a prologue and five scenes. New York, London: Samuel French, cop. 1925. 2 p.l., 42 p. illus. 8°.

Produced at the National Cathedral School, Washington, D. C., Dec. 13, 1924.

Brown, Nell K. A story of old Bethlehem. ₍In one act.₎ New York: The Abingdon Press ₍cop. 1930₎. 15 p. diagr. 8°.

Adapted from *Zerah,* by Montanye Perry.
Foreword by Montanye Perry.
The Biblical characters are Joseph, shepherds, and three wise men.

Bryan, Katharine C. The light; a service of worship for a white Christmas. New York: The Womans Press ₍cop. 1926₎. 21 p. 12°.

Buchanan, Fannie R. The first Noël; a Christmas masque with carols and children. ₍A synopsis of the action in four scenes.₎ (The Woman's home companion. Springfield, O., 1919. f°. v. 46, Nov., 1919, p. 49, 142.) ***DA**

Buckton, A. M. Eager heart; a Christmas mystery-play. New York: Chappell and Co., Ltd. ₍cop. 1905.₎ 4 p.l., 40 p. 12°. **NAFM**

Cammaerts, Émile. Le mystère des trois rois. The mystery of the three kings. (In his: New Belgian poems. London, 1916. 12°. p. 83–123.) **BTZI**

Text in English and French on opposite pages.
English translation by Tita Brand-Cammaerts.

New Testament Plays — The Nativity, cont'd

Modern Plays, continued

Cantello, Joseph. The star of Bethlehem, a sacred drama in five acts and a prelude. Los Angeles, Cal.: Commercial Printing House ₁cop. 1907₁. 131 p. illus. 8°.
Title from Library of Congress.

Carpenter, S. G., and E. H. WELSFORD. "The Christmas mystery." A series of Bethlehem tableaux with prologue, carols, hymns and dialogue arranged for parish players. Cambridge: W. Heffer & Sons, Ltd., 1921. 22 p. sq. 12°.   **NAC p.v.69**

Cavanah, Frances. The transfiguration of the gifts; a pageant play ₁in one scene₁ for Christmas. New York: The Womans Press ₁cop. 1923₁. 16 p. 12⁹.

Chapman, John Jay. Christmas once more; a sacred cantata for children. (In his: Neptune's Isle, and other plays for children. New York, 1916. 12°. p. 163–196.) **NASH**
Part I or Prelude. A drama without music. Cologne on the Rhine, about the year 400 A. D. Part II. Cantata, a morality with music and singing. The stable at Bethlehem.

A **Christmas** play. Ditchling. Sussex ₁:S. Dominic's Press, 1928₁. 15 p. 48°.

Clarke, Lois W. No room in the inn, a Christmas play. New York: Fitzgerald Pub. Co., cop. 1928. 12 p. 12°.   **NBL p.v.196**

Clements, Claudine E. The first Nowell; a play for Christmastide, in three scenes, which are adapted from the mediaeval Nativity plays, and with a prologue and epilogue. New York: The Womans Press ₁cop. 1926₁. 38 p. 12°.
The persons in the prologue and epilogue are represented as being at an inn in Salisbury, England.

—— A troubadour's dream. (A play for Christmas-tide in one act with three episodes and an epilogue.) (Drama. Chicago, 1925. 4°. v. 16, p. 57–58.)   **NAFA**
The scene of the play is Toulouse on a Christmas eve in the twelfth century. The scene of the episodes is Bethlehem, also on a Christmas eve.

Clements, Florence (Ryerson), and C. C. CLEMENTS. The littlest shepherd; a Christmas interlude ₁in one scene₁. (Emerson quarterly. Boston, 1929. 4°. v. 10, Nov., 1929, p. 11–12, 14.)   **† NANA**

Cole, Edna Earle. Two journeys to Bethlehem. ₁In two acts.₁ (In her: The good Samaritan and other Bible stories dramatized. Boston ₁cop. 1915₁. 12°. p. 63–73.)
Based on Luke II:8–20 and Matthew II:1–12.

Collins, Jacob Guy. The Saviour's advent. A pastoral — Hebrew-Greek. (In his: Poems. Memphis, 1883. 8°. p. 79–83.) **NBI**
The speakers: Hillel and Idius.

Conger, Margaret Lynch. The brightness of his rising, a Christmas miracle play ₁in

two prologues and three scenes₁. New York: Womans Press ₁1926, cop. 1924₁. 23 p. 12°.
First presented in 1921 by the Master School of Music, Brooklyn.

—— St. Francis of Assisi; a Christmas masque in one act...given first by Greenwich House, New York. New York: The Womans Press ₁1925₁. 16 p. 12°.
The characters are birds, animals, and the usual Nativity figures.

Connelly, H. G. White gifts for the King. ₁In three parts.₁ illus. (Church school. New York, 1921. 4°. v. 3, p. 119–120.)
Copy in Library of Union Theological Seminary.

Converse, Florence. The blessed birthday, a Christmas miracle play. New York: E. P. Dutton & Company ₁cop. 1917₁. 2 p.l., 68 p. 12°.   **NBM**
Also printed in her *Garments of praise*, New York, 1921, p. 1–48, *NAFM*.

Cooper, Miriam Denness. The canticles of Mary; a Christmas mystery play... New York: The Century Co. ₁cop. 1930.₁ 1 p.l., 26 p. 12°.
"Suggested by a story in *Men of the way*, by Louis Tucker." The chief speakers are Luke, the physician, and the Virgin Mary, who tells him the incidents of the Nativity, so that he may set them down in writing. Jerusalem, in the home of the beloved disciple, near the close of the life of Mary.

Corliss, Leon R. "The Messiah." ₁In ten scenes.₁ Aurora, Ill., cop. 1926. 1 p.l., 13 p., 1 l. 12°. (Advent Christian pamphlets. B-G.)   **ZXRD n.c.2**
A sort of a modern Prophetae play.

Cotton, Stéphanie. The legend of Baboushka. A Nativity play in two acts and an epilogue. Adapted from two Russian legends — the legend of "Baboushka" (the Russian "Father Christmas") and the legend that S. Andrew the Apostle preached the Gospel in Russia gaining many converts there. London: H. F. W. Deane & Sons, 1928. 28 p. 12°. (Village Drama Society. Plays.)   **NCO (Village)**
Scenes: a peasant's hut, and a market-place in south Russia. Within this play is a Nativity play.
Cf. *A Christmas ballad: the legend of Baboushka*, by Julia C. R. Dorr. New York [188–?]. 13 f. 16°. *NBF p.v. 26.*

Coxe, Arthur Cleveland. Advent, a mystery. New-York: John S. Taylor, 1837. x p., 1 l., 13–132 p. 12°.   **NBHD**

Craig, Grace E. The spirit of Christmas. ₁In one act.₁ New York: The Womans Press ₁1928₁. 15 p. 12°.

Cropper, Margaret. ...The next-door house; a Christmas play. ₁In three scenes.₁ London: Society for Promoting Christian Knowledge, 1920. 16 p. 12°. (Parish plays.)
Another ed., 1925.   **NCO p.v.459**
The Virgin and her baby as visitors on Christmas eve in the cottage of Down in the Dust.

—— Two sides of the door. ₁In two scenes.₁ New York: The Century Co., cop. 1926. 15 p. 8°.
Cover-title.

New Testament Plays — The Nativity, cont'd

Modern Plays, continued

Cuthbert, Father. The shepherds; a Nativity representation [in seven scenes and an epilogue]. With three illustrations by Gabriel Pippet. London: Burns & Oates, Ltd., 1919. 68 p. illus. 12°.

Davies, C. Beverley. ...The cradle king; a Nativity play [in a prologue and five acts]. London: Society for Promoting Christian Knowledge [1930?]. vii(i), 9–64 p. 12°. (Parish plays. no. 30.)
The usual Nativity personages, and other Biblical and fictitious characters.

Davis, Dorothy Marie. The street of hearts; a Christmas fantasy [in one act] for children. Los Angeles: Pageant Publishers, cop. 1928. 12 p. 8°.
Notes on production, p. 11–12.
"Joseph and Mary on Christmas eve seek haven for the night in the hearts of men."

Dearmer, Mabel (White). The soul of the world. A mystery play [in a prologue and three acts] of the Nativity and the Passion, by Mrs. Percy Dearmer. London: A. R. Mowbray & Co., Ltd., 1911. 65 p. illus. 8°. **NCR**
Reprinted in her *Three plays*, London, 1916, p. 203–255, *NCR*.

Denton, Clara Janetta (Fort). While shepherds watched. A Christmas drama in one scene. (In: Sunday school and church entertainments. Philadelphia, 1914. 12°. p. 127–131.) **ZICS**

Dunham, Helen. The Nativity of the manger; a Christmas tableau. New York: The Womans Press [1928]. 22 p. 12°.

Durell, J. C. V. On the road to Bethlehem; a miracle play of the Nativity of Christ [in eight scenes]; with full instructions for acting and introductory essays... [London: Faith Press, Ltd., 192–?] 12, 19 p. music. 4°.

—— When Christ was born; a miracle play of the Nativity of Our Lord [in eleven scenes]. London: Faith Press, Ltd., 1920. 32 p. 12°.

Erskine, John. Noel: a mystery. [A dramatic poem.] (In his: Actaeon, and other poems. New York, 1907. 12°. p. 78–96.) **NBI**

Farrar, John. Worship the Nativity, a masque for Christmastide [in one scene]. illus. (In his: The magic sea shell, and other plays. New York [cop. 1923]. 8°. p. 133–155.) **J793-F**

Finn, Sister Mary Paulina. The star of Bethlehem. (In her: Alma Mater...and other dramas. Washington, D. C.: Georgetown Visitation Convent, 1913. 12°. p. 211–219.) **NBM**
A drama in one act.

Fite, W. A. The birth of Our Lord, a Christmas drama [in five acts]. Cincinnati: Powell & White [cop. 1921]. 15 p. 8°. **NBL p.v.223**

Flecker, James Elroy. The miracle of Bethlehem. [A dramatic poem.] (In his: Forty-two poems. London, 1911. 12°. p. 62–69.) **NCM**
Reprinted in his *Collected poems*, London [1921], p. 110–118, *NCM*.

Folmsbee, Beulah. The gift of love, a Nativity play in one act. illus. (In her: Guki, the moon boy and other plays... New York [cop. 1928]. 8°. p. 127–157.) **J793-F**

Fulton, Esmé. ...A Nativity play [in seven scenes]. London: Society for Promoting Christian Knowledge [192–?]. vi, 7–23 p. 12°. (Parish plays. no. 2.)

Getz, Arthur H. The story ever new; a Christmas pageant, with tableaux vivant and carols. [In six scenes.] Philadelphia: The United Lutheran Publication House [cop. 1926]. 23 p. 12°. **NCO p.v.540**

Githens, Harry W. The star of the East. [In eight scenes.] (In his: New Testament stories dramatized. Cincinnati [cop. 1929]. 12°. p. 11–22.)

Goodwin, V. D. I was a stranger; a Nativity play [in five scenes]. London: Selwyn & Blount, Ltd., 1923. 63 p. illus. 8°. **NCR**

Goold, Marshall N. Good will among men; a Christmas service for all the church, arranged by Marshall N. Goold. Boston: The Pilgrim Press, cop. 1925. 18 p. music. 8°.
Prophetic voices, p. 8–9.

—— The shepherds. [A play in three scenes.] (In: Religious dramas. New York: Century Co. [cop. 1926.] 8°. v. 2, p. 283–315.) **NAFM**
Scene: plains north of Bethlehem. Characters: Jethro, Joseph, Mary the mother of Jesus, etc.
Also reprinted as a separate: cop. 1926. 1 p.l., 285–315 p., 2 l.

Gosselink, Sara. The star of hope. [In four acts.] (In: Church plays and entertainments for young people. Franklin, Ohio, cop. 1924. 12°. p. 62–81.)

Gregg, Marjorie True. A Christmas miracle play. (Education. Boston, 1917. 8°. v. 38, p. 91–101.) **SSA**

Grimball, Elizabeth B. The waif; a Christmas morality of the twentieth century [in one act]. New York: Womans Press [cop. 1923]. 16 p. 12°.
Place: the street corners of the world. Time: the eve before Christmas.

Griswold, Virginia A. The Christmas story; a play in four scenes. New York: Samuel French, cop. 1921. 26 p. 12°.

New Testament Plays — The Nativity, cont'd

Modern Plays, continued

Haas, Harlow Edgar. When Christmas came. ₍In four acts.₎ Franklin, O.: Eldridge Entertainment House, Inc., cop. 1923. 18 p. 12°. (Eldridge popular plays.)
Three wise men, four shepherds, King Herod, and others.

Hamilton, Cicely Mary. The child in Flanders; a Nativity play in a prologue, five tableaux and an epilogue. Music arranged by Theodore Flint. London: Samuel French, Ltd., cop. 1922. 35(1) p. 12°. (French's acting edition. no. 398.)
The action in the prologue and epilogue is supposed to pass on a Christmas day during the great war. The dialogue in the prologue and the epilogue is partly in French.

—— —— London: S. French, Ltd.; New York: S. French, cop. 1922. 35(1) p. illus. 12°. (French's international copyrighted... edition of the works of the best authors. no. 450.)   **NCO p.v.494, no.2**
Reprinted in J. W. Marriott, *One-act plays of to-day, Second series,* London [1925], p. 237–266, *NCO.*

Hanzsche, William Thomas. The inn at Bethlehem; a Christmas pageant ₍in five scenes₎. Music and verses by Lyman R. Bayard. Los Angeles: Pageant Publishers, cop. 1930. 23 p. illus. music. 8°.
Suggestions [for production], p. 20–23.

Hare, Walter Ben. The white Christmas; a Christmas morality play in one act ₍of three scenes₎. (In his: The white Christmas, and other merry Christmas plays. Chicago ₍cop. 1917₎. 12°. p. 11–45.)   **NASH**
Originally produced by the Quadrangle Club of the University of Missouri, Christmas, 1909.

Henderson, Alice (Corbin). The star of Bethlehem; a Nativity play for children. (In her: Adam's dream, and two other miracle plays. New York, 1909. 12°. p. 13–26.)   **NASH**
Scene: about midnight, in the stable of the Inn at Bethlehem.

Hewetson, George Benson. The desired of all nations. A drama of the Holy Nativity in three acts with prologue. St. Paul: Webb Publishing Co. ₍1918.₎ 16 p. 8°. **NBF p.v.20**
Produced by the College of St. Catharine, St. Paul, Minn., Dec. 16, 1917.

Hibbert, Francis Aidan. A Christmas miracle play; together with an introductory note on the miracle play, and some suggestions for staging. The music (vocal, instrumental) arranged by A. Rawlinson Wood... Manchester ₍Eng.₎: The Faith Press, 1919. 20 p. illus. 4°.   **NAFM**
Running-head reads: A miracle play of the Christ Mass.
Performed at Denstone, England, December, 1917.

Hinkson, Katharine (Tynan). The Nativity. ₍In two scenes.₎ illus. (In her: Miracle plays. London, 1895. 12°. p. 39–56.)   **NCR**

Holland, Norah M. When half gods go, a mystery play ₍in three scenes₎. (In her: When half gods go, and other poems. New York, 1924. 12°. p. 1–21.)   **NBI**

Holley, Margaret S. A Christmas mystery; an out-of-doors Christmas pageant ₍in one scene₎. (International journal of religious education. Mt. Morris, Ill., 1927. f°. v. 4, Dec., 1927, p. 25–26.)
Produced on the campus of the Hartford Seminary Foundation, Hartford, Conn., December, 1926.

Holt, Laura Davies. The Christmas angel choir; a one-act play with hymns by hidden voices. Franklin, O.: Eldridge Entertainment House, Inc., cop. 1927. 13 p. 12°. (Eldridge Christmas material.)

Home, Georgina. The children's pilgrimage; a Christmas play ₍in seven scenes₎. London: A. R. Mowbray & Co., Ltd. ₍1926.₎ 27 p. 12°.   **NAFH p.v.15**

Housman, Laurence. Bethlehem; a Nativity play...performed with music by Joseph Moorat under the stage-direction of Edward Gordon Craig, December, MCMII. London: Macmillan and Co., Ltd., 1902. 44 p. 8°.
In two scenes.

—— —— New York: Macmillan Co., 1902. 3 p.l., 3–76 p. 16°.   **NCR**
Reprinted in Le Roy Phillips and Theodore Johnson, *Types of modern dramatic composition,* Boston [cop. 1927], p. 139–173, *NCO.*
Also reprinted separately, with imprint, Boston: Baker International Play Bureau, 1927. 1 p.l., 141–173 p.
Reviewed by N. N. in *Nation,* New York, 1903, v. 76, p. 49–50, * *DA.*

SWIFT, Thomas. Bethlehem; a Nativity play by Laurence Housman. A study. (Champlain educator. New York, 1903. 8°. v. 22, p. 419–426.)   **ZLF**

Hunter, Mable. Christmas gifts. ₍In one scene.₎ (Normal instructor and primary plans. Dansville, N. Y., 1925. f°. v. 35, Dec., 1925, p. 67–68.)   **† SSA**

Hutchison, Isobel W. The calling of Bride. Stirling: Eneas Mackay ₍1926?₎. vi, 7–32 p. 12°.   **NCR**
"Founded upon the Gaelic legend that St. Bride was transported by the angels from the Hebrides to Bethlehem on the first Christmas Eve, to become the foster-mother of Christ." A symbolic play.

Hyde, Douglas. The Nativity. ₍In one scene.₎ (In: Isabella Augusta, lady Gregory, Poets and dreamers. Dublin, 1903. 8°. p. 244–254.)   **NDM**
Reviewed by Francis Hackett in *The Reader,* Indianapolis, 1906, v. 7, p. 214, * *DA.*

MERRILL, John, and MARTHA FLEMING. The production of The Nativity in the eighth grade. (In their: Play-making and plays. New York, 1930. 8°. p. 116–121.)   **NASH**
"Exquisite telling of the story of two Irish peasant women who sought the cradle of the Christ child." — *p. 516.*

New Testament Plays — The Nativity, cont'd

Modern Plays, continued

Inglis, Ruth P. "The true Christmas gift." Story and dialogue. (Normal instructor and primary plans. Dansville, N. Y., 1916. f°. v. 26, Dec., 1916, p. 26, 77.) † **SSA**

Jenkins, Mary. The gospel of Bethlehem, an easy play for children. London: Society for Promoting Christian Knowledge ₁192–?₁. 16 p. 12°.
In seven scenes: The vision of Zacharias, The Annunciation, The visitation, The circumcision of John Baptist, The shepherds of Bethlehem, The wise men and Herod, The adoration.

Johnson, Charles. The Nativity pageant ₁in nine scenes₁. ₁London:₁ Faith Press, Ltd. ₁1924.₁ 23 p. illus. 8°. **NAC p.v.126**

Johnson, Mabel Hubbard. The light upon the way, a Christmas play ₁in two acts₁. (In: Eleven short Biblical plays. New York, 1929. 12°. p. 155–182.) **NBL p.v.216**
Christmas Eve several centuries after the Nativity. Christ appears as a stranger and an old man, and again seven years later as an unknown lad.

Judge, Jane, and LINWOOD TAFT. A Christmas mystery... given in Forsythe Park, Savannah, Ga., Dec. 25, 1919. (Drama. Mt. Morris, Ill., 1920. 4°. v. 11, p. 60–62.) **NAFA**

Kaye-Smith, Sheila. A child born at The Plough. A Nativity play in four scenes. (In her: Saints in Sussex. New York ₁1927₁. 8°. p. 33–82.) **NCM**
The Biblical circumstances in a modern setting. Herod is the county squire, "with Semitic hints about him"; Mrs. Herod, who is frankly American, secured her divorce in Idaho; the three wise men are from Oxford and Cambridge. The patriarchs and the prophets and all the conventional figures of the Nativity are come to worship the Child born at The Plough, "village of Udimore, province of Canterbury."

Kelly, Norah. St. Brigit of the Mantle. A Christmas mystery play. London: Society for Promoting Christian Knowledge, 1924. vi, 7–31 p. 12°. **NCO p.v.515, no.3**
In eight scenes.
A Nativity play based on the "Legend of St. Brigit of the Mantle." "The author is indebted to Mrs. William Sharp for leave to use the legend of St. Brigit of the Mantle, from 'The Washer at the ford' by 'Fiona Macleod' (William Sharp)." Produced at the Chapter House of Gloucester Cathedral just before Christmas, 1923.

Kennedy, Katherine (Mrs. Alfred Shirley). Angels at Bethlehem; a Nativity play ₁in six scenes₁. London: Society for Promoting Christian Knowledge, 1923. 15(1) p. 12°.

Kenyon, Katharine. The shepherds; a Christmas play. London: Society for Promoting Christian Knowledge, 1922. 14 p. 12°. **NCO p.v.490, no.2**
The dramatis personae are the members of a Jewish family near Bethlehem, and a strange traveller.
New edition, 1928.

Ketchum, Arthur. Bethlehem, a Christmas mystery play ₁in one act₁... Milwaukee, Wis.: Morehouse Pub. Co. ₁cop. 1928.₁ 2 p.l., 12 p. 12°. **NAFH p.v.46**
Another printing [1930].
First published in 1913.

Kimball, Rosamond. The Nativity; a Christmas service ₁in four scenes₁. n. p. ₁192–?₁ 16 p. 8°.
Composed of selections from the Bible, arranged in dramatic form on the plan of the mystery play.
Reprinted in her *The wooing of Rebekah, and other Bible plays*, New York, 1925, p. 219–239, ZICS.

Kingsford, H. The fulness of time; a Nativity play of the altar and the manger... London: Published for the Catholic Play Society at the Faith Press, 1921. 11(1) p. 12°.

Knight, William Allen. A Bethlehem scenario ₁in three scenes₁. illus. (Church school. New York, 1921. 4°. v. 3, p. 101–103.)
Copy in Library of Union Theological Seminary.

Knox, Janet. The shepherd of Bethlehem; a one-act Christmas play. Chicago: T. S. Denison & Co. ₁cop. 1928.₁ 34 p. 12°. (Denison's Christmas plays.)
The home of a shepherd on the night of the Nativity.

Lamers, William Mathias. Bethlehem, a drama of the first Christmas, in three acts... Sleepy Eye, Minn.: Catholic Dramatic Company, cop. 1928. 32 p. illus. 12°.

Langdon, William Chauncy. The Amherst Christmas mystery, 1916. Amherst, Mass. ₁1916.₁ 15 p. 8°. **NAC p.v.23**
"Primarily a service of community worship and only secondarily a dramatic performance." — *Foreword.*
Performed at Amherst, Dec. 23, 1916.

—— A Christmas mystery of the war. Urbana-Champaign: University of Illinois, 1918. 22 p. 8°. **BTZI p.v.13**
The characters are both modern and Biblical.

Lawson, McEwan. The coming; a Christmas play ₁in seven scenes₁. London: Congregational Union of England & Wales ₁1925₁. 48 p. 12°. **NCO p.v.522, no.2**
Among the characters is Herod.

Lea, Kathleen M. A Nativity play... Illustrated by Isoult M. Bennett. London: Swarthmore Press, Ltd. ₁1922.₁ 12 l., 3 col'd illus. sq. 8°. **NCR**

Letchworth, Ruth A. The star of Bethlehem; a play of the first Christmas long ago in the land of Judea... Boston: American Unitarian Association, n.d. 12 l. 4°.
In three scenes.
Mimeographed.
Reprinted in Marie W. Johnson, compiler, *Plays and pageants for the church school*, Boston ₁cop. 1929₁, p. 47–63.
First presented by First Unitarian Church School, Buffalo, N. Y.

New Testament Plays — The Nativity, cont'd

Modern Plays, continued

Lindsay, Maud McKnight. The first Christmas morning. ₁In one scene.₁ (In: Christmas plays. Boston, Chicago ₁cop. 1927₁. 12°. p. 5–8.)

Longfellow, Henry Wadsworth. The golden legend. Boston: Ticknor, Reed, and Fields, 1851. 2 p.l., 3–301 p. 12°.   * **KL**
First edition.
Reprinted as part II of *Christus, a mystery.* Boston, 1872. * *KL.*
It contains the Nativity, a miracle play in seven episodes, based on "the old record of the Protoevangelion," the Arabic Gospel of the Infancy, the Gospel of Pseudo-Matthew, the History of Joseph the Carpenter, and others of the Apocryphal gospels.
The first five episodes are reprinted in Lesley Frost, editor, *Come Christmas*, New York, 1929, p. 123–134, *NAEM.*
Reviews: *American Whig review,* New York, 1852, v. 15, p. 431–439, * *DA; The Athenæum,* London, 1851, p. 1303–1304, * *DA; Blackwood's magazine,* London, 1852, v. 71, p. 212–225, * *DA; British quarterly review,* London, 1864, v. 39, p. 42–50, * *DA; Carpetbag,* Boston, v. 1, Jan. 3, 1852, p. 2, * *DA; Eclectic review,* London, 1852, v. 95, p. 455–467, * *DA; Fraser's magazine,* London, 1853, v. 47, p. 371–379, * *DA; Graham's magazine,* Philadelphia, 1852, v. 40, p. 214–216, * *DA; New Englander,* New Haven, 1852, v. 10, p. 90–101, * *DA;* and *English review,* London, 1852, v. 17, p. 435–442, *ZPD.* Longfellow called it "a furious onslaught."

—— —— Boston: Ticknor, Reed, and Fields, 1852. 1 p.l., 301 p. ₁2. ed.₁ 12°.

—— —— Boston: Ticknor, Reed, and Fields, 1853. 2 p.l., 3–301 p. 12°.   **NBI**

—— —— Illustrated...from designs by Birket Foster and Jane E. Hay. London: David Bogue, 1854. vi p., 1 l., 224 p. 12°.

—— —— Boston: Ticknor and Fields, 1855. vi p., 1 l., 224 p. 12°.   **Stuart 9587**

—— The golden legend. Boston: Ticknor and Fields, 1857. 2 p.l., 3–326 p. 12°.

—— —— Boston: Ticknor and Fields, 1859. 2 p.l., 3–326 p. 12°.

—— —— Boston: Ticknor and Fields, 1864. 1 p.l., 326 p. 12°.

—— —— With notes by Samuel Arthur Bent. Boston, New York: Houghton, Mifflin and Company, 1887. vi, (1)8–194 p. 12°. (The Riverside literature series. no. 25–26.)

C., P. A. Longfellow's 'Golden legend' and its analogues. (Poet lore. Boston, 1892. 8°. v. 4, no. 2, p. 91–100.)   * **DA**

MUENZNER, F. Die Quellen zu Longfellow's Golden legend. (In: Festschrift der 44. Versammlung deutscher Philologen. Dresden, 1897.)
Reprinted separately, Dresden, 1898. 37 p. 8°.
Reviewed by O. Glöde in *Englische Studien*, Leipzig, 1900, Bd. 27, p. 148–150, *RNA.*

SPRENGER, Robert. German legends and customs in Longfellow's Golden legend. (International Folk-Lore Congress, 3d, Chi-

cago, 1893. ₁Papers and transactions.₁ Chicago, 1898. 8°. p. 510–512.)
ZBA (International)

McCann, John. Christmas; a pastoral. (Globe. New York, 1895. 8°. v. 5, p. 59–66.)
* **DA**
Dramatic poem. The speakers are Rachel and Nathan, on Christmas morn.

McChesney, Dora Greenwell. Outside the gate; a pilgrim play. (Fortnightly review. London, 1903. 8°. v. 80, p. 1035–1040.) * **DA**
Shepherds, a Roman soldier; the Greek, the Egyptian, and the Indian as the three wise men.

McGavran, Grace W. The shepherd who stayed behind. ₁In two scenes.₁ Boston: W. H. Baker Company, cop. 1927. 19 p. 12°.
On cover: Baker's royalty plays.
A Christmas play which tells the story of the sacrifice of the one shepherd who stayed behind to guard the sheep and denied himself the joy of worshipping at the manger.
Produced by the Dramatic Department of Boston University School of Religious Education.

MacKaye, Percy. The evergreen tree. New York, London: D. Appleton and Company, 1917. xviii p., 1 l., 81(1) p. illus. 8°.
NCR
Added t.-p.: The evergreen tree; a masque of Christmas time for community singing and acting, by Percy MacKaye, with scenic and costume designs by Robert Edmond Jones; together with three monographs on the masque written by the author, the scenic designer, and Arthur Farwell, composer of the music.
Theme from Matthew II.

Manley, Marian. The message of the Christ-child. ₁In three scenes.₁ New York: The Abingdon Press ₁cop. 1920₁. 16 p. 8°.
NAC p.v.39
Cover-title. Designed primarily for Chinese children. A special ending is given for Christmas season, with the Holy Family in tableau.
Another ed. [1926.]

Manley, William Ford. The first gift; a Christmas miracle. ₁In four scenes.₁ his: A second book of Bible dramas. New York ₁cop. 1930₁. 8°. p. 11–28.)   **NBM**

Marquis, Marjorie. The first Christmas; a play in one act of two scenes. Illustrated by Gertrude A. Kay. (Ladies' home journal. Philadelphia, 1930. f°. v. 47, Dec., 1930, p. 14–15, 51, 53.)   * **DA**

Martínez Sierra, Gregorio. Holy night, a miracle play in three scenes. English version by Philip Hereford, — with wood-engravings by Gabriel Pippet. London: Sheed and Ward ₁1928₁. 4 p.l., 56 p. illus. 8°.

—— New York: E. P. Dutton & Co., Inc. ₁1929.₁ 4 p.l., 55(1) p. illus. 8°.   **NPO**

Masefield, John. The coming of Christ. ₁In one act.₁ London: William Heinemann, Ltd. ₁1928.₁ 4 p.l., 3–48 p. 12°.
The spirits of Peter and Paul, the three kings, three shepherds, and Mary mother of Jesus are the characters in the play.

—— New York: The Macmillan Company, 1928. 3 p.l., 57 p. 8°.   **NCR**
Reviewed in the *New York Herald-Tribune, Books,* July 29, 1928, p. 9, † *NAA.*

New Testament Plays — The Nativity, cont'd

Modern Plays, continued

Miller, Jane Taylor. The Christmas story; a group of ₍six₎ tableaux... New York: National Board of Young Women's Christian Association, 1915. 35 p. 12°.　**MZB p.v.4**

———————— New York: Womans Press ₍cop. 1926₎. 46 p. 12°.

" 'The Christmas story' had its birth and beginning in 'Ben Hur — a tale of the Christ.' " — *Preface.*

Molloy, Lida Lisle. The day of taxing. ₍In two scenes.₎ illus. (International journal of religious education. Chicago, 1930. f°. v. 7, Dec., 1930, p. 27–28, 36, 47.)

Time decreed by Augustus for taxing, Luke ii:1. Joseph and Mary among the characters.

Moment, John J. The throne of David; a Christmas pageant ₍in four scenes₎, in rhythmic prose... New York, London: Century Co. ₍cop. 1929.₎ vii, 9, 8 p. music. 4°.

Morley, George Howard, and JOHN WYLDE. The Saviour's birth; a Nativity play ₍in a prologue and nine scenes₎. London: Faith Press, Ltd. ₍1925.₎ viii, 24 p. 12°.　**NAC p.v.149, no.1**

Written for and performed by the parish of St. Saviour, Leeds, England.

Mudge, E. Leigh. Oh come, all ye faithful; a Christmas service ₍in five scenes₎ for all departments of the church school. illus. (Church school. New York, 1922. 4°. v. 4, p. 122–123.)

Copy in Library of Union Theological Seminary.

Murray, E. The quest of the three kings. (In: Holiday entertainments. Edited by Charles C. Shoemaker. Philadelphia, 1909. 12°. p. 146–150.)　**NAC p.v.99**

Also printed in the Philadelphia, 1913, edition, *NACG-HE.*

The **Mystery** of Christmas. A festival Christmas play with songs. In one act. St. Cloud, Minn.: Catholic Dramatic Company, 1923. 16 p. 12°. (Collection of Catholic theatrical. no. 3.)

A **Nativity** play. (As acted at Hall Green in 1922 by children aged 4 to 9.) (Torchbearer. London, 1924. 8°. v. 1, p. 150–151.)　***DA**

In a prologue and nine scenes.

Nielsen, Eilert C. The Prince of Peace; a Christmas pageant ₍in nine scenes₎. illus. Philadelphia: The United Lutheran Publication House ₍cop. 1928₎. 36 p. diagrs. 12°.　**MV p.v.107**

O'Donnell, Charles L. The Nativity, a miracle play ₍in three scenes₎. (Lippincott's magazine. Philadelphia, 1908. 8°. v. 82, p. 713–716.)　***DA**

Ott, Susanna Clayton. A masque — the story of the Nativity for the commonwealth of Los Angeles. Los Angeles: The Fred S. Lang Company ₍cop. 1915₎. 2 p.l., 25 p. illus. 8°.

Produced at Los Angeles on Christmas Eve, 1915. Reviewed by Paul Henry Dowling in *American city,* New York, 1916, v. 15, p. 655–657, *SERA.*

Overton, Grace Sloan. The eternal quest, a Christmas pageant ₍in three episodes₎, illus. (International journal of religious education. Mt. Morris, Ill., 1926. f°. v. 3, Nov., 1926, p. 32–36.)

Reprinted in her *Dramatic activities for young people,* New York [cop. 1927], p. 47–65.

Owen, Ruth (Bryan). Bethlehem; a children's pageant of Christmas, illustrated ₍in colors₎ by Herbert Paus. (Woman's home companion. Springfield, O., 1928. f°. v. 50, Dec., 1928, p. 22–23.)　***DA**

Los **Pastores.** Los Pastores, a Mexican play of the Nativity; translation, introduction and notes by M. R. Cole; with illustrations and music. Boston and New York: For the American Folk-lore Society by Houghton, Mifflin and Company, 1907. xxxi p., 1 l., 234 p., 1 l., 9 pl. 8°. (American Folk-lore Society. Memoirs. v. 9, 1907.)　**NPX**

Spanish and English texts on opposite pages.

Reviewed in *American historical review,* Lancaster, Pa., 1907, v. 12, p. 935, *IAA.*

BOURKE, John G. The miracle play of the Rio Grande. (Journal of American folk-lore. Boston and New York, 1893. 8°. v. 6, p. 89–95.)　**HBA**

CALLAWAY, Dorothy Elizabeth. "Los Pastores." A survival of the ancient miracle play in America. illus. (Rosary magazine. New York, 1925. 4°. v. 67, no. 6, p. 1–4.)　**† ZLF**

GARRISON, Winfred Ernest. A surviving mystery play: primitive religious drama on the American frontier. (Journal of religion. Chicago, 1927. 8°. v. 7, p. 225–243.)　**ZAA**

KING, Sarah S. The Pastores, an interpretation... San Antonio, Texas: Passing Show Pub. Co. ₍cop. 1908.₎ 22 p. illus. sq. 16°.　*** C p.v.1803**

Patterson, Stephen Van Rensselaer, and WILLIAM PATTERSON. A pastoral of the Nativity. ₍A dramatic poem.₎ (In their: Poems of twin graduates of the College of New Jersey. Newark, N. J., 1882. 8°. p. 30–37.)　**NBI**

Patton, Marion Keep. The gift of gifts; a Christmas mystery play ₍in one scene₎. (Delineator. New York, 1914. f°. v. 85, Dec., 1914, p. 20–21.)　**† VSA**

Paull, Harry Major, and LAURENCE HOUSMAN. The unknown star, a Christmas mystery play in prose and verse, in **three acts and four scenes.** (Nineteenth century. London, 1919. 8°. v. 86, Dec., 1919, p. 1065–1095.)　***DA**

Listed in the annual index of the periodical as Christ versus Jupiter.

The verse passages of the play are largely the work of Housman.

New Testament Plays — The Nativity, cont'd

Modern Plays, continued

Pearn, Violet A. Their angels; a modern miracle play ₍in three acts₎ for children... London: S. French, Ltd., cop. 1927. 58, 7 p. music. 8°. (French's standard library ed.)
NCO p.v.551
Music of incidental songs by Barbara Thorley, 7 p. at end. Act ii, scene 2, the stable scene. First produced at Guildford, England, Christmas, 1925.

Pepler, Hilary Douglas C. Bethlehem; a tableau of the Nativity for presentation by children. Ditchling, Sussex: S. Dominic's Press, 1927. 2 p.l., 27 p. music. 8°.
"This tableau originated in *Christmas gifts*, first printed in 1916, it was performed as *A Christmas play* in 1924, this was revised and included in *Pertinent and impertinent*, 1926. In its present form it was acted during the Christmas Octave 1926–7."

—— The ox and the ass. ₍In one scene.₎ 7 l. (In his: Plays for puppets. Ditchling, Sussex, 1929. 24°.)　*** KP (S. Dominic's)**
Reprinted in Reed Moorhouse, editor, *Plays for middle forms*, London [1930], p. 63–80, NCO (*Moorhouse*).
Scene: Stable at Bethlehem. The players: a broom, two pails, an ox, an ass, and a girl.

Perin, Lydia C. The little angels, a legend of the first Christmas night. ₍In one scene.₎ Cincinnati: Powell & White ₍192–?₎. 8 p. 12°.

Pound, Ezra. Christmas prologue ₍with scenes "in the air," and "in heaven," and "on earth"₎. (Sunday school times. Philadelphia, 1910. f°. v. 52, p. 613 ₍cover₎.)　**† ZICN**
One of the magi and a shepherd speak.
Reprinted in his *Canzoni*, London, 1911, p. 34–36, NBI.

Powell, A. L. The spirit of the Christ; a Christmas eve story ₍in nine scenes₎. illus. (International journal of religious education. Mt. Morris, Ill., 1924. f°. v. 1, Nov., 1924, p. 40–43.)
Copy in Library of Union Theological Seminary.

Race, Martha. At the door of the inn; a Christmas pantomime ₍in five parts₎. illus. (Church school. New York, 1921. 4°. v. 3, p. 108–113, 145.)
Copy in Library of Union Theological Seminary.

—— They who weave. ₍In one scene.₎ (In her: They who weave. Gold, silver and precious stones; portraying in dramatic form the religious contribution of the home to the life of the child. Boston ₍cop. 1926₎. 12°. p. 1–9.)　**NBL p.v.152, no.12**
The characters are four mothers, of whom the first is a Hebrew mother, and the second is Mary, mother of Jesus.

—— What child is this? a Christmas pageant ₍in one scene₎. (In: Christmas plays. Boston, Chicago ₍cop. 1927₎. 12°. p. 9–16.)

—— When the Prince cometh. A Christmas play ₍in one scene₎. illus. music. (Church school. New York, 1923. 4°. v. 5, p. 68–72.)

Raine, James Watt. The babe of Bethlehem. ₍In four scenes.₎ (In his: Bible dramatics. New York & London ₍cop. 1927₎. 12°. p. 277–292.)

Riesner, Rebecca. Children of Bethlehem, a Christmas dramatization ₍in one scene₎. Cincinnati: Powell & White, n.d. 8 p. 12°.

Roberts, Walter Charles. The light; a Christmas pageant in three episodes and nine scenes... New York, London: Century Co. ₍cop. 1930.₎ xvi, 42 p., 1 l. diagr. 12°.
First produced by the Dramatics I–B Classes of the Binghamton, N. Y., Central High School, Dec. 16, 18, 19, 1929.

Rockwell, Ethel Gesner. The way, a Christmas pageant of peace ₍in three parts₎. (International journal of religious education. Mt. Morris, Ill., 1927. f°. v. 4, Nov., 1927, p. 28–31.)
Part I. Waiting for the Christ. Characters: The Voice, Abraham, Moses, Elijah, and Isaiah.
Part II. The coming of the Christ. The usual Nativity characters and the Voice.
Part III. The Christ among us. The Voice and the nations.
Reprinted: Boston: W. H. Baker Co., cop. 1927. 23 p. 12°.

Russell, Mary M. The first Christmas. ₍In two scenes.₎ (In her: Dramatized Bible stories for young people. New York, 1921. 12°. p. 88–92.)
The Annunciation story.

—— The message of the star. (In her: How to produce plays and pageants. New York ₍cop. 1923₎. 12°. p. 125–137.)　**MZB**

Rutledge, Lyman Vincent. Bethlehem; a Christmas play ₍in four acts₎. (In: Marie W. Johnson, compiler, Plays and pageants for the church school. Boston ₍cop. 1929₎. 12°. p. 17–32.)

Sanderson, Virginia. Long ago in Judea; a Christmas play in two scenes. New York and London: Samuel French, cop. 1925. 35 p. 12°. (French's international copyrighted... edition of the works of the best authors. no. 528.)　**NBL p.v.142, no.12**

Schenck, Dorothy R. The little princess who traveled far to worship the King. ₍In one act.₎ New York: The Womans Press ₍cop. 1928₎. 15 p. 12°.

Seccombe, Charles Edward. Round the manger; being ₍four₎ scenes representing the Nativity of Our Lord... London: Chapman & Hall, Ltd., 1917. 88 p. 16°.　**NCR**

The **Sheepfold;** a Nativity play ₍in four scenes₎. A pax book. London, Oxford: A. R. Mowbray & Co., Ltd. ₍1930.₎ 28 p. music. 12°.

Simons, Evelyn. The Bethlehem babe. ₍In three scenes.₎ (In her: The favorite Christmas book, by Marie Irish ₍pseud.₎. Chicago ₍1917₎. 12°. p. 94–99.)　**NANV**

New Testament Plays — The Nativity, cont'd
Modern Plays, continued

Skidmore, Harriet M. The Nativity. ₁In four scenes.₁ (In her: Beside the western sea. New York, 1877. 2. ed. 12°. p. 135–149.) **NBI**
The usual Biblical characters and Rabbi Simon.

Smith, Roy L. Joseph and the inn-keeper, a Christmas conversation ₁in one scene₁. (In his: Pantomimes and pageants for pulpit use. Cleveland ₁cop. 1928₁. 8°. p. 72–76.)

Snyder, Margaret I. The Nativity; a Christmas pageant ₁in four episodes₁. New York: Abingdon Press ₁1926₁. 22 p. music. 8°.

Speare, Florence Lewis. The star gleams; a community X-mas choral, "the story of the star" told entirely by use of community singing ₁accompanied by several tableaux₁. New York, London: Samuel French, cop. 1922. 1 p.l., 5–31 p. illus. 8°. **NBL p.v.97**
Plate printed on both sides.
Produced at the Emmanuel Church, Baltimore.

Spencer, Elizabeth. Christmas eve in the land of Nod. ₁In one scene.₁ illus. (Normal instructor and primary plans. Dansville, N. Y., 1924. f°. v. 34, Dec., 1924, p. 74.) † **SSA**
Among the characters are the wise men and the shepherds.

Stackhouse, Perry J. The babe of Bethlehem. A Christmas drama ₁in four scenes₁. (In his: Bible dramas in the pulpit. Philadelphia ₁cop. 1926₁. 8°. p. 59–68.) **NBM**
Characters: Herod, Levi his adviser, the High Priest.

Steedman, C. M. The inn of the star; a Christmas mystery play, in eight scenes (with songs, carols, and incidental music), by C. M. Steedman... London: Society for Promoting Christian Knowledge ₁1924₁. 24 p. 12°. **NAC p.v.125, no.2**

Stenger, Georgia. On the road to Bethlehem; a Nativity play for young folks ₁in two scenes₁. Franklin, O.: Eldridge Entertainment House, cop. 1930. 23 p. 12°. (Eldridge Christmas material.)

Stevens, Edmund H. The holy night; a mystery play for Christmas-tide. ₁In one act.₁ Milwaukee: Morehouse Pub. Co. ₁cop. 1930.₁ 2 p.l., 16 p. 8°.

Stevens, Thomas Wood. The Duquesne Christmas mystery, a Nativity play ₁in one scene₁. (In his: The nursery-maid of heaven, and other plays... New York, 1926. 12°. p. 167–177.) **NBM**
"Written for the municipal Christmas celebration of Duquesne, Pa."

Stocks, Mary Danvers (Brinton). Everyman of everystreet; a Nativity play. London: Sidgwick & Jackson, Ltd. ₁1929.₁ xxiii, 48 p. illus. 8°. **NCR**
In a prologue, four scenes, and epilogue. Produced by the Manchester University Settlement.
Reviewed in *The Times literary supplement*, London, Dec. 12, 1929, p. 1060, † *NAA.*

Sundelof-Asbrand, Karin. Follow the star; a Christmas pageant with words and music. Denver, Colo., Franklin, O.: Eldridge Entertainment House, Inc. ₁cop. 1929.₁ 20 p. music. 12°.

Sutton, Vida Ravenscroft. Christ is born in Bethlehem; a play ₁in four scenes₁ of the Nativity. New York: The Womans Press ₁1928₁. 15 p. 12°.

Swire, S. In honour of the Christ child; a Nativity play ₁in a prologue, five scenes, and an epilogue₁. (With carols taken from "An Italian carol book"). London: Faith Press, Ltd. ₁1928.₁ 2 p.l., 15(1) p. 12°.

Symons, Arthur. Mary in Bethlehem: a nativity. (In his: The fool of the world, & other poems. London, 1906. 8°. p. 109–118.) **NCM**

Tappert, Wilfried C. H. The holy night. A Christmas pageant ₁in four parts₁. Philadelphia: United Lutheran Publication House ₁cop. 1925₁. 26 p. 12°. **NAC p.v.143**

Trask, Mrs. Kate (Nichols). The little town of Bethlehem, a play for the Christmas-tide in three parts by Katrina Trask. New York, Los Angeles: S. French; London: S. French, Ltd., 1929. 5 p.l., 3–88 p. 8°. **NBM**
Part I, Nativity. Part II, The interlude. Part III, The revelation.
First presented in New York by the Ben Greet Players, Christmastide, 1909.

Van Dyke, Henry. The other wise man; a vision of the East, dramatized by the author from the story of that name. New York and London: Harper & Brothers, 1927. xii p., 1 l., 44 p. 12°. **NBM**
In four acts.

Van Rensselaer, Alexander, and FRANK BUTCHER. Yule light; a Christmas pageant, in two parts ₁of seven and ten episodes each₁ based upon folk songs and ancient carols. New York, London: The Century Co. ₁cop. 1930.₁ xviii p., 2 l., 5–41 p. diagr. 12°.
Part 1, the manger; part 2, the Christmas revels.
The authors acknowledge the influence of the Boar's Head and Yule Log pageant annually produced at Hoosac School, Hoosick, N. Y.

Wallace, Emma Gary, and ADELAIDE B. MEAD. ...Glad tidings to all people... Syracuse, N. Y.: W. N. Bugbee Co., cop. 1928. 12 p. 12°. (Bugbee's popular plays.)
The characters of the play are gathered at the home of Amos, cousin of Luke, to hear Theophilus read the letter received by him from Luke, some time about 70 A. D. See Luke I: 1–4.

Ward, Lucile Ahrens. Wherever the star shines; a Christmas pageant ₁in one act₁. Franklin, O.: Eldridge Entertainment House, Inc., cop. 1929. 11 p. 12°. (Eldridge Christmas material.)

Whiting, Isabel Kimball. The Nativity. ₁In one scene.₁ (In her: Dramatic services of worship. Boston, 1925. 8°. p. 69–89.) **NBM**

New Testament Plays — The Nativity, cont'd

Modern Plays, continued

Wilson, Dorothy Clarke. "They that sit in darkness," a Christmas play ₍in four scenes₎. (International journal of religious education. Chicago, 1929. f°. v. 6, Nov., 1929, p. 25–26, 46–48.)

The Shepherds' Play

Miracle Plays

The **Angels** and the shepherds. The chaundelers play. ₍York play no. 15. 131 lines.₎ (In: Lucy T. Smith, editor, York plays. Oxford, 1885. 8°. p. 118–122.)
NAFM (Smith)
Also printed in S. B. Hemingway, editor, *English Nativity plays,* New York, 1909, p. 147–151, *NAFM.* Adapted in P. E. Osgood, *Old-time church drama adapted,* New York, 1928, p. 146–152, *NAFM.*

Prima pagina pastorum. ₍The first Shepherds' play. Towneley play no. 12.₎ (In: The Towneley mysteries. London, 1836. 8°. p. 84–97.)
CA (Surtees)
Surtees Society. Publications. [v. 3.]
Also printed in 1897 (ed. England) in Early English Text Society, Publications no. 71 (*The Towneley plays*), p. 100–116, *NCE (Early),* and in S. B. Hemingway, editor, *English Nativity plays,* New York, 1909, p. 170–187, *NAFM.*

EATON, Horace A. A source for the Towneley "Prima Pastorum." (Modern language notes. Baltimore, 1899. 4°. v. 14, col. 265–268.)
RAA

Secunda pagina pastorum. ₍The Second Shepherds' play. Towneley play no. 13.₎ (In: The Towneley mysteries. London, 1836. 8°. p. 98–119.)
CA (Surtees)
Surtees Society. Publications. [v. 3.]
First published in J. P. Collier, *Five miracle plays,* London, 1836 with the title "The adoration of the shepherds."
Also printed in William Marriott, *A collection of English miracle-plays,* Ba₋el, 1838, p. 109–136, *NAFM;* in 1897 (ed. England) in Early English Text Society, Extra series no. 71 (*The Towneley plays*), p. 116–140, *NCE (Early);* J. M. Manly, *Specimens of the pre-Shaksperean drama,* Boston, 1897, v. 1, p. 94–119, *NCO;* S. B. Hemingway, editor, *English Nativity plays,* New York, 1909, p. 188–214, *NAFM;* J. S. P. Tatlock and R. G. Martin, editors, *Representative English plays,* New York, 1916, p. 19–30, *R – NCO;* J. Q. Adams, editor, *Chief pre-Shakespearean dramas,* Boston, 1924, p. 145–157, *R – NCO;* Brander Matthews and P. R. Lieder, editors, *Chief British dramatists,* Boston, 1924, p. 11–25, *NCO;* "Everyman," *with other interludes including eight miracle plays,* London [1909], p. 52–73; W. R. Duffey, editor, *Acting versions of Everyman and the Second shepherds' play,* Milwaukee, 1925, p. 51–88, *NAC p.v. 130; Everyman and other plays,* London, 1925, p. 140–201, *NAFM;* J. B. Hubbell and J. O. Beaty, *An introduction to drama,* New York, 1927, p. 86–98, *NAFH;* under title "A Wakefield Nativity" in H. F. Rubinstein, editor, *Great English plays,* London, 1928, p. 9–26, *NCO;* H. C. Schweikert, *Early English plays,* New York [cop. 1928], p. 104–127, *NCO;* and F. J. Tickner, editor, *Earlier English drama from Robin Hood to Everyman,* New York [cop. 1929], p. 148–171, *NCO.*
Published in abridged form in A. W. Pollard, *English miracle plays,* Oxford, 1890, p. 31–43, 188–191, *NAFM* (other editions of this work issued in 1904, 1923, and 1927). An adapted form is printed in *The Second shepherds' play, Everyman, and other early plays,* Boston, 1910, p. 27–64, *NCO p.v. 556.* A short selec-

tion, entitled "Around the manger — the shepherds' address," is printed in A. L. J. Gosset, *Lullabies of the four nations,* London, 1915, p. 210–211, *NAEM (Gosset).*

Moorman, Frederic William. The ewe lamb, a farce ₍in two acts, and in Yorkshire dialect₎ (based upon the Nativity scene in the Wakefield mystery plays.) (In his: Plays of the Ridings. London, 1919. 12°. p. 73–98.)
NCR

The **Nativity** ₍in four scenes₎ adapted by Randall Cayford Burrell. illus. (Golden book magazine. New York, 1930. 4°. v. 12, Dec., 1930, p. 77–80.)
* DA

The **Shepherds'** play. (In: W. Dyfed Parry, editor, Old plays for modern players, selected and modernized by W. Dyfed Parry. London ₍1930₎. 12°. p. 37–46.)

Das **Zweite** Hirtenspiel der Wakefielder Spiele. Übersetzt von F. Holthausen. (Englische Studien. Leipzig, 1929. 8°. Bd. 63, p. 193–219.)
RNA
A translation into modern German, with an introduction and notes.

BAUGH, Albert C. The Mak story. (Modern philology. Chicago, 1918. 8°. v. 15, p. 729–734.)
NAA

CADY, Frank W. The maker of Mak ₍one of the shepherds in the Towneley Second shepherds' play₎. (University of California chronicle. Berkeley, Cal., 1927. 8°. v. 29, p. 261–272.)
STG (California)

CAREY, Millicent. ₍Phraseology. Sources in dramatic and non-dramatic literature and folk-lore; and the contribution of the Wakefield author.₎ (In her: The Wakefield group in the Towneley cycle. Göttingen, 1930. 8°. p. 109–210.)
NAFM

CARGILL, Oscar. The authorship of the "Secunda Pastorum." (Modern Language Association of America. Publications. Menasha, Wis., 1926. 8°. v. 41, p. 810–831.)
RAA

COOK, Albert Stanburrough. Another parallel to the Mak story. (Modern philology. Chicago, 1916. 8°. v. 14, p. 11–15.)
NAA

FOSTER, Frances A. Was Gilbert Pilkington author of the Secunda Pastorum? (Modern Language Association of America. Publications. Menasha, Wis., 1928. 8°. v. 43, p. 124–136.)
RAA

MALONE, Kemp. A note on the Towneley Secunda Pastorum. (Modern language notes. Baltimore, 1925. 8°. v. 40, p. 35–39.)
RAA

STRUNK, William, Jr. Two notes on the Towneley Second shepherd play. (Modern language notes. Baltimore, 1930. 8°. v. 45, p. 151.)
RAA
On lines 352 and 391.

New Testament Plays — The Nativity, cont'd

The Shepherds' Play: Miracle Plays, continued

The **Play** of the Shepherds. The paynters and glasiors playe... ₁Chester play no. 7.₁ (In: The Chester plays, ed. by Wright. London: Shakespeare Society, 1843. 8°. v. 1, p. 119–145.) **NAFM (Chester)**

Also printed in 1893 (ed. Deimling) in Early English Text Society, Extra series no. 62 (*The Chester plays*), p. 132–160, *NCE (Early)*; in S. B. Hemingway, editor, *English Nativity plays*, New York, 1909, p. 36–67, *NAFM;* and in F. J. Tickner, editor, *Earlier English drama from Robin Hood to Everyman*, New York [cop. 1929], p. 134–148, *NCO.*
Produced at the Old Vic Theatre, London, December, 1923. Reviewed in *The Spectator*, London, 1923, v. 131, p. 989–990, * *DA.* See also reminiscences of its rehearsal in Doris Westwood, *These players*, London, 1926, p. 112–115; the cast is given on p. 93, *NCOM.*

The **Adoration** of the shepherds. ₁Coventry play no. 16.₁ (In: Ludus Coventriæ, ed. Halliwell. London: Shakespeare Society, 1841. 8°. p. 156–160.) **NAFM (Coventry)**

Also printed in S. B. Hemingway, editor, *English Nativity plays*, New York, 1909, p. 113–118, *NAFM*, and in 1922 (ed. Block) in Early English Text Society, Extra series no. 120 *(Ludus Coventriæ)*, p. 146–151, *NCE (Early).*

The **Angels** and the shepherds. ₁Shrewsbury fragment no. 1.₁ (Academy. London, 1890. 4°. v. 37, p. 27–28.) ***DA**

Also printed in J. M. Manly, *Specimens of the pre-Shaksperean drama*, Boston, 1897, v. 1, p. xxviii–xxx, *NCO*, and in 1909 (ed. Waterhouse) in Early English Text Society, Extra series no. 104 *(The non-cycle mystery plays)*, p. 1–2, notes, p. xix–xx, *NCE (Early).*

MILLER, Frances H. Metrical affinities of the Shrewsbury *Officium Pastorum* and its York correspondent. (Modern language notes. Baltimore, 1918. 8°. v. 33, p. 91–95.) **RAA**

Pastores. <Christmas>. (In: J. Q. Adams, editor, Chief pre-Shakespearean dramas. Boston, New York ₁cop. 1924₁. 8°. p. 25–27.) ***R – NCO**

Latin text and English translation.
"Printed from A. Gasté, *Les drames liturgiques de la cathédrale de Rouen*, 1893, p. 25. The text is found in two manuscripts (Rouen MSS. y110 and y.108) of the fourteenth and fifteenth centuries respectively."

Modern Plays

Clarke, George Herbert. "And there were ...shepherds." ₁A dramatic poem.₁ (In his: Wayfarings. Chicago, 1901. 8°. p. 33–36.) Based on Luke II: 8ff. **NBI**

Esdaile, Katharine Ada. The shepherds' children; a Nativity play ₁in five scenes₁. London: Society for Promoting Christian Knowledge ₁192–?₁. 15 p. 12°. (Parish plays. no. 20.)

Gayley, Charles Mills. The star of Bethlehem, a miracle play of the Nativity, reconstructed from the Towneley and other old English cycles (of the XIIIth, XIVth and XVth centuries) and supplemented and adapted to modern conditions by Charles Mills Gayley. As composed for Mr. Ben Greet, and presented by his company. New York: Fox, Duffield and Company ₁1904₁. xix(i), 70 p. illus. 8°. **NAFM**

Harvey, G. Rowntree. The shepherds; a Nativity play. Aberdeen: W. and W. Lindsay, 1927. 16 p. 12°. **NCO p.v.554, no.9**

Written in the dialect of the north-east of Scotland.

McKeon, Thomas J. The Messiah; a Christmas play ₁in one scene₁. (Catholic world. New York, 1924. 8°. v. 120, p. 321–334.) ***DA**

The characters are six shepherds.

Ordway, Priscilla. The shepherd lad's gift. ₁In two acts.₁ (International journal of religious education. Mount Morris, Ill., 1925. f°. v. 2, Dec., 1925, p. 15–17.)

Osgood, Phillips Endecott. Shepherds all? (a little miracle play of Christmas Eve) ₁in a prologue, three scenes, and an epilogue₁. illus. (In his: The sinner beloved, and other religious plays. New York and London, 1928. 12°. p. 74–98.) **NAFM**

INFANCY AND CHILDHOOD OF JESUS

Kennedy, Anna R. Locusts and wild honey. ₁In three scenes.₁ (In her: Bible plays out of the East. New York, 1929. 8°. p. 29–38.)

In the twelfth year of the life of Jesus. The story is not Biblical.

Mary Agnes, Sister. Children of Nazareth, by S. M. A. ₁Winnipeg, Man.: St. Mary's Academy, cop. 1926.₁ 13 p. 12°.

Cover-title.

VISIT OF THE MAGI

Miracle Plays

The **Coming** of the three kings to Herod. The masonns play. ₁York play no. 16, 59 lines.₁ (In: Lucy T. Smith, editor, York

plays. Oxford, 1885. 8°. p. 123–125.) **NAFM (Smith)**

An adaptation of this and lines 73–216 of no. 17 is printed in P. E. Osgood, *Old-time church drama adapted*, New York, 1928, p. 155–162, *NAFM.*

The **Coming** of the three kings to Herod; the Adoration. Golde smythis play. ₁York play no. 17, 336 lines.₁ (In: Lucy T. Smith, editor, York plays. Oxford, 1885. 8°. p. 126–137.) **NAFM (Smith)**

An adaptation of lines 1–72 is printed under the title "The meeting of the three kings" in P. E. Osgood, *Old-time church drama adapted*, New York, 1928, p. 152–155, *NAFM*, while an adaptation of lines 217–304 and lines 26–36 of play no. 18 is printed in the

*New Testament Plays — Infancy and Child-
hood of Jesus, continued*

Visit of the Magi, continued

same work, p. 163–167, under the title "The Adoration
of the three kings."
   An extract is printed in Allardyce Nicoll, *Readings
from British drama,* New York [1928], p. 29–32,
* R–NCO.

Oblacio magorum. [Towneley play no. 14.]
(In: The Towneley mysteries. London, 1836.
8°. p. 120–134.)   **CA (Surtees)**
Surtees Society. Publications. [v. 3.]
   Also printed in 1897 (ed. England) in Early English
Text Society, Extra series no. 71 (*The Towneley plays*),
p. 140–160, *NCE (Early)*.

The **Three** kings. The vintneres playe...
[Chester play no. 8.] (In: The Chester plays,
ed. Wright. London: The Shakespeare Society, 1843. 8°. v. 1, p. 146–161.)
                                NAFM (Chester)
   Also printed in 1893 (ed. Deimling) in Early English Text Society, Extra series no. 62 (*The Chester
plays*), p. 160–176, *NCE (Early)*.

The **Adoration** of the magi. (In: Three
Chester Whitsun plays, introduction and
notes by Joseph C. Bridge. Chester: Phil-
lipson and Golder, 1906. 12°. p. 33–49.)
   "Condensed, and the language slightly modernized
for dramatic presentation by the English Drama Society, under the direction of Mr. Nugent Monck."

The **Offering** and return of the three kings.
The marcers playe... [Chester play no. 9.]
(In: The Chester plays, ed. Wright. Lon-
don: Shakespeare Society, 1843. 8°. v. 1,
p. 162–171.)   **NAFM (Chester)**
   Also printed in 1893 (ed. Deimling) in Early English
Text Society, Extra series no. 62 (*The Chester plays*),
p. 177–186, *NCE (Early)*.

Adoration of the magi. [Coventry play no.
17.] (In: Ludus Coventriæ, ed. Halliwell.
London: Shakespeare Society, 1841. 8°.
p. 161–171.)   **NAFM (Coventry)**
   Also printed in 1922 (ed. Block) in Early English
Text Society, Extra series no. 120 (*Ludus Coventriæ*),
p. 151–162, *NCE (Early)*.

Auto de los Reyes Magos. A Spanish mystery play of the twelfth century [in seven
scenes]. Translated by Willis Knapp-Jones.
(Poet lore. Boston, 1928. 8°. v. 39, p. 306–
309.)   * **DA**

Herodes. <Twelfth day.> (In: J. Q.
Adams, editor, Chief pre-Shakespearean
dramas. Boston, New York [cop. 1924]. 8°.
p. 32–40.)   * **R – NCO**
Latin text and parallel English translation.
   "From a twelfth-century manuscript of the Abbey
Saint-Benoit-sur-Loire, preserved in the library at
Orléans... I have reproduced the text from E. de
Coussemaker, *Drames liturgiques du moyen âge,* 1861.
p. 143."

Magi. <Twelfth day.> (In: J. Q. Adams,
editor, Chief pre-Shakespearean dramas.
Boston, New York [cop. 1924]. 8°. p. 28–31.)
                              * **R – NCO**
Latin text and parallel English translation.
   "The text comes from a manuscript of the fourteenth
century entitled Ordinarium seu liber ordinarius Ecclesiae Rothomagensis (reproduced by Armand Gasté,
Les drames liturgiques de la cathédrale de Rouen, 1893,
p. 49)."

Modern Plays

Armstrong, Anna Rebecca. The Epiphany, a religious service in the nature of a
mystery play...arranged by Anna Rebecca
Armstrong... [New York: H. Emmerson,
printer,] cop. 1920. 24 p. 12°.
                           NAC p.v.50, no.1

Bowen, Francis J. The three kings; a
mystery play in five acts by Francis J.
Bowen. With music by Miss Dorothy God-
win-Foster. Edinburgh and London: Sands
and Co., 1928. 59 p. 12°.   **NAFH p.v.37**
On cover: The three kings; a Christmas play.
Words only.

Fitzgerald, George S. The three kings.
[In one scene.] (Holy Cross purple. Worcester, Mass., 1922. 8°. v. 35, p. 184–187.)
                                    STG

Flecker, James Elroy. The masque of the
magi. [A dramatic poem.] (In his: Forty-two
poems. London, 1911. 12°. p. 18–20.) **NCM**
   Reprinted in his *Collected poems,* London [1921],
p. 72–74, *NCM*.

Lamers, William Mathias. A new scene
for Bethlehem. [In one scene.] (Practical
stage work. Milwaukee, 1929. 4°. v. 4, Nov.,
1929, p. 9–10.)   **MWA**
   The scene represents the house top of Melchior the
Babylonian.

McBride, Maxine. The three wise men and
the star. (A miracle play) [in one scene].
(Mount Holyoke monthly. South Hadley,
Mass., 1923. 8°. v. 32, p. 119–129.) **STG**

Pepler, Hilary Douglas C. A Nativity
play. The three wise men. [In three acts.]
Ditchling, Sussex: St. Dominic's Press
[1929]. 7 p.l., 46 p. 16°.

Polding, Elizabeth. The dawn of redemption; or, The adoration of the magi kings, a
Christmas play in four acts... Chicago: The
Dramatic Publishing Company, cop. 1899.
1 p.l., 11 p. 12°. (Sergel's acting drama.
no. 576.)

Smith, Mary Brainard, and EDITH H.
SMITH. "The Christmas spirit": an exercise
for the Sunday-school [in one scene]. (Sunday-school times. New York, 1910. f°. v. 52,
p. 548, 558–559.)   † **ZICN**
   Children of various nationalities, St. Nicholas, and
Balthazar.

Stoddard, Richard Henry. The masque of
the three kings [in two scenes]. (In his:
Poems...complete edition. New York, 1880.
12°. p. 412–420.)   **NBI**

Wilson, Dorothy Clarke. The lost star; a
fantasy of the first Christmas [in five epi-
sodes]. (International journal of religious
education. Chicago, 1930. f°. v. 7, Nov.,
1930, p. 25–27, 47–48.)
   The three magi, in Parthia, Damascus, and on the
road outside Jerusalem.

*New Testament Plays — Infancy and Child-
hood of Jesus, continued*

THE FLIGHT INTO EGYPT

Miracle Plays

The **Flight** into Egypt. The marchallis
play. ₁York play no. 18, 231 lines.₁ (In: Lucy
T. Smith, editor, York plays. Oxford, 1885.
8°. p. 138–145.) **NAFM**

Fugacio Joseph et Mariæ in Ægyptum.
₁Towneley play no. 15.₁ (In: The Towneley
mysteries. London, 1836. 8°. p. 135–139.)
CA (Surtees)
Surtees Society. Publications. [v. 3.]
Also printed in 1897 (ed. England) in Early English
Text Society, Extra series no. 71 (The Towneley plays),
p. 160–165, NCE (Early).

Modern Plays

Davidson, Mary Richmond. On the road
to Egypt, a play for the Christmas season
₁in one scene₁. Boston: Walter H. Baker
Company ₁cop. 1928₁. 15 p. 12°.
The place is given as a cave near Beersheba, two
weeks after the birth of Christ.

Hinkson, Katharine (Tynan). The flight
into Egypt. ₁In two scenes.₁ illus. (In her:
Miracle plays. London, 1895. 12°. p. 71–84.)
NCR

Kennedy, Anna R. The Virgin's tree. ₁In
one scene.₁ (In her: Bible plays out of the
East. New York, 1929. 8°. p. 25–28.)

O'Seasnain, Brian P. On the road to
Egypt. ₁In four scenes.₁ (Catholic world.
New York, 1925. 8°. v. 121, p. 21–30.) *DA

Wilder, Thornton Niven. The flight into
Egypt. (In his: The angel that troubled the
waters, and other plays. New York, 1928.
12°. p. 135–141.) **NBM**

THE SLAUGHTER OF THE INNOCENTS

Miracle Plays

The **Massacre** of the Innocents. The
gyrdillers and naylers play. ₁York play no.
19, 281 lines.₁ (In: Lucy T. Smith, editor,
York plays. Oxford, 1885. 8°. p. 146–155.)
NAFM

Magnus Herodes. ₁Towneley play no. 16.₁
(In: The Towneley mysteries. London, 1836.
8°. p. 140–153.) **CA (Surtees)**
Surtees Society. Publications. [v. 3.]
Also printed in 1897 (ed. England) in Early English
Text Society, Extra series no. 71 (The Towneley
plays), p. 166–181, NCE (Early).

De **Occisione** innocentium. The Gould-
smythes playe. ₁Chester play no. 10.₁ (In:
Chester mysteries. De deluvio Noe. De occisione innocentium. London, 1818. 4°.
p. 39–70.) **NAFM (Chester)**
Also printed in The Chester plays, ed. by Wright,
London, 1843, v. 1, p. 172–188, NAFM (Chester); ed.

by Deimling in Early English Text Society, Extra
series no. 62 (The Chester plays), p. 186–205, NCE
(Early); and, in abbreviated form, in F. J. Tickner,
editor, Earlier English drama from Robin Hood to
Everyman, New York [cop. 1929], p. 171–181, NCO.

The **Slaughter** of the innocents. ₁Coventry
play no. 19.₁ (In: Ludus Coventriæ, ed. Halliwell. London: Shakespeare Society, 1841.
8°. p. 179–188.) **NAFM (Coventry)**
Also printed in 1922 (ed. Block) in Early English
Text Society, Extra series no. 120 (Ludus Coventriæ),
p. 169–177 (lines 1–154: The massacre of the innocents;
lines 155–284: The death of Herod), NCE (Early).

Candlemas-Day, or The killing of the children of Israel. A mystery. ₁The Digby
play.₁ (In: Thomas Hawkins, editor, The
origin of the English drama. Oxford, 1773.
12°. v. 1, p. 1–26.) **NCO**
"The following mystery is preserved in the Bodleian
Library amongst the mss. bequeathed to the University
by Sir Kenelm Digby: it was written by one Ihan
Parfre in 1512." According to Halliwell, Dictionary of
old English plays, John Parfre was the transcriber of
the ms., which he calls an interlude on the subject of
the slaughter of the innocents.
Also printed in William Marriott, editor, Collection
of English miracle-plays or mysteries, Basel, 1838,
p. 197–219, NAFM; in New Shakespeare Society, Publications, series 7, no. 1 (The Digby mysteries), London, 1882, p. xxxi–xxxii, 1–24, * NCK; in Early
English Text Society, Extra series, no. 70 (The Digby
mysteries), p. xxxi–xxxii, 1–23, NCE (Early); and
with introductory note in Journal of sacred literature,
London, 1867, series 4, v. 10, p. 415–429, * DA.

THE PRESENTATION IN THE TEMPLE

Miracle Play

The **Presentation** in the Temple: a pageant, as originally represented by the Cor-
poration of Weavers in Coventry. Now first
printed from the books of the company.
With a prefatory notice ₁by Thomas Sharp₁.
Edited by J. B. Gracie. Edinburgh: Printed
for the Abbotsford Club, 1836. 3 p.l., 86 p.
4°.
First edition, prepared from the ms. which later was
destroyed.
Also printed in Early English Text Society, Extra
series no. 87 (Two Coventry Corpus Christi plays,
edited by Hardin Craig), p. 33–71, NCE (Early), and
in Anglia, Halle a. S., 1902 (ed. Holthausen), Bd. 25,
p. 209–250, RNA. Prof. Holthausen follows the London, 1836 edition and attempts to rectify the text and
metre without the aid of the ms. which had been
burned in 1879.

Davidson, Charles. The play of the Weavers of Coventry. (Modern language notes.
Baltimore, 1892. 4°. v. 7, col. 184–185.) **RAA**
It is pointed out that the second part of the Weaver's
play is identical with the twentieth York play. Comment on this article by A. R. Hohlfeld appears in
v. 7, col. 308–310.

Modern Play

Hinkson, Katharine (Tynan). The presentation in the temple. ₁In two scenes.₁ illus.
(In her: Miracle plays. London, 1895. 12°.
p. 57–70.) **NCR**

New Testament Plays — Infancy and Childhood of Jesus, continued

JESUS AND THE DOCTORS

Miracle Plays

GREG, Walter Wilson. Christ and the doctors: inter-relation of the cycles. 1 folded table. (Library. London, 1914. 8°. series 3, v. 5, p. 280–319.)   * HA
Reprinted in his *Bibliographical and textual problems of the English miracle cycles*, London, 1914, p. 69–108, *NAFM*.

Christ with the doctors in the Temple. The sporiers and lorimers play. ₁York play no. 20, 288 lines.₁ (In: Lucy T. Smith, editor, York plays. Oxford, 1885. 8°. p. 156–171.)
                                        NAFM
Also printed in M. S. Mooney, *A rosary of mystery plays*, Albany, 1915, p. 52–61, *NAFM*.

Pagina doctorum. ₁Towneley play no. 18.₁ (In: The Towneley mysteries. London, 1836. 8°. p. 158–164.)   CA (Surtees)
Surtees Society. Publications. [v. 3.]
Also printed in 1897 (ed. England) in Early English Text Society, Extra series no. 71 *(The Towneley plays)*, p. 186–194, *NCE (Early)*.

Christ disputing in the Temple. ₁Coventry play no. 20.₁ (In: Ludus Coventriæ, ed. Halliwell. London: Shakespeare Society, 1841. 8°. p. 189–198.)   NAFM (Coventry)
Also printed in 1922 (ed. Block) in Early English Text Society, Extra series no. 120 *(Ludus Coventriæ)*, p. 178–187, *NCE (Early)*.

Modern Play

Hinkson, Katharine (Tynan). The finding in the temple. ₁In two scenes.₁ illus. (In her: Miracle plays. London, 1895. 12°. p. 85–98.)   NCR

MINISTRY OF JESUS

This section is arranged according to the "Synopsis of Gospel history" in the *Cambridge companion to the Bible*, 1905, p. 334–346

JOHN THE BAPTIST

Modern Plays

Bale, John, bishop of Ossory. A brefe comedy, or enterlude, of Iohan Baptystes preachynge in the wyldernesse, openynge the craftye assaultes of the hypocrytes, with the gloryouse baptyme of the Lord Jesus Christ. Compyled by Iohan Bale, Anno M.D.XXXVIII. (Harleian miscellany. London, 1808. 8°. v. 1, p. 202–216.)   CBA
Also in the quarto edition of 1808, v. 1, p. 101–114, † *CBA*.
Reprinted in his *Dramatic writings, edited by J. S. Farmer*, London, 1907, p. 127–150, *NCO (Early)*.

Barry, Philip. John, a play. New York, Los Angeles: S. French; London: S. French, Ltd., 1929. 6 p.l., 3–173 p. 12°. NBM
Produced by the Actors' Theatre at the Klaw Theatre, New York, Nov. 4, 1927, with Jacob Ben-Ami as John and Anna Duncan as Salome. For reviews see *Collection of newspaper clippings for dramatic criticism, 1927–28*, vol. H–L, † *NBL*.

Boyd, Zachary. Historie of John the Baptist. ₁A dramatic poem. Excerpt of about 200 lines out of about 800 lines of the ms. "Flowers of Zion."₁ (In: Gabriel Neil, Biographical sketch of the Rev. Mr. Zachary Boyd. Glasgow, 1832. 8°. Appendix, p. xxx–xxxii.)   A p.v.144
Eleven speakers.

Boyton, Neil. "John the Baptist." ₁In one scene.₁ (Holy Cross purple. Worcester, Mass., 1912. 8°. v. 24, p. 443–446.)   STG

Buchanan, George. Tyrannicall-government anatomized; or, A discourse concerning evil-councellors. Being the life and death of

John the Baptist... ₁A tragedy in five acts.₁ London: Printed for John Field, 1642. 4°.
Title from British Museum Catalogue.
Ordered printed by the Committee concerning Printing of the House of Commons, Jan. 30, 1642.
First English translation, anonymous, of the Latin text published 1578. This 1642 translation is reprinted, together with a blank verse transcription by J. T. T. Brown, in *George Buchanan; Glasgow quatercentenary studies, 1906*, Glasgow, 1907, p. 91–173, *AN*. F. Peck in 1740 was the first to ascribe the 1642 translation to John Milton, and published it with a long preface, 29 p., and notes, 31 p., together with the Latin text, as:

——— Baptistes: a sacred dramatic poem, in defence of liberty: as, written in Latin, by Mr. George Buchanan: translated into English, by Mr. John Milton: and first published in 1641. By order of the House of Commons. (In: Francis Peck, New memoirs of the life and poetical works of John Milton. London, 1740. 8°. p. 265–428.)   * NCC (Peck)

BROWN, J. T. T. An English translation of George Buchanan's Baptistes attributed to Milton. (In: George Buchanan; Glasgow quatercentenary studies, 1906. Glasgow, 1907. 8°. p. 61–90.)   AN
In support of F. Peck's contention that the 1642 translation is by John Milton.

Buchanan, George. The Jephtha, and Baptist... Translated by Alexander Gibb. Edinburgh, 1870. 8°.
Title from British Museum Catalogue.
On the outside paper cover the translator's name is given as Alexander S. Gibb. The metre chosen is blank verse, and no mention is made of Peck's earlier version.

——— John the Baptist (1576); a drama translated from the Latin of George Buchanan by A. Gordon Mitchell. Paisley: Alexander Gardner, 1904. 127 p. 12°.
Reviewed in *Academy and Literature*, London, 1904, v. 66, p. 350, * *DA*.

New Testament Plays — Ministry of Jesus,
continued

John the Baptist, continued

Buchanan, George, *continued*

—— The Baptist; or, Calumny. (In his:
Sacred dramas. Translated into English
verse by Archibald Brown. Edinburgh, 1906.
8°. p. 89–162.) **NCP**

"Written as a political allegory... The dramatis
personae are to be sought among English men and
women — Henry VIII [Herod], Anne Boleyn [Hero-
dias], Sir Thomas More [John the Baptist]."
For a bibliography of the early Latin editions, English and foreign translations of the "Baptistes" see
George Buchanan; Glasgow quatercentenary studies,
1906, cited above, p. 447–449, *AN.*

Fries, Carl. Quellenstudien zu George
Buchanan. (Neue Jahrbücher für klassische
Altertum, Geschichte und Litteratur. Leipzig, 1900. 8°. Jahrg. 3, Bd. 6, p. 177–192, 241–
261.) † **NAA**

Grimald, Nicholas. The archprophet; a
tragedy. (In: L. R. Merrill, The life and
poems of Nicholas Grimald. New Haven,
1925. 8°. p. 229–357.) **NCF**

Yale studies in English no. 69.
A Latin tragedy in five acts, composed in 1546 and
published at Cologne by Gymnicus in 1548. The
author's own manuscript is in the British Museum
(Royal MS. 12 A 46). The text is reprinted, together
with a parallel English translation.
There are fifteen characters, among them Jehovah,
John the Baptist, King Herod, a court fool, Herodias,
and three choruses. The daughter of Herodias is here
called Tryphera (the voluptuous); two "representative"
Pharisees are named Philautus and Typhlus.
Cf. Preface, *ibid.,* p. 219–226, where it is stated that
"the source of the plot is not the Bible, but rather
Josephus' *Antiquities of the Jews.*"
For a synopsis of the drama see F. S. Boas, *Uni-*
versity drama in the Tudor age, Oxford, 1914, p. 33–
41, *NCOD.*

Heywood, Joseph Converse. Salome, the
daughter of Herodias; a dramatic poem.
New York: Putnam, 1862. 251 p. 12°. **NBM**

An entirely different play from the author's "Salome," published in 1867.

—— Herodias. A dramatic poem. New
York: Hurd and Houghton, 1867. 251 p.
12°. * **PSQ**

First edition, New York, 1862, published under title:
Salome, the daughter of Herodias.
Reviewed in *The Athenæum,* London, June 29, 1867,
p. 847–848, * *DA.*

Horne, Richard Henry. John the Baptist;
or, The valour of the soul. In two acts. (In
his: Bible tragedies. London [1881?]. 12°.
p. 1–46.)

Osgood, Phillips Endecott. In Herod's
dungeon. [In one scene.] (In his: Pulpit
dramas. New York and London, 1929. 12°.
p. 59–73.) **NAFM**

Sudermann, Hermann. Johannes. [Trans-
lated by W. H. Harned and Mary Harned.]
(Poet lore. Boston, 1899. 8°. v. 11, p. 161–
236.) * **DA**

—— John the Baptist; a play [in five acts]
by Hermann Sudermann. Translated by
Beatrice Marshall. London: J. Lane; New
York: J. Lane Company, 1909. vi p., 1 l.,
202 p. 8°. **NGE**

Time of action: the year 29 after Christ. Scene of
action: Jerusalem, and a town of Galilee.
Reprinted in Kuno Francke and W. G. Howard,
editors, *The German classics,* New York, 1913–14,
v. 17, p. 168–249, *NFF (Francke).*
Produced at the Lyric Theatre, New York, Jan. 21,
1907 with Frank Reicher as Herod Antipas, Julia Mar-
lowe as Salome, and E. H. Sothern as John. Reviewed
in *New York dramatic mirror,* New York, v. 57, Feb.
2, 1907, p. 3, * *DA,* and in *Theatre magazine,* New
York, v. 7, March, 1907, p. xvi, *NBLA.*

BAPTISM

Miracle Plays

The **Baptism** of Jesus. The barbours play.
[York play no. 21, 175 lines.] (In: Lucy T.
Smith, editor, York plays. Oxford, 1885. 8°.
p. 172–177.) **NAFM**

Johannes baptista. [Towneley play no. 19.]
(In: The Towneley mysteries. London, 1836.
8°. p. 165–171.) **CA (Surtees)**

Surtees Society. Publications. [v. 3.]
Also printed in 1897 (ed. England) in Early English
Text Society, Extra series no. 71 *(The Towneley plays),*
p. 195–203, *NCE (Early).*

The **Baptism** of Christ. [Coventry play no.
21.] (In: Ludus Coventriæ, ed. Halliwell.
London: Shakespeare Society, 1841. 8°.
p. 199–204.) **NAFM (Coventry)**

Also printed in 1922 (ed. Block) in Early English
Text Society, Extra series no. 120 *(Ludus Coventriæ),*
p. 188–193, *NCE (Early).*

THE TEMPTATION

Miracle Plays

The **Temptation** of Jesus. The smythis
play. [York play no. 22, 210 lines.] (In: Lucy
T. Smith, editor, York plays. Oxford, 1885.
8°. p. 178–184.) **NAFM**

The **Temptation,** and the woman taken in
adultery. The bowchers playe... [Chester
play no. 12.] (In: The Chester plays, ed. by
Wright. London: Shakespeare Society,
1843. 8°. v. 1, p. 201–211.) **NAFM (Chester)**

Also printed in 1893 (ed. Deimling) in Early English Text Society, Extra series no. 62 *(The Chester*
plays), p. 217–229, *NCE (Early).*

The **Temptation.** [Coventry play no. 22.]
(In: Ludus Coventriæ, ed. Halliwell. London: Shakespeare Society, 1841. 8°. p. 205–
212.) **NAFM (Coventry)**

Also printed in 1922 (ed. Block) in Early English
Text Society, Extra series no. 120 *(Ludus Coventriæ),*
p. 193–200, *NCE (Early).*

Modern Plays

Bale, John. "The temptacyon of our
Lorde"...now first re-printed and edited
by the Rev. Alexander B. Grosart. (In: A. B.

New Testament Plays — Ministry of Jesus,
continued

The Temptation, continued

Grosart, editor, Miscellanies of the Fuller
worthies' library. London, 1870–76. 16°. v. 1,
p. 123–155.)
    The Fuller worthies' library. [v.] 36.
    Reprinted as a separate, large paper ed., 1870.

—— A brefe comedy or enterlude con-
cernynge the temptacyon of Our Lorde and
Sauer Jesus Christ by Sathan in the desert.
Compyled by Johan Bale, Anno M.D.XXXVII.
(In his: Dramatic writings, edited by J. S.
Farmer. London, 1907. 16°. p. 151–170.)
    Early English dramatists.   **NCO (Early)**
    Title-page is a reduced facsimile of that of the
Bodleian copy.

—— ...The temptation of Our Lord, by
John Bale...1538. London and Edinburgh:
Issued for subscribers by T. C. & E. C. Jack,
1909. v p., facsim. (1 l., [18] p.) 4°. (The
Tudor facsimile texts...)   **NCO (Tudor)**
    "A single copy only of this play is known to be extant
(Bodleian, Douce B, Subst. 164)." The page of script
at the beginning of the printed copy is included in the
facsimile. — *cf. p.v.*

—— John Bales Drama, A brefe comedy or
enterlude concernynge the temptacyon of
our lorde and sauer Iesus Christ by Sathan in
the desert. Inaugural-Dissertation...vorge-
legt von Paul Schwemmer. Nürnberg:
Friedr. Schwemmer, 1919. xvi, 26 p., 1 l. 8°.
    NCO p.v.518, no.9
Dissertation, University of Erlangen.

Kummer, Frederic Arnold. The temptation; a play in one act. (In his: Phryne, Finer
Clay, and Temptation. Philadelphia [cop.
1924]. 12°. p. 115–128.)   **NBM**
    Dramatized by the author from his story of the same
name in *Delineator,* v. 102, April, 1923, p. 2, 71–73.
† *VSA.*

First Call of Disciples

Modern Play

Graves, Frederick D. ...Simon Peter's
brother... [In three acts.] Hartford: Church
Missions Pub. Co. [1928.] 26 p. 8°. (The
church in story and pageant. Publication
no. 19.)
    First call to discipleship, with incidents from the
second call. Based on John I: 35–51 and Luke V: 1–11.

Nicodemus

Modern Plays

Bates, Katharine Lee. Pharisees. (In her:
The pilgrim ship. New York, 1926. 8°.
p. 77–86.)   **NBI**
    Nicodemus and a rabbi are the two chief characters.

Osgood, Phillips Endecott. The fears of
Nicodemus, a sermon-substitute in dialogue
[in one scene]. (In his: The sinner beloved,
and other religious plays. New York and
London, 1928. 12°. p. 161–171.)   **NAFM**
    The other speaker is Joseph of Arimathea.

Stackhouse, Perry J. The disciple of the
night. A drama sermon [in four scenes]. (In
his: Bible dramas in the pulpit. Philadelphia
[cop. 1926]. 8°. p. 69–85.)   **NBM**
    Characters: Jesus, Jonathan, president of the San-
hedrin, Nicodemus, a Pharisee and member of the
Sanhedrin.

The Woman of Samaria

Modern Plays

Glover, Lydia May. The living water. [In
two scenes.] Based on John 4. 4–42. (In her:
Friends of Jesus. New York [cop. 1923]. 8°.
p. 24–34.)   **NAC p.v.113, no.5**
    Scene: Samaria, 51 A. D.

Rostand, Edmond. The woman of Sa-
maria; an evangel in three parts, in verse.
(In his: Plays. Translated by H. D. Norman.
New York, 1921. 8°. v. 1, p. 141–206.) **NKP**

The Pool of Bethesda

Modern Play

Hagedorn, Hermann. The pool of Beth-
esda. [In one act.] (Outlook. New York,
1914. 8°. v. 108, p. 782–785.)   * **DA**
    A prelude to a three-act play entitled "Greater works
than these."

Jesus Teaches at Nazareth

Modern Play

Osgood, Phillips Endecott. Rejected of
Nazareth. The keeper of the Nazareth synagogue...tells of the expulsion of the village
carpenter. [A monologue.] (In his: Pulpit
dramas. New York and London, 1929. 12°.
p. 41–57.)   **NAFM**
    Based on Luke IV: 16–30.

The Calling of Peter, Andrew, James and John

Modern Plays

Manley, William Ford. James of Galilee.
(In his: Bible dramas. New York [cop. 1928].
8°. p. 10–25.)   **NBM**
    In three scenes.

Moulton, Arthur W. On the Galilean lake.
[James and John, and Zebedee.] (In his: It
came to pass. Boston, 1916. 12°. p. 23–35.)
    ZFHK

Peter's Wife's Mother

Modern Play

Glover, Lydia May. Simon's wife's mother.
[In three scenes.] New York: Abingdon
Press [cop. 1926]. 19 p. 8°.
    Matthew VIII: 14–17.

New Testament Plays — Ministry of Jesus,
continued

THE SERMON ON THE MOUNT

Modern Play

Benton, Rita. Coming down the Mount.
ₜA play in four acts.ₗ (In her: Franklin, and
other plays. New York, 1924. 12°. p. 109–
173.)   **NBM**
Scene is laid on the shores of Galilee and at Jerusalem, before and after the Crucifixion. The Sermon on the Mount is discussed throughout by adherents and opponents as ideal or impractical.

THE HEALING OF THE PARALYTIC

Modern Play

Githens, Harry W. Down through the
roof. ₜIn three scenes.ₗ (In his: New Testament stories dramatized. Cincinnati ₜcop.
1929ₗ. 12°. p. 76–83.)
Mark ᴵᴵ: 1–12, the healing of the paralytic.

HEALING OF THE CENTURION'S SLAVE

Modern Play

Osgood, Phillips Endecott. Under authority; the centurion of Capernaum begs the
elders of that town to go for him with a
message to the Carpenter of Nazareth. ₜIn
one scene.ₗ illus. (In his: Pulpit dramas.
New York and London, 1929. 12°. p. 26–39.)
                                        NAFM
Based on Matt. ᵛᴵᴵᴵ: 5–13 and Luke ᵛᴵᴵ: 1–10.

FEEDING OF THE FIVE THOUSAND

Modern Plays

Kennedy, Anna R. A boy finds the kingdom. ₜIn two scenes.ₗ (In her: Bible plays
out of the East. New York, 1929. 8°. p. 39–
46.)

Ritchey, Belle MacDiarmid. There is a lad
here. ₜIn three acts.ₗ New York: Womans
Press ₜ1926, cop. 1925ₗ. 28 p. 12°.
The first two acts are at the time of the feeding of the five thousand; the third, after the Resurrection.

THE TRANSFIGURATION

Miracle Play

The **Transfiguration.** The coriours play.
ₜYork play no. 23, 240 lines.ₗ (In: Lucy T.
Smith, editor, York plays. Oxford, 1885. 8°.
p. 185–192.)   **NAFM**

THE WOMAN TAKEN IN ADULTERY

Miracle Plays

The **Woman** taken in adultery. The raising
of Lazarus. The cappemakers, etc. play.
ₜYork play no. 24, 209 lines.ₗ (In: Lucy T.
Smith, editor, York plays. Oxford, 1885. 8°.
p. 193–200.)   **NAFM**

The **Woman** taken in adultery. ₜCoventry
play no. 23.ₗ (In: Ludus Coventriæ, ed. Halliwell. London: Shakespeare Society, 1841.
8°. p. 213–222.)   **NAFM (Coventry)**
Also printed in 1922 (ed. Block) in Early English Text Society, Extra series no. 120 *(Ludus Coventriæ)*, p. 200–209, *NCE (Early).*
A short extract, modernized, is printed in Norman Ault, *The poet's life of Christ*, London, 1923, p. 129–131, *NCI (Ault).*
Both plays are based on the disputed text of John ᵛᴵᴵᴵ: 1–11.

THE MAN BORN BLIND

Modern Plays

Githens, Harry W. Opened eyes. ₜIn five
scenes.ₗ (In his: New Testament stories
dramatized. Cincinnati ₜcop. 1929ₗ. 12°.
p. 48–64.)
Based on John ᴵˣ: 1–41. Philip, the young blind man.

Glover, Lydia May. Nason, the blind
disciple; a sermon drama ₜin two scenesₗ
with suggestions for a Sunday evening's worship service. New York: Abingdon Press
ₜcop. 1927ₗ. 31 p. illus. 8°.
Presented at the Evanston, Ill., Summer School of Religious Education, August, 1926.

Stackhouse, Perry J. Facts are stubborn
things. ₜA play in four scenes.ₗ (In his: Bible
dramas in the pulpit. Philadelphia ₜcop.
1926ₗ. 8°. p. 101–112.)   **NBM**
Place: Jerusalem. Time: a Sabbath day, ᴀ. ᴅ. 29.
Characters: Jesus, Gideon, and the blind man. John ᴵˣ: 1–41.

THE GOOD SAMARITAN

Modern Plays

Baker, Clara. The good Samaritan. ₜIn
three acts.ₗ (In: T. W. Galloway, The dramatic instinct in religious education. Boston
ₜcop. 1922ₗ. 12°. p. 49–57.)

Bennett, Clara Marion. The good Samaritan: a Biblical drama. Emporia, Kan.: Press
of the Rowland Printing Company ₜcop.
1907ₗ. 35 p. 16°.

Benton, Rita. The good Samaritan. (In
her: Shorter Bible plays. New York ₜcop.
1922ₗ. 8°. p. 122–128.)   **NASH**

Cole, Edna Earle. The good Samaritan.
ₜIn two acts.ₗ (In her: The good Samaritan
and other Bible stories dramatized. Boston
ₜcop. 1915ₗ. 12°. p. 11–17.)
Based on Luke ˣ: 30–37.

Cropper, Margaret. The good Samaritan.
ₜIn three scenes.ₗ London: St. Christopher
Press ₜ1930?ₗ. 16 p. 12°. (Saint Nicolas
plays. no. 4.)

Ferris, Anita Brockway. The good Samaritan. (In: Religious dramas. New York:
Century Co. ₜcop. 1923.ₗ 8°. v. 1, p. 69–75.)
                            NAFM (Religious)

New Testament Plays — Ministry of Jesus, continued

The Good Samaritan, continued

Gairdner, William Henry Temple. The good Samaritan; a New Testament morality play in four scenes... London: Society for Promoting Christian Knowledge, 1923. 30 p. 12°. **NAC p.v.99, no.3**
"This play was originally represented, in Arabic, by the boys of the Old Cairo School, Egypt, in the open air, without curtain, stage furniture, or stage scenery."
"The Pilgrim hymn in Scene IV, is taken from Max Bruch's beautiful fantasia on Hebrew melodies, entitled 'Kol Nidrei.'"

Lobingier, Mrs. Elizabeth Erwin (Miller). The good Samaritan. [A dramatization in two scenes by the Dramatic Club of the Hyde Park Church of Disciples, Chicago, Ill.] (In her: The dramatization of Bible stories. Chicago [cop. 1918]. 12°. p. 103–105.) *** YIR**

Noble, Patricia. As the twig is bent; children's day pageant [in three scenes]. (International journal of religious education. Mt. Morris, Ill., 1925. f°. v. 1, June, 1925, p. 28–29.)
In Judah, about 25 A. D.

Russell, Mary M. A neighbor and his work. [In two scenes.] (In her: Dramatized Bible stories for young people. New York [cop. 1921]. 12°. p. 74–77.)

Whitney, Mary Ellen. The parable of the good Samaritan. [A play in two scenes.] (In her: Bible plays and how to produce them. New York [cop. 1927]. 12°. p. 104–108.)

MARTHA AND MARY

Modern Plays

Glover, Lydia May. The seeing heart. [In two scenes.] Based on Luke 10. 38–42; John 12. 2, 3. (In her: Friends of Jesus. New York [cop. 1923]. 8°. p. 17–23.) **NAC p.v.113, no.5**

Raine, James Watt. [Martha and Mary. In one scene.] (In his: Bible dramatics. New York & London [cop. 1927]. 12°. p. 84–88.)

JESUS TEACHES THE DISCIPLES HOW TO PRAY

Modern Play

Raine, James Watt. [Seek, and ye shall find. In one scene.] (In his: Bible dramatics. New York & London [cop. 1927]. 12°. p. 94–101.)
Based on Luke XI: 1–13.

PARABLE OF THE RICH FOOL

Modern Play

Parker, Mary Moncure. "The soul of the rich man." A morality play. Luke XII: 16–20. (In her: New monologues and dialect stories. Chicago [cop. 1908]. 16°. p. 116–119.) **NANV**

THE LOST COIN

Modern Play

Wood, Letitia W., and LENA P. MARTIN. The lost coin. [In two acts.] Franklin, O.: Eldridge Entertainment House, Inc., cop. 1929. 12 p. 12°. (Eldridge church entertainments.)
Based on Luke XV: 8–10.

THE PRODIGAL SON

Modern Plays

Finnegan, Edward. The prodigal son; a play in four acts. Boston: W. H. Baker Co., 1925. 74 p. 12°.
Produced at the St. Mary's Theatre, Boston, during the Lenten season of 1924.

Githens, Harry W. The wanderer. [In seven scenes.] (In his: New Testament stories dramatized. Cincinnati [cop. 1929]. 12°. p. 36–47.)

Glick, Carl. Ten days later; a comedy in one act. New York: Samuel French [cop. 1928]. 2 p.l., 34 p. 12°. **NBL p.v.192**
Scene: not far from Jerusalem, about the year 1 A. D. The prodigal son story used as a satire on the modern notion regarding the social revolution.
First printed in *Drama*, Chicago, 1921, v. 11, p. 159–165, *NAFA*.

Kemp, Harry. The prodigal son; a comedy in one act, as played at the Little Thimble Theatre. New York: E. Arens, 1919. 28 p. 16°. (The flying stag plays for the little theatre. no. 8.)
First printed in the *Smart set*, New York, v. 52, no. 3, July, 1917, p. 83–93, *NBA*.
First produced by the Provincetown Players at the Playwrights' Theatre, New York, March 10, 1917.

Kimball, Rosamond. The prodigal son. [In three scenes.] illus. (In her: The wooing of Rebekah, and other Bible plays. New York, 1925. 8°. p. 241–249.) **ZICS**

Knowles, Ava Beatrice. The prodigal son. [In six scenes.] (In her: Prodigal son; The beginning of the Church. New York [1925]. 12°. p. 2–13.)

Kruckemeyer, Erna. And he came to his father: religious play in one act... New York: S. French, cop. 1927. 25 p. 12°. (World's best plays.) **NBL p.v.167, no.7**
Near Jerusalem, about 32 A. D. The belief in, and doubts raised about, Jesus are echoed in the conversation of some of the characters.

Levinger, Elma C. Ehrlich. The return of the prodigal; a one-act play based on a certain parable in Luke. With an introduction by Mrs. A. Starr Best... Boston, Chicago: Pilgrim Press [cop. 1927]. xi(i), 27 p. illus. 12°. **NBL p.v.170, no.4**
The story of the prodigal son in a Jewish setting, in the days when the Temple stood, on an estate in Galilee. The "Return of the prodigal" was awarded the first prize in the 1925 Religious Drama Contest held by the Drama League of America. The play was produced by the Pilgrim Players of Evanston, Ill.

New Testament Plays — Ministry of Jesus, continued

The Prodigal Son, continued

Lobingier, Mrs. Elizabeth Erwin (Miller). The prodigal son. [A dramatization in three acts by the Dramatic Club of the Hyde Park Church of Disciples, Chicago, Ill.] (In her: The dramatization of Bible stories. Chicago [cop. 1918]. 12°. p. 105–108.)   ***YIR**

Manley, William Ford. The prodigal. [In three scenes.] (In his: A second book of Bible dramas. New York [cop. 1930]. 8°. p. 61–81.)   **NBM**
Scene placed in a modern community.

Parker, Mary Moncure. The prodigal comes home; a Biblical drama, in one act... Chicago: T. S. Denison & Co. [cop. 1930.] 24 p. 12°.
Time: between 30 and 33 A. D., "in ancient Palestine." Five men and three women. The prodigal is here called Joel; the father, Manasseh.

Raine, James Watt. The lost son. [In four scenes.] (In his: Bible dramatics. New York & London [cop. 1927]. 12°. p. 28–38.)

Samuels, Maurice Victor. The wanderer; the play of the month. [Extracts from the text.] illus. (Hearst's magazine. New York, 1917. f°. v. 31, p. 380–382, 437.)   ***DA**
The scenes are laid in Hebron and Jerusalem. Many extra characters are introduced.
Produced at the Manhattan Opera House, New York, Feb. 1, 1917, with William Elliott as the wanderer; James O'Neill as Jesse the father; Nance O'Neill as Huldah the mother; and Florence Reed as Tisha. Founded on Wilhelm Schmidtbonn's "Der verlorene Sohn."
Reviewed by Montrose J. Moses in *Book news monthly*, Philadelphia, 1917, v. 35, p. 282, illus., v. 36, p. 64, * *DA;* by Channing Pollock in *Green book magazine,* Chicago, 1917, v. 17, p. 581–584, illus., *NAFA;* by J. S. Metcalfe in *Life,* New York, 1917, v. 69, p. 268, * *DA;* in the *New York dramatic mirror,* New York, 1917, Feb. 10, p. 7, * *DA; New York Herald,* New York, 1917, Feb. 2, p. 5, col. 4–6, * *A; The Sun,* New York, 1917, Feb. 2, p. 7, col. 1–2, * *A; New York Times,* New York, 1917, Feb. 2, p. 9, col. 1, and Feb. 18, section ii, p. 6, col. 1, * *A;* by Arthur Hornblow in *Theatre,* New York, 1917, v. 25, p. 151, illustrations p. 134, 141, † *NBLA.* See also *ibid.,* p. 232.

Williams, Charles Richard. The return of the prodigal; a monodrama. (In his: The return of the prodigal, and other religious poems. Indianapolis [1927]. 12°. p. 1–33.)   **NBI**

DIVES AND LAZARUS

Modern Plays

Dives and Lazarus: a droll acted at Bartholomew Fair in the seventeenth century. It is mentioned in *Wit and drollery,* 1682, and in the *Second Part of the Pleasant Musical Companion,* 1687.
See W. C. Hazlitt, *Manual,* p. 65.

Holdsworth, Philip Joseph. Death and Dives (a Scriptural paraphrase) [in dramatic form]. (In his: Station hunting on the Warrego: Australia: At the valley of the Popran: and other poems. Sydney, 1885. 12°. p. 64–67.)   **NCM**

Lesley, or **Lesly,** George. Dives' doom; or, The rich man's misery. [In verse.] (In his: Divine dialogues. London, 1684. 2. ed. 8°.
Title from British Museum Catalogue.
First printed separately in 1675.

Radcliff, Ralph. Dives and Lazarus: a comedy by Ralph Radcliff. Not printed.
See W. C. Hazlitt, *Manual,* p. 65.

Vogl, Virginie Douglas (Hyde). Dives and Lazarus; a dramatic poem of the proletariat. (In her: Echoes and prophecies. [Westwood, Mass., cop. 1909.] 12°. p. 179–193.)   **NBM**
The motif from Luke xvi: 19–31.

LAZARUS

Miracle Plays

Lazarus. [Towneley play no. 31.] (In: The Towneley mysteries. London, 1836. 8°. p. 322–327.)   **CA (Surtees)**
Surtees Society. Publications. [v. 3.]
Out of the chronological order; later in origin than the other Towneley plays.
Also printed in 1897 (ed. England) in Early English Text Society, Extra series no. 71 *(The Towneley plays),* p. 387–393, NCE *(Early),* and, in abbreviated form, in F. J. Tickner, editor, *Earlier English drama from Robin Hood to Everyman,* New York [cop. 1929], p. 184–189, *NCO (Tickner).*

Lazarus. The glovers playe... [Chester play no. 13.] (In: The Chester plays, ed. Wright. London: Shakespeare Society, 1843. 8°. v. 1, p. 212–231.)   **NAFM (Chester)**
Also printed with title "Christ, the adulteress, Chelidonius" in Early English Text Society, Extra series nos. 62 and 115 *(The Chester plays),* NCE *(Early).* Lines 1–282 were edited by Deimling and published in 1893 in no. 62, p. 229–240. Lines 283–489 were edited after Deimling's death by Matthews and printed in 1916 in no. 115, p. 241–249.
Reprinted under the title "Christ's ministry" in J. Q. Adams, editor, *Chief pre-Shakespearean dramas,* Boston [cop. 1924], p. 167–174, * *R – NCO.*

Lazarus. [Coventry play no. 24.] (In: Ludus Coventriæ, ed. Halliwell. London: Shakespeare Society, 1841. 8°. p. 223–238.)   **NAFM (Coventry)**
Also printed in 1922 (ed. Block) in Early English Text Society, Extra series no. 120 *(Ludus Coventriæ),* p. 210–225, NCE *(Early).*

Modern Plays

Bale, John. Lazarus rais'd from the dead: a comedy by Bishop Bale.
This is one of the pieces mentioned in his own list of his writings.
See W. C. Hazlitt, *Manual,* p. 129.

Lawrence, Charles Edward. The message of Lazarus. (Nineteenth century. London, 1922. 8°. v. 91, Jan., 1922, p. 170–176.) * **DA**
The characters are Mary of Bethany, Martha, and a priest.

O'Neill, Eugene Gladstone. Lazarus laughed (1925–1926); a play [in four acts] for an imaginative theatre. New York: Boni and Liveright, 1927. 179 p. 8°.   **NBM**
Act i, complete in itself, is printed in *The American caravan,* New York, 1927, p. 807–833, *NBA.*
Reviewed, by G. F. H., in *The Curtain,* London,

New Testament Plays — Ministry of Jesus,
continued

O'Neill, E. G.: Lazarus laughed, *continued*

August, 1928, v. 7, p. 103, *NAFA;* by Joseph Wood Krutch in *The Nation,* New York, 1928, v. 126, p. 19, * *DA;* by Edwin Bjorkman in *New York Sun,* Nov. 26, 1927, p. 9, * *A;* and by J. Brooks Atkinson in *New York Times book review,* New York, Nov. 27, 1927, v. 32, p. 5, † *NAA.*
First produced at the Community House, Pasadena, Cal., April 9, 1928, with Irving Pichel as Lazarus, Lenore Shanewise as his wife Miriam. Reviewed in *Drama,* New York, 1928, v. 18, p. 244–246, *NAFA,* and in *New York Times,* April 10, 1928, p. 33, * *A.* See also review in *Arts & decorations,* New York, Sept., 1927, v. 27, p. 68–69, *MAA,* with photographs of models for sets and costumes for the production of the play designed by Norman Bel-Geddes.

Osgood, Phillips Endecott. Lazarus tells of his death. ₁In one scene.₁ (In his: Pulpit dramas. New York and London, 1929. 12°. p. 89–105.)   **NAFM**

THE TEN LEPERS

Modern Plays

Darlington, Anne Charlotte. The nine. ₁In one act.₁ (In her: The lady Joanna; By the roadside; The nine. New York ₁cop. 1928₁. 12°. p. 25–37.)

Hitchcock, Mary S. One of the nine; a drama in three acts. Franklin, Ohio, Denver, Colo.: Eldridge Entertainment House, Inc., cop. 1926. 35 p. 12°. (Eldridge church entertainments.)
Time: 33 A. D. Place: Jerusalem. Founded on the story of the ten who were cleansed. Luke xvii: 12–19.

THE YOUNG RICH RULER

Modern Plays

Kingsbury, Sara. ...The rich young man, a play in three acts. New York, Cincinnati: The Abingdon Press ₁cop. 1924₁. 42 p. 8°. (Biblical drama series.)
Time: within the ministry of Jesus. Place: in the garden of the summer palace of Rabbi Amos, the rich young man.

Stackhouse, Perry J. The rich young ruler. ₁A play in three scenes.₁ (In his: Bible dramas in the pulpit. Philadelphia ₁cop. 1926₁. 8°. p. 113–125.)   **NBM**
Based on Matthew xix: 16–29.
Time: Feast of the Tabernacles. Place: Bethany, two miles from Jerusalem.
Characters: Jesus, Lazarus, a rich young ruler.

CURE OF THE BLIND AT JERICHO

Modern Play

Russell, Mary M. The outcome of a secret. ₁In two scenes.₁ (In her: Dramatized Bible stories for young people. New York ₁cop. 1921₁. 8°. p. 35–38.)
Based on Matthew xx: 29–34 and Mark x: 46–52. Bartimeus, the main character.

ZACCHÆUS

Modern Plays

Claggett, Ralph P. "The half of my goods"; an Easter play ₁in three acts₁. (International journal of religious education. Chicago, 1930. f°. v. 6, March, 1930, p. 27–30, 52.)

———— New York ₁cop. 1930₁. 24 p. 8°.

Githens, Harry W. An unexpected guest. ₁In three scenes.₁ (In his: New Testament stories dramatized. Cincinnati ₁cop. 1929₁. 12°. p. 65–75.)
Zaccheus, chief character.

Moulton, Arthur W. Across the table. ₁Jesus and Zaccheus.₁ (In his: It came to pass. Boston, 1916. 12°. p. 9–21.)   **ZFHK**
Based on Luke xix: 1–10.

Osgood, Phillips Endecott. Outcast; the hated chief publican of Jericho entertains a self-invited guest at his richly laden table. ₁In one scene.₁ illus. (In his: Pulpit dramas. New York and London, 1929. 12°. p. 75–88.)
NAFM

Stackhouse, Perry J. The conversion of a dishonest tax-collector. ₁A play in four scenes.₁ (In his: Bible dramas in the pulpit. Philadelphia ₁cop. 1926₁. 8°. p. 87–99.) **NBM**
Time: 30 A. D. Place: Jericho.
Characters: Jesus, Zaccheus, commissioner of taxes, and others.

THE TALENTS

Miracle Play

Processus talentorum. ₁Towneley play no. 24.₁ (In: The Towneley mysteries. London, 1836. 8°. p. 233–243.)   **CA (Surtees)**
Surtees Society. Publications. [v. 3.]
Also printed in 1897 (ed. England) in Early English Text Society, Extra series no. 71 *(The Towneley plays),* p. 279–292, *NCE (Early).*

HOOPER, E. S. Processus torturum; a suggested emendation. (Athenæum. London, 1904. 4°. Aug. 27, 1904, p. 284.)   * **DA**
Points out that the play has no connection with the Parable of the Talents, but deals with the disposal of the seamless robe of Christ. W. A. Geldart in the *Athenæum* for Sept. 3, p. 321, offers "Processus talorum" and "Processus aleatorum" as two other possible emendations.

Modern Plays

Edland, Elisabeth. The parable of the talents. ₁In two scenes.₁ (In her: Children's dramatizations. Boston ₁cop. 1926₁. 12°. p. 39–47.)

Whitman, Eleanor Wood. Bible parables in pantomime. Boston: Walter H. Baker Co., 1924. 23 p. 16°.
Contents: Moral courage. The use of talents.
"The use of talents" is reprinted from *Church school,* New York, 1923, v. 4, p. 506–508.

New Testament Plays — Ministry of Jesus,
  continued

THE TRIUMPH OF PALM SUNDAY

Miracle Plays

The **Entry** into Jerusalem upon the Ass.
The skynners play. ₍York play no. 25, 545
lines.₎ (In: Lucy T. Smith, editor, York
plays. Oxford, 1885. 8°. p. 201–218.)
NAFM

Christ's entry into Jerusalem. The cor-
vysors playe... ₍Chester play no. 14.₎(In:
The Chester plays, ed. Wright. London:
Shakespeare Society, 1847. 8°. v. 2, p. 1–17.)
NAFM (Chester)

Also printed in 1916 with title "Christ's visit to
Simon the Leper" (ed. Matthews) in Early English
Text Society, Extra series no. 115 *(The Chester plays,
part 2),* p. 249–265, *NCE (Early).*

The **Entry** into Jerusalem. ₍Coventry play
no. 26.₎ (In: Ludus Coventriæ, ed. Halliwell.
London: Shakespeare Society, 1841. 8°.
p. 252–258.) **NAFM (Coventry)**

Also printed in 1922 (ed. Block) in Early English
Text Society, Extra series no. 120 *(Ludus Coventriæ),*
p. 237–243, lines 179–337, *NCE (Early).*

Modern Plays

Githens, Harry W. The magic touch. ₍In
three scenes.₎ (In his: New Testament
stories dramatized. Cincinnati ₍cop. 1929₎.
12°. p. 84–96.)

Healing of two lepers.
The author places this narrative, which is not Biblical,
during the time of Christ's entry into Jerusalem.

Smith, H. Augustine. The city beautiful.
₍A historical pageant in six scenes.₎ New
York: Centenary Conservation Committee,
Methodist Episcopal Church ₍cop. 1919₎. 15 p.
8°.

The first two scenes are Biblical: Jerusalem of King
David and Jerusalem on Palm Sunday. Presented at
the centenary celebration, Columbus, Ohio, June 20 to
July 13, 1919.

Whiting, Isabel Kimball. On the road of
Jerusalem. ₍In three scenes.₎ (In her: Dramatic services of worship. Boston, 1925. 8°.
p. 137–164.) **NBM**

TRIBUTE TO CÆSAR

Modern Play

Smith, Roy L. As Mary told it. ₍In one
scene.₎ (In his: Pantomimes and pageants
for pulpit use. Cleveland ₍cop. 1928₎. 8°.
p. 51–55.)

Mary, a Judaean peasant, relates to a neighbor
woman the story of the dispute in the temple between
Jesus and his enemies over the question, "Is it lawful
to pay tribute to Caesar?"

THE WIDOW'S MITE

Modern Play

Glover, Lydia May. Love's utmost. ₍In two
scenes.₎ Based on the story found in Mark
12. 41–44. (In her: Friends of Jesus. New
York ₍cop. 1923₎. 8°. p. 35–44.)
NAC p.v.113, no.5

Jerusalem, close to the Temple, during the latter
part of Jesus' earthly life.

THE WISE AND FOOLISH VIRGINS

Modern Plays

Crew, Helen Coale. The door. ₍In one act.₎
(In: Eleven short Biblical plays. New York,
1929. 12°. p. 45–69.) **NBL p.v.216**

Edland, Elisabeth. The wise and foolish
virgins. ₍In one scene.₎ (Church school. New
York, 1923. 4°. v. 4, p. 463–464.)

Fisher, Fay. The wise and foolish virgins,
in one act. (In: T. W. Galloway, The dramatic instinct in religious education. Boston
₍cop. 1922₎. 12°. p. 60–67.)

Lacey-Baker, Marjorie. The wise and the
foolish virgins, a dramatization of the parable
as found in the twenty-fifth chapter of St.
Matthew. ₍In one scene.₎ New York: Womans Press ₍cop. 1927₎. 12 p. 12°. (Program
series. no. 19.)

Lobingier, Mrs. Elizabeth Erwin (Miller).
The wise and foolish virgins. ₍A dramatization in one scene by the Dramatic Club of
the Hyde Park Church of Disciples, Chicago,
Ill.₎ (In her: The dramatization of Bible
stories. Chicago ₍cop. 1918₎. 12°. p. 99–100.)
* YIR

Russell, Mary M. The value of preparation. ₍In two scenes.₎ (In her: Dramatized
Bible stories for young people. New York
₍cop. 1921₎. 8°. p. 59–62.)

Based on Matthew xxv: 1–13.

THE SUPPER AT BETHANY

Modern Plays

Bale, John. Simon the Leper: a drama by
Bishop Bale, named only in his catalogue
of his own works.

See W. C. Hazlitt, *Manual,* p. 211.

Moulton, Arthur W. The precious ointment. ₍Jesus and the woman.₎ (In his: It
came to pass. Boston, 1916. 12°. p. 51–61.)
ZFHK

New Testament Plays, continued

THE PASSION OF JESUS

Miracle Plays

The Conspiracy

The **Conspiracy** to take Jesus. The cutteleres ₁play₁. ₁York play no. 26, 294 lines.₁ (In: Lucy T. Smith, editor, York plays. Oxford, 1885. 8°. p. 219–232.) **NAFM**

Conspiracio et capcio. ₁Towneley play no. 20.₁ (In: The Towneley mysteries. London, 1836. 8°. p. 172–189.) **CA (Surtees)**
Surtees Society. Publications. [v. 3.]
Also printed in 1897 (ed. England) in the Early English Text Society, Extra series no. 71 *(The Towneley plays)*, p. 204–227, NCE *(Early)*.

The **Council** of the Jews. ₁Coventry play no. 25.₁ (In: Ludus Coventriæ, ed. Halliwell. London: Shakespeare Society, 1841. 8°. p. 239–251.) **NAFM (Coventry)**
Also printed in 1922 (ed. Block) in Early English Text Society, Extra series no. 120 *(Ludus Coventriæ)*, p. 225–237, NCE *(Early)*. In Block's edition the play is divided into three separate episodes: Prologue of Demon, lines 1–124; Prologue of John the Baptist, lines 1–40; and The Council of the Jews, lines 1–178.

The Last Supper

The **Last** Supper. The baxteres ₁play₁. ₁York play no. 27, 187 lines.₁ (In: Lucy T. Smith, editor, York plays. Oxford, 1885. 8°. p. 233–239.) **NAFM**

FRANK, Grace. St. Martial of Limoges in the York plays. (Modern language notes. Baltimore, 1929. 4°. v. 44, p. 233–235.) **RAA**

Christ betrayed. The bakers playe... ₁Chester play no. 15.₁ (In: The Chester plays, ed. Wright. London: Shakespeare Society, 1847. 8°. v. 2, p. 18–32.) **NAFM (Chester)**
Also printed in 1916 (ed. Matthews) in Early English Text Society, Extra series no. 115 *(The Chester plays, part 2)*, p. 265–279, NCE *(Early)*, and in F. J. Tickner, editor, *Earlier English drama from Robin Hood to Everyman*, New York [cop. 1929], p. 191–200, NCO *(Tickner)*.

The **Passion**. ₁In ten scenes.₁ ₁Chester plays 15–17, adapted.₁ (In: Chester miracle plays, done...by I. and O. Bolton King. London ₁1930₁. 12°. p. 119–155.) **NAFM**

The **Last** Supper. ₁Coventry play no. 27.₁ (In: Ludus Coventriæ, ed. Halliwell. London: Shakespeare Society, 1841. 8°. p. 259–279.) **NAFM (Coventry)**
Also printed in 1922 (ed. Block) in Early English Text Society, Extra series no. 120 *(Ludus Coventriæ)*, p. 243–262, lines 338–892 (The Last Supper and The Conspiracy of the Jews and Judas), NCE *(Early)*.

Gethsemane

The **Agony** and the betrayal. The cordewaners ₁play₁. ₁York play no. 28, 301 lines.₁ (In: Lucy T. Smith, editor, York plays. Oxford, 1885. 8°. p. 240–253.) **NAFM**
Lines 1–152 are printed with the title "Christ's agony in the garden" in M. S. Mooney, *A rosary of*

mystery plays, Albany, 1915, p. 63–68, **NAFM** *(Mooney)*.

The **Betraying** of Christ. ₁Coventry play no. 28.₁ (In: Ludus Coventriæ, ed. Halliwell. London: Shakespeare Society, 1841. 8°. p. 280–287.) **NAFM (Coventry)**
Also printed in 1922 (ed. Block) in Early English Text Society, Extra series no. 120 *(Ludus Coventriæ)*, p. 262–269, lines 893–1084, NCE *(Early)*, and in J. Q. Adams, editor, *Chief pre-Shakespearean dramas*, Boston, 1924, p. 175–178, * R–NCO.

Jesus Before Caiaphas

Peter denies Jesus. Jesus examined by Caiaphas. The bowers and flecchers ₁play₁. ₁York play no. 29, 398 lines.₁ (In: Lucy T. Smith, editor, York plays. Oxford, 1885. 8°. p. 254–269.) **NAFM**

Coliphizatio. ₁Towneley play no. 21.₁ (In: The Towneley mysteries. London, 1836. 8°. p. 190–202.) **CA (Surtees)**
Surtees Society. Publications. [v. 3.]
Also printed in 1897 (ed. England) in Early English Text Society, Extra series no. 71 *(The Towneley plays)*, p. 228–242, NCE *(Early)*.

The **Passion**. The flechars, bowyers, coopers, and stringers playe... ₁Chester play no. 16.₁ (In: The Chester plays, ed. Wright. London: Shakespeare Society, 1847. 8°. v. 2, p. 33–50.) **NAFM (Chester)**
Also printed in 1916 (ed. Matthews) in Early English Text Society, Extra series no. 115 *(The Chester plays, part 2)*, p. 280–296, lines 1–384, NCE *(Early)*.

The **Trial** of Christ. ₁Coventry play no. 30.₁ (In: Ludus Coventriæ, ed. Halliwell. London: Shakespeare Society, 1841. 8°. p. 293–307.) **NAFM (Coventry)**
Also printed in 1922 (ed. Block) in Early English Text Society, Extra series no. 120 *(Ludus Coventriæ)*, p. 274–287, NCE *(Early)*. The Block edition divides the play into five episodes: lines 70–172 (The trial of Christ before Annas and Caiaphas), lines 173–204 (Peter's denial), lines 205–236 (The death of Judas), lines 237–356 (The trial of Christ before Pilate), and lines 357–465 (The trial of Christ before Herod).
Reprinted in J. Q. Adams, editor, *Chief pre-Shakespearean dramas*, Boston, 1924, p. 179–186, * R–NCO, and in F. J. Tickner, editor, *Earlier English drama from Robin Hood to Everyman*, New York [cop. 1929], p. 200–212, NCO *(Tickner)*.

Jesus Before Herod

Trial before Herod. The lytsteres ₁play₁. ₁York play no. 31, 406 lines.₁ (In: Lucy T. Smith, editor, York plays. Oxford, 1885. 8°. p. 292–306.) **NAFM**

King Herod. ₁Coventry play no. 29.₁ (In: Ludus Coventriæ, ed. Halliwell. London: Shakespeare Society, 1841. 8°. p. 288–292.) **NAFM (Coventry)**
Also printed in 1922 (ed. Block) in Early English Text Society, Extra series no. 120 *(Ludus Coventriæ)*, p. 269–273, NCE *(Early)*. Block prints the play in two episodes: lines 1–40 (Prologue of the doctors) and lines 1–69 (King Herod).

New Testament Plays — The Passion of Jesus,
continued

Miracle Plays, continued

Pilate's Wife

The **Dream** of Pilate's wife: Jesus before
Pilate. The tapiteres and couchers [play].
[York play no. 30, 546 lines.] (In: Lucy T.
Smith, editor, York plays. Oxford, 1885. 8°.
p. 270–291.)   **NAFM**

FREEMAN, Eva. A note on play xxx of the
York cycle. (Modern language notes. Baltimore, 1930. 8°. v. 45, p. 392–394.)   **RAA**

Pilate's wife's dream. [Coventry play no.
31.] (In: Ludus Coventriæ, ed. Halliwell.
London: Shakespeare Society, 1841. 8°.
p. 308–310.)   **NAFM (Coventry)**
Also printed in 1922 (ed. Block) in Early English
Text Society, Extra series no. 120 *(Ludus Coventriæ)*,
p. 287–289, lines 466–542, NCE (Early).

Judas Iscariot

Second accusation before Pilate: remorse
of Judas, and purchase of Field of Blood.
The cokis and watirlederes [play]. [York play
no. 32, 389 lines.] (In: Lucy T. Smith, editor,
York plays. Oxford, 1885. 8°. p. 307–319.)
                                          NAFM

Suspentio Judæ. [Towneley play no. 32.]
(In: The Towneley mysteries. London, 1836.
8°. p. 328–330.)   **CA (Surtees)**
Surtees Society. Publications. [v. 3.]
Also printed in 1897 (ed. England) in Early English Text Society, Extra series no. 71 *(The Towneley
plays)*, p. 393–396, NCE (Early).
"This poem is added in a more modern hand, apparently about the commencement of the sixteenth century."

The Condemnation

The **Second** trial before Pilate continued;
the Judgment of Jesus. The tyllemakers
[play]. [York play no. 33, 485 lines.] (In:
Lucy T. Smith, editor, York plays. Oxford,
1885. 8°. p. 320–336.)   **NAFM**
Reprinted in two separate episodes: lines 1–386 (The
scourging of Jesus by Pilate's order) and lines 387–
485 (The crowning of Jesus with thorns) in M. S.
Mooney, *A rosary of miracle plays*, Albany, 1915,
p. 69–86, NAFM (Mooney).

Flagellacio. [Towneley play no. 22.] (In:
The Towneley mysteries. London, 1836. 8°.
p. 203–215.)   **CA (Surtees)**
Surtees Society. Publications. [v. 3.]
Also printed in 1897 (ed. England) in Early English
Text Society, Extra series no. 71 *(The Towneley plays)*,
p. 243–257, NCE (Early).

The **Condemnation** and crucifixion of
Christ. [Coventry play no. 32.] (In: Ludus
Coventriæ, ed. Halliwell. London: Shakespeare Society, 1841. 8°. p. 311–328.)
                                NAFM (Coventry)
Also printed in 1922 (ed. Block) in Early English
Text Society, Extra series no. 120 *(Ludus Coventriæ)*,
p. 289–305, NCE (Early). Printed by Block in four
episodes: lines 543–657 (The trial of Christ and thieves
before Pilate), lines 658–677 (The condemnation and

scourging), lines 678–725 (The procession to Calvary),
and lines 726–970 (The crucifixion).
Reprinted in F. J. Tickner, editor, *Earlier English
drama from Robin Hood to Everyman*, New York [cop.
1929], p. 212–224, NCO (Tickner).

The Bearing of the Cross

Christ led up to Calvary. The shermen
[play]. [York play no. 34, 350 lines.] (In: Lucy
T. Smith, editor, York plays. Oxford, 1885.
8°. p. 337–348.)   **NAFM**
Reprinted in M. S. Mooney, *A rosary of mystery
plays*, Albany, 1915, p. 87–98, NAFM (Mooney).

The Crucifixion

Crucifixio Cristi. The pynneres (and paynters) play. [York play no. 35, 300 lines.] (In:
Lucy T. Smith, editor, York plays. Oxford,
1885. 8°. p. 349–358.)   **NAFM**
"The words 'and paynters' are added in a later hand."
Reprinted in M. S. Mooney, *A rosary of mystery
plays*, Albany, 1915, p. 99–108, NAFM (Mooney).

WALLIS, J. P. R. The miracle play of 'Crucifixio Cristi' in the York cycle. (Modern language review. Cambridge, 1917. 8°. v. 12,
p. 494–495.)   **NAA**

Crucifixio. [Towneley play no. 23.] (In:
The Towneley mysteries. London, 1836. 8°.
p. 216–232.)   **CA (Surtees)**
Surtees Society. Publications. [v. 3.]
Also printed in William Marriott, *A collection of
English miracle-plays*, Basel, 1838, p. 137–160, NAFM;
in 1897 (ed. England) in Early English Text
Society, Extra series no. 71 *(The Towneley plays)*,
p. 258–278, NCE (Early); and in "Everyman" with
other interludes including eight miracle plays, London
[1909], p. 99–119, NAFM.

KIRTLAN, Ernest J. B. A little drama of the
crucifixion, being a modernization of the
"Crucifixion" in the Towneley mystery plays
circa 1400 A. D. London: Epworth Press
[1920]. 45 p. 16°.   **NCO p.v.471, no.3**

The **Crucifixion.** The iremongeres playe.
[Chester play no. 17.] (In: The Chester plays,
ed. Wright. London: Shakespeare Society,
1847. 8°. v. 2, p. 51–70.)   **NAFM (Chester)**
Also printed in 1916 (ed. Matthews) in Early English Text Society, Extra series no. 115 *(The Chester
plays, part 2)*, p. 296–317, lines 385–892, where it is
printed as part of no. 16, NCE (Early).

The **Passion** of Our Lord Jesus Christ.
Journey to Jerusalem. — Healing the blind
and lame. — Simon the Leper. — Caiaphas
receives Judas. — The Last Supper. — The
betrayal. — Peter denies Christ. — Judas
hangs himself. — Jesus before Pilate. —
Beelzebub goes to Pilate's wife. — The Condemnation. — The Smith. — Crucifixion. —
Terror of Lucifer. — Descent from the Cross.
[3242 lines.] (In: Edwin Norris. editor. Ancient Cornish drama. Oxford, 1859. 8°. v. 1,
p. 222–470.)   **NAFM**
The history of Jesus from the Temptation to the
Crucifixion.
For an analysis of the drama see Henry Jenner in
the *Celtic review*, Edinburgh, 1907, v. 4, p. 46–50,
NDK.

*New Testament Plays — The Passion of Jesus,
continued*

Miracle Plays, continued

The Burial

Mortificacio Cristi <and burial of Jesus>.
The bocheres [play]. [York play no. 36, 416
lines.] (In: Lucy T. Smith, editor, York
plays. Oxford, 1885. 8°. p. 359–371.)
NAFM

The **Burial** of Christ. [Coventry play no.
34.] (In: Ludus Coventriæ, ed. Halliwell.
London: Shakespeare Society, 1841. 8°.
p. 331–337.)   **NAFM (Coventry)**
Also printed in 1922 (ed. Block) in Early English
Text Society, Extra series no. 120 *(Ludus Coventriæ)*,
p. 307–312, *NCE (Early)*. Block prints the play in
three episodes: lines 1018–1110 (The embassy to Pilate
of Joseph of Arimathea), lines 1111–1131 (The episode
of Longeus), and lines 1132–1175 (The descent from
the cross and the burial).

Modern Plays

GRANT, Percy Stickney. The Passion play
on the American stage. illus. (Theatre. New
York, 1902. 4°. v. 2, May, 1902, p. 10–12.)
† **NBLA**

Allotte de la Fuÿe, Marguerite. The Lord
of death. (Le Maitre de la Mort.) A play in
a prologue and three acts. Translated by
Louis N. Parker... London, New York:
Longmans, Green and Co., 1923. 95 p., 1 pl.
12°.   **NKP**
The action takes place at Capernaum in Galilee, and
Jerusalem.

Bates, Esther Willard. The two thieves;
a play in one act for Easter even... Boston:
Walter H. Baker Co., 1925. 17 p. 12°.
Also printed in *Religious dramas,* New York [cop.
1926], v. 2, p. 53–65, *NAFM.*

Bellamy, Frederica Lefevre. Darkness and
dawn; a mystery play for Easter even...
[In three episodes.] New York: The Womans Press [cop. 1925]. 38 p. 12°.
"Deals with the thoughts and experiences of children and
humble folk during...the Crucifixion...Entombment
and...Resurrection."
Reprinted in R. H. Schauffler and A. P. Sanford,
editors, *Plays for our American holidays,* New York,
1928, [v. 1], p. 273–292, *NASH.*

Benson, Robert Hugh. The upper room;
a drama of Christ's passion. With illustrations. London: Longmans, Green & Co.,
1914. 72 p. illus. 12°.
In a prologue and three acts.

———— —— London: Longmans, Green and
Co., 1915. 72 p. illus. 12°.   **NAFM**
Introduction by Cardinal Bourne.

———— —— London: Longmans, Green and
Co., 1924. 72 p. illus. 12°.
Produced at Columbia, Mo., by students of Stephens
College and the University of Missouri, Easter season,
1928. See notice, accompanied with illustrations, in
Drama, Mount Morris, Ill., Oct., 1928, v. 19, p. 19,
NAFA.

Bergen, Francis. The death of Pilate. [In
one scene.] (Yale literary magazine. New
Haven, 1911. 8°. v. 76, p. 282–291.)   **STG**
Pilate and his servant, Ananias, near a mountain
side in Switzerland.

Boulter, Benjamin Consitt. The mystery
of the Passion. [In ten scenes.] London: Society for Promoting Christian Knowledge,
1923. viii, 9–63 p. 12°.
"Every Good Friday the Mystery is played in the
Church of St. Silas — the Martyr, Kentish Town, for
which it was written."

Browne, Maurice, and ELLEN (VAN VOLK-
ENBURG) BROWNE. The King of the Jews; a
Passion play. (The Drama. Chicago, 1916.
8°. v. 6, p. 496–529.)   **NAFA**
Among the characters are Caiaphas, Judas, and
Pilate.
First produced at the Chicago Little Theatre, June
20, 1916.
Design for "The King of the Jews" by C. Raymon
Johnson on p. 1 of the magazine.

Cleveland, Mrs. Harlan. At the tomb. [A
dramatic poem.] (In her: Vigil of the first
Easter. Milwaukee [cop. 1927]. 12°. p. 19–
25.)   **NBF p.v.98**
Midnight, at the Garden of the Sepulchre; one of
the twelve, speaking.

Constantine, grand duke of Russia. The
King of the Jews, a sacred drama, from the
Russian of "K. P." (the Grand Duke Constantine) by Victor E. Marsden, M.A. [In four
acts and in verse.] London, New York: Cas-
sell and Company, Ltd., 1914. viii p., 1 l.,
159(1) p. 12°.   ** **QDK**
The action takes place at Jerusalem and occupies
one week, from the entry of Jesus into Jerusalem to
the day of His resurrection.

Creagh-Henry, May. "Greater love hath
no man"; a Passion play. [In three scenes.]
London: Society for Promoting Christian
Knowledge, 1930. 31 p. new ed. 12°.
Previously printed in her *Four mystical plays,* Lon-
don, 1924, p. 19–38, *NCR.*

Ehrmann, Max. Jesus; a Passion play.
New York, London: The Baker & Taylor
Co. [cop. 1915.] 282 p. 12°.   **NBM**
Act I. The cleansing of the Temple. Act II. Dispu-
tations in the Temple. Act III. Gethsemane. Act IV.
The trial before Pilate. Act V. The Resurrection.
"The persons who founded Christianity are here
stripped of supernatural embellishment; and they are
represented as simple, real, ardent Orientals in the
throes of a great and impending tragedy."

Felix, F. Pontia: the daughter of Pilate.
Drama in IV acts. Baltimore: John Murphy
Co., 1899. 52 p. 12°.   **NBL p.v.18, no.15**
Among the characters are Petronilla, Jewish maiden
(St. Pertronilla), Ruth and Miriam, Jewish girls.

Ferris, Ralph Hall. Tempted in all points;
a historical play in three acts and three
visions. Boston: The Gorham Press [cop.
1915]. 157 p. 12°. (American dramatists
series.)   **NBM**
A play on the Passion of Christ who is here called
Jeshua bar-Joseph. A love story is woven into the
drama, with Ruth, niece of Annas, hopelessly in love
with Jeshua. Judas, Peter, John, James, Caiaphas,
Annas, and others not mentioned in the Bible, figure
in the play.

New Testament Plays — The Passion of Jesus,
continued

Modern Plays, continued

Fromme Arbeiter vom hl. Joseph Cala-sanctius, Vienna. The Passion and death of Our Lord; a Biblical drama in five acts, translated from the German by Joseph W. Berg. Milwaukee, Wis.: Catholic Dramatic Company, 1927. 47 p. 12°.
This Passion play by the Congregation for Christian Workmen of St. Joseph of Calasanz, Vienna, was produced in German in St. Joseph's Parish Hall, Milwaukee, during Lent, 1927.

Gairdner, William Henry Temple. The last Passover night. London: Society for Promoting Christian Knowledge; New York: The Macmillan Co., 1921. 16 p. 12°.
Drama in one act. **ZAE p.v.130, no.4**
The scene is in Jerusalem on Good Friday eve.

Glover, Lydia May. In his strength. ₁In three scenes.₁ (Based on Matthew 4. 18–20; 16. 15–20; John 13. 14; Mark 14. 66–72; John 21.) (In her: Friends of Jesus. New York ₁cop. 1923₁. 8°. p. 68–80.) **NAC p.v.113, no.5**
Scene: Jerusalem and Capernaum, immediately before and after the crucifixion.

Goold, Marshall N. Saint Claudia; a religious drama; with an introduction by Mrs. A. Starr Best, drawings by F. Liley Young ... Boston, Chicago: The Pilgrim Press ₁cop. 1925₁. xiii, 62 p. illus. 12°.
In three acts. **NBF p.v.74, no.5**
Characters: Pilate, Judas, Miriam a sweet Hebrew singer, etc.
Reprinted in *Religious drama*, New York ₁cop. 1926₁, v. 2, p. 149–207, *NAFM*.
Intended to show the influence of the life of Jesus on the Roman mind. First produced by the Pilgrim Players of Evanston, Ill. Prize play of the 1924 Religious Drama Contest held by the Drama League of America.

Gosselink, Sara Elizabeth. The light of the cross. ₁In two scenes.₁ A sacred drama ... Franklin, Ohio, Denver, Colo.: Eldridge Entertainment House, Inc., cop. 1925. 15 p. 12°. (Eldridge church entertainments.)

Greene, Henry Copley. Pontius Pilate; a mystery play ₁in three acts₁. (In his: Pontius Pilate, Saint Ronan of Brittany, Théophile; three plays in verse. New York, 1903. 8°. p. 1–47.)
Reviewed by E. L. Halliwell in *Holy Cross purple,* Worcester, Mass., 1903, v. 15, p. 369–373, *STG.*

Gregory, Isabella Augusta (Persse), lady. The story brought by Brigit: a Passion play in three acts. London & New York: G. P. Putnam's Sons ₁1924₁. 3 p.l., 97 p. 12°. **NCR**
"Our [Irish] tradition and that of Gaelic Scotland, speak of St. Brigit as the foster-mother of Christ... She succoured both Blessed Mother and Child when they were brought here by a Heavenly Messenger for safety in Herod's time." The play was first produced at the Abbey Theatre, Dublin, in April, 1924, during Holy Week.

Groot, Hugo de. Christs Passion. A tragedie. ₁By Hugo de Groot.₁ With annotations. ₁Translated by George Sandys.₁ London: J. Legatt, 1640. 6 p.l., 124 p. 8°. **Reserve**

—— Christ's Passion. A tragedy. With annotations. By George Sandys. London: Printed by J. R. for T. Basset, 1687. 7 p.l., 107(1) p., 2 l., 6 pl. 2. ed. 8°. **NHM**

—— Christ's Passion. A tragedy. With annotations. ₁By George Sandys.₁ London: Printed, and are to be Sold by Jos. Blare, 1698. 8 p.l., 107(1) p., 2 l., 1 pl. 12°. **NHM**
Also printed in George Sandys, *Poetical works,* London, 1872, v. 2, p. 407–502, *NCL (Sandys).*

Harnwell, Anna Jane (Wilcox), and ISA-BELLE J. MEAKER. The alabaster box. ₁A play in three acts.₁ (In: Religious drama. New York ₁cop. 1926₁. 8°. v. 2, p. 209–234.) **NAFM (Religious)**
Time: Good Friday, A.D. 34.

Harris, Frank. The King of the Jews. ₁A playlet in one act.₁ (English review. London, 1911. 8°. v. 8, p. 8–12.) ***DA**
Reprinted in his *Stories of Jesus the Christ,* New York, 1919, p. 24–27.

Hitchcock, Mary S. Follow thou me; a Biblical drama, in four acts... Chicago: T. S. Denison & Co. ₁cop. 1929.₁ 90 p. 12°.
Time: 33 A. D. Plot deals with the adventures of one Daniel, a follower of Jesus, in his efforts to remain true to his faith. In the background lurks the shadow of the Crucifixion. Among the characters are Pontius Pilate and Caiaphas.

Hoge, Peyton Harrison. The divine tragedy; a drama of the Christ... New York, Chicago: Fleming H. Revell Company ₁cop. 1905₁. 146 p. 8°. **NBM**
In five acts and in verse.
Notes, p. 127–146.

Kaye-Smith, Sheila. The shepherd of Lattenden; a Passion play in six scenes. (In her: Saints in Sussex. New York ₁1927₁. 8°. p. 83–136.) **NCM**
Cf. "A study in Passion plays," by Stanley B. James in *Month,* London, 1927, v. 149, p. 309–312, ** DA.*

Kennedy, Charles Rann. The terrible meek; a one-act stage play for three voices; to be played in darkness... New York and London: Harper & Bros., 1912. 4 p.l., 44 p., 1 port. 8°. **NCR**
The three voices are those of a mother mourning her son, a captain wondering why he had been chosen to murder the son, and a soldier-executioner, who insists that he but obeyed orders. The son in question is Jesus Christ.
Reprinted in his *A repertory of plays for a company of seven players and two short plays for smaller casts,* Chicago [1930], p. 607–636, *NCR.*
Produced by Winthrop Ames at the Little Theatre, New York, March 19, 1912, with Edith Wynne Matthison as the mother.
For notices of the production see Louis Lipsky in the *American Hebrew,* New York, 1912, v. 90, p. 614, ** PBD;* the *Theatre magazine,* New York, 1912, v. 15, p. 139–140, *NBLA;* and the *New York dramatic mirror,* New York, March 27, 1912, v. 67, p. 6, ** DA.*

SIBLEY, H. Norman. "The terrible meek." An instance of the use of drama in an Easter service built around specific problems. (Religious education. Chicago, 1927. 8°. v. 22, p. 775–780.) **SSA**

New Testament Plays — The Passion of Jesus,
continued

Modern Plays, continued

Kenzel, Francis L. Calvary; a play of the Passion of Our divine Saviour for male characters. Boston: Redemptorist Fathers, 1908. 72 p. 16°. **NAC p.v.99, no.1**

In seven acts.

—— The mystic rose; or, Pilate's daughter, a scriptural drama for female characters. Boston: Redemptorist Fathers, 1905. 3 p.l., (1)6–62 p. 16°.

Title from Library of Congress.

Produced at Parson's Theatre, Hartford, Conn., March 19, 1914, by the Alban Company. See *New York dramatic mirror,* New York, March 25, 1914, v. 71, p. 17, * *DA.*

Produced in New York at the Century Opera House, Nov. 25, 1914. For reviews see *New York dramatic mirror,* Dec. 2, 1914, v. 72, p. 8–9, * *DA,* and *The Theatre,* New York, v. 21, 1915, p. 44. In the latter magazine on p. 14 is an illustration of a scene from the play.

For reviews of various productions see the Warren C. Cawley collection of about 100,000 clippings on plays, box Pa-Pit, *MWE.*

Klein, John W. Pontius Pilate; Biblical drama in five acts. London: Arthur H. Stockwell ₁1923₁. 267 p. 12°. **NCR**

GORDON, Franklin. Pontius Pilate whitewashed. To make a Biblical drama author warps history to suit his bias. (The American Hebrew. New York, 1923. f°. v. 114, p. 217, 222.) ***PBD**

Lamers, William Mathias. Calvary, a drama of the sacred Passion of Our Lord, in three acts. Sleepy Eye, Minn.: Catholic Dramatic Company, 1928. 35 p. 12°.

Besides the usual Biblical characters, Joachim, a rich Jew, and his son Daniel are introduced.

Mansel, Ronald. The third shepherds' play ₁in one act₁. (In: Eleven short Biblical plays. New York, 1929. 12°. p. 205–222.) **NBL p.v.216**

Elias, who was present at the Crucifixion, tells what he then saw to his fellow shepherds.

Marquis, Don. The dark hours; five scenes from a history. Garden City, N. Y.: Doubleday, Page & Company, 1924. 6 p.l., 155 p. 8°. **NBM**

A play based on the betrayal, the trial, and calvary of Jesus of Nazareth.

Reviewed by D. de Sola Pool in *Jewish forum,* New York, 1925, v. 8, p. 378, * *PBD;* in *New York Times book review,* v. 30, p. 16, †† *NAA.*

Marson, Gerald Francis. ...Jerusalem & Bethany. A Passion play ₁in a prologue and twenty scenes₁. Written and arranged by G. F. Marson. London: Society for Promoting Christian Knowledge ₁1928₁. viii, 9–63 p. 12°. (Parish plays. no. 14.) **NAFH p.v.42**

Masefield, John. Good Friday; a dramatic poem. (Fortnightly review. London, 1915.

8°. new series, v. 98 ₁v. 104₁, p. 993–1018.) ***DA**

The subject of the play is the story of the Crucifixion, from the moment when Jesus has been sent back to Pilate by Herod for trial, to the death on the Cross. The prisoner, Jesus, is not shown on the stage, but only suggested. The scene is outside the Roman citadel in Jerusalem. One of the characters, the leader of the rabble, is designated as a Jew.

—— Good Friday; a play in verse. Lollingdon Cholsay, Berkshire: the author, 1916. 77 p. 12°. **NCR**

—— —— London: William Heinemann ₁cop. 1917₁. vii, 79 p. 12°.

Also printed in his *Good Friday, and other poems,* New York, 1916, p. 1–64, *NCM; Poems and plays,* New York, 1918, v. 2, p. 581–640, *NCG;* and *Verse plays,* New York, 1925, p. 1–52, *NCR.*

Reviewed (by William Archer) in *The Nation,* New York, 1917, v. 104, p. 487, * *DA;* and in *The Spectator,* London, 1917, v. 119, p. 771–772, * *DA.*

—— The trial of Jesus. ₁In three acts.₁ London: William Heinemann, Ltd. ₁1925.₁ 4 p.l., 116 p. 12°.

The play was privately performed at the Music Room, Boars Hill, on May 9, 1925.

Reviewed (by John Freeman) in *The Bookman,* London, 1925, v. 69, p. 104–105, †* *GDD; The Mask,* Florence, Italy, 1926, v. 12, p. 163, *NAFA; The Nation & The Athenæum,* London, 1925, v. 38, p. 152, * *DA;* by Mary Willcox in *New York Herald-Tribune, Books,* New York, v. 2, Feb. 7, 1926, p. 18, † *NAA; New York Times book review,* Oct. 4, 1925, p. 5, † *NAA; Times literary supplement,* London, 1925, v. 24, p. 671, † *NAA.*

—— —— New York: The Macmillan Company, 1925. 4 p.l., 116 p. 8°. **NCR**

Oberammergau Passion Play. The Ober-Ammergau Passion play: illustrated. Giving the origin of the play, and history of the village and people, a full description of the scenes and tableaux of the seventeen acts of the drama, and the songs of the chorus, in German and English. By John P. Jackson... London: Sold by W. H. Smith & Son, etc., 1880. x, 86 p. illus. 8°.

—— The Passion play as it is played today, at Ober Ammergau in 1890, by William T. Stead... London: "Review of Reviews" ₁1890₁. viii, (1)10–130 p. illus. 4°. **NAFH p.v.32**

Text in German and English in parallel columns. "Specimens of the music," p. 18–21.

—— The story that transformed the world; or, The Passion play at Ober Ammergau in 1890 by William T. Stead. The complete German and English text of the Passion play in parallel columns... London: Office of the "Review of Reviews" ₁pref. 1890₁. 160 p. illus. sq. 4°. † **NAFM (Stead)**

The Passion play, p. 31–154.

—— Passion play at Ober-Ammergau with the whole drama translated into English, and the songs of the chorus, in German and English by the author of "Charles Lowder" ₁Maria Trench₁. London: W. H. Allen & Co., 1890. xiii p., 1 l., 128 p., 1 map. sq. 8°. **NAFM**

New Testament Plays — The Passion of Jesus,
continued

Modern Plays, continued

Oberammergau Passion Play, *continued*

—— The Ober-Ammergau Passion play:
giving the origin of the play, and history of
the village and people, a full description of
the scenes and tableaux of the seventeen
acts of the drama, and the songs of the
chorus, in German and English by John P.
Jackson... Munich: Wm. Hummel, 1890.
iv p., 3 l., 105(1) p., 1 l. illus. 8°.

—— —— Munich: C. A. Seyfried & Co.,
1900. 140 p. illus. 8°. **NAFM (Jackson)**

—— Complete official-text of the Oberammergau Passion play. From the manuscript
of the Very Rev. J. A. Daisenberger, and
published for the first time... Dialogue
translated by Frances Manette Jackson.
Oberammergau: G. Lang, 1900. 157 p. illus.
8°. **NAFM (Jackson)**
Bound with: J. P. Jackson, The Ober-Ammergau
Passion play. Munich, 1900.

—— The Passion play at Ober Ammergau.
1900. The complete German text of the play
with English translation printed side by
side... Copiously illustrated, with a complete series of the photographs of 1890.
[Edited by W. T. Stead.] London: Mewbray
House [pref. 1900]. viii, 309 p. illus. 12°.
NAFM

—— The Passion play at Ober-Ammergau; translated into English and the songs
of the chorus in German and English, with a
history of the play, by Maria Trench... London: K. Paul, Trench, Trübner & Co., Ltd.,
1900. (i)iv–xv, 128 p. sq. 8°.
NAFM (Oberammergau)

—— The Passion-play of Oberammergau;
translated from the German text with an
historical introduction by Montrose J. Moses.
New York: Duffield and Company, 1909.
lxviii p., 1 l., 218 p., 1 port. 8°.

—— The Passion play at Ober Ammergau,
1910. The complete official German text of
the play, with English translation printed
side by side... Copiously illustrated with a
complete series of the photographs of the
players of 1910, tableaux, scenes, &c. London: Stead's Pubg. House. Munich and Ober
Ammergau: C. A. Seyfried & Comp. [1910.]
384 p. illus. 12°. **NAFM**
"The English version is not only a translation. It
gives a running description of the scenes."

—— The Passion play at Ober Ammer-
gau. A sacred play in three divisions with
24 tableaux. With employment of the old
texts written by J. A. Daisenberger...
Oberammergau: Verlag der Gemeinde Ober-
ammergau [1910]. 144, 32 p. illus. 12°.
NAC p.v.159
On cover: The complete official text of the Passion
Play at Oberammergau.
"Ober Ammergau and its environs:" p. 1–32 at end.

—— The Passion play at Ober-Ammergau.
Translated into English and the songs of the
chorus in German and English, by Maria
Trench. London: Kegan Paul, Trench,
Trübner & Co., Ltd., 1910. 3 p.l., (i)x–xv(i),
96 p. sq. 8°.
Arranged in seventeen acts.

—— —— London: K. Paul, Trench, Trübner & Co., Ltd. [1930.] 2 p.l., 96 p. 8°.

—— The Passion play of Oberammergau.
Revised edition of the 1930 celebration.
Translated from the original German text,
with an introduction by Montrose J. Moses.
New York: Duffield & Co. [cop. 1930.]
lxxxvi p., 1 l., 222 p., 1 port. 8°.
NAFM (Oberammergau)
Bibliography, p. 205–222.
Casts of characters for the 1890–1930 productions,
p. vii–xv.

—— ...The Passion play at Oberammergau, 1930. The complete English text of the
play... London: Ernest Benn, Ltd.;
Munich: C. A. Seyfried & Co. [1930.] 309 p.
illus. 12°. **NAFM (Oberammergau)**
At head of title: Stead's guide.
The text of the play, p. 113–247.
For a full bibliography of the Oberammergau Passion play see Maximilian J. Rudwin, *A historical and
bibliographical survey of the German religious drama,*
Pittsburgh, 1924, p. 118–143, NGA.

BOGENRIEDER, Franz Xaver. Oberammer-
gau and its Passion play, 1930. Munich:
Knorr & Hirth [1929]. 171 p. illus. 8°.
NAFM
"Official guide, edited by the community."
Synopsis, p. 120–138.

BUTLER, William Allen. Oberammergau,
1890... New York: Harper & Brothers,
1891. 46 p. illus. 4°.
A poem descriptive of the play.
Notes, p. 41–46.
"I have...endeavored to give, in simple English
verse...the impressions created by witnessing its performance."

EPSTEIN, Mordecai. The Passion play at
Oberammergau. Reflections of a Jewish
spectator. illus. (The American Hebrew.
New York, 1922. f°. v. 111, p. 650, 659.)
* PBD

Is the Passion play [at Oberammergau]
anti-Semitic? (Literary digest. New York,
1930. 4°. v. 106, Sept. 13, 1930, p. 21.) *** DA**
An abstract of several articles.

KRAUSKOPF, Joseph. A Rabbi's impressions of the Oberammergau Passion play;
being a series of six lectures. — With three
supplemental chapters bearing on the subject.
Philadelphia: E. Stern & Co., Inc., 1908.
4 p.l., 11–226 p. 12°. *** PGB**
Reviewed by Israel Abrahams in *Jewish chronicle,*
London, Aug. 23, 1901. p. 20. *PBE,* and by A. H.
Japp in *London quarterly review,* London, 1902, v. 97,
p. 304–305, *DA.*

New Testament Plays — The Passion of Jesus,
continued

Modern Plays, continued

MacColl, Malcolm. The Ober-Ammergau
Passion play (reprinted by permission from
"The Times"). With some introductory remarks on the origin and development of
miracle plays... 4th ed., with a new appendix... London: Rivingtons, 1871. 112 p.
16°.   **NAFM (MacColl)**
"Appendix...Description of the scenes and tableaux
of the play," p. 89–112.

—— —— Oxford and Cambridge: Rivingtons, 1880. viii, 104 p. 6. ed. 12°.

The "MYSTERY play" in the mountains.
(Jewish chronicle. London, 1880. 4°. May
21, 1880, p. 10; May 28, 1880, p. 10.) **＊PBE**

RICHARDS, Louise Parks-. Oberammergau;
its Passion play and players. A 20th century
pilgrimage to a modern Jerusalem and a new
Gethsemane... Munich: Piloty & Loehle,
1910. 258 p., 1 l. illus. 2. ed. 12°.
                              NAFM (Richards)
"Synopsis with running commentary," p. 48–106.

—— Oberammergau; its Passion play and
players. A xx century pilgrimage to a
modern Jerusalem and a new Gethsemane...
Revised and enlarged with a complete synopsis of the play, stories of the actors, official photographs... Munich: Piloty &
Loehle, July, 1922. 120 p., 1 l. illus. 3. ed.
12°.   **NAFM (Richards)**
Synopsis, p. 15–74.

SCHOEBERL, Franz. The Passion-play at
Ober-Ammergau... Translated by Cath-
erine Thompson. Eichstätt, Stuttgart:
Kruell, 1871. 1 p.l., 94 p. 16°.
                              NAFM (Schoeberl)

SCHROEDER, Joseph.   ...Oberammergau
and its Passion play... 2nd revised edition
from official sources... Translated from the
German by Reginald Maxse. Munich: Heinrich Korff, 1910. 168 p. illus. 12°.
                              NAC p.v.160
At head of title: Guide to Oberammergau.
Synopsis of the play, p. 138–162.

SHORT, Josephine Helena. Oberammergau... New York: T. Y. Crowell & Co.
₍cop. 1910.₎ x, 84 p. illus. 12°.
                              NAFM (Short)
Synopsis of the play, p. 41–80.

SNOWMAN, Leonard Victor. The Oberammergau Passion play. A Jewish view. (Jewish chronicle. London, 1922. f°. Sept. 1,
p. 17.)   **†＊PBE**

Oldfield, Claude Houghton. In the house
of the high priest; a drama in one act, by
Claude Houghton. London: The C. W.
Daniel Company ₍1923₎. 57 p. 12°. (Plays
for a people's theatre. 23.) **NCO p.v.501, no.3**
Time: day of the Crucifixion, in the house of
Caiaphas.

Osborn, Laughton. Calvary. ₍A tragedy
in five acts.₎ (In his: Calvary — Virginia.
New York, 1867. 12°. p. 1–80.)   **NBM**
Also printed in his *Dramatic works,* New York,
1868, v. 1, p. 1–80, *NBM.*

—— The new Calvary. MDCCCLXIX. (In his:
Meleagros; The new Calvary; tragedies...
New York, 1871. 8°. p. 59–164.)   **NBM**
"I have written one Calvary to suit the prejudices...
of others. It failed to attract attention. I write one now
to satisfy myself." — *From the Preface.*
Notes to New Calvary, p. 111–164.

Osgood, Phillips Endecott. Gabbatha;
Procula upbraids her husband Pontius Pilate, for his craven betrayal of a righteous
man. ₍In one scene.₎ (In his: Pulpit dramas.
New York and London, 1929. 12°. p. 129–
139.)   **NAFM**

—— Naked evil. Gamaliel the Rabban
studies Barabbas the robber. ₍In one scene.₎
(In his: Pulpit dramas. New York and London, 1929. 12°. p. 141–158.)   **NAFM**

—— "Without a city wall." Simeon of
Cyrene at last returns to his two lads ₍and
tells them his impressions of the Crucifixion₎.
₍In one scene.₎ (In his: Pulpit dramas. New
York and London, 1929. 12°. p. 159–176.)
                                  NAFM
Palmer, A. W. Washington. Evangel
scenes. No. 1, Palm Sunday. London: Faith
Press, Ltd. ₍192–?₎ 12 p. 12°.

—— Evangel scenes. No. 2, Passion. London: Faith Press, Ltd. ₍192–?₎ 19 p. 12°.

Palmer, F. C. Pilate; a tragedy in four
acts. ₍London:₎ E. J. Burrow & Co., Ltd.,
1923. 149 p. 12°.   **NCR**

Palmieri, Aurelio. On the slopes of Cal-
vary; a religious drama in three acts and in
prose, dealing with the passion of Our Lord
Jesus Christ. Translated from the Italian
by Henry Grattan Doyle... Philadelphia,
Pa.: Our Lady of Good Counsel Printing
School, 1917. 4 p.l., (1)12–73 p., 1 l. 8°.
Title from Library of Congress.
The latest revised and only authorized version of the
drama, "On the slopes of Calvary" (Sulle pendici del
Calvario). It was originally copyrighted in manuscript
(but never printed) under title, "A child of Judea."

Roberts, Kenneth Lewis. One of the early
ones. ₍In one scene.₎ (In his: Antiquamania
... Garden City, N. Y., 1928. 8°. p. 191–
198.)   **MAVC**
Scene is laid in an "old antique-shop in old Jerusalem." A few years after the Crucifixion, the antique-
dealer in an effort to sell a piece of the cross to pros-
pective buyer.

Rockwell, Ethel Gesner. It is I; a Biblical
drama... Boston: Walter H. Baker Co.,
cop. 1927. 27 p. 12°.
Time: Passion week. Place: Jerusalem.

New Testament Plays — The Passion of Jesus, continued

Modern Plays, continued

Roosmale-Cocq, Reginald Edmund Charlton. Yesterday and to-day; a mystical play [in a prologue and two acts] of the Passion ... With a preface by P. N. Waggett... London: A. R. Mowbray & Co., Ltd. [1927.] 55(1) p. 12°.

Presented by the Guild of S. Mary, at S. James', Islington, England.

Sandkuehler, Henry G. "The Leper"; a new scriptural Passion play in a prologue, four acts, and an epilogue... Based on the narrative poem "The Leper" by Nathaniel Parker Willis... Baltimore: Redemptorist Fathers, cop. 1926. 64 p. 12°.

NBL p.v.147, no.15

Shiner, Mrs. L. M. "The son of man"; a sacred drama [in a prologue, three scenes and an epilogue]... London: Faith Press; Milwaukee: Morehouse Pub. Co. [1930.] 4 p.l., 23 p. 12°.

Sundelof-Asbrand, Karin. The kingdom; a presentation of the Easter story. [In three episodes.] New York: The Womans Press [cop. 1929]. 20 p. 4°.

Entry into Jerusalem; Betrayal; Crucifixion and Resurrection.

Thomas, John Allen. The trees, a fantasy [in one scene]. (Yale literary magazine. New Haven, 1921. 8°. v. 86, p. 187–192.) **STG**

David and Rachel, children, in a forest. The trees in conversation as to which of them is to serve as the cross for the Crucifixion.

Torrence, Frederic Ridgely. Simon the Cyrenian. (In his: Graany Maumee, The rider of dreams, and Simon the Cyrenian. New York, 1917. 8°. p. 77–111.) **NBM**

Based on the incident narrated in Luke 23:26. "It has been the author's design that all the characters in this play [all Biblical] should be represented by persons entirely or partly of Negro blood; and this intention has been carried out in the original stage production."

Trask, Mrs. Kate (Nichols). Without the walls; a reading play, by Katrina Trask... New York: The Macmillan Company, 1919. 3 p.l., 3–196 p. 12°. *** PSQ**

Scene: in and near the house of Jahdiel the Pharisee in Jerusalem. Time: the year 33 A.D.

Wallace, William. The divine surrender, a mystery play. London: Elliot Stock, 1895. 2 p.l., 77 p. 8°.

In three parts. "In the first, 'the Paschal eve,' will be found the Jewish opinion. The second, 'Pilate's wife,' shows the realistic bend of the Roman mind. In the third, 'the Resurrection,' the mystic element is set forth." The action takes place at Jerusalem, between the Paschal eve and the morning of the Resurrection.

Wilder, Thornton Niven. Now the servant's name was Malchus. (In his: The angel that troubled the water, and other plays. New York, 1928. 12°. p. 105–113.) **NBM**

Woods, William Hervey. The dream of Pilate's wife. [In one act and three scenes.] [Richmond: Published for the author by Presbyterian Committee of Publication, cop. 1922.] 24 p. 8°.

Among the characters is Rachel, a Jewish maid, nurse to Procula's son.

Yates, Elizabeth Hall. The laughing child. (In her: Small plays for small casts. Philadelphia, 1926. 12°. p. 55–69.) **NBM**

Three children and the stranger (Jesus), at Gethsemane just before the Crucifixion.

Yeats, William Butler. Calvary. (In his: Four plays for dancers. New York, 1921. 12°. p. 69–82.) **NCR**

Note on Calvary, p. 133–138.
The persons of the play are: three musicians, Jesus, Lazarus, Judas, and three Roman soldiers all masked.
Reprinted in his *Plays and controversies*, London, 1923, p. 399–411, *NCR*.

Judas Iscariot

Chait, Sabbatia. "Illusion and grave"; or, "Reign in heaven and reign on earth." A drama in four acts. 75 l. 4°. **† NCOF**

Typewritten ms.

De Kay, John Wesley. The maid of Bethany; a tragedy in three acts. Munich: K. Wolff [1929]. 155 p., 1 port. 12°. **NBM**

"My conception of the leading characters...was published in my book 'The weaver' in 1908. The story was again written...in the form of a drama, which in 1910 was printed [as Judas by J. de Kay, with a version in French by J. Coudurier de Chassaigne. New York: F. Rullman.] and produced...under the title of 'Judas' [in French, at the Globe Theatre, New York, Dec. 29, 1910 with Sarah Bernhardt in the title role]."

Reviewed in *New York dramatic mirror*, New York, 1911, v. 65, Jan. 4, p. 11, * *DA*. "The drama is a little more than a string of episodes... Mr. De Kay, in the fashion of Paul Heyse, represents Judas animated by jealous love for Mary Magdalene."

Githens, Harry W. For thirty pieces of silver. [In three scenes.] (In his: New Testament stories dramatized. Cincinnati [cop. 1929]. 12°. p. 97–104.)

Gleason, Charlotte. Judas Iscariot, a play arranged in a prologue and three acts, by Charlotte Gleason, with an introduction by Clara Fitch. New York: George H. Doran Company [cop. 1922]. xiii p., 1 l., 17–46 p. 12°. (The Drama League series.)

NBL p.v.86, no.4

"The prologue introduces us to Judson Burke, an American business man, in love with Anne Hartnett, a lovely product of the twentieth century, who, during her work in France, gained a vision. The author cleverly links the present time and place to the time of Christ, 31 A.D., and to the wonders that happened on the Sea of Galilee. The similarity of the man of power to-day and that of Judas Iscariot, the rich merchant and rug buyer of Jerusalem, is skillfully depicted." — *From Introduction.*

Goodman, Kenneth Sawyer. Dust of the road, a play in one act. Chicago: The Stage Guild [cop. 1912]. 21 p. 12°. (Stage Guild plays.) **NBL p.v.28**

Judas Iscariot, disguised as a tramp, is one of the characters.
Produced by the Wisconsin Dramatic Society, 1913, with Thomas Wood Stevens as the Tramp.
Also printed in George A. Goldstone, compiler, *One-*

New Testament Plays — The Passion of Jesus,
    continued

Modern Plays, continued

act plays, Boston [cop. 1926], p. 247–265, *NAFH*, and
in Fred Eastman, compiler, *Modern religious dramas*,
New York [1928], p. 179–195, *NBL*.

Horne, Richard Henry. Judas Iscariot, a
miracle play, in two acts. (In his: Judas
Iscariot...with other poems. London, 1848.
8°. p. 1–43.)
    See the introduction for the author's comments on
the character of Judas.
    "The crime of Judas is revolting enough without
supposing him to have been actuated by thirty pieces of
silver." The author embraces the view of Archbishop
Whately that Judas believed Jesus to be the true Messiah, who was about to establish a splendid and powerful
kingdom. Judas believed that Jesus, when brought before the Romans, would assert himself as leader of the
temporal kingdom and thus fulfil the hopes of the multitude. It was most natural for Judas to expect that
Jesus would so conduct himself. This departure, in the
interpretation of the character of Judas, has lately
been adopted in numerous works, both theological and
literary, but Horne, among dramatists, was the first to
represent Judas in this more sympathetic view.
    Also printed in his *Bible tragedies*, London [1881],
p. 105–191.
    Reviewed in *The Athenæum*, London, April 29, 1848,
p. 431–432, * *DA; The Examiner*, London, 1849, p. 820–
821, * *DA;* and in *Howitt's journal*, London, 1848, v. 3,
p. 316–318, * *DA.*

Jeffers, John Robinson. Dear Judas. (In
his: Dear Judas, and other poems. New
York, 1929. 8°. p. 9–49.)   **NBI**
    Reviewed by Frederick W. Dupee in *Miscellany*,
New York, March, 1930, v. 1, p. 34–36, * *DA;* by
Rolfe Humphries in *The New republic*, New York, 1930,
v. 61, p. 228–229, * *DA;* by Yvor Winters in *Poetry*,
Chicago, 1930, v. 35, p. 278–281, * *DA;* and by Eda
Lou Walton in *Symposium*, New York, 1930, v. 1,
p. 135–136, * *DA.*

Kemp, Harry. Judas. [A drama.] New
York: M. Kennerley, 1913. 3 p.l., 5–254 p.
12°.   **NBM**
    In four acts.
    Reviewed in the *Boston Evening Transcript*, June
14, 1913, part 3, p. 4, col. 5–6, * *A,* and in *New York
Times book review*, New York, Aug. 3, 1913, v. 18,
p. 421, † *NAA.*

Kendon, Frank. A life and death of
Judas Iscariot. [A dramatic poem.] London:
John Lane, The Bodley Head, Ltd. [1926.]
x, 111 p. 12°.   **NCM**

Lawrence, Charles Edward. Poor Judas.
[In one scene.] (Cornhill magazine. London,
1929. 8°. v. 66, p. 503–510.)   * **DA**

Manley, William Ford. Judas Iscariot; a
dramatic poem in six scenes. (In his: A
second book of Bible dramas. New York
[cop. 1930]. 8°. p. 29–43.)   **NBM**

Milligan, J. Lewis. Judas Iscariot; a poetic
play [in three scenes]. Toronto: The Ryerson Press, 1929. 31 p. 8°.
    Produced at the Westminster-Central United Church,
Toronto, on Good Friday, 1929.

Moore, Thomas Sturge. Judas. London:
G. Richards, Ltd., 1923. 110 p., 1 l. 8°.
    In verse.
    Reviewed by R. C. Trevelyan in *Nation & The
Athenæum*, London, 1923, v. 33, p. 812, * *DA;* in the

Saturday review, London, 1923, v. 136, p. 362–363,
* *DA;* and by John Freeman in *The Spectator*, London,
1923, v. 131, p. 391, * *DA.*

—— —— Chicago: Covici-McGee Co.,
1924. 109 p., 1 l. 8°.   **NCM**

Moulton, Arthur W. The silver pieces.
[The woman and Judas Iscariot.] (In his: It
came to pass. Boston, 1916. 12°. p. 63–77.)
    ZFHK

Nagle, Brother Urban. Barter; a drama in
four acts, by Urban Nagle, o. P., with an introduction by Mrs. A. Starr Best; the winning Biblical play of the 1928 Drama League-
Longmans, Green and Co. playwriting contest. London, New York: Longmans, Green
and Co., 1929. xiv, 92 p. 12°.   **NCR**
    The action of the play begins on the afternoon of
Holy Thursday and ends just after Jesus Christ dies
on the Cross — twenty-four hours later.

Norwood, Robert Winkworth. The man of
Kerioth. [A play in five acts.] With an in-
troduction by Robert Johnston... New
York: George H. Doran Co. [cop. 1919.] xxiii,
23–138 p. 12°.   **NCR**
    The Man of Kerioth is Judas, the central figure of
the play.
    Selections are printed in *Robert Norwood*, by Albert
Durrant Watson, Toronto [1923], p. 67–69, *NCM*
(Norwood).

Oldfield, Claude Houghton. Judas; a
tragedy in three acts, by Claude Houghton
... London: C. W. Daniel, Ltd., 1922.
127(1) p. 12°. (Plays for a people's theatre.
17.)   **NCO p.v.486, no.4**

—— —— Boston: The Four Seas Company [cop. 1923]. 133 p. 8°.   * **PST**

Osgood, Phillips Endecott. Judas of
Kerioth drives a bargain. [In one scene.] illus.
(In his: Pulpit dramas. New York and Lon-
don, 1929. 12°. p. 107–128.)   **NAFM**

Pepler, Hilary Douglas C. Judas; or, The
betrayal, a play in one act, with prologue and
epilogue... Ditchling, Sussex: St. Dominic
Press, 1926. 3 p.l., 15 p., 1 l. 8°.
    no. 60 of an edition limited to 200 copies.
    Confines itself to Judas's temptation by Caiaphas.
    Reviewed in *Times literary supplement*, London,
1926, v. 25, p. 341, † *NAA.*
    Cf. "A study in Passion plays," by Stanley B.
James in *Month*, London, 1927, v. 149, p. 314–315,
* *DA.*

—— —— Pilate. A Passion play [in two scenes].
Ditchling [Eng.]: St. Dominic's Press, 1928.
4 p.l., 47 p. 24°.   * **KP (St. Dominic's)**
    The characters are from the New Testament: four
Romans, four Judeans, Conscience, and the Reader.
The recitative parts assigned to the Choir are in Latin.
Includes much of the text of *Judas*, 1926.

Rowley, Samuel, and WILLIAM BORNE.
Judas: a play written by Samuel Rowley and
William Borne. Acted in 1601. Not printed.
    See W. C. Hazlitt, *Manual*, p. 123.

Stackhouse, Perry J. The man of Kerioth.
A tragedy [in four scenes]. (In his: Bible

New Testament Plays — The Passion of Jesus,
continued

Modern Plays, continued

dramas in the pulpit. Philadelphia [cop.
1926]. 8°. p. 127–138.) **NBM**
Place: house of Shaphan, a priest connected with the
Temple at Jerusalem. Characters: Judas, "The man
of Kerioth," Shaphan, friend of Judas, Simon, a
disciple of Jesus, the Voice of Jesus, etc.

Starkey, Digby Pilot. Judas; a tragic mystery [in five acts]. Dublin: W. Curry, Jr., and
Co., 1843. xxxi p., 2 l., 230 p. 8°.
Notes, p. 183–230.

Tavani, F. The tragedy of Judas Iscariot;
a modern drama in a prologue and five acts
by Gregorio d'Arci [pseud.]. Amersham: R.

Norrie, The Mascot Press [1926]. 72 p. 12°.
NCR
The appendix, p. 63–72, is the author's explanation
of his conception of Judas.
Place: Capernaum and Jerusalem.

Thurston, Ernest Temple. Judas Iscariot;
a play in four acts. London and New York:
G. P. Putnam's Sons [1923]. 6 p.l., 3–122 p.
8°. **NCR**
Produced by the Repertory Players at the New Scala
Theatre, London, Nov. 23, 1924, with Campbell Gullan
as Judas Iscariot. See *The Era, London,* Nov. 26, 1924,
v. 88, p. 1, † *NAFA.*

Van Norman, C. Elta. Betrayal, a play [in
one act]. (In: Eleven short Biblical plays.
New York, 1929. 12°. p. 1–23.) **NBL p.v.216**

Wilder, Thornton Niven. Hast thou considered my servant Job? (In his: The angel
that troubled the waters, and other plays.
New York, 1928. 12°. p. 127–133.) **NBM**
The characters are Christ, Satan, and Judas.

THE DESCENT INTO HELL

Miracle Plays

Burstein, Sona Rosa. The Harrowing of
Hell. (Folk-lore. London, 1928. 8°. v. 39,
p. 113–132.) **ZBA**

Mall, Eduard. Zu "The Harrowing of
Hell." (Jahrbuch für romanische und englische Sprache und Literatur. Leipzig, 1874.
8°. Bd. 13, p. 217–221.) **NAA**

Young, Karl. The Harrowing of Hell in
liturgical drama. (Wisconsin Academy of
Sciences, Arts & Letters. Transactions.
Madison, 1910. 8°. v. 16, part 2, p. 889–947.)
* EA

The Harrowing of Hell. The sadilleres
play. [York play no. 37, 408 lines.] (In: Lucy
T. Smith, editor, York plays. Oxford, 1885.
8°. p. 372–395.) **NAFM**

Extractio animarum ab Inferno. [Towneley
play no. 25.] (In: The Towneley mysteries.
London, 1836. 8°. p. 244–253.) **CA (Surtees)**
Surtees Society. Publications. [v. 3.]
Also printed in William Marriott, *A collection of
English miracle-plays,* Basel, 1838, p. 161–174, *NAFM;*
in 1897 (ed. England) in Early English Text Society,
Extra series no. 71 *(The Towneley plays),* p. 293–305,
NCE (Early); in Lucy T. Smith, editor, *York plays,*
Oxford, 1885, p. 372–395, *NAFM;* and in "*Everyman,*"
with other interludes including eight miracle plays,
London [1909], p. 137–152, *NAFM.*

The **Harrowing** of Hell. The cookes plaie
... [Chester play no. 18.] (In: The Chester
plays, ed. Wright. London: Shakespeare
Society, 1847. 8°. v. 2, p. 71–83.)
NAFM (Chester)
Introduces the idea that Enoch and Elijah inhabited
Paradise during the interval of their vanishing from
earth and descent of Christ into Hell.
Also printed in 1916 (ed. Matthews) in Early English Text Society, Extra series no. 115 *(The Chester
plays, part 2),* p. 318–331, *NCE (Early);* in J. Q.
Adams, editor, *Chief pre-Shakespearean dramas,* Boston, 1924, p. 187–190, ** R – NCO;* and in F. J. Tickner,
editor, *Earlier English drama from Robin Hood to
Everyman,* New York [cop. 1929], p. 224–232, *NCO
(Tickner).*

The **Descent** into Hell. [Coventry play no.
33.] (In: Ludus Coventriæ, ed. Halliwell.
London: Shakespeare Society, 1841. 8°.
p. 329–330.) **NAFM (Coventry)**
Also printed under title "The Descent into Hell of
Anima Christi" in 1922 (ed. Block) in Early English
Text Society, Extra series no. 120 *(Ludus Coventriæ),*
p. 305–307, lines 971–1017, *NCE (Early).*

The **Harrowing** of Hell; a miracle play.
Now first printed from Ms. Harl. 2253. [London,] 1836. 16 p. 12°. (In: J. P. Collier, Five
miracle plays.)

The **Harrowing** of Hell, a miracle-play
written in the reign of Edward the Second,
now first published from the original manuscript in the British Museum, with an introduction, translation, and notes by James Orchard Halliwell. London: J. R. Smith, 1840.
33 p. 8°. **NAFM**
Middle English text and modern version on opposite
pages.

The **Harrowing** of Hell. Das altenglische
Spiel von Christi Höllenfahrt. Neu herausgegeben von Dr. Eduard Mall. Breslau:
Maruschke & Berendt, 1871. 2 p.l., 55 p. 12°.
NAFH p.v.38
The text of the Harl. ms. is given, with the textual
variants in the Bodl. Digby and the Auchinleck ms.
Adapted and translated into modern English in
F. M. Capes, "The poetry of the early mysteries,"
Nineteenth century, London, 1883, v. 14, p. 664–673,
* DA. Reprinted in *Eclectic magazine,* New York,
1884, new series, v. 39, p. 10–16, ** DA.*

The **Middle-English** Harrowing of Hell,
and Gospel of Nicodemus. Now first edited
from all the known manuscripts, with introduction and glossary, by William Henry
Hulme. London: K. Paul, Trench, Trübner
& Co., Ltd., 1907 [issued in 1908]. lxx, 150 p.,
1 l. 8°. (Early English Text Society. Extra
series no. 100.) **NCE (Early)**
Contains in three parallel columns the texts of three
manuscripts: Bodleian Digby 86(O); Harl. 2253 ff.

New Testament Plays — The Descent into Hell, continued

Miracle Plays, continued

55b–56b(L); and Auchinleck W. 4I in the Advocates' Library, Edinburgh.

A variant of the prologue in Digby ms. 86, discovered by Halliwell, is given by him in *Reliquiæ antiquæ*, London, 1841, v. 1, p. 253, *NCE.*

The Harl. text is also printed in A. W. Pollard, *English miracle plays*, Oxford, 1890, p. 166–172, *NAFM.* Library also has the 1904, 1923, and 1927 editions of Pollard.

Reviewed by A. Schröer in *Englische Studien*, Leipzig, 1909, Bd. 40, p. 263–265, *RNA.*

The **Harrowing** of Hell, a miracle play, printed from the Auchinleck manuscript.

[Edinburgh, 1835?] 16 p. 12°. (In: J. P. Collier, Five miracle plays. London, 1836.)

CRAMER, Julius. Quelle, Verfasser und Text des altenglischen Gedichtes "Christi Höllenfahrt." Halle a.S.: Bernhardt Karras, 1896. 1 p.l., 38 p., 1 l. 8°.

That "Cynewulf is not the author of 'the Harrowing of Hell,'" is the conclusion of Cramer concerning the authorship of this dramatic poem.

Modern Play

Chamberlin, Henry Harmon. The harrowing of Hell. A mystery. [A dramatic poem.] (In his: Poems. Worcester: Privately printed [Commonwealth Press], 1911. 8°. p. 71–79.)   **NBI**

THE RESURRECTION

Miracle Plays

The Four Great Cycle Plays

POLLARD, Alfred William. Easter plays. (Guardian. London, 1889. f°. v. 44, part 1, p. 799–800.)   † **ZPD**

The **Resurrection**; fright of the Jews. The carpenteres play. [York play no. 38, 453 lines.] (In: Lucy T. Smith, editor, York plays. Oxford, 1885. 8°. p. 396–420.)   **NAFM**

Reprinted in J. M. Manly, *Specimens of the pre-Shaksperean drama*, Boston, 1897, v. 1, p. 153–169, *NCO.* This and no. 39 are printed in M. S. Mooney, *A rosary of mystery plays*, Albany, 1915, p. 109–127, *NAFM (Mooney).*

Jesus appears to Mary Magdalene after the Resurrection. The wynedrawers play. [York play no. 39, 149 lines.] (In: Lucy T. Smith, editor, York plays. Oxford, 1885. 8°. p. 421–425.)   **NAFM**

Resurrectio Domini. [Towneley play no. 26.] (In: The Towneley mysteries. London, 1836. 8°. p. 254–269.)   **CA (Surtees)**

Surtees Society. Publications. [v. 3.]

Also printed in 1897 (ed. England) in Early English Text Society, Extra series no. 71 (*The Towneley plays*), p. 306–325, *NCE (Early)*, and in J. Q. Adams, editor, *Chief pre-Shakespearean dramas*, Boston, 1924, p. 191–198, * *R* – *NCO.*

The lines of this play which partly parallel the York play no. 38 are given in Lucy T. Smith, editor, *York Plays*, Oxford, 1885, p. 396–420, *NAFM.*

The **Resurrection**. The skynners playe... [Chester play no. 19.] (In: The Chester plays, ed. Wright. London: Shakespeare Society, 1847. 8°. v. 2, p. 84–100.) **NAFM (Chester)**

Also printed in 1916 (ed. Matthews) in Early English Text Society, Extra series no. 115 (*Chester plays, part 2*), p. 331–351, *NCE (Early).* Lines 433–527 of this edition do not appear in the Shakespeare Society edition of 1843–47.

Lines 1–420 are again printed in F. J. Tickner, editor, *Earlier English drama from Robin Hood to Everyman*, New York [cop. 1929], p. 232–244, *NCO (Tickner).*

The **Resurrection**. [Coventry play no. 35.] (In: Ludus Coventriæ, ed. Halliwell. Lon-

don: Shakespeare Society, 1841. 8°. p. 338–353.)   **NAFM (Coventry)**

Also printed in 1922 (ed. Block) in Early English Text Society, Extra series no. 120 (*Ludus Coventriæ*), p. 312–327, lines 1176–1343 (The guarding of the Sepulchre), lines 1344–1415 (The harrowing of Hell), lines 1416–1479 (The Resurrection and appearance to the Virgin), and lines 1480–1647 (The compact of the soldiers and Pilate), *NCE (Early).*

The **Three** Maries. [Coventry play no. 36.] (In: Ludus Coventriæ, ed. Halliwell. London: Shakespeare Society, 1841. 8°. p. 354–359.)   **NAFM (Coventry)**

Also printed under title "The announcement to the three Maries" in 1922 (ed. Block) in Early English Text Society, Extra series no. 120 (*Ludus Coventriæ*), p. 327–333, *NCE (Early).*

Christ appearing to Mary. [Coventry play no. 37.] (In: Ludus Coventriæ, ed. Halliwell. London: Shakespeare Society, 1841. 8°. p. 360–363.)   **NAFM (Coventry)**

Also printed in 1922 (ed. Block) in Early English Text Society, Extra series no. 120 (*Ludus Coventriæ*), p. 333–337, *NCE (Early).*

Ancient Cornish Drama

The **Resurrection** of Our Lord Jesus Christ. Imprisonment of Nicodemus and Joseph. — Harrowing of Hell. — Soldiers guard the tomb. — Resurrection. — Soldiers inform Pilate. — The three Maries at the tomb. — Mary Magdalene informs the Apostles. — Disciples going to Emmaus. — Thomas's unbelief. — Appearance of Jesus. — Death of Pilate. — Ascension. [2646 lines.] (In: Edwin Norris, editor, Ancient Cornish drama. Oxford, 1859. 8°. v. 2, p. 2–199.)   **NAFM**

Lines 679–892 are reprinted in *"Everyman," with other interludes including eight miracle plays*, London [1909], p. 120–127, *NAFM.*

For an analysis of the play see Henry Jenner in *Celtic review*, Edinburgh, 1907, v. 4, p. 50–55, *NDK.*

The Digby Play

Christ's burial and resurrection. A mystery. In two parts, in the Northern dialect. From the Bodleian MS. E Museo 160... (In:

New Testament Plays — The Resurrection,
continued

Miracle Plays, continued

The Digby mysteries. London, 1882. 8°.
p. 169–228.) * **NCK (New)**
New Shakespere Society. [Publications.] Series 7,
[no. 1].
Also printed in 1896 (ed. Furnivall) in Early English Text Society, Extra series no. 70 *(The Digby plays),*
p. 169–226, *NCE (Early).*

SCHMIDT, Karl. Die Digby-Spiele. 3. The
Burial and resurrection of Christ. (Anglia.
Halle a.S., 1885. 8°. Bd. 8, p. 393–404.) **RNA**

A **Mystery** of the burial of Christ. (Reliquiæ antiquæ. Edited by Th. Wright and
J. O. Halliwell. London, 1843. 8°. v. 2,
p. 124–143.) **NCE**

A **Mystery** of the Resurrection. (Reliquiæ
antiquæ. Edited by Th. Wright and J. O.
Halliwell. London, 1843. 8°. v. 2, p. 144–
161.) **NCE**

The Shrewsbury Fragment

The **Three** Maries at the sepulchre.
[Shrewsbury fragment no. 2.] (The Academy.
London, 1890. 4°. v. 37, p. 28.) * **DA**
Also printed in 1897 in J. M. Manly, *Specimens of
the pre-Shaksperean drama,* v. 1, p. xxxi–xxxiii, *NCO;*
in 1909 (ed. Waterhouse) in Early English Text
Society, Extra series no. 104 *(The Non-cycle mystery
plays),* p. 3–4, notes, p. xx–xxiii, *NCE (Early);*
and under the title "The sepulchre" in J. Q. Adams,
editor, *Chief pre-Shakespearean dramas,* Boston, New
York [cop. 1924], p. 73–74, * *R – NCO.*

Quem Quaeritis

Quem quaeritis. The English Quem
Quaeritis from the Regularis Concordia
Monachorum. (In: The Second shepherds'
play; Everyman and other early plays. Boston [cop. 1910]. 16°. p. 1–6.) **NCO p.v.556**

Sepulchrum. <Easter.> (In: J. Q.
Adams, editor, Chief pre-Shakespearean
dramas. Boston, New York [cop. 1924]. 8°.
p. 9–10.) * **R – NCO**
Latin text and parallel English translation.
The Latin text is also given by W. S. Logeman
in *Anglia,* Halle a S., 1891, Bd. 13, p. 427–428, *RNA;*
by J. M. Manly in his *Specimens of pre-Shaksperean
drama,* Boston, 1897, p. xix–xxi, *NCO;* and by Sir
E. K. Chambers in his *The mediaeval stage,* Oxford,
1903, v. 2, p. 306–309, * *R – NAFM.*

The **Ancient** trope called the "Quem
Quæritis" the earliest form of mystery play
combined with the contemporary "Depositio
Crucis" and "Elevatio Crucis." Translated
and adapted [from the Latin]. (In: P. E.
Osgood, Old-time church drama adapted.
New York, 1928. 12°. p. 81–97.) **NAFM**
"The 'Quem Quæritis' is the very earliest form of
liturgical drama... The particular documents of the
'Quem Quæritis' which provide the following version
are the Regularis Concordia of St. Ethelwold, A.D. 965,
a manuscript of the thirteenth century of Orléans,
France, and a Sarum Processional of the fourteenth
century from Dublin." — *p. 84.*

Sepulchrum. <Easter.> (In: J. Q.
Adams, editor, Chief pre-Shakespearean

dramas. Boston, New York [cop. 1924]. 8°.
p. 11–14.) * **R – NCO**
Latin text and parallel English translation.
"From Bodleian ms. 15,846, described as 'a Sarum
processional written in the fourteenth century, and
belonging in the fifteenth century to the Church of
St. John the Evangelist, Dublin.' "

FLOOD, W. H. Grattan. The Irish origin of
the Easter play. (Month. London, 1923. 8°.
v. 141, p. 349–352.) * **DA**

Quem-Quaeritis trope. (In: J. Q. Adams,
editor, Chief pre-Shakespearean dramas.
Boston, New York [cop. 1924]. 8°. p. 3.)
* **R – NCO**
Latin text and parallel English translation.
From the St. Gall ms. 484, of the ninth century.

Semi-dramatic trope <Easter>. (In: J. Q.
Adams, editor, Chief pre-Shakespearean
dramas. Boston, New York [cop. 1924]. 8°.
p. 6.) * **R – NCO**
Latin text and parallel English translation.
From Carl Lange, *Die lateinischen Osterfeiern,* 1887,
p. 24. Performed at Tours, France.

Sepulchrum. <Easter>. (In: J. Q. Adams,
editor, Chief pre-Shakespearean dramas.
Boston, New York [cop. 1924]. 8°. p. 15–
20.) * **R – NCO**
Latin text and parallel English translation.
"The manuscript, of the thirteenth century, is from
Orléans, France. Text from Carl Lange, *Die latein-
ischen Osterfeiern,* 1887, p. 160."

Resurrection of Our Lord

The **Resurrection** of Our Lord... [Lon-
don: Printed for the Malone Society by H.
Hart at the Oxford University Press,] 1912.
viii, 42 p., 2 facsims. ob. 8°. (...The Malone
Society reprints.) **NCO (Malone)**
Fragments of a Protestant Resurrection play "here
printed for the first time." — *cf.* p. v–vi.
"This edition...has been prepared by J. Dover Wilson
and Bertram Dobell with the assistance of the general
editor [W. W. Greg]."
The date of composition of this play is assigned by
the editors to the period of 1530–1560, before the Puri-
tans had arisen to stamp out Miracles. "It is tempting
to father this Resurrection play on him [Bishop Bale]."
Simeon the Zealot is one of the characters.

The **Resurrection** of Our Lord; a Protestant miracle play of the XVI century, found
in the Malone Society Papers, 1912, and
adapted by May Pashley Harris. [In three
scenes, with elaborate directions for staging.]
New York: The Womans Press [cop. 1923].
23 p. 12°.

SCHARPFF, Paulus. Ueber eine englisches
Auferstehungsspiel; ein Beitrag zur Ge-
schichte des Dramas und der Lollarden...
Winnenden, Württ.: Lämmle & Müllerschön
[1920]. 63 p. 8°. **NAC p.v.133, no.5**
Benützte Literatur, p. 58–61.

Modern Plays

YOUR Easter program [with a brief list of
Easter plays and pageants]. (Church school.
New York, 1922. 4°. v. 3, p. 320–321.)

New Testament Plays — The Resurrection, continued

Modern Plays, continued

Agius, Ambrose. The resurrection. (In his: Two mystery plays. London ₁1927₁. 12°. p. 33–59.)   **NCO p.v.554, no.7**
In seven scenes.

Ashton, Leonora Sill. The Resurrection; a mystery play ₁in four scenes₁. Milwaukee: Young Churchman Co. ₁192–?₁ 14 p. 8°.

Bain, Ethel. He is risen, a play for Easter week, in six scenes, with prologue. New York: Avondale Press ₁cop. 1929₁. 31 p. obl. 12°.   **NBM**

Bates, Esther Willard. The tree of life, an Easter pageant ₁in one scene₁. (In: R. H. Schauffler, and A. P. Sanford, editors, Plays for our American holidays. New York, 1928. 12°. ₁v. 1₁, p. 253–271.)
    NASH (Schauffler)
Bayard, Lyman R. The dawning; a pageant of the Resurrection ₁in three scenes₁. ₁Los Angeles: Pageant Publishers,₁ cop. 1921. 46 p., 1 l. illus. 4°.   *** MRH**
Reprinted from *Church school,* New York, 1921, v. 2, p. 209–220.

—— Into Galilee. A pageant of the Easter story carried to Capernaum. ₁In one act.₁ music. (Church school journal. Cincinnati, 1927. 4°. v. 59, p. 145–149.)

—— —— Los Angeles: Pageant Publishers, cop. 1927. 17 p. illus. 8°.
Sequel to the author's *The tidings.*
Capernaum. How the news of the Crucifixion and the Resurrection spread through Palestine.

—— The tidings; a pageant ₁in three acts₁ of the Resurrection. Los Angeles: Pageant Publishers, cop. 1926. 26 p. illus. music. 4°.
Inserted with it is "Directions and suggestions for producing 'The tidings'," cop. 1926. 8 p.

Camp, Constance Willis. The open tomb; an Easter pageant-play, in four short episodes. San Francisco: Banner Play Bureau, Inc., cop. 1928. 20 p., 1 l. music. 8°.
"Depicts…the outstanding incidents of the four-gospel story of the trial, the crucifixion, the burial, and the resurrection."

Chase, Arthur. …Witnesses of the Resurrection; a church play ₁in one act, with prologue and epilogue₁ for Easter. Hartford: Church Missions Pub. Co., 1924. 16 p. illus. 8°. (The church in story and pageant. Publication no. 3.)
Cover-title.

Clarke, George Herbert. "But Mary stood without…weeping." ₁A dramatic poem.₁ (In his: Wayfarings. Chicago, 1901. 8°. p. 29–32.)   **NBI**
Based on John xx: 11ff.

—— "So they ran both together." ₁A dramatic poem.₁ (In his: Wayfarings. Chicago, 1901. 8°. p. 27–28.)   **NBI**
Based on John xx: 4ff.

Conger, Margaret Lynch. Night and morning, an Easter miracle play ₁in one scene₁. New York: Womans Press ₁1925, cop. 1924₁. 16 p. 12°.

Converse, Florence. Thy Kingdom come, a dream for Easter even. ₁In one act.₁ (Atlantic monthly. Boston, 1921. 8°. v. 127, p. 352–362.)   *** DA**
Reprinted in her *Garments of praise,* New York ₁cop. 1921₁, p. 49–96, *NAFM.*

Cooper, Miriam Denness. …He liveth; an Easter mystery. Hartford, Conn.: Church Missions Publishing Co., 1927. 19 p. 8°. (The church in story and pageant. Publication no. 14.)

Copenhaver, Laura Scherer. The children's first Easter. ₁In one scene.₁ music. (In her: Short pageants for Sunday school. Garden City, N. Y., 1929. 8°. p. 94–102.)   **MWF**

Creagh-Henry, May, and D. MARTEN. The unknown warrior; a mystical play ₁in two parts₁. London: Society for Promoting Christian Knowledge ₁1926₁. iv, 5–30 p. 12°.
Scene 2 of part I is the vision, in which the speakers are the Madonna, Mary Magdalene, Peter, and John.

Dallas, Marguerite. Dawn of the third day; an Easter pageant ₁in four parts₁. music. (In: H. Heron, compiler, Pageants for the year. Cincinnati, 1928. 8°. p. 55–68.) **NAFM**

Darling, Annie M. Easter morn. ₁In three scenes.₁ (In: Mary M. Russell, Dramatized Bible stories for young people. New York ₁cop. 1921₁. 12°. p. 39–46.)

Debenham, A. H. Light of the world; a drama of Christ's life and passion in nine episodes ₁with prologue and epilogue₁. London, New York: S. French, Ltd., cop. 1930. 57 p. 12°. (French's acting ed. no. 444.)
Produced at St. Barnabas' Church Hall, London, N. W., April 10 and 13, 1930.

Edland, Elisabeth. Life more abundant; a junior pageant service for Easter. ₁In one scene.₁ illus. (International journal of religious education. Mt. Morris, Ill., 1925. f°. v. 1, March, 1925, p. 52–54.)

Gosse, Edmund William. The tomb in the garden. ₁A dramatic poem.₁ (In: J. A. Blaikie, and E. W. Gosse, Madrigals, songs and sonnets. London, 1870. 16°. p. 93–129.)
    NCM

Grimald, Nicholas. The resurrection of Christ; a new sacred tragi-comedy. (In: L. R. Merrill, The life and poems of Nicholas Grimald. New Haven, 1925. 8°. p. 91–215.)
Yale studies in English. 69.   **NCF**
A Latin tragi-comedy "of the distinctly lyrical type," in a prologue and five acts, prefaced by a long dedicatory letter to a patron. Composed at Brasenose College, Oxford, played there before the students and townsmen, and printed at Cologne, 1543, through the probable effort of John Bale, an exile there at that time. The Latin dedicatory epistle and the text of the

New Testament Plays — The Resurrection, continued

Modern Plays, continued

play are here reprinted with a parallel English translation.
Cf. the editor's preface, *ibid.*, p. 57–89, where he points out that the Ober-Ammergau Passion play is a recasting of Grimald's present piece.
Two copies of the 1543 edition exist in England; one in this country (J. M. Hart, Ithaca, N. Y.).
Among the characters, 23 in number, are four swaggering soldiers of the *miles gloriosus* type, who supply the comic element.
For a synopsis of the play and facsimile reproduction of the original 1543 title-page see F. S. Boas, *University drama in the Tudor age*, Oxford, 1914, p. 26–33, *NCOD*.

TAYLOR, George Coffin. The Christus Redivivus of Nicholas Grimald and the Hegge Resurrection plays. (Modern Language Association of America. Publications. Menasha, Wis., 1926. 8°. v. 41, p. 840–859.)
RAA
"The present discussion is concerned primarily with pointing out those particular portions of the *Christus Redivivus* which are strikingly like the portions of the Hegge [Coventry] plays."

Henderson, Alice (Corbin). Easter morning; a play of the Resurrection for children. (In her: Adam's dream, and two other miracle plays. New York, 1909. 12°. p. 27–40.)
NASH
Scene: before the tomb of Jesus, the third day after the Crucifixion, very early in the morning.

Hinkson, Katherine Tynan. Resurrection: a miracle play [in prologue and two scenes]. (In her: Cuckoo songs. London, 1894. 12°. p. 3–16.)
NCM

Holloway, Pearl. The Lord is risen; a drama of the Resurrection [in two scenes]. With parts for eleven boys or young men and two girls or young women... Cincinnati, O.: Fillmore Music House, cop. 1924. 8 p. 12°.

—— The women's Easter; a drama of the Resurrection for young women or girls [in one scene]... Cincinnati, O.: Fillmore Music House, cop. 1924. 7 p. 12°.

Holt, Laura Davies. The King of the Jews. [An Easter pageant in five scenes, with interludes of popular hymns.] Franklin, O.: Eldridge Entertainment House, Inc., cop. 1926. 15 p. 12°. (Eldridge church entertainments.)

Joplin, Frances Grigsby. Those who saw him living, an Easter service [in one scene]. (International journal of religious education. Mount Morris, Ill., 1926. f°. v. 2, March, 1926, p. 49–51.)
A church service in which there is choir and congregational singing. The judge, a reader, and the witnesses of the Resurrection such as Mary Magdalene, Peter, John, and Thomas, are among the characters.

Kennedy, Anna R. The women from Galilee. [In two scenes.] (In her: Bible plays out of the East. New York, 1929. 8°. p. 55–58.)

Kimball, Rosamond. The Resurrection. An Easter service. (In: Religious dramas. New York: Century Co. [cop. 1923.] 8°. v. 1, p. 103–115.)
NAFM
Reprinted in her *The wooing of Rebekah, and other Bible plays*, New York, 1925, p. 251–266, *ZICS*.

Leamon, Dorothy. Barabbas. (In: Religious dramas. New York: Century Co. [cop. 1926.] 8°. v. 2, p. 267–282.)
NAFM
Time: early dawn of Resurrection day. Place: Jerusalem — road leading to the tomb of Jesus.
Reprinted as a separate: 267–282 p., 1 l.
1 l., at end, Notes on production.

McMaster, A. E. In old Jerusalem. [In one act.] (Sunday school times. Philadelphia, 1928. f°. v. 70, p. 137–138.)
† **ZICN**

Manley, William Ford. The unconquered. [In five scenes.] (In his: A second book of Bible dramas. New York [cop. 1930]. 8°. p. 44–60.)
NBM

Masefield, John. ...Easter, a play for singers. London: William Heinemann, Ltd. [1929.] 4 p.l., 14 p. 8°.
NCR
Reviewed in *Times literary supplement*, London, 1929, v. 28, p. 680, † *NAA*.

Overton, Grace Sloan. The light of life; a dramatic worship service for Easter [in two parts]. (International journal of religious education. Mount Morris, Ill., 1928. 4°. v. 4, March, 1928, p. 24–25, 47.)

—— The living Christ, a dramatic worship service for Easter [in five episodes]. (In her: Dramatic activities for young people. New York [cop. 1927]. 12°. p. 1–22.)
First printed in *International journal of religious education*, Mount Morris, Ill., v. 2, Feb., 1926, p. 28–32.

Palmer, A. W. Washington. Evangel scenes. No. 3, Easter. London: Faith Press, Ltd. [192–?] 22 p. 12°.

Parker, Sara Emily. The last beatitude, an Easter drama [in two acts]. Cincinnati: Powell & White [n.d.]. 14 p. 12°.

Race, Martha. The silent harp; a service for Easter. [In three parts.] illus. (Church school. New York, 1922. f°. v. 3, p. 314–318.)
A man and a youth are the speaking characters, with the Biblical characters in a *tableau*. Part 1, Prologue; part 2, Old Testament scenes; part 3, The Nativity and Resurrection scenes.

Raine, James Watt. The stone rolled away. [In one scene.] (In his: Bible dramatics. New York & London [cop. 1927]. 12°. p. 203–212.)

Russell, Mary M. Easter morning. [In one scene.] (In her: Dramatized Bible stories for young people. New York [cop. 1921]. 12°. p. 47–52.)

Stackhouse, Perry J. Thomas, the twin: An Easter drama [in three scenes]. (In his: Bible dramas in the pulpit. Philadelphia [cop. 1926]. 8°. p. 139–153.)
NBM
Place: Jerusalem. Time: Saturday, the day after the Crucifixion. Characters: Thomas, Mary, John, Mary Magdalene, etc.

New Testament Plays — The Resurrection,
continued

Modern Plays, continued

Stevenson, Mrs. Christine Wetherell. ₍The
pilgrimage play; life of the Christ.₎ illus.
(Art and archaeology. Washington, 1923.
4°. v. 15, p. 14–21.)   **MTA**
A Resurrection spectacle annually produced, since
1920, in the El Campino Real Canyon, at Hollywood,
Cal. The present account is by Harvey M. Watts of
the 1922 production. Henry Herbert as Jesus; Helen
Freeman as the Magdalene; Rosamond Joyzelle as
Mary, mother of Jesus.

Stott, Kathleen. The triumph of the cross;
an Easter play ₍in one act₎. Franklin, O.:
Eldridge Entertainment House, cop. 1930.
16 p. 12°. (Eldridge church entertainments.)

Sundelof-Asbrand, Karin. ...The way of
the cross, a religious play for Easter...

Syracuse, N. Y.: W. N. Bugbee Co., cop.
1928. 16 p. 8°. (Bugbee's popular plays.)

Williamson, Eugene F. Miriam: a drama
in three scenes. Pittsburgh: Stevenson, Foster & Co., 1879. xxxii p. 24°.   **NBM**
The action of the drama occurs soon after the death
of Jesus, and deals with the fortunes of a Jewish
Pharisee family, the members of which gradually become converted to the new faith.

Wilson, Dorothy Clarke. From darkness
to dawn, an Easter play ₍in two acts₎. (International journal of religious education.
Mount Morris, Ill., 1929. f°. v. 5, Feb., 1929,
p. 24–26, 36.)

Yeats, William Butler. The Resurrection.
(Adelphi. London, 1927. 8°. v. 4, p. 714–
729.)   * **DA**
Characters: The Hebrew, The Egyptian, The Syrian,
and Jesus.

MARY MAGDALENE

Miracle Plays

B., G. "Maria von Magdala" und das Ju-
denthum. (Dr. Bloch's Oesterreichische
Wochenschrift. Wien, 1903. 4°. Jahrg. 20,
p. 265–266.)   * **PBC**

Lewin, M. Maria von Magdala. (Allge-
meine Zeitung des Judentums. Berlin, 1903.
Jahrg. 67, p. 340–341.)   * **PBC**

The **Cornish** mystery-play of Mary Magdalene ₍lines 893–1188 of the Cornish Resurrection play₎. (In: "Everyman" with other
interludes, including eight miracle plays.
London ₍1909₎. 16°. p. 128–136.)   **NAFM**
The text is the same as that in the Norris edition.

Mary Magdalene, in two parts. Part 1,
in 20 scenes... Part 2, in 31 scenes... ₍Dig-
by play.₎ (In: The Digby mysteries... Lon-
don, 1882. 8°. p. 53–136.)   * **NCK (New)**
New Shakespere Society. Publications. series 7,
[no. 1].
Previously printed in *Ancient mysteries from the
Digby manuscripts, preserved in the Bodleian Library,
Oxford,* Edinburgh, 1835 (published by the Abbotsford
Club). Also issued in Early English Text Society,
Extra series no. 70 (The Digby plays), NCE (Early).
Printed in abridged form in A. W. Pollard, *English
miracle plays,* Oxford, 1890, p. 49–63, 193–197, *NAFM*
(other editions issued in 1904, 1923, and 1927). Part 1
is printed in J. Q. Adams, editor, *Chief pre-Shakes-
pearean dramas,* Boston, 1924, p. 225–242, * R – NCO.

Schmidt, Karl. Die Digby-Spiele. I.
Maria Magdalena. (Anglia. Halle a.S., 1885.
8°. Bd. 8, p. 371–390.)   **RNA**

Modern Plays

Bishop, John Peale. The funeral of St.
Mary Magdalene. illus. (In: J. P. Bishop,
and Edmund Wilson, Jr., The undertaker's
garland. New York, 1922. 12°. p. 39–53.)
                                     NBW
A satire. The speakers represent two sections of the
Jerusalem populace: Christian folk, and those from
the Roman and Latin quarters of the holy city of that
time.

Broadhurst, Thomas William. The holy
city; a drama ₍in five acts₎, with an intro-
ductory note by William Allan Neilson.
Philadelphia: G. W. Jacobs & Co. ₍1904.₎
214 p., 8 pl. 12°.
First presented March 31, 1903 at the Collingwood
Opera House, Poughkeepsie, N. Y. See a review,
accompanied by illustrations, in *Theatre magazine,*
New York, 1903, v. 3, p. 295–296, † *NBLA.*
First New York production at the Fifth Avenue
Theatre, Jan. 30, 1905, with Iva Merlyn as the Mag-
dalene and Hugh Ford as Judas. See *New York dra-
matic mirror,* New York, Feb. 11, 1905, v. 53, p. 16,
* *DA.*
First London presentation at the Comedy Theatre,
May 5, 1914, with Nancy Price as Mary Magdalene.
Reviewed in the *London Times,* May 6, 1914, p. 6, * *A;*
in the *Era,* London, May 6, 1914, v. 77, p. 12, † *NAFA;*
The Graphic, London, 1914, v. 89, p. 874, * *DA;* and
in the *Illustrated London news,* 1914, v. 144, p. 746,
* *DA.*

Cergrinn, H. H. Mary ₍a dramatic poem in
two scenes₎. (In his: Mary, and other poems.
New York and London, 1895. 12°. p. 1–28.)
                                     NBI

Commer, Clara. Mary Magdalen; a lyric-
dramatic Passion-play in four acts. ₍In
verse.₎ English translation by Dr. Francis
Xavier Kern. Munich: V. Höfling ₍cop.
1914₎. 96 p. 16°.   **NAFH p.v.2, no.3**

Evans, Florence (Wilkinson). Mary Magdalen. ₍A play in four acts.₎ (In her: Two
plays of Israel. New York, 1904. 8°. p. 203–
333.)   * **PSQ**

Heyse, Paul Johann Ludwig von. Mary
of Magdala; a drama in five acts, from the
German of Paul Heyse, by A. I. du P. Coleman. New York: E. Lederer, 1900. 22 p.
8°.   **NGB p.v.241, no.9**

—— Mary of Magdala; an historical and
romantic drama in five acts, the original in
German prose by Paul Heyse, the translation
freely adapted and written in English verse

New Testament Plays — Mary Magdalene,
continued

Modern Plays, continued

by William Winter... New York: The
Macmillan Company, 1903. 135 p. 8°. **NGE**
"It is suggested to the readers and spectators of the
drama of 'Mary of Magdala' that it aims to depict a
fanciful state of facts and circumstances, such as might
have existed anterior to the establishment of Christianity, at a time when Jesus of Nazareth — around
whom, although he is not introduced, the action circu-
lates — was viewed exclusively as a man, and had not
yet, in the eyes of any considerable number of persons,
been invested with a sacred character." — *Preface.*
Time: A.D. 14–37. Place: Jerusalem.
W. W. Whitelock gives a synopsis of the play in
Theatre, New York, Sept., 1902, v. 2, p. 12–13,
† *NBLA.*
First produced by Harrison Grey Fiske in Milwaukee, on Oct. 23, 1902. First New York presentation at the Manhattan Theatre, with Mrs. Fiske as
Mary, Nov. 19, 1902. See review in *Theatre*, v. 3,
p. 4–5, 249. Also reviewed in *New York Times*, Nov.
20, 1902, p. 9, * A.

E., R. Dr. ₍Emil G.₎ Hirsch on modern
plays. (American Hebrew. New York, 1904.
f°. v. 74, p. 415–416.) * **PBD**

LEVY, Joseph Leonard. Plays with a pur-
pose. VI₍–VIII₎. Mary of Magdala. (In his:
A Sunday lecture by the Rabbi of Rodef
Shalom Congregation, Pittsburgh, Feb. 25,
March 4, 11, 1917. 8°. series 16, no. 16–18,
p. 167–270.) * **PLM**

Maeterlinck, Maurice. Mary Magdalene, a
play in three acts. Translated by Alexander
Teixeira de Mattos. New York: Dodd, Mead
and Company, 1910. vii, 179 p. 8°. **NKP**

————— London: Methuen & Co., Ltd.
₍1911.₎ vii, 179 p. 3. ed. 8°.
"I have borrowed from Mr. Paul Heyse's drama
Maria von Magdala, the idea of two situations in my
play, namely, at the end of the first act, the intervention of Christ, who stops the crowd raging against
Mary Magdalene...and, in the third, the dilemma in
which the great sinner finds herself, of saving or
destroying the Son of God, according as she consents
or refuses to give herself to a Roman." — *From
author's note.*
Reviewed by Richard Burton in *The Dial*, Chicago,
1910, v. 49, p. 522, * *DA.*
Produced at the New Theatre, New York, Dec. 5,
1910, with Olga Nethersole in the title role. Reviewed
in *The Billboard*, Cincinnati, Dec. 17, 1910, v. 22,
p. 10, 50, † *MZA*; *New York dramatic mirror*, New
York, Dec. 7, 1910, v. 64, p. 7, * *DA;* and in *Theatre
magazine*, New York, 1911, v. 13, p. 2–3, † *NBLA.*

LEVY, Joseph Leonard. ...Mary Magdalene. (In his: A Sunday lecture by the Rabbi
of Rodef Shalom Congregation, Pittsburgh,
Feb. 20, 1916. 8°. series 15, no. 16, p. 149–
185.) * **PLM**

Mary Agnes, sister. Mary Magdalen, a
Biblical drama ₍in three acts₎. By S. M. A.
₍Winnipeg, Man.: St. Mary's Academy, cop.
1918.₎ 31 p. 12°.

Mary Magdalen: a masque performed at
Court, temp. James I. Some of the music is
preserved in Addit. MS. B. M. 10,444.
See W. C. Hazlitt, *Manual*, p. 152.

Mary Magdalene, religious play for young
ladies, in 3 acts. St. Cloud, Minn.: Catholic

Dramatic Company, 1924. 39 p. 12°. (Collection of Catholic theatrical. no. 15.)

Nicolson, John U. The sainted courtezan.
Illustrations by Boris Riedel. Chicago: P.
Covici, 1924. 6 p.l., 167 p. illus. 4°.

Osgood, Phillips Endecott. The first day
of the week. ₍In one scene.₎ (In his: Pulpit
dramas. New York and London, 1929. 12°.
p. 177–191.) **NAFM**

Rockwell, Ethel Gesner. Magda; a Biblical drama in seven scenes. Boston: Walter
H. Baker Company, 1925. 25 p. 12°.
Scene: Jerusalem, during Passion week.
The theme of the play lies in the slow comprehension
of, and final devotion to, the reality of Christ's spiritual
kingdom, as it is learned by Magda, a young Greek
girl, and her betrothed, the doubting disciple, Thomas.
— *From publisher's announcement.*

Russell, Charles Wells. L'adultera ₍a dramatic poem₎. (In his: Poems. New York,
1921. 8°. p. 156–175.) **NCM**

Taft, Linwood. He is the son of God, a
play ₍in four acts₎ for Holy Week, showing
the effect of the personality and deeds of
Jesus upon a Jewish woman of orthodox
training. (Church school. New York, 1923.
4°. v. 4, p. 212–216, 236–237.)

————— Boston, Chicago: Pilgrim Press
₍cop. 1923₎. 32 p. 12°.
Produced by the Pilgrim Players of Evanston, Ill.,
during Holy Week of 1921.

Thompson, Theodosia. Easter evening.
₍In one act.₎ (In: Edward and Theodosia
Thompson, Three Eastern plays. London
₍1927₎. 12°. p. 1–38.) **NCR**
The action is supposed to take place four years after
the death of Christ in a Syrian town of the Lebanon.
Reviewed in *The Times literary supplement*, Lon-
don, July 21, 1927, v. 26, p. 503, *NAA.*

Wager, Lewis. The life and repentaunce
of Marie Magdalene, by Lewis Wager. A
morality play reprinted from the original edition of 1566–67; edited with introduction,
notes and glossarial index, by Frederic Ives
Carpenter... Chicago: The University of
Chicago Press, 1902. xxxv, 91 p. 8°. (University of Chicago. The decennial publications. series 2, v. 1.)
Reviewed ·by A. Brandl in Deutsche Shakespeare-
Gesellschaft, *Jahrbuch*, Berlin, 1903, Bd. 39, p. 316–
319, * *NCK;* and by H. Logeman in *Englische Studien*,
Leipzig, 1903, Bd. 32, p. 408–410, *RNA.*

————— Chicago: University of Chicago
Press, 1904. xl, 99 p. new ed. 8°. (University of Chicago. Decennial publications.
series 2, v. 1.) **NCP**

————— ...The life and repentance of Mary
Magdalene, by Lewis Wager. 1567. London:
Issued for subscribers by T. C. & E. C. Jack,
1908. vi p., facsim. (1 p.l., ₍68₎ p.) 4°. (The
Tudor facsimile texts...) **NCO (Tudor)**
Original title: A new Enterlude, neuer before this
tyme imprinted, entreating of the Life and Repentaunce
of Marie Magdalene... Made by the learned clarke
Lewis Wager... Imprinted at London, by Iohn Charle-
wood...1567.
"Date of earliest known edition, 1566; reproduced in
facsimile, 1908."

New Testament Plays, continued

THE PILGRIMS AND THOMAS

Miracle Plays

The **Travellers** to Emmaus meet Jesus. The Sledmen ₁play₁. ₁York play no. 40, 194 lines.₁ (In: Lucy T. Smith, editor, York plays. Oxford, 1885. 8°. p. 426–432.) **NAFM**

A **Pageant** play, copied from an original mss. amongst the archives at Guildhall, York. ₁York play no. 42.₁ (In: John Croft, Excerpta antiqua; or, A collection of original manuscripts. York, 1797. 8. p. 105–110.)
Acted at York long before 1415. Indulgence granted by Pope Urban IV. Sixth part of the pageant acted by the scriveners, limners, questers, and dubbors.

The **Skryveners'** play, The incredulity of St. Thomas. ₁York play no. 42.₁ From a manuscript in the possession of John Sykes, Esq. M. D. of Doncaster. Edited by J. Payne Collier. Printed for the Camden Society, 1859. 18 p. 8°. (In: The Camden miscellany. v. 4, ₁no. 3.₁)   **CA (Camden)**
Camden Society. [Publications.] v. 73.
"Although the manuscript from which the ensuing miracle-play is printed is not, perhaps, earlier than the reign of Henry VI., there is ground for believing... that, if not the oldest, it is one of the oldest dramas existing in our language... It is now printed for the first time." — *From the Introduction.*

The **Incredulity** of Thomas. The escreueneres ₁play₁. ₁York play no. 42, 198 lines.₁ (In: Lucy T. Smith, editor, York plays. Oxford, 1885. 8°. p. 448–455.) **NAFM**
Also printed under the title "The mystery of the disbelief of Thomas" in J. O. Halliwell-Phillipps, *Yorkshire anthology*, London, 1851, p. 198–204, † *NCI.*

Peregrini. ₁Towneley play no. 27.₁ (In: Towneley mysteries. London, 1836. 8°. p. 270–279.)   **CA (Surtees)**
Surtees Society. Publications. [v. 3.]
Also printed in 1897 (ed. England) in Early English Text Society, Extra series no. 71 (*The Towneley plays*), p. 325–337, *NCE (Early).*

Thomas Indiæ. ₁Towneley play no. 28.₁ (In: The Towneley mysteries. London, 1836. 8°. p. 280–293.)   **CA (Surtees)**
Surtees Society. Publications. [v. 3.]
Also printed in 1897 (ed. England) in Early English Text Society, Extra series no. 71 (*The Towneley plays*), p. 337–352, *NCE (Early).*

The **Pilgrims** of Emaus. The saddlers playe... ₁Chester play no. 20.₁ (In: The Chester plays, ed. Wright. London: Shakespeare Society, 1847. 8°. v. 2, p. 101–112.)   **NAFM (Chester)**
Also printed under the title "Christ appears to two disciples" in 1916 (ed. Matthews) in Early English Text Society, Extra series no. 115 (*Chester plays, part 2*), p. 352–362, *NCE (Early).*

The **Fourth** play, or epilogue. ₁On the road to Emmaus, Chester play.₁ (In: Chester plays, done...by I. and O. Bolton King. London ₁1930₁. 12°. p. 157–162.)   **NAFM**

The **Pilgrim** of Emaus. ₁Coventry play no. 38.₁ (In: Ludus Coventriæ, ed. Halliwell.

London: Shakespeare Society, 1841. 8°. p. 364–376.)   **NAFM (Coventry)**
Also printed in 1922 (ed. Block) in Early English Text Society, Extra series no. 120 (*Ludus Coventriæ*), p. 337–349, *NCE (Early).*

The **Two** disciples going to Emmaus. ₁Shrewsbury fragment no. 3.₁ (Academy. London, 1890. 4°. v. 37, p. 28.)   ***DA**
Also printed in 1897 in J. M. Manly, *Specimens of pre-Shaksperean drama*, v. 1, p. xxxiii–xxxvii, *NCO*, and in 1909 (ed. Waterhouse) in Early English Text Society, Extra series no. 104 (*The non-cycle mystery plays*), p. 4–7, notes, p. xxiii–xxiv, *NCE (Early).*

The **Appearance** of our Lady to Thomas. The wefferes <weavers> ₁play₁. ₁York play no. 46.₁ (In: Lucy T. Smith, editor, York plays. Oxford, 1885. 8°. p. 480–490.) **NAFM**

Peregrini. <Monday of Passion week.> (In: J. Q. Adams, editor, Chief pre-Shakespearean dramas. Boston, New York ₁cop. 1924₁. 8°. p. 21–24.)   ***R–NCO**
Latin text and parallel English translation.
"I have selected the Rouen text (printed from A. Gasté, Les drames liturgiques de la Cathédrale de Rouen, 1893, p. 65) as being the most interesting one available."

Modern Plays

Abercrombie, Lascelles. The sale of Saint Thomas. ₁In verse.₁ Ryton: The author, 1911. 29 p. 12°.   **NCI p.v.29**
Reprinted in *Georgian poetry, 1911–1912*, London, 1914, p. 3–21, *NCI.*

Kennedy, Anna R. Easter night. ₁In one scene.₁ (In her: Bible plays out of the East. New York, 1929. 8°. p. 59–62.)
Cleopas and his friend tell the events of the journey to Emmaus to the ten apostles in the "upper room."

Joseph of Arimathea

Moulton, Arthur W. Joseph of Arimathea. ₁Pontius Pilate and Joseph of Arimathea.₁ (In his: It came to pass. Boston, 1916. 12°. p. 79–90.)   **ZFHK**

Smith, Edward Percy. Joseph of Arimathæa; a romantic morality in four scenes, by Edward Percy; with a preface by E. A. Baughan. London: Burns, Oates & Washbourne, Ltd., 1920. ix, 37(1) p. 8°.   **NAC p.v.44, no.11**
The characters are ten Romans and fourteen Jews.
"The action of the play takes place in and near the city of Jerusalem 'between the evenings' of the fifteenth and sixteenth days and on the mornings of the sixteenth and seventeenth days of the month Nisan, in the year A.D. 29, at the House of Pilate, in the upper room of a lodging in Jerusalem, in the garden of Joseph of Arimathæa at daybreak, and, again, at Pilate's House."
"He has depicted...the characters of the Apostles, and the attitude of the Jews and Romans towards the great reformer." — *Preface.*

Taylor, G. Winifred. Joseph of Arimathea; a Passion play... ₁In four acts.₁ London: A. H. Stockwell ₁1928₁. 64 p. 12°. **NCR**
"Act iii has been published under the title 'Pilate' as a separate play."
The characters are the chief heroes of the Crucifixion and Resurrection episodes, with Joseph of Arimathea as the central figure.

New Testament Plays, continued

THE ASCENSION

Miracle Plays

The **Ascension.** The tailoures ₁play₁. ₁York play no. 43, 278 lines.₁ (In: Lucy T. Smith, editor, York plays. Oxford, 1885. 8°. p. 456–464.) **NAFM**
Reprinted in M. S. Mooney, *A rosary of mystery plays*, Albany, 1915, p. 128–136, *NAFM (Mooney)*.

Ascencio Domini. ₁Towneley play no. 29.₁ (In: The Towneley mysteries. London, 1836. 8°. p. 294–304.) **CA (Surtees)**
Surtees Society. Publications. [v. 3.]
Also printed in 1897 (ed. England) in Early English Text Society, Extra series no. 71 *(The Towneley plays)*, p. 353–366, *NCE (Early)*.

The **Ascension.** The taylors playe... ₁Chester play no. 21.₁ (In: The Chester plays, ed. Wright. London: Shakespeare Society, 1847. 8°. v. 2, p. 113–121.) **NAFM (Chester)**
Also printed in 1916 (ed. Matthews) in Early English Text Society, Extra series no. 115 *(The Chester plays, part 2)*, p. 363–371, *NCE (Early)*.

The **Ascension.** ₁Coventry play no. 39.₁ (In: Ludus Coventriæ, ed. Halliwell. London: Shakespeare Society, 1841. 8°. p. 377–380.) **NAFM (Coventry)**
Also printed in 1922 (ed. Block) in Early English Text Society, Extra series no. 120 *(Ludus Coventriæ)*, p. 349–352, *NCE (Early)*.

Modern Plays

Barton, Alice L. Cleopas. ₁In one act.₁ (In: Eleven short Biblical plays. New York, 1929. 12°. p. 25–43.) **NBL p.v.216**

Demarest, Ada Rose. "Go ye into all the world." (In her: Junior pageants. Cincinnati ₁cop. 1927₁. 8°. p. 49–51.)
Pageant no. 6. In one scene.

Palmer, A. W. Washington. Evangel scenes. No. 4, Ascension. London: Faith Press, Ltd. ₁192–?₁ 22 p. 12°.

GOSPELS, ACTS AND EPISTLES

St. Mark

Osgood, Phillips Endecott. John Mark, his witness. ₁In one act.₁ (In his: The sinner beloved, and other religious plays. New York and London, 1928. 12°. p. 153–160.)
Two persons in Mark's audience. **NAFM**

St. Luke

Darlington, Anne Charlotte. The lady Joanna. ₁In one act.₁ (In her: The lady Joanna; By the roadside; The nine. New York ₁cop. 1928₁. 12°. p. 3–13.)
Lady Joanna grieves because her Master has been crucified. She is disconsolate until a traveler brings word from Jerusalem about His resurrection.
Joanna of this play is the wife of Chuza, Herod's steward. Mentioned in Luke VIII:3 and XXIV:10.

St. John

Bowen, Clayton R. The Fourth Gospel as dramatic material. (Journal of Biblical literature. New Haven, 1930. 8°. v. 49, p. 292–305.) *** DA**

Purinton, Herbert Ronelle, and C. E. **Purinton.** Dramatic presentation of the Gospel; a new study of the contents of the fourth Gospel. (In their: Literature of the New Testament. New York, 1928. 12°. p. 150–158.)
The contents of the Gospel are detailed into a synopsis outlining a drama of five acts, with prologue and epilogue.

Strachan, Robert Harvey. The Fourth evangelist, dramatist or historian... London: Hodder and Stoughton ₁1925₁. 324 p. 8°.
"The Gospel is conceived in dramatic form."

Glover, Lydia May. Whom Jesus loved. ₁In two scenes.₁ (In her: Friends of Jesus. New York ₁cop. 1923₁. 8°. p. 45–57.) **NAC p.v.113, no.5**
Home of John in Bethany, a few miles from Jerusalem, shortly after John and Peter's journey to Samaria.

Hrotsvit, of Gandersheim. Callimachus; a play by Roswitha, the nun of Gandersheim. Translated from the original Latin into English prose by Richard S. Lambert, and illustrated by Agnes Lambert. ₁Wemblay Hill:₁ Stanton Press, 1923. 4 p.l., (1)6–35 p., 1 l. illus. 8°. *** KP (Stanton)**
Colophon: Printed and sold by Richard Stanton Lambert and Elinor Lambert at their Stanton Press at 32 Chalfont Avenue, Wembley Hill, Middlesex. Finished on July 22nd, 1923.
"The text from which the...translation was made is that of C. Mangin published at Paris, 1842."
no. 51 of 75 copies printed.
The precursor of the various types of the Romeo and Juliet theme. St. John the apostle appears for a few moments to perform a miracle.
A translation was published by Evangeline W. Blashfield in her *Portaits and backgrounds*, New York, 1917, p. 59–82, *SNE*.
Produced in a translation by Arthur Waley at the Art Theatre, London, Dec. 7, 1919 with Ernest Thesiger as St. John. Reviewed in *The Athenæum*, London, Dec., 1919, p. 1348, * *DA*.

—— Callimachus. (In: Plays of Roswitha. Translated by Christopher St. John ₁pseud.₁. London, 1923. 16°. p. 49–68.) **NGA**

—— Callimachus. (In her: Plays. Translated by H. J. W. Tillyard, 1923. sq. 8°. p. 40–55.) **NGA**

Binsse, Henry B. The birth of the Christian drama. (Catholic world. New York, 1916. 8°. v. 103, p. 340–348.) *** DA**

New Testament Plays — Gospels, Acts, and Epistles, continued

DALE, Darley. Roswitha, nun and dramatist. (American Catholic quarterly review. Philadelphia, 1914. 8°. v. 39, p. 442–457.)

*DA

John the Evangelist. The interlude of Johan the Evangelist. The Malone Society reprints, 1907. ₁London: Printed for the Malone Society by C. Whittingham & Co. at the Chiswick Press, 1907.₁ vii p., 1 l., ₁2₁ p., 1 l., ₁20₁ p., 1 l. incl. 2 facsim. ob. 8°.

NCO (Malone)

With reproduction of original t.-p.: "Here begynneth the enterlude of Johan the Euangelyst."

"This reprint of 'Johan the Evangelist' has been prepared by the general editor and checked by Arundell Esdaile." Signed: W. W. Greg.

Facsimiles by Horace Hart, M. A., at the Oxford University Press.

Reviewed by F. Holthausen in *Anglia: Beiblatt*, Halle a. S., 1918, Bd. 29, p. 372–375, *RNA*.

—— ...John the Evangelist. ₁n. p.;₁ Privately printed for subscribers only, 1907. 3 p.l., facsim. (1 p.l., ₁21₁ p.) 4°. (Tudor facsimile texts...)   **NCO (Tudor)**

Also printed in John S. Farmer, editor, *Recently recovered "lost" Tudor plays, with some others*, London, 1907, p. 349–368, *NCO (Early)*. Issued as one of the volumes of the series Early English dramatists.

BRADLEY, Henry. Textual notes on 'The enterlude of Johan the Evangelist.' (Modern language review. Cambridge, 1907. 8°. v. 2, p. 350–352.)   **NAA**

Reprinted in his *Collected papers*, Oxford, 1928, p. 254–255, *NDH*.

WILLIAMS, W. H. 'Irisdision,' in the interlude of 'Johan the Euangelyst.' (Modern language review. Cambridge, 1908. 8°. v. 3, p. 369–371.)   **NAA**

ACTS

Currie, Carleton H. Whither goest thou? Religious play in one act. New York: S. French; London: S. French, Ltd. ₁1926.₁ 21 p. 8°.   **NBL p.v.162, no.4**

Prisca and his wife Aquila, Jewish Christians. Time: A. D. 64, during the persecution of the Christians by Nero. Place: outside the city of Rome on the Appian way.

Reprinted in *Religious dramas*, New York ₁cop. 1926₁, ₁v. 2₁, p. 235–248, *NAFM*.

Farquhar, Edward. Christianity in the apostles. ₁A dramatic poem.₁ (In: Libyssa. Washington, 1898. 8°. p. 6–13.)

NBI (Libyssa)

The speakers: Paul, Mark, and Barnabas. From Acts XV.

Reprinted in his *Poems*, Boston, 1905, p. 30–38, *NBI*.

Githens, Harry W. At the beautiful gate. ₁In two scenes.₁ (In his: New Testament stories dramatized. Cincinnati ₁cop. 1929₁. 12°. p. 114–121.)

Acts III and IV: 1–22.

—— At the feet of the apostles. ₁In two scenes.₁ (In his: New Testament stories dramatized. Cincinnati ₁cop. 1929₁. 12°. p. 138–141.)

Ananias and Sapphira.

—— Delivered from prison. ₁In three scenes.₁ (In his: New Testament stories dramatized. Cincinnati ₁cop. 1929₁. 12°. p. 105–113.)

Acts V: 17–42.

Knowles, Ava Beatrice. The beginning of the church. ₁In five scenes.₁ (In her: Prodigal son; The beginning of the church. New York ₁1925₁. 12°. p. 15–32.)

Manley, William Ford. Diana of the Ephesians. (In his: Bible dramas. New York ₁cop. 1928₁. 8°. p. 43–62.)   **NBM**

In five scenes.

Mason, Harry Silvernale. At the gate beautiful; religious drama in one act. New York: S. French, Ltd., cop. 1926. 29 p., 1 l. music. 8°.   **NBL p.v.162, no.5**

Tunes of incidental music, p. [30].

Reprinted in *Religious dramas*, New York ₁cop. 1926₁, v. 2, p. 249–265, *NAFM*.

Place: a street in Jerusalem in front of the Temple, soon after the ministry of Christ. The characters, with one exception, are all Jews. The believers in Christ preach Him to the sceptical ones.

Pace, William. Lydia; or, Conversion; a sacred drama; inscribed to the Jews, by a clergyman of the Church of England ₁William Pace₁... London: J. G. and F. Rivington ₁etc.₁, 1835. vii(i), 75 (1) p. 8°.

Plot laid at Antioch in the first century A. D. In the preface the author declares the purpose of the play to be to promote conversion of the Jews to Christianity.

Whitney, Mary Ellen. The imprisonment of Peter and John. ₁In three scenes.₁ illus. (In her: Bible plays and how to produce them. New York ₁cop. 1927₁. 12°. p. 126–134.)

Descent of the Holy Spirit

Miracle Plays

The **Descent** of the Holy Spirit. The potteres ₁play₁. ₁York play no. 44, 224 lines.₁ (In: Lucy T. Smith, editor, York plays. Oxford, 1885. 8°. p. 465–472.)   **NAFM**

Reprinted in M. S. Mooney, *A rosary of mystery plays*, Albany, 1915, p. 137–144, *NAFM (Mooney)*.

The **Emission** of the Holy Ghost. The fishemongeres playe... ₁Chester play no. 22.₁ (In: The Chester plays, ed. Wright. London: Shakespeare Society, 1847. 8°. v. 2, p. 122–138.)   **NAFM (Chester)**

Also printed in 1916 (ed. Matthews) in Early English Text Society, Extra series no. 115 *(The Chester plays, part 2)*, p. 371–387, *NCE (Early)*.

The **Descent** of the Holy Ghost. ₁Coventry play no. 40.₁ (In: Ludus Coventriæ, ed. Halliwell. London: Shakespeare Society, 1841. 8°. p. 381–382.)·   **NAFM (Coventry)**

Also printed in 1922 (ed. Block) in Early English Text Society, Extra series no. 120 *(Ludus Coventriæ)*, p. 352–354, *NCE (Early)*.

New Testament Plays — Gospels, Acts, and Epistles, continued

The **Representation** ₍or descent₎ of the Holy Ghost, translated from the Italian ₍by the editor, Thomas Holcroft₎. (Theatrical recorder. London, 1805. 8°. v. 2, p. 17–26.)
NCOA

This is a translation of *Lo spirito santo,* Siena, 1616, in a volume of Italian miracle plays, sold in London in 1789, as item no. 3576 of M. Pinelli's library.

"It [the translation] is a faithful picture of the verbosity, insipidity, and irreverend manner, which pervade these pieces."

A list of dramatis personae is supplied by the translator; there being none in the original.

Modern Play

Wilson, Dorothy Clarke. The Pentecost of youth; a pageant of religious education. ₍In four episodes.₎ (International journal of religious education. Chicago, 1930. f°. v. 6, Sept., 1930, p. 25–27, 36, 44.)

Episode one takes place on the first Pentecost, and the characters are the twelve disciples. Based on Acts II.

Copy in Library of Union Theological Seminary.

Stephen

Githens, Harry W. The first martyr. ₍In four scenes.₎ (In his: New Testament stories dramatized. Cincinnati ₍cop. 1929₎. 12°. p. 128–137.)

The stoning of Stephen, Acts VII.

Whitney, Mary Ellen. The martyrdom of Stephen. ₍A play in two scenes.₎ (In her: Bible plays and how to produce them. New York ₍cop. 1927₎. 12°. p. 135–139.)

Paul

Miracle Plays

The **Conversion** of Saul: a mystery of the early part of the sixteenth century, MS. Digby 133, in the Bodleian Library. (In: Ancient mysteries from the Digby manuscripts preserved in the Bodleian Library, Oxford. ₍Edited by T. Sharpe.₎ Edinburgh, 1835. 4°.)

One of the Abbotsford Club publications.

Also printed with the title "The Conversion of St. Paul" in New Shakspere Society, Publications, series 7, [no. 1] *(Digby mysteries),* p. 25–52, * NCK; Early English Text Society, Extra series no. 70 *(The Digby plays),* p. 25–52, *NCE (Early);* J. M. Manly, *Specimens of the pre-Shaksperean drama,* Boston, 1897, v. 1, p. 215–238, *NCO;* J. Q. Adams, editor, *Chief pre-Shakespearean dramas,* Boston, 1924, p. 212–224, * R–NCO; F. J. Tickner, editor, *Earlier English drama from Robin Hood to Everyman,* New York [cop. 1929], p. 248–266, *NCO (Tickner).*

Conversio Beati Pauli Apostoli. ⟨Festival of the convertion of St. Paul.⟩ (In: J. Q. Adams, editor, Chief pre-Shakespearean dramas. Boston, New York ₍cop. 1924₎. 8°. p. 51–54.)
*** R – NCO**

Latin text and parallel English translation.

From a thirteenth-century Fleury manuscript. Text based on that of E. de Coussemaker, *Drames liturgiques du moyen âge,* 1861, p. 210.

Modern Plays

Arpee, Leon. The Lord is risen indeed; an Easter play ₍in one act₎. Cincinnati: Powell & White ₍cop. 1921₎. 15 p. 8°.

Paul's defense before Felix as recorded in Acts XXIV. The story of the Resurrection is verified by a number of witnesses introduced as characters.

Boulter, Benjamin Consitt. Paul and Silas, a play in four scenes. London: Society for Promoting Christian Knowledge ₍1923₎. vii, 9–31 p. 12°.   **NCO p.v.497, no.4**

Boyd, Charles Arthur. Paul the farsighted. ₍In five acts.₎ (In his: Worship in drama. Philadelphia ₍cop. 1924₎. 8°. p. 93–119.)
NAFM

In five acts.

Boyle, Douglas Jackson. Paul of Tarsus; a tragedy, illustrated by Violet Dinsdale. n. p.: Published by the author, 1923. 52 l. illus. 16°.   **NCE p.v.44, no.6**

In three acts.

Time: 62–68 A. D. Place: Rome.

Chase, Alice C. ...The whole armor of God; a mystery play ₍in one act₎ of the Christian year. Hartford: Church Missions Pub. Co., 1923. 14 p. illus. 8°. (Soldier and servant series. Publication no. 131.)

The Biblical characters are Paul, Timothy, and Onesimus. First given on Easter evening, 1922, in Trinity Church, Ware, Mass.

Cole, Edna Earle. Paul and the jailer. ₍In three acts.₎ (In her: The good Samaritan, and other Bible stories dramatized. Boston ₍cop. 1915₎. 12°. p. 19–29.)

Based on Acts XVI: 12–40.

Crafer, Thomas Wilfrid. Scenes in drama from St. Paul's life, to illustrate the writings of his epistles... With a foreword by A. H. McNeille. London: Society for Promoting Christian Knowledge ₍1923₎. 46 p. 12°.

Reconstructs the occasions when some of S. Paul's Epistles were written. The play, in four scenes, was produced by the students of St. Christopher's College, Blackheath, England.

Crigler, John Fielding. Saul of Tarsus; a religious drama ₍in seven acts₎... Boston: Sherman, French & Co., 1914. 5 p.l., 226 p. 12°.   **NBM**

Act I, Saul in Tarsus; Act II, Saul in Jerusalem; Act III, Saul in Damascus; Act IV, Paul in Antioch; Act V, Paul in Corinth; Act VI, Paul in Ephesus; Act VII, Paul in Rome.

Dearmer, Geoffrey. St. Paul, an historical play, in three acts. London: William Heinemann, Ltd. ₍1929.₎ xiii, 76 p. illus. 12°.
NCO p.v.581

Reviewed in *The Times literary supplement,* London, 1929, v. 28, p. 586, † *NAA.*

Eastman, Fred. The triumph of the defeated; an Easter pageant. New York: Samuel French, cop. 1929. 23 p. 8°. **NAFH p.v.46**

New Testament Plays — Gospels, Acts, and Epistles, continued

Fite, W. A. Blindness, a Biblical play emphasizing evangelism. [In two acts.] [Cincinnati:] Powell & White, n. d. 12 p. 8°.

Based on Acts XIII: 4–13.

—— The conquest of a continent (a dramatization of the 16th chapter of Acts). [In four acts.] Cincinnati: Powell & White [192–?]. 18 p. 12°.

Gairdner, William Henry Temple. Saul and Stephen; a sacred drama. London: Society for Promoting Christian Knowledge, 1921. viii, 56 p. 12°. **NCO p.v.472, no.2**

In three acts.

The dramatis personae are divided into groups: 1, Saul of Tarsus, a young graduate of Gamaliel's school; 2, Christians; 3, Non-Christian Jews; 4, Pagans.

שאול ואסטפנוס מחזה מראשית ימי המשיחיות, מאת ו. ח. גרדנר'. העתקה עברית מאת דר. פ. פ. לבר־טוב.
London and Jerusalem: The Sheldon Press, 1930. 62 p., 1 l. 12°.

Githens, Harry W. An ambassador in bonds. [In eight scenes.] (In his: New Testament stories dramatized. Cincinnati [cop. 1929]. 12°. p. 192–206.)

Acts XXI–XXVI.

—— A herald of the cross. [In eight scenes.] (In his: New Testament stories dramatized. Cincinnati [cop. 1929]. 12°. p. 174–184.)

Acts XVI: 12–14.

—— An interrupted coronation. [In two scenes.] (In his: New Testament stories dramatized. Cincinnati [cop. 1929]. 12°. p. 167–173.)

Acts XIV: 1–20.

—— A labor riot. [In one scene.] (In his: New Testament stories dramatized. Cincinnati [cop. 1929]. 12°. p. 185–191.)

Acts XIX: 23–41.

—— The last journey. [In six scenes.] (In his: New Testament stories dramatized. Cincinnati [cop. 1929]. 12°. p. 207–216.)

Acts XXVII–XXVIII.

—— A stricken traveler. [In five scenes.] (In his: New Testament stories dramatized. Cincinnati [cop. 1929]. 12°. p. 154–166.)

The conversion of Saul, Acts IX.

—— The wrath of Israel. [In four scenes.] (In his: New Testament stories dramatized. Cincinnati [cop. 1929]. 12°. p. 142–153.)

The great persecution, Acts VIII.

Hale, Harris G., and N. M. HALL. ...Paul the prisoner of the Lord. Arranged by Harris G. Hale and Newton M. Hall. Boston: The Pilgrim Press, 1907. iv, 22 p. 12°. (Biblical dramas. [no. 12.])

Higgins, Aileen Cleveland. Thekla; a drama. Boston: Poet Lore Co., 1907. 62 p. 12°. **NBM**

Scene: Iconium (the modern Konieh), A. D. 50. The apostle Paul is one of the characters.

Holcomb, Carlysle Henry. Saul of Tarsus. [In four acts.] Cincinnati: Standard Publishing Company, cop. 1918. 23(1) p. illus. 8°.

Kimball, Ruth Putnam. Lydia; or, The seller of purple, a pageant for Easter... Boston: Walter H. Baker Company, cop. 1928. 17 p. 12°. (Baker's royalty plays.)

Based on the incident narrated in Acts XVI.

Manley, William Ford. Saul of Tarsus. (In his: Bible dramas. New York [cop. 1928]. 8°. p. 80–95.) **NBM**

In seven scenes.

Masters, Edgar Lee. Berenice. [A dramatic poem.] (In his: The open sea. New York, 1921. 8°. p. 202–211.) **NBI**

Among the speakers, besides Berenice, are Agrippa and Paul.

Moore, George. The apostle; a drama in three acts. Dublin: Maunsel and Co., Ltd. [cop. 1911.] 4 p.l., 100 p. 8°. **NCR**

—— The apostle; a drama in a prelude and three acts. London: William Heinemann, Ltd., 1923. 3 p.l., 125 p. 8°. **NCR**

Printed in *The Dial*, New York, 1923, v. 74, p. 537–561; v. 75, p. 43–72, * *DA.* The scenario accompanied by a prefatory note was published in the *English review*, London, 1910, v. 5, p. 564–576, * *DA.*

Reviewed by Percy Lubbock in *The Nation and Athenæum*, London, 1923, v. 33, p. 428, * *DA,* and in *The Spectator*, London, 1923, v. 131, p. 160, * *DA.*

Based on the author's novel *The Brook Kerith.*

GEORGE Moore's daring dramatic travesty of the gospel. (Current literature. New York, 1911. 8°. v. 51, p. 423–424.) *** DA**

A summary of various reviews.

Moore, George. The passing of the Essenes; a drama in three acts... London: William Heinemann, Ltd., 1930. 4 p.l., 3–96 p., 1 l. 8°. *** KP (Riverside, Edinburgh)**

Printed at the Riverside Press, Limited, Edinburgh.

Music, 1 l. at end.

"This edition is limited to 775 copies, of which 750 are for sale...and 25 are for presentation. This is no. 374."

—— —— New York: The Macmillan Company, 1930. 5 p.l., 3–96 p. 8°.

no. 43 of edition limited to 500.

A further dramatization of the author's well-known theory as to what happened to Jesus after the Crucifixion. The main characters are Jesus and Paul.

Reviewed in *Times literary supplement*, London, 1930, v. 29, p. 802, † *NAA.* Cf. letter by George Moore, *ibid.*, p. 890.

Produced at the Arts Theatre, London, Oct. 1, 1930, with Ian Fleming as Jesus and John Laurie as Paul. Reviewed in *Era*, London, 1930, v. 94, Oct. 8, p. 1, † *NAFA; Curtain*, London, 1930, v. 9, p. 142, *NAFA;* and in *Jewish chronicle*, London, 1930, Oct. 10, p. 27, * *PBE.*

New Testament Plays — Gospels, Acts, and Epistles, continued

Morley, Louis J. "The acceptable time"; a play in five scenes and an epilogue... London: Arthur H. Stockwell, Ltd. ₁1930.₁ 48 p. 12°.

Time: about 40 A. D.

Scene: Athens, Bethany, El Arish, and Macedonia. The plot leads up to the arrest of Paul by the Roman procurator Sejanus. Stirring of Christianity among the Romans and the Jews.

Nickles, Alice Belmer. A study of St. Paul in dialogue. Philadelphia: Lutheran Publication Society ₁cop. 1910₁. 74 p., 1 l. 8°.   **NBL p.v.24, no.1**

With music.

A dramatic presentation of the life of the apostle Paul in eight parts. First part is dated 12 A. D. when Paul is 7 to 11 years old, in Judaea; the eighth part in Rome, 67 A. D.

Opal, pseud. St. Paul in Athens. (Drama IV) Acts XVII: 18–34. (In his: The cloud of witnesses. New York, 1874. 12°. p. 62–69.)   **NBM**

Parish, Rebecca M. Saul in the desert; or, Preparation. ₁In eleven scenes.₁ (In: H. Heron, compiler, Pageants for the year. Cincinnati ₁cop. 1928₁. 8°. p. 121–130.)   **NAFM**

Prepared for use in a church at Tarlac, Philippine Islands.

Raine, James Watt. Delivered from the lion's mouth. ₁In one scene.₁ (In his: Bible dramatics. New York & London ₁cop. 1927₁. 12°. p. 311–330.)

Rome, 63 A. D. Paul is the main character.

Riesner, Rebecca. The desire of all nations. ₁In nine episodes.₁ Cincinnati: Powell & White ₁192–?₁. 12 p. 12°.

Cover-title.

A historical pageant of missionary activities. Paul is a character in the first two episodes.

Roberts, Charles V. H. Myrrha: a tragedy in five acts. Illustrated by Blanche Brink. Boston: Four Seas Co., 1922. 140 p. illus. 12°.   **NBM**

The action takes place in Rome, A. D. 54.

—— Thaisa: a tragedy in prologue and five acts... New York and Cedar Rapids, Ia.: Torch Press, 1918. 181 p. illus. 12°. **NBM**

Rome, A. D. 54–60. Paul of Tarsus. All characters, according to the author, are historical.

Todd, Helen L. For His name's sake. ₁In one act.₁ (In: Eleven short Biblical plays. New York, 1929. 12°. p. 89–104.)   **NBL p.v.216**

Turner, Elizabeth E. Paul's nephew; a dramatization. ₁In four scenes.₁ illus. (Church school. New York, 1922. 4°. v. 3, p. 472–474.)

Based on Acts XXIII.

Copy in Library of Union Theological Seminary.

Walkerdine, W. E. At Damascus' gate, a drama of the conversion of St. Paul. London: Simpkin, Marshall, Hamilton, Kent & Co., Ltd., 1923. x, 11–93 p. 8°.

Based on Acts IX.

Werfel, Franz. ...Paul among the Jews (a tragedy). Authorised translation from the German by Paul P. Levertoff. London: Diocesan House ₁1928₁. 150 p. 8°.   **NGE**

In six "pictures."

The scene is laid in Jerusalem in the time of Caesar Caligula.

Deals with the psychologic conflict between St. Paul and his former teacher, Rabbi Gamaliel.

Also printed in **Menorah journal,** New York, 1928, v. 15, p. 195–214, 317–332, 428–443, * PBD.

Reviewed by A. W. G. Randall in *Monthly criterion,* London, 1927, v. 5, p. 352–353, * DA (Criterion).

Presented by the Incorporated Stage Society at the Prince of Wales Theatre, London, July 8, 1928. Reviewed in *The Era,* London, July 11, 1928, v. 91, p. 4, † *NAFA,* and in *New York Times,* Aug. 5, 1928, section 7, p. 1, * A.

LEVERTOFF, Paul P. A Jewish dramatist's presentation of St. Paul. (In his: St. Paul in Jewish thought; three lectures. London, 1928. 8°. p. 27–47.)

A synopsis of the story with copious extracts.

SCHAPIRO, Eva. „פאולוס בין היהודים" (הדאר) New York, 1928. 4°. v. 8, p. 330.)   *** PBA**

A review.

White, Edward Joseph, and X. P. WIL-FLEY. Paul of Tarsus; a religious drama in five parts, adapted for the screen. ₁St. Louis, cop. 1924₁ 100 p. 4°.

Time: 33–65 A. D.

Whitney, Mary Ellen. The conversion of Saul. ₁A play in four scenes.₁ (In her: Bible plays and how to produce them. New York ₁cop. 1927₁. 12°. p. 140–144.)

Place: court of the high priest. Characters: Saul, Annas, Ananias.

—— Paul and Silas at Philippi. ₁In four scenes.₁ illus. (In her: Bible plays and how to produce them. New York ₁cop. 1927₁. 12°. p. 145–153.)

—— The shipwreck of Paul. ₁In four scenes.₁ illus. (In her: Bible plays and how to produce them. New York ₁cop. 1927₁. 12°. p. 154–161.)

Peter

Clinton, Inez Funk. The resurrection of Peter; a short drama for Easter... ₁in two scenes₁. Written for the young people of the Pilgrim Congregational Church, Oak Park, Ill., with an order of worship to be used when the drama is presented. Boston, Chicago: Pilgrim Press ₁cop. 1925₁. 1 p.l., 17 p. 12°.

The short drama begins on the morning after the Crucifixion.

First appeared, with an introduction by Ernest Bourner Allen, in *Church school,* New York, 1921, v. 2, p. 248–250, 287.

First scene: the remorseful Peter; second scene: the resolute Peter.

Cole, Edna Earle. Peter and the Roman captain. ₁In three acts.₁ (In her: The good Samaritan and other Bible stories dramatized. Boston ₁cop. 1915₁. 12°. p. 53–61.)

Based on Acts x: 1–9, 17–48.

New Testament Plays — Gospels, Acts, and Epistles, continued

Copenhaver, Laura Scherer. "Nothing common or unclean." ₁In one scene.₁ music. (In her: Short pageants for Sunday school. Garden City, N. Y., 1929. 8°. p. 35–42.)
MWF

Cropper, Margaret. St. Peter is delivered from prison. ₁In one act.₁ London: St. Christopher Press, Society for Promoting Christian Knowledge ₁1930₁. 16 p. 12°. (Saint Nicolas plays. no. 5.)
Among the characters are Mark, his mother Mary, and the apostles Andrew, John, Philip, and Peter.

Doran, Marie. Quo vadis; a play in five acts and seven scenes, adapted from the novel of Henryk Sienkiewicz. New York: Samuel French, cop. 1928. 102 p., 4 l. diagrs. 12°.   **NBL p.v.181, no.9**
Place: Rome. Time: during the reign of Nero, 54–68 A. D.
Produced at the Castle Square Theatre, Boston, April 16, 1900, with Lindsay Morison as the apostle Peter. A previous dramatization by Chas. W. Chase was produced on Nov. 21, 1899, and was seen in New York, with Wm. H. Elliott as Peter, at the Star Theatre, Aug. 11, 1900.
A six-act version by Stanislaus Stange was staged at McVicker's Theatre, Chicago, Dec. 12, 1899; at the New York Theatre, New York, April 9, 1900, and at the Adelphi, London, May 5, 1900. A dramatization by Jeannette L. Gilder was produced at the Herald Square Theatre, New York, April 9, 1900. Another adaptation by Wilson Barrett was staged at the Edinburgh Lyceum, Edinburgh, May 29, 1900.

Githens, Harry W. A captain's confession. ₁In one scene.₁ (In his: New Testament stories dramatized. Cincinnati ₁cop. 1929₁. 12°. p. 122–127.)
Based on Acts x; Simon Peter a character.

—— The fisherman. ₁In three scenes.₁ (In his: New Testament stories dramatized. Cincinnati ₁cop. 1929₁. 12°. p. 23–35.)
The fisherman is Simon Peter.

Glover, Lydia May. Simon of Cyrene. ₁In four scenes.₁ Based on Mark 15. 21 and Romans 16. 13. (In her: Friends of Jesus. New York ₁cop. 1923₁. 8°. p. 58–67.)
NAC p.v.113, no.5
Near Jerusalem, two months before, and a week after, the Crucifixion.

Hamlin, Mary P. The Rock; a play in three acts showing the character develop-

ment of Simon Peter. Boston, Chicago: The Pilgrim Press ₁cop. 1921₁. 37 p. 8°.
NBF p.v.41, no.4
Prize play — Drama League of America.
Time of the Crucifixion. The Jewish ideology of the new Christians is constantly made obvious.
First appeared in *Church school*, New York, 1921, v. 3, p. 23–35.
Reprinted in *Religious dramas*, New York [cop. 1923], v. 1, p. 3–67, *NAFM (Religious)*.
The first public performance of the play was given by the Pilgrim Players of Evanston, Ill., during Holy Week, 1921.

Hornsey, Evelyn Grant. Denial. ₁In one act.₁ Boston: Walter H. Baker Company ₁cop. 1927₁. 26 p. diagr. 12°.
Time: the night of the taking of Jesus at the Garden of Gethsemane.

Hummel, Margaret. Simon the Cyrenian; an Easter play... Boston: Walter H. Baker Co., cop. 1927. 14 p. 12°. (Baker's royalty plays.)
Place: near Jerusalem. Time: five days after the Crucifixion.

Kemper, Robert C. The mark of the Master; a Biblical drama in one act. Cincinnati: Powell & White ₁cop. 1929₁. 29 p. 12°.

Moulton, Arthur W. Tears of a man. ₁Simon Peter and the Apostles.₁ (In his: It came to pass. Boston, 1916. 12°. p. 37–50.)
ZFHK

I. CORINTHIANS

Bruton, Iva Purdum. The test of the thirteenth; a missionary presentation ₁in one act₁. Cincinnati: Powell & White ₁cop. 1922₁. 7 p. 8°.   **NBL p.v.223**
Cover-title.
The characters are modern. The test in the title is i. Corinthians, XIII.

PHILEMON

Haines, Helen R. The test. ₁A dramatization, in one act, of the story of Philemon and Onesimus.₁ (International journal of religious education. Mount Morris, Ill., 1927. 4°. v. 3, Sept., 1927, p. 35–37.)

Tupper, Wilbur S. Onesimus, a Biblical play ₁in one act₁. (In his: Six short plays. Boston, 1922. 12°. p. 45–58.)   **NBM**
The action takes place at Colossae, 63 A. D.

REVELATION — LAST THINGS

PURINTON, Herbert Ronelle, and C. E. PURINTON. The drama of Revelation. (In their: Literature of the New Testament. New York, 1928. 12°. p. 116–122.)
The contents of chapters IV–XIX:22 are outlined in a synopsis for a drama of five acts. The first three chapters constitute the prologue.

Bayard, Lyman R. A legend of Saint John ...in three acts. Los Angeles: Pageant Publishers, cop. 1926. 25 p. illus. music. 4°.
Based on the narrative of St. John and the robber, as given by Clement of Alexandria. "Nearly every word as spoken by St. John in this play is either from

the Scripture, or is in the words of Clement." Time: in the latter years of the first Christian century. Jewish characters are the disciple John and two youths, Lemuel and Enon.
Also printed in *Church school journal*, Cincinnati, 1927, v. 59, p. 77–85.

Bowles, William Lisle. St. John in Patmos: a ₁dramatic₁ poem. By one of the old living poets of Great-Britain ₁W. L. Bowles₁. London: J. Murray, 1832. x p., 1 l., 133 p. 8°.   **NCM**
Also in his *Poetical works*, New York, 1855, v. 2, p. 143–220, *NCM*.

New Testament Plays — Revelation — Last Things, continued

Guthrie, Kenneth Sylvan. The angelic mysteries of the nine heavens, a drama of interior initiation, embodying Dionysius the Areopagite's ninefold celestial hierarchy, a vision of judgment and heaven, an evocation of the historic lawgivers, the reincarnatory career of a famous soul, a passage through hell, purgatory & heaven and the mystery of the twenty-four elders. Yonkers, N. Y.: Platonist Press, cop. 1926. 217 p. illus. 12°.
NBM
In the fourth scene of the "Ninth Heaven," which contains the Seraphim and the "Twenty-four elders," numerous Biblical characters are introduced.

Thompson, James Westfall. The lost oracles, a masque ₁in six acts₁... Chicago: Walter M. Hill ₁1921₁. xi, 143 p. 8°. **NAFM**

Antichrist

Ezechiel. The clothe workers playe... ₁Chester play no. 23.₁ (In: The Chester plays, ed. Wright. London: Shakespeare Society, 1847. 8°. v. 2, p. 139–149.) **NAFM (Chester)**
Previously printed, under the title "The Advent of Antichrist," in J. P. Collier, *Five miracle plays,* London, 1836.
Also printed, with the title "The prophets and Antichrist," in 1916 (ed. Matthews) in Early English Text Society, Extra series no. 115 *(The Chester plays, part 2),* p. 387–399, *NCE (Early),* and with the title "Antichrist" in J. M. Manly, *Specimens of the pre-Shaksperean drama,* Boston, 1897, v. 1, p. 170–197, *NCO.*

Antichrist. The dyars playe... ₁Chester play no. 24.₁ (In: The Chester plays, ed. Wright. London: Shakespeare Society, 1847. 8°. v. 2, p. 150–177.) **NAFM (Chester)**
Also printed in William Marriott, *A collection of English miracle plays,* Basel, 1838, p. 16–38, *NAFM,* and in 1916 (ed. Matthews) in Early English Text Society, Extra series no. 115 *(The Chester plays, part 2),* p. 400–427, *NCE (Early).*

GREG, Walter Wilson. The coming of Antichrist: relation of the manuscripts in the Chester cycle. (Library. London, 1914. 8°. series 3, v. 5, p. 168–205.) ***HA**
Reprinted in his *Bibliographical and textual problems of the English miracle cycles,* London, 1914, p. 32–69, *NAFM.*

The **Early** play of Antichrist. ₁Translated by William H. Hulme from the original

Latin according to the Froning edition.₁ (In: The Mediaeval religious plays Antichrist and Adam. Cleveland, 1925. 8°. p. 13–32.)
NAC p.v.142, no.5
Western Reserve University. Bulletin, v. 28, no. 8. Western Reserve studies, v. 2, [no. 1?].
"The author of this drama was a German poet and he wrote it...about the year 1160, during the reign of Frederick Barbarossa. The immediate source of this drama seems to have been the tenth century tract by Adso of Toul, entitled *Libellus de Antichristo.* 'Into this Libellus' says Chambers, 'the author of the drama has worked the central theme of the prophetae and the debating figures from the very popular débat, the Altercatio Ecclesiae et Synagogae.' " — *From the prefatory introduction.*
Reviewed by George R. Coffman in *Modern language notes,* Baltimore, 1927, v. 42, p. 129–133, *RAA.*

The Judgment

The **Judgment** Day. The merceres ₁play₁. ₁York play no. 48, 380 lines.₁ (In: Lucy T. Smith, editor, York plays. Oxford, 1885. 8°. p. 497–513.) **NAFM**
Also printed in J. M. Manly, *Specimens of the pre-Shaksperean drama,* Boston, 1897, v. 1, p. 198–211, *NCO;* J. Q. Adams, editor, *Chief pre-Shaksperean dramas,* Boston, 1924, p. 199–204, * *R-NCO;* and in H. C. Schweikert, *Early English plays,* New York [cop. 1928], p. 128–138, *NCO.*

Juditium. ₁Towneley play no. 30.₁ (In: The Towneley mysteries. London, 1836. 8°. p. 305–321.) **CA (Surtees)**
Surtees Society. Publications. [v. 3.]
Also printed in William Marriott, *A collection of English miracle-plays,* Basel, 1838, p. 175–195, *NAFM,* and in 1897 (ed. England) in Early English Text Society, Extra series no. 71 *(The Towneley plays),* p. 367–387, *NCE (Early).*

Doomsday. The websters playe... ₁Chester play no. 25.₁ (In: The Chester plays, ed. Wright. London: Shakespeare Society, 1847. 8°. v. 2, p. 178–201.) **NAFM (Chester)**
Also printed in 1916 (ed. Matthews) in Early English Text Society, Extra series no. 115 *(The Chester plays, part 2),* p. 427–453, *NCE (Early).*

Doomsday. ₁Coventry play no. 42.₁ (In: Ludus Coventriæ, ed. Halliwell. London: Shakespeare Society, 1841. 8°. p. 401–405.) **NAFM (Coventry)**
Also printed in 1922 (ed. Block) in Early English Text Society, Extra series no. 120 *(Ludus Coventriæ),* p. 373–377, *NCE (Early),* and in F. J. Tickner, editor, *Earlier English drama from Robin Hood to Everyman,* New York [cop. 1929], p. 244–248, *NCO (Tickner).*

THE FALL OF JERUSALEM

Boyle, Douglas Jackson. Titus and Berenice. A romance ₁in one act₁. ₁Leeds:₁ The Author, 1926. 35 p. 12°. **NCO p.v.543, no.6**
Scene: palace of Titus in Rome.
Portrays the struggle in Titus' heart between his love for the Jewish princess Berenice and his duty to Rome which forbids it.

Carvalho, Naomi Nunes. The death of Philo, the Graeco-Judaic philosopher. ₁A dialogue between Philo and a student.₁ (In her: Vox humana. London, 1912. 12°. p. 147–152.) **NRD p.v.9**

Crowne, John. The destruction of Jerusalem by Titus Vespasian. In two parts. — As it is acted at the Theatre Royal. London: Printed for James Magnes and Richard Bentley...1677. 2 parts. 8°. **NCP**

—— —— London: Printed for R. Wellington and E. Rumball, 1703. 5 p.l., 106 p. 8°.
8 – NCP
Bound with his: Juliana. London, 1671. 8°.
The play is in two parts of five acts each, the dramatis personae being the same for both parts. The

The Fall of Jerusalem, continued

second part commences with the siege and terminates with the destruction of the city.

Mr. Winship calls the author the first Harvard man who succeeded in making a living by practising a recognized form of literature, Crowne having attended Harvard College while his father resided in Boston during the Protectorate.

Reprinted in his *Dramatic works*, Edinburgh, 1873, v. 2, p. 215–396, *NCP*.

For a historical discussion of the play see A. F. White, *John Crowne; his life and dramatic works*, Cleveland, 1922, p. 92–103, *NCC (Crowne)*.

Heming, William. ₁The Jewes tragedy, or, Their fatal and final overthrow by Vespatian and Titus his son. Agreeable to the authentick and famous history of Josephus. Never before published. By William Hemings, Master of arts of Oxon. London: Printed for Matthew Inman and sold by Richard Gammon over-against Excestor-House in the Strand, 1662.₁ 2 p.l., 78 p. 4°.

Title from Library of Congress.

—— The Jewes tragedy von William Hemings, nach der quarto 1662, hrsg. von Heinrich A. Cohn. Louvain: A. Uystpruyst, 1913. xi, 106 p., 3 l., 91 p. 4°. (Materialien zur Kunde des älteren englischen Dramas... Bd. 40.)   *** PSQ**

A short extract is printed in Allardyce Nicoll, editor, *Readings from British drama*, New York [1928], p. 110–112, * R – NCO.

Holland, John. The cottage of Pella, a tale of Palestine; with other poems. By John Holland, author of Sheffield Park, &c. London: Longman, Hurst, Rees, Orme, and Brown, 1821. 80 p. 8°.

Reviewed in *Imperial magazine*, London, 1821, v. 3, col. 668–671, * *DA*.

A dramatic poem, not given in British Museum Catalogue nor mentioned in D. N. B., under Holland. See W. C. Newsam, *The poets of Yorkshire*, London, 1845, p. 202: " 'The cottage of Pella'...dedicated to the Rev. H. H. Milman, whose 'Fall of Jerusalem' celebrated that memorable catastrophe in Jewish history, of which Mr. Holland's 'Tale' is but an episode."

Kaenders, P. Lucius Flavus; a drama in five acts. (Adapted from Father Spillmann's story.) St. Louis, Mo.: B. Herder, 1908. 70 p. 12°.   **NBL p.v.9, no. 12**

Time: just before the fall of Jerusalem.

Latter, Mrs. Mary. The siege of Jerusalem, by Titus Vespasian; a tragedy. ₁By Mrs. Mary Latter.₁ To which is prefixed, by way of introduction, An essay on the mystery and mischiefs of stage-craft. London: C. Bathurst, 1763. 1 p.l., xxxvii, 87 p. 8°.

Title from Library of Congress.

Milman, Henry Hart. The fall of Jerusalem. A dramatic poem. London: J. Murray, 1820. vii, 167(1) p. new ed. 8°.   **NCR**

—— —— New-York: L. and F. Lockwood, 1820. vii p., 2 l., 13–180 p. 16°.   **NCR**

—— —— London: J. Murray, 1822. iii–vii, 167(1) p. new ed. 8°.   **NCR**

"Though their children are fictitious characters, the leaders of the Jews, Simon, John, and Eleazar are historical." — *p. vi.*

"The ground work of the poem is to be found in Josephus... It has been my object also to show the full completion of prophecy in this great event." — *Introduction.*

Also printed in his *Poetical works*, London, 1839, v. 1, p. 1–114, *NCM* (also edition of 1840), and in *Poetical works of Milman, Bowles, Wilson, and Barry Cornwall*, Paris, 1829, p. 155–180, *NCI*, and *The Poetical works of Howitt, Milman, and Keats*, Philadelphia, 1847, p. 407–433, *NCI*.

Printed in abridged form in G. A. Kohut, editor, *A Hebrew anthology*, Cincinnati, 1913, v. 2, p. 1111–1146, * *PSO*.

Reviewed in *British critic*, London, 1820, v. 56, p. 32–40, * *DA; Literary gazette*, London, 1820, v. 4, p. 241–244, * *DA;* and *London magazine*, London, 1820, v. 1, p. 679–686, * *DA*.

Mones, Leon. Jochanan ben Saccai. A historical playlet for reading or presentation, based on the treachery of Joseph, later Josephus, and the heroism of Jochanan. (Temple tidings. Newark, N. J., 1927. 8°. v. 3, no. 4, Oct. 7, 1927, p. 2–3.)

Otway, Thomas. Titus and Berenice, a tragedy ₁in five acts and in verse₁... With a farce called The Cheats of Scapin. London: Printed for Richard Tonson at his Shop under Grays-Inn-Gate, next Grays-Inn-Lane, 1677. 62 ₁i. e. 70₁ p., 1 l. 4°.

Title from British Museum Catalogue.

—— —— London: Printed for M. Tonson, and are to be sold by T. Chapman, 1701. 4 p.l., 26, 23(1) p. 4°.

Title from British Museum Catalogue.

—— —— London: T. Davis, S. Bladon, etc., 1771. 70 p., 1 l. 16°.

Also printed in his *Works*, London, 1712, v. 1, p. 135–174; London, 1757, v. 1, p. 201–252, *NCP*; London, 1812, v. 1; London, 1813, v. 1, p. 161–201, *NCP*; and his *Complete works, edited by Montague Summers*, Bloomsbury, 1926, v. 1, p. 141–179, * *KP (Nonesuch)*.

SPIES, Joseph. Otway's Titus and Berenice and Racine's Bérénice, a parallel. (In: Wetzlar, Germany. — Königliches Gymnasium. Programm für 1890/1. Wetzlar, 1891. 4°. p. 1–11.)

Pinski, David. The stranger (or, "The eternal Jew"); a legend-drama in one act. Authorized translation from the Yiddish by Isaac Goldberg, with an introductory appreciation by the translator, David Pinski: master dramatist. (Menorah journal. New York, 1918. 4°. v. 4, p. 214–227.)   *** PBD**

Time: 70 A. D., in the city of Beris Arva.

The story is based on a legend from Midrash Eicha Rabothi, the text of which is given as comment on Lamentations 1:16.

Reprinted in Isaac Goldberg, translator, *Six plays of the Yiddish theatre: second series*, Boston [1918], p. 25–69, * *PTP*, and in the author's *Ten plays*, New York, 1920, p. 177–209, * *PTP*.

Produced by the Pathfinders-Reviewers, San Francisco, May 23, 1929.

Racine, Jean Baptiste. Berenice. (In his: Dramatic works. A metrical English version by Robert Bruce Boswell. London, 1889–90. 12°. v. 1, p. 325–386.)

Also issued in 1913, *NKO*, and 1918.

The Fall of Jerusalem, continued

—— Berenice, a tragedy. Translated from the French of Jean Racine by John Masefield. London: William Heinemann, 1922. 4 p.l., 61 p. 12°.

In five acts and in verse. Translated for the use of the Hill Players and produced by them Nov. 24, 1921, with John Lanyon as Titus and Mrs. Keatinge as Berenice.

Reprinted in Masefield's *Esther and Berenice,* New York, 1922, p. 109–205 and in his *Verse plays,* New York, 1925, p. 157–207, *NCR.*

Reviewed by George S. Hellman in *Menorah journal,* New York, 1922, v. 8, p. 250–251, * *PBD;* by F. L. Lucas in *New statesman,* London, 1922, v. 19, p. 489–490, * *DA;* and by O. W. Firkins in *Yale review,* New Haven, 1922, v. 12, p. 192–193, * *DA.*

VILLARD, Léonie. Bérénice en Angleterre. (Revue de l'Université de Lyon. Lyon, 1928. 8°. no. 2, p. 105–113.)

The **Stork** and the lion. ₁A playlet in one scene.₁ (Jewish child. New York, 1917. 4°. v. 5, no. 29, p. 2, 4.)   * **PBD**

When the rebellious Jews, in 120 A. D., in defiance of Rome, begin to rebuild the Temple, the tanna Joshua b. Hananiah reminds them of the fable of the stork and the lion, and that Rome is the lion.

Strathmore, Mary Eleanor Lyon Bowes, countess of. The siege of Jerusalem. ₁A dramatic poem, in five acts.₁ London, 1774. 8°.

Title from British Museum Catalogue.

THE WANDERING JEW

ZIRUS, Werner. ...Der ewige Jude in der Dichtung, vornehmlich in der Englischen und Deutschen. Leipzig: Mayer & Müller, G.m.b.H., 1928. xi, 159 p. 8°. (Palaestra 162...)   * **PZB p.v.1**
Literaturverzeichnis, p. vii–xi.

Reviewed in *Jewish quarterly review,* Philadelphia, 1929, new series, v. 20, p. 106–107, * *PBE.*

Carman, Mrs. The Wandering Jew, an adaptation of Sue's novel, was produced at the Bowery Theatre, New York, Jan. 14, 1850, with Mr. Bowes as the Jew.

Noticed in *Spirit of the times,* New York, 1850, v. 19, p. 576, 588, †† *MVA.*

Evans, Albert Eubule. The curse of immortality. ₁A dramatic poem in three acts.₁ London, Cambridge ₁printed₁, 1873. 8°.

Title from British Museum Catalogue.

Reviewed in *The Athenæum,* London, June 14, 1873, v. 61, p. 754–755, * *DA.*

Also reviewed by R. G. Moulton in *Poet-lore,* Philadelphia, 1891, v. 3, p. 326–335, * *DA.* "He [the author] supposes Theudas to be *unrepentant,* and that a single moment's submission to the power he defied sixteen centuries before will bring the longed-for rest of death. The problem becomes thus a struggle of human will against divine." — *p. 326.*

Franklin, Andrew. The wandering Jew; or, Love's masquerade A comedy, in two acts... London: George Cawthorn, 1797. 55 p. 8°.   **NCO p.v.147**

Three other editions were also printed the same year.

Reviewed in *Monthly review,* London, 1797, second series, v. 24, p. 465, *NAA,* and in *Monthly visitor,* London, 1797, v. 1, p. 451–452; v. 2, p. 383–384, * *DA.*

First produced at the Drury Lane Theatre, London, in May, 1797. The production was reviewed in the *Monthly mirror,* London, 1797, v. 3, p. 309–310, * *DA.* Produced for the first time in America at the New Park Theatre, New York, May 2, 1798.

The first stage representation of the legend of the Wandering Jew.

Heywood, Joseph Converse. Antonius. A dramatic poem. New York: Hurd and Houghton, 1867. 272 p. 16°.   **NBM**

Kaliphilus, the wandering Jew, in Gaul.

Judd, Sylvester. Philo: an evangeliad. By the author of "Margaret; a tale of the real and ideal." Boston: Phillips, Sampson and Co., 1850. 244 p. 8°.   **NBHD**

A Christological dramatic poem, with interlocutors

human, allegorical, angelic, and divine. In the mouth of Philo are put ideas and phrases of the historical Philo.

Reviewed in *North American review,* Boston, 1850, v. 70, p. 433–443, * *DA.* Cf. Arethusa Hall, *Life and character of the Rev. Sylvester Judd,* Boston, 1854, p. 342–343, 362–370, *AN.*

Klingemann, Ernst August Friedrich. ₁Ahasver, a tragedy in five acts. 1827. Selections. Synopsis.₁ (Foreign quarterly review. London, 1827. 8°. v. 1, p. 578–595.)   * **DA**

The scene of the play is on the Bohemian frontier of Saxony and at the battle of Lutzen, 1632. The plot is taken from Franz Horn's *Der ewige Jude.* Not mentioned in Zirus.

Reviewed in *Foreign review,* London, 1829, v. 3, p. 106–107, * *DA.*

Lawrence, Charles Edward. Spikenard. ₁In one act.₁ (Cornhill magazine. London, 1921. 8°. new series, v. 50, p. 413–420.) * *DA*

Scene laid in Assyria. The Wandering Jew, Judas, the impenitent thief, and Mary Magdalene, are the characters.

—— Spikenard, a play in one act... London and Glasgow: Gowans & Gray, Ltd., 1929. 23 p. 16°. (Repertory plays. no. 74.)

"The present edition has been revised by the author."

Lewis, Leopold. The Wandering Jew, a dramatization of Eugene Sue's novel, was produced at the Adelphi Theatre, London, April 14, 1873, with H. Russell as the Jew.

Reviewed in *The Athenæum,* London, April 19, 1873, p. 513, * *DA; The Era,* London, April 20, 1873, v. 35, p. 10–11, † *NAFA;* and the *London Times,* April 15, 1873, p. 8, col. 1, * *A.*

Machado de Assis, Joaquim Maria. Life. Translated from the original Portuguese by Isaac Goldberg. (Stratford journal. Boston, 1919. 8°. v. 5, no. 3, p. 119–129.)   * **DA**

Ahasverus the wandering Jew and Prometheus are the two characters.

Medwin, Thomas. Ahasuerus, the wanderer: a dramatic legend, in six parts. By the author of Sketches in Hindoostan, and other poems... London: Printed for G. and W. B. Whittaker, 1823. xvi, 112 p. 8°.

Title from British Museum Catalogue.

Reviewed in *New monthly magazine,* London, 1823, v. 9, p. 319, * *DA.*

The Wandering Jew, continued

Mitchell, Silas Weir. Barabbas; a dramatic poem. (Book news monthly. Philadelphia, 1914. 4°. v. 32, p. 361–365.)   *** DA**

Characters: Amplias, Barabbas, and two Jews, Yacob and David, father and son, who succor Barabbas on his wanderings.

Also printed in his *Complete poems,* New York, 1914, p. 234–256, *NBI.*

Paulton, T. G. The Wandering Jew, a dramatization of Sue's novel, was produced at the Marylebone Theatre, London, July 7, 1873.

Reviewed in *The Era,* London, July 13, 1873, v. 35, p. 11, † *NAFA.*

Shelley, Percy Bysshe. Hellas, lyrical drama... London: Charles and James Ollier, 1822. xi, 60 p. 8°. (In his: Poetical pieces. London, 1823. 8°.)   *** KL**

—— Hellas, a lyrical drama by Percy Bysshe Shelley; a reprint of the original edition published in 1822, with the author's prologue and notes by various hands, edited by Thomas J. Wise. London: Published for the Shelley Society by Reeves and Turner, 1886. lviii p., reprint (xi, 60 p.), 1 l. 8°. (The Shelley Society's publications. series 2, no. 5.)

Reprinted in various editions of his poetical works.

Landa, Myer Jack. Shelley's undying Jew. (Jewish times. Baltimore, 1927. f°. v. 17, p. 224, 224A–224B.)   **†* PBD**

Richter, Helene. "Hellas." (In her: Percy Bysshe Shelley. Weimar, 1898. 8°. p. 570–593.)   **AN**

Todhunter, John. "Hellas." (In his: A study of Shelley. London, 1880. 12°. p. 261–268.)   **NCC (Shelley)**

Thurston, Ernest Temple. The wandering Jew; a play in four phases. New York and London: G. P. Putnam's Sons, 1920. viii, 156 p. 12°.

Phase I, Jerusalem, time of Jesus; Phase II, period of first crusade; Phase III, Palermo, 1290; Phase IV, Seville, 1560.

—— New York and London: G. P. Putnam's Sons, 1921. ix, 156 p. 12°.   **NCR**

Extracts are printed in *Hearst's international,* New York, Jan., 1922, v. 41, p. 21–23, 58–59, * *DA.*

Reviewed in *Saturday review,* London, 1920, v. 130, p. 233–234, * *DA,* and by Joseph Krauskopf in *Talmud magazine,* Boston, 1922, v. 1, no. 3, p. 54–66, * *PBD.*

First produced at Manchester, England, Aug. 23, 1920. First London production at the New Theatre, London, Sept. 9, 1920. For reviews see *The Athenæum,* London, Sept. 17, 1920, p. 385–386, * *DA; The Graphic,* London, 1920, v. 102, p. 434, * *DA;* and the *Play pictorial,* London, 1921, v. 38, no. 227, p. 17–32, † *NCOA.*

Cf. "The legend of the Wandering Jew" by Moses Gaster and Regina M. Bloch in *Jewish Chronicle,* London, 1920, Sept. 17, p. 17, 26, and Sept. 24, p. 13, * *PBE.* Reviewed also *ibid.,* Sept. 17, p. 26, and by J. Light in *Jewish guardian,* London, 1920, Sept. 10, p. 11, * *PBE.*

Produced in New York at the Knickerbocker Theatre, Oct. 26, 1921, with Tyrone Power as the wandering Jew. See *American Hebrew,* New York, 1921, v. 109, p. 658, 688, * *PBD; Jewish tribune,* New York, Nov. 4, 1921, v. 38, p. 3, * *PBD; Theatre magazine,* New York, 1922, v. 35, p. 30–31, † *NBLA.* For additional reviews see *Collection of newspaper clippings of dramatic criticism, 1921–22,* vol. S–Z, † *NBL.*

JEWISH FESTIVAL PLAYS

GENERAL WORKS

Soltes, Mordecai. ...Two hundred and fifty (250) questions and answers on the Jewish festivals... New York City: Jewish Publication Society of America for the Jewish Welfare Board [cop. 1931]. iii–[iv], 5–74 p. 8°. (Jewish Welfare Board. Publications.)

[A **Symposium** on dramatics.] (Jewish center. New York, 1925. 4°. v. 3, March, 1925, p. 4–21.)   *** PYR**

Dramatics in the Jewish center program, S. S. Grossman. The administration of dramatics in the Jewish center, A. W. Rosenthal. Producing the play, Max Lieberman. Staging and scenery for amateurs, Percy Shostac. Bibliography of works on dramatics, Monroe B. Hack and A. W. Rosenthal.

Young Judaea. Festival program series. Chamisho Osor b'Shevat and Purim. New York: Young Judaea [192–?]. 63 p. 12°.

—— Festival programs for Young Judaeans. How to use the festival material. Rosh ha-Shonah and Yom Kippur. Sukkoth. Chanukah. New York: Issued by Young Judaea [192–?]. 64 p. 16°.

SPECIAL OCCASIONS

Passover

Jewish Education Committee, Chicago. Portfolio for the observance of Passover. Chicago: Bureau of Jewish Education, Tzofim Headquarters [1929]. 28 f. 4°.   *** PKB**

Partial contents: The child Moses, P. H. Dowling. Five Passover tableaux, E. C. E. Levinger.

Cover-title.
Mimeographed.

Jewish Welfare Board. Bulletin on the observance of Passover. [Compiled by M. Soltes.] New York: Jewish Welfare Board, March, 1930. 28 f. diagr. 4°.   *** PKB**

Cover-title.
Mimeographed.
Tableaux, games and plays, f. 17–21.

Zionist Organization of America. — Department of Education. ...Passover envelope for young Judaeans... [New York, 1920.] 29 l. 4°.   *** PBM p.v.76, no.15**

Typewritten.

Bien, Herman M. Easter Eve; or, The "New Hagodoh shel Pesach." A metrical family-feast service. Consisting of a pro-

Jewish Festival Plays, continued

Special Occasions — Passover, continued

logue and one character poem; including the old traditions, legends and melodies, with supplement illustration from Oppenheim's celebrated painting, "The Passover Feast." Cincinnati: Bloch Pub. and Prtg. Co., 1886. 28 p., 1 pl. 8°.   *** PKO**
Text interspersed with Hebrew passages from the Haggadah.
The Passover Seder service arranged in form of a drama. The characters represented are the members of a family, the prophet Elijah, and Nancy, the colored girl. The setting is in an American city. A sort of a miracle play.

Burstein, Abraham. The Passover rehearsal; a comedy. New York: Bloch Pub. Co., 1924. 12 p. 12°.
Time: the present. A farce showing children rehearsing for a Passover play.

Chad gadya (one only kid) tableau; adapted from Alexander M. Dushkin. (In: Jewish festival books; Passover. New York: Bureau of Jewish Education [19—?]. 8°. p. 40–42.)
"A Jewish nursery rime...borrowed from, or fashioned after, a popular German ballad, the prototype of which seems to have been an old French song."

Deitchman, Emily. Elijah's promise. (A Passover play.) (In: Jewish festival books: Passover. New York: Bureau of Jewish Education [19—?]. 8°. p. 26–37.)

A **Game** of nuts. (Jewish child. New York, 1914. f°. v. 2, no. 11, p. 3–4.) *** PBD**

Gerson, Emily Goldsmith. The Matzoh shalet, a Passover sketch [in one act]. New York: Bloch Pub. Co. [cop. 1911.] 12 p. 16°.
Time: modern.

Grossman, Samuel S. The crumb conspiracy; (Seder humoresque.) (In: Jewish festival books: Passover. New York: Bureau of Jewish Education [19—?]. 8°. p. 15–25.)
A fantastic comedy of the Seder service.

—— The glad maker. (A dolly dialogue for Erev Pesach, for young children.) (Jewish child. New York, 1920. f°. v. 8, no. 11, p. 2–3, 6–7.) *** PBD**

—— —— [New York: Young Judaea, 1920?] 5 l. 4°.
Mimeographed.
The prophet Elijah in the role of a "glad-maker."

Isaacs, Meir. The trial of Passover. [New York: Young Judaea, 19—?] 5 l. 4°.
Mimeographed.
The characters are the Jewish holidays, who ask for an injunction against Passover being a holiday.

Jewish Welfare Board. ...Fifty questions on Passover. [Compiled by M. Soltes.] New York: Jewish Welfare Board, March, 1927. 1 p.l., 10 f. 4°.   *** PKB**
Cover-title.
Mimeographed.
A sort of a how-many-can-you-answer game in which the celebrants of the Seder service participate.

Levinger, Elma C. (Ehrlich). Five Passover tableaux, adapted from E. C. Ehrlich. (In: Jewish Education Committee, Chicago, Portfolio for the observance of Passover. Chicago [1929]. 4°. 2 f.)   *** PKB**

—— The gift of Elijah. A Passover sketch in two scenes. (The Ark. Cincinnati, 1913. 8°. v. 3, no. 4, April 25, 1913, p. 223–226.)   *** PBD**

—— —— [New York: Young Judaea, 1913?] 5 l. 4°.
Mimeographed.
Time: the present. Place: the dining room of the Jacobs family a few hours before the Seder service.

—— Out of Egypt. A Passover play for senior students in three acts. (In her: Jewish festivals in the religious school. Cincinnati, 1923. 8°. p. 465–502.)   *** PSY**

—— The Passover guest; a realistic fairy tale [in three acts]. [New York: Young Judaea, 19—?] 20 l. 4°.
Mimeographed.
Time: the present, a month before Passover. Place: any American city. Elijah brings peace to an unhappy family.

—— The silver cup; a Passover folk play in one act... Cincinnati: Dept. of Synagog and School Extension of the Union of American Hebrew Congregations [cop. 1923]. 16 p. 12°.
Also printed in her *Jewish festivals in the religious school*, Cincinnati, 1923, p. 449–464, *** PSY**.
Time: about 100 years ago. Place: in a deep forest. The prophet Elijah performs a miracle.

—— The trumpet blast. A Passover play for young people. (Jewish forum. New York, 1921. 8°. v. 4, p. 821–823, 825–826, 830–831.)   *** PBD**
Simon Golden, an American-Jewish doughboy from Texas, with his two American pals as guests at the Passover Seder meals at the home of M. Levi in a small town behind the lines in France in 1918.

Mizrachi Hatzoir. The Seder. [In one scene.] (In: Envelope on Passover. New York, 1922. 4°. f. 22–25.)   **†* PBM p.v.112**
Mimeographed.
The "characters" are the four cups of wine and the dishes peculiar to the Seder meal.

Roth, Samuel. "Uncle Leiser." A Passover play for children [in two acts]. (The Ark. Cincinnati, 1913. 8°. v. 3, p. 243–249.)   *** PBD**

Sampter, Jessie Ethel. Some dates; a sketch for Pesach. [New York: Young Judaea, 19—?] 5 l. 4°.
Mimeographed.
Scene: in the sitting room of the Cohen family on the eve of Passover, 1919. The characters are the five Cohen children.

Segal, Hyman. The new Passover. [In one scene.] (Maccabaean. New York, 1911. 8°. v. 20, p. 152.)   *** PBD**

Jewish Festival Plays, continued

Special Occasions, continued

SHAVUOTH

JEWISH EDUCATION COMMITTEE, Chicago. Portfolios for holy days and festivals; Shovuoth. Chicago: Board of Jewish Education, Dramatics Dept. ₁1929?₁ 46 f. 4°.   **∗ PKB**
Partial contents: Marchers in the sun, S. S. Grossman. Near Sinai, A. Burstein. Ruth. "Sammy blintzes" and "professor," S. S. Grossman.
Cover-title.
Mimeographed.
Suggestions for plays, f. 46.

JEWISH WELFARE BOARD. Bulletin for the observance of Shovuoth. ₁Compiled by M. Soltes.₁ New York: Jewish Welfare Board, May, 1930. 23 f. 4°.   **∗ PKB**
Cover-title.
Mimeographed.
Tableaux and plays, p. 17–21. Twenty questions and answers, p. 22–23.

—— ...The Jewish ideal of learning. ₁Compiled by M. Soltes.₁ New York: Jewish Welfare Board ₁1928?₁. 28 f. 4°. (Club programs. series 1.)   **∗ PKB**
Cover-title.
Mimeographed.
Selected bibliography, f. 20–21.
Outline of historical and ceremonial aspects of Shovuoth, f. 25–28.

Blatt, William M. The treasure in the trunk. ₁In one act.₁ New York: Bloch Pub. Co., 1919. 12 p. 24°.
Scene in a modern American Jewish home. The treasure is the Bible found in grandfather's trunk.

Burstein, Abraham. Mounting Mount Sinai; a Shabuouth comedy. New York: Bloch Pub. Co., 1924. 12 p. 12°.

—— Near Sinai; Shevuoth dialogue for two boys. ₁New York: Young Judaea, 19—?₁ 2 l. 4°.
Mimeographed.

Grossman, Samuel S. Marchers in the sun; recitation and tableau. ₁Five tableaux and orations."₁ (In: Jewish festival books; Shovuoth. New York: Bureau of Jewish Education ₁19—?₁. 8°. p. 39–47.)
Reproduced in shortened form in Jewish Education Committee, Chicago, *Portfolios for holy days and festivals; Shovuoth,* Chicago [1929?], ∗ PKB.

—— ...Playlet game for Shovuos...₁in one scene.₁ ₁Philadelphia? 192–?₁ 3 f. 4°.   **†∗ PBM p.v.112, no.4**
At head of title: Board of Jewish Education.
Mimeographed.

—— "Sammy Blintzes" and "Professor." (A novelty monologue.) ₁New York: Young Judaea, 192–?₁ 2 l. 4°.
Mimeographed.
A dialogue for two boys.
Also printed in Zionist Organization of America. — Department of Education, *Lag ba'Omer-Shabuoth envelope for young Judaeans,* New York [1920?], p. 21–23, ∗ PBM p.v.
Reproduced in shortened form in Jewish Education Committee, Chicago, *Portfolios for holy days and festivals,* Chicago [1929?], ∗ PKB.

Ish-Kishor, Judith. A day off the exile; a Shabuoth fancy to be played outdoors. New York: Issued for Young Judea by the Department of Education of the Zionist Organization of America ₁19—?₁. 7 l. 4°.
Scene: anywhere in a park.

—— In our closet; a sketch for students (Ivris b'Ivris). ₁In one scene.₁ (Jewish child. New York, 1917. f°. v. 5, no. 14, p. 3–4.)   **∗ PBD**

—— The slave from Egypt; a Sh'vous play. (Jewish advocate. Boston, 1924. f°. June 5, 1924, section 2, p. 6, cols. 1–3.) ∗ **PBD**

—— —— New York: National Young Judaea ₁1924?₁. 4 l. 4°.
Mimeographed.

—— The slave from Egypt; a play in one act... New York: Samuel French, cop. 1930. 3 ₁p.l., 8 p. 12°.
Six nations refuse the Law; Israel, the slave from Egypt, accepts it.

Levinger, Elma C. (Ehrlich). The heathen who stood on one foot. ₁In one scene.₁ (In her: Entertaining programs for the assembly. Cincinnati ₁cop. 1930₁. 8°. p. 94–97.)   **∗ PSY**
The characters are Hillel, Shammai, and Gaius, a young heathen. Based on a Talmudic legend.

—— The man with empty hands; a Shevuoth play. ₁New York: Young Judaea, 192–?₁ 9 l. 4°.
Mimeographed.
Deals with the duty of making a pilgrimage to Jerusalem on Shavuoth day and bringing an offering.

Teiser, Ruth. Confirmation for girls. ₁In three acts.₁ illus. (Young Israel. Cincinnati, 1930. 4°. v. 22, May, p. 4–5.)   **∗ PBD**
The scene of the play is laid in Hamburg, Germany, in the year 1821.

SUCCOTH

JEWISH EDUCATION COMMITTEE, Chicago. Portfolios for the holy days and festivals; Succoth and Simchath torah. Chicago: Bureau of Jewish Education, Dramatics Dept. ₁1929.₁ 46 f. 4°.   **∗ PKB**
Cover-title.
Mimeographed.
Suggested plays, f. 46.

JEWISH WELFARE BOARD. Bulletin on the observance of Succoth, including program material and twenty-five questions and answers. ₁Compiled by M. Soltes.₁ New York: Jewish Welfare Board, Sept., 1929. 35 f. 4°. ∗ **PKB**
Cover-title.
Mimeographed.
Plays and tableaux, p. 13–15.

Abramowitz, Louis. The fruit of the land; a Succoth tableau in two scenes. ₁New York: Young Judaea, 19–?₁ 2 l. 4°.
Mimeographed.
Reproduced in Jewish Education Committee, Chicago, *Portfolios for holy days and festivals; Succoth and Simchath torah,* Chicago [192–?], ∗ PKB.
Scene 1 — in the wilderness in the days of Moses; scene 2 — in Eretz Israel in 1920.

Jewish Festival Plays, continued

Special Occasions — Succoth, continued

Binstock, Ruth Atlas. Harvest festival; a pageant in four scenes. Cincinnati: Department of Synagog and School Extension of the Union of American Hebrew Congregations [cop. 1925]. 13 p. 8°.

Blum, Rose. Harvest scene of old Judea. [In three scenes.] [New York: Bureau of Jewish Education, 192–?] 4 f. 4°.

Typewritten.
Time: "Judea's golden age," in the reign of King Josiah. Huldah, the prophetess (see II. Kings, XXII: 14–20) is one of the characters. Suggested costumes, f. 4.

Burstein, Abraham. Life in a Succah; a Succoth comedy [in one act]. New York: Bloch Pub. Co., 1924. 12 p. 12°.

Time: the present.

Cavanah, Frances. Thanksgiving wonders. [In one scene.] Illustrated by Hazel Frazee. (Child life. Chicago, 1924. f°. v. 3, p. 656–659, 687–689.)

Rebecca is the doll of ancient Jerusalem. She tells her sister dolls, Greece, Rome, Egypt, Puritan England, of the ancient Hebrew feast of ingathering.

Ehrlich, Ida Lublinski. In booths. (Young Israel. Cincinnati, 1928. f°. v. 21, Sept., 1928, p. 10–12.)   *** PBD**

Goldberg, Israel. The ancient fortress. [In one act.] [New York: Young Judaea, 1919?] 5 l. f°.

Mimeographed.
A war play. On the Russo-German border on the eve of Succoth, during the Great War. The sukkah is the fortress.

Grossman, Samuel S. "Hiding in the Sukkah." A playlet for Sukkot in one act. [New York: Young Judaea, 19—?] 4 l. 4°. (In his: [Holiday and other plays for Jewish children.])   **NASH**

Mimeographed.

—— Who built the Sukkoh? A modern farce-comedy for Jewish children [in two scenes]. [New York: Young Judaea, 19—?] 13 l. 4°. (In his: [Holiday and other plays for Jewish children.])   **NASH**

Ish-Kishor, Judith. "Can he do it?" A Succos phantasy in two scenes and an epilogue. [New York: Young Judaea, 19—?] 15 l. 4°.

Mimeographed.
The Feinstein family in a dream of Russia, dream of Spain, and dream of Palestine.

Levinger, Elma C. Ehrlich. How Succoth came to Chayim. A modern play, in one act. (In her: Jewish festivals in the religious school. Cincinnati, 1923. 8°. p. 263–278.)   *** PSY**

Time: the present. Place: a farm-house in northern Minnesota. How a foreign-born boy influences an American family to observe Succoth.

—— The Jewish community. [In one scene.] (In her: Entertaining programs for the assembly. Cincinnati [cop. 1930]. 8°. p. 59–63.)   *** PSY**

Intended for the occasion of the dedication of a synagogue.

—— Pilgrims to Palestine; a travelogue in pictures to music and poetry. (In her: Entertaining programs for the assembly. Cincinnati [cop. 1930]. 8°. p. 73–78.)   *** PSY**

Among the characters are Judah ha-Levi, Nachmanides, Joseph Caro, Moses Montefiore, and Theodor Herzl. The Israelites were enjoined to make three annual pilgrimages to Jerusalem, on Succoth, Passover and Shavuoth.

Linsky, Fannie Barnett. America and the Jew; a pageant for Thanksgiving day. Cincinnati, O.: Department of Synagog and School Extension of the Union of American Hebrew Congregations [cop. 1923]. 20 p. 12°.   **NBL p.v.107, no.8**

Thanksgiving pageant suitable for Succoth.
Performed by the children of the Temple Israel Sunday Schools, Boston, October, 1922.

What's the rush? (A dialogue for Succoth.) [In one scene.] (In: Jewish Education Committee, Chicago. Portfolios for holy days and festivals. Succoth and simchath torah. Chicago [192–?]. 3 f. 4°.)   *** PKB**

Mimeographed.

PURIM

Abrahams, Israel. Lost Purim joys. (In his: The book of delight, and other papers. Philadelphia, 1912. 8°. p. 266–272.)   *** PBT**

—— Purim parodies. (In his: Festival studies. London, 1906. 12°. p. 32–39.)   *** PKA**

Gaster, Moses. Minstrelsy and Purim play. (Jewish chronicle supplement. London, 1921. f°. no. 4, April, 1921, p. i–ii.)   *** PBE**

Jewish Education Committee, Chicago. Purim portfolio. Chicago: Board of Jewish Education, Dramatics Dept. [192–?] 43 f. 4°.   *** PKB**

Partial contents: The jolly jester, E. C. E. Levinger. Shadows of Purim.
Cover-title.
Mimeographed.
Purim plays, f. 42–43.

Jewish Welfare Board. Bulletin for the observance of Purim. [Compiled by M. Soltes.] New York: Jewish Welfare Board, Feb., 1930. 26 f. 4°.   *** PKB**

Cover-title.
Mimeographed.
Plays and tableaux, p. 12–18. Twenty-five questions and answers, p. 23–24.

Lipsky, Louis. The Purim plays. (The New era. New York, 1905. 4°. v. 6, no. 4, March/April, 1905, p. 385–387.)   *** PBD**

Zionist Organization of America. — Department of Education. ...Suggestions for Purim program, for young Judaeans... New York: Young Judaea [192–?]. 6 f., 1 l. 4°.   *** PBM p.v.112, no.7**

Typewritten.

Jewish Festival Plays, continued

Special Occasions — Purim, continued

Benedict, George. The masterpiece. A Purim comedietta in two acts. (London Jewry sketches. VI.) (Jewish exponent. Philadelphia, 1901. f°. v. 32, no. 19, March 1, 1901, p. 1–2.)   †* **PBD**
Place: house in Whitechapel back street. Time: present.

Bergman, Ruth, and DAVID DE SOLA POOL. A Purim carol. With apologies to Charles Dickens. (Alav Hashalom). [In three scenes.] (Young Judaean. New York, 1923. 8°. v. 13, no. 2, p. 44–50, 59, 62, 64.)   * **PBD**
A Zionist Purim play. The character of the Kamsan modelled after that of Scrooge, in Dickens' *A Christmas carol.*

Bertie's Purim party. [A burlesque Purim play.] (American Hebrew. New York, 1881. f°. v. 6, p. 30, 42.)   * **PBD**

Burstein, Abraham. Casting of lots (a Purim party in one act). (Young Judaean. New York, 1914. 8°. v. 4, March, 1914, p. 17–22.)
Copy in Dropsie College.

—— —— New York: Young Judaean Pub. Association, cop. 1914. 7 p. 8°. * **PSQ p.v.1**

—— —— New York: Bloch Pub. Co., 1922. 15 p. new and rev. ed. 12°.
Jewish children of modern times get together and impersonate the characters in the Book of Esther.

—— A dream of Purim. n. p., n. d. 8 p. 8°.   * **PSQ p.v.1**
The action of the play, the characters of which are all from the book of Esther, takes place in a dream of two children, Aaron and Miriam.

Burstein, Abraham, and JULIUS BACHER. Haman of today; a Purim play [in three scenes] about a play. New York: Bloch Publishing Company, 1931. 12 p. 12°.

Burstein, Elliot M. A Purim surprise, a comedy [in two acts]. New York: Bloch Publishing Company, 1930. 24 p. 12°.
Depicts the way in which two modern families celebrate Purim.

Fuchs, J. "Mordechai's triumph" — a Purim play. [Second act] from "The Comedy of Queen Esther and the wicked Haman." (American Hebrew. New York, 1910. f°. v. 86, p. 529–531.)   * **PBD**

Gerson, Emily Goldsmith. The Purim basket. [In two acts.] (Young Israel. Cincinnati, 1910. 8°. v. 5, p. 390–394.)   * **PBD**

—— —— New York: Bloch Pub. Co., cop. 1914. 12 p. 16°.
Time: the present.

—— Ten years after; a Purim play [in two acts]. Philadelphia: J. H. Greenstone [19—?]. 4 l. 8°.   * **PSQ p.v.1**
Caption-title.
Time: the present.

Goldberg, David. Purim drama [in eleven scenes] founded on the book of Esther. [Brockton, Mass.: Standard-Modern Prtg. Co., 1931.] 11 l. 12°.
Caption-title.
"Undertaken...for the benefit of Temple Israel Sunday School."

Goldberg, Israel. The last of Haman; a play in one act for Purim by Rufus Learsi [pseud.]. n. p., n. d. 9 l. 4°.
Time: the present. Place: the United States.

Gordin, Jacob. A Purim injunction. (Adapted from the Yiddish of Jacob Gordin.) [New York: Young Judaea, 19—?] 3 l. 4°.
Mimeographed.
The Jewish holidays appear as plaintiffs before the judge for an injunction against Purim.

Grossman, Samuel S. "The Jester's gift." A Purim playlet [in five scenes] for young children... [New York:] Bureau of [Jewish] Education, n. d. 1, 11 f. 4°.
Mimeographed.
Also in his *[Holiday and other plays for Jewish children]*, *NASH*.
Produced by the Free Synagogue, Bronx Schools, Feb. 24, 1918, at the Community Building Auditorium.

—— The Purim players. [New York: Young Judea, 1911?] 6, 13 f. 4°.
Mimeographed.   †* **PBM p.v.112**
A drama in two scenes and in verse.

—— The Purim players; a Purim play in one act. [In verse.] Philadelphia: J. H. Greenstone, 1911. 8 l. 12°.   * **PSQ p.v.1**
Presented by the pupils of the Philadelphia Hebrew Sunday School, March 3, 1912, at Touro Hall, Philadelphia.

—— —— Philadelphia: J. H. Greenstone, 1925. 14 p. 8°.

—— Purim prologue. [In one scene]... [Philadelphia? 192–?] 3 f. 4°.
Mimeographed.   †* **PBM p.v.112**

—— "Vote for Haman!" A Purim humoresque. [New York: Young Judaean, n. d.] 5 l. 4°. (In his: [Holiday and other plays for Jewish children.])   **NASH**
Mimeographed.

—— —— [New York: Young Judean, n. d.] 4 l. 4°.
Mimeographed.
A variant edition.
Haman, on Purim day, protests against the way he is treated.

Hoffman, Rebekah B. Judah's new deliverer. A Purim allegory [in three scenes]. (Jewish exponent. Philadelphia, 1918. f°. v. 66, no. 21, Feb. 22, 1918, p. 1, 9.)   * **PBD**
Public opinion is the King of the play, and Zionism is a beautiful maiden. The King puts away his queen, Commercialism, and enthrones Zionism in her place.

Judaism's triumph. [A Purim sketch, in one scene.] [New York: Bureau of Jewish Education, 192–?] 6 f. 4°.
Typewritten.

Jewish Festival Plays, continued

Special Occasions — Purim, continued

Kates, James A. Purim on trial. [In one act.] New York: Bloch Publishing Company, 1931. 10 p. 12°.
The other Jewish holidays object to Purim as being one of them. The jury decides in favor of Purim.

Kraft, Louis. A daughter of her people. [In one act.] [New York: Jewish Welfare Board, 1927.] 8 f. 4°.
Caption-title.
Typewritten.
Scene is laid in modern Poland, where another Esther intervenes on behalf of her people.

Krentzler, Daisy, and W. W. SCHORR. "Purim Shpiel"; or, "The glorification of the Hamantasch," a comic operetta in two acts. Written by Daisy Krentzler, in collaboration with William W. Schorr. New York: Central Jewish Institute [1928]. 29 (1) p. diagr. 8°.
Produced at the Central Jewish Institute, March 4, 1928.

Leiser, Joseph. Evelyn dreams of Purim. [In three scenes.] New York: Bloch Publishing Company, 1930. 12 p. 12°.

Leonard, Oscar. A grown up children's Purim play. General suggestions. (Arranged by S. S. Grossman.) [New York: Young Judaea, 19—?] 5 l. 4°.
Mimeographed.
A burlesque on the manner in which children present a play.

—— A new Esther. [A play in one act.] (From the Jewish life in modern Russia.) Cincinnati: Young Israel, cop. 1911. 5 p. 8°.
                                                    * PSQ p.v.1
Reprinted from *Young Israel*, Cincinnati, 1911, v. 7, p. 372–376, * PBD.
An episode of Russian Jewish life.

—— The spirit of Purim; a fairy play for Jewish children. (Jewish tribune. New York, 1924. f°. v. 43, March 14, 1924, p. 18, 29–30, 32.)   * PBD
Time: the present. Scene: a hovel in the poorest Jewish district of a small town in Poland.

Levinger, Elma C. Ehrlich. The jolly jester. [In one scene.] (In: Jewish Education Committee, Chicago. Purim portfolio. Chicago [192–?]. 1 f. 4°.)   * PKB
Mimeographed.

—— Purim prologue — "My basket." [In one scene.] (In her: Jewish festivals in the religious school. Cincinnati, 1923. 12°. p. 126–127.)   * PSY

—— The Purim robe; a little episode of mediaeval Jewry [in one act]. illus. (American Hebrew. New York, 1920. f°. v. 106, p. 458, 488–489.)   * PBD
Love story of a Jewish maiden and a Christian Humanist, in the Judengasse of a German city, about 1500. The incident takes place on Purim eve.

—— A sick Purim. A modern Purim play in one act. (In her: Jewish festivals in the religious school. Cincinnati, 1923. 8°. p. 351–374.)   * PSY
Little orphans, confined to bed in a hospital, dramatize the story of Esther.

Levinger, Elma C. (Ehrlich), and LILLIAN ROSENBAUM. The Purim pussy. Story by E. C. E. Levinger; dramatized [in three acts] by Lillian Rosenbaum. [New York: Bureau of Jewish Education, 192–?] 3 f. 4°.
Typewritten.

Levinson, Herman D. The spirit of Purim. New York: Bloch Pub. Co., cop. 1916. 12 p. 16°.
The characters are Esther and Ahasuerus, both masked as such at a Purim masked ball, given by a Reform Temple. A satire on modern American Reform Rabbinate.

Linsky, Fannie Barnett. The paper hat; a play for Purim in two acts and an entr' act. Cincinnati, O.: Department of Synagog and School Extension of the Union of American Hebrew Congregations [cop. 1924]. 39 p. 12°.   **NBL p.v.106, no.9**
Deals with the problem of anti-Semitism; at the same time presents the atmosphere of Purim.

A **Modern** Purim. [In three acts.] New York: Jewish Welfare Board [1925]. 7 f. 4°.
Caption-title.
Typewritten.
The Purim story told under a modern setting.

Morris, Esther. The story of Purim [in a prologue and two acts]. (In her: Tears and laughter. London, 1926. 12°. p. 41–56.)
                                                       NCR

A **Purim** sketch. (Jewish child. New York, 1912. 4°. v. 1, no. 18, p. 2.)   * PBD
Queen Esther and nine little girls of to-day.

Reinhart, Harold F. The trial of Haman; a Purim farce. (Young Israel. Cincinnati, 1930. f°. v. 22, no. 7, March, 1930, p. 3–4, 10–12.)   * PBD

Restored to life. Adapted from the Hebrew by Chas. Blumenthal. (Maccabaean. New York, 1906. 8°. v. 10, p. 73–75.) * PBD
In one act.

Roth, Samuel. The double demand. A Purim play. (The Ark. Cincinnati, 1914. 8°. v. 4, no. 2, Feb. 27, 1914, p. 101–111.) * PBD

Segal, Benny. The holiday Jack likes best. (Young Israel. Cincinnati, 1928. f°. v. 21, Sept., 1928, p. 19.)   * PBD
A playlet by a ten year old boy. The holiday, Purim.

Seligman, Florence C. The call of his people; a Purim play. [In two acts.] illus. (The guardian, ha-Shomer. New York, 1918. 8°. v. 1, Feb., 1918, p. 7–8.)
Copy in Library of Union Theological Seminary.

Shadows of Purim. [In five scenes and epilogue.] (In: Board of Jewish Education. — Dramatics Department, Chicago. Purim portfolio. Chicago [192–?]. 3 f. 4°.) * PKB
Mimeographed.

Jewish Festival Plays, continued

Special Occasions — Purim, continued

Simon, Carolyn. The under-dog; a one-act play. [New York: Jewish Welfare Board, 1925.] 15 f. 4°.
Typewritten.
Deals with anti-Jewish discrimination in an American college community. Intended for Purim presentation.

Wolf, Ruth E. Levi. The king's choice; a Purim sketch. New York: Bloch Pub. Co., cop. 1910. 11 p. 12°.   * **PSQ**
From among the numerous women of the Bible who appear before the king, Esther is chosen.

Woolf, Henry. The cute little king; a Purim play in one act. (Jewish tribune. New York, 1926. f°. v. 45, Feb. 26, 1926, p. 2–3, 42–43, 46–47.)   * **PBD**

———— Haman's conspiracy, a Purim play ... A drama in two acts. (Young Israel. Cincinnati, 1910. 8°. v. 5, p. 325–332, 358–363.)   * **PBD**

———— The Purim tale; a story in rhyme [in one act]. Cincinnati: Department of Synagogue and School Extension of the Union of American Hebrew Congregations [cop. 1929]. 23 p. music. 12°.
In the style of a comic opera. Several songs interspersed. Six main characters and a chorus.

HANUKKAH

JEWISH EDUCATION COMMITTEE, Chicago. Portfolios for holy days and festivals; Chanukah. Chicago: Bureau of Jewish Education [192–?]. 36 f. 4°.   * **PKB**
Partial contents: Chanukah lights, S. Ish-Kishor. Over the Chanukah lights, M. Myers. Candle drill for Hanukka, J. E. Sampter.
Cover-title.
Mimeographed.

———— Programs for Jewish youth clubs; Chanukah program. Chicago: Jewish Youth League [1929]. 21 f. 4°.   * **PKB**
Cover-title.
Mimeographed.
"Chanukah plays," f. 18.

JEWISH WELFARE BOARD. Bulletin on the observance of Chanukah, including supplementary material and thirty-five questions and answers. [Compiled by M. Soltes.] New York: Jewish Welfare Board, Nov., 1929. 30 f. 4°.   * **PKB**
Cover-title.
Mimeographed.
Annotated list of plays, tableaux, dances and games, p. 15–21.

Benjamin, Irma A. Shadows of our past; a Hanukah entertainment. A prologue, shadowgraphs, an epilogue   New York: Bloch Pub. Co., 1924. 11 p. 12°.
Two Christian boys and one Jewish boy.

Bien, H. M. The feast of lights, or Chanukoh, three character poems and grand tableau finale; containing the story of the Book Maccabees, and designed for representation by Sabbath Schools and Y. M. L. A. A companion piece to "Purim" the Feast of Esther... Vicksburg, Miss.: Vicksburg Printing & Pub. Co., 1885. 27 p. 8°.
                    * **PSQ** p.v.1
Part first: Traitor and patriot; part second: Martyrs and tyrant; part third: The victory of freedom; Grand tableau finale: Chanukoh.

Broido, Louis. The enemies of Israel; a Hanukkah fantasy in one act. Cincinnati, O.: Department of Synagog and School Extension of the Union of American Hebrew Congregations [cop. 1917]. 26 p. 12°.
                    * **PBM** p.v.1, no.7
A second ed. 29 p. * *PBM p.v.98.*
A picture of present Jewish home life.

Bursetown, G. "Old Mattathias' home during Maccabean War." (A Chanukah play in one act.) n. p., cop. 1925. 16 p. 8°.
Deals with the period following the death of Mattathias.

Burstein, Abraham. Too much noise; a Chanukah play [in one act] for boys. New York: Bloch Pub. Co., 1924. 12 p. 12°.
Time: the present.

Ehrlich, Ida Lublinski. A Hanukkah play. illus. (Young Israel. Cincinnati, 1929. 4°. v. 22, no. 4, Dec., 1929, p. 3–5.)   * **PBD**

Fineberg, Solomon. By the light of Chanukah; a play in three acts... Cincinnati: Department of Synagog and School Extension of the Union of American Hebrew Congregations [cop. 1924]. 28 p. 12°.
                    * **PBM** p.v.98, no.5
Place: modern America.
The story of Hanukkah as background for the ambition of a young boy anxious to matriculate at a Rabbinical college.

Frank, Florence. Chanukkah night. A Chanukkah play in one act. (The Ark. Cincinnati, 1912. 8°. v. 2, p. 814–818.)   * **PBD**

Freehof, Fanny Evelyn. Forever and — a Chanukah play [in three scenes]. New York: Bloch Publishing Company, 1929. 11 p. 12°.

Frisch, Ruth. Kindle the lights. [In one act] illus. (Young Israel. Cincinnati, 1923. 4°. v. 16, Dec., 1923, p. 5, 15.)   * **PBD**

Fuhrman, J. M. Struggle and victory; a Chanukah program [in two acts] by J. M. Fuhrman...in collaboration with Howard L. Fineberg... New York: Bloch Pub. Co., 1925. 16 p. 12°.
The characters are in two groups: Hostile forces, Pharaoh, Torquemada, Czar Nicholas; Saving forces, Abraham, Moses, Prophets, and the Temple.

Jewish Festival Plays, continued

Special Occasions — Hanukkah, continued

Gerson, Emily Goldsmith. The brass candelabra. A Hanucca sketch. (Jewish exponent. Philadelphia, 1908. f°. v. 48, no. 6, Nov. 20, 1908, p. 5, 8.)   †† * **PBD**
In two acts.

—— —— Philadelphia: J. H. Greenstone ₁1908₁. 3 l. 12°.   * **PSQ p.v.1**
Scene: in Russia.
Sentimental story with a Russian and American setting.

—— A delayed birthday, a Chanukkah play ₁in one act₁. (Young Israel. Cincinnati, 1909. 8°. v. 5, p. 70–73.)   * **PBD**

—— New lamps for old. A Chanukkah playlet. (The Ark. Cincinnati, 1915. 8°. v. 5, no. 12, Dec., 1915, p. 574–578.)   * **PBD**
Place: modern America.
Reprinted in *Jewish exponent*, Philadelphia, v. 62, no. 9, Dec. 3, 1915, p. 5, * *PBD.*

Goldberg, Israel. "The capture"; a one act play for Chanukah by Rufus Learsi ₁pseud.₁. New York: Department of Education, Zionist Organization of America, cop. 1918. 7 l. 4°.
Mimeographed.
Time: the present. Place: Russia.
Black Vasily, an agent provocateur and pogrom-organizer, is one of the characters. He is captured by a girl.

—— —— New York: Jewish Welfare Board ₁1930₁. 7 l. 4°.
Mimeographed.

Grossman, Samuel S. Chanuckah tableaux with recitations, adapted and arranged... ₁Philadelphia? 192–?₁ 3 f. 4°
Typewritten.   †* **PBM p.v.112, no.6**

—— The light of love. A Chanukah play for seniors. ₁New York: Young Judaea, 19—?₁ 7 l. 4°. (In his: ₁Holiday and other plays for Jewish children.₁)   **NASH**
Typewritten.
Place: modern America.

—— "Then and now;" tableaux for Chanuckah. ₁Philadelphia? 192–?₁ 2 f. 4°.
Typewritten.   †* **PBM p.v.112, no.5**

—— What's tonight? A Chanukkah farce comedy in two acts. (The Ark. Cincinnati, 1911. 8°. v. 1, no. 1, Nov. 24, 1911, p. 621–637.) ·   * **PBD**

—— Philadelphia: Julius H. Greenstone, 1925. 26 p. 8°.
In the Greenbaum home, Sunday afternoon, before Hanukkah. Modern America.

Ish-Kishor, Judith. "When the candle smoked"; a Chanukah jumble, in a prologue, an act, and an epilogue. ₁New York: Young Judaea, 19—?₁ 16 l. 4°.
Mimeographed.
In the prologue, a number of boys forming the entertainment committee of "Kol Yisroel Club" arrange for a Hanukkah play which follows.

Ish-Kishor, Sulamith. Chanukah lights. ₁A poem dramatized.₁ (In: Jewish Education Committee, Chicago, Portfolios for holy days and festivals; Chanukah. Chicago ₁192–?₁. 4°. 2 f.)   * **PKB**

Jacobson, Janie. Chanukkah Eve; or, Jacob Mendoza's dream and what came of it. (A Chanukkah fantaisie in four acts.) A play for school and home. ₁Cincinnati:₁ Young Israel, cop. 1909. 4 l. 8°.

Kraft, Irma. A Maccabean cure. (In her: The Power of Purim, and other plays. Philadelphia, 1915. 12°. p. 55–91.)   * **PSQ**
Time: the eve before Hanukkah, the present era.
Place: the living-room of Mrs. Philip Beckman, Homestead, Pa.
Presented by the Alliance Drama Circle, Los Angeles, Cal., Dec. 28, 1924.

Landman, Isaac. Their own people. A Chanukah play ₁in one act₁. Cincinnati, cop. 1927₁. 20 p. 12°.

Leibson, Jacob J. David of Modin; a Chanukah play. ₁In a prologue and three acts.₁ (Jewish home. New York, 1903. 8°. v. 10, p. 87–98.)   * **PBD**

Levinger, Elma C. Ehrlich. The Chanukah lights. ₁In one scene.₁ (In her: Jewish festivals in the religious school. Cincinnati, 1923. 12°. p. 75–77.)   * **PSY**

—— Light in the darkness; a play for Hanukah ₁in one act₁. (American Hebrew. New York, 1920. f°. v. 108, p. 70, 95.) * **PBD**
Time: the middle ages. Place: any country in Christian Europe.

—— The unlighted menorah; a Chanukah fantasy of the time of Felix Mendelssohn in one act... Cincinnati: Department of Synagog and School Extension of the Union of American Hebrew Congregations ₁cop. 1923₁. 12 p. 12°.   * **PBM p.v.98, no.7**
The characters are Felix Mendelssohn-Bartholdy, his father, his mother, and his grandfather Moses Mendelssohn (seen in a dream). The time is a November evening in the year 1835.
Also printed in her *Jewish festivals in the religious school*, Cincinnati, 1923, p. 305–316, * *PSY.*

—— ₁New York: Young Judaea, n. d.₁ 6 l. 4°.
Mimeographed.

Lewis, Rena. A Hanukka surprise. New York: Bloch Pub. Co., 1922. 8 p. 12°.
Scene is in a modern home during the Hanukkah week.

Linsky, Fannie Barnett. The end of the story; a Hanukkah play. Cincinnati: Department of Synagogue and School Extension of the Union of American Hebrew Congregations ₁cop. 1928₁. 20 p. 12°.

Jewish Festival Plays, continued

Special Occasions — Hanukkah, continued

Lipkind, Goodman. What happened on Chanuka; a play·for adults (in one act). New York: Bloch Pub. Co., 1924. 40 p. 12°.
* PBM p.v.97, no.9
Time: the present. Place: a small town.
The action of the play has nothing to do with the historical facts of Hanukkah.

Lipsky, Louis. "Vice-versa!" A Chanuka play for Purim. Published for the Junior Literary Branch of the B'nai and Benoth Zion Kadimah of New York. New York: Maccabean Pub. Co., 1907. 17 p. 16°.
* PSQ p.v.1

Lyons, Alexander. Chanukah evening. (Jewish home. New York, 1903. 8°. v. 10, p. 99–102.)   * PBD
A modern sketch, in verse.

Lyons, Mabel. Chanuka in camp. ₁In two scenes.₁ (Helpful thoughts. New York, 1900. 8°. v. 6, p. 134–136.)   * PBD
Celebration of Hanukkah in camp, during the Cuban campaign of the Spanish-American war.

Meyer, Jeanne L. A modern Hanukkah play ₁in six scenes₁. illus. (Young Israel. Cincinnati, 1931. 4°. v. 23, Feb., 1931, p. 3– 5, 27, 30.)   * PBD

Myers, Miriam. Over the Chanukah lights; a dialogue for eight little boys. (In: Elma C. E. Levinger. Jewish festivals in the religious school. Cincinnati, 1923. 12°. p. 78–79.)   * PSY
Reprinted from the *Hebrew standard.*

—— Over the Chanukah lights. ₁In one scene.₁ (In: Jewish Education Committee, Chicago. Portfolios for holy days and festivals. Chanukah. Chicago ₁192–?₁. 2 f. 4°.)
Mimeographed.   * PKB

Perlman, David H. A war-time Chanukah. ₁New York: Jewish Welfare Board, 191–?₁ 9 l. 4°.
Mimeographed.
The play is staged in the sitting room of an inn in any of the countries at war in Europe.

Poppea, a Chanukah play in three acts, by Judas Maccabeus ₁pseud.₁. ₁In three acts.₁ ₁New York: Bureau of Jewish Education, 1921.₁ 15 f. 4°.
Typewritten.
"Deals with Judas Maccabeus and pre-war developments."

Sampter, Jessie Ethel. Candle drill for Hanukka for nine girls, whose ages do not matter, but whose sizes are important. New York: Bloch Pub. Co., 1922. 8 p. 12°.
Reproduced in Jewish Education Committee, Chicago, *Portfolios for holy days and festivals; Chanukah,* Chicago [192–?], * PKB.
The nine girls impersonate the 8 candles and the service candle (shamesh) of the Hanukkah candelabrum.

—— Hannah; a Hanukkah play in two acts. ₁New York: Young Judaea, 19—?₁ 5 l. 4°.
Mimeographed.
Time: the present. Place: America.
Hannah, sewing teacher, tells Mrs. Brown the story of Hannah and her seven children.

—— The last candles; a dramatic sketch for Chanukah. New York: Department of Education, Zionist Organization of America, cop. 1918. 4 p. 8°.
Time: early evening, Dec. 10, 1917. Soon after the capture of Jerusalem by Lord Allenby. Place: a Jewish house on the outskirts of Jerusalem.

Segal, Samuel M. One Hanukkah Day. Philadelphia: J. H. Greenstone, 1923. 12 p. 12°.
Modern setting, with the Feast of Lights as the theme.

Shalom Alechem, pseud. of Shalom Rabinowitz, and Isaac Dob Berkowitz. Chanukah gelt; a Chanukah play in 3 scenes. Story by Sholom Aleichem; dramatic version by I. D. Berkowitz. Translated from the Yiddish by Riva Rudy. ₁New York: Bureau of Jewish Education, 192–?₁ 7 f. f°.
Typewritten.
Deals humorously with the custom of exchanging gifts on Purim day. See Esther IX:19.

Simon, Sidney Jacob. "The college play." From fun to earnest. A Chanukah play. By S. J. S. (Jewish Daily News. New York, 1927. f°. v. 43, no. 263, Nov. 17, p. 8; no. 264, Nov. 18, p. 16.)   * PBB
November afternoon in a dormitory at an Eastern college.

Spitz, Leon. Hannah of today. (A Hanukah playlet) ₁in one scene₁. (Young Judaean. New York, 1922. 8°. v. 12, p. 352–353.)   * PBD
The characters represent a group of Sunday school girls.

Witt, Louis. Pictures out of the past; a Chanukah play ₁in one act₁. Cincinnati, Ohio: Department of Synagog and School Extension of the Union of American Hebrew Congregations ₁cop. 1918₁. 18 p. 12°.
* PBM p.v.100, no.8

Wolf, Ruth E. Levi. Chanukah sketch. New York: Bloch Pub. Co., 1921. 8 p. 12°.
Time: the present.

—— "A thought for Chanukah." ₁In two parts and three scenes.₁ (Young Israel. Cincinnati, 1922. 4°. v. 15, Dec., 1922, p. 5–7.)   * PBD

Woolf, Henry. "Dreambook." Story of Chanukkah. A one act playlet. (The Ark. Cincinnati, 1915. 8°. v. 5, no. 11, Nov., 1915, p. 531–543.)   * PBD

—— —— ₁Cincinnati:₁ Ark Pub. Co. ₁cop. 1915.₁ 15 p. 8°.
A modern home. The characters, representing the historical figures of Hanukkah, step out from the pages of a book.

Jewish Festival Plays, continued

Special Occasions — Hanukkah, continued

—— A unique Chanukkah party. A one-act comedy, with music. (The Ark. Cincinnati, 1911. 8°. v. 1, no. 1, Nov. 24, 1911, p. 582–592.)   *** PBD**
Words only.

—— —— n. p. ₍cop. 1911.₎ 12 p. music sheet, 8 p. 8°.
Scene: a modern home. Time: the present.

Young Judaea. Playlet. (Choose your own name.) ₍In one scene.₎ (In its: 20th anniversary program. New York, 1930. 4°. p. 10–11.)
The characters are ten boys and girls. Produced in Philadelphia, 1928, as its annual Hanukkah entertainment.

Lag Ba'Omer

Jewish Education Committee, Chicago. Portfolio for the observance of Lag b'Omer. Chicago: Bureau of Jewish Education, Dramatics Dept. ₍1929?₎ 30 f. illus. 4°.   *** PKB**
Partial contents: Israel's arrow, E. C. E. Levinger. For love of Torah, J. E. Sampter. "Arrows to the east," S. S. Grossman.
Cover-title.
Mimeographed.

Jewish Welfare Board. Bulletin on Achad ha-Am. ₍Compiled by M. Soltes.₎ New York: Jewish Welfare Board, Jan., 1930. 30 f. 4°.   *** PKB**
Cover-title.
Mimeographed.
Selected references, f. 30.

—— Lag ba'Omer; program material and suggestions. ₍Compiled by M. Soltes.₎ New York: Jewish Welfare Board, Feb., 1929. 1 p.l., 21 f. 4°.   *** PKB**
Cover-title.
Mimeographed.
List of plays, p. 7–8. Twenty-five questions and answers, p. 20–21.

Grossman, Samuel S. "Arrows to the east." (A fantasy for Lag Ba'Omer.) ₍New York: Young Judea, 19—?₎ 3 l. 4°. (In his: ₍Holiday and other plays for Jewish children.₎)   **NASH**
Mimeographed.
First appeared in *Young Judaean,* New York, 1920, v. 10, p. 207, 210–211, * *PBD.*
Reproduced in Jewish Education Committee, Chicago, *Portfolio for the observance of Lag b'Omer,* Chicago [1929?], * *PKB.*
Characters: Abey, Manny, and the little old man with arrows.
Place: any part of the woods, or any part of the world for that matter, on the way to Palestine.

—— Lag B'omer stars. A mood play for Jewish children. illus. (Young Judaean. New York, 1922. 8°. v. 12, p. 225–228, 240–245.)   *** PBD**

Levinger, Elma C. (Ehrlich). The golden ring, a play about Rabbi Akiba and Lag b'Omer. ₍In one scene.₎ (In her: Entertaining programs for the assembly. Cincinnati ₍cop. 1930₎. 8°. p. 162–166.)   *** PSY**
A sketch about Rabbi Akiba.

—— Israel's arrow; a Lag Ba'Omer playlet. By E. C. Ehrlich. New York: Issued for Young Judea by the Department of Education, Zionist Organization of America ₍1920?₎. 3 l. 4°.

—— —— (In: Zionist Organization of America. — Department of Education. Lag ba'Omer-Shabuoth envelope for young Judaeans. New York ₍1920?₎. 8°. p. 17–19.)
*** PBM p.v.**
Reproduced in Jewish Education Committee, Chicago, *Portfolio for the observance of Lag b'Omer,* Chicago [1929?], * *PKB.*

Linsky, Fannie Barnett. The counting of days; a Lag b'Omer cycle. Cincinnati: Department of Synagogue and School Extension of the Union of American Hebrew Congregations ₍cop. 1929₎. 27 p. 8°.

Sampter, Jessie Ethel. For love of Torah. ₍In two scenes.₎ (In: E. C. E. Levinger, Jewish festivals in the religious school. Cincinnati, 1923. 12°. p. 242–245.)   *** PSY**
Characters: Akiba and Pappus ben Judah.
Reproduced in Jewish Education Committee, Chicago, *Portfolio for the observance of Lag b'Omer,* Chicago [1929?], * *PKB.*

Chamisha Oser

Jewish Education Committee, Chicago. Portfolios for holy days and festivals; Chamishoh Osor bi-shevat. (Palestine arbor day.) Chicago: Board of Jewish Education, Dramatics Dept. ₍1929?₎ 77 p. 4°.   *** PKB**
Partial contents: "Here and there," E. C. E. Levinger. "Wandering," S. S. Grossman. The carob tree, E. C. E. Levinger. "Homeless," "the wanderer," "wandering," and "return." The burden of his race, H. Segal. The parable of the trees and its prophecy. What the trees said, S. S. Grossman. A dancing lesson. New year of the trees. What grows in Palestine.
Cover-title.
Mimeographed.

Jewish Welfare Board. Bulletin for the observance of Chamisho Osor bishevat, including program material and twenty questions and answers. ₍Compiled by M. Soltes.₎ New York: Jewish Welfare Board, Jan., 1929. 2 p.l., 2–39 f. 4°.   *** PKB**
Cover-title.
Mimeographed.
Plays and pageants, p. 9–11.

Bril, Isaac L. The Jewish trees: a Chamisho Oser b'Shvat playlet ₍in one scene₎. (Jewish daily news. New York, 1928. f°. Jan. 22, 1928, p. 14.)   *** PBB**

Burstein, Abraham. Palestine spring song. ₍In pantomime.₎ (In: Elma C. E. Levinger, Entertaining programs for the assembly. Cincinnati ₍cop. 1930₎. 8°. p. 115–117.)   *** PSY**
Translated from the Hebrew.

Jewish Festival Plays, continued

Special Occasions — Chamisha Oser, cont'd

A **Dancing** lesson. ₍In one scene.₎ (In: Jewish Education Committee, Chicago. Portfolios for holy days and festivals. Chamishoh Osor bi-Shevat. Chicago ₍1929?₎. 2 f. 4°.   *** PKB**
Mimeographed.

David, Edward. The trees of Lebanon. ₍A Chamisho Osor playlet.₎ ₍New York:₎ Bureau of Education, Department of Social Activities ₍19—?₎. 6 l. 4°.
Mimeographed.
In a modern sitting room. A fanciful appeal for Palestine relief.

Dushkin, Alexander Mordecai. The parable of the trees and its prophecy. (In: Jewish Welfare Board. Bulletin for Chamisho Osor bishevat. New York, 1929. 4°. f. 32–34.)   *** PKB**
Based on Judges ix. A slight variant of the entry listed under Judges anonymously under its title, on p. 59 of this bibliography.

Friedland, Abraham H. A guest for Chamisha Osor. A sketch for Chamisha Osor B'Shevat. Written by H. A. Friedland, for the Young Judaea Organization. Translated from the Hebrew by Menahem Sobel. ₍New York: Young Judea, 19—?₎ 5 l. 4°.
Mimeographed.
School celebration in a Palestinian colony.

Goldberg, Israel. The new planting. A play for "Chamisho Osor" by Rufus Learsi ₍pseud.₎. Illustrated by William Camerer. (Young Judaean. New York, 1927. f°. v. 17, no. 1, p. 8–11.)   *** PBD**
In two acts.

Grossman, Samuel S. "Wandering." Poem dramatization ₍in one scene₎. (In: Jewish Education Committee, Chicago. Portfolios for holy days and festivals. Chamishoh Osor bi-Shevat. Chicago ₍1929?₎. 2 f. 4°. *** PKB**
Mimeographed.

—— What the trees said. (A Chamisho Oser B' shvat fantasio) ₍in one act₎. ₍New York: Young Judaea, 19—?₎ 5 l. f°.
Mimeographed.
Reproduced in Jewish Education Committee, Chicago, *Portfolios for holy days and festivals; Chamishoh Osor bi-Shevat,* Chicago [1929?], * *PKB.*

Harman, Harry. The fairies of the Jordan; a fantasy for children ₍in one scene₎. (Jewish child. New York, 1917. f°. v. 5, no. 39, p. 2–4.)   *** PBD**

"**Homeless,**" "The wanderer," "Wandering," and "Return." ₍In one scene.₎ (In: Jewish Education Committee, Chicago. Portfolios for holy days and festivals. Chamishoh Osor bi-Shevat. Chicago ₍1929?₎. 2 f. 4°.   *** PKB**
Mimeographed.

Ish-Kishor, Judith. Here and there. A Chamisho Osor playlet. (Young Judaean. New York, 1923. 8°. v. 13, p. 12–13.) *** PBD**
Also printed in *Jewish advocate,* Boston, Feb. 5, 1925, section 2, p. 3, col. 3–4, * *PBD.*

—— —— ₍New York: Young Judea, 1923?₎ 3 l. 4°.
Mimeographed.
Reproduced in Jewish Education Committee, Chicago, *Portfolios for holy days and festivals; Chamishoh Osor bi-Shevat,* Chicago [1929?], * *PKB.*

Kolodney, William, and REBECCA WEISS. Palestine mandate dance, song and dramatic tableau. ₍In five scenes.₎ (In: Jewish Welfare Board. Bulletin for Chamisho Osor bishevat. New York, 1929. 4°. f. 37–39.)   *** PKB**

Levinger, Elma C. Ehrlich. The carob tree. ₍In two scenes.₎ Based on a Talmudic story. ₍New York: Young Judaea, 19—?₎ 2 l. 4°.
Mimeographed.
Reprinted in her *Entertaining programs for the assembly,* Cincinnati ₍cop. 1930₎, p. 118–120, * *PSY.*
Reproduced in Jewish Education Committee, Chicago, *Portfolios for holy days and festivals; Chamishoh Osor bi-Shevat,* Chicago [1929?], * *PKB.*

—— The tree song. ₍In one scene.₎ (In her: Entertaining programs for the assembly. Cincinnati ₍cop. 1930₎. 8°. p. 121–123.)   *** PSY**

New year of the trees. (Taken from story of the same name by Mamie Gamoran.) ₍In one scene.₎ (In: Jewish Education Committee, Chicago. Portfolios for holy days and festivals. Chamishoh Osor bi-Shevat. Chicago ₍1929?₎. 5 f. 4°.)   *** PKB**
Mimeographed.

Segal, Hyman. The burden of his race. ₍New York: Young Judaea, 1917.₎ 1 l. f°.
Mimeographed.
Reproduced in Jewish Education Committee, Chicago, *Portfolios for holy days and festivals; Chamishoh Osor bi-Shevat,* Chicago [1929?], * *PKB.*

—— The burden of his race. ₍In one scene.₎ (In: Jewish Education Committee, Chicago. Portfolios for holy days and festivals. Chamishoh Osor bi-Shevat. Chicago ₍1929?₎. 2 f. 4°.   *** PKB**
Mimeographed.

Jewish Festival Plays, continued

Special Occasions — Chamisha Oser, cont'd

What grows in Palestine; a map dialogue. (In: Jewish Education Committee, Chicago, Portfolios for holy days and festivals; Chamishoh Osor bi-shevat. Chicago [1929?]. 5 f. 4°.   *****PKB**

MISCELLANEOUS

JEWISH WELFARE BOARD. Bulletin on the observance of the high holidays, including twenty-five questions and answers on Rosh Hashonah and Yom Kippur. [Compiled by M. Soltes.] New York: Jewish Welfare Board, August, 1929. 2 p.l., 2–22 f. 4°. *****PKB**
Cover-title.
Mimeographed.
Selected references, p. 10–10a.

—— Summer activities in the Jewish center including Jewish programs for summer camps. [Compiled by M. Soltes.] New York: Jewish Welfare Board, July, 1930. 1 p.l., 26 f. 4°.   *****PKB**
Cover-title.
Mimeographed.
Twenty questions and answers on the significance and observance of Tishah b'Ab, f. 21–22.
Jewish library, f. 17–20.

Abraham, Nanette. Queen Sabbath. (A one-act playlet.) New York: Bloch Publishing Company, 1931. 11 p. 12°.
Several Sabbath poems, p. 9–11.

Bril, Isaac L. Everyjew; a Jewish morality play [in one scene]. (Young Judaean. New York, 1915. 8°. v. 5, May, 1915, p. 18–20, 29.)
Copy in Dropsie College Library.

—— —— [New York: Young Judaean, 1915?] 5 p. illus. 8°.
Reproduced in Jewish Welfare Board, *Bulletin for the observance of Chamisho Osor bishevat.* New York, 1929, * PKB.

Cohen, Saul J. David's Bar-mitzvah. [In one act.] (Young Judaean. New York, 1921. 8°. v. 11, p. 163–164, 178.)   *****PBD**

Eckhouse, Mrs. Elmer L. "Dust"; a play [in one act]. New York: National Council of Jewish Women, Dept. of Farm and Rural Work [1927?]. 10 f. 4°.   **NBF p.v.107**
Mimeographed.
The day before the New Year, in a farm house kitchen.

Edlavich, Betty. En kelohenu. (Young Israel. Cincinnati, 1928. f°. v. 21, Oct., p. 18.)   *****PBD**
On the meaning of the concluding prayer in the Sabbath services. The characters are Rabbi Stein, four children and their two parents.

—— House of holidays. [In one scene.] (Young Israel. Cincinnati, 1929. 4°. v. 22, Oct., 1929, p. 19.)   *****PBD**

Goldberg, Israel. The Kehillah-spirit (a dramatic fragment) [in one scene]. Dedicated to the Jewish Community (Kehillah) of New York, by Rufus Learsi [pseud.]. (Jewish child. New York, 1918. 4°. v. 5, no. 50, p. 2–3.)   *****PBD**

Grossman, Samuel S. A dolly play; for the younger "Jewish children." (Jewish child. New York, 1917. f°. v. 5, no. 22, p. 1–2, 4.)   *****PBD**

Hess, Harold. Jack's dream. [A juvenile playlet in three acts.] (Jewish exponent. Philadelphia, 1915. f°. v. 61, May 28, 1915, p. 5.)   *****PBD**
About a sick boy who can't go to Sunday school. The second act is in six scenes, each representing a Biblical episode.

Ish-Kishor, Judith. Waking; a newspageant for the year 5678. [In one scene.] (Jewish child. New York, 1917. f°. v. 5, no. 34, p. 1–4.)   *****PBD**

The **Judgment** of the days. A dramatic sketch in rhyme for Rosh Hashanah. [New York: Young Judaea, n. d.] 8 l. 4°.
Mimeographed.
The characters are ten Jewish holidays who stand in judgment on New Year's Day.

Kissin, Ritta. The holidays. (The Ark. Cincinnati, 1916. 8°. v. 6, p. 195–196.)   *****PBD**
Five Jewish holidays are the characters.

Levinger, Elma C. (Ehrlich). A day in a Jewish home. [In one scene.] (In her: Entertaining programs for the assembly. Cincinnati [cop. 1930]. 8°. p. 21–27.) *****PSY**
The characters are religious ceremonial objects used at home.

—— The Hebrew's Friday night. (Based on the poem by Israel Zangwill, to be read to music and illustrated by tableaux [in five pictures]. (In her: Entertaining programs for the assembly. Cincinnati [cop. 1930]. 8°. p. 12–14.)   *****PSY**

—— In our synagogue. [In one scene.] (In her: Entertaining programs for the assembly. Cincinnati [cop. 1930]. 8°. p. 29–34.)   *****PSY**
Ceremonial objects at the synagogue.

—— The magic circle, a series of pictures to illustrate how Thanksgiving came to be. [In one scene.] (In her: Entertaining pro-

Jewish Festival Plays, continued

Special Occasions — Miscellaneous, continued

grams for the assembly. Cincinnati ₁cop. 1930₁. 8°. p. 51–56.)   * PSY
Among the historical characters are Moses and Elder Brewster.

—— The prayers of Israel. ₁In five pictures.₁ (In her: Entertaining programs for the assembly. Cincinnati ₁cop. 1930₁. 8°. p. 65–71.)   * PSY
Among the symbolic characters are the historical Rabbi Akiba and Maimonides.

Levy, Clifton Harby. The harvest of prayer; a pageant. (Jewish tribune. New York, 1923. f°. v. 42, Sept. 28, 1923, p. 4.)   * PBD

—— The spirit of prayer; a pageant in which the prayers of the Sabbath ritual are personified. New York: Bloch Pub. Co., 1925. 4 l. 8°.

Linsky, Fannie Barnett. Happy New Year! illus. (Young Israel. Cincinnati, 1925. f°. v. 18, no. 1, p. 7–8, 23.)   * PBD
The characters are the thirteen months of the Hebrew leap year.

—— Old pictures in new frames; a group of tableaux for any holiday. Cincinnati: Department of Synagogue and School Extension of the Union of American Hebrew Congregations ₁cop. 1929₁. 11 p. 8°.
Foreword by Harry Levi, p. 3–4.

—— The Sabbath angel, a play in two acts. Cincinnati: Department of Synagogue and School Extension of the Union of American Hebrew Congregations ₁cop. 1929₁. 19 p. 8°.

Rosenbaum, Yetta. The poor little rich girl. (Jewish child. New York, 1918. f°. v. 6, no. 32, p. 3.)   * PBD
The little rich girl is poor because she had been deprived of the opportunity of reading all the beautiful Jewish stories and attending the Jewish children's entertainments.

INDEX OF AUTHORS

Numbers refer to pages.

Titles of anonymous books are also included in this index,
but not those of anonymous magazine articles.

Bale, John, bishop of Ossory, 1495–1563, *continued*
The interlude of "God's promises," 33.
Lazarus rais'd from the dead, 125.
Simon the Leper, 127.
"The temptacyon of our Lorde," 121.
A tragedye or enterlude, manyfestyng the chefe promyses of God unto man, 33.
Balmforth, Ramsden:
Bernard Shaw's metabiological plays, 41.
The drama of Job, 78.
Barbee, Lindsey, 1876–   :
The making of a king, 67.
Barbor, Herbert Reginald:
Jezebel, 74.
Barlow, Joseph:
Jesus of Nazareth, 98.
Barlow, N. P.:
The Shunemite maid in the court of David and Solomon, 80.
Barnard, Percy Mordaunt, 1868–   :
Jezebel, 74.
Barnum, Madalene Demarest, 1874–   :
Brethren, 48.
Barry, Philip, 1896–   :
John, 120.
Bartlett, Edward R., and E. Ruth Bartlett:
The child of prophecy, 107.
Followers of the star, 107.
Release, 90.
Barton, Alice L.:
Cleopas, 145.
Bates, Esther Willard:
The Christmas flowers, 107.
The city of God, 98.
The promise of peace, 107.
The tree of life, 140.
The two thieves, 130.
Bates, Katharine Lee, 1859–1929:
The English religious drama, 21.
The healing of Tobit, 90.
Joanna the wife of Chuza, 98.
Outlines and references, 20.
Pharisees, 122.
Bates, William Oscar, 1852–   :
In the light of the manger, 107.
Battine, William:
Another Cain, 42.
Baugh, Albert Croll, 1891–   :
The Chester plays and French literature, 30.
The Mak story, 116.
Baughan, E. A.:
"Back to Methuselah," 41.
Baum, Paull Franklin:
Samson Agonistes again, 63.
Bayard, Lyman R.:
The dawning, 140.
Into Galilee, 140.
A legend of Saint John, 150.
"Out of the Bible," 34.
The tidings, 140.
"When the stars shone," 107.
See also Tarrant, William George, and Lyman R. Bayard.
Bayle, Pierre, 1647–1706:
[Ezekiel, a Jewish poet], 55.
Bayne, Peter, 1830–1896:
The days of Jezebel, 74.
Beale, William Thomas:
The chancellor of Egypt, 51.
Beardsley, Harry J.:
Joseph, 51.
Beer-Hofmann, Richard, 1866–   :
Jaákobs Traum, 50.
Bellamy, Frederica Lefevre:
Darkness and dawn, 130.
The jongleur's story, 34.
Benacense, Troilo Lancetta:
[Analysis of the drama entitled Adam and Eve], 39.

Bendz, Ernst:
A propos de la Salomé d'Oscar Wilde, 97.
Benedict, George:
The masterpiece, 158.
Benjamin, Irma A.:
Shadows of our past, 160.
Bennett, Arnold, 1867–1931:
Judith, 91.
Bennett, Clara Marion:
The good Samaritan, 123.
Benson, Robert Hugh, 1871–1914:
A mystery play in honour of the Nativity of Our Lord, 107.
The upper room, 130.
Bentley, John:
The royal penitent, 67.
Benton, Rita, 1881–   :
Bible plays, 15.
The burning fiery furnace, 88.
The call of Samuel, 64.
The Christmas story, 107.
Coming down the Mount, 123.
Daniel, 89.
The daughter of Jephthah, 60.
David and Goliath, 67.
Esther, 84.
The golden calf, 56.
The good Samaritan, 123.
Joseph and his brethren, 51.
The judgment of Solomon, 72.
Moses in the bulrushes, 56.
Noah's flood, 46.
The proving of Abraham, 48.
Ruth and Boaz, 82.
Shorter Bible plays, 15.
Up, up from Egypt to the promised land, 56.
Berenberg, David P.:
Glaucon & Sarai, 98.
Bergen, Francis:
The death of Pilate, 130.
Bergman, Ruth, and David De Sola Pool, 1885–   :
A Purim carol, 158.
Berkowitz, Isaac Dob, 1885–   ., joint author. *See* Shalom Alechem, pseud. of Shalom Rabinowitz, 1859–1916, and Isaac Dob Berkowitz, 1885–   .
Betzner, Era, 1891–1931:
Bringers of gifts, 107.
Beverley, Robert Mackenzie:
Jubal, 36.
Beverley, England:
[Orders for the governance of the Corpus Christi play], 21.
Bèze, Théodore de, 1519–1605:
A tragedie of Abrahams sacrifice, 48.
Bible. — Song of Solomon, 80.
Bickerstaff, Isaac:
Judith, 91.
Bien, Herman M.:
Easter eve, 154.
The feast of lights, 160.
"Purim," 84.
Binsse, Henry B.:
The birth of the Christian drama, 145.
Binstock, Ruth Atlas:
Harvest festival, 157.
Birt, Henry Norbert, 1861–1919:
The ancient mystery plays of Coventry, 31.
Bishop, John Peale:
The funeral of St. Mary Magdalene, 142.
Bland, John, d. 1788:
A grammatical version...of the Song of Solomon, 80.
Blatt, William M.:
The treasure in the trunk, 156.
Bliss, Frank Chapman:
Queen Esther, 84.
Bloch, Regina Miriam:
Samson and Delilah, 62.
The witch of En-Dor, 65.

INDEX OF PLAYS

INDEX TO SPECIAL TOPICS

This index is designed primarily to enable the reader to locate the more important characters and episodes upon which plays have been based. The books of the Bible and the apocryphal books are also listed here, with references to the pages where the plays based upon each are enumerated.

INDEX TO ENGLISH TRANSLATIONS
OF FOREIGN PLAYS

INDEX TO A SURVEY OF RECENT MAJOR PLAYS